Dictionary of Literary Biography • Volume Thirty-two

Victorian Poets Before 1850

Edited by
William E. Fredeman
University of British Columbia
and
Ira B. Nadel
University of British Columbia

A Bruccoli Clark Book
Gale Research Company • Book Tower • Detroit, Michigan 48226

Advisory Board for
DICTIONARY OF LITERARY BIOGRAPHY

Louis S. Auchincloss
John Baker
D. Philip Baker
A. Walton Litz, Jr.
Peter S. Prescott
Lola L. Szladits
William Targ

Matthew J. Bruccoli and Richard Layman, *Editorial Directors*
C. E. Frazer Clark, Jr., *Managing Editor*

Manufactured by Edwards Brothers, Inc.
Ann Arbor, Michigan
Printed in the United States of America

Copyright © 1984
GALE RESEARCH COMPANY

Library of Congress Cataloging in Publication Data
Main entry under title:

Victorian poets before 1850.

(Dictionary of literary biography; v. 32)
"A Bruccoli Clark book."
Includes index.
1. English poetry—19th century—History and criticism. 2. English poetry—19th century—Bio-bibliography. 3. Poets, English—19th century—Biography—Dictionaries. I. Fredeman, William E. (William Evan), 1928- . II. Nadel, Ira Bruce. III. Series.
PR591.V53   1984   821'.7'09   84-18781
ISBN 0-8103-1710-9

For Luke and Ryan

Contents

Plan of the Series ix

Foreword xi

Acknowledgments xv

Matthew Arnold (1822-1888) 3
William Robbins

William Edmondstoune Aytoun (1813-1865) 28
Mark A. Weinstein

Philip James Bailey (1816-1902) 33
Mark A. Weinstein

William Barnes (1801-1886) 39
Peter Quartermain

Emily Brontë (1818-1848) 46
Victor A. Neufeldt

Elizabeth Barrett Browning (1806-1861) 53
Gardner B. Taplin

Robert Browning (1812-1889) 68
Thomas J. Collins

Edward Caswall (1814-1878) 88
G. B. Tennyson

Arthur Hugh Clough (1819-1861) 91
Patrick Scott

Sydney Dobell (1824-1874) 108
Mark A. Weinstein

Frederick William Faber (1814-1863) 112
G. B. Tennyson

Sir Samuel Ferguson (1810-1886) 114
Tirthankar Bose

Edward FitzGerald (1809-1883) 118
Joseph Sendry

David Gray (1838-1861) 132
Christopher Murray

Thomas Gordon Hake (1809-1895) 134
John R. Reed

Arthur Henry Hallam (1811-1833) 138
Jack Kolb

Robert Stephen Hawker (1803-1875) 150
John R. Reed

Richard Henry (Hengist) Horne (1802 or 1803-1884) 154
Robert G. Laird

Ebenezer Jones (1820-1860) 160
William B. Thesing

Ernest Jones (1819-1868) 166
Nicholas Coles

John Keble (1792-1866) 170
G. B. Tennyson

Fanny Kemble (1809-1893) 176
Lionel Adey

Charles Kingsley (1819-1875) 182
Nicholas Coles

Edward Lear (1812-1888) 190
Ina Rae Hark

William James Linton (1812-1897) 197
Tirthankar Bose

Edward Robert Bulwer Lytton (Owen Meredith) (1831-1891) 202
Michael Darling

Thomas Babington Macaulay (1800-1859) 209
Richard Tobias

Gerald Massey (1828-1907) 214
Tirthankar Bose

Richard Monckton Milnes (Lord Houghton) (1809-1885) 218
David Latham

John Henry Newman (1801-1890) 225
Lionel Adey

Adelaide Anne Procter (1825-1864) 232
Susan Drain

William Bell Scott (1811-1890) 235
William E. Fredeman

Alexander Smith (1830-1867) 249
Mark A. Weinstein

Charles Swain (1801-1874) 254
Dorothy W. Collin

Sir Henry Taylor (1800-1886) 257
Lawrence Poston

Contents

Alfred Tennyson (1809-1892)..........................262

Frederick Tennyson (1807-1898).....................282
Rowland L. Collins

Martin F. Tupper (1810-1889) 288
Patrick Scott

Charles (Tennyson) Turner (1808-1879) 298
Rowland L. Collins

Charles Jeremiah Wells (circa 1800-1879).........303
Ira Bruce Nadel

Isaac Williams (1802-1865)...............................306
G. B. Tennyson

Appendix

On Some of the Characteristics of
    Modern Poetry..313
Arthur Henry Hallam

Thoughts on Poetry and Its Varieties...............324
John Stuart Mill

The Hero as Poet. Dante; Shakspeare 334
Thomas Carlyle

Essay on Chatterton..349
Robert Browning

Introductory Essay...359
Robert Browning

The Novel in "The Ring and the Book".........367
Henry James

Preface to *Poems* (1853) 376
Matthew Arnold

Books for Further Reading..............................383
Contributors...387
Cumulative Index..391

Plan of the Series

... Almost the most prodigious asset of a country, and perhaps its most precious possession, is its native literary product—when that product is fine and noble and enduring.

Mark Twain*

The advisory board, the editors, and the publisher of the *Dictionary of Literary Biography* are joined in endorsing Mark Twain's declaration. The literature of a nation provides an inexhaustible resource of permanent worth. It is our expectation that this endeavor will make literature and its creators better understood and more accessible to students and the literate public, while satisfying the standards of teachers and scholars.

To meet these requirements, *literary biography* has been construed in terms of the author's achievement. The most important thing about a writer is his writing. Accordingly, the entries in *DLB* are career biographies, tracing the development of the author's canon and the evolution of his reputation.

The publication plan for *DLB* resulted from two years of preparation. The project was proposed to Bruccoli Clark by Frederick G. Ruffner, president of the Gale Research Company, in November 1975. After specimen entries were prepared and typeset, an advisory board was formed to refine the entry format and develop the series rationale. In meetings held during 1976, the publisher, series editors, and advisory board approved the scheme for a comprehensive biographical dictionary of persons who contributed to North American literature. Editorial work on the first volume began in January 1977, and it was published in 1978.

In order to make *DLB* more than a reference tool and to compile volumes that individually have claim to status as literary history, it was decided to organize volumes by topic or period or genre. Each of these freestanding volumes provides a biographical-bibliographical guide and overview for a particular area of literature. We are convinced that this organization—as opposed to a single alphabet method—constitutes a valuable innovation in the presentation of reference material. The volume plan necessarily requires many decisions for the placement and treatment of authors who might properly be included in two or three volumes. In some instances a major figure will be included in separate volumes, but with different entries emphasizing the aspect of his career appropriate to each volume. Ernest Hemingway, for example, is represented in *American Writers in Paris, 1920-1939* by an entry focusing on his expatriate apprenticeship; he is also in *American Novelists, 1910-1945* with an entry surveying his entire career. Each volume includes a cumulative index of subject authors. The final *DLB* volume will be a comprehensive index to the entire series.

With volume ten in 1982 it was decided to enlarge the scope of *DLB* beyond the literature of the United States. By the end of 1983 twelve volumes treating British literature had been published, and volumes for Commonwealth and Modern European literature were in progress. The series has been further augmented by the *DLB Yearbooks* (since 1981) which update published entries and add new entries to keep the *DLB* current with contemporary activity. There have also been occasional *DLB Documentary Series* volumes which provide biographical and critical background source materials for figures whose work is judged to have particular interest for students. One of these companion volumes is entirely devoted to Tennessee Williams.

The purpose of *DLB* is not only to provide reliable information in a convenient format but also to place the figures in the larger perspective of literary history and to offer appraisals of their accomplishments by qualified scholars.

We define literature as the *intellectual commerce of a nation*: not merely as belles lettres, but as that ample and complex process by which ideas are generated, shaped, and transmitted. *DLB* entries are not limited to "creative writers" but extend to other figures who in this time and in this way influenced the mind of a people. Thus the series encompasses historians, journalists, publishers, and screenwriters. By this means readers of *DLB* may be aided to perceive literature not as cult scripture in the keeping of cultural high priests, but as at the center of a nation's life.

DLB includes the major writers appropriate to each volume and those standing in the ranks immediately behind them. Scholarly and critical counsel has been sought in deciding which minor figures to include and how full their entries should be.

---

*From an unpublished section of Mark Twain's autobiography, copyright © by the Mark Twain Company.

Plan of the Series

Wherever possible, useful references will be made to figures who do not warrant separate entries.

Each *DLB* volume has a volume editor responsible for planning the volume, selecting the figures for inclusion, and assigning the entries. Volume editors are also responsible for preparing, where appropriate, appendices surveying the major periodicals and literary and intellectual movements for their volumes, as well as lists of further readings. Work on the series as a whole is coordinated at the Bruccoli Clark editorial center in Columbia, South Carolina, where the editorial staff is responsible for the accuracy of the published volumes.

One feature that distinguishes *DLB* is the illustration policy—its concern with the iconography of literature. Just as an author is influenced by his surroundings, so is the reader's understanding of the author enhanced by a knowledge of his environment. Therefore *DLB* volumes include not only drawings, paintings, and photographs of authors, often depicting them at various stages in their careers, but also illustrations of their families and places where they lived. Title pages are regularly reproduced in facsimile along with dust jackets for modern authors. The dust jackets are a special feature of *DLB* because they often document better than anything else the way in which an author's work was launched in its own time. Specimens of the writers' manuscripts are included when feasible.

A supplement to *DLB*—tentatively titled *A Guide, Chronology, and Glossary for American Literature*—will outline the history of literature in North America and trace the influences that shaped it. This volume will provide a framework for the study of American literature by means of chronological tables, literary affiliation charts, glossarial entries, and concise surveys of the major movements. It has been planned to stand on its own as a vade mecum, providing a ready-reference guide to the study of American literature as well as a companion to the *DLB* volumes for American literature.

Samuel Johnson rightly decreed that "The chief glory of every people arises from its authors." The purpose of the *Dictionary of Literary Biography* is to compile literary history in the surest way available to us—by accurate and comprehensive treatment of the lives and work of those who contributed to it.

The *DLB* Advisory Board

Foreword

The two *Dictionary of Literary Biography* volumes on *Victorian Poets* (volumes 32 and 35) are intended as companions to *DLB 21, Victorian Novelists Before 1885* and *DLB 18, Victorian Novelists After 1885;* indeed, six of the fiction writers treated in those volumes also appear as poets—Emily Brontë, Robert Buchanan, George Meredith, Mortimer Collins, George Eliot, and William Morris. For many Victorian novelists, such as George Eliot and Emily Brontë, the writing of verse was more or less incidental to their primary talent; for others, such as Morris, fiction was a kind of polyphonic prose extension of their poetry; still others, such as Buchanan, engaged in both genres indiscriminately, with only moderate success in either. Only Meredith and Hardy among the great Victorian novelists had successful parallel careers as poets, and Hardy has been included in *DLB 19, British Poets, 1880-1941* because his creatively poetic period commenced only at the very end of the century with the publication of *Wessex Poems and Other Verses* in 1898.

Compartmentalizing the Victorian Age has always posed problems for the literary historian, not only because so many of the great Victorians were indefatigable writers who refuse to submit to taxonomical pigeonholing, but because any definition of the age must accommodate major and prodigious achievements in three distinct literary genres—poetry, the novel, and nonfictional prose. The scope of these genres is amply demonstrated by the three critical surveys devoted to them, edited by Frederic Faverty (poetry), George Ford (the novel), and David DeLaura (nonfictional prose).

While it is not really possible to identify the age as dominated by a single genre, there is no question that the novel attained its majority during the 1800s. Paradoxically—or perhaps predictably—the social advances of the century, which included the growth of the middle classes, the universalization of public education, and an increase in leisure time, resulted not in an elevation in aesthetic sensitivity but in a democratization of the arts; from this the novel, more than any other literary form, benefited. The nineteenth-century aesthetic equivalent of television, the novel, because of its wide appeal and readership, was subject to the same kind of "prime-time" restrictions that operate today in "family oriented" TV programming. While these strictures were often self-imposed, as in the case of Trollope in England and W. D. Howells in the United States—both prided themselves on never having written anything that could not be read aloud in mixed company—the stranglehold that the great lending libraries exerted on popular taste and on both the economics and the format of the novel enabled them to enforce a de facto censorship. Realism is evident in the treatment and style of many Victorian novels, but nowhere in the fiction of the period is there so explicit a sexual passage as the consummation scene in the Ottima-Sebald section of Robert Browning's *Pippa Passes* (1841) or domestic dialogue comparable to that in George Meredith's *Modern Love* (1862).

The novel, however, was destined to thrive because its very nature made it more accessible to the average reader, and because the relaxed grip of the libraries in the late 1880s freed novelists and publishers to experiment more widely with both form and content. As it became more mature and sophisticated in terms of technique and style, arrogating to itself most of the self-reflexive qualities associated with poetry and becoming ever more prominently a nondiscursive form, the novel tended to usurp virtually all other literary genres. No modern writer—and probably not even Browning today—coming across the materials of *The Old Yellow Book* would cast them into a poem of over 21,000 lines; the material itself, with its inherent potential for an experimental and complicated handling of point of view, coupled with the impact on sales, would lead him instinctively to write *The Ring and the Book* (1868-1869) as a novel.

The Victorians may have been the last poets who will ever successfully compete with novelists for a fair share of readers' attention, and while even they were no longer regarded, in Shelley's terms, as the "unacknowledged legislators of the world," certainly they were the last whose message was taken seriously by their contemporaries, and the last to be overly concerned about the aesthetic and moral responsibility of the poet as a spokesman for and interpreter of his age. Of course, most Victorian poets posed no real threat in terms of sales to the leading Victorian novelists—Dickens, Thackeray, George Eliot, Hardy, Meredith, and Trollope—but Tennyson raked off a fair share of the market: *Enoch Arden,* for example, sold over 17,000 copies on the first day of publication in August 1864; the entire first impression of 60,000 copies was exhausted by year's end, and the half-year profits on that book alone netted the laureate £6,664.4s.2d. It could be argued that *Enoch Arden,* as a verse narrative, capitalized on a certain spillover from the popularity of the novel, but many of Tennyson's other works could also be considered "bestsellers" in nineteenth-century terms; and the demand for even so eccentric a book as Philip James Bailey's *Festus* (1839) sent it through more than sixty editions in half a century. The point, however, is not so much that poetry in the Victorian period managed to survive against the competition of the novel, or that the major poets could make a living practicing their craft, but that there was still a sizable and literate audience concerned with the poet's perception of his world. The isolation that has characterized the poet since the 1880s—for which the poets themselves, by insisting on the privateness of their individual vision and language and disclaiming all responsibility save to art itself, must assume a large part of the blame—was not the condition of the Victorian poet. The tension between the private and public roles of the poet is readily evident in Tennyson, Browning, and Arnold, as E. D. H. Johnson pointed out several decades ago; but the major Victorians, at least, were unwilling to surrender one for the other and consciously sought and adopted strategies which would allow them to pursue private visions and values without alienating themselves from their readers.

The divisions between historical eras are always somewhat arbitrary, but it is more difficult to assign boundaries to the Victorian age than to do so for some other literary periods. The limits of the queen's reign, 1837 and 1901, while convenient, are inadequate. For 1837, there is no single event or work associated with the date, beyond her ascendancy, that signals a clear transition—as do, say, the death of Dryden and the publication of his *The Secular Masque* in 1700, which brings the curtain down with a nice finality on the Restoration; or the publication in 1798 of Wordsworth's *Lyrical Ballads,* whose preface and practice launch a dramatic shift in poetic theory that heralds the literature of Romanticism. Similarly, if the Victorians ever did refer to themselves by that epithet, by the year of the first Jubilee (1887), and certainly by 1901, most nineteenth-century intellectuals could have mustered half a dozen more appropriate labels for themselves. And, of course, neither date accounts for those last leaves upon the tree at either end of the Victorian spectrum. Even as a chronological denominator *Victorian* is ambiguous; but as a critical term, it is in a sense even more vague, since it can hardly be said to describe a body of writing that has any distinguishing homogeneity (though there are certain identifiable traits and characteristics among the poets belonging to the Oxford Movement, the Spasmodics, or the Pre-Raphaelites, who shared, to a degree at least, common aims and practices). In conventional usage, the term *Victorian* is often used pejoratively to refer to a set of social, cultural, and moral attitudes that by the standards of the twentieth century are regarded as narrow-minded, hypocritical, and chauvinistic; but such distinctions, which dominated the period of reaction in the first two decades following the death of the queen, have been undercut by systematic research into all aspects of the period in recent years.

The inherent inadequacies of the above applications of the term have led a number of modern critics to attempt to make the Victorians respectable by demonstrating that they were either post-Romantics or premoderns. But as Michael Timko pointed out in his important essay on "The Victorianism of Victorian Literature" in *New Literary History* (1975), such attempts, while a tribute to the skill of the critics and to the versatility of the literature of the period, ignore palpable distinctions that are unique to the condition of the Victorians, stemming from the twin influences of Darwinism, on the one hand, and the substitution of epistemological for metaphysical concerns on the other, both of which altered significantly the ways in which the Victorians viewed civilized man's relationship to nature and God. And they also overlook the literary innovations, such as the development of new, or combinations of traditional, genres, devised by the Victorians to meet the challenge of their times. Victorian literature, and especially the poetry, is a literature of personal, social, and moral engagement, often cast in the imagery of struggle or battle, which is characterized by dialogue, duality, conflict, quest, and uncertainty—about the human situation, the social condition, and the responsibility of the artist in confronting these important issues. While all periods are to some degree transitional, it is not a particularly useful generalization to apply to the Victorians. As Timko says, "To talk of the period from 1825 to 1890 as post-Romantic or pre-modern . . . is to fail to recognize these unique characteristics that constitute the paradigmatic experience and contribute to the style or charter of the period."

In selecting a dividing line for the poetry of the period, the editors have been guided by practical as well as theoretical considerations. While any date would inevitably be arbitrary, a genuine case can be made for 1850 on several different grounds: the death of the Romantic poet laureate, Wordsworth, and the publication of his *Prelude;* the appointment of Tennyson as the Victorian poet laureate and the publication of his *In Memoriam.* The year 1850 has always been regarded as Tennyson's annus mirabilis, but because it forces immediate comparisons between the two poets and their two major works, it is perhaps of even greater importance to the history of Victorian poetry. The year, however, hardly marks the end or even the beginning of an era—Wordsworth had long been a living anachronism, a fact to which in some ways *The Prelude* is a literary testament; and Tennyson's personal triumphs in 1850 only climaxed the new career he had launched after the "Ten Years' Silence" with the publication of *Poems* in 1842.

The two laureates' works are striking examples of Romantic and Victorian poetic sensibilities. Notwithstanding the obvious similarities in *The Prelude* and *In Memoriam* as poetic autobiographies—Rossetti's term *autopsychologies* might be more apt—the works are inherently different. Not only do they proceed from different world views but their respective personae speak for two generations that have little in common, intellectually or spiritually. *The Prelude* is essentially a personal and highly subjective document, archetypically romantic in its treatment of the "growth of a poet's mind." In some ways equally subjective, anchored as it is in personal grief and loss, *In Memoriam* manages to transcend the personality of the narrator and to generalize the experience of the poet into a universal grief, tempered by hope. The narrational "I" in *The Prelude* is always Wordsworth; in *In Memoriam,* Tennyson said, "I is not always the author speaking of himself, but the voice of the human race speaking through him." In this elementary distinction lies one of the major contrasts between the poetry of the Romantics and the Victorians.

Thus, 1850 does provide a convenient transition between early and late Victorian poetry. The editors have imposed broad guidelines to assist in assigning individual poets to one volume or the other, and these have had the fortunate result of roughly equalizing the contents of the two volumes, both in terms of the number of poets and the major poets of the period, though the three giants—Browning, Tennyson, and Arnold—all appear in the first volume. Obviously, the poetic careers of many of the poets in this volume, including Browning, Tennyson, and Arnold, extend well beyond 1850; but the division into two volumes at 1850 does provide some insight into the scope and the chronological development of Victorian poetry.

Finally, we would like to thank our contributors, many of them recognized authorities on their respective figures and on Victorian poetry in general, who have generously given of their time and knowledge to compose entries of the highest caliber. Inevitably, differences of opinion arise in a project of this kind and magnitude over matters of emphasis, perspective, and length. Our editorial decision has been—except in matters of house style and format, which are determined by the *DLB* editorial offices—to allow the authors themselves to be the final arbiters of these questions.

–William E. Fredeman and Ira B. Nadel

Acknowledgments

This book was produced by BC Research. Karen L. Rood is senior editor for the *Dictionary of Literary Biography* series. Philip B. Dematteis was the in-house editor.

Art supervisor is Claudia Ericson. Copyediting supervisor is Joycelyn R. Smith. Typesetting supervisor is Laura Ingram. The production staff includes Mary Betts, Rowena Betts, Kimberly Casey, Patricia Coate, Mary Page Elliott, Lynn Felder, Kathleen M. Flanagan, Joyce Fowler, Judith K. Ingle, Angelika Kourelis, Vickie Lowers, Judith McCray, and Jane McPherson. Jean W. Ross is permissions editor. Joseph Caldwell, photography editor, did photographic copy work for the volume.

Walter W. Ross did the library research with the assistance of the staff at the Thomas Cooper Library of the University of South Carolina: Lynn Barron, Daniel Boice, Sue Collins, Michael Freeman, Gary Geer, Alexander M. Gilchrist, Jens Holley, David Lincove, Marcia Martin, Roger Mortimer, Jean Rhyne, Karen Rissling, Paula Swope, and Ellen Tillet.

Dictionary of Literary Biography • Volume Thirty-two

Victorian Poets
Before 1850

Dictionary of Literary Biography

Matthew Arnold

William Robbins
University of British Columbia

BIRTH: Laleham-on-Thames, England, 24 December 1822, to Thomas and Mary Penrose Arnold.

EDUCATION: Second class degree, Oxford University, 1844.

MARRIAGE: 10 June 1851 to Frances Lucy Wightman; children: Thomas, William Trevenen, Richard Penrose, Lucy Charlotte, Eleanor Mary, Basil Francis.

DEATH: Liverpool, England, 15 April 1888.

BOOKS: *Alaric at Rome: A Prize Poem* (Rugby: Combe & Crossley, 1840);
Cromwell: A Prize Poem (Oxford: Vincent, 1843);
The Strayed Reveller and Other Poems, as A. (London: Fellowes, 1849);
Empedocles on Etna and Other Poems, as A. (London: Fellowes, 1852); republished as *Empedocles on Etna: A Dramatic Poem* (Portland, Maine: Mosher, 1900);
Poems: A New Edition (London: Longman, Brown, Green & Longmans, 1853);
Poems: Second Series (London: Longman, Brown, Green & Longmans, 1855);
Merope: A Tragedy (London: Longman, Brown, Green, Longman & Roberts, 1858);
England and the Italian Question (London: Longman, Green, Longman & Roberts, 1859); edited by Merle M. Bevington (Durham, N.C.: Duke University Press, 1953);
The Popular Education of France, with Notices of That of Holland and Switzerland (London: Longman, Green, Longman & Roberts, 1861);
On Translating Homer: Three Lectures Given at Oxford (London: Longman, Green, Longman & Roberts, 1861);
On Translating Homer: Last Words: A Lecture Given at Oxford (London: Longman, Green, Longman & Roberts, 1862);
Heinrich Heine (Philadelphia: Leypoldt/New York: Christern, 1863);
A French Eton; or, Middle Class Education and the State (London & Cambridge: Macmillan, 1864);
Essays in Criticism (London & Cambridge: Macmillan, 1865; Boston: Ticknor & Fields, 1865);
On the Study of Celtic Literature (London: Smith, Elder, 1867); with *On Translating Homer* (New York: Macmillan, 1883);
New Poems (London: Macmillan, 1867; Boston: Ticknor & Fields, 1867);
Schools and Universities on the Continent (London: Macmillan, 1868); republished in part as *Higher Schools and Universities in Germany* (London: Macmillan, 1874);
Culture and Anarchy: An Essay in Political and Social Criticism (London: Smith, Elder, 1869); with *Friendship's Garland* (New York: Macmillan, 1883);
St. Paul and Protestantism; with an Introduction on Puritanism and the Church of England (London: Smith, Elder, 1870; New York: Macmillan, 1883);
Friendship's Garland: Being the Conversations, Letters and Opinions of the Late Arminius, Baron von Thunder-ten-Tronckh; Collected and Edited with a Dedicatory Letter to Adolescens Leo, Esq., of "The Daily Telegraph" (London: Smith, Elder, 1871); with *Culture and Anarchy* (New York: Macmillan, 1883);

Literature and Dogma: An Essay towards a Better Apprehension of the Bible (London: Smith, Elder, 1873; New York: Macmillan, 1873);

God and the Bible: A Review of Objections to "Literature and Dogma" (London: Smith, Elder, 1875; Boston: Osgood, 1876);

Last Essays on Church and Religion (London: Smith, Elder, 1877; New York: Macmillan, 1877);

Mixed Essays (London: Smith, Elder, 1879; New York: Macmillan, 1879);

Irish Essays, and Others (London: Smith, Elder, 1882);

Discourses in America (New York & London: Macmillan, 1885);

Education Department: Special Report on Certain Points Connected with Elementary Education in Germany, Switzerland, and France (London: Eyre & Spottiswoode, 1886);

General Grant: An Estimate (Boston: Cupples, Upham, 1887); republished as *General Grant. With a Rejoinder by Mark Twain*, edited by J.Y. Simon (Carbondale: Southern Illinois University Press, 1966);

Essays in Criticism: Second Series (London & New York: Macmillan, 1888);

Civilization in the United States: First and Last Impressions of America (Boston: Cupples & Hurd, 1888);

Reports on Elementary Schools 1852-1882, edited by Sir Francis Sandford (London & New York: Macmillan, 1889);

On Home Rule for Ireland: Two Letters to "The Times" (London: Privately printed, 1891);

Matthew Arnold's Notebooks (London: Smith, Elder, 1902); republished as *The Note-Books of Matthew Arnold*, edited by Howard Foster Lowry, Karl Young, and Waldo Hilary Dunn (London & New York: Oxford University Press, 1952);

Arnold as Dramatic Critic, edited by C. K. Shorter (London: Privately printed, 1903); republished as *Letters of an Old Playgoer*, edited by Brander Matthews (New York: Columbia University Press, 1919);

Essays in Criticism: Third Series, edited by Edward J. O'Brien (Boston: Ball, 1910);

Thoughts on Education Chosen from the Writings of Matthew Arnold, edited by L. Huxley (London: Smith, Elder, 1912; New York: Macmillan, 1912);

Five Uncollected Essays of Matthew Arnold, edited by Kenneth Allott (Liverpool: University Press of Liverpool, 1953);

Essays, Letters, and Reviews by Matthew Arnold, edited by Fraser Nieman (Cambridge, Mass.: Harvard University Press, 1960).

Matthew Arnold at about the time of his first trip to America in 1883 (Elliott and Fry)

Collections: *The Works of Matthew Arnold*, edited by G. W. E. Russell. 15 volumes (London: Macmillan, 1903-1904);

The Poetical Works of Matthew Arnold, edited by C. B. Tinker and H. F. Lowry (London & New York: Oxford University Press, 1950);

Complete Prose Works, edited by R. H. Super, 11 volumes (Ann Arbor: University of Michigan Press, 1960-1977);

The Poems of Matthew Arnold, edited by Kenneth Allott (London: Longmans, 1965);

Culture and the State, edited by P. Nash (New York: Teachers College Press, 1965).

OTHER: *A Bible-Reading for Schools: The Great Prophecy of Israel's Restoration (Isaiah, Chapters 40-66) Arranged and Edited for Young Learners,*

edited by Arnold (London: Macmillan, 1872);
Isaiah XL-LXVI, with the Shorter Prophecies Allied to It, Arranged and Edited with Notes, edited by Arnold (London: Macmillan, 1875);
The Six Chief Lives from Johnson's "Lives of the Poets," with Macaulay's "Life of Johnson," edited by Arnold (London: Macmillan, 1878);
The Hundred Greatest Men: Portraits of the One Hundred Greatest Men of History, introduction by Arnold (London: Low, Marston, Searle & Rivington, 1879);
Poems of Wordsworth, edited by Arnold (London: Macmillan, 1879);
Letters, Speeches and Tracts on Irish Affairs by Edmund Burke, edited by Arnold (London: Macmillan, 1881);
Poetry of Byron, edited by Arnold (London: Macmillan, 1881);
Isaiah of Jerusalem in the Authorised English Version, with an Introduction, Corrections and Notes, edited by Arnold (London: Macmillan, 1883);
"Charles Augustin Sainte-Beuve," in *Encyclopaedia Britannica,* ninth edition (London: Black, 1886), IX: 162-165;
"Schools," in *The Reign of Queen Victoria,* edited by T. H. Ward (London: Smith, Elder, 1887), II: 238-279.

Among the major Victorian writers sharing in a revival of interest and respect in the second half of the twentieth century, Matthew Arnold is unique in that his reputation rests equally upon his poetry and his prose. Only a quarter of his productive life was given to writing poetry, but many of the same values, attitudes, and feelings that are expressed in his poems achieve a fuller or more balanced formulation in his prose. This unity was obscured for most earlier readers by the usual evaluations of his poetry as gnomic or thought-laden, or as melancholy or elegiac, and of his prose as urbane, didactic, and often satirically witty in its self-imposed task of enlightening the social consciousness of England.

Assessing his achievement as a whole, G. K. Chesterton said that under his surface raillery Arnold was, "even in the age of Carlyle and Ruskin, perhaps the most serious man alive." A later summary by H. J. Muller declares that "if in an age of violence the attitudes he engenders cannot alone save civilization, it is worth saving chiefly because of such attitudes"—a view of Arnold's continuing relevance which emphasizes his appeals to his contemporaries in the name of "culture" throughout his prose writings. It is even more striking, and would have pleased Arnold greatly, to find an intelligent and critical journalist telling newspaper readers in 1980 that if selecting three books for castaways, he would make his first choice *The Poetical Works of Matthew Arnold* (1950), because "Arnold's longer poems may be an acquired taste, but once the nut has been cracked their power is extraordinary." Arnold put his own poems in perspective in a letter to his mother on 5 June 1869: "It might be fairly urged that I have less poetical sentiment than Tennyson, and less intellectual vigour and abundance than Browning; yet, because I have perhaps more of a fusion of the two than either of them, and have more regularly applied that fusion to the main line of modern development, I am likely enough to have my turn, as they have had theirs."

The term *modern* as used by Arnold about his own writing needs examining, especially since many readers have come to see him as the most modern of the Victorians. It is defined by Arnold in "On the Modern Element in Literature," his first lecture as professor of poetry at Oxford in 1857. This lecture, the first to be delivered from that chair in English, marked Arnold's transition from poet to social as well as literary critic. Stating that the great need of a modern age is an "intellectual deliverance," Arnold found the characteristic features of such a deliverance to be a preoccupation with the arts of peace, the growth of a tolerant spirit, the capacity for refined pursuits, the formation of taste, and above all, the intellectual maturity to "observe facts with a critical spirit" and "to judge by the rule of reason." This prescription, which he found supremely fulfilled in Athens of the fifth century B.C., is of course an idealized one when applied to any age, as is obvious when Arnold writes that Athens was "a nation the meanest citizen of which could follow with comprehension the profoundly thoughtful speeches of Pericles."

Such an ideal Arnold saw as peculiarly needful if his own age was to become truly modern, truly humanized and civilized. The views he developed in his prose works on social, educational, and religious issues have been absorbed into the general consciousness, even if what his contemporary W. R. Greg called "realisable ideals" are as far as ever from being realized. The prospect of glacially slow growth never discouraged Arnold. He could harshly satirize the religious cant which would have the "festering mass" of "half-sized, half-fed, half-clothed" children in London's miserable East End "succour one another if only with a cup of cold water"; he could more gently satirize the suicide of a

Arnold's parents, Dr. Thomas Arnold and Mary Penrose Arnold (picture of Dr. Thomas Arnold from the painting in Oriel College, photo by H. W. Taunt)

Puritan businessman obsessed with the two fears of falling into poverty and of being eternally lost. But he believed above all in the need for a vision of perfection if faith in the possibility of a better society for all were to be maintained. The vision, as an eloquent conclusion to a call for practical reforms in education, suffuses the final paragraph of heightened prose in *A French Eton* (1864). The belief that sustained him and motivated his crusade on behalf of "culture" is soberly expressed in the late essay "A French Critic on Milton": "Human progress consists in a continual increase in the number of those, who, ceasing to live by the animal life alone and to feel the pleasures of sense only, come to participate in the intellectual life also, and to find enjoyment in the things of the mind."

When Arnold's poetry is considered, a different meaning must be applied to the term *modern* than that applied to the ideas of the critic, reformer, and prophet who dedicated most of his life to broadening the intellectual horizons of his countrymen—of, indeed, the whole English-speaking world. In many of his poems can be seen the psychological and emotional conflicts, the uncertainty of purpose, above all the feeling of disunity within oneself or of the individual's estrangement from society which is today called alienation and is thought of as a modern phenomenon. As Kenneth Allott said in 1954: "If a poet can ever teach us to understand what we feel, and how to live with our feelings, then Arnold is a contemporary."

The recurring themes of man's lonely state and of a search for an inner self; the rejection in "The Scholar-Gipsy" of "this strange disease of modern life,/With its sick hurry, its divided aims"; the awareness, at the end of the early poem "Resignation," "In action's dizzying eddy whirled" of "something that infects the world" make an impact a century and more later. Readers of the jet age may find wryly amusing these lines from "Stanzas in Memory of the Author of 'Obermann'" (1849):

Like children bathing on the shore
Buried a wave beneath,
The second wave succeeds before
We have had time to breathe.

But the speed of the destabilizing process of change is, after all, relative. On the other hand, no reader can fail to respond to Arnold's well-known lines in "Stanzas from the Grande Chartreuse" describing himself as "Wandering between two worlds, one dead,/The other powerless to be born." Romantic nostalgia for idealized older worlds, or for simpler states of being, is at the emotional core of many of his poems, with the insistent pressure of the present creating a conflict only to be resolved by a shift to prose and to the role of midwife, or at least prophet, of a better world in the future.

Chesterton's view of Arnold as, in spite of his fun with the Philistines, basically the most serious man of his times was supported by the publication in 1952 of the complete *Note-Books*. This "breviary of a humanist" contains quotations in six languages, copied from books over a period of thirty-six years, that caught Arnold's attention, passages which held profound meaning for him and invited meditation and reconsideration. The Bible bulks largest, followed by moral, religious, and philosophical thinkers. Even an hour a day of serious as against mere desultory reading was, in Arnold's experience, immensely "fortifying." In a letter of 1884 to Charles Eliot Norton he characteristically blends observation and prediction: "You are quite right in saying that the influence of poetry and literature appears at this moment diminishing rather than increasing. The newspapers have a good deal to do with this. The *Times,* which has much improved again, is a world, and people who read it daily hardly feel the necessity for reading a book; yet reading a book—a good book—is a discipline such as no reading of even good newspapers can ever give. But literature has in itself such powers of attraction that I am not over anxious about it."

The emphasis on religion and morality in the *Note-Books* is what one might expect of a son of Dr. Thomas Arnold, that strenuous Christian and scholarly clergyman-historian who fulfilled a prophecy that if elected headmaster of Rugby he would change the face of education "all through the Public Schools of England." But son Matthew was a more complex being, partly perhaps by virtue of genetic inheritance from his Cornish mother, Mary Penrose. There is evidence that the good doctor, whose avowed aim in education was to place moral and religious edification above mere intellectual attainment in order to turn schoolboys into young Christian gentlemen, felt some disappointment at times over the behavior of Matthew, who was less amenable, apparently, than were his brothers and sisters. Some of this "worldly" behavior, which puzzled and alarmed family and friends and caused great surprise at the serious tone and substance of his first published poems, was probably a sign of incipient polarities and conflicts. It marked his school and university days and to some extent his

Rugby School, where Dr. Arnold was headmaster and Matthew Arnold was one of his students (photo by H. W. Taunt)

earlier years in the larger world, years illuminated not only by his poems but even more by his letters to Arthur Hugh Clough; the important collection of these letters published in 1932 gave fresh stimulus and direction to Arnold studies.

Following five years under tutors at Laleham and at Rugby, Arnold was sent for a year to his father's old school, Winchester College, presumably for discipline as well as instruction. At Winchester he won a prize for verse recitation with a passage from Byron and a barrage of potato peelings from horrified schoolmates who heard him casually telling the headmaster that the work of the school was really quite light. The fifth and sixth forms he spent at Rugby, where he did well without obvious effort, and where on one occasion he delighted his friends by making faces at them over his father's head from the position behind Dr. Arnold's chair that served for punishment. He won prizes for Latin verse and for English essay and verse—his prize poem *Alaric at Rome* (1840) was printed at Rugby—and climaxed his public school career with a scholarship to Balliol College, Oxford, in 1840. At Oxford he established an intimate friendship with Clough, the former Rugby student who had most completely fulfilled Dr. Arnold's aim of intellectual brilliance crowned by Christian fervor and moral earnestness. "I verily believe," Clough said, "my whole being is soaked through with the wishing and hoping and striving to do the school good"; he later transferred this compulsion to society, earning from Arnold the mocking title of "Citizen" Clough. There was a whole other side to Clough, as the satirical wit and realistic substance of many of his poems were to show, but his hyperactive conscience and often paralyzing dissection of desires and motives have frequently been adduced as the effect on sensitive natures of Dr. Arnold's standards of prayer and purity.

There was little evidence at this time of a similar influence on Matthew Arnold. The touches of mischief and resistance displayed in boyish years developed at Oxford into outright dandyism and independence, entertaining but also at times disturbing his more conventional friends. Clough records with amusement and reproach that "Matt is full of Parisianism; Theatre in general, and Rachel in special: he enters the room with a chanson of Beranger's on his lips—for the sake of French words almost conscious of tune: . . . his hair is guiltless of English scissors: he breakfasts at 12 . . . and in the week . . . he has been to Chapel *once*." This Frenchiness extended to the reading of George Sand's novels, no doubt with a sense of daring in the Victorian atmosphere of rectitude and distrust of things foreign. In part it was a romantic response to vivid descriptions of nature and to a passionate gospel of freedom in human relations; in larger part it was a response to the element of social idealism based on a belief in equality, as recalled in his generous obituary tribute of 1877 to George Sand's greatness of spirit and her civilizing influence. Visiting her at her home in Nohant in 1846 and following the actress Rachel to Paris to see every performance for six weeks must have been seen by his friends, however, as Byronic and dangerous adventures.

In the years at Balliol a deeper source of concern to his friends than his rather extravagant dress and behavior was his careless attitude to his studies in the formally required subjects. Only prodding and coaching got him even a second class degree, though his general performance was apparently good enough to let him join Clough as a fellow of Oriel College. Clough had been expected on all sides to get a first instead of the second he also received, but in his case the distractions were part of that period of hectic religious strife. Young men at Oxford were, as Clough described himself, caught "like a straw drawn up the draught of a chimney" in the anguished debates swirling around the Tractarian or Oxford Movement and the dominant figure of John Henry Newman, who was soon to move on with some disciples to the Roman Catholic church. Differences between the Roman and Anglican positions and difficulties in subscribing to the articles of faith required of communicants in the Church of England were only the chief among problems exercising sensitive young minds at Oxford in those days. But the soul-searching and tormented inner debate which later led Clough, unwilling to subscribe to the Thirty-nine Articles, to resign his Oriel fellowship, were even then foreign to Arnold's cool and skeptical consideration of religious dogma. He was moved by the imaginative and spiritual eloquence of Newman, but he was after all the son of an aggressively liberal reformer in matters of Church and State. (Dr. Arnold, who died suddenly in 1842, had been appointed professor of modern history at Oxford in 1841, at a time when echoes of his searing attack on Newman and the "Oxford Malignants" in the *Edinburgh Review* were still reverberating.) The tone of a letter from Arnold to John Duke Coleridge in 1845 is noncommittal, even playful. Telling his friend not to let admiration for the sermons of Thomas Arnold reduce his admiration for Newman, Arnold said: "I should be unwilling to think that they did so in my own case, but owing to my utter want of prejudice . . . I find it perfectly possible to admire them both."

Arnold's behavior during those early years was a mask, enabling him to keep others at arm's length while he tried to make up his own mind, to explore his own nature and needs. His preferred reading is revealing. He shared the general enthusiasm of his friends for Carlyle's attacks on materialism and sham, and the exalting of great men and of character in *Heroes, Hero-Worship, and the Heroic in History* (1841) may have inspired his own Oxford prize poem on Cromwell (1843). His preferences included Emerson, with his themes of "Self-Reliance" and "Trust thyself!"; Goethe, who taught that the main thing for man is to learn to master himself; and Spinoza, whose philosophy contains the idea that man's need is to affirm his own essence, to follow the law of his being. He had developed a strategy of detachment, as against Clough's commitment to the issues of the day; and the introspective analysis of his own nature and of his relations to men and ideas permeates the correspondence with Clough. He wrote to Coleridge in 1843 protesting against the general impression "as to my want of interest in my friends which you say they have begun to attribute to me. It is an old subject" and "the accusation, as you say, is not true. I laugh too much and they make one's laughter mean too much. However, the result is that when one wishes to be serious one cannot but fear a half suspicion on one's friends' parts that one is laughing, and, so, the difficulty gets worse and worse." When, seven years later, Charlotte Brontë met Arnold in Crabb Robinson's home, she found him striking and even prepossessing in appearance, but foppish, and added: "Ere long a real modesty appeared under his assumed conceit, and genuine intellectual aspirations, as well as high educational acquirements, displaced superficial affectations."

Arnold's drive to self-understanding and self-control may suggest a wish for a detached and self-sufficient position from which to contemplate human events and the historical flow, and could explain a change in the story of the young Egyptian king Mycerinus in Arnold's early poem of that name. Having heard from an oracle that he is to die in six years, although he has tried to atone for his father's selfish and unjust reign by a virtuous life and justice for his subjects, Mycerinus turns in scorn from his gods and his "sorrowing people" to spend the last years of his life in revelry. The possibility Arnold adds to that decision in lines 107-111 may be self-revealing:

> It may be on that joyless feast his eye
> Dwelt with mere outward seeming; he, within,
> Took measure of his soul, and knew its strength,
> And by that silent knowledge, day by day,
> Was calmed, ennobled, comforted, sustained.

Arnold's appointment as private secretary to the elderly Whig statesman Lord Lansdowne in 1847, after a term as assistant master at Rugby School, gave him over the next four years a vantage point for observation of the "joyless feast" of nineteenth-century industrialism and class discontent and the revolutionary upheavals of 1848 throughout Europe. The striving to take "measure of his soul" is evident in poems and in the letters to Clough, as is the struggle to attain a state of peace and calm, a balance between withdrawal and commitment, a reconciliation of the claims of reason and the feelings and of the "two desires" which "toss about the poet's feverish blood./One drives him to the world without/And one to solitude." Clough had committed himself to action and wrote Arnold from Rome describing his situation during bombardment of the city by the French armies. Arnold's reaction to Clough's reforming zeal appears in his two sonnets "To a Republican Friend." The first sonnet declares: "God knows it, I am with you" for "if to despise the barren, optimistic sophistries of comfortable moles" and "If thoughts, not idle, while before me flow/The armies of the homeless and unfed—/If these are yours, if this is what you are,/Then am I yours, and what you feel, I share." The second sonnet counsels a longer view, for "When I muse on what life is, I seem/Rather to patience prompted" than to the hope proclaimed by France "so loud." Necessity spares us "narrower margin than we deem," and the day when "liberated man" will burst through "the network superposed by selfish occupation" will not "dawn at a human nod."

Such sympathy with revolutionary aims but distrust of precipitate action could be expected of the young man whose "respect for the reason" sent him to Locke and Spinoza, and who already was turning from Beranger's "fade" Epicureanism to the stoic philosopher Epictetus. Arnold was especially attracted to the tragic dramatist Sophocles, whose "even-balanced soul," in the famous line from Arnold's sonnet "To a Friend," made him preeminently the writer "who saw life steadily and saw it whole." But though a philosophical overview, strengthened by classical art, could steady relations with the outer world, it was put to a much more severe test by the new experience that came Arnold's way on his travels. The powerful force of romantic love threatened to frustrate entirely the longing to take "measure of his soul" and so to be "calmed, ennobled, comforted, sustained."

The long dispute over whether Marguerite, the French girl Arnold fell in love with in Switzerland, was real or imaginary was settled by the publication of the letters to Clough. In a letter of 29 September 1848 he will "go to Thun" and "linger one day at the Hotel Bellevue for the sake of the blue eyes of one of its inmates." On 23 September 1849 he is in Thun "in a curious and not altogether comfortable state: however tomorrow I carry my aching head to the mountains and to my cousin the Bhunlis Alp." Research has failed to provide further clues, but adding these to the names and places of physical details in the poems has allowed the majority view to prevail: the Marguerite of the Switzerland lyrics was indeed real, as was the anguish of the lover who could not surrender himself to passion. For a man who believed above all in self-control and integrity, the outcome of a conflict between the Platonic and the Byronic (or between the shades of Dr. Arnold and of George Sand) could not be long in doubt. There is as much of relief as of desolation in the poem "Self-Dependence." Standing at the prow of the ship bearing him back to England, "Weary of myself, and sick of asking/ What I am, and what I ought to be," Arnold sends "a look of passionate desire" (the only one on record) to the stars, and asks that they "Calm me, ah, compose me to the end!" The Socratic answer comes, that to live "self-poised" as the stars do, there is only one prescription: " 'Resolve to be thyself; and know that he,/Who finds himself, loses his misery!' "

Having survived exposure to the storms of passion in the Alps, Arnold still felt the need for a love and companionship compatible with the needs of ordinary human nature, and before long he was attracted by the charms of a more suitable English girl, the daughter of a judge. The conventional courtship which followed, and which produced some charming lyrics, was prolonged until Arnold could obtain a position with an income that would support a wife. He achieved this when Lord Lansdowne had him appointed inspector of schools in April 1851, and the marriage to Frances Lucy Wightman took place in June. Though his first volume of poetry, *The Strayed Reveller and Other Poems* (1849), and the second, *Empedocles on Etna and Other*

Arnold's wife, Frances Lucy Wightman Arnold (courtesy of Mrs. M. C. Moorman)

Poems (1852), both published under the pseudonym "A.," received limited attention and were soon withdrawn from circulation in spite of praise from a discerning few, Arnold continued writing poetry. His reputation was established with his third volume, *Poems: A New Edition* (1853), the first published under his name. It omitted "Empedocles on Etna" and the early poem "The New Sirens," but contained two new poems which have been widely known and liked ever since, "Sohrab and Rustum" and "The Scholar-Gipsy." Most of Arnold's best poems are in these volumes—except "Dover Beach," which, though not published until 1867, has been convincingly assigned to 1851 by Kenneth Allott.

During this period in which Arnold moved from a studied aloofness through turbulence to the desired calm, though with an awareness that *"Calm's not life's crown, though calm is well"* ("Youth and Calm"), the letters gradually change in tone from the early touches of extravagance and badinage to exhortation and even reproach. Clough, unable to settle down to any one job, including those found for him by Arnold, is finally told that he is "the most conscientious man I ever knew" but "on some lines morbidly so." A letter commenting on this high-minded (or irresolute) inability to find anything worth doing for long is both anxious and pointed: "The mental harass of an uncertain life must be far more irksome than the ennui of the most monotonous employment." That such concern for his old friend was a way of checking similar tendencies in himself seems apparent from a letter of 1849, when Arnold was breaking away from Marguerite: "What I must tell you is that I have never yet succeeded in any one great occasion in consciously mastering myself. . . . at the critical point I am too apt to hoist up the mainsail to the wind and let her drive."

Though he could generously concede in looking back "an invincible languor of spirit" compared with Clough's "genuineness and faith," Arnold by 1852 had arrived at a point where he could say firmly, "Nothing can absolve us from the duty of doing all we can to keep alive our courage and activity." A lightness of touch still appeared at times, as when he wrote from Fox How, the Arnold family home in the Lake District, while on holiday from the wearying routine of school inspecting and marking papers: "I for my part find here that I could willingly fish all day and read the newspapers all the evening and so live—but I am not pleased with the results in myself of even a day or two of such life." The words *courage, duty,* and *activity* suggest the voice of Dr. Arnold helping to point the direction Matthew was to follow after 1853. Yet the early poem "The Voice," attributed by Allott to the impact of Newman's sermons, should be related to the late essay on Emerson in which Arnold recalls the effect of Newman's eloquence, those "words and thoughts which were a religious music—subtle, sweet, mournful." The response to both sensuous and spiritual beauty which made Arnold a poet, and emerged at times throughout his prose, appears in the lines which tell of

> Those lute-like tones which in the bygone year
> Did steal into mine ear—
> Blew such a thrilling summons to my will,
> Yet could not shake it;
> Made my tossed heart its very life-blood spill,
> Yet could not break it.

Arnold's poetics, as revealed in the letters to Clough, show a gradual shift from a predominantly aesthetic to a predominantly moral emphasis. In criticizing Clough's poems he warns against a striving after "individuality" and, even more, against attempting to "solve the Universe." There is a "deficiency of the *beautiful* in your poems," which alone is "properly *poetical* as distinguished from rhetorical, devotional, or metaphysical" and which makes him "doubt your being an *artist.*" The "sincerity" in all of Clough's poems must produce "a powerful effect on the reader," for "the spectacle of a writer striving evidently to get breast to breast with reality is always full of instruction and very invigorating." But these merits are not such as to produce the effect of "naturalness . . . an absolute propriety—of form, as the sole *necessary* of Poetry as such: where the greatest wealth and depth of matter is merely a superfluity in the Poet *as such.*" When form of conception and form of expression achieve congruity one has "the poet's highest result," but Clough's "mode of expression" seems to be "arbitrarily adopted." He seems to be trying "to get to the bottom of an object instead of grouping objects," which is "fatal to the sensuousness of poetry," and Arnold quotes a line from his own poem "Resignation" to affirm that "not deep the Poet sees, but wide." The end of poetry is to "attain the *beautiful,*" which is realized when a poem "gives PLEASURE, not excites curiosity and reflexion."

As with the urging to self-mastery and to useful activity, Arnold is again talking to himself as much as to Clough. The italicized and capitalized earnestness hides a growing suspicion that for him a pure and autonomous aesthetic is not possible. He offers as one reason for the contemporary failure to reach poetic heights the feeling of "how deeply *unpoetical* the age and all one's surroundings are," an age he elsewhere describes as arid, blank, and barren, with our "spread of luxury, our physical enervation, the absence of great *natures,* the unavoidable contact with millions of small ones." The *Architectonicè* of form he speaks of can only be found among the ancients, because, as he says in the 1853 preface to *Poems: A New Edition,* "They, at any rate, knew what they wanted in Art, and we do not." The exquisite bits and images and the exuberance of the Romantics and the Elizabethans will not help us; only the grandly simple overall harmony of form, style, and substance will.

Arnold finally faces up to the fact that his classical ideal embraces much more than the aesthetic values he has been insisting on with Clough. Modern poetry, to serve the age well, "can only subsist by its contents: by becoming a complete magister vitae as the poetry of the ancients did: by including, as theirs did, religion with poetry." Poetry is something more than Keats's "Beauty is Truth, Truth Beauty," of which Arnold was later to say that it is *not* "all ye need to know," though it is much. It is a source of moral therapy for the age and a surrogate for the weakening Christian faith. These views anticipate Arnold's lectures *On Translating Homer* (1861), in which "nobility" is seen as a major characteristic of Homer, and "The Study of Poetry" (1880), which proclaims that "the strongest part of our religion today is its unconscious poetry."

A parallel shift in emphasis is apparent in the definitions of style. It is at first simply "saying in the best way *what you have to say*," though Arnold adds that "what you have to say depends on your age." The thoughts expressed in an article by Carlyle are "every newspaper's"; it is "the style and feeling by which the beloved man appears" which make it "solemn" and "deeply restful." (A year later Carlyle becomes a "moral desperado," presumably because of his increasingly strenuous demands that we must *do* something and do it with all our might.) The new emphasis appears when Arnold declares that "there are two offices of Poetry—one to add to one's store of thoughts and feelings—another to compose and elevate the mind by a sustained tone, numerous allusions, and a grand style." Milton is mentioned, but the main points are the dismissal of Keats as an impetuous "style and form seeker," and the praise of Sophocles as exhibiting "the grand moral effects of style. For the style is the expression of the nobility of the poet's character, as the matter is the expression of the richness of his mind: but on men character produces as much effect as mind."

Arnold's perception of beauty and greatness in art has shifted from the aesthetic impact of a unity in form of conception and form of expression to the moral impact of a unity of style and substance which exhibits and influences character. Poetry must convey the emotional warmth and spiritual power that religion was losing in an era of sectarian strife on the one hand and agnostic indifference on the other. "If one loved what was beautiful and interesting in itself [the collocation of terms is noteworthy] *passionately* enough, one would produce what was excellent without troubling oneself with religious dogmas at all. As it is, we are *warm* only when dealing with the last," and because warmth is a blessing and frigidity a curse, Arnold would have "most others" stay "on the old religious road."

This letter of 6 September 1853 foreshadows the Arnold of the 1870s who tried by humanistic reinterpretation to preserve the Bible and Christianity for the masses. What is pertinent here is the attempt to find in great poetry a supreme moral and spiritual influence as well as an ideal aesthetic form. In a letter written three months later, Arnold's rejection of Clough's praise for "The Scholar-Gipsy" is almost Carlylian in tone. "I am glad you like the Gipsy Scholar," he says, "but what does it *do* for you? Homer *animates*—Shakespeare *animates*—in its poor way I think Sohrab and Rustum *animates*—the Gipsy Scholar at best awakens a pleasing melancholy." But what men want is "something to *animate* and *ennoble* them . . . I believe a feeling of this kind is the basis of my nature—and of my poetics."

The names of Homer and Shakespeare here, like the frequent praise of Sophocles elsewhere, suggest that for Arnold the high calling of poetry for the age could only be realized in the classical forms of epic and drama. Clearly set forth in the 1853 preface, the preference is further refined in his first Oxford lecture when he says that "the great poets of the modern period of Greece are . . . the dramatic poets." Indeed, Arnold tried at that time to offer his English readers an example of the kind of poetry he still wished to write, and felt ought to be written. In a letter to his sister Jane he admitted that he had not succeeded, and could not succeed. *Merope* (1858) might exhibit perfection of form, but "to attain or approach perfection in the region of thought and feeling, and to unite this with perfection of form, demands not merely effort and labour, but an actual tearing of oneself to pieces." Though he blames the age and his occupation for not letting him devote his whole life to poetry as Wordsworth could, he adds that Shelley and Byron could also do this, "and were besides driven by their demon to do so." Driven by no such demon, but by a need to control impulse by reason (and later anarchy by culture), Arnold produced poems reflecting conflicts that were a genuine part of his emotional and intellectual experience, but not the poem of his ideal that would both illuminate and transcend experience in the artistic perfection of classical form.

How much this ideal embraced was later to be seen in his praise of the Sophoclean power of "imaginative reason" and in his lectures *On the Study of Celtic Literature* (1867). He credits the Celts not with "great poetical works" but with poetry having "an air of greatness," for in poetry "emotion counts for so much," but "reason, measure, sanity, also count for so much." In a letter to his mother, referring to the poems of Jean Ingelow, he gives the simplest summary of his poetical creed: "It is a great deal to give one true feeling in poetry, and I think she seemed to be able to do that; but I do not at present very much care for poetry unless it can give me true *thought* as well. It is the alliance of these two that makes great poetry, the only poetry really worth very much."

Arnold noted in the preface to the second edition of *Poems: A New Edition* (1854) the charge that he had neglected the lyric, "that region of the poetical field which is chiefly cultivated at present." In his *On Translating Homer: Last Words* (1862) he was to make handsome amends. After asserting, and trying to illustrate by his own specimens, that English hexameters were best for translating Homer into English verse, he rejected the ballad as inadequate, saying of two lines from Macaulay's *Lays of Ancient Rome* (1842) that they were "hard to read without a cry of pain." But a case is then made for "purely emotional poetry," to which the question of suitability for narrative is irrelevant because it is "so powerful and absorbing in itself." He continues: "When there comes in poetry what I may call the *lyrical cry*, this transfigures everything, makes everything grand; the simplest form may be here even an advantage, because the flame of the emotion glows through and through it more easily." In Wordsworth and Keats the "lyrical cry" may transform a simple stanza or even a passage from an "ampler form." From this concession, Arnold's flexibility and growth as a critic were to carry him on to the isolating of lines revealing "natural magic" in his essay on Maurice de Guérin, to the "Celtic note" in his lectures, and finally to his famous "touchstone" method of detecting supreme poetic quality in single lines and short passages. Such lines or passages (one thinks again of the *Note-Books*) Arnold found from his own experience were capable of setting up aesthetic, moral, and spiritual resonances which echo in the mind and soul, achieving through style and interpretative power something of the "grand" effects he found in epic and drama, and blending into his final definition of poetry as a "criticism of life" under the laws of "poetic truth" and "poetic beauty."

Arnold's criticism of Clough's poems, that they were arbitrary rather than inevitable in form, can be applied in large degree to his own poems, in terms of structure or pattern. For instance, there seems no good reason for a ballad type of stanza in the Obermann poems, or the Anglo-Saxon verse stresses in "Consolation," or in most cases for the choice of the sonnet form. Yet his patterns were original at times and could be appropriate to theme and mood, as is the adapted stanza from Keats's odes to the lonely musings and loving natural descriptions in "The Scholar-Gipsy" and "Thyrsis."

Arnold at about the age of thirty-eight (Wordsworth Library, Grasmere)

The conventional structure of four octosyllabic lines followed by a couplet is effective where the pressure of emotion, usually elegiac, is strong enough, as in the two poems "To Marguerite" and in "Stanzas from the Grande Chartreuse." Where the poem is essentially argumentative or rhetorical, as often in the sonnets, rhythms and sounds can result which read like Macaulay's revenge ("Who prop, thou ask'st, in these bad days, my mind?" or "A prop gave way! crash fell a platform! lo"). Exclamation marks and italics and the intrusive "Ah" are sometimes stumbling blocks for readers. Against such evidence that Arnold had no ear for euphony, much less music, one can place "The Forsaken Merman" and "Dover Beach," lyrics like "Longing" and "Requiescat," the ending of "Sohrab and Rustum," and the last section of "The Church of Brou."

Arnold's characteristic verse structures tend to depart from the traditional. Stanzas or verse paragraphs of varying length and of varying line length make him a forerunner of free verse practice, as in

"A Summer Night" and "Dover Beach," in the romantically melancholy and melodiously rhymed "The Forsaken Merman," and in unrhymed poems such as "The Strayed Reveller" and "The Future." This last poem, and others of more conventional form such as "Human Life," "Self-Deception," and "Morality," all reflecting upon the human condition, help to explain the view of Arnold's poetry as thought-laden or "gnomic" or even, among hostile critics like Edith Sitwell and T. S. Eliot, as academic versifying. Such a view is confirmed for some readers by the solemn march of unrhymed three-stress lines in Arnold's "Pindarics": "Heine's Grave," "Rugby Chapel," "Haworth Churchyard," and, to a large extent, in "The Youth of Man" and "The Youth of Nature." (Clough, leaving for a temporary stay in America, advised his fiancée to console herself during his absence by reading Matt Arnold on "Morality," moving one to ponder the curious nature of Victorian courtship.) But perhaps the most Arnoldian verse form is that mixture of modes or genres which made it difficult for him to classify some of his own poems. The lyrical drama "The Strayed Reveller," the dramatic narrative "The Sick King of Bokhara," the diversity of verse patterns in his major work "Empedocles on Etna" all suggest a creative and original element in Arnold's poetics as well as an urge to "animate" and "ennoble" mankind. Of "Empedocles on Etna" Swinburne said: "Nothing can be more deep and exquisite in poetical tact than this succession of harmonies, diverse without a discord."

Arnold's twofold search for knowledge of himself and of the world was from the beginning philosophical in nature. Modern poets, Arnold told Clough, "must begin with an Idea of the world in order not to be prevailed over by the world's multitudinousness: or if they cannot get that, at least with isolated ideas." One must begin with a controlling principle or be overwhelmed by experience. But experience resisted this rational commitment to "the high white star of truth" and compelled the honest poet to record his frustrations and mental sufferings. To achieve understanding by embracing or surrendering to experience was for Arnold a dangerous course, for it involved risking the sacrifice of the reason to the senses and feelings. Yet any answer arrived at without the sanction of emotion was, he said, arid and incomplete. This conflict runs through much of Arnold's poetry, with his deepest feelings attaching to the unresolved debate, to the anxious questions and the ambiguous or dusty answers. Ideas in his case were to come from his own kind of immersion in experience, through professional work in education and the extension of criticism from literature to society and religion. The view of truth as multifaceted, the attempt at a synthesis in the phrase "the imaginative reason," the definition of religion as "morality, touched with emotion"—all these later formulations suggest acceptance and interpretation of experience as a better way than prior commitment to an Idea of coping with the world's multitudinousness.

A useful approach can be made to Arnold's poetry by recognizing three broad divisions. First, there is that large body of reflective or gnomic verse, where the poet's voice is freely heard but which shows varying degrees of detachment, in tones of questioning or stoicism or contemplation. Second, there are the lyric poems of intense personal engagement in the human situation, especially the love poems with their burden of longing and suffering and the elegies with their milder melancholy. Third, there are the narrative and dramatic poems, which attempt to achieve objectivity and distance by form, character, and plot, and by the remoteness of myth and legend. Qualities marking these categories respectively are notably present in "In Utrumque Paratus," in the lyric "Absence" from the Switzerland group, and in "The Strayed Reveller."

The first category most obviously anticipates Arnold's later development as critic, consisting as it does of poems in which differing views on man, nature, or art are balanced or contrasted, advanced or rejected. "In Utrumque Paratus" shows that as early as 1846 Arnold could contemplate with equanimity alternative answers to man's cosmic questions. The idealist hypothesis of the first three stanzas ("If, in the silent mind of One all-pure/At first imagined lay/The sacred world") is balanced by the materialist hypothesis of the last three stanzas ("But, if the wild unfathered mass no birth/In divine seats hath known"). What emerges is a twofold moral reflection on the unifying theme of man's lonely state.

According to the idealist hypothesis, compatible with religious belief, man can achieve self-transcendence and a return to the divine by virtue of the divine element in himself, but only if a "lonely pureness" enables him to remount "the coloured dream of life." According to the materialist hypothesis, compatible with scientific thinking, man's unique self-consciousness, his "sun-bathed head," will separate him from his "still-dreaming brother-world" and make him "when most self-exalted most alone," in need of the sober warning "Be not too proud!" This is the Arnold who was later to stress the multiple approach to truth, to say in his literary and religious criticism that both physical science and metaphysics are inadequate to account for the nature and needs of man. The dominant emotion here is akin to that in the Marguerite poems. But there the echoing "alone" and "lonely" and "loneliness" are charged with the lyric cry of personal suffering; here, with the imagination employed in contemplative mood on the cosmic scale, the loneliness attaching to each philosophical alternative has a grave serenity.

Two of the more interesting themes considered in this exploratory and critical way are the relationship of man and nature and the conflicting claims of reason and feeling, the latter indeed omnipresent in Arnold's poetry. The first theme can best be examined with reference to several poems, the second within the limits of one poem, "The New Sirens," a poem which also makes a convenient transition to the second category.

In an age of increasingly complex views of man's relationship with nature, with the extremes marked by Wordsworth's "Let Nature be your teacher" and Tennyson's "Nature red in tooth and claw," it is not surprising that Arnold should express himself in the noncommittal terms of "In Utrumque Paratus." His later commitment to a dualistic psychological doctrine of two selves, with a higher human nature being the area of moral and religious truths, got him into difficulties reflected in his exclamation in *Literature and Dogma* (1873), "What pitfalls are in that word Nature!" In his poetry, however, the question of relationship with nature is generally dealt with by assuming a distinctive (not necessarily a higher) human nature, allowing man to select for emulation those aspects of nature which will promote his moral growth.

An angry outburst in one sonnet, "In Harmony with Nature," asserts that man can never be "fast friends" with a "cruel" Nature, but must "pass her" or else "rest her slave." Yet Arnold gave little heed to the ruthless aspect of nature as the scene of a struggle for survival, a theme in imaginative writing from *In Memoriam* to *Jean Christophe* and the subject of an essay, "Wordsworth in the Tropics," by his grandnephew Aldous Huxley. In fact, another sonnet entitled "Quiet Work" apparently contradicts the first by beginning "One lesson, Nature, let me learn of thee." The contradiction is resolved when the sonnet goes on to say that the lesson is one of "Toil unsevered from tranquillity," learned from "thy sleepless ministers." This is the nature of cosmic grandeur, of eternal law, compatible with the concluding lines of "Religious Isolation": "To its own impulse every creature stirs;/Live by thy light, and earth will live by hers." The lesson can be that learned in "Self-Dependence" from the stars and waters, from God's works "In their own tasks all their powers pouring." Or it can be that in "A Summer Night," where the pure heavens remain "A world above man's head, to let him see/How boundless might his soul's horizons be,/How vast, yet of what clear transparency." Though "The Youth of Man" and "The Youth of Nature" stress the separateness of man and nature, other poems convey a sense of oneness in terms of soul or spirit. In "Lines Written in Kensington Gardens" the poet, relaxing in the air of a "lone, open glade," begs an inner peace from the "Calm soul of all things." The elegy to Arnold's brother and sister-in-law, "A Southern Night," ends with an invocation to nature:

Mild o'er her grave, ye mountains, shine!
Gently by his, ye waters, glide!
To that in you which is divine,
They were allied.

When in "A Wish" the poet pleads, "There let me gaze, till I become/In soul, with what I gaze on, wed!" the reader may feel that, as in some earlier poems, elements from the *Bhagavad Gita* have mingled with those from the Stoics and Spinoza—an appropriate response in view of Arnold's admission that he lacked philosophical consistency and his nonchalant attitude that it did not matter.

The emotions in these poems that find peace or inspiration in a spiritual union do not derive from a resolving of the moral and philosophical ambivalences about man's relationship with nature. They come rather from one of Arnold's deepest sources of poetical feeling, his sheer pleasure in natural beauty, whether as bringing peace or joy, or as fit symbols for the imagination. Whether it is pictorial—"Pale, dew-drenched, half-shut roses gleam" ("Resignation"), or touched with metaphor—"old oaks, whose red wet leaves/Are jewelled with bright drops of rain" (*Tristram and Iseult*), or whether it blends the senses in a lyrical evocation of the loved one's voice—"has some wet bird-haunted English lawn/Lent it the music of its trees at dawn?" ("Parting")—Arnold's imagery shows a genuine delight in the world of physical objects. It is the source for his tribute to Wordsworth as one who "laid us as we lay at birth/On the cool flowery lap of earth."

On the level of symbolic fitness, Arnold could "yearn to the greatness of Nature" in her power to uplift man by his contemplation of the stars and the "cold lunar beams" and the "high mountain-platforms." Her gift of water, of dews and rain and clear-flowing streams, could suggest both a purity free of the world's contaminations and an appropriate symbol for the life of man. In his letters he speaks of his "passion for clear water" and of the "positive pain" of dry water-courses in Italy sending his mind back to the clear rivers of Scotland, of a charm "so infinite to me." He complained to Clough of the "curse" of dirty water, of "the real pain it occasions one who looks upon water as the Mediator between the inanimate and man."

Two letters are especially relevant to the kind of writing in this division of Arnold's poems, poems so often intellectual in impact and bare in style. A letter to Clough describes these poems as having "weight" but "little or no charm," and wonders whether "I shall ever have heat and radiance enough to pierce the clouds that are massed around me." Yet escape or isolation was impossible—"woe was upon me if I analyzed not my situation" and "the modern situation in its true *blankness* and *barrenness* and *unpoetrylessness*." The other letter, to his mother on 3 March 1865, refers to the success of his newly published *Essays in Criticism,* and continues: "No one has a stronger and more abiding sense than I have of the daemonic element—as Goethe called it—which underlies and encompasses our life; but I think, as Goethe thought, that the right thing is, while conscious of this element, and of all that there is inexplicable around one, to keep pushing on one's posts into the darkness, and to establish no post that is not perfectly in light and firm." The dominant effect conveyed by these letters is of an independent mind, the primacy of reason, and the compulsion to understand the world as well as oneself. The shift from poetry to prose, and from introspection to action of a suitable kind, was mainly a shift in emphasis. Yet reason and the moral will were never to have it all their own way. In the many-sided search for truth, the critic was never to lose entirely the poet's sense of the "daemonic" and the "inexplicable," the mystery of the buried life, or the darkness beyond the last lighted post.

If the poems Arnold is obviously referring to tend to be overly intellectual (one notes the word "analyzed"), they often compensate by a feeling of intimacy. They are poems of the speaking voice, sharing thoughts with the reader as he walks or stands or sits with the speaker, and if not intense in expression, the best of them awaken a response to ideas that have evoked emotion as well as thought in the poet. "Resignation," to his sister Jane—here called Fausta—is a sort of verse epistle. It considers diverse patterns in the life of man, theorizes about the nature of the poet in relation to his fellows, and comments rather bleakly on man's environment. Yet the reader finds it no mere academic exercise in verse, as he follows the poet's eye from the brook with its "clear, shallow, turf-fringed bed" down to the noisy town "capped with faint smoke," or sees the Gypsy children who "in dark knots crouch round the wild flame," or feels man's isolation from "the strange-scrawled rocks, the lonely sky," or shares the Vergilian mood when the poet contemplates the human and rural scene: "Leaned on his gate, he gazes—tears/Are in his eyes, and in his ears/The murmur of a thousand years."

This blend of participation and detachment, an aloof and considering stance modified by an engaged sympathy, is characteristic of Arnold, and is often a source of that charm which, in a depressed moment, he told Clough he lacked. Yet although Swinburne praised the poetic power of concrete imagery and modernized myth in "The New Sirens" and successfully urged its reprinting, Arnold's agreement with Clough that it was a "mumble" indicates his wish to be clearly understood in his line of thought. The poem presents opposing cases for judgment and comes reluctantly to a decision. It projects the dialogue in the mind, or externalizes it, without objectifying it in narrative or drama. It is tempting to see Arnold here as a kind of Greek chorus commenting on the processional movement and contrasting attitudes which he has evoked, but the effect is rather that of the poet interpreting the scenes and figures in a tapestry, finding allegorical meaning for the life of man and, ironically, for the state of his own mind. (Arnold rejects, in the 1853 preface, art which seeks to provide an "allegory of the state of one's own mind.") A more attractive and compelling poem than Arnold first thought it to be, "The New Sirens" nevertheless does have enough of a stage-managed debate about it to come marginally within this first category of his poems, as it weighs the opposing claims of feeling and reason to a dominant role in the life of man.

The new Romantic sirens are not the cruel sirens of old, luring men to destruction, but they are as seductive. They persuade men that there is "as staunch adherence/Due to pleasure as to pain," that the heart "gleans rarer secrets than the toiling head," and that "only, what we feel, we know." The poet has been a joyful member of their train. Yet he has heard "sounds of warning" as "the hoarse boughs labour in the wind," and even though before their pleading "all/Man's grave reasons disappear," they have nothing to offer when their "flowers are overblown" but the "folded palms" of ennui, or at best, in "mad succession/Fits of joy and fits of pain." Rejection does not bring serenity. The poet's thoughts stray "to where at sunrise" he had seen the sirens playing, and "if the dawning into daylight never grew," the roses and lilies need never be exchanged for yew and cypress. But the "cold night-air" and "north-wind blowing," bringing thoughts of "old age, youth's fatal morrow," cannot be countered by this "earthward-bound devotion."

This poem anticipates the essay "Pagan and Medieval Religious Sentiment" in its turning away from a life of "scent, and song, and flowers" because these will not suffice to bring "brightness" to the "sorrow-stricken day." It also stands in stark contrast to Keats's tribute to the fullness of pagan life, "rich in the simple worship of a day," which concludes his *Ode to Maia*, a passage Arnold was himself to offer as a specimen of one kind of greatness in poetry. The romanticism of feeling in Arnold's poem takes the form of regret that what the new sirens have to offer is inadequate, a feeling hardly able to offset the insistent classical morality in the searching questions of the poem, but strong enough to keep him a practicing poet for a number of years. It appears in a letter of 25 January 1851, a letter that is virtually a commentary on "The Forsaken Merman": "The aimless and unsettled, but also open and liberal state of our youth we *must* perhaps all leave and take refuge in our morality and character: but with most of us it is a melancholy passage from which we emerge shorn of so many beams that we are almost tempted to quarrel with the law of nature which imposes it on us." When the dream sirens had so firmly been put in their place by the young moralist some half-dozen years before, this letter's continuing lament suggests the influence of a more tangible siren. Not only did Marguerite give substance to the shadow, the experience of love brought into sharper focus and painful reality the balanced musings of the earlier poem.

To make of the love poems and the elegies a second major division among Arnold's poems is to see them, first, as dominated by the need for self-discovery and for wholeness of personality, and secondly, as poems in which the contrasting claims on man's nature of passion and reason, and of solitude and society, find their most intense and personal expression. They are poems of confessional suffering and fractured sensibility, where the poet is too much involved in the emotional struggle to interpret experience in the light of philosophical alternatives or a dialectical process. They show the divided or alienated mind which so many, including Arnold himself, have seen as the marks of his early writing.

If all love poems are egotistical in seeing the loved one as the fulfillment in reality of the lover's dreams, Arnold's Switzerland lyrics are supremely egotistical in seeing the loved one as a means to the end of self-fulfillment. They are a study in attraction and repulsion, sometimes unfortunate in their effect as the poet blames God or Fate or Marguerite or himself for their inability to get together. In the lyric "Parting" the lover's gaze swings between the warm beauty of Marguerite coming in at the door and the snowy purity of the mountains seen through the window, until he flees with a cry of "our different past" from her arms to those of Mother Nature. He finds in "A Farewell" his "true affinities of soul" in "The hush among the shining stars/The calm upon the moonlit sea." Marguerite was a victim of Arnold's romantic attachment to a classical ideal of wholeness in life and art, and of his hope that sexual love might prove a way to find this intellectual integrity without sacrificing emotional vitality. The failure to achieve this transcendent union, to feel even the illusory happiness of men who have "*dreamed* two human hearts might blend in one," inspired the best and best-known of the Marguerite poems, with the true theme evident in the title "Isolation. To Marguerite," and in the uncompromising and paradoxical line of the companion poem, "We mortal millions live *alone*" ("To Marguerite—Continued"). The struggle itself, however, is most clearly seen in "Absence," where the necessary choice between feeling and reason, and the pain of making it, elicit a cry of anguish:

> This is the curse of life! that not
> A nobler, calmer train
> Of wiser thoughts and feelings blot
> Our passions from our brain.
>
> But each day brings its petty dust
> Our soon-choked souls to fill,
> And we forget because we must
> And not because we will.
>
> I struggle towards the light; and ye,
> Once-longed-for storms of love!
> If with the light ye cannot be,
> I bear that ye remove.
>
> I struggle towards the light—but oh,
> While yet the night is chill,
> Upon time's barren, stormy flow,
> Stay with me, Marguerite, still!

Of the lyrics belonging to the Switzerland group, this is the strongest in its diction and feeling, though the "longing like despair" in the two poems "To Marguerite" and the climactic power of "the unplumbed, salt, estranging sea" make them the more melodious and memorable. The repetition of "struggle," the bitterness that the "petty dust" of daily trivia and not "wiser thoughts" should blot out our feelings, the cold and painful choice, the longing for love free of those storms which are no help against the storms that whirl around modern man, all give an urgency and immediacy of impact. By comparison, the poem "Longing" from the "Faded Leaves" series tends to suggest the sighing lover and unkind mistress of the conventional sonnet cycle. But then, this whole group of lyrics addressed to the future Mrs. Arnold has something of the conventional about it: Arnold brooding on the fated parting of lovers in "Too Late"; Arnold the forbidden suitor gazing sorrowfully at "My queen" from among the idlers on the pier in "Calais Sands"; Arnold trying manfully to say in "Separation" that if parting must come let it be clean and quick, but spoiling the effect by the anapestic jingling quatrain to which he was, unhappily, occasionally inclined.

This is not to say that his love for Lucy was not genuine, or something caught on the rebound; it was rather that Arnold had revised his expectations. Having failed to transform Marguerite into an Alpine Beatrice, he was now at the more realistic level of seeking emotional security in marriage, in the Wordsworthian ideal of the perfect woman who is yet "not too good/For human nature's daily food." The most vital lyric in this series is "The River," where the lovers glide in their boat down the Thames. The unusually loving and lingering description of Lucy's physical appearance and movements conveys a yearning and a need that find expression in the last three stanzas, with even a decorous Arnoldian variant on the old carpe diem theme. Most revealing of all, however, is "A Dream," which is not part of either series. As Arnold and his friend Martin sail "down a green Alpine stream" through scenes of rich natural beauty, Marguerite and her companion Olivia greet them from a balcony, with "white arms, waved eagerly," while "more than mortal impulse filled their eyes." Suspended for a moment's longing gaze, their boat poised "on the rapid's top," the poet and his friend are swept away by the "darting river of life." But this is no rationalized turning away from the symbolic new sirens of romanticism to the superior wisdom of reason; this is the melancholy memory of a flight from the warm promise of real sirens, down a river leading to "burning plains, bristled with cities."

Two other poems which stand apart from both groups of love lyrics, and yet may be related to them, are "The Buried Life" and "Dover Beach." The former reveals more of the need and the search in Arnold's love poems. As the lovers hold hands and exchange bantering words, "a nameless sadness" overcomes the poet. He gazes into the beloved's eyes with "A longing to inquire/Into the mystery of this heart which beats/So wild, so deep in us," to see whether love will disclose to him something of his hidden or "genuine self." For once, the hope is not seen as utterly futile, as Arnold develops his favorite image of the flowing stream. At "rare" times "a beloved hand" and "the tones of a loved voice" will help us, through "another's eyes," to become aware of our "life's flow" and of its "winding murmur" in the meadows, bringing an air of coolness and "an unwonted calm." The poet's experience is an illusion: "And then he thinks he knows/The hills where his life rose,/And the sea where it goes." But he is content to leave it at that and to be for a moment one of those "happier men" envied in the poems to Marguerite, who "at least/Have *dreamed* two human hearts might blend/In one," and so to be released from "isolation without end/Prolonged."

If "The Buried Life" illuminates one side of Arnold's dual search, hinting at a fleeting possibility of happiness through self-discovery in love, "Dover Beach" offers a somber picture of a world that has defeated all attempts at comprehension. The words "Ah, love, let us be true to one another!" are a heartfelt cry in the surrounding darkness where "ignorant armies clash by night." Against the Sophoclean echo of "the turbid ebb and flow of human misery," and hearing the retreating sea of faith, Arnold in his most modern poem finds himself in the dead end of a wasteland. "Dover Beach" is only momentarily a love poem, in the single cry which gives it pathos. It is the supreme expression of Arnold's elegiac mood, induced by the failure of oracles old and new to help modern man escape the "confused alarms of struggle and flight," or to enunciate a principle to help in understanding the causes of the darkness and in promoting growth toward the light.

The elegies in general extend the theme of struggle between withdrawal and commitment from the love relationship to the relationship of the individual and the world, from the need for self-discovery to the need for a certainty of some kind as a base for operations in life. In "Stanzas in Memory of the Author of 'Obermann,'" the self-imposed solitude appeals to one desire in the poet's "feverish blood," but the claims of duty are too strong for one "who in the world must live." In "Stanzas from the Grande Chartreuse" the poet begs forgiveness of the "rigorous teachers" who showed him the "high white star of Truth," yet there is the yearning for another kind of truth as he asks the "cowled forms" to "fence me round/Till I possess my soul again," and as he nostalgically catches the "accents of another sphere." And in "The Scholar-Gipsy" the reproach to modern life with its "sick hurry, its divided aims" reflects the appeal of a time when it was possible to have "*one* aim, *one* business, *one* desire."

In the elegies as in the love poems can be seen how congenial to Arnold were themes of loss and longing—of the light that failed, the frustrated search, and the love that never was. But the compulsions that drove him can also be seen—the ingrained call to duty that made him bid "a sad farewell" to Sénancour, the need for calmness of spirit that allows a feeling of kinship with the Carthusian monks, the search for unity of mind and purpose in the fellow-feeling for the Scholar-Gipsy (a theme recurring in "Thyrsis" when Arnold recalls the symbolic force for him and Clough in Oxford days of "that lone, sky-pointing tree").

What must also be seen in the elegies, however, is the recognition of man's need for happiness, something radically different from a moral or philosophical principle by which one may order or understand experience. In the Obermann poem it is "the glow, the thrill of life." In "Stanzas from the Grande Chartreuse" it is a future "gay without frivolity." In "The Scholar-Gipsy" it is the nostalgic dream of "days when wits were fresh and clear/And life ran gaily as the sparkling Thames." And in "Memorial Verses" what stands out is that Wordsworth's "soothing voice" brought to our dead spirits "the freshness of the early world." A limited tribute, but in striking contrast is the tribute paid to Goethe, "Europe's sagest head," that "he was happy, *if* to know/Causes of things, and far below/His feet to see the lurid flow/Of terror, and insane distress,/And headlong fate, be happiness."

Nature, love, solitude, the church, the past, even knowledge on the Olympian level—none of these could yield the Idea that Arnold told Clough the poet must search for. The attendant conflicts and frustrations produced his best lyrical poems, where patterns of imagery throughout—the stars, the mountains, a world above man's head, the struggle toward the light—point to a need for self-transcendence as well as self-fulfillment. At the same time he was learning that he could only resolve the conflict of reason and emotion by an effort of will carrying him along the paths of duty, and that although the life of the feelings and the aim of happiness might be deleterious if allowed to dominate one's mind, they were vitally necessary to man's well-being. Two elegies composed near the beginning of the 1860s, the first decade of Arnold's lectures and essays, suggest purpose and affirmation growing out of self-analysis, as he moved on to participate in his own way in the life of his age. "Rugby Chapel" praises his father as a servant of God and "a helper and friend of mankind"; "Haworth Churchyard" hails the "steadfast soul" of Harriet Martineau, "which, unflinching and keen,/Wrought to erase from its depth/Mist and illusion and fear."

In 1849 Arnold had told his sister Jane that he felt himself to be "a reformer in poetical matters" against the modern habit, too much encouraged by Wordsworth, of using poetry as "a channel for thinking aloud." This declaration points to the third division of his poems: poems of narrative or dramatic form and substance meant to exhibit classical objectivity and wholeness, poems whose timeless stories would have more power and meaning for modern man than writing marked by personal peculiarity and contemporary distractions. This aim he realized most fully in the early dramatic sketch "The Strayed Reveller" and in the tragedy *Merope*, the latter intended to offer through traditional form and conventions "a specimen of the world created by the Greek imagination." What in fact is missing is the creative imagination, as might be expected of a tragedy written "rather to inaugurate my Professorship with dignity than to move deeply the present race of humans." The only interesting conflict to a modern reader is that between old and new ideas, between an Aeschylean and a Euripidean temper, between the sacred and rigid duties of revenge and the humanely rational spirit evident in certain speeches of Merope herself and, especially, of Polyphontes the usurper. But these utterances, by rather wooden characters, are incidental and rhetorical in effect, with little if any dramatic force.

In "The Strayed Reveller," which tends to be lyrical and pictorial rather than dramatic in impact, the poet's imagination is engaged with the creative process itself. Though presented with concrete and delicate detail, the three characters of Circe, Ulysses, and the youth are static and symbolic, giving the effect of a classical frieze come to life. What emerges through the sensuous texture of the poem, in balance but not in conflict, are the major poetic responses to man's experiences. There is of course the Olympian indifference of the gods, who look down with "shining" eyes on man in all his activities. But the aesthetic balance lies between a classical, tragic involvement and a romantic escapism. The "wise bards" behold and sing the adventures and sufferings of the heroes and of ordinary men, but with labor and pain, paying the "price/The Gods exact for song:/To become what we sing." The youthful reveler, though told these things by the old Silenus, has his visions of the mythological and natural worlds of man granted him "Without pain, without labour" by the Circean wine that in this case inspires and does not degrade. Unlike the "proud procession" of the new sirens which leads us to an "unlovely dawning" and a regretful dismissal, the reveler's intoxicated possession is a recurrent release of creative energy. His imaginative insights lack the empathic suffering of the wise bards and the active experience of the "proved, much enduring/Wave-tossed Wanderer" Ulysses, but they are neither challenged nor judged. In balancing the young reveler and the wise bards, Arnold not only achieves objectivity by allowing the senses to lead man to a vision of truth, he also foreshadows the recognition in his critical essays that the poetical power of interpreting life lies in natural magic as well as in moral profundity.

The story of Tristram and Iseult was derived from a French source and from Malory; Arnold's was "the first modern treatment of the Tristram legend in English," according to Allott. As a story requiring the poet to see tragic grandeur in lives dominated and destroyed by passion, it was not a happy choice for Arnold. Unity is lacking in feeling and in form, with a mixture of dialogue and description, narrative and commentary, quatrains and couplets, that is far from the "succession of harmonies" praised by Swinburne in *Empedocles on Etna*. There are vivid and dramatic scenes, as in the opening lines where the dying and delirious Tristram looks eagerly for Iseult of Ireland, and in the recollected drinking of the fatal love potion. There are striking descriptive passages, as of the arras with its huntsman figure and of the hollow and glen where the children play. There is a moving tenderness, too sentimental for some readers, in the lingering description of the sleeping children, and in the sympathetic portrayal of their mother, the second Iseult, that "snowdrop by the sea." In short, there are fine passages—the very thing Arnold would have poets avoid in order to gain a total artistic effect. They hardly compensate, by his own criteria, for the stilted and stichomythic quatrains of Part Two between the lovers, united at last in a passionless Liebestod; for the complete shift of focus in the lengthy Part Three to the mother and children; or for the intrusion of the narrator when he bursts out, "And yet, I swear, it angers me to see/How this fool passion gulls men potently." Though passion here includes "ambition, or remorse, or love," it is clear that the theme of "all for love or the world well lost" was not for Arnold.

The reason for relative failure was probably Arnold's ambivalent feelings about Marguerite. He was fascinated by the story of Tristram and Iseult and yet unable to accept it, to immerse himself in the destructive element (as old Stein advises in Conrad's *Lord Jim*); finally, growing increasingly impatient with it, he enters as a kind of moralistic Puck with his own "what fools these mortals be!" Yet the conflict is there, in a poet who knew that "Calm's not life's crown," and that a doomed young man should be able to say "Let me live, let me feel, *I have lived!*" ("Early Death and Fame"). Of Iseult of Brittany, who possessed only Tristram's "waning time," Arnold says that "Joy has not found her yet, nor ever will." The coda to the poem, the story of Merlin and Vivien as told to the children by their mother, has perhaps a rueful personal echo in the escape of the lively Vivien from her sage lover: "For she was passing weary of his love."

On the surface it seems curious that Arnold should have retained *Tristram and Iseult* and withdrawn *Empedocles on Etna* until persuaded by Browning to restore it. Star-crossed lovers are, to be sure, more popular than depressed philosophers. The reasons for the withdrawal of *Empedocles on Etna* were given in the 1853 preface—that it was painful, not tragic; that it lacked the power to inspire man because the prolonged distress found no outlet in action; that consequently it was unable to offer the profound "joy" that accompanies true tragedy. A more convincing reason for the different impact of the two works may well be, however, that the conflict in *Empedocles on Etna* was of far greater importance. The storms of love drove Arnold to the Tristram story, but the "modern problems" and "the discouragement of Hamlet and Faust," which inspired the imaginative blending of his own thoughts with those of Empedocles, were of larger significance for his times and made for a heavier responsibility to his art and his reader, with the resultant self-criticism that he had failed both.

In spite of the objectivity achieved by historical remoteness and by the classicality of characters, conventions, and allusions, "the dialogue of the mind with itself" in *Empedocles on Etna* derives from the poet's own experience and his reflections upon it. As an allegory of Arnold's search until that time, it is a study in sterile oscillation and a rejection of exclusively intellectual solutions to human problems. Following "the high white star of truth" has brought Empedocles to a state of unbearable loneliness, to the point where he is "Nothing but a devouring flame of thought/But a naked, eternally restless mind." The songs of Callicles offer only a nostalgic memory, the well-meaning attentions of Pausanius serve only to recall the "sophist-brood" world of men whose tormenting "friendly chatter" drove him to "that other torment," the solitude of his restless mind. Proceeding upward alone, he attains the isolation of the peak, where there are no companions but the inhumanly remote and shining stars, and no step forward but into the destroying flames. Apollo is now the "young, implacable God," whose service has come to mean a bondage of the mind, "Forged by the imperious lonely thinking power."

In this hopeless situation the inner conflict is suddenly resolved by a clear conviction of his own intellectual integrity, rousing in Empedocles the only joyful emotion possible to him. He has not after all been entirely "the slave of thought," for he has "loved no darkness,/Sophisticated no truth,/Nursed no delusion,/Allowed no fear!" Whether this conviction is itself a delusion, or a form of hubris, or a redeeming truth, the emotion it awakens motivates the decisive action at the climax. Before the moment of joy can pass from his soul, and "the mists/Of despondency and gloom/Rush over it again," Empedocles plunges into the crater. Ironically, the great philosopher finally puts his trust in feeling: "I feel it in this hour. The numbing cloud/Mounts off my soul; I feel it, I breathe free." The last song of Callicles fittingly concludes the drama in classical fashion with a hymn of Apollonian worship that evokes a scene of calm and moonlit beauty.

The advice given Pausanius to "moderate desire" and to "trust the joys there are" is not cynical. Musing alone, Empedocles feels that now "the good, learned, friendly, quiet man/May bravelier front his life, and in himself/Find henceforth energy and heart." But it is not advice he can apply to his own case. Nor was Arnold as yet capable of following such a course, though the letters to Clough show him moving toward it. He was still enough the victim of his inner conflicts, his feeling of futile "elasticity," to create with sympathetic insight and imaginative power the central figure of Empedocles as the tragically alienated intellectual. The suicide of the hero represents a turning point in Arnold's own thinking. There was nothing more he could do in treating dramatically the consequences of a one-sided development that divorced one from humanity. What he did next, in the epical "Sohrab and Rustum," of less painful relevance, was to attempt a dramatic confrontation of different values inherent in differing attitudes to life.

This Persian story on the Homeric model has long been the best known and most popular of the major poems, even if some critics have found Arnold's epic similes long and digressive, his use of local color overdone, or his simplicity of style studied. Unlike *Tristram and Iseult* or *Empedocles on Etna* it satisfies Arnold's own criteria as found in the 1853 preface. On the one hand, it has a noble action involving "primary affections"; it aims at a single action and moral impression through overall careful construction or *Architectonicè*, "that power of execution, which creates, forms, and constitutes"; it is objective in allowing the action to speak directly to the reader without commentary or intrusion. On the other hand, it is not painful or depressing in

Arnold's daughters, Lucy and Eleanor ("Nell") (courtesy of Mrs. M. C. Moorman)

outcome; compassion and reconciliation make for a catharsis of emotion, even if to some readers the effect is more pathetic than tragic. Yet all this is merely to say it is a well-told story and to explain its perennial choice for school texts. There are other reasons why mature readers have found the poem of continuing interest, if not as complex or compelling as *Empedocles on Etna*. One is the "shadowy personal significance" that Lionel Trilling saw in the father-son struggle. Another is the contrast of character between the two heroes, which allows for a larger interpretation.

A major theme in Arnold's prose, notably different from the feeling for simpler past ages in many of the elegies, is the contrast between "the modern spirit" and attitudes derived from the past in politics, social values, and religious beliefs. The former is ardent, inquiring, liberal, adaptable, aware above all of the need for a sensitive and clear-eyed approach to growth and change and new facts, the spirit he believed marked the fifth century B.C. in Greece. The latter, a legacy of feudal aristocracy, for all its virtues of strength and resolution and accepted codes and standards, is marked by fixity and conservatism of ideas, by resistance to and distrust of any departure from the established order.

It is not fanciful to see this pattern of conflicting attitudes in the contrasts of character, appearance, and behavior developed by Arnold from the primitive originals. Rustum is "vast and clad in iron," his main weapon a huge, unlopped tree trunk; he broods like Achilles over what he conceives to be a slight to his honor by the king; his pride makes him fight "unknown, and in plain arms" lest men should say that he was matched in fight "with any mortal man"; he is suspicious of Sohrab's eager response to his own mild opening words, seeing only a wily maneuver to gain fame by sharing honors; his bitter speech over the fallen Sohrab and his "cold, incredulous voice" when Sohrab again affirms their kinship show a mind completely closed to the true cause of his lucky victory, in Sohrab's instinctive helplessness at the shout of "that beloved name." In short, he is capable of a magnanimous gesture, befitting a great man, when he first sees Sohrab coming, and even of feeling pity, but he is unable to feel new truth in a familiar situation. The pity returns as grief at the sight of a dying youth, and to despair when the seal proves Sohrab's claim to be his son—but he has to have the visible proof. By this natural movement to pity and grief, however, Arnold has humanized the larger-than-life Rustum and created sympathy for an old warrior whose ironclad inhibitions have prevented recognition of the truth until too late, leaving him only an enduring sadness, and a weary disgust with the outcome of a life "full of blood and battles."

Everything about Sohrab is in contrast to the mighty Rustum, that "giant figure planted on the sand,/Sole, like some single tower, which a chief/Hath builded on the waste in former years/Against the robbers. . . ." Sohrab is "the unknown, adventurous youth," slender and "of spirited air," motivated by love, not pride. He quickly responds to a new element in the situation—"for never was my heart so touched before"—as he feels the reality of Rustum behind the plain arms and deviceless shield. His magnanimity is tactful when he tries to console Rustum by blaming his death on Fate and considerate in requesting safe departure for the men who have followed him. Above all, it is Sohrab who thinks in larger terms at the end, restraining Rustum's attempt at suicide by opposing the reality of their few moments of loving union to such a gesture, by a reminder that the difference between great fame and an obscure and early death is a matter of destiny and by a prophecy of ultimate peace for the soul of Rustum.

To see Rustum and Sohrab as representatives of old and new orders, as archetypal figures in a struggle between the questing idealism of youth and a liberal modern spirit on the one hand, and a resisting conservatism, inflexible and inhibited, on the other, cannot diminish the tragic power of a colorful story in which a father in ignorance kills his own son. But it offers another level of meaning, consonant with Arnold's later ideas as they developed out of literary into social criticism. And its parable force, with rigid barriers of pride and archaic values rejecting a freely offered love and peace, may help to explain the hold of the poem over several generations as something more than a moving heroic tale.

Arnold attempted the epic form again in "Balder Dead" (1855), drawing his materials from Scandinavian mythology, but readers have not shared his preference for this poem over "Sohrab and Rustum." The shadowy world of magical powers and eternally renewed fighting and feasting among the gods is too remote to arouse human interest and feeling. Toward the end of the poem, however, a theme appears which anticipates the prophetic strain in Arnold's writing over the coming years. Balder will "return to light,/In times less alien to a spirit mild" with "a small remnant of the gods" (the term *remnant* which was to be central in

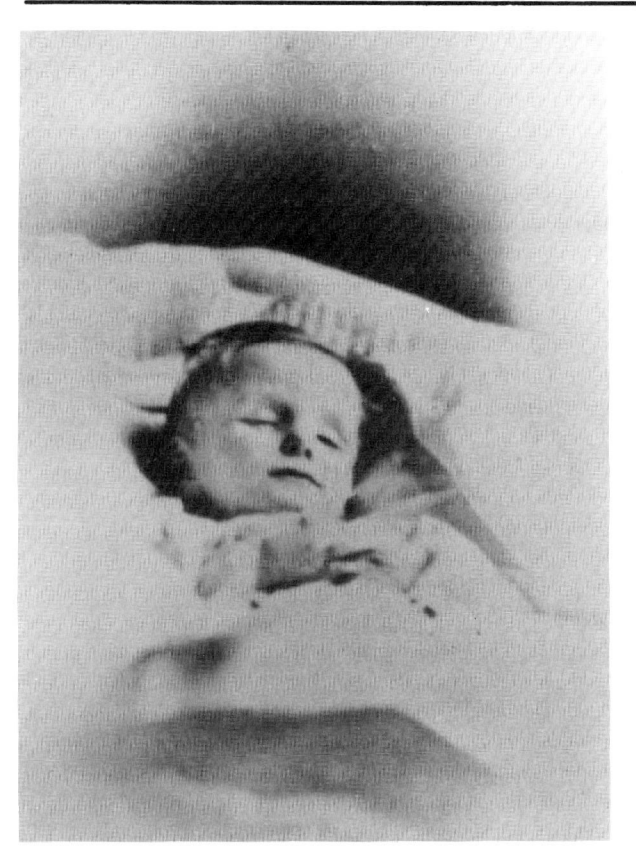

A photograph by Arnold of his dead infant son, Basil, who died in January 1868. Two of his other three sons died as teenagers (courtesy of Mrs. M. C. Moorman).

Arnold's lecture "Numbers" on his American tour), and they with "wise discourse" will "live in peace, as now in war."

This theme is enlarged in "Obermann Once More" in Arnold's *New Poems* (1867), the last body of his poetry to be published before the collected editions. In this poem the recluse Obermann (Sénancour) reveals that the time has come to translate into appropriate action his earlier humane insight: "But now the old is out of date,/The new is not yet born,/And who can be *alone* elate/While the world lies forlorn?" The summons to the poet, symbolized by a fresh vision of the Alps, then comes: "What still is left of strength, employ/That end to help attain:/*One common wave of thought and joy/Lifting mankind again!*"

"Obermann Once More" is one of the new poems in the 1867 edition, which contains seven poems from earlier volumes and five previously published in magazines. Two strains emerge in these new poems, one apparent in the broadening from Balder's "remnant" to Obermann's "the world" and "mankind." Arnold's inspectoral trips around England and his professional visits to the Continent as a commissioner for the Department of Education made him a knowledgeable educational reformer, and his strategic concentration on state education for the middle classes as the most necessary reform at that time should not, as it too often has, obscure the fact of his awareness of and concern for the educational needs of the poor. He saw the poor when his duties took him into London's East End and when he visited rural districts and small towns as assistant to Judge Wightman on circuit. How far a desire to get below the surface took him is seen in a letter of January 1879 to his sister Susy, who was evidently engaged in a Victorian lady's good works. "I heard with great interest of your Christmas, and perhaps . . . nothing . . . brings one . . . so much happiness as beneficence. But do not you feel sometimes anxious to attack the condition of things which seems to bring about the evils on which your beneficence has to be exercised? When once you have got it into your head that this condition *does* in great measure bring the evils about, and that it is in great measure remediable, I think one can hardly rest satisfied with merely alleviating the evils that arise under it."

In the new volume the sonnet "West London" shows a rare kind of sensitive insight as part of a vision for the future. Observing a "tramp" with "a babe in her arms" sending her little girl across the square to beg of "some labouring men" while letting "the rich pass by with frozen stare," Arnold concludes:

> Thought I: "Above her state this spirit towers;
> She will not ask of aliens, but of friends,
> Of sharers in a common human fate.
> She turns from that cold succour, which attends
> The unknown little from the unknowing great,
> And points us to a better time than ours."

This is the Arnold who, when a retirement banquet was held in his honor, took his greatest pleasure from the tributes to his just treatment of the teachers and his unfailing kindness to the children.

A second strain suggests, however, that not only will the new day not "dawn at a human nod," but that discouragement can only be avoided by having a fixed star to guide one over the turbulent waters of change. "The light we sought is shining still," Arnold is told by the shade of Clough in "Thyrsis," and in the sonnet "East London" a dedicated and overworked preacher in the squalid streets of Bethnal Green is told that he has set up his "mark of everlasting light." The self-control longed for in poems and letters of the 1840s and 1850s has become in the quest for self-fulfillment a belief in the need for self-transcendence. Like the image of Pallas high above Troy and the battles swirling around it, in the new poem "Palladium,"

> Still doth the soul, from its lone fastness high,
> Upon our life a ruling effluence send.
> And when it fails, fight as we will, we die;
> And while it lasts, we cannot wholly end.

As the central images in these poems indicate, Arnold was on his way, via *Culture and Anarchy,* to his books on religious subjects. Two sonnets show the nature of his religious liberalism, which tried to placate the orthodox by retaining the names and forms of Christian worship, and at the same time to attract the growing number of unbelievers by giving them a moral equation requiring no more for acceptance than a transcending of the ordinary self. "The Better Part" concludes simply, "Was Christ a man like us? *Ah! let us try/If we then, too, can be such men as he!*" Impatience with theological quibbling over God's attributes sums it all up as "*Wisdom and goodness, they are God!*—what schools/Have yet so much as heard this simpler lore?" Italicized vigor will not turn rhetoric into poetry, but it does firmly proclaim the ideas which Arnold was to pursue in essay after essay. They are compatible with a faith in evolutionary human and social development, even the tenuous faith wistfully expressed in his essay "Marcus Aurelius." Arnold, no friend to either Victorian "progress" in its cruder forms or to sudden doctrinaire change, presents with aphoristic compression in "Westminster Abbey" (1881) his humanistic view of historical and social man. The elegy to his friend Arthur Stanley—fellow Rugbeian, biographer of Dr. Arnold, and dean of Westminster—contains these lines: "For this and that way swings/The flux of mortal things/Though moving inly to one far-set goal."

This passage can be seen as a formulation of that Idea of the world that Arnold had long before told Clough the poet must have. In working his way out of the "flux of things" that had destroyed Empedocles and had left Arnold "tired at last of my own elasticity," he had found something to do that brought with it a sense of purpose. The vision of perfection that emerged, conceivable though unattainable, could give meaning to the search for "the mysterious goddess" of truth, provided the searcher remained open-minded and cosmopolitan in outlook. The move to the persuasive rhetoric of prose, interrupted by longings "to busy myself with poetry only," was a move toward clarifying the Idea that gave unity to his life and work.

The young Arnold of "extravagant" waistcoats and "Parisianism" was never wholly submerged, as is shown in a letter home from Brussels: "It is a white, sparkling, cheerful, wicked little place, which, however, one finds rather good for one's spirits." When his favorite sister and critic, Jane, accused him of becoming as dogmatic as Ruskin, he blandly replied that "the difference was that Ruskin was dogmatic and *wrong*." When reviewers, annoyed by his preaching the gospel of sweetness and light and so staying aloof from the heat and struggle of the day, called him an elegant Jeremiah in kid gloves, he coolly remarked that he objected to being compared to the Old Testament prophet whose style he least admired.

Such remarks, defended by Arnold as "vivacities" when he was reproached for undue levity, were the signs of a sociable man and witty writer who liked to dine out and was a popular guest. They show one side of the coin, as does a letter of March 1881 approving the revolution against puritan restrictions on such amusements as theater and dancing. They are evidence that a man can be serious without being solemn. The other side of the coin is shown by the tribute to his father in "Rugby Chapel," and by a letter to his mother in 1868, one of several assessing his father's influence on himself. Allowing for differences, "Still, on the whole, I

Arnold in later years, with one of the family pets

Arnold's grave in Laleham Churchyard. His wife and three of his sons are also buried here (photo by Ralph Lane).

think of the main part of what I have done, and am doing, as work which he would have approved and seen to be indispensable." How serious Arnold was in search for serenity and wisdom in the company of great minds is amply shown in the *Note-Books* and in his reaction to the deaths of three of his four sons. The infant Basil died in 1868, as did Thomas, a semi-invalid, aged sixteen, and the letters at the time are full of tender and pathetic details. But when Trevenen, or "Budge" as he was called, died in 1872 at age eighteen in the midst of good health and with a promising future, stoical self-control was all that could help. His young friend George Russell, the future editor of his letters, called on the morning after the death to find Arnold trying to console himself by reading Marcus Aurelius. A letter to his mother a week later begins, "I can hardly bear to write about him," offers some information and a few brief reminiscences, and concludes, "I cannot write his name without stopping to look at it in stupefaction at his not being alive."

What weaves the two aspects of Arnold's personality into the complexity of the whole man is a resilience—or to use his favorite term, a "flexibility"—that enabled him to grow with experience, never to see the whole truth as expressed in a summary judgment or in an opinion based on personal preference. The romantic strain that produced "The Forsaken Merman" and *Tristram and Iseult* was still there when he could tell his mother, "I have a great *penchant* for the Celtic races with their melancholy and unprogressiveness"; yet he could say in his lectures on Celtic literature that the Celts lack "the true art, the *Architectonicè* which shapes great works, such as the *Agamemnon* or the *Divine Comedy*." He scourged the philistine middle class for its lack of culture, for its devotion to business and newspapers and chapel-house meetings; yet he praised its achievements in the field of "direct practical utility" and described it as, all in all, "the best stuff in this nation." He shared a mid-Victorian dislike for all things American, but his trips to America in 1883 and 1886 completed a gradually changing assessment to the point where he could write essays praising Americans, see in America's social equalitarianism the hope for the future, and serenely welcome an American son-in-law. He showed a fastidious distaste for the life of Shelley and the love letters of Keats; yet on Keats the final verdict was that his deep insight into Beauty as Truth and his "fascinating felicity" of expression entitled him to a place with Shakespeare. As for Shakespeare, Arnold showed that he could dismiss his early reservations about unfortunate influences on form and style and surrender to sheer poetic and dramatic power when he said, "We do well to place our pride in the Elizabethan age and Shakespeare, as the Greeks placed theirs in Homer," a tribute recapturing the mood of exalted praise in the early sonnet "Shakespeare." Even in the novel, held by the classically educated to be an inferior form of literature, Arnold had read widely and could say in his late essay on Tolstoy that though "the crown of literature is poetry," the novel had become "that form of literature which in our day is the most popular and the most possible"—a reserved statement, but prophetic and positive.

An attractive aspect of Arnold's personality was his fondness, which expressed itself in whimsical elegiac verses when they died, for the family pets. His devoted affection for his children was not without humor. He wrote to his wife from Italy: "I saw a little duck of a girl running about stark naked (the best costume for her) at Maddaloni yesterday, who made me think of our Nell." And when Budge, reminded by the governess that he must "love God more than any one, more even than your papa and mama," stoutly replied, "No, I shan't," Arnold remarked approvingly, "Jolly little heathen." Nor was he without humor about himself, a grace some have denied him. In a last letter to his married daughter in America, Mrs. F. W. Whitridge, he tells her he has sent "an absurd newspaper" with "a picture of me; mama thinks it very weak-looking, but upon my part I am well pleased to be made to look amiable."

He had many warnings, increasingly severe from 1883 on, of the heart disease that had struck his father down in the prime of life. It was perhaps fitting that Matthew Arnold, who enjoyed life in so many ways, should have died suddenly, while he was happily hurrying to meet his "darling Lucy" and his granddaughter "the Midget" on their arrival in Liverpool from America on 15 April 1888. The entries in the *Note-Books* for the following Sunday reflect the mind and spirit of a man who extended his search for the inner self to a concern for the outer world. One is from Ecclesiastes: "When the dead is at rest, let his remembrance rest; and be comforted for him when his spirit is departed from him"; another is from an article on Karl Marx: "Society is a sort of organism on the growth of which conscious efforts can exercise little effect"; a third is from *De Imitatione Christi*: "Si est gaudium in mundo, hoc utique possidet puri cordis homo."

Letters:

Letters of Matthew Arnold, 1848-1888, edited by G. W. E. Russell, 2 volumes (London: Macmillan, 1895);

Unpublished Letters of Matthew Arnold, edited by Arnold Whitridge (New Haven: Yale University Press, 1923);

The Letters of Matthew Arnold to Arthur Hugh Clough, edited by H. F. Lowry (London & New York: Oxford University Press, 1932);

Matthew Arnold's Letters: A Descriptive Checklist, edited by A. K. Davis, Jr. (Charlottesville: University of Virginia Press, 1968).

Bibliographies:

Thomas B. Smart, *Bibliography of Matthew Arnold* (London: Davy, 1892);

Theodore G. Ehrsam, Robert H. Deily, and Robert M. Smith, eds., *Bibliographies of Twelve Victorian Authors* (New York: Wilson, 1936).

Biographies:

George Saintsbury, *Matthew Arnold* (New York: Dodd, Mead, 1899);

Lionel Trilling, *Matthew Arnold* (New York: Meridian Books, 1939);

A. L. Rowse, *Matthew Arnold: Poet and Prophet* (London: Thames & Hudson, 1976);

Park Honan, *Matthew Arnold, A Life* (New York: McGraw-Hill, 1981).

References:

W. D. Anderson, *Matthew Arnold and the Classical Tradition* (Ann Arbor: University of Michigan Press, 1965);

P. F. Baum, *Ten Studies in the Poetry of Matthew Arnold* (Durham, N.C.: Duke University Press, 1958);

E. K. Brown, *Matthew Arnold: A Study in Conflict* (Toronto & Chicago: University of Chicago Press, 1948);

Vincent Buckley, *Poetry and Morality* (London: Chatto & Windus, 1959);

Douglas Bush, *Matthew Arnold: A Survey of his Poetry and Prose* (New York: Collier, 1971);

W. F. Connell, *The Educational Thought and Influence of Matthew Arnold* (London: Routledge & Kegan Paul, 1950);

A. D. Culler, *The Imaginative Reason* (New Haven, Conn.: Yale University Press, 1966);

D. J. DeLaura, *Hebrew and Hellene in Victorian England* (London & Austin: University of Texas Press, 1969);

DeLaura, "Matthew Arnold," in *Victorian Prose: A Guide to Research,* edited by DeLaura (New York: Modern Language Association, 1973), pp. 249-320;

T. S. Eliot, "Matthew Arnold," in his *The Use of Poetry and the Use of Criticism* (London: Faber & Faber, 1933), pp. 103-120;

F. E. Faverty, "Matthew Arnold," in *The Victorian Poets: A Guide to Research,* edited by Faverty (Cambridge: Harvard University Press, 1968), pp. 164-226;

Faverty, *Matthew Arnold the Ethnologist* (Evanston: Northwestern University Press, 1951);

H. W. Garrod, *Poetry and the Criticism of Life* (New York: Russell & Russell, 1931);

L. E. Gates, "Matthew Arnold," in his *Three Studies in Literature* (New York & London: Macmillan, 1899), pp. 124-211;

Leon Gottfried, *Matthew Arnold and the Romantics* (London: Routledge & Kegan Paul, 1963);

John Holloway, *The Victorian Sage* (London: Macmillan, 1953);

R. H. Hutton, *Literary Essays* (London & New York: Macmillan, 1892);

E. D. H. Johnson, *The Alien Vision of Victorian Poetry* (Princeton, N.J.: Princeton University Press, 1952);

Isobel MacDonald, *The Buried Self* (London: Peter Davis, 1949);

W. A. Madden, *Matthew Arnold: A Study of the Aesthetic Temperament in Victorian England* (Bloomington: Indiana University Press, 1967);

P. J. McCarthy, *Matthew Arnold and the Three Classes* (New York: Columbia University Press, 1964);

S. M. Parrish, ed., *A Concordance to the Poems of Matthew Arnold* (Ithaca, N.Y.: Cornell University Press, 1959);

J. H. Raleigh, *Matthew Arnold and American Culture* (Berkeley: University of California Press, 1957);

William Robbins, *The Ethical Idealism of Matthew Arnold* (London & Toronto: Heinemann, 1959);

Ruth Roberts, *Arnold and God* (Berkeley: University of California Press, 1983);

Alan Roper, *Arnold's Poetic Landscapes* (Baltimore, Md.: Johns Hopkins Press, 1969);

S. P. Sherman, *Matthew Arnold: How to Know Him* (Indianapolis: Bobbs-Merrill, 1917);

Robert Stange, *Matthew Arnold: The Poet as Humanist* (Princeton, N.J.: Princeton University Press, 1967);

A. C. Swinburne, "Matthew Arnold's New Poems," in his *Essays and Studies* (London: Chatto & Windus, 1901), pp. 123-183;

C. B. Tinker and H. F. Lowry, *The Poetry of Matthew Arnold: A Commentary* (London & New York: Oxford University Press, 1940);

Mrs. Humphry Ward, *A Writer's Recollections* (London & Glasgow: W. Collins, 1918).

Papers:

The major manuscript repositories for Arnold are the Beinecke Library at Yale and the Arthur Kyle Davis Papers at the University of Virginia. The Yale material includes notebooks, diaries, commonplace books, literary manuscripts, and over 200 letters. The Virginia materials consist mainly of letters. For a detailed summary of the location of Arnold's literary manuscripts and letters, see Barbara Rosenbaum and Pamela White, *Index of English Literary Manuscripts,* Volume 4: *1800-1900, Part 1: Arnold to Gissing* (London: Mansell/New York: Wilson, 1982).

William Edmondstoune Aytoun

(21 June 1813-4 August 1865)

Mark A. Weinstein
University of Nevada, Las Vegas

BOOKS: *Poland, Homer, and Other Poems*, anonymous (London: Longman, Rees, Orme, Brown, Green & Longman, 1832);

The Life and Times of Richard the First, King of England (London: Tegg, 1840);

Our Zion; or, Presbyterian Popery, by Ane of That Ilk, anonymous (Edinburgh: Constable, 1840);

The Drummond Schism Examined and Exposed, by a Layman of the Church, anonymous (Edinburgh: Grant, 1842);

The Book of Ballads, by Aytoun and Theodore Martin, as Bon Gaultier (London: Orr, 1845; New York: Redfield, 1852);

Lays of the Scottish Cavaliers and Other Poems (Edinburgh: Blackwood, 1849; New York: Redfield, 1852);

Firmilian; or, The Student of Badajoz. A Spasmodic Tragedy, as T. Percy Jones (Edinburgh: Blackwood, 1854; New York: Redfield, 1854);

Bothwell: A Poem (Edinburgh: Blackwood, 1856; Boston: Ticknor & Fields, 1856);

Inaugural Address (Edinburgh: Blackwood, 1861);

Norman Sinclair: A Novel, 3 volumes (London: Blackwood, 1861);

Nuptial Ode on the Marriage of His Royal Highness The Prince of Wales (Edinburgh: Blackwood, 1863);

The Burial March of Dundee and the Island of the Scots, edited by W. K. Leask (London: Blackie, 1897).

Collections: *Poems of William Edmondstoune Aytoun*, edited by Frederick Page (London & New York: Oxford University Press, 1921);

Stories and Verse, edited by W. L. Renwick (Edinburgh: Edinburgh University Press, 1964).

OTHER: *The Ballads of Scotland*, edited by Aytoun, 2 volumes (Edinburgh & London: Blackwood, 1858);

Poems and Ballads of Goethe, translated by Aytoun and Theodore Martin (Edinburgh: Blackwood, 1859; New York: Holt & Williams, 1871);

"Endymion; or, A Family Party of Olympus," in *Ixion in Heaven and Endymion: Disraeli's Skit and Aytoun's Burlesque*, edited by E. Partridge (London: Scholartis, 1927).

PERIODICAL PUBLICATIONS: "Ancient and Modern Ballad Poetry," *Blackwood's*, 61 (May 1847): 622-644;

"The Two Arnolds," *Blackwood's*, 75 (March 1854): 303-314;

"Firmilian—A Tragedy," *Blackwood's*, 75 (May 1854): 533-551.

(An engraving by J. C. Armytage from a bust by Patrick Park)

William Edmondstoune Aytoun is remembered today for his brilliant parody *Firmilian; or, The*

Student of Badajoz. A Spasmodic Tragedy (1854), rather than for his more serious writings. Begun as an attempt to define and demolish the contemporary "Spasmodic School of Poetry," *Firmilian* developed into an imaginative satire against all forms of romantic extravagance. Enormously successful, *Firmilian* helped to chasten mid-Victorian critical standards; it still constitutes Aytoun's chief claim to a place in literature.

Aytoun was the only son of a prosperous Edinburgh family. The fierce Jacobitism and love of ballads of his mother, Joan Keir Aytoun, had a lasting influence upon Aytoun's own political and literary preferences. His father, Roger Aytoun, was a leading writer to the Signet; this was a superior order of solicitors peculiar to Scotland, among whose privileges was that of appearing before the Court of Sessions, the supreme civil court of the kingdom. Roger Aytoun planned William's education carefully, preparing him with a private tutor for three years before sending him to the newly opened Edinburgh Academy in 1824 and to Edinburgh University in 1828. The university curriculum was basically classical, but Aytoun followed his own interests, reading widely in British literature and history, and becoming a member of the Speculative Society. His chief concern, however, was already the writing of poetry.

Aytoun finished *Poland, Homer, and Other Poems* in 1830, but the six poems were not published until 1832. Although "Poland" expresses sympathy for the Poles' struggle to regain their independence from Russia, the other poems reflect Aytoun's increasing conservatism. In them, he contrasts the virtue and nobility of the "bright ages" with the vice and sordidness of the present. This contrast became a recurrent theme in Aytoun's poetry.

After he had completed his university studies, Aytoun complied reluctantly with his father's wishes and entered the legal profession. He became a writer to the Signet in 1835 and was admitted to the Faculty of Advocates in 1840. But his first love was literature. He had spent seven months in Germany in 1833-1834 studying the language and German literature. His first contributions to *Blackwood's*, in 1836, were translations of German ballads. In the early 1840s he had three prose works published—two pamphlets on topical religious controversies and a biography of Richard I. More importantly, from 1841 to 1844, Aytoun and Theodore Martin wrote for *Tait's* and *Fraser's* a series of parodies that were to develop into a remarkably popular book.

The Book of Ballads, written with Theodore Martin, was published in 1845 under the pseudonym Bon Gaultier. It included, in the phrase of George Kitchin, "a mannequin's parade of Victorian modes": parodies of national ballads, of the Eastern tale, of the philosophical poem, of the reflective poem, of the "poetical puff," of the epigram, of thieves' literature, of young ladies' literature, and of the leading stylists of the day. Superior to his coauthor Martin as a parodist, Aytoun took special delight in deflating the romantic sensibility of much contemporary poetry. Today, Bon Gaultier's humor seems rather broad, but it is difficult to overrate the historical importance of the book. Saintsbury characterized it as "that admirable book of light verse, the equal of anything earlier and certainly not surpassed since." *The Book of Ballads* ran through thirteen editions from 1845 to 1877 in England alone; the number of pirated editions in America was at least as large. Blackwood sold over 32,000 copies from 1857 to 1909. The number of ballads increased from thirty-nine in the first edition to fifty-six in the sixteenth. Because of its enormous scope, it served as a textbook for later parodists, showing what subjects could be legitimately exposed to laughter. Its success also encouraged Aytoun to write *Firmilian*.

In 1844, in the most important act of his business career, Aytoun formally joined the staff of *Blackwood's Edinburgh Magazine*. He found in the conservative *Blackwood's* the ideal organ for his deepest feelings and beliefs. In politics, society, and literature, he looked back to the past with an admiration approaching reverence. He disliked the new and unusual; he identified the status quo with order. Aytoun soon became *Blackwood's* most prolific writer and, after the death of "Christopher North" (John Wilson) in 1854, was acknowledged to be its best. His writings were in many forms, including prose, poetry, and translation, and on many subjects, including politics, literature, railways, magic, boxing, art, and wines. For his efforts in the debate over free trade, the Derby administration rewarded him with the honorary position of sheriff and lord admiral of Orkney and Zetland. In 1845 Aytoun became professor of rhetoric and belles lettres at the University of Edinburgh, a position he raised to new importance. But Aytoun's annus mirabilis was 1849. On 11 April, he married Jane Emily Wilson, the youngest daughter of "Christopher North." It became a marriage of great contentment. Also in 1849, Edinburgh University conferred the honorary degree of M.A. upon Aytoun (four years later, Oxford was to make him a D.C.L.). Finally, 1849 was the publication date of the book that became Aytoun's most famous work among his contemporaries and a Victorian best-seller.

Lays of the Scottish Cavaliers and Other Poems reached its fifteenth British edition in fifteen years and its thirty-second in thirty-two years. Blackwood sold over 60,000 copies during the Victorian period alone, and, with foreign editions, the final total approaches the 100,000 mark. Although the book attained considerable popularity in America, Australia, and Germany, its greatest vogue was in Scotland, where selections were included in school reading books and recited by students. Its appeal is obvious. At their best, such ballads offer blood and fire in a "cut-and-thrust" style; they have a nervous energy that appeals immediately to the heart. They lie on that thin line between admirable rhetoric and genuine poetry, neither too low nor too high for the mass of educated readers. For example, "The Island of the Scots" describes the plight of Dundee's Scottish force, fighting for France because it is the home of their exiled King James:

> What mattered it that men should vaunt and loud and fondly swear,
> That higher feat of chivalry was never wrought elsewhere?
> They bore within their breasts the grief that fame can never heal—
> The deep, unutterable woe which none save exiles feel.
> Their hearts were yearning for the land they ne'er might see again—
> For Scotland's high and heathered hills, for mountain, loch and glen—
> For those who haply lay at rest beyond the distant sea,
> Beneath the green and daisied turf where they would gladly be!

As the title indicates, the Scottish cavalier is the hero of Aytoun's ballads. This romantic loyalist has been defeated in earthly terms: he has either been killed, like James IV, Montrose, Sir James Douglas, Dundee, and the Old Scottish Cavalier; or lost loved ones, like the Widow of Glencoe; or been exiled, like Charles Edward and Dundee's regiment. But he triumphs spiritually. Therefore, the movement of Aytoun's lays is frequently from earth's fitful fever toward the calm of Heaven.

Aytoun departs from standard ballad practice by making the narrator an active participant in four of the eight lays. By such a change, he makes the ballad a more partisan vehicle, establishing a sympathetic point of view for the cavaliers; Aytoun is the deeply committed minstrel. Herein lies the

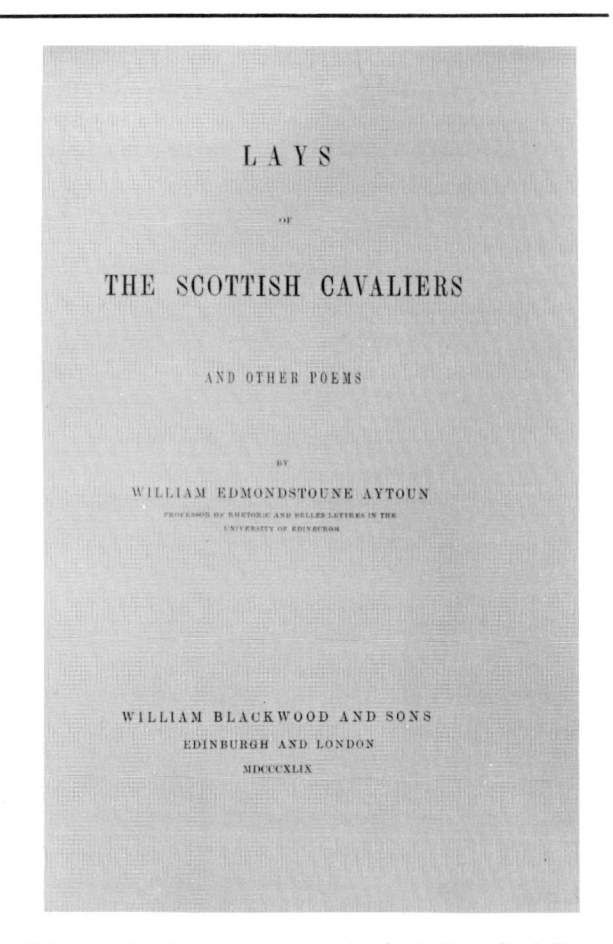

Title page for Aytoun's most popular book (Rare Book Room, Thomas Cooper Library, University of South Carolina)

emotional appeal of these poems. Two of the lays are nationalistic in theme; six deal with the fortunes of the Stuarts and their followers. Much of Aytoun's emotional being had become concentrated on that unhappy family. His religious faith, the Episcopalian, and his political party, the Tory, had been the last defenders of the Stuarts. Perhaps most importantly, his cherished notions about the past, about chivalry, and about loyalty to the sovereign found their focal point in his devotion to the Stuarts. Aytoun wrote in an article on "Ancient and Modern Ballad Poetry" that the ballad "is the simplest, and at the same time the sublimest form of poetry, nor can it be written except under the influence of that strong and absorbing emotion, which bears the poet away from the present time, makes him an actor and a participator in the vivid scenes which he describes, and which is, in fact, inspiration of the very loftiest kind...."

Aytoun, the conservative balladist, was disturbed by the increasing extravagance of romantic poetry. When *A Life-Drama* (1853) by Alexander

Smith and *Balder* (1853) by Sydney Dobell won critical acclaim, Aytoun felt the need to act. In May 1854 *Blackwood's* published his "review," with copious "extracts," of *Firmilian; or, The Student of Badajoz. A Spasmodic Tragedy,* by "T. Percy Jones." The reviewer attacks vigorously the "Spasmodic" school, which includes the critic George Gilfillan and the poets Smith, Dobell, Philip James Bailey, and T. Percy Jones. The imaginary Jones is contrasted favorably with his real-life counterparts; still, *Firmilian* serves as an excellent example of Spasmodic practice, for "in it he has portrayed the leading features of the poetical school to which he belongs with so much fidelity and effect." Lengthy excerpts from the latest Spasmodic tragedy follow, interspersed with the reviewer's criticisms, which are both humorous and serious and mix praise with censure. The reviewer, for example, admires the picture of Firmilian's large soul but has reservations about "an occasional floridness, or even warmth of expression," in the poetry:

> He had a soul beyond the vulgar reach,
> Sun-ripened, swarthy. He was not the fool
> To pluck the feeble lily from its shade
> When the black hyacinth stood in fragrance by.
> The lady of his love was dusk as Ind,
> Her lips as plenteous as the Sphinx's are,
> And her short hair crisp with Numidian curl.
> She was a negress. You have heard the strains
> That Dante, Petrarch, and such puling fools
> As loved the daughters of cold Japhet's race,
> Have lavished idly on their icicles.
> As snow melts snow, so their unhasty fall
> Fell chill and barren on a pulseless heart.
> But, would you know what noontide ardour is,
> Or in what mood the lion, in the waste,
> All fever-maddened, and intent on cubs,
> At the oasis waits the lioness—
> That shall you gather from the fiery song
> Which that young poet framed, before he dared
> Invade the vastness of his lady's lips.

Aytoun did his job too well. To the lovers of Spasmody, the poetic extracts seemed no more suspicious than the serious productions of their favorites. Aytoun was surprised to learn that they were eagerly awaiting the entire tragedy. So he incorporated the published extracts, introduced "a good many hits," provided the necessary connections, and in late July 1854 the complete 153-page "Spasmodic Tragedy," *Firmilian,* was published.

Firmilian is more than an attack upon local eccentricity; it is a classical protest against extravagance. In literature it goes beyond the Spasmodic school to expose exorbitant prose, the *Faust* tradition, and all ultraromantic drama; it extends beyond the realm of literature to expose excess in religion, social criticism, science, and popular belief. *Firmilian* is a plea for sanity.

It was tremendously successful. It not only gained great critical acclaim but also helped to effect a critical revolution in the mid-1850s. The Spasmodics had been unusually popular poets; after *Firmilian*, they were widely condemned. Their violent language, nonfunctional imagery, emotional extravagances, and poetic digressions were censured. Classical conceptions of unity and coherence appeared more frequently in criticism; heroes of dubious morality were examined more strictly. Moreover, this extreme reaction against Spasmodic poetry also affected those works suspiciously close to it. Distinctions were not often made, and even significant works such as Tennyson's *Maud* (1855), Robert Browning's *Men and Women* (1855), and Elizabeth Barrett Browning's *Aurora Leigh* (1856) were condemned as "Spasmodic."

After this series of triumphs, Aytoun's last decade was less successful and less happy. In *Bothwell* (1856), this Jacobite tried to vindicate Queen Mary

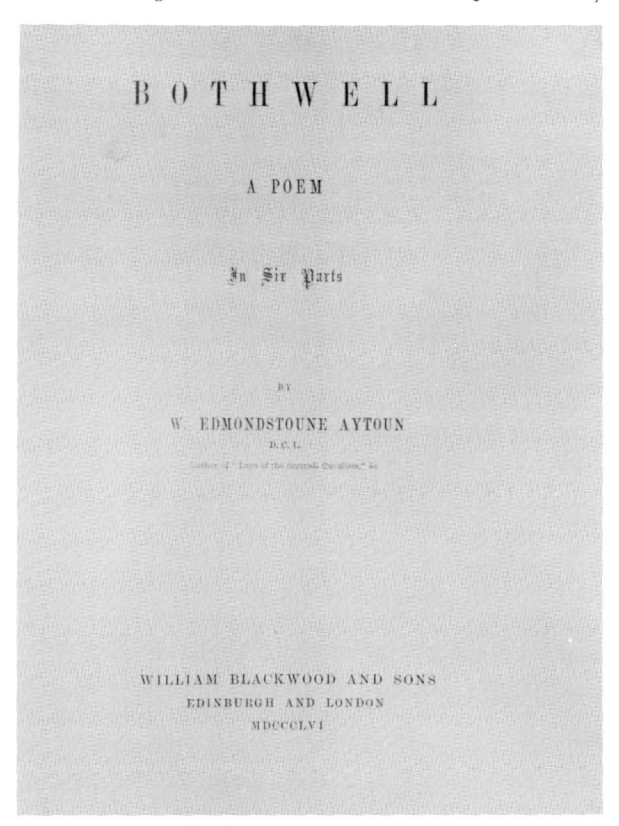

Title page for Aytoun's 1856 historical poem, which was not successful (Rare Book Room, Thomas Cooper Library, University of South Carolina)

and to show that Bothwell was the unfortunate dupe of Scottish nobles and the English queen. Challenging comparison with the Spasmodics, the monologue tells a clearly defined story, the material of which was drawn from history. Unfortunately, its chief virtue—"no spasm"—is negative, and its ballad measure becomes monotonous in a lengthy poem.

In June 1858, Aytoun's two-volume edition of *The Ballads of Scotland* was published. He aimed to present in their original forms all 139 Scottish ballads of "real intrinsic merit" that had been composed before the union of the kingdoms. Both contemporary and twentieth-century critics have praised the collection. In December 1858 Aytoun's and Martin's *Poems and Ballads of Goethe* was published (the year of publication is given as 1859 on the title page); this was a revision and expansion of their earlier translations for *Blackwood's*. It is an uneven collection.

Suddenly, Aytoun's quiet domestic life was shattered: his wife died on 15 April 1859, four days after their tenth wedding anniversary. Aytoun was left a childless, lonely man. He told Martin, "The great calamity of life has fallen upon me." Aggravating Aytoun's sorrow was his disappointment over public affairs, particularly the resignation of the Conservative ministry. He tried to lighten his gloom by writing the novel *Norman Sinclair* (1861). Thinly disguised as fiction, it is an objective review of his life, an attempt to distance and find pattern in the past. Valuable as autobiography and perhaps as therapy, it has little merit as literature.

Aytoun never recovered his genial spirits. A chronic stomach ailment made eating and sleeping difficult. The sedentary professor who had lived almost exclusively in Edinburgh was forced to seek relief in the health resorts of France, Switzerland, and Germany. His literary output was curtailed: he produced only occasional articles for *Blackwood's* and a *Nuptial Ode on the Marriage of His Royal Highness The Prince of Wales* (1863). In his loneliness, Aytoun married for a second time on Christmas Eve, 1863. Although his mother and two sisters all lived to be over ninety, Aytoun died on 4 August 1865 at the age of fifty-two.

A minor talent and largely forgotten today, Aytoun made one lasting contribution to literature. *Firmilian* was so successful an attack on the Spasmodic School of Poetry that it seemingly undermined its own reason for existence; but the kind of excessive romanticism exemplified by that early Victorian school is a recurrent literary phenomenon.

Biography:
Theodore Martin, *Memoir of William Edmondstoune Aytoun* (Edinburgh: Blackwood, 1867).

References:
George Kitchin, *A Survey of Burlesque and Parody in English* (Edinburgh: Oliver & Boyd, 1931), p. 295;

Rosaline Masson, *Pollok and Aytoun* (Edinburgh: Oliphant, Anderson & Ferrier, 1898), p. 153;

Mark A. Weinstein, *William Edmondstoune Aytoun and the Spasmodic Controversy* (New Haven: Yale University Press, 1968).

Philip James Bailey
(22 April 1816-6 September 1902)

Mark A. Weinstein
University of Nevada, Las Vegas

SELECTED BOOKS: *Festus: A Poem*, anonymous (London: Pickering, 1839; Boston: Mussey, 1845);

The Angel World, and Other Poems (London: Pickering, 1850; Boston: Ticknor, Reed & Fields, 1850);

The Mystic, and Other Poems (London: Chapman & Hall, 1855; Boston: Ticknor & Fields, 1856);

The Age; a Colloquial Satire (London: Chapman & Hall, 1858; Boston: Ticknor & Fields, 1858);

The International Policy of the Great Powers (London: Sounders, Otley, 1861);

Universal Hymn (London: Bell & Daldy, 1867).

OTHER: "The Author of 'Festus' and the Spasmodic School," in *Literary Anecdotes of the Nineteenth Century*, edited by William R. Nicoll and Thomas J. Wise, volume 2 (London: Hodder & Stoughton/New York: Dodd, Mead, 1896), pp. 411-418.

Philip James Bailey is best, if not solely, remembered as the author of *Festus* (1839). He became so identified with the poem that he was popularly referred to as "Festus" Bailey; and because *Festus* influenced several poets of the next generation, Bailey was accused of fathering the "Spasmodic School of Poetry."

Bailey was born in Nottingham, where he spent much of his life. He was the only son of Thomas Bailey, a jack-of-all-trades, and Mary Taylor Bailey. Thomas began in business as a silk-hosier, ran unsuccessfully for Parliament, was a member of the Nottingham town council from 1836 to 1843, and in 1845 became the proprietor and editor of the Nottingham *Mercury*. He was a liberal, writing on political revolutions and the rights of labor, but his greatest loves seem to have been his topographical and poetical endeavors. The latter—volumes of speculative poems such as *What is Life? and Other Poems* (1820) and *The Carnival of Death* (1822)—anticipate the more famous work of his son.

Thomas Bailey was also an indulgent father.

When Philip showed an early interest in writing poetry—"From the time I was ten years old I have always been writing verse more or less," he said years later—his father encouraged him, even taking him to see Byron's lying-in-state and asking him to memorize the nearly 5,000 lines of *Childe Harold*. As his friend Sir Edmund Gosse said, Philip James Bailey was educated to "the vocation of a poet."

33

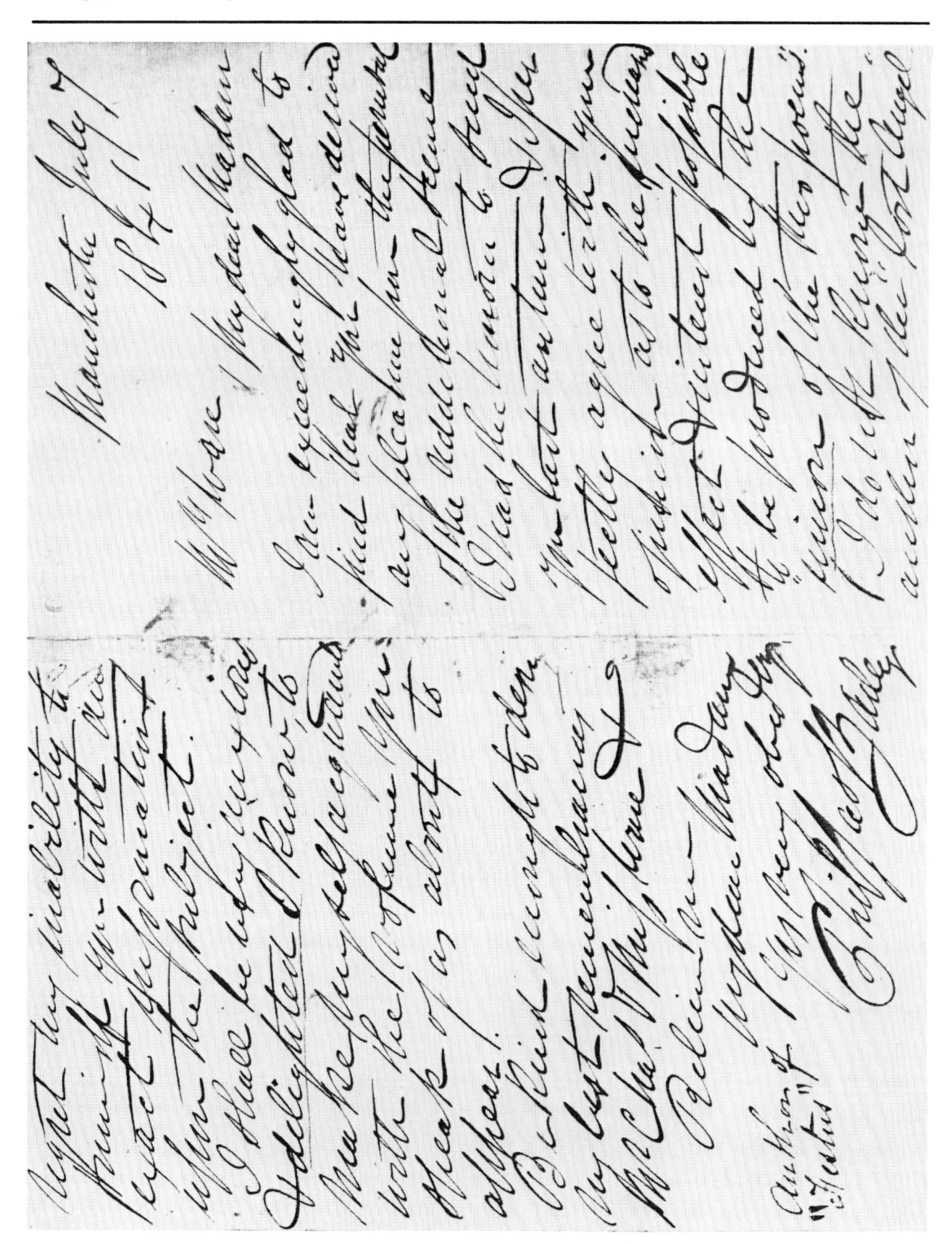

An 1841 letter from Bailey discussing the composition of Festus *(Rare Book Room, Thomas Cooper Library, University of South Carolina)*

we leave I met with
the production).
Mr Pickering is certainly
celebrated for the excellent
typographical execution
of the works he publishes
but I speak advisedly
when I add that I am
unable to recommend
him on account of any
interest which he has
exhibited in producing
or stimulating the circu-
lation of the volume com-
mitted to his charge
by my printer; to whose
exertions the appearance

of the poem & its success
as far as it goes, is en-
tirely attributable.
Nevertheless if upon re-
consideration you desire
an introduction to Mr
P. I shall have great
pleasure in complying
with your request.
As to the cost of the pro-
duction of Festus I am
almost ashamed to
confess my ignorance. The
business part of the
matter has entirely
rested between my Father
& the Printer and I

Formally, he studied under tutors in Nottingham and matriculated at Glasgow University in his sixteenth year. In 1833 he went to London to study law but, although he became a solicitor in 1840, his most intense life revolved around poetry, reading the Romantics and writing endless verses. He grew increasingly arrogant, writing to his father at the end of 1834, "As to the poem I may be I confess somewhat opinionated. When I dismissed the piece it seemed to me perfect." The poetry was abstract, theological, and speculative. Bailey expressed little interest in people: "I shrink from the mass of men. I should love to go into the desert. I think of absconding." In 1835 he began to plan his epic; in 1836 he sequestered himself in his father's house at Old Basford, near Nottingham, to begin writing it; in 1838 he finished the first draft; and in 1839, when Bailey was twenty-three, *Festus: A Poem* was published in London.

In a letter of 26 April 1836, Bailey described his original conception of *Festus* to his father: "It is a poem; a dramatic poem (if that may be termed dramatic which boasts no plot, no action; and only a few characters) on a scheme almost the reverse of that of the Devil and Doctor Faustus. The plan is this. A young man delivered over to Lucifer, who devotes himself entirely to the mortal's gratifications. The body of the poem is occupied with meditations, arguments, and reflections upon all sorts of subjects and sentiments, principally an hereafter, a future state, rewards and punishments for sin, and happiness to come. Ends with his gradual repentance and Death—and salvation." The overall scheme and several particular episodes in *Festus* reveal the influence of *Faust*. Bailey has followed the advice of Goethe's stage manager to "show the whole circle of creation, and travel with reasonable speed from Heaven through the world to Hell." The original version of *Festus* opens dramatically in Heaven. Just as in *Faust*, the choral singing of the angels alternates with God's discussion with Lucifer, in which they agree to a test of the hero's soul. No dramatic suspense is raised, however, for it is immediately asserted that the hero is secure:

> though he dip his soul in sin like a wick
> In wax, it shall be glory still to God.
> And he shall shine in robes wet through with light
> In Heaven at last.
>   The child is chosen!

Thus, Bailey makes clear at the start that *Festus* does not deal with the struggle between good and evil, but with the increasing experience and understanding of the protagonist.

Festus himself belongs in the tradition of the Byronic hero. He is the superior, solitary, passionate, disillusioned young man. In his moments of ecstasy he feels that he can become one with his surroundings, but more frequently he appears as the malcontent. Although a young man, he has suffered everything:

> My bosom, like the grave, holds all quenched passions.
> It is not that I have not found what I sought—
> But, that the world—tush! I shall see it die.
> I hate, and shall outlive the hypocrite.

Such outbursts are generally not the result of any external stimulus but proceed from the action of his mind upon itself; the motivation is temperamental rather than logical.

Festus not only remains apart from other men but generally despises them. One of his thoughts "is clearly worth a thousand lives/Like many men's." It follows naturally that "I live but for myself—/The whole world but for me." The Byronic hero, now developing into the more extreme Spasmodic hero under the hand of Bailey, turns away from people and seeks solace in nature. Festus addresses frequent paeans to nature. The natural man and the natural world can never go wrong by themselves. It is society which sins, and as for the hero, "Yes! if I have sinned, I have sinned sublimely."

Festus goes to the extremes of experience in love as in everything else. He swears eternal fidelity to Angela, and Clara, and Marian, and Helen, and Elissa, stealing the last away from Lucifer himself. Making love at a party to another woman, he assures the dead Angela in an aside that "If on her breast I lay my head,/My heart on thine is fixed." Generally, however, he does not play the hypocrite with himself:

> Oh! Why was woman made so fair? or man
> So weak as to see that more than one had beauty?
> It is impossible to love but one.

After all, if such promiscuity was a fault in him, "Twas one which made him do the sweetest wrongs/Man ever did."

As Bailey's letter to his father suggests, however, the events of the poem exist to provide occasions for "meditations, arguments, and reflections." *Festus* offers theological speculation clothed in Technicolor imagery. It is a sentential, didactic, comforting work, whose keynote is spiritual optimism. Festus, who has retained his religious faith throughout the most sinful experiences, achieves salvation—and so does everyone else, including Lucifer, according to the comforting doctrine of universal redemption. It was because of his solution of "such vexed questions as the nature, origin, end, and endurance of evil" that Bailey contrasted *Festus* favorably with what he considered the shortsighted works of Milton, Byron, Shelley, and Goethe.

Many readers agreed. *Festus* enjoyed an unbelievable popularity throughout the nineteenth century. It is uncertain just how many editions there have been, but the number exceeds 100. T. W. Higginson claimed in 1900 that "No English poem, it was said, ever sold through so many American editions as 'Festus.'" Mussey, the publisher of the first American edition in 1845, sold over 22,000 copies of *Festus* within a decade. But Bailey "never got a sixpence" from the more than thirty American reprints. Undoubtedly, the majority of readers can be explained away as a nonliterary group who read the book for its didacticism and doctrine. Still, several literary men and intelligent readers gave high praise to *Festus*. Tennyson, for example, is quoted in the publisher's notices as saying, "I can scarcely trust myself to say how much I admire it, for fear of falling into extravagance."

Two factors combine to explain this popularity among the literati. First, the original *Festus* of 1839 is a finer poem than the editions that followed in rapid succession. It consists of 8,000 lines of Bailey's best work and makes some pretense to form, while later editions have up to 40,000 lines of the most incongruous bombast. Bailey not only kept adding to *Festus* itself but also included in it huge parts of his later, unsuccessful poems. He was simply following the advice of his own hero on the writing of poetry:

> But once
> Begun, work thou all things into thy work;
> And set thyself about it, as the sea
> About earth, lashing at it day and night,
> And leave the stamp of thine own soul in it.

Second, *Festus* appeared at the perfect moment. Criticism had been dominated in the 1830s by utilitarians and rationalists; highly passionate and personal poetry had been forced underground. Then came *Festus*, and ardent young spirits, feeling a sense of liberation, tended to confuse its intent with its merit. Bailey soared and sank into Heaven, Hell, Everywhere, and Nowhere. He wrote of "feeling stars" and "moons and planets ... gibbous-faced." He employed violent and grandiloquent imagery, which may have recalled that of Byron. Elizabeth Barrett perceived how terrible a poet Bailey was at times, but she could still shout out, "what poet-stuff remains! what power! what fire of imagination!"

Festus exerted a strong influence over the poetry of the next generation. Alexander Smith's *A Life-Drama* (1853) and Sydney Dobell's *Balder* (1853) were both indebted to it and called forth a reaction against it. In 1854, William Edmondstoune Aytoun's *Firmilian; or, The Student of Badajoz: A Spasmodic Tragedy*, a brilliant parody of the "Spasmodic School of Poetry," was published. Aytoun made Bailey the father of the Spasmodics and ridiculed his pruriency, grandiloquent imagery, and emotional extravagance. The critical tide shifted: classical standards of unity and coherence were invoked more frequently; heroes of dubious morality were examined more scrupulously. Although *Festus* re-

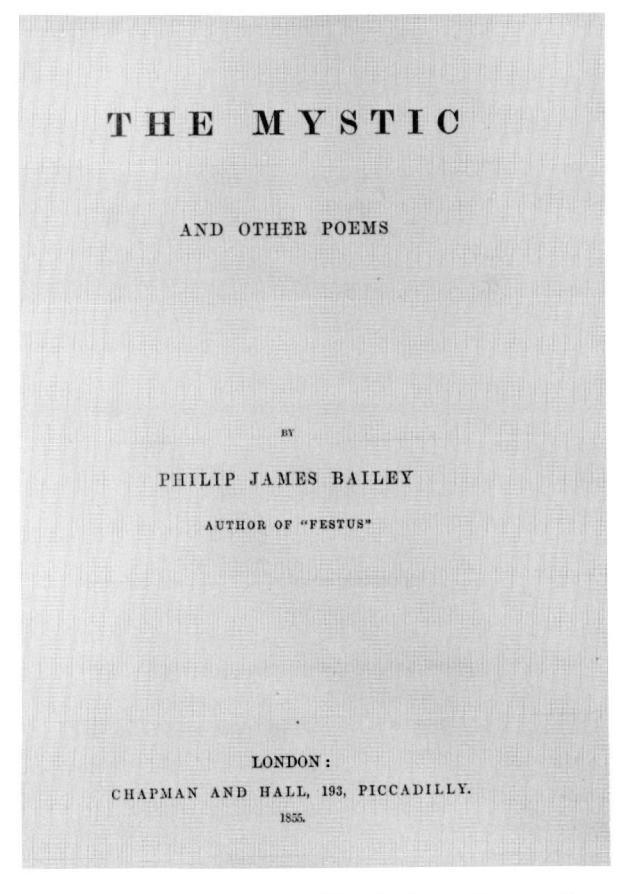

THE MYSTIC

AND OTHER POEMS

BY

PHILIP JAMES BAILEY

AUTHOR OF "FESTUS"

LONDON:
CHAPMAN AND HALL, 193, PICCADILLY.
1855.

Title page for Bailey's third published volume of poetry (Rare Book Room, Thomas Cooper Library, University of South Carolina)

tained its popularity among a large group of nonliterary people, it lost forever its reputation among the literati.

The rest of Bailey's career was an anticlimax, a story of what Gosse calls "arrested development and successive mishaps." *The Angel World* (1850), a celestial romance in blank verse, was a great disappointment to Bailey's admirers. It repeated the *Festus* doctrine of universal redemption, but in far less exhilarating poetry. Only the Pre-Raphaelites expressed interest in the work. So Bailey put huge parts of it, with necessary adaptations, into the next edition of *Festus*. As he said later, he perceived the original outline of *Festus* "to be sufficiently extensive and elastic to admit almost every variety of classifiable thought." *The Mystic, and Other Poems* (1855) contains three poems: "The Mystic," an allegory of the progress of the human mind through various spiritual beliefs to the perfect faith of Christianity; "A Spiritual Legend," a history of the Earth and its inhabitants and their connection with the angelic orders; and "A Fairy Tale," an insipid

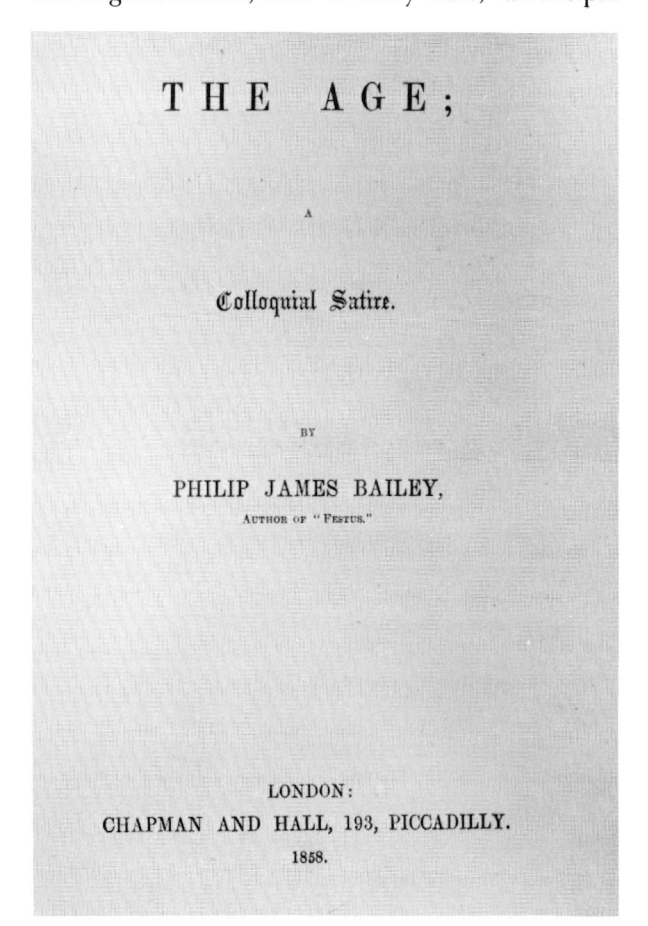

Bailey in old age

story of a little girl who propounds the theory of universal salvation to soulless fairies. The critics, reacting against Spasmodic poetry because of the success of Aytoun's *Firmilian*, condemned *The Mystic* for obscurity and took the opportunity to re-examine *Festus* more critically. Bailey again injected fragments of his latest failure into *Festus*. But he did realize the need for new directions in his poetry. *The Age* (1858) is a colloquial satire, in heroic couplets, on the manners and morals of the day; but no subject could be less appropriate for Bailey. His imagination was stimulated by theological, speculative, visionary matters, not by concrete human concerns. *The Age* was another dismal failure.

Bailey's personal life, however, changed for the better. After divorcing his first wife, of whom virtually nothing is known but by whom he had a son (Philip Festus James Bailey) and a daughter, Bailey married Anne Sophia Carey, the daughter of a Nottingham alderman, in 1863. This marriage of thirty-three years was relatively happy, apparently because of his wife's devotion to Bailey and her interest in poetry. Bailey, who had lived mostly in Nottingham, began to see more of the world. In 1864 he settled on the island of Jersey, from which he took frequent trips to the Continent, witnessing

Title page for Bailey's satirical 1858 poem, which was a failure (Rare Book Room, Thomas Cooper Library, University of South Carolina)

the famous eruption of Vesuvius in 1872. In 1876 he returned to England for good, settling first at Lee in Devonshire, moving to Blackheath in 1885, and finally retiring to The Elms in the Ropewalk of his native Nottingham. There, his beloved second wife died in 1896.

He never regained the public ear. *Universal Hymn* (1867), a return to his earlier subject matter and blank verse, failed and was, predictably, dismembered to feed *Festus. Nottingham Castle* (1878) was an unsuccessful attempt at the historical ode in the grand style. But there were compensations. Bailey had been receiving a civil list pension of £100 since 1856. In 1892, upon Tennyson's death, there was even some talk of giving Bailey the laureateship. In 1901, Glasgow University awarded him an honorary LL.D. degree. But the long end of his life is silence. As Gosse summed up, "For the last quarter of a century Mr. Bailey gave up the vain attempt to attract readers to his miscellaneous writings. He frankly abandoned them, and we need not dwell upon them." Bailey died of influenza in 1902.

Bailey was neither modest nor perceptive about *Festus*. Late in life, he still maintained that "no more orderly and methodical poem is to be found in the whole range of English literature; no vaster nor more comprehensive theme." But he did tell a visitor "that he was the author of one book, and that is what he will remain in the chronicle of literature." Here he was correct. Bailey is remembered solely as the author of *Festus*, a poem that is read today not for its intrinsic merits but for its historical importance.

References:
Elizabeth Barrett Browning, *Letters to Richard Hengist Horne*, edited by S. R. Townshend Mayer (New York: Miller, 1877), pp. 223-224;

Sir Edmund Gosse, "Philip James Bailey," in his *Portraits and Sketches* (New York: Scribners, 1912), pp. 59-93;

T. W. Higginson, *Studies in History and Letters* (Boston: Houghton Mifflin, 1900), p. 262;

Alan D. McKillop, "A Victorian Faust," *PMLA*, 40 (1925): 743-768;

Mark A. Weinstein, *William Edmondstoune Aytoun and the Spasmodic Controversy* (New Haven: Yale University Press, 1968).

William Barnes
(22 February 1801-7 October 1886)

Peter Quartermain

BOOKS: *Poetical Pieces* (Dorchester, U.K.: Clark, 1820);

Orra: A Lapland Tale. The Wood-Cuts engraved by the Author (Dorchester, U.K.: Criswick, 1822);

The Etymological Glossary, or Easy Expositor, for the Use of Schools and Non-Latinists (Shaftesbury, U.K.: Rutter/London: Whittaker, Teacher & Arnot, 1829);

The Solution of the Problem to Tri-Sect the Arc of a Circle (London: Whittaker, 1832);

A Catechism of Government in General, and of England in Particular (Shaftesbury, U.K.: Bastable, 1833);

The Mnemonical Manual (N.p., 1833);

A Few Words on the Advantages of a More Common Adoption of the Mathematics as a Branch of Education (London: Whittaker, 1834);

A Mathematical Investigation of the Principle of Hanging Doors, Gates, Swing Bridges and Other Heavy Bodies (Dorchester, U.K.: Simonds & Sydenham, 1835);

A Corrective Concordance; or, Imposition Book (Dorchester, U.K.: Clark, 1839?);

An Arithmetical and Commercial Dictionary (London: Longman, Whittaker, Hamilton & Adams, 1840);

An Investigation of the Laws of Case in Language, Exhibited in a System of Natural Cases (London: Longman, Whittaker, Hamilton & Adams, 1840);

The Elements of English Grammar, with a Set of Questions and Exercises (London: Longman, Whittaker, Hamilton & Adams, 1842);

The Elements of Linear Perspective and the Projection of Shadows (London: Longman, Brown, Hamilton & Adams, 1842);

Exercises in Practical Science (Dorchester, U.K.: Clark, 1844);

Sabbath Lays: Six Sacred Songs, by Barnes with music by F. W. Smith (London: Chappell, 1844);

Poems of Rural Life, in the Dorset Dialect: with a Dissertation and Glossary (London: Smith, 1844);

Poems, Partly of Rural Life (in National English) (London: Smith, 1846);

Outlines of Geography and Ethnography for Youth (Dorchester, U.K.: Barclay, 1847);

Humilis Domis: Some Thoughts on the Abodes, Life and Social Conditions of the Poor (London: Privately printed, 1849?);

Se Gefylstá (The Helper): An Anglo-Saxon Delectus, Serving as a First Class-Book of the Language (London: Smith, 1849);

A Philological Grammar, Grounded upon English, and Formed from a Comparison of More than Sixty Languages: Being an Introduction to the Science of Grammar and a Help to Grammars of All Languages (London: Smith, 1854);

Notes on Ancient Britain and the Britons (London: Smith, 1858);

Views of Labour and Gold (London: Smith, 1859);

Hwomely Rhymes. A Second Collection of Poems in the Dorset Dialect (London: Smith, 1859); republished as *Poems in the Dorset Dialect* (Boston: Crosby & Nichols, 1864);

Tiw; or, A View of the Roots and Stems of English as a Teutonic Tongue (London: Smith, 1861);

Poems of Rural Life in the Dorset Dialect. Third Collection (London: Smith, 1862);

A Grammar and Glossary of the Dorset Dialect, with the History, Outspreadings and Bearings of South-Western English (Berlin: Philological Society, 1863);

A Guide to Dorchester (Dorchester, U.K.: Foster, 1864);

Poems of Rural Life in Common English (London: Macmillan, 1868); republished as *Rural Poems* (Boston: Roberts, 1869);

Early England and the Saxon-English, with Some Notes on the Father-stock of the Saxon-English, the Frisians (London: Smith, 1869);

A Selection from Unpublished Poems (Dorchester, U.K.: Published at the School, Winterborne Monkton, 1870);

An Outline of English Speech-Craft (London: Kegan Paul, 1878);

An Outline of Rede-Craft (Logic), with English Wording (London: Kegan Paul, 1880);

Ruth, A Short Drama from the Bible (Dorchester, U.K.: Henry Ling, 1881?);

A Glossary of the Dorset Dialect, with a Grammar of Its Word Shaping and Wording (London: Trübner, 1886).

William Barnes

Collections: *Poems of Rural Life in the Dorset Dialect* (London: Kegan Paul, 1879);

Select Poems of William Barnes, edited by Thomas Hardy (London: Frowde, 1908);

A Selection from Poems of Rural Life in the Dorset Dialect, arranged by the Reverend William Miles Barnes (London: Kegan Paul, Trench, Trübner, 1909);

Twenty Poems in Common English by William Barnes, edited by John Drinkwater (Oxford: Blackwell, 1925; New York: Duffield, 1925);

Poems Grave and Gay, edited by Giles Dugdale (Dorchester, U.K.: Longmans Dorchester, 1949);

Selected Poems of William Barnes, edited by Geoffrey Grigson (London: Routledge & Kegan Paul, 1950);

The Poems, edited by Bernard Jones, 2 volumes (London: Centaur Press/Carbondale: Southern Illinois University Press, 1962);

William Barnes: One Hundred Poems, with an essay by E. M. Forster (Blandford Forum, Dorset, U.K.: Dorset Bookshop, 1971);

William Barnes: A Selection of his Poems, edited by

Robert Nye (Oxford: Carcanet Press, 1972).

OTHER: *The Song of Solomon in the Dorset Dialect,* translated by Barnes (London: Privately printed, 1859);

J. Poole, *Introductory Observations, Additions from Various Sources, and Notes to a Glossary, with Some Pieces of Verse, of the Old Dialect of the English Colony in the Baronies of Forth and Bargy,* edited by Barnes (London: Smith, 1867).

SELECTED PERIODICAL PUBLICATIONS:
"The Pyrrhonism of Joseph Glanvill," *Retrospective Review,* 1 (February 1853): 105-119;

"Thoughts on Beauty and Art," *Macmillan's,* 4 (May 1861): 126-137;

"Rariora of Old Poetry," *Macmillan's,* 8 (May 1863): 36-42;

"On the Credibility of Old Song-History and Tradition," *Fraser's,* 68 (September 1863): 394-401;

"Plagiarism and Coincidence; or Thought-thievery and Thought-likeness," *Macmillan's,* 15 (November 1866): 73-80;

"The Old Bardic Poetry," *Macmillan's,* 16 (August 1867): 306-317.

In 1823, at the start of what was to be a thirty-nine-year career as a schoolmaster, William Barnes was studying Latin, Greek, French, Italian, and German. "I began Persian with Lee's grammar," he wrote years later in an autobiographical notebook for his daughter, "and for a little time Russian, which, as being wanting in old lore, I soon cast off." The anecdote says much about the whole of his life and work: pressing financial necessity which drove him to a defunct school at Mere in Wiltshire, where he did not want to go; a quick, ready, and practical mind which, coupled with a taste for hard work, gave him mastery of a prodigious variety of skills and subjects; a taste for the exotic, the old, and the arcane which ran counter to worldly interest; and a complete trust in nature and the domestic passions which enabled him patiently to wait four years to marry. Through his knowledge of mathematics he helped improve the design of Gen. Henry Shrapnel's howitzers, mortars, and small arms; he invented collapsible swimming shoes like frogman's flippers (which did not work) and an instrument to describe ellipses (which did); he was instrumental in establishing the Dorset County Museum, retrieving, preserving, and cataloguing Roman and other antiquities. "Old lore" and the latest in science were equally fascinating to him: absolutely of his time yet determined to preserve tradition; poet; draughtsman; engraver; painter; mechanic; political commentator; mathematician; staunch defender of the rural working class; carpenter; musician; cabinetmaker; gardener; playwright; clockmaker; archaeologist; amateur astronomer; schoolteacher; priest; parent; journalist; at ease in fourteen languages, including French, Italian, Greek, German, Latin, Russian, Persian, Spanish, Welsh, Hindustani, and Hebrew. Almost completely self-taught, Barnes was—in the words of Sir Frederick Treves—"a man who lived in the past and the future rather than in the present." As his daughter Lucy Baxter put it in her *Life of William Barnes* (1887): "In action he was behind the world. . . ; in thought he was far before his time."

In the course of a writing career which began when he was nineteen and ended with his death at eighty-five, Barnes produced some ten books of verse, twenty-seven books on a wide variety of subjects (including school texts which he wrote because there were none adequate for his needs), and over seventy-five articles and essays. The great source of his energy was the belief that the world can be understood through intense study and is amenable to reason. He thought grammar (and hence philology) an exact science and allied it in his mind to "politics," what nowadays is called social science: the order of nature is the order of reason; the task of reason is to discover the order of nature. This is why, as his daughter records, he would "eschew all the evil in newspapers; no theft or murder could ever be read to him." His mind leaned toward order, and the craft of poetry was to him a celebration. "There is no art without love," he said. "Every artist who has produced anything worthy has had a love of his subject."

William Barnes was born on 22 February 1801, one of six children of John and Grace Scott Barnes, at Rush-hay, a tenant farm near Sturminster-Newton, Dorset. The experiences of his first fifteen or so years set the pattern of his life. The interests he passionately followed and the social causes he ardently espoused came from his mother, from the countryside around him, and from his rural neighbors—both those whose example he might follow, and those whose plight he might observe. His mother fostered in him a passion for the beautiful in nature and in art; as an old man he clearly remembered her voice reciting poetry to him, telling him about the paintings and other works of art she had seen in such local houses as Thornhill (where Hogarth's father-in-law had lived). She encouraged him to draw, and by the age of ten the child was determined to be an artist.

After his mother died in 1806, Barnes spent much of his time at his uncle Charles Roberts's Pentridge Farm on the river Stour; he told his daughter Laura that his chief delight in childhood was to wander over the common and the fields. His feeling for the country of his childhood is directly portrayed in such poems as "Pentridge," "Trees Be Company," "Rustic Childhood," and the lovely "Pentridge by the River," but trees, mills, and streams pervade the whole of his work. If in his poetry there is little or no contemplation of evil, it is because the goodness of God was evident to him in nature and the pursuit of good was ill served by negative thought. Thus in *Philological Grammar* (1854) he defends the twelve cases he gives to the declension of nouns by calling them "natural cases": "All the logical relations of things are in nature, and if they are manifold there is no help for it." So, too, in "Thoughts on Beauty and Art" (1861) he says: "The beautiful in Nature is the unmarred result of God's first creative or forming will, and the beautiful in Art is the result of an unmistaken working of man in accordance with the beautiful in Nature." But the countryside was not wholly idyllic: the effects of enclosures on the rural laborer in Barnes's childhood and later, and the dreadful agricultural depression following the Battle of Waterloo in 1815, in which his uncle Charles went bankrupt—recounted in *Views of Labour and Gold* (1859)—fed Barnes's political conscience. The first series of *Poems of Rural Life, in the Dorset Dialect* (1844) includes a number of poems notable for their bitter sympathy for the plight of the rural poor. Not the least of these are the "Eclogues"—his first poems in dialect. "Bread is so high an' wages be so low," says Tom in one poem; and John says in another: "I'd keep myself from parish, I'd be bound,/If I could get a little patch o' ground." It was indeed for its political impact that the 1844 volume was welcomed by reviewers.

Barnes was educated first at a dame's school in Sturminster-Newton, then at the church school. His education was "nothing but elementary," says Lucy Baxter, "but this was of little importance, for the learning which made his name was no grammar-school knowledge." When he was seven or eight years old Barnes was irresistibly attracted (despite his father's prohibition) to Jemmy Jenkins, a local necromancer whose collection of over 200 old books on astrology, magic, and the black arts not only fostered in the child a love of reading but also taught him to satisfy his curiosity about anything unusual or uncommon, and to pursue old lore and learning. As Giles Dugdale has said, his instinct for "exact reasoning" kept him from falling into such superstitions as those he later recorded in "A Witch" (1844).

At thirteen or fourteen he became copying-clerk to a local solicitor, Thomas Henry Dashwood, who died in 1817. In 1818, after working with Dashwood's successor, George Score, Barnes went to Dorchester, where he became engrossing clerk for the solicitor Thomas Coombs. Some of his work from that job, decorated with engravings of cottages and animals, still exists. In 1818 he met Julia Miles, to whom he was betrothed in 1822; her father was hostile to the marriage and insisted on his future son-in-law's being solvent, so in 1823 he took up schoolmastering at Mere, in Wiltshire, in order to get enough money together to marry. In 1827 he took the Chantry House at Mere as his residence and school, and married Julia. The couple had six children. They lived at Mere under considerable financial strain until 1835, when Barnes went to Dorchester to found his own school; it is clear from Trevor Hearl's 1966 account that Barnes was one of the great schoolmasters of his century.

Barnes's poetic career falls into three distinct phases: his apprenticeship, which ended in 1833-1834, was followed by a period ending roughly in 1866 in which he wrote almost exclusively in the Dorset dialect. In the final period, from 1866 to 1886, he returned almost completely to writing in standard English. His best-known work is generally from the second period, though there are such notable exceptions as the very fine dialect poem "The Geäte A-vallèn To," dictated on 13 October 1885. The poems of his apprenticeship are all in rather consciously literary standard English and offer mainly personal and conventional reflection; poems like "The Farewell" or "A Father to His Child" are like occasional poems, written to demonstrate the writer's social accomplishment.

The great breakthrough which marks the end of Barnes's apprenticeship is embodied in the "Eclogues," particularly "The 'Lotments," "Rusticus Emigrans," "Rusticus Res Politicas Animadvertens. The New Poor Laws," and "The Common A-Took In." Written during 1833-1834, these were Barnes's first dialect poems, and in them he discovered not only the characteristic voice for his poetry thereafter (in which he preserves the tones and word order of common speech) but also his subject. The six "Eclogues" reveal a close and clear observation of the daily lives, needs, pains, hopes, fears, and pleasures of country folk. As Bernard Jones observes in his edition of the *Poems*, they are "a most true and

An engraver's card made by Barnes while he was a schoolmaster at Mere, Wiltshire, from 1823 to 1835

detailed picture of social conditions and of the society of the landfolk."

What triggered the breakthrough for Barnes, with his adaptation of a pastoral form and his adoption of a local and rural dialect, was the visit he made to Abergavenny, Wales, in 1831. In Welsh he thought mistakenly that he had found a British language which was free of foreign taint, especially from Latin, and which at the same time was readily accessible to and used by all classes of society—rich and poor, aristocrat and laborer. So he began to see, as William Turner Levy has said, that his childhood dialect was a purer form of English than the national language because it was uncorrupted both by Latin and Greek on the one hand and by social snobbery on the other: in it he could write poetry accessible to all. It was this conviction that fed his intense philological studies, which in turn, during the second phase of his poetic career, fed his poetry. Thus as he studied Welsh he discovered *cynghanedd*—matching consonants, as in "Ellen Brine ov Allenburn"—and *cymmeriad*—using the same vowel or consonant sound for the beginnings of two, four, or more lines (a device he also found in Hebrew). The most celebrated example of Barnes's use of *cynghanedd* is in the refrain of "My Orcha'd in Linden Lea" (which has been set to music by Ralph Vaughan Williams), where the apple tree "Do lean down low in Linden Lea," playing the pattern DLNDNL/NLNDNL; it can also be found in such lines as "An' love to roost, where they can live at rest" and "In our abode in Arby Wood." This last line is close to a device Barnes adopted from Persian, which he called "ornamental punning" or "full-matching": a likeness in sounds of words which differ in meaning, such as "Ah! Well-a-dae! O wall adieu." Such wordplay is reminiscent of verbal parlor games popular in the early years of the nineteenth century and can be found in the quite execrable puns which are the pretext for Barnes's very early poem "Solution of the Charade from *The Crypt*."

In 1837 Barnes registered in St. John's College, Cambridge, as a ten-year man; in 1847 he was ordained deacon and pastor of Whitcombe; in 1848 he was priested, and in 1850 he received his B.D. degree. Barnes resigned from his pastorate after his wife died in June 1852. In 1858 he read his poetry to the members of the Working Men's Institute in Dorchester Town Hall, which was "thronged almost to suffocation with rich and poor.... It was the first time a Dorset audience heard its feeling, language, and daily life portrayed in common speech." It was by no means the last, for during the following years Barnes read his work to packed audiences throughout Dorset and Wiltshire. His financial difficulties were somewhat alleviated in 1861, when he was granted a civil list pension of £70 a year, and resolved in 1862, when he was granted the living of Winterborne Came with Whitcombe. He moved into the rectory at Came and retired from schoolteaching.

Barnes's study of Anglo-Saxon in 1846 led him to adaptations of Anglo-Saxon alliteration, as in "God's glistning glare/And glow-gleaming glance round glimpses"; and his extensive linguistic and philological studies—which led to his *Philological Grammar*, in which he discusses many of the poetic devices he found in other languages—make his poetry of the second period (1834-1866) remarkable for its technical experimentation, inventiveness, and variety. "A poet," he wrote in the *Philological Grammar*, "may impose upon himself any task—as that he will introduce some forechosen word into every distich or line, or exclude it from his poem; or that every line shall end with a noun; or that his poem shall take a chosen form to the sight; or he may bind himself to work out any unusual fancy."

Barnes had written his first dialect poems in 1833-1834 in the belief that "the Dorset dialect is a broad and bold shape of the English language, as the Doric was of the Greek. . . . It is . . . purer and more regular than the dialect which is chosen as the

Barnes in 1880 (from a photograph by Walter Pouncy)

national speech, purer, inasmuch as it uses many words of Saxon origin, for which the English substitutes others of Latin, Greek, or French derivation; and more regular, inasmuch as it inflects regularly many words which, in the national language, are regular. *In English, purity is in many cases given up for the sake of what is considered to be elegance*" (italics added). Later Barnes began to strip his own language of all save words of Anglo-Saxon origin, thus coining such terms as *bookling* for pamphlet, *redecraft* for logic, *breath-pennings* for consonants, *matewordings* for synonyms. His taste for such language, close as it is to Old English kennings, would lead to such remarkable lines in his poetry as "the souserush-brush-hollow-bulgy-hopping-top" (describing the surface of the sea), a clear anticipation of Gerard Manley Hopkins.

The poetry of the final period is almost all in national English—some of the poems, usually the less satisfactory ones, are translations of those earlier written in dialect. It is quite clear, however, that in this period Barnes's poems, with their fairly secure mastery of the techniques he had acquired

Barnes in about 1845, while he was studying at Cambridge (from the oil painting by John Thorne, in the possession of Col. Lawrence Barnes)

Barnes (seated) with family and friends in front of Came Rectory in 1882

from other languages, are notable for an increased simplicity of language and thought which make for freshness of vision. They are also notable for their exploitation of a larger sense of structure than that afforded by the earlier experiments: the later poems tend to be formally organized around a color, a shape (as "Rings"), or some similar abstraction rather than around a theme or a simple narrative thread. Bernard Jones has pointed out that some time in middle life Barnes made a detailed study of colors, shapes, and movements as they are found in nature, and that "whereas the poetry written up to almost 1860 might well be illustrated from the paintings of Morland, much of the later poetry has the visionary innocence of the work of Samuel Palmer." Barnes himself said of the dialect poems written before 1866 that writing them was "like the playing of music, the refreshment of the mind from care or irksomeness." The later poems sprang from a deeper emotional source.

In June 1885, Thomas Hardy, who had met Barnes in 1856 in Dorchester, moved into his new house, Max Gate, only a few hundred yards from the Came rectory, in order to be close to his old friend. But Barnes died in October 1886.

The fact that he came to be known as "William Barnes of Dorset" has told against him, for he came to be thought of, and dismissed, as a regional poet. Yet his work has had a wide appeal; some of it has always been in print. He has been disparagingly thought of as an eccentric, and the celebrated picture of him in his characteristic clothing, which he designed according to his theories of fitness and utility and habitually wore from 1862 onward, confirms that; but as a result his gentleness, his versatility, his learning, his intense love of the rural and of the past accompanied by political and moral passion, and his sheer poetic ability have all been discounted. As Hardy said, "a more notable example of self-help has seldom been recorded." Yet he is still severely underrated as a poet. While not a major writer, he is, as John Heath-Stubbs has suggested, "a true and highly original poet in his own right . . . , in the main stream of poetic development." His profound influence on Hopkins and on Hardy (both of them forward-looking poets) stands as testimony to his virtues as an experimenter in verse and an authentic and original, though limited, voice. Hardy summarized Barnes's work succinctly in his preface to the *Select Poems* (1908): "Primarily spontaneous, he was academic closely after; and we find him warbling his native wood-notes with a watchful eye on the predetermined score."

Biographies:
Lucy Baxter ("Leader Scott"), *The Life of William Barnes* (London: Macmillan, 1887);
Giles Dugdale, *William Barnes of Dorset* (London: Cassell, 1953);
Bernard Jones, *William Barnes* (Dorchester: Dorset County Museum, 1962);
Trevor W. Hearl, *William Barnes the Schoolmaster* (Dorchester: Longmans, 1966).

References:
C. C. Abbott, ed., *Further Letters of Gerard Manley Hopkins* (London: Oxford University Press, 1938);
Abbott, ed., *The Letters of Gerard Manley Hopkins to Robert Bridges* (London: Oxford University Press, 1933);
Thomas Hardy, "The Rev. William Barnes, B.D.," *Athenaeum*, No. 3055 (16 October 1886): 501-502;
John Heath-Stubbs, "William Barnes," in *Great Writers of the English Language,* volume 2, *Poets,* edited by James Vinson (London: Macmillan, 1979), pp. 59-61;
Willis D. Jacobs, *William Barnes, Linguist* (Albuquerque: University of New Mexico Studies in Language and Literature, 1952);
William Turner Levy, *William Barnes: The Man and the Poems* (Dorchester, U.K.: Longmans, 1960);
F. T. Palgrave, "William Barnes and His Poems of Rural Life in the Dorset Dialect," *National Review,* 8 (February 1887): 818-839;
Coventry Patmore, "An English Classic," *Fortnightly Review,* n.s. 40 (November 1886): 659-670;
Sir Frederick Treves, "William Barnes, the Dorset Poet," *The Dorset Year Book 1915-1916* (London: Society of Dorset Men, 1916), pp. 3-10;
C. J. Wallis, "The Early Manhood of William Barnes the Dorset Poet," *Gentleman's Magazine,* 265 (July 1888): 23-40.

Papers:
William Barnes's papers, with a virtually complete collection of his published work, are in the Dorset County Museum, Dorchester. No copies are known to exist of three of his works: *The Solution of the Problem to Tri-Sect the Arc of a Circle* (1832), *The Mnemonical Manual* (1833), and *Outlines of Geography and Ethnography for Youth* (1847).

Emily Brontë
(30 July 1818-19 December 1848)

Victor A. Neufeldt
University of Victoria

See also the Brontë entry in *DLB 21, Victorian Novelists Before 1885.*

BOOKS: *Poems by Currer, Ellis and Acton Bell,* by Charlotte, Emily, and Anne Brontë (London: Aylott & Jones, 1846; Philadelphia: Lea & Blanchard, 1848);
Wuthering Heights: A Novel, as Ellis Bell (2 volumes, London: Newby, 1847; 1 volume, Boston: Coolidge & Wiley, 1848);
Gondal Poems, edited by Helen Brown and Joan Mott (Oxford: Blackwell, 1938);
The Complete Poems of Emily Jane Brontë, edited by C. W. Hatfield (New York: Columbia University Press, 1941; London: Oxford University Press, 1941);
Five Essays Written in French by Emily Jane Brontë, translated by Lorine White Nagel, edited by Fannie E. Ratchford (Austin: University of Texas Press, 1948);
Gondal's Queen: A Novel in Verse, edited by Fannie E. Ratchford (Austin: University of Texas Press, 1955).

An aura of mystery has surrounded all the Brontë sisters ever since "Currer (Charlotte), Ellis (Emily), and Acton (Anne) Bell" had a volume of poetry published in 1846, followed the next year by

Emily Brontë

Jane Eyre, Wuthering Heights, and *Agnes Grey,* but Emily has always been the most enigmatic of the three. Despite the research and critical attention she has received, she remains a remote figure. As Mrs. Humphry Ward says in her preface to the Haworth edition of *Wuthering Heights:* "The artist remains hidden and self-contained.... She has the highest power . . . the power which gives life, intensest life, to the creatures of the imagination, and, in doing so, endows them with an independence behind which the maker is forgotten." Emily was an extremely private individual both as an artist and as a person. She was, according to Charlotte's friend Ellen Nussey, a "law unto herself, and a heroine in keeping to that law." The act of creation was essential to her, but it was a private act—in the words of Mrs. Ward, "a high talent working solely for its own joy and satisfaction, with no thought of a spectator, or any aim but that of an ideal and imaginative whole." She left behind one of the most widely read novels in the English language (for which the manuscript has been lost), some 193 poems and verse fragments (for most of which manuscripts are extant), seven French exercises, a few birthday notes, and three brief letters. Given this scarcity of personal records, public or private, and the questionable reliability of secondhand sources of information about her life and personality, the poems become extremely important to anyone who would try to understand her as a person and as an artist.

Yet this immediately leads to another problem, for much of the mystery and lack of understanding that surround Emily Brontë stem from the fact that the real nature of her poetry—and of her youthful writing as a whole—remained undiscovered until well into this century. Only twenty-one of her poems were published in her lifetime. After her death, Charlotte and others had some more tantalizing bits of her poetry published until, in 1895, T. J. Wise and Clement Shorter obtained the bulk of the Brontë manuscripts. Wise and Shorter had much of the material published; but their texts turned out to be unreliable and were sometimes ascribed to the wrong author because the editors were careless and because the characteristically small script in which most of the manuscripts are written makes them difficult to transcribe and identify. Wise then divided much of the manuscript material into small lots—sometimes again with incorrect ascriptions and sometimes breaking up coherent units—and sold it, resulting in the dispersal of manuscript materials over Britain and the United States. As a result, it was not until 1923 that Madeline Hope Dodds drew attention to the peculiar relationships of some of Emily's poetry to adolescent plays she and Anne had created about their mythical kingdom of Gondal. In 1941 C. W. Hatfield produced the first complete and reliable edition of the poems, and Fannie Ratchford made a fuller exploration of the Brontë children's games, plays, and related compositions in *The Brontës' Web of Childhood.* For the genesis of those plays and compositions one has to turn to Brontë family history.

In April 1820 the Reverend Patrick Brontë brought his wife, Maria Branwell Brontë, and six children—Maria, Elizabeth, Charlotte, (Patrick) Branwell, Emily Jane, and Anne—to the remote Yorkshire village of Haworth. In November 1821 Mrs. Brontë died; the children were brought up by their aunt, Elizabeth Branwell, who left her home in Penzance to live in Haworth. That the aunt was a staunch Methodist is well known; how strong her Calvinist tendencies were is a matter of dispute. However, the literature of all three girls contains a clear and strong rejection of Calvinist doctrines. Because the family's life was socially circumscribed

A drawing by Branwell Brontë of himself and his sisters (left to right) Anne, Charlotte, and Emily

by Mr. Brontë's vocation—the Brontë children were not encouraged to mix with the Haworth children—and because both the father and the aunt valued their privacy, the children led a comparatively free but isolated existence and were driven in on themselves to create their own entertainment.

In 1824 Maria, Elizabeth, Charlotte, and six-year-old Emily were sent to the Clergy Daughters' School at Cowan Bridge. The two older sisters became ill and returned home to die within a year; Mr. Brontë ordered Charlotte and Emily home in June 1825.

In 1826 Mr. Brontë brought home for nine-year-old Branwell a box of wooden soldiers, which became the dramatis personae for a series of plays influenced by the children's reading of such works as Aesop's *Fables, The Arabian Nights,* and the Reverend J. Goldsmith's *A Grammar of General Geography* (1803). Inspired by Goldsmith's section on Africa, the children eventually sent their heroes to settle in the land of the Ashantis (the Gold Coast), creating the "Glasstown Confederacy," the most sophisticated and complex of their imaginative constructions. From these plays sprang the Brontë juvenilia. Charlotte and Branwell, presumably with the help of the younger Emily and Anne, recorded, in minute script on tiny pages stitched together and covered with wrapping paper, the accounts and activities of their imaginary kingdoms—the exploits and tragedies of their leaders, with their feuds, battles, and love affairs.

When Charlotte departed for Roe Head School in 1831, Emily and Anne struck out on their own to create and develop the world of Gondal and its epic, while Charlotte and Branwell—collaborating during Charlotte's vacations and working independently while she was away—developed their kingdom of Angria. In 1835 Emily went to Roe Head School, where Charlotte had recently been appointed as a teacher. After only three months Emily returned home; she needed the noiseless, secluded, unrestricted, and unartificial existence and close contact wth nature that Haworth could offer. On only two subsequent occasions did she leave home again: to teach at Law Hill near Halifax from September 1838 until around March 1839, and with Charlotte to study in Brussels in February 1842. When she returned home in November 1842 for Aunt Branwell's funeral, she decided not to go back to Brussels. In the solitude and security of the moors and her home, she looked after much of the cooking and housework while Charlotte and Anne were away studying and governessing.

Charlotte took formal leave of her Angrian world in 1839 and turned to writing novels, but Emily maintained her involvement with Gondal until she died. Her earliest known poem suggests that the Gondal cycle was underway by 1832, and her last poem, begun after the completion of *Wuthering Heights,* marked a return to the cycle, which seems to have been set aside during the writing of the novel. The cycle included dialogue, lyric poetry, verse narrative, and prose history. Much of Emily's poetry is related to Gondal, yet exactly how many poems this includes and where they fit into the saga are not known with any certainty because all of the prose framework has been lost. In 1844 Emily began to copy the best of her poems into two notebooks, one labeled "Gondal Poems," the other "E. J. B. Transcribed February, 1844." The first contains forty-five poems, the second thirty-one; this leaves 117 poems, many of which cannot be identified definitely as either personal or Gondal. Thus the various attempted reconstructions of the Gondal saga—principally those by Laura Hinckley, Fannie Ratchford, and W. D. Paden—have to be regarded as speculative; all that is known about Gondal is based on Emily's and Anne's poems and a few brief references in their birthday notes. The poems themselves provide no clear pattern: the complex Gondal epic is full of situations that echo each other. Gondal functioned as a set of myths, out of which any action, situation, or passion could be taken up according to mood and inclination.

By late 1844 all the sisters were at home again, looking after their father and—following his dismissal as tutor in 1845—after Branwell in his pathetic addiction to alcohol and opium. It was in 1845 that Charlotte accidentally discovered a manuscript notebook of Emily's verse. Although Charlotte had known that her sister was writing poetry, she only then became aware of the nature and quality of Emily's work. The result was the publication of the Bells' volume of poems in 1846. Of the twenty-one poems Emily very reluctantly contributed, fifteen were from the non-Gondal notebook; the other six were from the Gondal notebook but were adapted to remove all traces of Gondal. Although no definite date can be established, it seems she began *Wuthering Heights* sometime in 1845. By July 1846 the manuscripts of *Wuthering Heights,* Charlotte's *The Professor,* and Anne's *Agnes Grey* were making the rounds of publishers. *Wuthering Heights* and *Agnes Grey* were published together in December 1847; Charlotte's novel remained unpublished until 1857, two years after her death.

In trying to come to terms with Emily's poetry, one is confronted with a number of obstacles. On the one hand, one must dismiss the myth of the uneducated, spontaneous, rustic creator, and recognize that she composed with care and delibera-

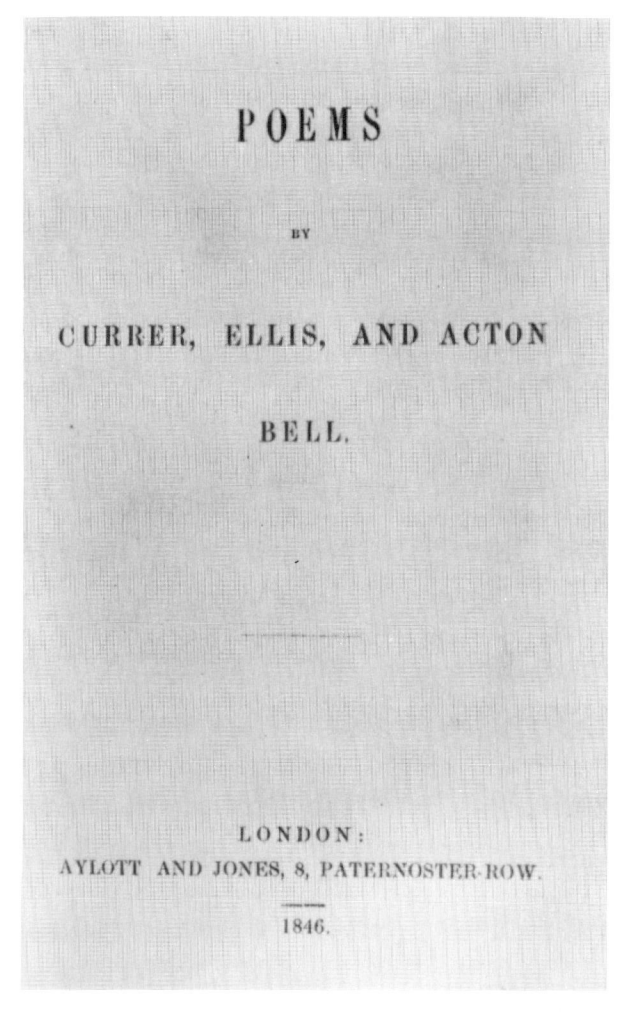

Title page for the Brontë sisters' first published work, under their masculine-sounding pseudonyms (courtesy of the Brontë Parsonage Museum)

tion. At the same time one remains acutely aware of the uneven quality of her poems and of certain undisciplined elements in them. Much of her poetry, especially the Gondal material, is melodramatic and pseudoheroic, filled with lurid Gothic trappings and themes—passionate and illicit love affairs; betrayals, hatred, and vengeance; desperate battles, flights, and exile; martyrdom and captivity; stoic defiance and lonely deaths; regret for the lost paradise of childhood innocence. The influence of Scott, Shelley, and Byron, especially the latter, is obvious. As a result, one often finds defiant gestures degenerating into emotional rant, and intensely felt, powerful lyric passages embedded in banal and melodramatic contexts ("Julian M. and A. G. Rochelle" is the best-known example). However, it must be remembered that Emily did not compose under the incentive to achieve form and coherence that is produced by writing for an audience. She was free to indulge herself, to return to and rework situations and states of feeling, to create a past that was accomplished and recurrent at the same time; it is this lack of restraint that produced much of the powerful intensity one feels in her poetry. One must also remember that the brevity of her creative life—she died at the age of thirty—precluded the possibility of much development. In the forty-three poems she had written by the end of 1837, Emily introduced every important theme she was to elaborate later.

Much of her poetry is dramatic, making use of a large number of personae and of various forms of direct speech and address. As Rosalind Miles has suggested: "Without in any way undervaluing her more reflective mood, it remains a remarkable feature of her work just how many of the poems plunge in in this direct and startling way, with direct address—and how central is this technique for stimulating and involving readers, not relaxing the poetic hold upon them even at the end." While one must be careful, therefore, not to read as autobiographical the experiences and actions of Gondal personae, one recognizes that Emily is no Robert Browning, even when she uses a form of dramatic dialogue. She plays the various roles and her characters all speak with much the same voice. Her chief interest is not character delineation; it is rather the investigation of attitudes, values, and states of feeling. Thus the "I" of her poems is often neither Emily nor a Gondalian, but a personified state of feeling. Clearly these investigations arise out of personal questions and experiences—it is not farfetched to suggest that Hatfield's number 96, by "R. Gleneden," laments the absence of Anne, who had left to go governessing a week earlier. But her characteristic reticence caused her to confront the world through a series of masks. Therefore much of her poetry remains impersonal, and her attraction to ballad themes and forms probably stems from the depersonalized patterns they offered, patterns that served to protect her from the chaotic flux of daily life and offered her a reassuring rhythmical order. Also, although references to the natural world Emily loved so much abound in her poems, she is not a nature poet. She does not delineate the relationship between a speaker and a particular landscape. Rather, in the tradition of the Romantic poets, a presented scene usually serves to raise an emotional problem, a background out of which the poem's reflections on some aspect of the meaning of human existence arise.

These reflections are largely of a philosophical or religious nature, calling into question the values that motivate human behavior. She is very much aware of the dark sides of both the natural world and human nature. Gondal is a moral wasteland in which normal values are perverted, and in which uncontrolled passion and ambition reign. After 1837 her depiction of a perverted and hellish world becomes increasingly vehement, emphasizing the awful consequences the deeds of the evil have on others and the sense of wasted and perverted potential. Gondal's wars, with all their attendant misery, violence, and cruelty, become Emily's chief metaphor for the world in which she lived; this interpretation is reinforced by her surviving devoirs. Decorum and social convention, designed to make behavior more humane, are too frequently used instead to make self-indulgence and its consequent inhumanity socially respectable. In such a world the ability to feel intensely is the only salvation, but it must be paid for in suffering (Hatfield, number 112). She is, therefore, acutely aware of the incongruity of pain and suffering with the splendor of nature, and also aware of the inadequacy of traditional Christianity to provide explanations and assurances. The angels are happy because they are ignorant (Hatfield, number 149). For Emily, hell is no place of retribution in the afterlife; it is life on earth. The Gondal love poems reveal a continual state of tension between passionate indulgence and morality. Passion can only be indulged at another's expense; such indulgence must be paid for, and retribution occurs in this world, not the next. "If I have sinned," says Fernando De Samara, "long, long ago/That sin was purified by woe" (Hatfield, number 133).

Not surprisingly, some poems depict the attractiveness of escape into imaginary worlds from which she could exclude the people and situations she found so distasteful:

Yes, as I mused, the naked room,
The flickering firelight died away
And from the midst of cheerless gloom
I passed to bright, unclouded day—
(Hatfield, number 92)

Yet the poems of the last ten years of her life show Emily fighting a battle over the proper use of the creative imagination. Her stance is often ambiguous and contradictory, but the general development is away from escapism and toward an attempt to come to terms with a world she detested. Her disgust with humanity becomes most vehement between 1842

A manuscript page for one of Brontë's poems about the imaginary kingdom of Gondal (by courtesy of the Trustees of the British Museum)

and 1845: "So hopeless is the world without, /The world within I doubly prize" (Hatfield, number 174). In a series of dialogue poems she tries to justify escape, but the dialectic remains unresolved because the longing to escape is frequently accompanied by a feeling of guilt and an admission that such escape is a delusion: "I trust not to thy phantom bliss" (Hatfield, number 174). This inner debate reaches a crisis in the poems of 1844: the commitment to the imagination is fervently repeated, but with increasing skepticism as Emily's intellect more and more rejects uncritical surrender. She begs the stars, Dreams, and Night to return and hide her from the hostile light of day "that does not warm, but burn," yet also admits "It would not do" (Hatfield, number 184). After 1844 she seems to have found a resolution, which is delineated more clearly in *Wuthering Heights* than in the poetry. "No Coward Soul," written concurrently with *Wuthering Heights,* demonstrates the confidence and clarity of vision she had achieved. Conflict, rebellion, lamentation, and death wish have been replaced by the rising affirmation of an imagination that has transcended rather than run away. Her last poem, although marking a return to Gondal, shows a clear attempt to link Gondal more directly with the real world, with any hope of salvation based on the possibility of a self-sacrificing love that can return love for hate:

> Yet not to thee, not even to thee
> Would I return such misery.
> Such is that fearful grief I know
> I will not cause thee equal woe
>
> (Hatfield, number 192)

On 24 September 1848, Branwell Brontë died. Emily caught a cold at Branwell's funeral; this aggravated a tubercular condition, and she died on 19 December.

Emily Brontë gave evidence of her lyric ability as early as 1836 with "High waving heather," but her greatest poems were produced between 1844 and 1846, when her doubts and inner conflict produced a sense of sustained power she had not achieved before. As Barbara Hardy has put it: "The achievement of [her] poetry at its best, is to join impassioned experience with a grasp of the significance of that experience. Emily Brontë occasionally writes love poetry, more frequently poetry expressing experiences of nature, religion and death, but she joins all these subjects or experiences in an exploration of the nature of Imagination." She was no great innovator in form and technique, but, as Charlotte said, neither was her poetry "at all like the poetry women generally write." Many of her ideas and attitudes were unconventional and disturbing, and her poetry is the closest thing available to an uncensored record of the growth of her mind; it cannot simply be dismissed as juvenilia that offers no useful insights. Yet serious attempts to make a coherent whole of her poems, of her artistic production, and indeed of her life have only recently begun and still go on.

Bibliographies:
Anthony C. Yablon and John R. Turner, *A Brontë Bibliography* (London: Hodgins, 1978);
Anne Passel, *Charlotte and Emily Brontë: An Annotated Bibliography* (New York: Garland, 1979).

Biographies:
John Hewish, *Emily Brontë: A Critical and Biographical Study* (London: Macmillan, 1969);
Winifred Gérin, *Emily Brontë* (Oxford: Oxford University Press, 1971).

References:
Edward Chitham and Tom Winnifrith, *Brontë Facts and Brontë Problems* (Atlantic Highlands, N. J.: Humanities Press, 1983);
Elizabeth Cleghorn Gaskell, *The Life of Charlotte Brontë,* 2 volumes (London: Smith, Elder, 1857);
J. Hillis Miller, *The Disappearance of God: Five Nineteenth-Century Writers* (Cambridge: Harvard University Press, 1963);
W. D. Paden, *An Investigation of Gondal* (New York: Bookman, 1958);
F. B. Pinion, *A Brontë Companion* (London: Macmillan, 1975);
Fannie E. Ratchford, *The Brontës' Web of Childhood* (New York: Columbia University Press, 1941);
Ratchford, *Gondal's Queen* (Austin: University of Texas Press, 1955);
Anne Smith, ed., *The Art of Emily Brontë* (London: Vision Press, 1976).

Elizabeth Barrett Browning

Gardner B. Taplin
Tulane University

BIRTH: Coxhoe Hall, Durham County, England, 6 March 1806 to Edward Barrett Moulton-Barrett and Mary Graham-Clarke Moulton-Barrett.

MARRIAGE: 12 September 1846 to Robert Browning; child: Robert Wiedemann Barrett.

DEATH: Florence, Italy, 29 June 1861.

BOOKS: *The Battle of Marathon: A Poem* (London: W. Lindsell, 1820);
An Essay on Mind, with Other Poems, anonymous (London: Duncan, 1826);
Prometheus Bound, Translated from the Greek of Aeschylus; and Miscellaneous Poems, anonymous (London: A. J. Valpy, 1833; Boston: J. H. Francis/New York: C. S. Francis, 1851);
The Seraphim and Other Poems (London: Saunders & Otley, 1838);
Poems, 2 volumes (London: Moxon, 1844); republished as *A Drama of Exile: and other Poems,* 2 volumes (New York: Langley, 1845);
Poems: New Edition, 2 volumes (London: Chapman & Hall, 1850); republished as *The Poems of Elizabeth Barrett Browning* (New York: C. S. Francis/Boston: J. H. Francis, 1850);
Casa Guidi Windows: A Poem (London: Chapman & Hall, 1851);
Poems: Third Edition, 2 volumes (London: Chapman & Hall, 1853);
Two Poems, by Browning and Robert Browning (London: Chapman & Hall, 1854);
Poems: Fourth Edition, 3 volumes (London: Chapman & Hall, 1856);
Aurora Leigh (London: Chapman & Hall, 1857; New York & Boston: C. S. Francis, 1857; revised, London: Chapman & Hall, 1859);
Poems before Congress (London: Chapman & Hall, 1860); republished as *Napoleon III in Italy, and Other Poems* (New York: C. S. Francis, 1860);
Last Poems (London: Chapman & Hall, 1862; New York: Miller, 1862);
The Greek Christian Poets and the English Poets (London: Chapman & Hall, 1863); republished as *Essays on the Greek Christian Poets and the English Poets* (New York: Miller, 1863);

Elizabeth Barrett Browning (National Portrait Gallery)

Psyche Apocalyptè: A Lyrical Drama, by Browning and Richard Hengist Horne (London & Aylesbury, U.K.: Privately printed, 1876);
New Poems by Robert and Elizabeth Barrett Browning, edited by Frederic G. Kenyon (London: Smith, Elder, 1914; New York: Macmillan, 1915);
The Poet's Enchiridion, edited by H. Buxton Forman (Boston: Bibliophile Society, 1914);
Elizabeth Barrett Browning: Hitherto Unpublished Poems and Stories, with an Unedited Autobiography, edited by H. Buxton Forman, 2 volumes (Boston: Bibliophile Society, 1914);
Diary by E. B. B.: The Unpublished Diary of Elizabeth Barrett Browning, 1831-1832, edited by Philip Kelley and Ronald Hudson (Athens: Ohio University Press, 1969).

Collections: *The Poetical Works of Elizabeth Barrett*

Browning, 6 volumes (London: Smith, Elder, 1889-1890);

The Poetical Works of Elizabeth Barrett Browning, edited by Frederic G. Kenyon (London: Smith, Elder, 1897);

The Complete Poetical Works of Elizabeth Barrett Browning, Cambridge Edition, edited by Harriet Waters Preston (Boston & New York: Houghton Mifflin, 1900);

The Complete Works of Elizabeth Barrett Browning, edited by Charlotte Porter and Helen A. Clarke, 6 volumes (New York: Crowell, 1900).

OTHER: "Queen Annelida and False Arcite" and "The Complaint of Annelida to False Arcite," in *The Poems of Geoffrey Chaucer, Modernized* (London: Whittaker, 1841), pp. 237-257;

Richard Hengist Horne, ed., *A New Spirit of the Age,* many anonymous contributions by Browning, 2 volumes (London: Smith, Elder, 1844);

Two versions of "The Daughters of Pandarus," translated from the *Odyssey* by Browning, in Mrs. Anna Jameson, *Memoirs and Essays Illustrative of Art, Literature, and Social Morals* (London: Bentley, 1846), pp. 137-138.

Among all women poets of the English-speaking world in the nineteenth century, none was held in higher critical esteem or was more admired for the independence and courage of her views than Elizabeth Barrett Browning. During the years of her marriage to Robert Browning, her literary reputation far surpassed that of her poet-husband; when visitors came to their home in Florence, she was invariably the greater attraction. Both in England and in the United States she had a wide following among cultured readers. An example of the reach of her fame may be seen in the influence she had upon the recluse poet who lived in the rural college town of Amherst, Massachusetts. A framed portrait of Mrs. Browning hung in the bedroom of Emily Dickinson, whose life had been transfigured by the poetry of "that Foreign Lady." From the time when she had first become acquainted with Mrs. Browning's writings, Dickinson had ecstatically admired her as a poet and had virtually idolized her as a woman who had achieved such a rich fulfillment in her life. When Samuel Bowles, a close friend of the Dickinson family and respected editor of the *Springfield Republican,* went to Europe for the first time, he took with him two books: the Bible and Mrs. Browning's *Aurora Leigh* (1857). So highly regarded had she become by 1850, the year of Wordsworth's death, that she was prominently mentioned as a possible successor to the poet laureateship. Her humane and liberal point of view manifests itself in her poems aimed at redressing many forms of social injustice, such as the slave trade in America, the labor of children in the mines and the mills of England, the oppression of the Italian people by the Austrians, and the restrictions forced upon women in nineteenth-century society.

As a child and a young woman Elizabeth Barrett was extremely fortunate in the circumstances of her family background and environment. Her father, whose wealth was derived from extensive sugar plantations in Jamaica, was the proprietor of "Hope End," an estate of almost 500 acres in Herefordshire, between the market town of Ledbury and the Malvern Hills. In this peaceful setting, with its farmers' cottages, gardens, woodlands, ponds, carriage roads, and mansion "adapted for the accommodation of a nobleman or family of the first distinction," Elizabeth—known by the nickname "Ba"—at first lived the kind of life that might be expected for the daughter of a wealthy country squire. She rode her pony in the lanes around the Barrett estate, went with her brothers and sisters for walks and picnics in the countryside,

Elizabeth Barrett's father, Edward Barrett Moulton-Barrett (from a painting by H. W. Pickersgill; courtesy of Mrs. Violet Altham)

"Hope End," the Barretts' estate in Herefordshire, where Elizabeth Barrett spent her early childhood

visited other county families to drink tea, accepted visits in return, and participated with her brothers and sisters in homemade theatrical productions. But, unlike her two sisters and eight brothers, she immersed herself in the world of books as often as she could get away from the social rituals of her family. "Books and dreams were what I lived in — and domestic life only seemed to buzz gently around, like bees about the grass," she said many years later. Having begun to compose verses at the age of four, two years later she received from her father for "some lines on virtue penned with great care" a ten-shilling note enclosed in a letter addressed to "the Poet-Laureate of Hope End."

Before Barrett was ten years old, she had read the histories of England, Greece, and Rome; several of Shakespeare's plays, including *Othello* and *The Tempest;* portions of Pope's Homeric translations; and passages from *Paradise Lost.* At eleven, she says in an autobiographical sketch written when she was fourteen, she "felt the most ardent desire to understand the learned languages." Except for some instruction in Greek and Latin from a tutor who lived with the Barrett family for two or three years to help her brother Edward ("Bro") prepare for entrance to Charterhouse, Barrett was, as Robert Browning later asserted, "self-taught in almost every respect." Within the next few years she went through the works of the principal Greek and Latin authors, the Greek Christian fathers, several plays by Racine and Molière, and a portion of Dante's *Inferno* — all in the original languages. Also around this time she learned enough Hebrew to read the Old Testament from beginning to end. Her enthusiasm for the works of Tom Paine, Voltaire, Rousseau, and Mary Wollstonecraft presaged the concern for human rights that she was later to express in her poems and letters. At the age of eleven or twelve she composed a verse "epic" in four books of rhyming couplets, *The Battle of Marathon,* which was privately printed at Mr. Barrett's expense in 1820. She later spoke of this product of her childhood as "Pope's Homer done over again, or rather undone." Most of the fifty copies that were printed probably went to the Barretts' home and remained there. It is now the rarest of her works, with only a handful of copies known to exist.

At the age of twenty Barrett offered to the public, with no indication of authorship, a slender volume entitled *An Essay on Mind, with Other Poems* (1826). Long afterwards in a letter to an American critic she called the book "a girl's exercise, nothing

An 1823 drawing of Barrett by her mother

more nor less!—not at all known to the public." The poem for which the volume was named was a pretentious and frigid effort to survey in some eighty-eight pages the history of science, philosophy, and poetry from ancient Greece to the present. The other fourteen poems were occasional pieces or verses of a personal nature which did not yet display the author's authentic voice. Of the two journals which noticed the volume, one objected to its obscurity of language and its "barren themes," and the other advised the poet to come down from the heights to look more closely at nature.

Shortly after the publication of this volume Barrett entered into one of the most important friendships of her life. Hugh Stuart Boyd, a totally blind, middle-aged dilettante scholar with private means, had published at his own expense several volumes of translations from the Greek patristic writings. Since the author of the "Essay on Mind" lived not far from him, he was eager to become acquainted with a poet of such extraordinary erudition. From his home in Malvern Wells he sent her copies of his works and invited her to pay him a visit. Starved as she was for intellectual companionship, she eagerly began to correspond with him and before long was making frequent visits to Ruby Cottage, where he lived with his wife and daughter. It was entirely owing to Boyd's influence that Barrett's enthusiasm for Greek studies was rekindled. During this period she read an astonishing amount of classical Greek literature—Homer, Pindar, the tragedians, Aristophanes, and passages from Plato, Aristotle, Isocrates, and Xenophon—as well as the Greek Christian Fathers Boyd had translated.

In 1832 the peaceful, secure lives of the Barretts in their Herefordshire retreat came to a distressing close. For a number of years the Jamaican plantations of the Barrett family had been mismanaged and Mr. Barrett had suffered serious financial losses. With the prospect of a greatly reduced income he could no longer afford to maintain the Hope End estate and suffered the embarrassment of its having to be sold at a public auction to satisfy creditors. The eleven children and their father (Mrs. Barrett had died in 1828) went to live temporarily in Sidmouth, on the southern coast of Devonshire. The reason for the choice of this town in the south of England may have been Mr. Barrett's concern for Elizabeth's health. At the age of fifteen she had injured her spine when she was attempting to saddle her pony. Seven years later the breaking of a blood vessel in the chest left her with a weakened constitution and a chronic cough. During the period of the Barretts' stay in Sidmouth, Boyd lived for a year and a half within a few minutes' walk from their home. To the detriment of her own poetic career she went to him daily and helped him to see

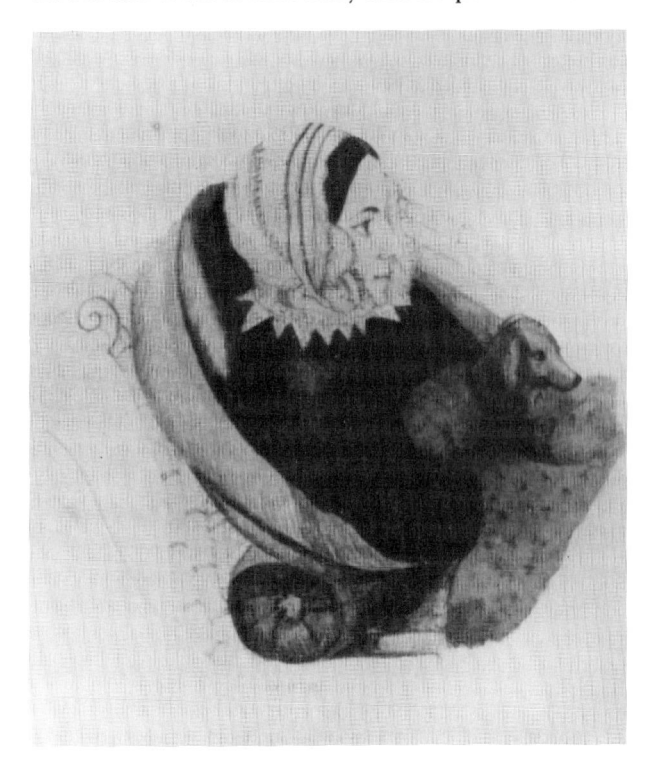

A drawing of Barrett by her brother Alfred (courtesy of Edward Moulton-Barrett)

through the press a bizarre volume on his favorite subject, Greek Christian Fathers. By the time she left Sidmouth Browning's feelings toward Boyd had changed: she now saw him as limited, naive, and even pathetic. The one volume that she produced while at Sidmouth was *Prometheus Bound, Translated from the Greek of Aeschylus; and Miscellaneous Poems,* published anonymously in 1833. Twelve years later in a letter to Boyd she called the translation "that frigid, rigid exercise," and after her marriage she made amends by writing a vastly improved version. The "miscellaneous poems" are all immature in content and expression and give little promise of their author's future distinction.

After living for three years in several rented houses in the coastal town, the Barretts moved in 1835 to London, which was to remain their permanent place of residence. At first Elizabeth missed the fresh sea breezes and the sound of the waves, and disliked her new setting because of the ever-present soot and fog and the long, narrow streets lined with attached stone or brick houses which all looked alike. But before long she was content to be living in a great metropolis, the center of the nation's literary and artistic activities. Barrett made her name known in literary circles with *The Seraphim and Other Poems* (1838). Except for the privately printed *Battle of Marathon,* this was the first work with her name on the title page. She said that the volume, despite some shortcomings, was "the first utterance of my own individuality." The many reviews that appeared both in England and America almost all hailed her as a young poet of extraordinary ability and still greater promise. The long poetic drama of seventy-eight pages for which the volume was named presents the conversation of two angels in the heavens retelling portions of the Old and New Testaments, and commenting on the Crucifixion then taking place. Although most of the critics considered the poem too mystical and too high-flown to be successful, they generally praised the shorter poems, most of which now seem sentimental and trite. A poem that soon became a great favorite with both professional critics and the general public was "Isobel's Child," with its depiction of the death of a three-month-old baby who has been lying all night in the mother's arms. The well-known critic John Wilson ("Christopher North") declared that there was beauty in all the poems and that some were "altogether beautiful."

Just as Barrett was being recognized as one of England's most original and gifted young poets, she was in such poor health because of the weakness of her lungs that her physician recommended that she

The Barretts' home at 50 Wimpole Street, London (City of Westminster Archives)

move away from London and live for a while in a warmer climate. Torquay, on the south coast of Devonshire, was selected, and there, together with various members of her family who took turns living with her, she remained for three years as an invalid under the watchful care of her physicians. Seriously ill as she was, she suffered a sudden shattering blow that left her prostrated for months. The death by drowning on 11 July 1840 of her favorite brother, Edward, who had been with her constantly at Torquay, was the greatest sorrow of her life. The memory of that tragic event remained with her as long as she lived and was so painful that she could never speak of it even to those closest to her.

When she returned to the family home at 50 Wimpole Street after the three terrible years at Torquay, she felt that she had left her youth behind and that the future held little more than permanent invalidism and confinement to her bedroom. For the following five years she remained mostly in her room, which she decorated with busts of Homer and Chaucer and later with engravings of Browning (whom she had not yet met), Tennyson, Carlyle, Harriet Martineau, and Wordsworth. Yet despite

The weakest thing.

Which is the weakest thing of all
   Mine heart can ponder?
The sun, a little cloud can pall
   With darkness yonder?—
The cloud, a little wind can move
   Where'er it listeth?
The wind, a leaf which hangs above,
   Tho' sere, resisteth?

What time that yellow leaf was green,
   My hopes were gladder:
Now on its branch each summer seen
   May find me sadder.
Ah me! a leaf with sighs can wring
   My lips asunder—
Then is mine heart the weakest thing
   Itself can ponder.

Manuscript page for one of the poems published in Barrett's The Seraphim and Other Poems *(Anderson Galleries, 4-5 April 1934)*

her frail health she was more fortunate in her circumstances than most women writers of her time. Thanks to inheritances from her grandmother and her uncle, she was the only one of the brothers and sisters who was independently wealthy. As the eldest daughter in a family without a mother, she normally would have been expected to spend much of her time supervising the domestic servants, but her weakness prevented her from leaving her room. Thus the members of her family came to visit with her and to bring her everything she desired. Relieved of all household burdens and financial cares, she was free to devote herself to reading English and French fiction and memoirs and to writing letters, essays, and poetry. Since the prospect of meeting strangers made her nervous, only two visitors besides her family had the privilege of seeing her in her room: John Kenyon, a minor poet and friend of many English poets, and the well-known writer Mary Russell Mitford. During her last year or two at Wimpole Street she also received the Reverend George B. Hunter, whom she had come to know during her years at Sidmouth, and the art critic Anna Jameson.

Protected from the outside world and surrounded by a loving family, Barrett resumed her literary career, which had been partially interrupted during her serious illness at Torquay. In addition to producing a continuous flow of poems for publication in both English and American journals, she wrote a series of articles on the Greek Christian poets and another series on the English poets, the latter originally begun as a critique of a recently published anthology of English verse. Also, in collaboration with the playwright Richard Hengist Horne, she made many anonymous contributions to a book of critical essays on eminent literary figures edited by him and entitled *A New Spirit of the Age* (1844). Within three years after her return to Wimpole Street she had many new poems in manuscript and others already published in journals, and she believed that the time was ripe for their appearance in book form—the first since *The Seraphim and Other Poems* of 1838. The critical reception of her *Poems,* published in two volumes in 1844, was such that the author was no longer merely a promising young poet but had suddenly become an international celebrity. On both sides of the Atlantic the leading journals came out with substantial reviews, and almost all found much to praise; Elizabeth Barrett was now acclaimed as one of England's great living poets. The poem which found least favor with the critics was "A Drama of Exile." For 119 pages the drama recounts the conversations and events of

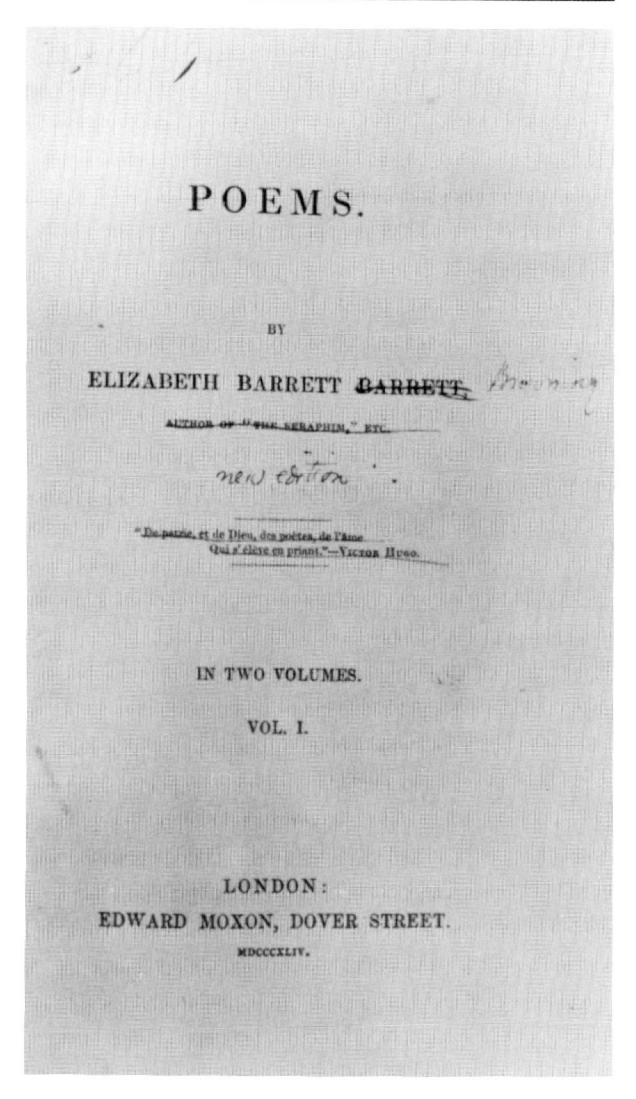

Title page for the volume of poems that made Barrett an international celebrity. After her marriage, she crossed out her maiden name and substituted "Browning."

the first day's exile from Eden, as various spirits alternately rebuke and console the fallen pair. In the judgment of most reviewers the drama was lacking in coherence, the language was obscure, and the characters were unreal.

None of the shorter poems caught the public fancy more than "Lady Geraldine's Courtship: A Romance of the Age." A young poet with slender financial resources falls in love with the daughter of an earl; but since her life is filled with luxuries, he has little hope that his love will be returned. Despite the social barriers, however, the romantic conclusion has the girl responding to her suitor's ardor. Another poem much admired by sentimental readers was "Bertha in the Lane." The heroine, though apparently in good health, dies suddenly after learning that her lover has jilted her in favor of her younger sister. The most influential poem in the volumes, and one of the best-known of all her works, was "The Cry of the Children," which had first appeared in *Blackwood's* a year earlier. Having read the reports from the parliamentary commissioners of the terrible conditions of children's employment in mines, trades, and manufactures, she tells of the hopeless lives of the boys and girls who are the victims of capitalist exploitation. Even though Barrett was a bookish, sheltered, upper-middle-class unmarried woman far removed from the scenes she was describing, she gives evidence here of her passionate concern for human rights. The critics reviewing *Poems* praised her for her intellectual power, originality, and boldness of thought; but most agreed that her weakness lay in her frequent vagueness of concept and obscurity of expression.

The two volumes found their way into the home of Robert Browning. Upon seeing a handsome tribute paid to him by name in "Lady Geraldine's Courtship," Browning in January 1845 wrote a letter which began, "I love your verses with all my heart, dear Miss Barrett." When Browning wrote that first of the many letters that were to be exchanged between the two poets, Barrett had already won an admiring public and was maintaining an extensive correspondence with writers and artists in England and the United States. Browning, on the other hand, was bitterly discouraged because his poetical career was not prospering and his productions on the London stage had proved to be hopeless failures. Six years younger than Barrett, he had abundant energy and good health, dressed as a young man of fashion, and enjoyed going to dinners and receptions where he conversed with many of the leading figures of the literary world. For almost all of his life he had been living at home with his parents and his sister—all three of whom adored him—and was financially dependent upon his father, since none of his volumes of verse had repaid the expenses of publication.

The courtship progressed despite the objections of Mr. Barrett, who wished his children to remain totally dependent on him. During the period of the exchange of letters and of Browning's visits to her room, she was composing the poems later to be named "Sonnets from the Portuguese." Most of the world's great love poetry has been produced by men; what is new about the sonnets is that the coming of love into the writer's life is described from the point of view of the woman. Among the finest love poems ever written by a woman, they are her most enduring poetic achievement. A chronic invalid, worn down by a succession of griefs, robbed of the bright-hued cheeks and resilience of youth, living without hope that a new life might someday be hers outside of her virtual prison, she expresses in the sonnets her sense of wonder that her life has been so transfigured. Filled with gratitude for her suitor's offer of love, she at first tells him that they must remain no more than friends because of the disparities in health and age. Marriage, she says, would place a severe burden upon him, for the care of an invalid wife six years older than he would necessarily take him away from the varied social life he has been enjoying. Will love that has come so quickly not fade just as quickly? Is her lover's suit based merely on pity? If she will promise to give up her home and the day-to-day associations with father, brothers, sisters, and friends, will he in turn be everything to her so that she will never miss the life she leaves behind? From the earnest look of her lover's eyes she finds the answers to these and other questions, so that her doubts and hesitations are

A somewhat inaccurate portrait of Robert Browning from R. H. Horne's A New Spirit of the Age *(1844), which hung on Barrett's wall at Wimpole Street. Before they met, this picture gave Barrett her only conception of Browning's appearance.*

dispelled. With the full assurance of the depth of his feelings for her, she responds to his love in the most inspired sonnet of the cycle, "How do I love thee? Let me count the ways."

The clandestine marriage ceremony took place on 12 September 1846 at St. Marylebone Parish Church, which was not far from the Barretts' house. Almost immediately the couple left for Italy, where they hoped the warmer climate might help Elizabeth to regain some of her strength. After one winter they moved to Florence, which was to remain their home until Elizabeth's death. Despite the responsibilities of marriage and motherhood—their only child, Robert Wiedemann Barrett Browning, called "Pen," was born in 1849—Mrs. Browning had no intention of discontinuing her literary career. Her first task was to revise her volumes of 1838 and 1844 for publication in a new edition.

For the three years following her marriage Mrs. Browning had kept the forty-four sonnets in a notebook; she did not show them to her husband until the summer of 1849. He was so impressed with their beauty that he insisted on their appearing in her forthcoming new edition of *Poems* (1850). In order to make it appear that the poems had no biographical significance, the Brownings selected the ambiguous title "Sonnets from the Portuguese," as if they were translations. "Catarina to Camoens," the poem immediately preceding the sonnets in the second volume of *Poems*, tells of the love of Catarina for the Portuguese poet Camoens. Since first reading "Catarina to Camoens" in Elizabeth's *Poems* of 1844, Browning had associated Elizabeth with the Portuguese Catarina. Most of the reviews of the *Poems* of 1850 paid little attention to the sonnets, but a writer in *Fraser's* magazine immediately appreciated their distinctive quality: "From the Portuguese they may be: but their life and earnestness must prove Mrs. Browning either to be the most perfect of all known translators, or to have quickened with her own spirit the framework of another's thought, and then modestly declined the honour which was really her own." The sonnets gradually gained critical acceptance and have become the most beloved of all Mrs. Browning's works.

Besides the "Sonnets from the Portuguese," the other major new work in the volumes was the retranslation of *Prometheus Bound*. This new version was an enormous improvement over the translation that had been published in 1833; it is faithful to the original without being pedantic and is expressed in lively, idiomatic English. The two volumes were fairly well received in England, where the reviewers praised her for the depth of her intellect, the earnestness of her thought, and the "pathetic beauty" of the romantic ballads. They believed, however, that Mrs. Browning's poetry still retained some of the deficiencies of her earlier books, such as diffuseness, obscure language, and inappropriate imagery.

Mrs. Browning had developed a passionate interest in Italian politics; during her first year in Italy she had written "A Meditation in Tuscany" and sent it to *Blackwood's*. The editor had declined it and returned the manuscript to her, and it became the first part of *Casa Guidi Windows* (1851). The poem deals with political events as seen by the poet from the windows of Casa Guidi, the great stone palace in Florence where the Brownings had an apartment. In 1846 the newly elected Pope Pius IX had granted amnesty to prisoners who had fought for Italian liberty, initiated a program looking forward to a more democratic form of government for the Papal State, and carried out a number of other reforms so that it looked as though he were heading toward the leadership of a league for a free Italy. Progressive measures had also been instituted in Tuscany by Grand Duke Leopold II, who arranged for a representative form of government and allowed the people to have a free press and to form their own civic guard. The first half of *Casa Guidi Windows* had been written when Mrs. Browning was filled with enthusiasm and was hopeful that the newly awakened liberal movements were moving toward the unification and freedom of the Italian states.

In the second half of the poem she voices her disillusionment and her bitter disappointment that liberalism had been crushed almost everywhere in Italy. Pope Pius had fled in disguise from the Vatican in the face of agitation for a republican government and had taken refuge at Gaeta under the protection of the king of Naples. Leopold, whom Mrs. Browning had at first admired, had proved to be a coward; and, rather than agree to the formation of a constituent assembly of the Italian states in Rome, he had left his Florentine palace and joined the exiled pope in Gaeta. Several months later the Austrian troops had occupied Florence, and Leopold had returned under their protection. In her poem Mrs. Browning expresses her disappointment with the pope, the grand duke, the English government for its failure to intervene on the side of the Italian patriots, and the Florentines themselves because they had been unwilling to make the necessary sacrifices. By the middle of 1849 the liberal impulses had been crushed; except for Piedmont all the Italian states were under the

Casa Guidi, the palace in Florence, where the Brownings had an apartment

domination of Austria and the papacy. For the next ten years there were no more uprisings or wars, and in the absence of stirring political events Mrs. Browning began the composition of a completely different kind of poem from anything she had written up to then.

As early as 1845 she had written to Browning that it was her intention to write a sort of novel-poem "running into the midst of our conventions, & rushing into drawing-rooms & the like 'where angels fear to tread'; & so, meeting face to face & without mask the Humanity of the age, & speaking the truth as I conceive of it, out plainly." For several years events in her own life and in the world about her distracted her from her purpose, so that the first mention of her new work appears in a letter written in 1853 to her friend Anna Jameson. Her poem would fill a volume when it was finished, she said; it was the romance she had been "hankering after so long, written in blank verse, in the autobiographical form." Named after the heroine of the poem, *Aurora Leigh* was published in 1857. In the dedication to her lifelong friend and benefactor John Kenyon she wrote that it was "the most mature of my works, and the one into which my highest convictions upon Life and Art have entered." In a narrative of some 11,000 lines the heroine tells of her birth in Italy, her early years in rural England, her successful literary career in London and later in Florence, and at the end her marriage to her one true love.

Orphaned at an early age and brought up by an aunt in the western county of Shropshire, the youthful Aurora finds herself in a cultural desert, with no one to share her enthusiasm for literature. Aurora's description of the kind of education imposed upon her by her conventional aunt illustrates the restricted, anti-intellectual attitudes of the English middle classes toward the upbringing of their daughters. Aurora memorizes the Collects of the Anglican Church, takes lessons in music and dancing, is given some superficial instruction in French, German, history, and geography, and is taught sewing and embroidery. Not only were young

John Kenyon, friend and benefactor of the Brownings (courtesy of the British Museum)

women discouraged from learning Greek and Latin and from reading "controversial" books, but they were denied a university education. Aurora has to seek her education at home, whereas her cousin Romney Leigh is sent to a university. Rebelling against her aunt's narrow regimen, Aurora finds her true life in the world of books. Discovering her father's private library hidden away in the attic, she reads widely in Greek and Latin literature and English poetry and begins to compose verses of her own.

At the age of twenty she rejects a proposal of marriage from Romney Leigh, who asks her to be his wife for the sole reason that he needs her to help him in his philanthropic activities. Women, he tells her, are lacking in the higher imaginative qualities that would enable them to be great writers or artists. Aurora moves away from the rural community which has so stifled her and makes her home in London, where she will be independent and strive for literary success. By dint of steady application she wins within six or seven years a place for herself in the London literary world. To help support herself she writes articles for encyclopedias and journals, but she finds her chief satisfaction in the publication of her volumes of poetry. The heroine of this novel-poem serves as Mrs. Browning's mouthpiece when she declares that the most fitting subjects for poetry are to be found in contemporary settings and that a poet should not reject his own times to seek inspiration from earlier civilizations. Aurora, though still in her middle twenties, has already produced books of poetry which are reaching a wide and admiring public.

In contrast to Aurora, who has lived a serene and rather sheltered life, the main figure of the subplot is a pathetic victim of the abuses of society. Marian Erle is the only child of an ignorant and abusive migrant farm worker and a wife cowed into submission by his drunken rages. The girl runs away from her parents in fear of their violence, is rescued from destitution by Romney Leigh, and even receives from him an offer of marriage. As a radical socialist he thus proposes to put into practice his utopian ideal of the destruction of the barriers that separate the rich from the poor and the educated from the ignorant. The marriage, however, does not take place, for Marian is treacherously spirited away from England by a woman who believes herself to be in love with Romney. Marian is taken to a house of ill fame in Paris, where she is drugged and sexually assaulted. As a result of this act of violence she becomes pregnant and after much ill-treatment gives birth to a son.

After nine years in London Aurora suddenly gives up her apartment and establishes a new home for herself in a villa in Florence. On the way she stops in Paris, where she encounters Marian and hears her story; she takes Marian and the baby to Florence with her. A few months after her arrival Aurora is asked once again by Romney to be his wife. This time, however, he is blind and much humbled by his misfortunes. Leigh Hall, which he had converted into a utopian community, had been set on fire and destroyed by the very people whom he had been aiding. At the time of the fire he had been struck on the forehead and blinded by a falling beam. Romney now sadly admits that doctrinaire socialism is a failure, for the people will rebel against any restrictions and reforms imposed upon them. Aurora says that she too has been wrong in her proud independence and her belief that her life could be complete without the companionship of a loved one. They pledge themselves to each other and look forward to a life of shared responsibilities. In the meanwhile Marian has told them that she will never marry and that when her child no longer needs her care she will devote herself to helping the "outcast orphans of the world."

In this long narrative poem Mrs. Browning has dealt with some of the major social problems of her age. In Victorian England an educated woman with unusual talents had almost no opportunity to make use of her skills in a world that was dominated by men. Nevertheless, as the poem shows in the example of its heroine, it was possible for a woman with great energy and sense of purpose to live by herself in London and become renowned on the strength of her own unaided efforts. Professional success alone, however, is not sufficient, for nothing can give more meaning to a woman's life than enduring love in marriage. Another theme is Mrs. Browning's distrust of the theories of contemporary French socialists, such as Charles Fourier, who advocated the division of society into communistic units. She believed that in the kind of state envisioned by the radical socialists there would be no place for artists and poets. Nothing stirred up more controversy than her frank treatment of the plight of "the fallen woman"—a subject that was considered by the Victorian public to be outside the purview of the serious novelist or poet. In mid-nineteenth-century England standards of sexual conduct were so rigid that any woman who bore a child out of wedlock, even if she had been a victim of male aggression, was shunned by "respectable" people and condemned to a life of penance and mortification. Eighteenth-century readers had allowed their novelists more freedom to depict sexual irregularities, but the great Victorian novelists dealt obliquely, or not at all, with such subjects. One of Mrs. Browning's most fundamental convictions was that sexual activity outside of marriage was immoral, but she believed that society should be more compassionate in its treatment of women who had been victims of seduction or sexual attacks. It is not surprising that the story of Marian Erle shocked a number of women readers, some of whom were reported to have said that the reading of *Aurora Leigh* had endangered their morals.

Most of the Brownings' literary friends were delighted with the poem and accorded it the highest praise; Swinburne, Leigh Hunt, Walter Savage Landor, Ruskin, and the Rossetti brothers all spoke of it with unrestrained enthusiasm. From a commercial point of view it proved to be by far the most successful of Mrs. Browning's works; by 1885, twenty-eight years after its first publication, it had gone through nineteen editions. Despite its great popularity with other poets and with the general public, it found little favor with professional reviewers. Most were in agreement that the poem was too long and lacking in coherence, that the characterization was weak, that the plot was melodramatic and implausible, that the imagery was often inappropriate and discordant, and that some of the material was so vulgar that it offended good taste. One reviewer declared that the coarseness of its language made Mrs. Browning's book "almost a closed volume for her own sex." The notices in the most influential journals, however, granted that despite its shortcomings the poem gave evidence of its author's vigorous intellect, her earnestness, and her wide and humane sympathies.

Browning in 1858

Two years after the publication of *Aurora Leigh* Mrs. Browning again became absorbed in current political events as the Italians, after a decade of truce, began once more their struggle for independence and unity. In June 1859 Italian troops under the leadership of King Victor Emmanuel of Piedmont, joined by Napoleon III, who had come to northern Italy with substantial French forces, won two battles against the Austrians in Lombardy. Then early in July Napoleon surprised and bitterly disappointed the Italians by agreeing at Villafranca to an armistice which would leave Venice under the domination of Austria. In response to these events Mrs. Browning's *Poems before Congress* was published in the spring of 1860; but by the time the volume appeared the title was misleading, for the congress of the leading powers that was to have been held in January had been indefinitely postponed. Seven of the eight poems deal with Italian politics, while the other, "A Curse for a Nation," is an antislavery poem that had earlier been published in an abolitionist journal in Boston. Although Mrs. Browning felt betrayed when she first heard of the truce initiated by the emperor whom she had long admired, she expressed her continuing faith in him in two of the poems, "A Tale of Villafranca" and "Napoleon III in Italy." In her view the emperor was not at fault, for his noble aims had been frustrated by selfish and small-minded statesmen. In "Italy and the World" Mrs. Browning prophesies that the states of central Italy in revolt against Austria will join Piedmont and Lombardy to form a united and independent kingdom, but the triumphant conclusion of the Italian cause will owe nothing to the English government, which she berates for its failure to provide military aid. The notices in the leading English journals were uniformly unfavorable toward the volume, which they found offensive because of its strident tone and anti-British bias.

In the spring of 1860 Mrs. Browning continued to write poems on the Italian situation, which to her great delight appeared to be moving toward a victorious outcome. Central and northern Italy had become a united kingdom under the leadership of Victor Emmanuel of Piedmont and his prime minister, Count Cavour. The theme of "King Victor Emmanuel Entering Florence, April, 1860" is the great joy of the people of Tuscany and their expressions of gratitude toward the king for the part he has played in helping them to their freedom. The tone of "Summing up in Italy," however, is bitter; here Mrs. Browning utters her fears that although the great powers of Europe will ratify the creation of the new kingdom of Italy, they will discredit its chief architects. Besides her political poems, at this time she wrote "A Musical Instrument," which has become one of her best-known poems. Based on the myth of Pan and Syrinx, the verses exemplify the doctrine that the true poet is destined to suffer much hardship and pain in the practice of his art.

Despite her extreme frailty Mrs. Browning followed with feverish excitement the rapidly unfolding events of the winter of 1860-1861. The peoples of Sicily, Naples, and the States of the Church had voted for annexation with Victor Emmanuel's new kingdom. With most of the Italian states united, a national parliament met at Turin early in 1861. Mrs. Browning felt that her faith in the Italian leaders had been justified. "There are great men here, and there will be a great nation presently," she declared. She had been in poor health for several years, suffering from weakness of the lungs and heart, and her obsession with Italian politics further weakened her nervous system. The final blow, which prostrated her emotionally and physically, was the unexpected and premature death on 6 June 1861 of Count Cavour, the great patriot who had been chiefly responsible for bringing the disparate states into a unified and independent kingdom. "I can scarcely command voice or hand to name *Cavour*," Elizabeth wrote; "if tears or blood could have saved him to us, he should have had mine." For the next two weeks she remained in seclusion, never going out and seeing almost no one at home. Then on 20 June she was stricken with a severe cold, cough, and sore throat, and was confined to her bed; she died in Browning's arms early in the morning of 29 June. Within a month Browning left Florence with his son to make his permanent home in London.

The many journals which reported Mrs. Browning's untimely death all spoke of her as the greatest woman poet in English literature. The highly respected *Edinburgh Review* expressed the prevailing view when it said that she had no equal in the literary history of any country: "Such a combination of the finest genius and the choicest results of cultivation and wide-ranging studies has never been seen before in any woman." In America the most extravagant of the obituary notices appeared in the *Southern Literary Messenger,* which called her "the Shakespeare among her sex" and placed her among the four or five greatest authors of all time. A year after her death Browning collected and arranged for publication her *Last Poems,* which included a number of translations from Greek and Latin poetry, personal lyrics, and poems on Italian politics. In the same year the fifth edition of her *Poems* was published. Both works were warmly received by the leading literary journals on both sides of the Atlantic as they reviewed her poetic career from its beginning and concluded that her gifts had been of the highest order. A writer in the *Christian Examiner* of Boston said that Tennyson's *In Memoriam* (1850) and Mrs. Browning's *Aurora Leigh* were the two greatest poems of the age and that the "Sonnets from the Portuguese" were the finest love poems in

Elizabeth Barrett Browning's tomb in the English Cemetery, Florence

English: "Shakespeare's sonnets, beautiful as they are, cannot be compared with them, and Petrarch's seem commonplace beside them."

In the decades following Mrs. Browning's death her poetry began to lose much of the appeal it had held for readers during her lifetime. The consensus of late-Victorian critics was that much of her writing would be forgotten in another generation but that she would be remembered for "The Cry of the Children," a few of the romantic ballads such as "Isobel's Child" and "Bertha in the Lane," and most of all for the "Sonnets from the Portuguese." During all this period and for the first three decades of the present century, *Aurora Leigh* largely dropped out of sight. In 1930, however, Virginia Woolf in an article in the *Times Literary Supplement* deplored the fact that Mrs. Browning's poetry was no longer being read and especially that *Aurora Leigh* had been forgotten. She urged her readers to take a fresh look at the poem, which she admired for its "speed and energy, forthrightness and complete self-confidence." "Elizabeth Barrett," Mrs. Woolf wrote, "was inspired by a flash of true genius when she rushed into the drawing-room and said that here, where we live and work, is the true place for the poet." In Mrs. Woolf's view, the heroine of the poem, "with her passionate interest in social questions, her conflict as artist and woman, her longing for knowledge and freedom, is the true daughter of her age."

Notwithstanding Mrs. Woolf's enthusiasm for *Aurora Leigh*, the poem continued to be ignored by the general public and by scholars until the recent advent of feminist criticism. None of Mrs. Browning's poems has received more attention from feminist critics than *Aurora Leigh*, since its theme is one that especially concerns them: the difficulties that a woman must overcome if she is to achieve independence in a world mainly controlled by men. In her *Literary Women* Ellen Moers writes that *Aurora Leigh* is the great epic poem of the age; it is "the epic poem of the literary woman herself." It now looks as though Mrs. Browning's literary reputation will remain secure with future critics who view her work from a feminist perspective. One may also prophesy that for the general public the "Sonnets from the Portuguese," despite some Victorian quaintness of imagery, will continue to hold their place among the most-admired love poems of world literature.

Letters:
Letters of Elizabeth Barrett Browning Addressed to

Richard Hengist Horne, edited by S. R. Townshend Mayer, 2 volumes (London: Bentley, 1877);

The Letters of Elizabeth Barrett Browning, edited by Frederic G. Kenyon, 2 volumes (London: Smith, Elder, 1897);

Letters to Robert Browning and Other Correspondents by Elizabeth Barrett Browning, edited by Thomas J. Wise (London: Privately printed, 1916);

Elizabeth Barrett Browning: Letters to Her Sister, 1846-1859, edited by Leonard Huxley (London: Murray, 1929);

Letters from Elizabeth Barrett to B. R. Haydon, edited by Martha Hale Shackford (New York: Oxford University Press, 1939);

"Twenty Unpublished Letters of Elizabeth Barrett to Hugh Stuart Boyd," edited by Bennett Weaver, *PMLA,* 65 (June 1950): 397-418;

"New Letters from Mrs. Browning to Isa Blagden," edited by Edward C. McAleer, *PMLA,* 66 (September 1951): 594-612;

Elizabeth Barrett to Miss Mitford: The Unpublished Letters of Elizabeth Barrett Barrett to Mary Russell Mitford, edited by Betty Miller (London: Murray, 1954);

Elizabeth Barrett to Mr. Boyd: Unpublished Letters of Elizabeth Barrett Browning to Hugh Stuart Boyd, edited by Barbara P. McCarthy (New Haven: Yale University Press, 1955);

Letters of the Brownings to George Barrett, edited by Paul Landis with the assistance of Ronald E. Freeman (Urbana: University of Illinois Press, 1958);

The Letters of Robert Browning and Elizabeth Barrett Barrett, 1845-1846, edited by Elvan Kintner, 2 volumes (Cambridge, Mass.: Harvard University Press, 1969);

Invisible Friends: The Correspondence of Elizabeth Barrett Barrett and Benjamin Robert Haydon, 1842-1845, edited by Willard Bissell Pope (Cambridge, Mass.: Harvard University Press, 1972);

Elizabeth Barrett Browning's Letters to Mrs. David Ogilvy, 1849-1861, edited by Peter N. Heydon and Philip Kelley (New York: Quadrangle/ New York Times Book Co. and the Browning Institute, 1973).

Bibliographies:

H. Buxton Forman, *Elizabeth Barrett Browning and Her Scarcer Books* (London: Privately printed, 1896);

Thomas J. Wise, *A Bibliography of the Writings in Prose and Verse of Elizabeth Barrett Browning* (London: Privately printed, 1918);

Wise, *A Browning Library. A Catalogue of Printed Books, Manuscripts, and Autograph Letters by Robert Browning and Elizabeth Barrett Browning, Collected by T. J. Wise* (London: Privately printed, 1929);

Theodore G. Ehrsam, Robert H. Deily, and Robert M. Smith, *Bibliographies of Twelve Victorian Authors* (New York: Wilson, 1936), pp. 48-66;

Warner Barnes, *A Bibliography of Elizabeth Barrett Browning* (Austin: University of Texas Press, 1967);

William S. Peterson, *Robert and Elizabeth Barrett Browning: An Annotated Bibliography, 1951-1970* (New York: Browning Institute, 1974);

Philip Kelley and Ronald Hudson, eds., *The Brownings' Correspondence: A Checklist* (New York & Arkansas City, Kans.: Browning Institute & Wedgestone Press, 1978).

Biographies:

Jeannette Marks, *The Family of the Barrett: A Colonial Romance* (New York: Macmillan, 1938);

Dorothy Hewlett, *Elizabeth Barrett Browning: A Life* (New York: Knopf, 1952; London: Cassell, 1953);

Gardner B. Taplin, *The Life of Elizabeth Barrett Browning* (New Haven: Yale University Press, 1957; London: Murray, 1957);

Edward C. McAleer, *The Brownings of Casa Guidi* (New York: Browning Institute, 1979);

Rosalie Mander, *Mrs. Browning: The Story of Elizabeth Barrett* (London: Weidenfeld & Nicolson, 1980).

References:

Alethea Hayter, *Mrs. Browning: A Poet's Work and Its Setting* (London: Faber & Faber, 1962; New York: Barnes & Noble, 1963);

Gladys W. Hudson, *An Elizabeth Barrett Browning Concordance,* 4 volumes (Detroit: Gale, 1973);

Mary Jane Lupton, *Elizabeth Barrett Browning* (Old Westbury, N.Y.: Feminist Press, 1972);

Ellen Moers, *Literary Women* (Garden City: Doubleday, 1976);

Virginia L. Radley, *Elizabeth Barrett Browning* (New York: Twayne, 1972);

Patricia Thomson, *George Sand and the Victorians: Her Influence and Reputation in Nineteenth-Century England* (New York: Columbia University Press, 1977).

Papers:
There are important collections of Elizabeth Barrett Browning's manuscripts and books at the Wellesley College Library, in the Berg Collection at the New York Public Library, the Huntington Library, the British Library, the Folger Library, the Harvard College Library, the Yale University Library, the Pierpont Morgan Library, the Library of the University of Texas, the Armstrong Browning Library at Baylor University, and the Boston Public Library.

Robert Browning

Thomas J. Collins
University of Western Ontario

BIRTH: Camberwell, England, 7 May 1812, to Robert and Sarah Anna Wiedemann Browning.

EDUCATION: London University, 1829.

MARRIAGE: 12 September 1846 to Elizabeth Barrett; child: Robert Wiedemann Barrett.

DEATH: Venice, Italy, 12 December 1889.

BOOKS: *Pauline: A Fragment of a Confession,* anonymous (London: Saunders & Otley, 1833);
Paracelsus (London: Wilson, 1835; edited by C. P. Denison, New York: Baker & Taylor, 1911);
Strafford: An Historical Tragedy (London: Longman, Rees, Orme, Brown, Green & Longmans, 1837);
Sordello (London: Moxon, 1840);
Bells and Pomegranates. No. I.–Pippa Passes (London: Moxon, 1841);
Bells and Pomegranates. No. II.–King Victor and King Charles (London: Moxon, 1842);
Bells and Pomegranates. No. III.–Dramatic Lyrics (London: Moxon, 1842; edited by J. O. Beatty and J. W. Bowyer, New York: Houghton, 1895);
Bells and Pomegranates. No. IV.–The Return of the Druses: A Tragedy in Five Acts (London: Moxon, 1843);
Bells and Pomegranates. No. V.–A Blot in the 'Scutcheon: A Tragedy in Five Acts (London: Moxon, 1843; edited by W. Rolfe and H. Hersey, New York: Harper, 1887);
Bells and Pomegranates. No. VI.–Colombe's Birthday: A Play in Five Acts (London: Moxon, 1844);
Bells and Pomegranates. No. VII.–Dramatic Romances & Lyrics (London: Moxon, 1845);
Bells and Pomegranates. No. VIII.–and Last. Luria; and A Soul's Tragedy: (London: Moxon, 1846);
Poems: A New Edition, 2 volumes (London: Chapman & Hall, 1849; Boston: Ticknor, Reed & Fields, 1850);
Christmas-Eve and Easter-Day (London: Chapman & Hall, 1850; Boston: Lothrop, 1887);
Two Poems by Robert Browning and Elizabeth Barrett Browning (London: Chapman & Hall, 1854);
Men and Women (2 volumes, London: Chapman & Hall, 1855; 1 volume, Boston: Ticknor & Fields, 1856);
Dramatis Personae (London: Chapman & Hall, 1864; Boston: Ticknor & Fields, 1864);
The Poetical Works of Robert Browning, 6 volumes (London: Smith, Elder, 1868);
The Ring and the Book (4 volumes, London: Smith, Elder, 1868-1869; 2 volumes, Boston: Fields, Osgood, 1869);
Balaustion's Adventure, Including a Transcript from Euripides (London: Smith, Elder, 1871; Boston: Osgood, 1871);
Prince Hohenstiel–Schwangau, Saviour of Society (London: Smith, Elder, 1871);
Fifine at the Fair (London: Smith, Elder, 1872; Boston: Osgood, 1872);
Red Cotton Night-Cap Country; or, Turf and Towers (London: Smith, Elder, 1873; Boston: Osgood, 1873);
Aristophanes' Apology, Including a Transcript from Euripides: Being the Last Adventures of Balaustion (London: Smith, Elder, 1875; Boston: Osgood, 1875);
The Inn Album (London: Smith, Elder, 1875; Boston: Osgood, 1876);
Pacchiarotto and How He Worked in Distemper, with

(National Portrait Gallery)

Robert Browning.

Other Poems (London: Smith, Elder, 1876; Boston: Osgood, 1877);
La Saisiaz, and The Two Poets of Croisic (London: Smith, Elder, 1878);
Dramatic Idyls (London: Smith, Elder, 1879);
Dramatic Idyls: Second Series (London: Smith, Elder, 1880);
Jocoseria (London: Smith, Elder, 1883; Boston & New York: Houghton Mifflin, 1883);
Ferishtah's Fancies (London: Smith, Elder, 1884; Boston: Houghton Mifflin, 1885);
Parleyings with Certain People of Importance in Their Day (London: Smith, Elder, 1887; Boston & New York: Houghton Mifflin, 1887);
Asolando: Fancies and Facts (London: Smith, Elder, 1889; Boston & New York: Houghton Mifflin, 1890);
Complete Poetic and Dramatic Works of Robert Browning, Cambridge Edition, edited by G. W. Cooke and H. E. Scudder (Boston & New York: Houghton Mifflin, 1895);
The Complete Works of Robert Browning, Florentine Edition, edited by Charlotte Porter and Helen A. Clarke, 12 volumes (New York & Boston: Crowell, 1898);
The Works of Robert Browning, Centenary Edition, edited by Frederic G. Kenyon, 10 volumes (London: Smith, Elder/Boston: Hinkley, 1912);
New Poems by Robert Browning and Elizabeth Barrett Browning, edited by Kenyon (London: Smith, Elder, 1914; New York: Macmillan, 1915);
Robert Browning: The Ring and the Book, edited by Richard D. Altick (London: Penguin/New Haven: Yale University Press, 1971);
Robert Browning: The Poems, edited by John Pettigrew, supplemented and completed by Thomas J. Collins, 2 volumes (London: Penguin/New Haven: Yale University Press, 1981).

OTHER: John Forster, *Lives of Eminent British Statesmen,* volume 2, undetermined contribution to biography of Thomas Wentworth, Earl of Strafford, by Browning (London: Longman, Orme, Brown, Green & Longmans, 1836);
Letters of Percy Bysshe Shelley, introduction by Browning (London: Moxon, 1852), pp. 1-44;
The Agamemnon of Aeschylus, translated by Browning (London: Smith, Elder, 1877);
Thomas Jones, *The Divine Order: Sermons,* introduction by Browning (London: Isbister, 1884);
"Sonnet: Why I Am a Liberal," in *Why I Am a Liberal,* edited by A. Reid (London: Cassell, 1885).

Robert Browning, with Alfred Lord Tennyson, is considered one of the two major poets of the Victorian age. His life (1812-1889) and the chronological span of his publishing career (from *Pauline* in 1833 to *Asolando* in 1889) place him firmly in the context of Victoria's reign (1837-1901); his major poetic achievements, including the development of his themes and techniques, simultaneously reflect and dominate the period in which he wrote. Although his early poetry was generally either ridiculed or ignored, as the century progressed Browning gained recognition for his mastery of the dramatic monologue form, for his skillful and penetrating method of character analysis, and for the enunciation of important Victorian themes—especially progress, imperfection, and optimism. Like Tennyson, Browning not only reflected his culture; because he seemed to offer a sense of the stable and the enduring in a dynamic and ever-changing world, he became an object of culture. Thus, by the early 1880s, members of the newly formed Browning Society thought of Browning not only as a major poetic force, but also as a prophet and a teacher who bore an inspired message to an unbelieving and materialistic age.

When one is faced with such a huge bulk of poetry, such major artistic achievements, and such varied and frequently contradictory reasons for admiration of the canon, it is prudent to engage in careful discriminations. From a twentieth-century perspective, Browning's development of the techniques of the dramatic monologue form is regarded as his most important contribution to poetry. His use of diction, rhythm, and symbol directly influenced Ezra Pound, T. S. Eliot, and Robert Frost, to cite only a few examples. But the dramatic monologue, although the most successful of Browning's endeavors, does not exhaust the variety or the scope of his creative efforts.

Browning was born in 1812 in Camberwell, a middle-class suburb across the Thames from the main part of nineteenth-century London, to Robert Browning, Sr., and Sarah Anna Wiedemann Browning. Mrs. Browning, of German-Scottish descent, was a musician, a lover of nature, and a devout evangelical Christian. She was no doubt the stronger of the two parents in guiding her son through his developmental stages. A woman of common sense and stability—qualities inherited by Browning's sister, Sarianna, who was born in 1814—she was later characterized by Thomas Carlyle as "the true type of Scottish gentlewoman." Like his father before him, Browning's father was employed as a clerk in the Bank of England. Robert Browning, Sr., a rather passive man, quietly labored at the bank and pursued his cherished interests in the home environment. He was an artist, a scholar, a collector of books and pictures, and an antiquarian. His rare book collection of over 6,000 volumes included works in Greek, Hebrew, Latin, French, Italian, and Spanish.

It is believed that Browning was already proficient at reading and writing by the age of five. He was then sent to a local dame school but was asked to leave after a short time, apparently because he was superior to the other students. He studied at home until the age of seven and about that time was sent to the lower school at Peckham run by the Ready sisters. When Browning was ten he passed from the lower school to the classes of the Reverend Thomas Ready, studying writing, arithmetic, English, history, Latin, and Greek. This narrow, conservative, and traditional training was doubtless augmented by the vast store of materials in Browning's father's library, in which the boy was encouraged to read; among the works consumed by the young Browning were Wanley's *Wonder of the Little World* (1678) and the fifty-volume *Biographie Universelle*. The esoteric nature of the library and his father's wide-ranging interests make it hardly surprising that Browning's poetry is so richly allusive. From fourteen to sixteen, the aspiring poet was educated at home, attended to by various tutors in music, drawing, dancing, and horsemanship. Since he was ineligible to attend Oxford or Cambridge because he was not a member of the Church of England, he attended London University for about one year, during which he was enrolled in a regular program of study in Greek and Latin, and also in beginning German. His sudden departure in 1829 perhaps indicates a firm decision to turn his attention to poetry as a vocation.

Given the circumstances of Browning's education, it is not surprising that he was especially precocious in his poetic development. At the age of twelve he wrote a volume of Byronic verse entitled "Incondita," which his parents attempted, unsuccessfully, to have published. The two poems which survive, "The Dance of Death" and "The First-Born of Egypt," clearly reflect the Byronic influences on and impulses of the early adolescent Browning. The most momentous occurrence for the young Browning was in 1825, when he was given a copy of Shelley's *Miscellaneous Poems* (1826) by his cousin, James Silverthorne. This volume, which contained poems pirated from Mrs. Shelley's edition of *Posthumous Poems* (1824), included all of the most important of Shelley's lyrics except "The Cloud" and "Ode to the West Wind." At his request, Browning's mother purchased most of Shelley's other works for his birthday that same year, thus enabling Browning to immerse himself in the Shelley canon. At the age of thirteen, Browning, strongly under the influence of Shelley, became a vegetarian and an atheist. As Mrs. Sutherland Orr, a confidante in his later years and one of his first biographers, records, he "gratuitously proclaimed himself everything that he was, and some things that he was not."

Browning seems to have written no poetry between the ages of thirteen and twenty; then, in 1832, he composed his first major published work, *Pauline*. Few details are available concerning the period leading up to the publication of *Pauline*, but it is evident from the poem that some time during this period Browning had come to terms with Shelley's influence; by 1832 he no longer accepted the

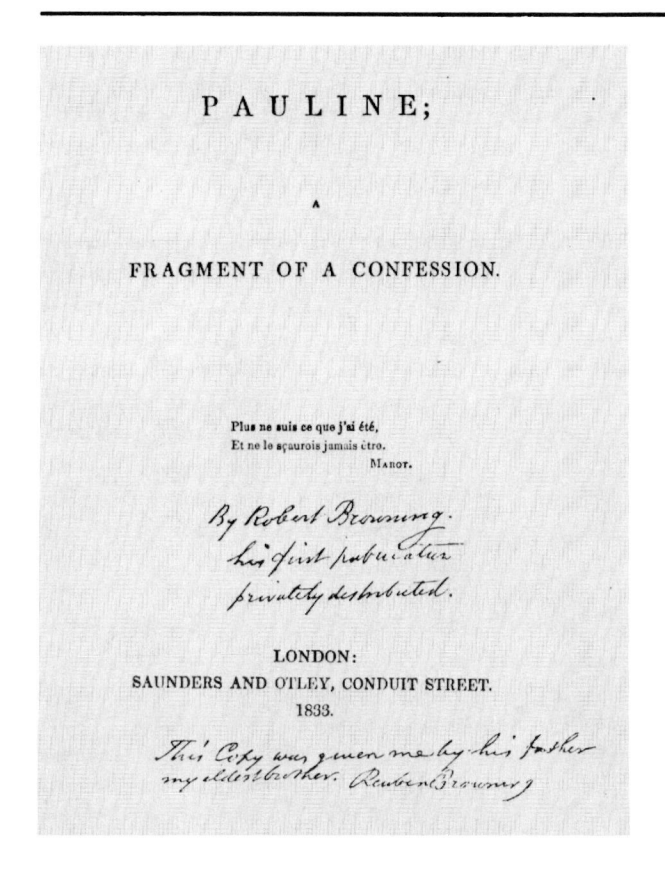

Title page for Browning's first published work, on which his name did not appear (Anderson Galleries, 13-16 May 1918)

apocalyptic impulse as the most important, and he also rejected Shelley's atheism and returned to more orthodox Christianity.

Published anonymously in 1833, *Pauline,* slightly over 1,000 lines in length, is, as its subtitle states, *A Fragment of a Confession.* The poem falls roughly into three divisions: in the first and third, the speaker addresses the imaginary Pauline, with whom he appears to be deeply infatuated, and complains that he can no longer be productive poetically, that he is in a state of deep depression and sadness, and that he wants desperately to try to understand his fragmented state. In the initial section, the speaker celebrates the influence upon his life and poetry of the "Sun-treader," whom most scholars identify as Shelley:

> Sun-treader, life and light be thine for ever!
> Thou art gone from us; years go by and spring
> Gladdens and the young earth is beautiful,
> Yet thy songs come not, other bards arise,
> But none like thee.

The "Sun-treader" has had an important influence on the speaker's early years, but that influence is now diminished; and the speaker sets out in the second third of the poem to try to understand the course of his own development. This section is heavily autobiographical, referring specifically in various places to aspects of Browning's youth and adolescence. The speaker then moves into a long lyric passage near the beginning of the third segment of the poem in which he attempts to revivify himself by traveling through nature with the fictional Pauline. He resolves his doubts and difficulties by affirming his faith in God and in the necessity of offering some allegiance to the spirit of orthodox Christianity, rather than to the spirit of his former poetic mentor. However, as the poem closes the speaker yokes Shelley and God:

> Sun-treader, I believe in God and truth
> And love; and as one just escaped from death
> Would bind himself in bands of friends to feel
> He lives indeed, so, I would lean on thee!

Consequently, the reader is left wondering whether or not the personal problems which evoked the poem's utterance have indeed been solved. John Stuart Mill, who was sent a copy of *Pauline* for review by Browning's friend W. J. Fox, wondered about precisely this. In the copy of the book sent to him (now housed in the Victoria and Albert Museum in London) Mill wrote: "With considerable poetic powers, the writer seems to me possessed with a more intense and morbid self-consciousness than I ever knew in any sane human being." His lengthy comments, many of which reflect this attitude to the poem and its speaker, have served as the focus of a good deal of the discussion about Browning's early work, particularly *Pauline, Paracelsus* (1835), and *Sordello* (1840).

Fox gave his copy of *Pauline,* with Mill's comments, to Browning shortly after publication. Browning added his own remarks to those of Mill by way of reply and explained, presumably in an attempt to downplay the autobiographical nature of the work, that the poem had "for its object the enabling me to assume and realize I know not how many different characters;—meanwhile the world was never to grasp that 'Brown, Smith, Jones, and Robinson' . . . the respective authors of this poem, the other novel, such an opera, such a speech etc. etc. were no other than one and the same individual." A similar explanation is added in the preface to the poem which Browning wrote for its republication in 1868. It is generally believed that Browning reacted with acute embarrassment to the self-revelation of *Pauline*. Deeply hurt by Mill's comments, he resolved to distance himself from the poem and to protect himself in the future by turning from lyrical expression to more dramatic forms. There is little doubt that Browning attempted to divorce himself from the persona of the poem, and there is equally little doubt that the poem is highly personal. And although the contention that his subsequent movement to more dramatic forms resulted solely from Mill's comments is an oversimplification, the attitude expressed by Mill was perhaps one of several factors which influenced his decision in his next published work, *Paracelsus*, to employ at least the external trappings of drama.

Paracelsus, a poem of over 4,000 lines, is divided into five sections which seem to function as scenes. Browning provides each scene with a specific time, cast of characters, and dialogue. But nothing of an external nature really happens in the poem. The minor characters, Festus and Michal, are simply foils for Paracelsus as he reflects upon the events of his life and on his problems in coming to an understanding of himself, his ambitions, and the nature of reality.

While *Paracelsus* is no greater a technical success than *Pauline*, there is one important point of contrast between the two poems. The ideas in *Pauline* are unclear, irresolute, and incomplete; in *Paracelsus*, the ideas are relatively clear, certain, and complete. This difference is significant, for in *Paracelsus* Browning is dealing with basically the same problems which concerned him in *Pauline*. Browning's development is described in *Pauline* as a series of stages: he desires greatness, pursues a utopian dream, fails, becomes a cynic, and finally announces that he is saved. But the conclusion of the poem, its religious resolution, is problematical and contradictory. In *Paracelsus*, Browning is one step removed from his problems and thus can work out, with a greater degree of objectivity, the moral dilemma left unsolved in *Pauline:* what is man's relationship to God and to his fellow man; how can unlimited aspiration be reconciled with limited ability; how can man reach God without succumbing to the fruitless idealism of Shelley; and how does one serve the human race without being dragged down into the quagmire of reality? Through the poem's five parts, each of which represents a different stage in the life of Paracelsus, Browning explores these problems; in Canto V, he offers solutions.

The character Paracelsus is based upon a real historical figure, a German who lived from 1490 to 1541. The original Paracelsus is only vaguely present in the poem; Browning recreates the character to suit his own particular purposes. The basic problem of Paracelsus is his desire to possess a kind of Godhead, to obtain some form of perfect knowledge. These desires are outlined in the expository first canto. In the second section of the poem, Paracelsus meets a poet, Aprile, modeled on Browning's conception of Shelley; Aprile explains that he, too, has tried to possess an absolute— perfect love—but that he has failed and has come to understand the nature of the imperfect world in which man must live and which man must accept. Paracelsus mistakes Aprile's message and sets off to combine the aspiration for perfect knowledge with the aspiration for perfect love, and thereby to possess the whole of existence. He is, of course, unable to realize his ambition, and inevitably falls into despair and cynicism.

It is only in Canto V, following his philosophical and personal setbacks, that Paracelsus is able to come to terms with his problems. He understands that infinites are unattainable to man in his present state of imperfection; that imperfection, qualified by the necessity and the inevitability of progress, is

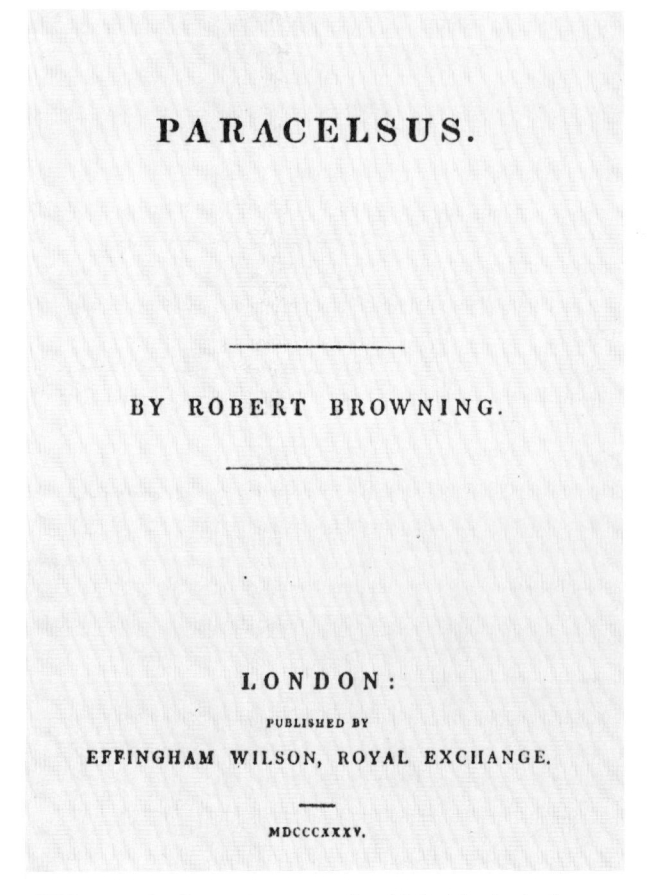

PARACELSUS.

BY ROBERT BROWNING.

LONDON:
PUBLISHED BY
EFFINGHAM WILSON, ROYAL EXCHANGE.

MDCCCXXXV.

Title page for Browning's second published book (Anderson Galleries, 14-15 April 1937)

the law of life; and that progress depends upon the recognition that the flesh is not a snare but a temporal element which can contribute to man's ultimate perfection. Finally, he learns that God rejoices and resides in all aspects of His creation, even to the extent of allowing man, in his weakness, to reflect His grandeur. Through *Paracelsus,* Browning is able to reconcile himself to the nature of limited aspiration, and is also able to work out some of the basic elements of his reflective thought on the fundamental problems of humanity.

Like *Pauline, Paracelsus* was an experimental poem. It was not well received critically, although some reviewers noted the presence of an embryonic dramatic talent. And Browning's dramatic impulse would soon be allowed to surface. Browning first met W. C. Macready, the great actor, at the home of W. J. Fox on 27 November 1835. On 16 February, 1836, he visited Macready to discuss an idea for a play. This meeting was unproductive, but on 26 May of the same year Browning met Macready again, with Walter Savage Landor and William Wordsworth, at a dinner given by Sergeant Talfourd in honor of the success of his play *Ion.* Macready is reported to have said to Browning, "Will you not write me a tragedy, and save me from going to America?" Browning took the challenge seriously and wrote a historical play, *Strafford,* which ran for five nights in 1837. That Browning was not to become the savior of the Victorian stage is clear in the failure of *Strafford;* this historical play could not engage its audience because, while Browning was able to deal skillfully with the internal conflicts of human beings, he was unable to represent on the stage the public, external drama of men acting and conflicting in the world of politics and business. This is true as well of the various plays published between 1841 and 1846 in the *Bells and Pomegranates* series. But Browning, in 1837, had another major project in mind.

Sordello was published in 1840, but it had been in the process of composition since 1833. During this period, the poem underwent four distinct stages of composition: the first stage, between March of 1833 and March of 1834, concerned the development of a poetic soul. The second period began after the completion of *Paracelsus* and continued into 1837. During this stage, the poem probably focused on events connected with war and passion. In the third stage, from September 1837 until the middle of April 1838, Browning added the historical element to the poem. In the final stage, which began in August 1838 and lasted until May 1839, Browning concentrated upon a dedication to humanity and the extension of his earlier Shelleyan liberalism. As a result of this constant revision, the poem became a conglomeration of psychology, love, romance, humanitarianism, philosophy, and history.

Upon publication, *Sordello* was regarded as a colossal failure. Harriet Martineau was so wholly unable to understand it that she supposed herself ill. Douglas Jerrold reportedly read *Sordello* when he was recovering from an illness and thought that he was going mad; and Mrs. Carlyle is said to have read it through without being able to ascertain whether Sordello was a man, a book, or a city. However, *Sordello* is worth brief comment because in it Browning enunciates theories of the poet and poetry which further refine statements made in *Pauline* and *Paracelsus.*

As in *Paracelsus,* the main character in the poem is historical in origin but adapted by Browning for his own purposes. Sordello is primarily a poet, and a most important aspect of the poem is his attempt to understand his role as a poet and the nature of poetic expression. Central to both of these elements in the poem, and most important for Browning's own career, is the recognition that poets must always temper their idealism with an understanding of reality, and that language as the vehicle for poetic expression can never adequately enunciate the poet's vision:

> Piece after piece that armour broke away,
> Because perceptions whole, like that he sought
> To clothe, reject so pure a work of thought
> As language: thought may take perception's place
> But hardly co-exist in any case,
> Being its mere presentment—of the whole
> By parts, the simultaneous and the sole
> By the successive and the many.

Participating in the poem as narrator who comments upon Sordello and the action of the work, Browning explains that the true poet can never accomplish what he desires in this grimy, imperfect society; he must not only find beauty in the ugly, the whole in the broken, but he must also be content to accomplish partial good. Similarly, poetry itself can never be perfect; at best it will be an inadequate verbal instrument which only partially expresses the total poetic vision. Sordello fails to grasp either of these principles. He is broken, rather than usefully changed or educated, by his attempt to bypass these restrictions on both the poet and his poetry. But Browning is clear about these ideas and they are, perhaps, the most central and important of the poem's various concerns.

Browning's three early long poems were not successes by any conceivable standard of judgment. But they are important for understanding Browning's poetic aspirations and for the opportunity they provide the reader to trace Browning's developing philosophy and his developing poetic techniques. In these poems Browning has learned to temper the Romantic idealism of Shelley, and has also begun to develop the techniques of representing action in character which would find their fruition in the dramatic monologue. In the work of the 1840s following the publication of *Sordello,* the impulse to a combination of dramatic and lyric expression can be traced.

Whatever the effect of Mill's comments about *Pauline,* the reaction to *Sordello* was so extremely negative that it must have caused Browning to reassess his poetic aims. Comments such as the following help explain why the damage done to Browning's reputation by the publication of *Sordello* was so severe: "the sins of [Browning's] verse are premeditated, willful, and incurable"; "the song of the bard falls dull and muffled on the ear, as from a fog"; and, perhaps more to the point in terms of mid-Victorian standards of taste, one critic complained that the poem is "offensive and vicious . . . apparently grounded on some conceited theory, at utter variance with all the canons of taste and propriety." When Browning moved with his family from Camberwell in December 1840 to New Cross Hatcham in Surrey, he turned his attention to the publication of a series of pamphlets entitled *Bells and Pomegranates.* Browning explained the meaning of his title for these pamphlets, the idea for which was suggested by Edward Moxon, the publisher of *Sordello,* between the two parts of *Bells and Pomegranates* number VIII: "I only meant by that title to indicate an endeavour towards something like an alternation, or mixture, of music with discoursing, sound with sense, poetry with thought; which looks too ambitious, thus expressed, so the symbol was preferred."

This series contained *Pippa Passes* (1841), *Luria* (1846), and *A Soul's Tragedy* (1846), all of which are closet dramas, and four other plays written expressly for the stage: *King Victor and King Charles* (1842), *The Return of the Druses* (1843), *A Blot in the 'Scutcheon* (1843), and *Colombe's Birthday* (1844). In addition, the third and seventh numbers in the series, *Dramatic Lyrics* (1842) and *Dramatic Romances & Lyrics* (1845), contained collections of short poems. Of all this work, the first number in the series, *Pippa Passes,* deserves particular attention, as do some of the short poems in the 1842 and 1845 collections. But the dramas written for the stage were unsuccessful, as *Strafford* had been in 1837, and for very much the same reason: Browning understood and was able to represent with great skill action in character, but he did not understand nor could he present effectively character in action. Taken as a collection, however, the seven plays show Browning experimenting with syntax, imagery, diction, and rhythm, gradually developing the techniques of characterization fully evident in the other monologues and, in the process of this development, confirming his growing sense that his true talent lay solely in character delineation. It is in *Pippa Passes* and two of the shorter poems written during this period that this experimentation becomes most clearly focused.

The numerous connections between *Pippa Passes* and *Sordello* indicate that *Pippa Passes* was written immediately after *Sordello* was completed on 1 May 1839, and that it was a direct by-product of the longer poem. Browning's travels in northern Italy in June 1838 had taken him to Asolo, and his observation of life there contributes to the materials which make up *Pippa Passes*. The topography of Asolo, the conditions in the silk mills, church and political affairs, as well as such character types as mill owners, workers, peasants, policemen, and itinerant students, all appear in the poem. An even more significant link between the two works is to be found in the relationship between Sordello and Pippa. They are both solitary individuals, both stolen children who are the offspring of wealthy parents, and both poets. Sordello's problem is that he attempts to involve himself too fully as a reformer both as a politician and as a poet. It is as a result of his failed aspirations that he learns about the necessity of compromise in life. *Pippa Passes* seems to be a turning away from *Sordello* in terms both of the nature of the poet figure and the techniques involved in presenting such figures.

Pippa, the poor young silkwinder, sets out on New Year's morning, her only holiday of the year, to wander through her environment. She seems committed to nothing except singing short lyrics from time to time, as she wanders from location to location. She does, however, have a striking effect as an instrument of God's mercy and justice on the lives of the various individuals who hear her songs. Each of the four parts of the poem—Morning, Noon, Evening, and Night—involves characters at points of crisis in their lives, who are moved to make significant moral decisions on overhearing Pippa's

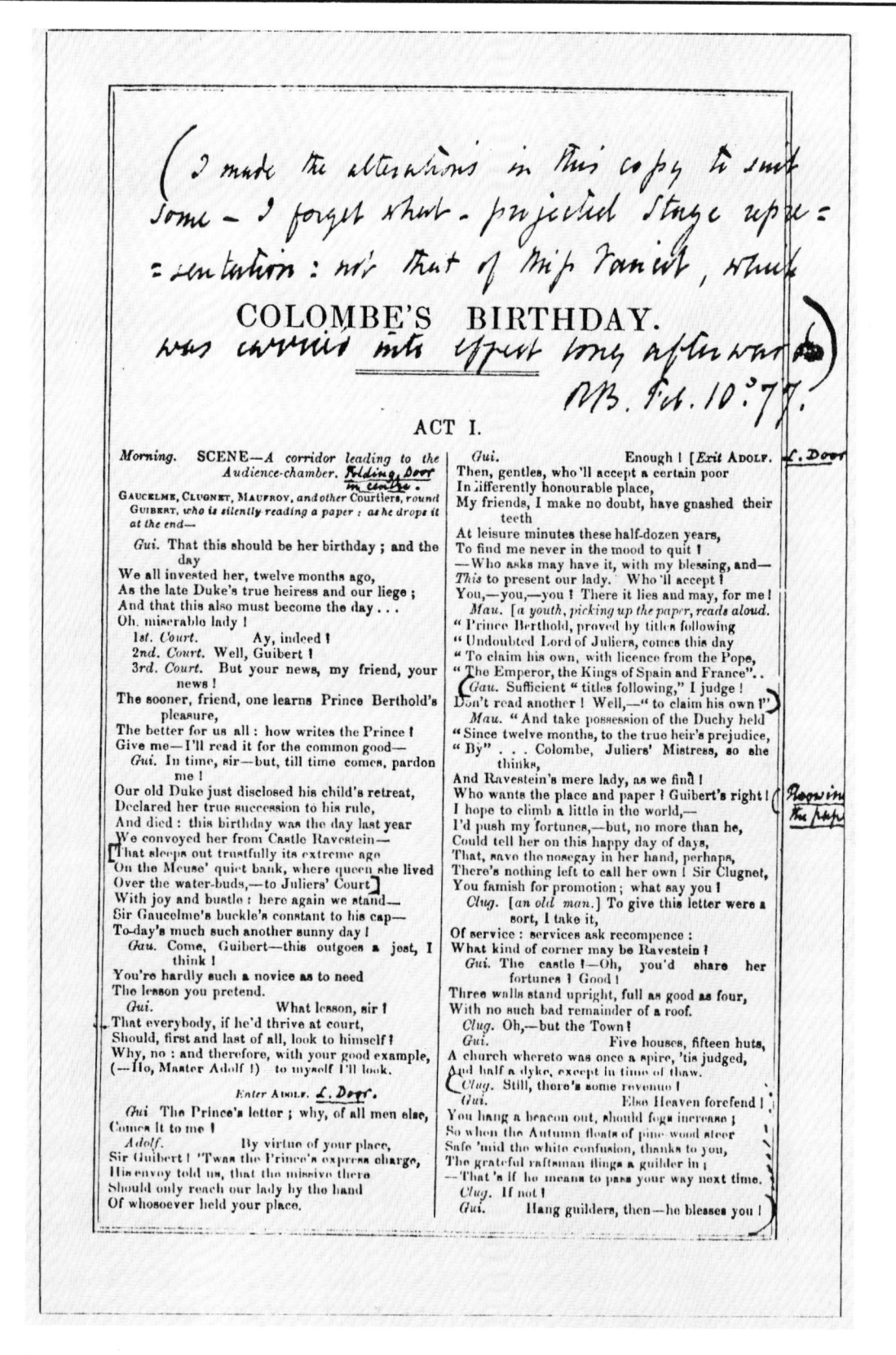

First page of Part VI of Browning's Bells and Pomegranates *(1844), with notations by Browning (David Magee/Antiquarian Books, Victoria Catalogue)*

songs. In these specific episodes Browning can be observed honing his dramatic skills and developing his verbal techniques.

The first scene involves Ottima and Sebald, lovers who have been responsible for the death of Ottima's husband Luca. Pippa's song seems to move them to feel some degree of guilt and perhaps even to suicide; there is, at any rate, a recognition on the part of the lovers that they have sinned. The second scene concerns Jules, a sculptor, and Phene, a young model whom he has recently been tricked into marrying. Phene recites a poem composed for the occasion by a group of Jules's confederates which informs him about the sham of his marriage; Pippa's song is heard immediately afterwards. Rather than rejecting Phene, as his peers had anticipated, Jules resolves to be loyal to her and to help her develop the fullness of her humanity. The two following scenes, one involving the revolutionary Luigi and his mother, and the other the Monsignor and the Intendant, are also concerned with moments of decision. The four scenes are connected by episodes which reflect on the action which has preceded or anticipate that which is to follow. In these linking episodes, Browning pays particular attention to the rhythms of conversation.

Of the short poems published in 1842 and 1845, the most important are "My Last Duchess" from the first collection and "The Bishop Orders His Tomb at St. Praxed's Church" from the second. "My Last Duchess," a poem of fifty-six lines in rhyming couplets, has been much discussed as an example of Browning's ability to concentrate and distill experience in the brief dramatic-lyric form. The speaker of the poem, the Duke of Ferrar, is overheard coolly explaining to an individual, who remains unidentified until near the end of the poem, the subject of a painting—his recently deceased wife. It becomes evident that the duchess had displeased her husband by her generous behavior toward others and also by her failure to recognize his superiority in even the most trifling of matters, and that this led to his order to have her executed:

> Oh sir, she smiled, no doubt,
> Whene'er I passed her; but who passed without
> Much the same smile? This grew; I gave commands;
> Then all smiles stopped together. There she stands
> As if alive.

The reader learns at the end of the poem that the duke is addressing his remarks to the envoy from the count whose daughter he next plans to wed. The duke treated his wife as an art object in life, and disposed of her when she displeased him; it is implied that he will treat his next wife the same way.

Robert Langbaum, in *The Poetry of Experience*, explains that this poem represents an important aspect of Browning's technique in the dramatic monologue; the poet is able to achieve in the reader a suspension of judgment concerning the odious behavior of the duke, and a degree of sympathy is engaged which allows the reader to attempt to understand the duke's character. This relationship between sympathy and judgment is accepted by most students of Browning's poetry as an important principle in understanding the dramatic monologue form. Other aspects of the dramatic monologue are also typified by "My Last Duchess": it has a single speaker who is not the poet, addressing an unspeaking audience within the poem. There is a psychological interplay between the speaker and the audience which, in various subtle ways, influences the progression of the speaker's thought patterns, which he then verbalizes. In addition, the poem is set in a particular place at a specific time. Most of Browning's successful mature monologues contain some combination of these elements.

It is, however, in "The Bishop Orders His Tomb at St. Praxed's Church" (1845) that Browning hits upon the synthesis of technique and form that he was later to exploit so fully in the dramatic monologues of *Men and Women* (1855). This poem, the first blank verse dramatic monologue, concerns the dying bishop's pleas to his assembled nephews concerning his placement in the church upon his death and the particular kind of tombstone he desires. His "nephews" are, of course, really his children, and his reactions to their facial expressions strongly suggest that they view both him and his wishes with some degree of disdain. As the poem unfolds, the bishop's mind wanders over his career and his relationship with his competitor in love and life, Fra Gandolf:

> Draw round my bed: is Anselm keeping back?
> Nephews—sons mine . . . ah God, I know not! Well—
> She, men would have to be your mother once,
> Old Gandolf envied me, so fair she was!

The poem offers brilliant insights into the psychology of a once lively and powerful, but now dying and dispirited, individual.

During this period in the early 1840s, Browning's correspondence indicates that while he might attempt to gain an audience by writing for the theater, he knew full well that his talents, and the possibility of gaining a larger audience, would probably have to result from different kinds of endeavors. Thus, in May 1842 he wrote his friend Alfred Domett that "these things [the dramas] done . . . , I shall have tried an experiment to the end, and be pretty well contented either way." Similarly, in 1844 he wrote Domett that, having seen the publication of most of his dramas, he will "begin again. I really seem to have something fresh to say." That is, following the recognized failures of his long poems in the 1830s and of the dramas in the early 1840s, he was resolved to concentrate his efforts on shorter poems. But some considerable time was to elapse, and events of momentous importance were to occur, before this ambition could be realized.

When Browning was traveling in Italy in 1844, Elizabeth Barrett's *Poems* was published. In "Lady Geraldine's Courtship," she links Browning with Wordsworth and Tennyson and praises his humanity: "or from Browning some 'Pomegranate,' which, if cut deep down the middle, /Shows a heart within blood-tinctured, of a veined humanity." Browning first wrote Barrett on 10 January 1845, and was allowed to see her on 20 May. The RB-EBB letters of 1845-1846, collected and fully annotated in the Harvard edition, are important documents which detail the development of their growing love relationship and of their mutual concern over issues of the day and their own poetic endeavors.

In his second letter, on 13 January, Browning proclaimed: "You *do* what I always wanted, hoped to do. . . . I only make men & women speak—give you truth broken into prismatic hues, and fear the pure white light, even if it is in me." He explains on 11 February that he has never undertaken "R. B. a poem." These letters indicate Browning's tendency to self-effacement in his poetry, as well as his parallel tendency to adopt poetic personae and have characters other than himself articulate the poems. Elizabeth continually urges him to speak out in his own person; but despite her encouragement, Browning seemed to be facing an artistic impasse at this time.

As he prepared the collection of *Dramatic Romances & Lyrics* for publication in 1845, Browning complained to Elizabeth that he was not satisfied with a poetic fragment, "Saul," which he felt unable to complete. In the first nine stanzas of the poem, David, the young singer, is sent to attempt to cure Saul's physical and spiritual inertia. David celebrates the natural joys of living and the stature and grandeur of the king as the pinnacle of natural creation; but Browning could not move the poem to a redemptive solution which would lead to a full spiritual regeneration for Saul. He sent the poem to Elizabeth and she commented, in a letter of 27 August, that he should have no doubts about the poem. She suggested that he either allow it to be published in its partial state or complete it without fully revealing the nature of the cure which is achieved for Saul's spiritual malaise. Browning chose the former alternative; the poem would not be finished until sometime after 1852, when Browning had come to terms with religious and poetic problems with which he was grappling during the late 1840s.

It was the influence of Elizabeth which doubtless assisted him in the resolution of these difficulties. Following their marriage in September 1846, against the wishes of her autocratic, overbearing father, the Brownings traveled to Pisa; they lived there for six months before moving to an apartment in the Casa Guidi in Florence, where they were to live for fourteen years. During this period their activities included reading, writing, visiting galleries and churches, and entertaining visitors from the United States and England. Robert Wiedemann Barrett Browning ("Pen") was born on 9 March 1849. His birth, after several miscarriages, brought joy and comfort to both the Brownings.

Browning's first collected edition appeared in 1849; it significantly omitted *Pauline* and *Sordello*. The poet's only original work during this period includes *Christmas-Eve and Easter-Day* (1850) and the "Essay on Shelley" written in 1851 and published in 1852. *Christmas-Eve and Easter-Day* represents a serious approach on Browning's part to religious problems he had neglected in his poetry up to this time. In these poems Browning considers a number of religious approaches—Evangelicalism, Roman Catholicism, and Biblical criticism in *Christmas-Eve;* and the cynical, relaxed approach to Christianity and its opposite, the narrowly aesthetic approach which stresses the difficulty of belief in *Easter-Day*—and singles out from these analyses elements of belief he could accept. The results of this liberal Christian survey by Browning may be summarized as follows: belief in the divinity of Christ and the power of divine love; the realization that through human love man in some way partakes of God's love; a growing awareness of the limitations of the power of reason, which, in *Paracelsus,* had been equated with the power of love; and finally, an understanding that the world must be seen not as an end in itself but as a means to a higher goal.

The "Essay on Shelley," in contrast, represents Browning's articulation of poetic principles which, coupled with the consolidation of his religious

Registration of the Brownings' marriage at St. Marylebone Parish Church (reproduced by permission of the Rector of St. Marylebone Parish)

views, would release his poetic energies in the two most important collections of short poems in his career: *Men and Women* in 1855 and *Dramatis Personae* in 1864. Browning begins the essay by defining and distinguishing between the terms *objective* and *subjective*. The objective poet is one who essentially deals with reality, while the subjective poet concerns himself with the ideal. The objective poet appeals to the "aggregate human mind" and so depicts the actions of men. Conversely, the subjective poet, who appeals to the "absolute divine mind," dwells on external appearances which serve to draw forth his own "inner light and power." There is an important function for each of the two kinds of poets, and the best poetry is that which fuses the objective and subjective modes. This combination of the real and the ideal, of the dramatic and lyric, is found in what Browning calls the "whole poet." He cites Shakespeare as an example of the objective or dramatic poet; judging from the depiction of the Shelleyan visionary tendency depicted in *Pauline* and *Paracelsus*, one might expect that Browning would name Shelley as an example of the subjective poet. However, he now seems to contradict the ideas enunciated in his youthful poetry, and he even appears to forget that he has unequivocally stated in the essay itself that there has never been an adequate fusion of the seer-fashioner roles. Shelley has, by some incomprehensible transformation, become the "whole poet." Browning seems to be identifying Shelley with himself: it is Browning, not Shelley, who will combine the roles of the objective and subjective poets, who will learn how to fuse the real and the ideal in his poetry, and who will unite the dramatic and lyric modes in the dramatic monologue form. The "Essay on Shelley" exhibits Browning working through his problems as a poet and coming to an understanding, even if a misrepresentation, of how poetic unity and some degree of redemptive vision can be achieved.

All of the available evidence indicates that Browning wrote no short poems between 1845 and 1852. By the latter date, having worked through the most important of his religious and poetic problems in the two long poems published in 1850 and in the "Essay on Shelley," Browning seems to have achieved a sense of balance which enabled him to turn his attention once again to the shorter form. Early in 1852 he completed "Women and Roses," "Childe Roland to the Dark Tower Came," and "Love among the Ruins." On 24 February 1853, he wrote to his friend Joseph Milsand from Florence: "I am writing—a first step towards popularity for me—lyrics with more music and painting than before, so as to get people to hear and see.... Something to follow, if I can compass it." Browning was at this time preparing poems for the two volumes of *Men and Women* to be published in 1855.

With the possible exception of *The Ring and the Book* (1868-1869), *Men and Women* is the most highly regarded of all Browning's works. Now agreed to be one of Victorian England's most distinguished poetic accomplishments, it had little impact at the time: of the fairly small pressrun of about 2,000, many copies were still available a decade later, and there was no second edition. Browning continued to be known as his wife's husband. However, in the fifty-one poems contained in these volumes, Browning achieved his widest ranging accomplishments in terms of characterization, techniques of

A letter from Browning to his sister-in-law, Henrietta Moulton-Barrett, announcing the birth of his son (Anderson Galleries, 14-15 April 1937)

presentation, psychological insight and penetration, ambiguity, irony, and topicality. The many excellent poems in these volumes include the completed "Saul," "Fra Lippo Lippi," "Andrea del Sarto," "Childe Roland to the Dark Tower Came," "Bishop Blougram's Apology," "Cleon," and "Karshish." They are among the most anthologized works in the Browning canon.

It was probably the completion of the fragmentary "Saul," first published in 1845, which helped Browning to achieve the full poetic release which enabled him to compose the other poems in *Men and Women*. He had been unable to complete "Saul" in 1845 because he was unsure of how to achieve the poem's religious and poetic resolution; the work's original version ended with a naturalistic celebration of the joys of life and praise of Saul as the epitome of creation, but could not move beyond that level. Having achieved the sense of certainty that resulted from his work between 1845 and 1852, Browning was able to effect a sense of resolution in "Saul" that was not possible earlier. David the singer, in the first version, acted primarily as a fashioner; he dealt with the real world and with things of everyday life. In the stanzas added in 1852 or 1853, David assumes the role of the subjective poet; he undergoes a revelatory experience culminating in a prophetic foreshadowing of the Incarnation:

> "He who did most, shall bear most; the strongest shall
>   stand the most weak.
> 'Tis the weakness in strength that I cry for! my
>   flesh, that I seek
> In the Godhead! I seek and I find it. O Saul, it
>   shall be
> A Face like my face that receives thee; a Man like
>   to me,
> Thou shalt love and be loved by, for ever: a Hand
>   like this hand
> Shall throw open the gates of new life to thee! See
>   the Christ stand!"

In this yoking of the concerns of the objective and subjective poets, and in the acceptance of Christ as a poetic symbol of the reconciliation of the real and the ideal, the human and the divine, the flesh and the spirit, Browning comes to understand how he can most effectively operate as a "whole poet." Similar concerns are explored in "Fra Lippo Lippi" and "Andrea del Sarto," both poems about artists.

"Fra Lippo Lippi" is one of Browning's finest character portraits. The poem concerns a licentious monk caught out late at night in streets "where sportive ladies leave their doors ajar." His amicable confrontation with the city guards causes the good monk to explain in some detail his past and present circumstances. With the auditors in the poem, the reader learns that at an early age he was taken by his aunt to a monastery and pressed into service. As he matured, his superiors discovered that he had artistic talents, and they instructed him to paint vague and spiritual pictures for the edification of the viewers. He has been instructed to paint "soul," but Fra Lippo Lippi knows that this view of art is invalid. The monk explains that his purpose in painting is not to glorify the flesh, but to employ it as a means through which man can more easily perceive soul. This view of art reflects his view of life. Fra Lippo celebrates the physical, and yet clearly understands the nature of the relationship between the physical and spiritual. He may paint, at times, as directed by his superiors, but he cannot, and does not, suppress the impulse toward the physical evident in his own life. Fra Lippo Lippi is both intriguing and beguiling. Despite his apparent self-indulgence, most readers view him as a sympathetic and entertaining character. Such is not the case with Andrea del Sarto.

This individual, called "The Faultless Painter" in the poem's subtitle, creates work which presents a perfect pictorial image of flesh but which has no soul. Andrea is a fine draftsman, but his work has no insight and no depth. The cause of his failure is his complete devotion to his wife, Lucrezia, who has proven herself to be a negative source of inspiration. His painting, for which Lucrezia always serves as the model, exactly parallels in its strength and its weakness the physical beauty and spiritual emptiness of his wife. Having sacrificed all for this empty spiritual vessel, he is now on the verge of losing her to the "cousin" who waits for her at twilight outside their residence. Andrea's present is empty of meaning and his future is devoid of hope. But he is resigned.

Four other poems depict a wide range of character types. In "Childe Roland," which seems to reflect a terrifying nightmare experience, the speaker feels that both man and nature are conspiring against him. As he journeys across a barren and sterile wasteland, Roland believes that he is guided by fate or the devil and that he has no hope of success in his quest. However, he persists through adversity, and the poem closes with his ringing assertion of self-identity, which shows that he has been able to overcome the obstacles thrown up by his own mind in his pursuit of self-knowledge.

Bishop Blougram has, perhaps, too much self-knowledge. In this long and complicated poem, Blougram converses with an individual whom he considers a third-rate journalist, Gigadibs. The argument of the poem concerns the nature of reality and the nature of the faith which is necessary to sustain oneself in the face of that reality. In his effort to assert his intellectual and moral superiority, Blougram offers lengthy disquisitions on each of these subjects and the manner in which they relate to his own accomplishments.

Gigadibs is an absolutist who insists that one must possess total faith or none at all, while the bishop explains that both life and faith are compromises and that absolutes simply cannot be grasped. The poem is highly ironic. Blougram is easily able to overcome the journalist in argumentation and takes considerable pride in doing so. But he has not deflated or demoralized the journalist as he had intended, nor does Gigadibs succeed in gathering information with which to publicly embarrass the bishop. Instead, as the poem closes the poetic speaker reveals that Gigadibs has been converted to Christianity and is setting off for a new life abroad:

> He did not sit five minutes. Just a week
> Sufficed his sudden healthy vehemence.

Something had struck him . . .
Another way than Blougram's purpose was:
And having bought, not cabin-furniture
But settler's-implements (enough for three)
And started for Australia—there, I hope,
By this time he has tested his first plough,
And studied his last chapter of Saint John.

"Cleon" and "Karshish" are unique in the Browning canon because they are epistolary monologues. Each of the title characters writes a letter to his superior describing his most recent experiences. With his highly trained intellect, Cleon, the Greek philosopher, has delved into the fundamental problems of existence and discovered the answer to the contradiction posed by the theory of progress which, for the non-Christian, can end only with regression and death. His answer to the questions of Protus concerning the nature of existence is that there is no final and clear answer. Cleon, the most highly gifted of Greek philosophers and poets, will die like Protus, and his works will serve only to mock him in death, not to grant him immortality. He explains that he has recently heard of doctrines being proposed by "a mere barbarian Jew" named "Christus," which offer hypothetical answers to the questions raised by Protus; but Cleon believes that "their doctrine could be held by no sane man." Karshish, the Arab physician, reports on his travels to his medical and academic superior, Abib. Wearied by his long and difficult journey from Jericho to Bethany, yet eager to share the experiences he has had, he records his thoughts haphazardly, as they come to him. He details matter of immediate interest, particularly pertaining to medical observations, and then proceeds to a discussion of the strange case of a man named Lazarus who, after being dead for three days, was cured by some medical means unknown to Arab science, and is now in good health. A trained observer should not become a superstitious gossip, so Karshish dismisses the matter, but not without some hopeful speculation that there might be some truth in the story. The poem thus closes on a somewhat more positive note than that struck by "Cleon."

The poems in *Men and Women* are chiefly concerned thematically with art, religion, and love. The characters depicted are fascinating in their variety and their complexity, and the nuances of language and tone render these poems among Browning's finest. But the remaining years of the decade were not to be highly productive for Browning. From 1855, when they visited London in order that Browning could oversee the publication of *Men and Women,* to June 1861, when Elizabeth died, the two poets and Pen lived a quiet social and literary life in Florence. Some poems might have been written by Browning during this period, but none were published.

In 1856 the Brownings were granted a degree of financial independence as a result of a bequest made to them by their friend John Kenyon. It was Kenyon who had encouraged Browning to write to Elizabeth in 1845. After Elizabeth's father had abandoned the management of her financial affairs because of her marriage, Kenyon had assumed those duties; following Pen's birth in 1849, Kenyon generously sent the poets an annual gift of £100. Although Elizabeth's poetry produced some funds which helped them to maintain their livelihood during the 1850s, and they also received £170 a year from English government bonds, Kenyon's bequest upon his death provided the first real relief for the Brownings from financial concerns. The £11,000 which he willed to them provided an income of about £550 per year.

Elizabeth Barrett Browning died in June 1861. Browning and Pen left Florence in August; after a holiday in France, they settled in London in October. Browning and his son moved into a house at 19 Warwick Crescent, where the poet resided for the next twenty-six years. Arabel Barrett, his wife's sister, was a neighbor with whom he visited frequently. Pen and his father were joined at 19 Warwick Crescent in 1866 by Browning's sister Sarianna, who was to remain with Browning until his death. These years prior to the publication of *Dramatis Personae* in 1864 were primarily devoted to raising Pen. Browning strove to give the boy a masculine sense of identity by changing the rather feminine haircut and clothing which had been imposed upon the child by his mother. The period is also marked by Browning's increasingly active social life. Perhaps the most mysterious event during this period was the offer to Browning in 1862 to succeed Thackeray as the editor of the *Cornhill* magazine. This was a financially advantageous opportunity, and considerable stature went with the position; but for some unknown reason Browning declined.

A good deal is known about the years from 1861 to the early 1870s because of Browning's letters to Isabella Blagden. Miss Blagden had been a close friend of the Brownings in Florence and had greatly assisted Browning in his bereavement in 1861. Following Elizabeth's death, Browning and Isa Blagden agreed to write each other regularly, she on the twelfth of each month and he on the nineteenth. These informative letters cover a period of ten years up to Blagden's death. During this time Browning began to make plans for another collection of poems like *Men and Women,* and also to work on the "old yellow book" he had purchased from a bookstall in June 1860 in Florence.

Dramatis Personae (1864) contains a number of important poems but is more abstract, less pictorial, more speculative, less vibrant, and more meditative than *Men and Women.* Nonetheless, it was the first of Browning's publications to go into a second edition. Sales were relatively good; in his fifties, Browning was beginning to attract a fair number of readers. (In 1868, however, Chapman and Hall still had 550 copies on hand.) This work, including such important pieces as "Abt Vogler," "Rabbi Ben Ezra," "A Death in the Desert," and "Caliban upon Setebos," was the last successful collection of Browning's short poems to be published.

From the publication of *Dramatis Personae* to the end of the 1860s, Browning especially concerned himself with three activities: the raising and education of his son; the composition of the poem considered by many to be his major contribution to English literature, *The Ring and the Book;* and the increasing social whirl, which Browning seemed to enjoy immensely.

Browning assiduously attempted to prepare his son for Balliol College, Oxford, but without much success: Pen was adept at drawing, fencing, and riding, but not at learning. He finally sat for matriculation on 2 April 1868, but failed. Browning's dream of sending his son to Balliol College was not realized, but Pen was finally matriculated at Christ's Church, the most popular and least demanding of the Oxford Colleges at the time. Browning's disappointment might have been partially offset by his progress with the old yellow book which he was transforming into *The Ring and the Book.*

The collection of materials which Browning had acquired in Florence in 1860 included legal briefs, pamphlets, and letters relating to a case involving a child bride, a disguised priest, a triple murder, four hangings, and the beheading of a nobleman. He resolved in October 1864 that he would write twelve books of the poem in six months, but by July 1865 he had completed only 8,400 lines, about a third of the eventual total. When it was finally printed in 1868-1869, its reception was better than that of any other work of Browning's published to that time. The *Athenaeum* for 20 March 1869 called it "beyond all parallel the supremest poetical achievement of our time . . . the most precious and profound spiritual treasure that England has produced since the days of Shakespeare."

The title of the poem contains multiple associations. It points to the poem's source, the old yellow book; to the pattern of the monologues, which is circular; to Browning's initials; and, in the ring, to the memory of Elizabeth. In the first and last books of the poem, the speaker, usually identified with Browning, addresses the British public and describes how he uncovered a book concerning a seventeenth-century Italian murder trial in a Florence bookstall. He explains why its subject attracted him, and how he has since imaginatively recreated every moment of the trial of Count Guido Franceschini, which took place in the courts of Rome in January and February 1698. The speaker portrays himself as a master craftsman who will fashion a poem out of the raw stuff of his old document.

Introducing the actors in the original case, he offers to bring them back to life through a poetic reproduction of their voices. He continually asserts the factual nature of his rendition, identifying himself with the skilled artist who shapes the metal (the facts), made malleable by the addition of an alloy (the poet's own fancy), until with the removal of the alloy the ring stands triumphant as a completed work of art. The speaker suggests that it is through the withdrawal of his personality that the truth emerges through the voices of the characters in the drama. While he insists upon the facts, he also indicates that the truth to be perceived by the reader lies beyond the simple factual level. Browning presents the basic material and its meaning three times in the opening book and says that he has found Guido guilty as charged; consequently, the reader is not to concern himself with who is right and who is wrong but is to examine the ten monologues with a view to understanding why objective reality appears so differently to different eyes.

In 1693 Guido Franceschini, a relatively poor nobleman of inferior rank, married a young woman, Francesca Pompilia, who had been raised in Rome by a couple named Comparini. When the Comparinis visited Guido's home in Arezzo three years after the marriage, they found that Guido had misrepresented his financial condition at the time of the marriage and, consequently, brought suit against him for the return of Pompilia's dowry. Violante Comparini had revealed to her husband that Pompilia was really the daughter of a whore, and that she had claimed her as her own in order to gain an inheritance left to them on condition of their having a child. As a result of their action, Guido became an even more impossible husband than he had been previously. Pompilia attempted to flee many times; she was eventually successful in escaping and taking flight for Rome with the assistance of a young canon, Giuseppe Caponsacchi. Guido followed, and Pompilia and her companion were captured about fifteen miles from Rome. According to the documents, Caponsacchi was charged with "adultery," and found guilty of "seduction" and of having "carnal knowledge" of Pompilia. Pompilia was sent during further inquiry to a nunnery for penitent women. But she was pregnant, and was shortly thereafter sent to the house of the Comparinis in Rome. Eight months after her flight from Arezzo, she gave birth to a boy, who was named Gaetano. Shortly after, Guido came with four of his henchmen pretending to bear a message from Caponsacchi, murdered and mutilated the Comparinis, and left Pompilia for dead with twenty-two wounds in her body. She died four days later. Guido was captured, charged with the crime, and tried.

There was no question that Guido had committed the deed; the legal quandary was whether a husband should be allowed to kill his adultress wife and her accomplices without incurring the ordinary penalty. This reopened the question, which the courts had never considered settled, as to whether or not Pompilia had committed adultery with Caponsacchi. Thus, the conduct and the characters of the Comparinis, Guido, Pompilia, and Caponsacchi were thrown open in order that the court might arrive at a decision as to whether Guido was justified in any way whatsoever in his triple murder. In February 1698 the court decided against Guido and condemned him to be beheaded and his fellow conspirators hanged. But Guido, who held a minor office in the church, appealed to Pope Innocent XII to set aside the judgment. The pope refused the appeal, and Guido and his companions were executed on 22 February 1698. Shortly thereafter, Pompilia was declared innocent, and Gaetano was declared the rightful heir to her property.

Browning took these materials, cast over them the light of his own imaginative power, and transmuted them into *The Ring and the Book*. Book I serves as the explanatory introduction. In Book II, "Half-Rome," the speaker is the first of three anonymous commentators upon the crime which Guido has committed. He is an older man who is having difficulty with his wife, and his sympathies are with Guido. The speaker in Book III, "The Other Half-Rome," is a younger man with finer instincts than those of "Half-Rome." He speaks on behalf of Pompilia. The speaker in Book IV, "Tertrum Quid," is relatively neutral. He sums up,

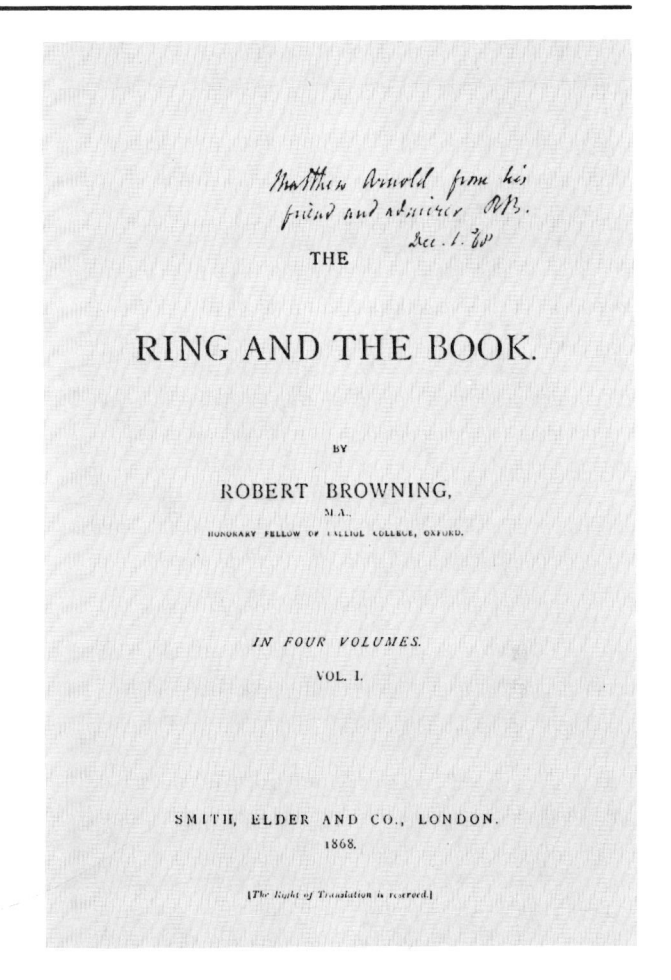

Title page for Browning's poem based on an actual seventeenth-century murder case, with an inscription by Browning to Matthew Arnold (Anderson Galleries, 30 April 1936)

weighs, and arranges the evidence of the two speakers who have gone before him, and of the whole case. In Book V, "Count Guido Franceschini," Guido's first monologue occurs just a few days after the crime. Guido is speaking to his judges and cleverly defends himself by reviewing his life, eliciting the sympathy of the hearers, and blaming the faithlessness of his wife for his present sorry condition. In Book VI, "Giuseppe Caponsacchi," the young priest addresses the judges about four days after the murders, while he is still in the throes of grief over the slaughter of Pompilia. His speech reflects his love for Pompilia, his hatred for Guido, and his scorn for the judges. Book VII is "Pompilia": in her deathbed monologue, Pompilia attempts, with considerable difficulty, to reconstruct the events which have lead to her present situation. She tries to explain her life to herself as well as to her confessor, Fra Celestino. Books VIII and IX present the two lawyers, Dominus Hyacinthus de Archangelis and Juris Doctor Johannes-Baptista Bottinus, the former the defender of Guido, and the latter his prosecutor. These monologues provide some humor, striking a note of relief following the intense monologues of Pompilia and Caponsacchi, and preceding the monologue of the pope in Book X, "The Pope." It has been generally assumed that the pope speaks on Browning's behalf, and this is to some extent true. The judgments rendered by the pope on Guido, Pompilia, and Caponsacchi are similar to those offered by Browning's speaker in Books I and XII of the poem. In the eleventh monologue "Guido," Guido is given a second chance to defend himself immediately before his death. He sheds the hypocritical mask worn in Book V and reveals that he has, all the time, been motivated by hatred of his superiors, of the church, and above all of Pompilia. The poem's final book, "The Book and the Ring," reintroduces the speaker closely identified with Browning himself. The poem concludes with important comments on the nature of art and on the uses of indirection and obliqueness in poetry, and offers the proposition that, although the poet employs facts, the meaning lies beyond them: "So write a book shall mean, beyond the facts, / Suffice the eye and save the soul beside." In the final few lines the poet makes reference to his "Lyric Love," Elizabeth, and to her gold ring of verse which links England and Italy:

> And save the soul! If this intent save mine,—
> If the rough ore be rounded to a ring,
> Render all duty which good ring should do,
> And, failing grace, succeed in guardianship,—
> Might mine but lie outside thine, Lyric Love,
> Thy rare gold ring of verse (the poet praised)
> Linking our England to his Italy!

The Ring and the Book combines the most important of Browning's thematic concerns—the nature of truth, the value and validity of human perception, the nature of poetry and poetic expression—with his greatest technical achievement in the extended monologue form. Most critics of Browning's poetry, as well as the general public, agree that *The Ring and the Book* represents the apex of Browning's career. He continued to write until his death in 1889, however, and many of the works published during this period are of considerable interest to Browning specialists because of the experiments with technique and form he undertook in them.

Of particular interest in this regard are *Prince Hohenstiel-Schwangau, Saviour of Society* (1871) and *Parleyings with Certain People of Importance in Their Day* (1887). *Prince Hohenstiel-Schwangau* is a long, complex interior monologue; the speaker is modeled on Napoleon III. The poem is basically one of self-examination and the contemplation of life's possibilities before the speaker decides upon a course of political action. Section I, to line 1231, focuses on the intellectual convolutions of the prince's attempt to explain himself to himself; in the second section, from line 1231 to the end of the poem, the prince posits and then undercuts an ideal conception of self. The characterization is precise although complex, and the style is dense, full of nuances and elliptical. In its difficulty, it is representative of much of Browning's poetry after *The Ring and the Book*. The essentially negative public reaction to it typifies the reaction to much of the poetry Browning wrote during this period.

Just as Browning's poetry during the last twenty years of his life was not as successful as he would have wished, so too his personal life, despite outward appearances, was not as happy as he might have desired. In 1870, at the age of twenty-one, Pen disappointed his father by failing the exams at Christ's Church. In a letter to George Barrett in June 1870, Browning remarks, somewhat despair-

Browning with his son, Pen, in 1870 (photograph courtesy of Frances Winwar)

Browning's life—philosophy, history, poetry, politics, painting, the classics, and music—this problem of Browning's double image remains unresolved.

But many of Browning's contemporaries regarded the poet as a sage who deserved recognition and praise in his declining years. In 1881, for example, Frederick James Furnivall, founder of the Early English Text Society (1864), the Chaucer and the Ballad Societies (1868), and one of the initial planners of the *Oxford English Dictionary,* instituted the Browning Society. He circulated a prospectus which read, in part: "The Browning student will seek the shortcomings [of Browning's obscure style] in himself rather than in his master. He will wish . . . to learn more of the meaning of the poet's utterances; and then, having gladly learnt, 'gladly wol he teche,' and bring others under the same influence that has benefited himself. To this end *The Browning Society* has been founded." Browning was understandably flattered by the formation of a society in his honor, but he was also rather skeptical about the intelligence and motivation of some of its members. He was much less reluctant about accepting the symbolic status conferred by honorary degrees

Browning in later years

ingly, "the poor boy is simply weak." Browning's perception of Pen's weakness would not be contradicted by his son's activities in the 1870s and 1880s. In 1874 he was sent to Antwerp to study painting and, aided by his father's rather shameless patronage, achieved some minor success as a painter-sculptor. But he was, finally, not much more than a dilettante, despite his father's affection and attention.

During the final two decades of his life Browning wrote, traveled, and became very much a part of the London social scene. As Henry James suggests in his short story "The Private Life" (1892), there seemed to be two Robert Brownings inhabiting one person during this period. James was especially fascinated by the contrast between the Browning who wrote poems and the Browning one met socially. It was difficult to reconcile the person who wrote the dense, difficult, and frequently high-sounding poetry with the plump, garrulous gentleman in white waistcoat who was such a favorite at London dinner parties. Although *Parleyings with Certain People of Importance in Their Day* offers a mental biography of the poet by delineating seven men who represent the seven major interests in

A photograph of Browning taken the year of his death

The Palazzo Rezzonico, Venice, where Browning died (photograph courtesy of Wellesley College Library)

from Oxford University in 1882 and the University of Edinburgh in 1884.

As these events suggest, Browning's final decade was active. In 1887 he was forced to vacate Warwick Crescent as a result of demolition by the Regent's Canal Bill; he moved with Sarianna to 29 DeVere Gardens, across the street from Henry James at No. 32. He continued to travel. He and Sarianna were in Venice in the fall of 1888, with Pen and his wife Fannie, to visit and inspect the Palazzo Rezzonico, a colossal derelict structure soon to be purchased and refurbished for Pen by Fannie, using her inheritance. Early in August 1889 Browning was quite ill, but he was sufficiently recovered by the end of the month to undertake a trip with his sister to Asolo, Italy, to be followed by another visit with Pen and Fannie. November and December were cold and damp months in Venice in 1889, and the poet's previous illness and advanced age made him particularly susceptible. He contracted a cold in late November and died during the evening of Thursday, 12 December. Browning was buried on 31 December in Westminster Abbey in the Poet's Corner, an appropriate and final public honor.

Browning's career falls roughly into three divisions. His early poetry of development to 1845 reflects his growing awareness of his own powers as a poet; it also illustrates the method by which he refined his poetic techniques in order to reach the stage during which he could perfect the dramatic monologue as a poetic form. From 1845 to 1869 Browning wrote the poems for which he is most popular today. The last part of his career involved a falling off poetically and was a time of much less personal satisfaction than the years of his marriage.

Browning's importance as a poet of the nineteenth century is unquestionable, as is the extent to which he influenced the major poets of the twentieth century, such as Ezra Pound and T. S. Eliot. Within the last thirty years, there has been an upsurge of critical activity aimed at coming to an understanding of all aspects of Browning's work. Significant advances have been made in the perception and elucidation of Browning's technical achievements, and in the relationship of these achievements to his aesthetic concerns. With the recent publication of the Penguin two-volume edition of Browning's *Poems,* a standard text now exists which will make his work even more accessible to scholars and to the general reading public.

Letters:

Letters of Robert Browning Collected by Thomas J. Wise, edited by Thurman L. Hood (New Haven: Yale University Press, 1933);

Robert Browning and Julia Wedgwood: A Broken Friendship as Revealed in Their Letters, edited by Richard Curle (London: Murray & Cape, 1937);

New Letters of Robert Browning, edited by William Clyde DeVane and Kenneth Leslie Knickerbocker (New Haven: Yale University Press, 1950);

Dearest Isa: Browning's Letters to Isa Blagden, edited by Edward C. McAleer (Austin: University of Texas Press, 1951);

Browning to His American Friends: Letters between the Brownings, the Storys, and James Russell Lowell, 1841-1890, edited by Gertrude Reese Hudson (London: Bowes & Bowes, 1965);

Learned Lady: Letters from Robert Browning to Mrs. Thomas FitzGerald 1876-1889, edited by McAleer (Cambridge: Harvard University Press, 1966);

The Letters of Robert Browning and Elizabeth Barrett, 1845-1846, edited by Evan Kintner, 2 volumes (Cambridge: Harvard University Press, 1969);

The Brownings to the Tennysons, edited by Thomas J. Collins (Waco, Tex.: Armstrong Brown Library, Baylor University, 1971);

"Ruskin and the Brownings: Twenty-five Unpublished Letters," edited by David J. DeLaura,

Bulletin of John Rylands Library, 54 (1972): 314-356.

Bibliography:

Warner Barnes, *Catalogue of the Browning Collection at The University of Texas* (Austin: University of Texas Press, 1966).

Biographies:

Mrs. Sutherland Orr, *Life and Letters of Robert Browning,* revised by F. G. Kenyon (London: Smith, Elder, 1908);

W. Hall Griffin and Harry Christopher Minchin, *The Life of Robert Browning* (London: Methuen, 1910);

Betty Miller, *Robert Browning: A Portrait* (London: Murray, 1952);

Maisie Ward, *Robert Browning and His World,* 2 volumes (London: Cassell, 1967-1969);

William Irvine and Park Honan, *The Book, the Ring, and the Poet: A Biography of Robert Browning* (New York: McGraw-Hill, 1974);

John Maynard, *Browning's Youth* (Cambridge, Mass.: Harvard University Press, 1977).

References:

Isobel Armstrong, "Browning and the Grotesque Style," in *The Major Victorian Poets: Reconsiderations,* edited by Armstrong (London: Routledge & Kegan Paul, 1969), pp. 93-123;

G. K. Chesterton, *Robert Browning* (New York & London: Macmillan, 1903);

Thomas J. Collins, *Robert Browning's Moral-Aesthetic Theory 1833-1855* (Lincoln: University of Nebraska Press, 1967);

Eleanor Cook, *Browning's Lyrics: An Exploration* (Toronto: University of Toronto Press, 1974);

A. Dwight Culler, "Monodrama and the Dramatic Monologue," *PMLA,* 90 (May 1975): 366-385;

William Clyde DeVane, *A Browning Handbook,* second edition (New York: Appleton-Century-Crofts, 1955);

DeVane, "The Virgin and the Dragon," *Yale Review,* new series, 37 (September 1947): 33-46;

Edward Dowden, *Robert Browning* (London: Dent, 1904);

Philip Drew, *The Poetry of Browning: A Critical Introduction* (London: Methuen, 1970);

F. J. Furnivall, ed., *The Browning Society's Papers,* 3 volumes (London: Browning Society, 1881-1891);

Roy E. Gridley, *The Brownings and France: A Chronicle with Commentary* (London: Athlone, 1983);

Donald S. Hair, *Browning's Experiments with Genre* (Toronto: University of Toronto Press, 1972);

Constance W. Hassett, *The Elusive Self in the Poetry of Robert Browning* (Athens: Ohio University Press, 1982);

Park Honan, *Browning's Characters* (New Haven: Yale University Press, 1961);

Robert Langbaum, *The Poetry of Experience* (New York: Random House, 1957);

William S. Peterson, *Interrogating the Oracle: A History of the London Browning Society* (Athens: Ohio University Press, 1970);

F. A. Pottle, *Shelley and Browning: A Myth and Some Facts* (Chicago: Pembroke Press, 1923);

Robert O. Preyer, "Robert Browning: A Reading of the Early Narratives," *ELH,* 26 (December 1959): 531-548;

Preyer, "Two Styles in the Verse of Robert Browning," *ELH,* 32 (March 1965): 62-84;

William O. Raymond, *The Infinite Moment and Other Essays in Robert Browning,* second edition (Toronto: University of Toronto Press, 1965);

Clyde L. Ryals, *Becoming Browning: The Poems and Plays of Robert Browning, 1833-1846* (Columbus: Ohio State University Press, 1983);

Ryals, *Browning's Later Poetry: 1871-1889* (Ithaca, N.Y.: Cornell University Press, 1975);

W. David Shaw, *The Dialectical Temper: The Rhetorical Art of Robert Browning* (Ithaca, N.Y.: Cornell University Press, 1968);

Lionel Stevenson, "Tennyson, Browning, and a Romantic Fallacy," *University of Toronto Quarterly,* 13 (1944): 175-195;

Arthur Symons, *An Introduction to the Study of Browning,* revised edition (London: Dent, 1906);

Michael Timko, "Ah, Did You Once See Browning Plain?," *Studies in English Literature,* 6 (Autumn 1966): 731-742;

Herbert F. Tucker, *Browning's Beginnings: The Art of Disclosure* (Minneapolis: University of Minnesota Press, 1980).

Papers:

There is no central depository for Robert Browning's papers. A listing of all manuscripts and their locations can be found in Philip Kelley and Betty A. Coley, *The Browning Collections* (Winfield, Kans.: Wedgestone Press, 1984).

Edward Caswall
(15 July 1814-2 January 1878)

G. B. Tennyson
University of California, Los Angeles

SELECTED BOOKS: *The Art of Pluck: Being a Treatise after the Fashion of Aristotle, Writ for the Use of Students in the Universities; to Which Is Added Fragments from the Examination Papers,* as Scriblerus Redivivus (Oxford: Vincent, 1836);

Pluck Examination Papers for Candidates at Oxford and Cambridge in 1836, as Scriblerus Redivivus (Oxford: Slatter, 1836);

Sketches of Young Ladies, in Which These Interesting Members of the Animal Kingdom Are Classified according to Their Several Instincts, Habits and General Characteristics, as Quiz (London: Chapman & Hall, 1837);

Characteristic Sketches of Young Gentlemen, as Quiz, Jr. (London: Kidd, 1838);

Sermons on the Seen and Unseen (London: Barnes, 1846);

The Masque of Mary and Other Poems (London: Burns & Lambert, 1858);

A May Pageant and Other Poems (London: Burns, Lambert, 1865);

Hymns and Poems, Original and Translated (London: Burns, Oates, 1872).

OTHER: *Lyra Catholica: Containing All the Breviary and Missal Hymns, with Others from Various Sources,* translated and edited by Caswall (London, 1849).

One of the younger members of the Tractarian or Oxford Movement, Edward Caswall exemplifies the spirit of Tractarian devotional poetry carried into the Roman Catholic communion. An ardent admirer of John Henry Newman, Caswall wrote hymns and poems that show the influence of Newman, John Keble, and other Tractarian poets even as they also exhibit a more intensely Roman commitment than is associated with the purely Tractarian experience.

Caswall came from a well-placed Anglican family. His father, Robert Clarke Caswall, was a vicar in Hampshire; his brother, Henry, was a prebendary of Salisbury Cathedral; and his uncle, Thomas Burgess, was the bishop of Salisbury. Caswall was educated at Marlborough School and at Brasenose College, Oxford, from which he graduated B.A. in 1836 and M.A. in 1838. He took holy orders in the Church of England in 1838 and accepted a living in Wiltshire in his uncle's diocese. But in 1847 he resigned his living and was received into the Roman Catholic church. After the death of his wife in 1849 he was free to join Newman's Oratory of St. Philip Neri in Birmingham, which he did in 1850. For the remainder of his life he worked as an Oratorian, and it was during these years that he wrote the great bulk of his poetry and hymns. He died in Birmingham and was buried, with Newman officiating, in the Oratory cemetery at Rednall.

As an Anglican, Caswall had produced a collection of sermons the very title of which reveals the influence of Newman—*Sermons on the Seen and Unseen* (1846). Likewise, his first published verse reflects in its title, *Lyra Catholica* (1849), the Newman and Tractarian influence exhibited in Newman's 1836 collection of his own and other Tractarians' verses, the *Lyra Apostolica*. Caswall's *Lyra Catholica*, however, is a gathering not of original poems but of translations of Latin hymns from the Breviary and Missal. The earliest efforts in this direction had been made in the 1830s by Newman and Isaac Williams, but Caswall's collection is the most extensive undertaken up to that time. His translations bear comparison with the work of the preeminent Victorian translator and adapter of ancient hymns, John Mason Neale.

Caswall's original poetry is found in *The Masque of Mary and Other Poems* (1858) and in *A May Pageant and Other Poems* (1865), both of which also contain additional translations of hymns. All of Caswall's poems and translations were gathered together in *Hymns and Poems, Original and Translated* (1872). Many of his translations have passed into common use in hymnbooks of all denominations, but his original hymns have been limited largely to Roman Catholic circles.

Caswall's original poetry, though not extensive, exhibits a number of arresting features, especially in terms of the Tractarian inheritance. On the one hand, Caswall intensifies the Tractarian devotion to the church as the visible source of poetic

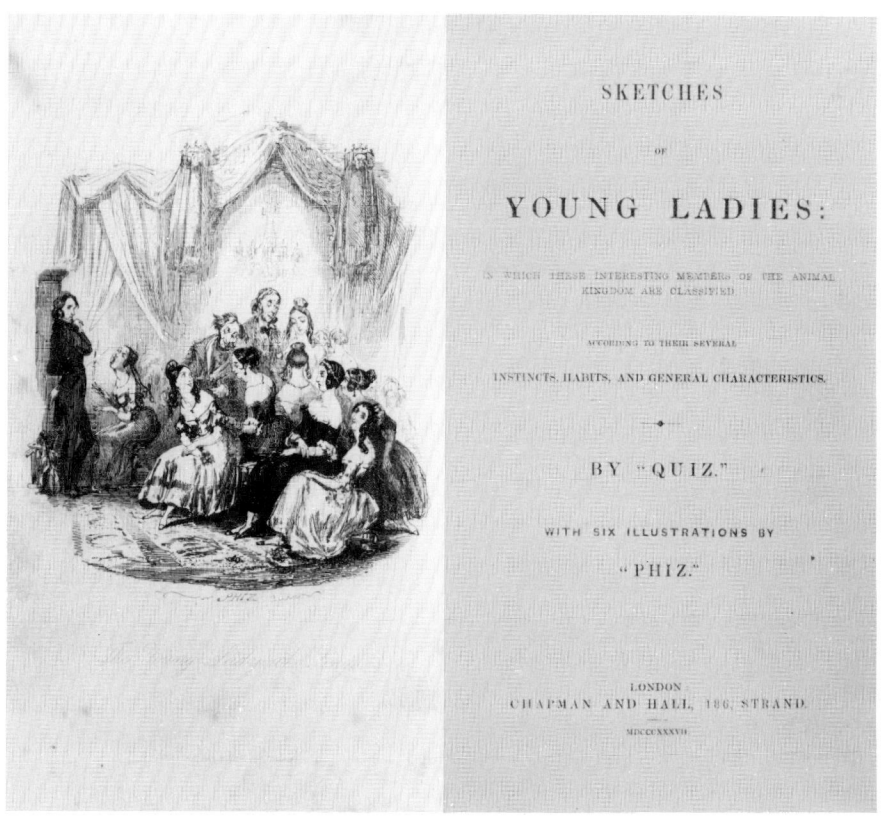

Cover, frontispiece, and title page for Caswall's satirical sketches, written while he was a student at Oxford University (Thomas Cooper Library, University of South Carolina)

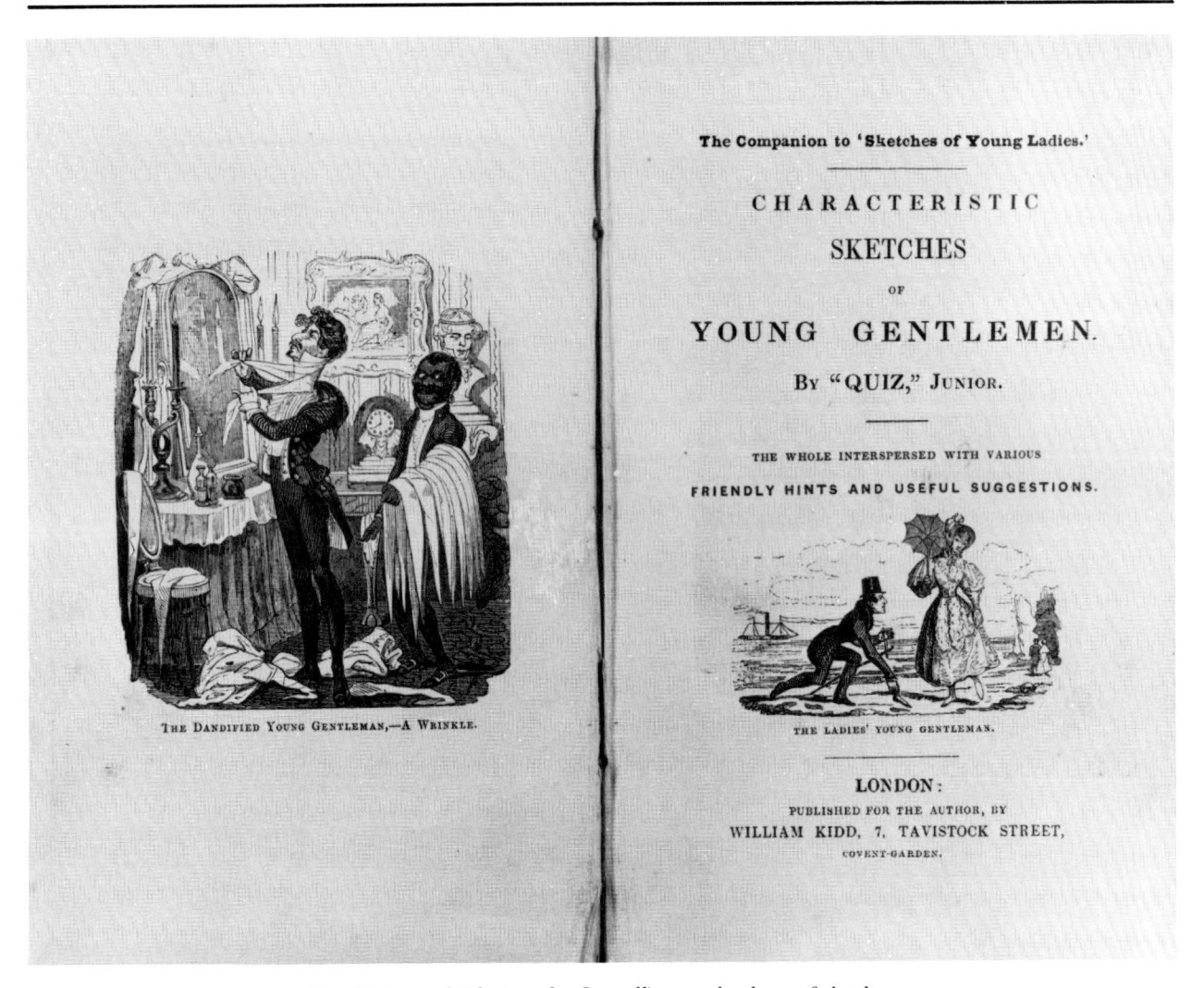

Frontispiece and title page for Caswall's second volume of sketches

subject matter and inspiration; on the other hand, he leaves no doubt that the church in question is solely the church of Rome. His *Masque of Mary,* for example, contains what has been called "an extraordinary mating of Milton and Roman triumphalism," featuring an "Angelic Guard" led by Ithuriel and language such as the following, spoken of Mary by the High Priest of the Temple:

> Daughter of Joachim and Anna blest!
> Of David's race the loveliest and the best!
> Scion of Jesse, in whose stem entwine
> The sacerdotal and the regal line;
> In whom, with ever-new delight, we trace
> New miracles of still increasing grace;—
> Accept the homage that we come to pay
> On the bright morning of thy natal day.

Many of the shorter pieces in *The Masque of Mary* and in *A May Pageant* are openly polemic poems on the issues that divided Anglicans and Roman Catholics. A notable example from the *Masque of Mary* volume is Caswall's "Belief of Anglicans in the Real Presence Tested." In this poem Caswall charges Anglicans with, at the least, insincerity in professing to believe in the Real Presence but failing to bow before it:

> Be honest; if Him truly there ye hold,
>   When next the Feast ye share,
> Bow down before the Mystery untold,—
>   Bow down, and worship there!

At the same time Caswall continues to exhibit the Tractarian concern for nature and for visible signs of God's superintending design, as expressed in the doctrine of Analogy. "Nature's Mysteries" proclaims the Tractarian belief that nature is but the external manifestation of God's greater hidden glory:

> O, might I but look behind,
> What a blaze of glory bright!
> In thy hidden depth enshrin'd,
> Would confound my dazzled sight!

At the Roman Catholic end of Caswall's poetic spectrum he can be found in "England's Future Conversion" offering a prayer that "After the wasting heresies/Of thrice a hundred years" England will yet come to acknowledge Roman supremacy and true Christianity:

> Thy desecrated shrines once more
> Shall their true God receive;
> And kneeling Englishmen adore,
> Where now they disbelieve.

Caswall has received almost no attention in the years following his death, although his translations continue to appear in many hymnals. His original poetry would repay investigation for its links with Newman's later Roman Catholic verse and for its points of contact with the poetry of Gerard Manley Hopkins. One can note, for example, Caswall's insistent nature emphasis: his "Temple of Nature" calls upon man to find in nature "a store, from whence His praise to sing/Who is above all praise, of all creation King!" and seems to anticipate Hopkins's "Pied Beauty"; his preoccupation with May imagery, calling to mind such Hopkins poems as "Spring" and "The May Magnificat"; and his intense incarnationalism, which is a pervasive aspect of Hopkins's poetry as well. Caswall does not originate these concerns, but he is the first in the Victorian age to express them in a body of verse that makes the transition from Tractarian to Roman Catholic devotional poetry.

References:

John Julian, ed., *A Dictionary of Hymnology*, volume 1 (London: Murray, 1907), pp. 214-215;

G. B. Tennyson, *Victorian Devotional Poetry: The Tractarian Mode* (Cambridge: Harvard University Press, 1981), pp. 183-185.

Arthur Hugh Clough

Patrick Scott
University of South Carolina

BIRTH: Liverpool, England, 1 January 1819, to James Butler and Ann Perfect Clough.

EDUCATION: B.A., Balliol College, Oxford, 1841; M.A., 1845.

MARRIAGE: 13 June 1854 to Blanche M. Smith; children: Florence, Arthur Hugh, Blanche Athena.

DEATH: Florence, Italy, 13 November 1861.

BOOKS: *The Close of the Eighteenth Century, A Prize Poem* (Rugby, U.K.: Rowell, 1835);
A Consideration of Objections against the Retrenchment Association at Oxford during the Irish Famine in 1847 (Oxford: Macpherson, 1847);
The Bothie of Toper-na-fuosich, A Long-Vacation Pastoral (Oxford: Macpherson/London: Chapman & Hall, 1848; Cambridge, Mass.: John Bartlett, 1849); revised as *The Bothie of Toberna-Vuolich* for *Poems, with a Memoir* (1862); 1848 text republished as *The Bothie*, edited by Patrick Scott (St. Lucia, Australia: Queensland University Press, 1976);
Ambarvalia, by Clough and Thomas Burbidge (London: Chapman & Hall, 1849); Clough's section separately bound as *Poems by Arthur H. [or A. H.] Clough* (privately distributed by Clough);
Poems, with a Memoir (memoir by F. T. Palgrave, London: Macmillan, 1862; memoir by C. E. Norton, Boston: Ticknor & Fields, 1862; 2nd edition, expanded, London: Macmillan, 1863);
Letters and Remains of Arthur Hugh Clough (London: Privately printed, 1865);
The Poems and Prose Remains of Arthur Hugh Clough, edited by Blanche Clough, 2 volumes (Lon-

don: Macmillan, 1869);
Poems, edited by Howard F. Lowry, A. L. P. Norrington, and F. L. Mulhauser (Oxford: Clarendon Press, 1951; partially republished as the Oxford Standard Authors edition, edited by Norrington, 1968);
Selected Prose Works, edited by Buckner B. Trawick (University: University of Alabama Press, 1964);
Amours de Voyage, edited by Patrick Scott (St. Lucia, Australia: Queensland University Press, 1974);
The Poems of Arthur Hugh Clough, edited by F. L. Mulhauser (Oxford: Clarendon Press, 1974).

TRANSLATIONS: *Plutarch's Lives, The Translations Called Dryden's, Corrected from the Greek and Revised,* 5 volumes (Boston: Little, Brown, 1859; London: Low, 1859);
Greek History from Themistocles to Alexander in a Series of Lives from Plutarch (London: Longman, Green, Longman & Roberts, 1860).

OTHER: "The Longest Day: A Poem...1836," in untitled collection of pamphlet poems gathered by G. F. Blandford, deposited at British Library; first published in *The Poems of Arthur Hugh Clough* (1974), pp. 479-480.

Arthur Hugh Clough has long been valued as a representative "Victorian doubter" who expressed through his poetry the bewildering religious controversies of the period. He has a reputation, too, as an accomplished lyric poet, and some of his shorter, more optimistic poems (such as the well-known "Say not, the struggle naught availeth") have found their way into the standard anthologies and even into several hymnbooks. But the publication of much more complete Clough editions in 1951 and 1974 has made it clear that religious doubt was only one among his many poetic concerns, and recent readers have come most to appreciate Clough's satiric wit and the ironic complexity of his work; his reputation now rests less on his shorter religious lyrics than on his three major poems—*The Bothie of Toper-na-fuosich, Amours de Voyage,* and *Dipsychus.* Clough's poems are far from perfect; they were often unfinished, drastically changed in idea and tone during composition, and fragmentary in structure. Yet from such rough and explorative writing he "edited" at various stages of his life a substantial body of poetry; and his personal voice, and the variety of techniques he used in its realization, make him far more than a minor poet. James

Arthur Hugh Clough

Russell Lowell was acute in prophesying, soon after Clough's early death in 1861, that he would "be thought a hundred years hence to have been the truest expression in verse of the moral and intellectual tendencies, the doubts and struggles toward settled convictions, of the period in which he lived."

Clough (pronounced "cluff") was born in Liverpool, in the north of England, in 1819, the second son of an intermittently unsuccessful cotton merchant from the North Wales landed gentry, and a much more middle-class mother from Yorkshire. In 1822, he moved with his family to Charleston, South Carolina. The Cloughs had a house in the trading area of East Bay Street; they spent the hot summers out on Sullivan's Island, and one of Clough's early poems is a recollection of that childhood:

Of my brother and my sister, and our rambles on the beach,
Of my mother's gentle voice, and my mother's beckoning hand,
And all the tales she used to tell of the far, far, English land;
....

And I longed for England's cool, and England's
   breezes then,
But now I would give full many a breeze to be back in
   the heat again.

When he was nine, the family made a visit to England, and Clough was left there to be educated—first at a private school in Chester, near his Welsh relatives; and from 1829 at Rugby School, which, under its new headmaster, Dr. Thomas Arnold, was becoming the prototypical Victorian public boarding school. Clough's family was conservative in politics and Evangelical in religion, while Dr. Arnold was liberal in both; a former fellow of Oriel College, Oxford, he could introduce his pupils to modern Germanic classical and historical scholarship (how many Victorian fifteen-year-olds, one wonders, were reading the historian Niebuhr or the philosopher Schleiermacher in German, as Clough was in 1834?), but Dr. Arnold's greatest effect lay in the moral education he gave, his instilling of a sense of moral purposiveness or "earnestness." Clough, in effect orphaned by distance from his parents, and early promoted into Arnold's own sixth (senior) form, became a favorite pupil and a loyal disciple; one of his Rugby contemporaries later recalled "the almost feminine expression of trust and affection" with which Clough "looked up to Arnold in answering his questions and hanging on his words."

While at Rugby, Clough collaborated on, and eventually edited, the *Rugby Magazine,* and the poetry he contributed shows various early influences and also the emergence of some of his later themes and tones. Dr. Arnold's strongly moral view of historical development forms the basis of Clough's 1835 prize poem, *The Close of the Eighteenth Century*; Clough presents the "crisis" of the French Revolution as the inevitable consequence of earlier irreligion, and closes with a sea-image that prefigures his later lyric "Where lies the land":

Lord, we are wandering on an unknown Sea
Whither we know not; yet we do not fear.

Other poems show direct imitation of Wordsworth, a neighbor of the Arnolds at their vacation home in the Lake District. For instance, in "Lines" (July 1836), which describes an evening walk in a country lane and the healthful spiritual effect of nature and memory, the opening and the meter are in the style of Wordsworth's poems in *Lyrical Ballads* (1798):

It was but some few nights ago
   I wandered down this quiet lane.

I pray that I may never know
   The feelings that I felt again.

Still other poems suggest that the young Clough had already been reading Tennyson (for instance, "Song of the Hyperborean Maidens"), Macaulay ("Count Egmont"), and the witty Byron of *Don Juan* (the opening of "The Poacher of Dead Man's Corner"). The lighthearted "An Apology" introduces a recurring theme in Clough's later work, the difficulty of writing honest poetry ("In these utilitarian days/Poetic fiction ne'er will answer"), and the more serious poem "To———, On Going to India" treats the theme of separation and ultimate reunion, to be taken up again in Clough's poems of the mid-1840s. The most interesting of these juvenile poems is "The Longest Day," written in 1836 while Clough was at Rugby but not printed until later. It was composed as a class-work assignment and uses the set topic of midsummer and seasonal turning points to express, at the public level, a questioning of historical progress or optimism, and at the personal level, Clough's fears that he will not be able to live up to others' expectations of him:

Is it not awful then to think
   How growth and progress now are o'er,
That we are on the mountain's brink,
   Where we have clomb to climb no more?
That each day now shall be more brief?

It is a reflection of the psychological pressure of Dr. Arnold's educational method that such lines could be written by a boy of only seventeen. In these early poems, such self-questioning is nearly always resolved by an appeal to religious faith, but the writing Clough did at Rugby shows, in its themes and variety of tone, the roots of his later poetic craftsmanship.

In 1837, Clough left Rugby for Balliol College, Oxford, where, the previous year, he had been elected in open competition to a classical scholarship. Here he entered a different intellectual world, where Dr. Arnold's earnest liberalism was only one among several fiercely canvassed religious and philosophical positions. Clough's mathematical tutor, W. G. Ward, while initially Arnoldian in religious outlook, soon introduced him to the utilitarian and skeptical ideas of Jeremy Bentham and John Stuart Mill, and then, having himself fallen under the influence of the religious leader John Henry Newman, pressed Clough to accept Newman's "Tractarian" position and so resolve all religious uncertainties by the authority of church tradition. Clough's undergraduate journals, now available in the Balliol library, show that he passed through periods of intensely religious self-distrust, but the language in which he wrote about his doubts was as much Evangelical as Tractarian, and he never really seems to have been sucked into the whirlpool of Tractarianism. His short poems "*Sic Itur*" and "*Qua Cursum Ventus*" record his break with Ward when the latter converted to Roman Catholicism in 1845. The Tractarians did influence Clough, however, in their teaching about the privateness of true spiritual feelings and the reserve with which these should be publicly discussed, and this teaching affected his ideas about poetry. Tractarian critics such as John Keble stressed the "instinctive delicacy" of the true poet, who, Keble claimed, "recoils from exposing" his feelings. Clough seems during his undergraduate years (as later) to have had an acute moral fear of false posturing or self-deception in writing poetry. He had been very put off by the emotional self-indulgence of his school-friend Thomas Burbidge's poems, published in 1838, and the poems he himself wrote while at Balliol are predominantly private, almost therapeutic, explorations of his inner conflicts, shared only with friends in letters. By contrast with the frequent publication of his school days, Clough had virtually none of his poetry published during his nine years in Oxford. In December 1839, however, he did send a copy of his old poem "The Longest Day" to a new Rugby School magazine, the *Rugbaean*, and in early 1840 the poem was printed in page form; but the magazine folded before its second issue could be published. In the late 1840s the page proof of "The Longest Day" was bound into a pamphlet along with a number of other poems by an enthusiastic collector, who added a title page to the pamphlet.

A few of Clough's undergraduate poems show that he still occasionally recurred to his earlier Arnoldian hopefulness. In an untitled poem of 1838 he asserts the continuity of belief, "invisible but sure," against the discontinuities of experience and feelings:

> Truth is a golden thread, seen here and there
> In small bright specks upon the visible side
> Of our strange being's party-coloured web.

The poems he wrote on vacation in Wales in 1839 ("When soft September comes again," "So I as boyish years went by") draw a Wordsworthian strength from the Welsh landscape. But the overwhelming theme of Clough's undergraduate poetry is much less Arnoldian: it is panic over personal failure—moral, spiritual, and poetic. In "Come back again, my olden heart!" he describes how "the doubting soul, from day to day/Uneasy paralytic lay," and other journal poems talk of his "palsying self-mistrust" or of irrevocable failure:

> O, I have done those things that my Soul fears
> And my whole heart is sick. My Youth hath flown,
> The talents thou hast given me are gone,
> And I have nought to pay thee but my tears.

Clough's spiritual and psychological crisis was made deeper by the immediate fear of academic failure—he kept postponing the final honors examinations on which his career would rest, and success became a financial necessity when his father went bankrupt, for the second time, in 1841. Clough's lyric sequence "Blank Misgivings of a Creature Moving about in Worlds Not Realized" was drafted in this period (though only edited into shape much later), and it shows how Clough's disruptive experience led him to poetic experimentation. In the first four sections, which are in standard sonnet form, Clough meditates on his spiritual shortcomings at age twenty-three:

> . . . sails rent,
> And rudder broken,—reason impotent,—
> Affections all unfixed; so forth I fare
> On the mid seas unheedingly. . . .

In the fifth section he revolts against this falsifying introspection and simplifies the versification in search of a simpler, truer self, "one feeling based on truth," seeking the "buried world below" his surface emotions. In the sixth section he abandons the initial discursive treatment for a more imagistic one, describing himself as "a child/In some strange garden left awhile alone," plucking flowers and fearing parental retribution; he pictures his intellectual speculations in the seventh section as a band of drunken fellow students whom he has foolishly admitted to his college room, and who will not leave when asked. In the eighth and ninth sections he approaches even the Wordsworthian consolations and stabilities of nature and landscape with suspicion, before returning in the tenth section to more formal verse and eventual stanzaic regularity and accepting his temporary skepticism and disorientation as the price he had to pay for higher philosophic truth. The "Blank Misgivings" sequence, made up of fragmentary, short poems and based on personal experience, illustrates well the way Clough's poetic development grew from a process of internal debate and self-contradiction.

After considerable emotional upheaval, during which (as his sister recalled) "his health suffered, he lost his hair, he was feverish and disquieted," Clough settled himself enough to take his narrowly classical examinations in May 1841, receiving second class honors instead of the first class predicted for him by others. When the results came out, he walked the fifty-odd miles from Oxford to Rugby and told Dr. Arnold, "I have failed." Nor did he fare any better in the competition for a Balliol fellowship in November. It was only after a year of free-lance tutoring work that he was elected, like Dr. Arnold and J. H. Newman before him, to a fellowship at Oriel College, Oxford, in the spring of 1842. To increase his income, he willingly took on college tutoring as well, even though college teaching was not then seen as a long-term career, and he was later to describe it as "a mere parenthetical occupation, uncontemplated in the past, and wholly alien to the future." It did, however, give him an assured social position, and it allowed him to help his mother and sister financially; and so for the next six years he threw himself into university life, lecturing on ancient history and Aristotle, contributing numerous entries to a *Dictionary of Greek and Roman Biography,* and writing on Latin metrics and classical translation. Though Oriel was not at the time a strong undergraduate college, Clough was good at his job and was well liked by such later-famous pupils as the novelist Thomas Hughes.

With this success came some renewal of his earlier confidence and optimism. The 1840s were a period of great social and political awareness; Clough eagerly absorbed Carlyle's writings on the "condition-of-England" question, set himself to study political economy, and wrote a series of articles on economic questions for a liberal workingmen's paper, the *Balance.* He also helped regularly with a soup kitchen and night shelter for transients run by the Oxford Mendicity Society, and wrote a pamphlet supporting the Retrenchment Association's efforts to aid victims of the Irish famine. His own family had, through his father's business failures, suffered from the vagaries of the early Victorian laissez-faire economy, and increasingly he came to believe that the privileges he enjoyed at Oxford, and the comforts of the moneyed classes generally, were excessive and unjust. As an undergraduate, Clough's satiric eye had been fixed chiefly on family pressures (as in "Duty, that's to say complying"), but his new political awareness widened his target to the larger society. "To the Great Metropolis" describes London as merely "Competition and Display . . . a huge bazaar/A railway terminus." "In the Great Metropolis" is a mock celebration of the free-market law that "The devil take the hindmost, O!" "The Latest Decalogue," a satiric modern version of the Ten Commandments, picks out particularly the economics of Victorian religion:

No graven images may be
Worshipped, except the currency:
. . . .
Thou shalt not kill; but needst not strive
Officiously to keep alive:
. . . .
Thou shalt not covet; but tradition
Approves all forms of competition.

Such opinions contributed also to the treatment of class in *The Bothie of Toper-na-fuosich*, and led Oxford students during the European revolutions of 1848 to announce an Oxford revolution in a broadsheet purporting to come from that dangerous radical "Citizen Clough." Indeed, Clough had traveled to Paris in the spring of 1848 to see revolution at first hand.

Clough's Oriel years also saw a new confidence in the sphere of religious debate. His letters to his friends and to his sister Anne show a continuing questioning of traditional religious formulas: "What is the meaning of 'Atonement by a crucified Saviour,' " he wrote in 1847; "Until I know, I wait." During vacation visits to his family in Liverpool, he came into contact with the American-influenced Unitarianism of James Martineau and his circle; he met Ralph Waldo Emerson during Emerson's visit to England in 1848; and he read further in German Biblical criticism. A short poem, "Epi-Strauss-ium," shows him accepting with apparent equanimity the German scholar David F. Strauss's argument about the mythic, unhistorical nature of the four Gospels:

Matthew and Mark and Luke and holy John
Evanished all and gone!
. . . .
Lost, is it? lost, to be recovered never?
However,
The place of worship the meantime with light
Is, if less richly, more sincerely bright. . . .

The poem "In a Lecture Room" rejects "vain Philosophy" in favor of the direct impulse of an Emersonian nature, "Wisdom at once, and Power." "The New Sinai" is a double exhortation against both total skepticism and any lazy or craven acceptance of the "gilded calves," "baby-thoughts" and traditional untruths: man's "adult spirit," Clough asserts, can "take better part, with manlier heart," and wait for a fuller revelation. One of the most effective, because most self-questioning, of these "religious" poems is "Why should I say I see the things I see not," which pictures religious conformists dancing to a music that the speaker cannot hear:

> Why should I say I see the things I see not,
>   Why be and be not?
> Show love for that I love not, and fear for what I fear not?
> And dance about to music that I hear not?

The speaker at first distrusts his own deafness, and vows to try conforming in the hope of coming to believe, and hear the music, later, but the question still nags at him: "What if all along / The music is not sounding?" Clough's later addition to the poem, distinguishing "two musics"—the coarse drumbeat of conventional belief and the purer sound of true revelation—seems forced, but it allows him finally to endorse religious unorthodoxy as the better, if lonelier, way:

> . . . the bare conscience of the better thing
> Unfelt, unseen, unimaged, all unknown,
> May fix the entranced soul 'mid multitudes alone.

It is worth noting that it is in the poems where Clough is most exploratory in ideas that he is also most innovative metrically, while his more safely Arnoldian liberal religious poems (such as "*Qui laborat orat*") are metrically more conventional.

Clough never abandoned the religious idealism of his youth, and he continued to assert that it is "impossible for any Man, to live, act, and reflect without feeling the significance and depth of the moral and religious teaching which passes amongst us by the name of Christianity," but by the later 1840s he had abandoned all specifically Christian doctrines.

The new confidence of the Oriel years showed in one further area of Clough's poetry—a newly confident treatment of sexuality. Clough's undergraduate journals suggest that he had been deeply disturbed by his own sexuality. Now, in "*Natura Naturans*," for instance, he could explore the "sensation strange" passing between a perfectly proper Victorian man and girl as they sit in a second-class railway carriage, and could even suggest that their feelings are an echo of the unfallen, unashamed sexuality of Eden, "the primal prime embrace." "Farewell, my Highland lassie!" is an appreciative, guilt-free tribute to a girl the speaker had danced with, and kissed, on a Scottish vacation. One poem Clough wrote on this theme was so misinterpretable that he deleted it from the proofs of his first collection: "*Homo sum, nihil humani*—" ("I am a man, nothing human is alien to me") describes kissing "for her carnalness" a beggar girl he had met on the road. Clough's treatment of sexuality, like his treatment of religious questions, remained idealistic, but it had moved far beyond prim conventionality.

Several of these themes from the shorter Oriel poems met in Clough's first attempt at a longer poem. *Adam and Eve* is a demythologizing drama about the Fall of Man, and reflects the openness and confidence of his religious speculations during the Oriel years. Though not published until 1869, after Clough's death, the poem was probably started late in 1845 as a response to Elizabeth Barrett's more orthodox poem on the same theme, *The Drama of Exile* (1844). It was after reading a review of Miss Barrett's poem in the Unitarian *Prospective Review* that Clough jotted in his notebook, "Is there anything in the notion of a Fall & a Redemption which is not conveyed in the common philos. expressions— . . . May not Adam & Christ & their stories be but a Time-Effigiation of the Untemporal Truth?" The poem grew from this idea.

The first half of Clough's work (scenes I-IV) centers on Adam and Eve themselves, as they look back on eating the fruit. Eve, crying "Oh, guilt, guilt, guilt!," represents the orthodox reaction, while, when talking to her, Adam brushes aside her story of a serpent-tempter as simply a "queasy dream," the result of sickness in her first pregnancy. He roundly dismisses the Biblical account as "the mighty Mythus of the Fall" (the word *Mythus* shows the link with German historical scholarship), and argues instead that everything the couple have done is from their innate nature, their need to move on, develop, and change. Instead of feeling regretful or guilty, they should simply get on with their work. Nonetheless, when Adam is alone, he reveals much more of the internal conflict behind his philosophy ("tortured in the crucible I lie,/Myself my own experiment"). On the birth of Cain, he tries to warn the jubilant Eve that her son, however perfect he may seem as a baby, will face the same difficulties, external and internal, as they have faced; from this she develops the new doctrine that Original Sin is to be inherited by all future men. These early scenes are a clever dramatization of the way German scholars were arguing that all religious and historical myths grew up—as the making of fables to give unquestioned explanations of real-life problems. Clough builds the dramatization very realistically on the tensions between husband and wife during a first pregnancy, including a subtext of sexual tension; there is considerable wit behind Adam's down-to-earth, modern debunking of Eve's fanciful fears (which are also the orthodox story). Clough's treatment of Scripture was too strong for immediate publication (even Matthew Arnold wrote to Clough that it "rather offended" him); when it was published twenty years later, Henry Sidgwick condemned the whole concept of giving "antique personages" modern self-consciousness as being "too whimsical" for success. Twentieth-century Clough critics have usually been much more sympathetic to his imaginative recreation of a world before orthodoxy.

The second half of the poem (scenes V-XIV) centers on Cain's murder of Abel and the contrasting reactions of Adam and Eve. Shifting focus from the psychological effects of imagined guilt to real violence and murder involved also a shift in tone; these scenes (probably drafted in 1849-1850) are much more melodramatic than the earlier ones and fit very uneasily with them, perhaps because Clough never completed his final revisions that would have fitted the two "acts" together. There is, though, a continuity of theme in the continuing contrast between the nobility of Adam's realism and Eve's insistent religiosity; and Adam's final deathbed speech, expressing "no sure trust in ought/Except a kind of impetus within," yet still asserting that "Life has been beautiful," probably represents the almost mystical confidence of Clough's own philosophical position in the later 1840s. Indeed, W. E. Houghton has argued that *Adam and Eve,* unrevised though it remained, is "the fullest expression" Clough "ever made of his religio-ethical philosophy."

But the expression of such religious attitudes was hardly consistent with Clough's position at Oriel, for Oxford was still officially a church-dominated university. To take his M.A., Clough had had to sign the Thirty-Nine Articles of Religion, which proclaimed "the Original, or Birth-Sin" of all men; and to continue in his fellowship beyond 1849 he would soon have to accept ordination as a clergyman, unless he turned to law or medicine—as he briefly considered doing. To these religious pressures was added the requirement that fellows remain unmarried, and as Clough neared thirty he wrote in his notebook, "Should one want to marry, and should one want children . . . desolate old age is sad." Clough's political ethos, too, was out of place in Oxford, and even though others of his liberal friends felt able to swallow their scruples and stay on, Clough decided in the fall of 1848 that he must resign his fellowship to retain his integrity.

The outcome of his decision to resign was his first major work, *The Bothie of Toper-na-fuosich,* a substantial narrative poem in nine books, written, printed, and published in a mere two months (mid-September to mid-November 1848). The subtitle was "A Long-Vacation Pastoral," and the poem describes a group of Oxford undergraduates on vacation in the remote Highlands of Scotland; one of them, the radical Philip Hewson, falls in love, marries the daughter of a Scottish crofter, and immigrates to the new country of New Zealand. One of Clough's aims was to illustrate English hexameter (he had been reading Longfellow's *Evangeline* aloud to his mother, and had found its heavy dactyls "monotonously regular"); much of *The Bothie*'s col-

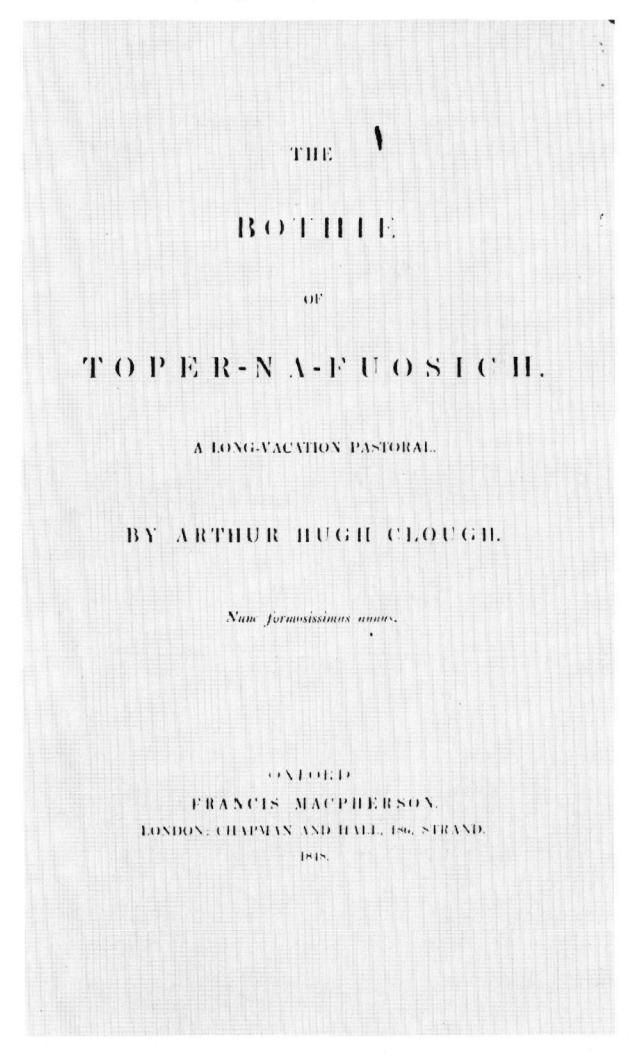

Title page for Clough's first major work

loquial freshness of tone, especially in the early books, comes from the ready availability of unstressed syllables in hexameters and the flexibility with which Clough handles the verse form. The subject matter of the poem is strongly autobiographical: as a college tutor, Clough had himself organized such Scottish "reading-parties" (study vacations) in 1846 and 1847; a close friend, Tom Arnold (the Doctor's younger son), had immigrated to New Zealand out of political idealism in 1847; and Clough, after one tentative flirtation at his own social level in 1846, may himself have contemplated in 1847 a marriage across the class barriers—certainly several of his poems over a number of years discuss love affairs between Oxford men and Highland lassies. He dedicated the poem to his former students in the hope that they might be "here and there reminded of times we enjoyed together." But to these technical and autobiographical beginnings, Clough added his larger political and philosophical concerns, and the result is the only major English poetic response to the hopes and frustrations of European radicalism in 1848.

The Bothie begins with almost novelistic realism, describing the English visitors at the Highland Games. At the ensuing dinner and dance, Philip has the bad taste to criticize the local landowners with a Carlylian sneer at their game-preserving. The next day, over breakfast, the students quarrel about the beauty of upper-class ladies as compared to that of the ordinary Scottish girls with whom they have been dancing, and the debate turns to the fashionable 1840s topic of the "proper" role of women. (Tennyson's 1847 poem *The Princess* deals with the same issue.)

Several of the students set off on a walking tour, and the poem gradually begins to offer a symbolic level as well as a realistic one: the journey, and their initially frivolous search for love, parallel the intellectual and spiritual journeyings of Clough's generation. Philip is attracted first to a Scottish peasant girl, Katie, and then to the idealized high-born Lady Maria at the Castle; after these false starts he comes to the remote Bothie (cottage) of Toper-na-fuosich and falls in love with Elspie Mackay. The sexual awareness in their courtship is narrated through the imagery of tidal movement up a freshwater mountain stream, and of the keystone coming in to complete the two parts of a bridge-arch, in Elspie's dream (Book VII). Through Philip's love for Elspie is symbolized his commitment to a life beyond the confines of his class and beyond mere debate. Philip, like Clough, is skeptical of the conventional wisdom about the various ranks and duties of the battle of life:

> If there is battle, 'tis battle by night: I stand in the darkness,
> ....
> Yet is my feeling rather to ask, where *is* the battle?
> ....
> Neither battle I see, nor arraying, nor King in Israel,
> Only infinite jumble and mess and dislocation,
> Backed by a solemn appeal, "For God's sake do not stir, there!"

Now, with the new commitment of love, he feels that the alienating and dislocated life of the growing Victorian cities can be "reaccepted, resumed to Primal Nature," and he leaves the old, class-divided England behind for a new life of honest work and simple living in New Zealand. "Which things," Philip's friend Hobbes writes to him, "are an allegory"; life, like marriage, is a compound, "one part heavenly-ideal, the other vulgar and earthy." In *The Bothie,* the radical dream of the 1840s and Clough's own idealism are presented as realizable visions, to be lived out in the real world.

The Bothie was the Victorian favorite among Clough's longer poems. Though some of his former Oxford colleagues thought it "indecent and profane, immoral and communistic," and Matthew Arnold condemned Clough privately for plunging and bellowing in the Time-Stream, most initial reaction was favorable. Reviewers such as Charles Kingsley were attracted by the freshness and colloquialism of Clough's style and the modernness of his subject matter, and W. M. Rossetti gave an extended appreciation of the poem's natural descriptions in the new Pre-Raphaelite magazine, *The Germ.* In America, Longfellow found it "fascinating"; Emerson, who had met Clough earlier that year, called it "a high gift from angels"; and it was soon reprinted by a New England publisher. After publication, however, Clough was told that *Toper-na-fuosich*, though an actual place-name on contemporary Scottish maps, was also an indecent Gaelic toast; when he revised the poem in the late 1850s he changed the title to *The Bothie of Tober-na-Vuolich,* as well as making other changes to reduce the satiric element in favor of the love-pastoral. *The Bothie,* especially in the revised text, is the most straightforward of Clough's longer poems, and its Victorian preeminence gave way in the twentieth century to some criticism of its later books for sentimentality. More recently, John Goode has given it

Title page for Clough's second major published work, written in conjunction with a friend from his school days

high praise as a "revolutionary" and "affirmative poem about love," a "radical critique of society and a vision of the possibilities of historical change."

In January 1849 *Ambarvalia* was published. This was a collection of shorter poems by Clough and his former school-friend, Thomas Burbidge. Clough's portion was essentially a selection and revision from his Oxford poems. One poem added at proof stage, however, indicates Clough's view of poetry. "Is it true, ye Gods" takes up the claim that poetic "inspiration" is simply a psychological, even a physiological, quirk or malfunction:

> Is in reason's grave precision,
> Nothing more, nothing less,
> Than a peculiar conformation,
> Constitution, and condition
> Of the brain and of the belly?

It is typical of Clough that he should subject his own poetry to such subversive analysis, yet still retain a stubborn idealism:

> If it is so, let it be so,
> . . . .
> Yet the plot has counterplot,
> It may be and yet be not.

Ambarvalia attracted some favorable comment for its more conventional lyrics, but several reviewers were puzzled by its "fragmentary state," "careless obscurity," and "hieroglyphical abruptness of expression." This very explorativeness in religious ideas, in language, and in poetic form, however, would help Clough attract later readers and modern revaluation. Clough had some copies of his sixty-four-page section of *Ambarvalia* bound separately for gifts to his family and friends, with a cover and title page reading "Poems by Arthur H. Clough" or "Poems by A. H. Clough." These copies have sometimes been mistaken for a distinct work.

Resignation from Oxford set Clough loose from those frameworks in which he had previously developed his life and ideas. The next three years were his most original and creative, but they were also years of frequent loneliness and much frustra-

Clough at about the time he left Oxford and moved to London (courtesy of Miss Katherine Duff)

tion. As in the undergraduate period, 1839 to 1842, Clough had very little work published, but out of the contradictions and shapelessness of his life and his poetic drafts in the years 1849 to 1852 grew what is now regarded as his greatest poetry.

Almost immediately after his resignation, he was able to secure an appointment as principal of the (Unitarian) University Hall, London; but before taking up that post, he set out alone to spend several months in Italy, where a new nationalist Roman Republic had been declared under Mazzini. Soon after Clough's arrival, the French government sent troops to rescue Rome for the papacy, and Clough was caught in the siege of the city from April to July 1849, when Mazzini's republic fell to the French. Clough's most famous lyric was originally drafted to express a liberal faith in the survival of the republic's ideals as he observed the smoke-obscured confusion of the first—unsuccessful—French attack on 30 April:

> Say not, the struggle nought availeth
> . . . .
>
> If hopes were dupes, fears may be liars;
>   It may be, in yon smoke concealed,
> Your comrades chase e'en now the fliers,
>   And, but for you, possess the field.
>
> For while the tired waves, vainly breaking,
>   Seem here no painful inch to gain,
> Far back, through creeks and inlets making,
>   Comes, silent, flooding in, the main.

Clough did not, however, go to Rome blind to the likelihood of Mazzini's failure: he had already confronted the very unideal outcome of the French revolution of the previous year, and had written to his radical friend Tom Arnold, "Put not your trust in republics." The major poetic outcome of the Roman months, much more complex and realistic than the famous lyric, was the long poem *Amours de Voyage,* which was mostly drafted during the siege, "edited" into shape over the next nine years, and first published in the American *Atlantic Monthly* from February to May 1858.

The new poem shared with *The Bothie* the novelistic modernness of its subject and the flexibility of the hexameter verse form. It is made up of a series of letters home from English visitors to Italy. Most are from Claude, an Oxonian uncertain over his future career, but some are from the two Trevellyn daughters, Georgina and Mary, who are touring with their parents. Claude's story provides the central plot of the poem, while the Trevellyn girls' alternative viewpoint on events allows the reader to put Claude's comments and character in perspective.

Amours de Voyage traces Claude's developing and interrelated attitudes to art or culture, politics, and love, and toward all three his attitudes go through distinct stages. In his opening letters he is the skeptical tourist fascinated by the classical and artistic monuments of Rome, but unwilling to be uncritically admiring like the Trevellyns:

> Rome disappoints me much; I hardly as yet
>   understand, but
> *Rubbishy* seems the word that most exactly would suit it.
> All the foolish destructions, and all the sillier savings,
> All the incongruous things of past incompatible ages,
> Seem to be treasured up here. . . .

Nor is he much impressed by the Trevellyn daughters ("middle-class people these . . . most worthy people"), and initially he claims to be completely apolitical. He is not excited by the prospect of fighting, however chivalrous the cause ("Am I prepared to lay down my life for the British female?"). Gradually, however, he comes to feel an "older, austerer worship" in the classical buildings, and he is haunted by the distant view across the Roman Campagna toward the Alban hills, where his favorite Roman poet, Horace, had lived in retreat on the Sabine Farm. Claude's attitude toward politics changes with the French attack; as a tourist, he is a bewildered spectator of the first battle and subsequent street fighting, but he writes, "I am thankful they fought, and glad that the Frenchmen were beaten." He also begins to think he might be falling in love with Mary Trevellyn; he moves from a simple wish for "the feminine presence" to the discovery that "it is a pleasure indeed to converse with this girl."

But with the start of Canto III, these developments are disrupted. Mary's matchmaking sister tries to force Claude to declare his "intentions," and scares him off; when the Trevellyns leave Rome for Florence, he stays behind and is caught in the siege, which ends any hopes of actually visiting his idealized Sabine Farm; and the republic itself seems doomed and its sacrifices purposeless. Claude is left to meditate on the chanciness of fate and love (he dismisses love as mere "juxtaposition"). With the end of the siege and the fall of Rome, he sets off rather doubtfully on an attempt to catch up with Mary in northern Italy, but misses her by a series of comic accidents and goes away regretfully to winter in the still more ancient cultures of Greece and Egypt.

By contrast with *The Bothie*, *Amours de Voyage* is a poem of apparent defeat and frustrated idealism. Clough's contemporaries were made uneasy by this. One friend criticized the first draft because "everything crumbles to dust beneath a ceaseless self-introspection and criticism," and when the poem was published in America, Emerson upbraided Clough for its "baulking end or no end." The modern revaluation of the poem has rested largely on inverting these criticisms, seeing in the poem's ironies and inconclusiveness a precursor of the alienated self-irony of T. S. Eliot's "The Love Song of J. Alfred Prufrock." But Clough did not mean the poem to end in "mere prostration and defeat"; he intended for the reader to find in Claude some "final Strength of Mind." It is not just a satirical or a psychological poem, but also a philosophical one:

> *Action will furnish belief,*—but will that belief be the true one?
> This is the point, you know. However, it doesn't much matter.
> What one wants, I suppose, is to predetermine the action,
> So as to make it entail, not a chance-belief, but the true one.

Through all of Claude's inner debates and self-doubt, the poem retains an intermittently lyrical idealism, especially in the "elegiac" sections that open and close each canto. It was the balance between these elements that Clough found so difficult to adjust for Victorian readers, and that delayed publication; but his revised poem can now be seen as what J. D. Jump calls "one of the finest and most readable longer poems of the Victorian age."

Back in London, Clough found that his new job was not all that he had hoped. University Hall was really only a small residence-house for about a dozen underprepared young students, and Clough found the Unitarianism of his new employers quite as oppressive as the more orthodox religion of Oxford. Within a few days he wrote to Tom Arnold: "I have no confidence in my own tenure. For intolerance, O Tom, is not confined to the cloisters of Oxford, or the pews of the establishment, but . . . is indeed in manner indigenous in the heart of the family man of the middle classes." He found London life lonely, and withdrew into himself, "secret as an oyster." He took on an additional part-time post as Professor of the English Language and Literature at University College, London; his lectures there show him stressing the values of restraint and plainness in literature over richly expressive language—he ranked Wordsworth highest among the English Romantics, and he made a notable tribute to the then-unfashionable eighteenth-century writers: "This austere love of truth; this rigorous abhorrence of illusion; the rigorous uncompromising rejection of the vague, the untested, the merely probable . . . such a spirit, I may say, I think, claims more than our attention,—claims our reverence." In his moral philosophy tutorials (Walter Bagehot was one of his pupils), he advised his students to avoid speculation: "Reconcile what you have to say with green peas, for green peas are certain."

The poetry Clough was writing reveals the complex of contradictory attitudes that still underlay this restrained surface. On the religious question, for instance, he wrote an extraordinary and powerful poem, "Easter Day, Naples, 1849," about the impossibility of the Resurrection:

> As circulates in some great city crowd
> A rumour changeful, vague, importunate, and loud,
> From no determined centre, or of fact,
>   Or authorship exact,
>   Which no man can deny
>   Nor verify;
>   So spread the wondrous fame;
>   He all the same
>   Lay senseless, mouldering, low.
> . . . .
> This is the one sad Gospel that is true,
>   Christ is not risen.

Yet a second part of the poem repudiates the skepticism of the first, and claims, rather blandly, that "in the true Creed. . . . /Hope conquers cowardice," and so Christ has a spiritual resurrection. Clough's next major poem begins with a more alienated self-repudiation—when "Easter Day" is quoted, it provokes the comment,

> H'm! and the tone then after all
> Something of the ironical?
> Sarcastic, say; or were it fitter
> To style it the religious bitter?

This new poem, *Dipsychus* (pronounced "die-*sike*-us"), demonstrates how unstable Clough's position was becoming. *Dipsychus* is a loosely structured dramatic poem in fourteen scenes set in Venice, where Clough had spent the autumn of 1850. While several of the scenes began in Clough's own internal debates, he soon came to structure the poem as a dialogue between Dipsychus ("the double-minded man") and a temptingly common-sense Spirit; the format is quite clearly modeled on Goethe's *Faust* (in early drafts of the poem in Clough's notebooks, the two characters were called Faustulus and Mephistopheles), and it is significant that Clough once described Goethe's opposed characters as meaning "contradictory elements of our own unity." At least in the early scenes, the idealistic protagonist is weak and ineffectual, while the worldly Spirit is both realistic and self-confidently witty. The story is very simple: for scene after scene, the Spirit deflates Dipsychus's pretentious speculations and advocates various man-of-the-world compromises about sexual morality, religious beliefs, and career ambitions; Dipsychus agonizes over every issue before finally deciding to submit to the Spirit's amoral realism. The drama is framed by a prose dialogue between the "author" and his commonsensical septuagenarian uncle, who criticizes the poem as "unmeaning, vague, and involved," and roundly asserts that "consciences are often much too tender in your generation."

What distinguishes Clough's work from the numerous other early Victorian "Spasmodic" *Faust*-imitations is its satiric perspective and its very wide range of poetic tones and forms. The opening scenes have Dipsychus tempted by the prostitutes of Venice, and his conventionally Victorian high-mindedness ("the coy girl/Turns to the flagrant woman of the street") is juxtaposed with the Spirit's enthusiastic debunking:

> Fiddle di diddle, fal lal lal!
> By candlelight they are pas mal;
> Better and worse of course there are,—
> Star differs (with the price) from star.

In the middle sections Clough uses several songs, originally written separately, to express the instability of moral attitudes. Dipsychus surrenders to the charm of irresponsible tourism: "How light it moves, how softly! Ah,/Were all things like the gondola!" The Spirit celebrates the pleasures of financial independence: "How pleasant it is to have money, heigh ho!/How pleasant it is to have money." Dipsychus has a frenetically surreal song of religious denial, where he dreams of a bell ringing in his head all night:

> Ting, ting, there is no God; ting, ting;
> Come dance and play, and merrily sing—
> Ting, ting a ding; ting, ting a ding!
> O pretty girl who trippest along,
> Come to my bed—it isn't wrong.
> Uncork the bottle, sing the song!
> . . . .
> Dong, there is no God; Dong!

In the later part of the poem, Dipsychus becomes stronger and is treated less ironically. In one of Clough's best pieces of taut, speculative poetry, Dipsychus compares unheroic modern life to a vast but purposeless factory with no one in charge:

> No individual soul has loftier leave
> Than fiddling with a piston or a valve
> . . . .
>   . . . We ask Action,
> And dream of arms and conflict; and string up
> All self-devotion's muscles; and are set
> To fold up papers. To what end? We know not.
> Other folks do so; it is always done;
> And perhaps it is right. And we are paid for it.

But Dipsychus never regains the stature he has lost in the early scenes, and even his final earnest submission to the "positive and present" is undercut when the Spirit mocks his religious apostasy by chanting the nursery rhyme "Little Bo Peep, she lost her sheep."

Dipsychus provokes the most critical disagreement of all of Clough's longer poems. Clough neither had it published nor put it into finished form, partly no doubt because the sexual explicitness would have been unacceptable to contemporary publishers, partly perhaps because he found the aesthetic problems in his scrappy drafts to be intractable. Certainly, his later short poem, "*Dipsychus* Continued," abandons the kaleidoscopic inventiveness of the earlier poem for a rather stodgily realistic situation-drama in conventional blank verse. Most of the early critics recognized the work's biographical significance and praised its style as "bold and novel," but they found it distressingly inconclusive. Recent critics such as W. E. Houghton have seen *Dipsychus* as "Clough's masterpiece," which presents "the complexity of modern experience" through the modernist techniques of "juxtaposition and symbolic implication." It is a poem of much local brilliance, yet it remains fundamentally unfocused, and R. K. Biswas argues that this was because Clough was too close to the conflicts of the poem to be able to control its multiple ironies. The self-irony, multiple perspectives, and self-division that made possible this most innovative and creative phase in Clough's career also prevented him from gaining aesthetic control over the insights he had gained.

In 1852 Clough left University Hall, where he had been in conflict with the council, and decided to try his luck in America. He had become engaged to Blanche Smith and needed to establish a more remunerative and stable career. He sailed for Boston in late 1852 (among his fellow passengers were Thackeray and James Russell Lowell) and settled in Cambridge, where, through Emerson, he already had friends. He was hoping for a Harvard professorship, but it never materialized; in the meantime he occupied himself tutoring private pupils and undertaking miscellaneous literary work, including articles on social questions and the art of translation, and a major new translation of Plutarch for the Boston publisher Little, Brown—a project that would occupy him off and on for the next six years.

His most important writings from this period are two prose articles in which he redefined his attitude to poetry. In the better-known essay, "Recent English Poetry" in the *North American Review* (July 1853), he compared recent volumes by Matthew Arnold and Alexander Smith rather to Smith's advantage, because Smith, unlike Arnold, had dealt with modern subjects such as city life: "The modern novel is preferred to the modern poem," he argued, because it can deal with "ordinary feelings, . . . the actual palpable things with which our everyday life is concerned." (Arnold's preface to his 1853 *Poems* is, in part, an answer to Clough's criticism.) Where Smith and other Victorian poets failed, though, according to Clough, was in an overrichness of metaphor; they were trying too hard to imitate "Elizabethan phraseology," and so "there is a whole hemisphere, so to say, of the English language" that Smith had "left unvisited." Obviously, these comments reflect Clough's preference for modern subjects and a plain style in his own poetry. But a less well-known essay, the first "Letter of Paripedemus" in *Putnam's* magazine (July 1853), penetrated closer to Clough's poetic dilemma. Here he discussed how the constantly changing nature of a writer's experience makes him constantly dissatisfied with his writing, and he illustrated this point with a poem, "Upon the water, in the boat," about an artist sketching while the river carries him inexorably away from his subject matter:

Still as we go the things I see,
E'en as I see them, cease to be;
Their angles swerve, and with the boat
The whole perspective seems to float
. . . .
Yet still I look, and still I sit,
Adjusting, shaping, altering it;
And still the current bears the boat
And me, still sketching as I float.

We write, he asserted, chiefly as release, to discover "the imperfection of our views," yet such writing is still "not impotent, not wholly unavailing," for it may help others gather a more permanent harvest in a future generation. This "letter" points strongly to the ambivalence, even dissatisfaction, Clough felt about many of the poems he had drafted so prodigally in the previous years in London.

But his tutoring and occasional literary work were not providing him with any substantial income, so in 1853, with the help of Thomas Carlyle, he got a post in the Education Office of the Privy Council. He returned to London to settle down as a civil servant and, on the strength of a regular salary, to marry Blanche. Several critics have pointed to this career move and the marriage as a kind of capitulation, a withdrawal from the personal and creative tensions of the University Hall years. Certainly, Clough's poetry seems to have been pushed aside for several years by his Plutarch translation and his new job (he served as an examiner for civil service examinations and as secretary to an investigative commission in addition to his regular office duties). He devoted a great deal of time also to helping his wife's cousin, Florence Nightingale, with her governmental lobbying over health and nursing policy and with her day-to-day business affairs. As his wife later observed, Clough found in all this activity freedom from "perplexing questions" and from "the enforced and painful communing with the self alone."

Yet Clough's married years were not entirely unproductive from a literary standpoint. The Plutarch translation (1859) ran to over 1,500 pages in five volumes; he put together a school-text, *Greek History from Themistocles to Alexander in a Series of Lives from Plutarch* (1860); and he wrote an article on Goethe's poems, illustrated with his own translations (1859). Above all, he found in the new stability of his personal life a perspective that enabled him to edit the often chaotic drafts of earlier poetry into publishable form. In 1857-1858 he revised *Amours de Voyage* for publication; with Charles Eliot Norton's encouragement, he also prepared a revision of *The Bothie* and a selection of his shorter poems for American readers (1862). Some have seen these

PLUTARCH'S LIVES.

THE TRANSLATION CALLED DRYDEN'S

CORRECTED FROM THE GREEK AND REVISED

BY

A. H. CLOUGH,

SOMETIME FELLOW AND TUTOR OF ORIEL COLLEGE, OXFORD, AND LATE
PROFESSOR OF THE ENGLISH LANGUAGE AND LITERATURE
AT UNIVERSITY COLLEGE, LONDON.

VOL. I.

BOSTON:
LITTLE, BROWN AND COMPANY.
1859.

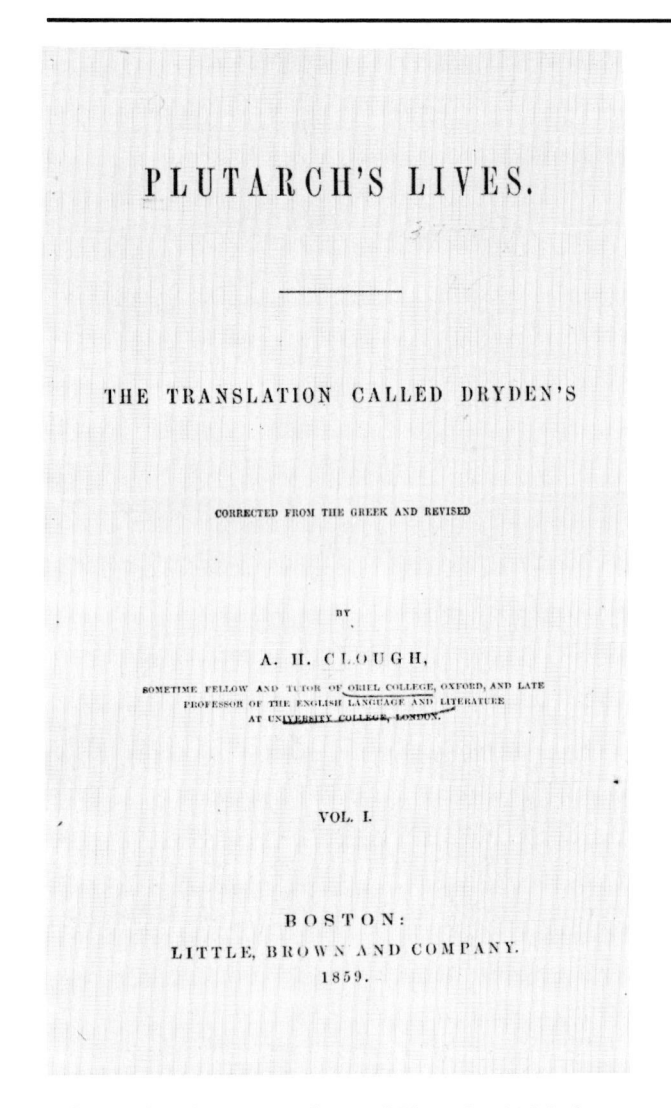

Title page for Clough's translation of Plutarch, which he began in America and worked on for six years

revisions as a bowdlerization of the more shocking and innovative elements in his writing, and it was probably at this time that he tried unsuccessfully to draft a version of *Dipsychus* without the prostitute incident, but many of his revisions represent a new aesthetic control rather than censorship, and parallel his new personal stability.

The change can be seen in the one new poetic project of this period. In 1860 he became ill, and for most of the next year he was on sick leave from his job, traveling in Greece, the French Pyrenees, Switzerland, and Italy in search of renewed health. For all except the last month he traveled alone, for his wife was expecting their third child. He turned back, as on previous Continental vacations, to poetry, embarking on a series of verse narratives told by a group of ship's passengers en route to America; he gave these the general title *Mari Magno* ("On the Great Ocean"). Some details of the journey are based on Clough's 1852 voyage with Thackeray and Lowell, and the whole project looks back to Chaucer's *Canterbury Tales*. All the tales, like one major group of Chaucer's, are concerned with love and marriage, and several return realistically to incidents Clough had dealt with more idealistically or problematically in earlier years. For instance, "The Lawyer's First Tale" is about meeting a former girl friend in the Alps—echoing the last part of *Amours de Voyage*—but discovering that she has married someone else and is on her honeymoon. "The Lawyer's Second Tale" discusses a love affair between an Oxford don and a Highland girl, as in *The Bothie*; but this time the lovers part, and it is only years later that he discovers that she has borne his illegitimate child after immigrating to Australia. "The Clergyman's Second Tale" recounts the guilt of a husband who, while traveling abroad alone, has a brief affair, and then separates himself from his wife and children for years afterwards, a guiltiness Clough clearly condemns as exaggerated. What has changed is the way such incidents are presented: Clough no longer uses fluid, colloquial hexameters but good-humored, rather jogging, Chaucerian couplets; and he seems to have been aiming also at a Chaucerian tone of middle-aged tolerance. The *Mari Magno* sequence was never completed, but it is a valuable clue to the spirit in which Clough had been revising his earlier, major works. As his wife noted, after his marriage Clough "did not cease to think about the problems which had hitherto occupied his leisure," but "he thought about them in a different way, and was able . . . to create a new treatment of old subjects, to turn them over and bring them out in the new light of his critical but kindly philosophy."

In November 1861, aged only forty-two, Clough died in Italy and was buried in the Protestant Cemetery in Florence. The cause of his death has been variously reported. He had been ill for over a year; he suffered an attack of malaria in October; and his wife writes of his "frightful neuralgia" in the head and "paralysis" of an eye and leg, which suggests a stroke. At first he was memorialized by his contemporaries as a good and sincere man who, because of Victorian religious disputes, never fulfilled his youthful promise; this is the theme of Matthew Arnold's elegy "Thyrsis" (1866), which depicts Clough as the "too quick despairer," whose "piping took a troubled sound, . . . of men contention-tost." But such patronizing praise became more difficult as more of Clough's work got into print. Within a few days of his death, his widow had initiated arrangements for a new British edition of his poetry, which made available for the first time to English readers *Amours de Voyage, Mari Magno,* and some of the songs from *Dipsychus.* Subsequently, she released some of Clough's more dangerously heterodox writings, such as the "Easter Day" poems, most of the *Dipsychus* dialogue (1865), and *Adam and Eve* (1869). It was these posthumous editions that established for Clough the poetic reputation that had evaded him during his lifetime, for younger Victorians found in his writing a role model for their own ambivalent emancipation from traditional beliefs; his poems went through more than twenty printings in various editions by the turn of the century, and a large agnostic hagiography grew up in the more progressive journals. Henry Sidgwick, the Cambridge philosopher who had found Clough's poems "the wine of life," judged him "ahead of his time" in his unaffected style and "the patient tenacity with which he refuses to quit his hold of any of the conflicting elements" in his experience, while the critic J. A. Symonds described how his generation looked "on Clough as the expression of their deepest convictions" and sought "in him a mirror of themselves." Late Victorians, then, responded to Clough as a thinker representative of the period.

Twentieth-century critics, at least since the 1930s, have stressed much more aesthetic questions, depicting Clough as an outsider to the Victorian cultural establishment, and delighting in his self-irony and his satirical writings on religion and sexuality. Graham Greene, in his novel *The Quiet American* (1955), commented that Clough was "an adult poet in the nineteenth century. There weren't so many of them." The landmark study in this critical revaluation, by W. E. Houghton (1963), concludes that Clough is "not only one of the best of Victorian poets, he is also perhaps the most modern." Other critics, drawing on the detailed biographical and textual scholarship that began in the 1950s, have preferred to downplay Clough's "anti-Victorianism," and to stress instead the moral idealism of his work and the similarities of poetic concern he holds with such contemporaries as Tennyson (in religion and psychology) or Robert Browning (in the ironic use of dramatic voices). But Clough's particular balance of irony and commitment, the detached and the lyrical, remains distinctive, and new readers continue to be surprised at the freshness of voice in his best poetry. While the initial critical consensus on Clough's "rediscovery" in the 1950s and 1960s has now broken down and his reputation has slipped back a little from the claims then made for him, he remains one of the most interesting, most significant, and most enjoyable of Victorian poets below the first rank.

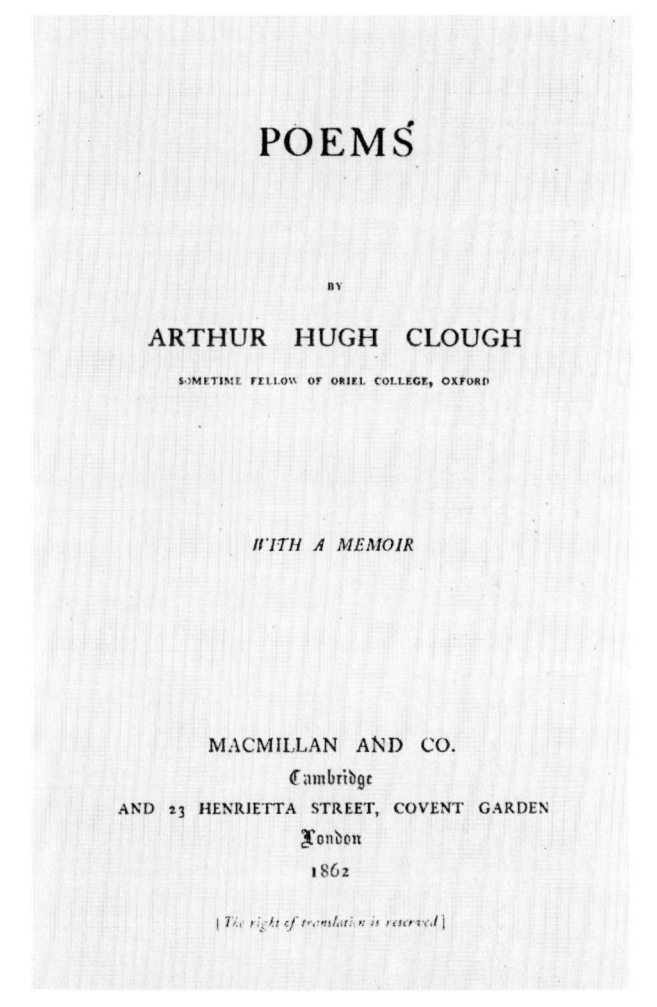

Title page for the first of the posthumously published collections of Clough's poems

Letters:
Letters of Matthew Arnold and Arthur Hugh Clough, edited by Howard Foster Lowry (Oxford: Clarendon Press, 1932);
Emerson-Clough Letters, edited by Lowry and R. L. Rusk (Cleveland: Rowfant Club, 1934);
Correspondence of Arthur Hugh Clough, edited by F. L. Mulhauser, 2 volumes (Oxford: Clarendon Press, 1957);
New Zealand Letters of Thomas Arnold the Younger, with . . . Letters of Arthur Hugh Clough, edited by James Bertram (London: Oxford University Press/Wellington, N. Z.: Auckland University Press, 1966).

Bibliographies:

Richard M. Gollin, Walter E. Houghton, and Michael Timko, *Arthur Hugh Clough: A Descriptive Catalogue* (New York: New York Public Library, 1967);

Patrick Scott, *The Early Editions of Arthur Hugh Clough* (New York: Garland, 1977).

Biographies:

James I. Osborne, *Arthur Hugh Clough* (Boston: Houghton Mifflin, 1920);

Goldie Levy, *Arthur Hugh Clough, 1819-1861* (London: Sidgwick & Jackson, 1938);

Katharine Chorley, *Arthur Hugh Clough: The Uncommitted Mind* (Oxford: Clarendon Press, 1962);

Paul Veyriras, *Arthur Hugh Clough (1819-1861)* (Paris: Didier, 1964);

David Williams, *Too Quick Despairer: The Life and Work of Arthur Hugh Clough* (London: Hart-Davis, 1969);

Robindra K. Biswas, *Arthur Hugh Clough: Towards A Reconsideration* (Oxford: Clarendon Press, 1972).

References:

Isobel Armstrong, *Arthur Hugh Clough* (London: Longmans for the British Council, 1962);

Eugene R. August, "*Amours de Voyage* and Matthew Arnold in Love: An Inquiry," *Victorian Newsletter*, 60 (1981): 15-20;

James Bertram, "Arnold and Clough," in *Matthew Arnold*, edited by Kenneth Allott (London: Bell, 1975), pp. 178-206;

Frederick Bowers, "Arthur Hugh Clough: The Modern Mind," *Studies in English Literature*, 6 (1966): 709-716;

Stopford Brooke, *A Study of Clough, Arnold, Rossetti, and Morris* (London: Pitman, 1908); republished as *Four Victorian Poets* (New York: Putnam's, 1908), pp. 30-55;

A. O. J. Cockshut, *The Unbelievers* (London: Collins, 1964), pp. 31-43;

Doris N. Dalglish, "Arthur Hugh Clough: The Shorter Poems," *Essays in Criticism*, 2 (1952): 38-53;

Dorothy Deering, "The Antithetical Poetics of Arnold and Clough," *Victorian Poetry*, 16 (1978): 16-31;

Hoxie Neale Fairchild, *Religious Trends in English Poetry, 4: 1830-1880* (New York: Columbia University Press, 1957), pp. 505-527;

H. W. Garrod, *Poetry and the Criticism of Life* (London: Oxford University Press, 1931), pp. 109-127;

R. M. Gollin, "The 1951 Edition of Clough's *Poems*: A Critical Re-examination," *Modern Philology*, 60 (1962): 120-127;

John Goode, "*Amours de Voyage*: The Aqueous Poem," in *The Major Victorian Poets*, edited by Isobel Armstrong (London: Routledge & Kegan Paul, 1969), pp. 275-297;

Goode, "1848 and the Strange Disease of Modern Love," in *Literature and Politics in the Nineteenth Century*, edited by John Lucas (London: Methuen, 1971), pp. 45-75;

Evelyn Barish Greenberger, *Arthur Hugh Clough: The Growth of a Poet's Mind* (Cambridge: Harvard University Press, 1970);

Barbara Hardy, "Clough's Self-Consciousness," in *The Major Victorian Poets*, edited by Isobel Armstrong (London: Routledge & Kegan Paul, 1969), pp. 253-274;

Wendell V. Harris, *Arthur Hugh Clough* (New York: Twayne, 1970);

Walter E. Houghton, *The Poetry of Clough: An Essay in Revaluation* (New Haven: Yale University Press, 1963);

Jeffrey M. Jeske, "Clough's *Mari Magno*: A Reassessment," *Victorian Poetry*, 20 (1982): 21-32;

G. P. Johari, "Arthur Hugh Clough at Oriel College and at University Hall," *PMLA*, 66 (1951): 405-425;

Jacqueline Johnson and Paul Dean, " 'Paradise Come Back': Clough in Search of Eden," *Durham University Journal*, 38 (1977): 249-253;

J. D. Jump, "Clough's *Amours de Voyage*," *English*, 9 (1953): 176-178;

E. S. Leedham-Greene, "Four Unpublished Translations by Arthur Hugh Clough," *Review of English Studies*, new series 23 (1972): 179-187;

Richard D. McGhee, " 'Blank Misgivings': Arthur Hugh Clough's Search for Poetic Form," *Victorian Poetry*, 7 (1969): 105-115;

P. S. McGrane, "Unpublished Poetic Fragments and Manuscripts of Arthur Hugh Clough," *Victorian Poetry*, 14 (1976): 359-364;

Masao Miyoshi, *The Divided Self: A Perspective on the Literature of the Victorians* (New York: New York University Press, 1969), pp. 161-176;

F. L. Mulhauser, "Clough's 'Love and Reason,' " *Modern Philology*, 42 (1945): 174-186;

Ira Bruce Nadel, "Thackeray and Clough," *Studies in the Novel*, 13 (1981): 64-78;

Simon Nowell-Smith, "An Unascribed Clough

Poem," *Times Literary Supplement,* 8 March 1974, p. 238;

John Purkis, introduction to *A Selection from Arthur Hugh Clough* (London: Longmans, 1967), pp. 1-17;

John M. Robertson, *New Essays Toward a Critical Method* (London: Lane, 1897), pp. 301-330;

William M. Rossetti, "*The Bothie of Toper-na-fuosich,*" *Germ,* 1 (January 1850): 36-48;

R. B. Rutland, "The Genesis of Clough's *Bothie,*" *Victorian Poetry,* 11 (1973): 227-284;

Rutland, "Some Notes on the Highland Setting of Clough's *Bothie,*" *Victorian Poetry,* 14 (1976): 125-133;

Clyde de L. Ryals, "An Interpretation of Clough's *Dipsychus,*" *Victorian Poetry,* 1 (1963): 182-188;

Patrick Scott, "The Editorial Problem in Clough's *Adam and Eve,*" *Browning Institute Studies,* 9 (1981): 79-104;

Scott, "The Victorianism of Clough," *Victorian Poetry,* 16 (1978): 32-42;

W. David Shaw, "The Agnostic Imagination in Victorian Poetry," *Criticism,* 22 (1980): 116-139;

Henry Sidgwick, "The Poems and Prose Remains of Arthur Hugh Clough," *Westminster Review,* 92 (1869): 363-389;

Lawrence J. Starzyk, " 'That Promised Land': Poetry and Religion in the Victorian Period," *Victorian Studies,* 16 (1973): 269-290;

Michael Thorpe, ed., *Clough: The Critical Heritage* (London: Routledge & Kegan Paul, 1972);

Thorpe, Introduction to *A Choice of Clough's Verse* (London: Faber & Faber, 1969), pp. 9-28;

Geoffrey Tillotson, "Clough's *Bothie,*" in Geoffrey Tillotson and Kathleen Tillotson, *Mid-Victorian Studies* (London: Athlone, 1965), pp. 118-144;

Michael Timko, "Arthur Hugh Clough: Palpable Things and Celestial Fact," in *The Victorian Experience: The Poets,* edited by Richard A. Levine (Athens: Ohio University Press, 1982), pp. 47-50;

Timko, *Innocent Victorian: The Satiric Poetry of Arthur Hugh Clough* (Athens: Ohio University Press, 1966);

Albert M. Turner, "A Study of Clough's *Mari Magno,*" *PMLA,* 44 (1929): 569-589;

Samuel Waddington, *Arthur Hugh Clough: A Monograph* (London: Bell, 1883);

Humbert Wolfe, "Arthur Hugh Clough," in *The Eighteen-Sixties,* edited by John Drinkwater (Cambridge: Cambridge University Press, 1932), pp. 20-50;

Frances J. Woodward, *The Doctor's Disciples* (London: Oxford University Press, 1954), pp. 127-179.

Papers:

The major collections of Arthur Hugh Clough's papers are at Balliol College, Oxford (manuscripts of *The Bothie,* early diaries, and later travel journals with poetic drafts); in the Bodleian Library, Oxford (extensive poetic drafts, undergraduate and later essays, and correspondence); and in the Houghton Library, Harvard University (correspondence, especially with C. E. Norton and J. R. Lowell, and poetic manuscripts, including *Amours de Voyage* and revisions for *Poems,* 1862). There is a microfilm of the Bodleian manuscripts in the Honnold Library, Claremont, California.

Sydney Dobell
(5 April 1824-22 August 1874)

Mark A. Weinstein
University of Nevada, Las Vegas

BOOKS: *The Roman: A Dramatic Poem,* as Sydney Yendys (London: Bentley, 1850);
Balder: Part the First (London: Smith, Elder, 1854);
Sonnets on the War, by Dobell and Alexander Smith (London: Bogue, 1855);
England in Time of War (London: Smith, Elder, 1856);
Poems (Boston: Ticknor & Fields, 1860);
Of Parliamentary Reform: A Letter to a Politician (London: Chapman & Hall, 1865);
The Poetical Works of Sydney Dobell, with introduction and memoir by John Nichol, 2 volumes (London: Smith, Elder, 1875);
Thoughts on Art, Philosophy, and Religion (London: Smith, Elder, 1876);
America (London, 1896).

Sydney Dobell wrote the popular dramatic poem *The Roman* (1850) and a number of lovely lyrics, including the haunting "Keith of Ravelston." But he is most often remembered for the notorious *Balder* (1854), a "Spasmodic" poem that ruined his poetic reputation.

Sydney Thompson Dobell was born in Cranbrook, Kent, the eldest son among the ten children of an old Sussex family. His father, John Dobell, a hide merchant, wrote a radical pamphlet on government, *Man Unfit to Govern Man* (1812). His mother, Julietta, was the daughter of Samuel Thompson, a well-known political reformer and religious leader, who advocated a freethinking, ecumenical Christianity. Thus, Dobell grew up in a literary, religious, and speculative household, with a bias toward radicalism.

Because his family was opposed to public schools and universities, Dobell was educated entirely at home by private tutors. He also showed a remarkable zeal for learning on his own and composed precocious juvenile verses. His biographers trace his later poetic eccentricities to this early period of intense and insulated study. In the mid-1830s his father became a wine merchant in Cheltenham; Sydney kept up his connection with this business until his death. In 1839 he became engaged to Emily Fordham, whom he married five years later. In thirty years of marriage, according to Dobell's biographer, they were never apart as long as thirty hours.

Their early married life was divided between Cheltenham, where Dobell superintended his father's business, and a couple of pleasant country places among the Cotswolds. At Coxhorne House in the valley of Charlton Kings, Dobell, James Stansfield, and George Dawson originated the "Society of the Friends of Italy." At Hucclecote on an old Roman road, Dobell began writing in 1848 *The Roman,* his poem on the liberation and unification of Italy.

Dobell got his poetic start in the world under

the auspices of the Reverend George Gilfillan of Dundee, an influential critic and extoller of aspiring poets. In 1849 Gilfillan had an extract from *The Roman* published in *Tait's Edinburgh Magazine* and whetted the public appetite with a glowing eulogy of the forthcoming author, "another Shelley, of a manlier Christian type." The young poet sent letters of gratitude to the critic, submitted the entire poem to Gilfillan for inspection, and amended all but one of the passages that the critic condemned.

The Roman was published under the pseudonym "Sydney Yendys" in April 1850. Ostensibly, it is a simple, partisan poem. Vittorio Santo, "a Missionary of Freedom," goes out "disguised as a monk, to preach the Unity of Italy, the Overthrow of Austrian Domination, and the Restoration of a great Roman Republic." His lengthy speeches display "the lavish wealth of infinite resource" and stir his hearers to patriotic self-sacrifice. As the noble Roman is led away to his death at the end, "great shouts" are heard outside: "Down with the Austrians! Arms! Blood! Charge! Death—death to tyrants! Victory! Freedom!"

A closer look at the protagonist, however, reveals ambiguous possibilities. One character says of Vittorio:

> this polyglot of prophets
> Roams like a manifold infection, shedding
> Through the sick souls of men the strange disease
> Of his own spirit.

Vittorio considers himself to be a godlike prophet. He inspires his brother, his lover, and "his chosen followers," including children, to die for his cause but shows no emotion over their fate. The cause seems all, the individual nothing. This element of disease in the self-proclaimed prophet was, of course, muted in this propagandistic poem, but it was to become prominent in the forthcoming *Balder*.

The Roman achieved instantaneous and remarkable success. Dobell's biographer claimed that "since Byron 'woke one morning to find himself famous' no young poet of this century had achieved so great and so unexpected a success." A second edition came out in early 1852. Much of its success is undoubtedly attributable to the political climate of the times. Popular feeling in Great Britain, which sympathized with the European uprisings of 1848, discovered its voice in *The Roman*. But the poem also has intrinsic merits—the emotional sweep of Vittorio's speeches, the beauty of the incidental lyrics, the challenging obliqueness of the imagery.

Fame encouraged Dobell to expand his horizons. He and his wife visited London, North Wales, and Switzerland. He was especially impressed by the Alps, which left their mark on his later poetry. He also became acquainted with many of the eminent figures of the time, including Tennyson, Browning, and Charlotte Brontë; Mazzini and Kossuth; Philip James Bailey, whose *Festus* (1839) was to have a deleterious effect upon *Balder*; and Carlyle, who may have helped to wean Dobell from his democratic views. Whatever the cause, after *The Roman* Dobell began to exchange his early radical sympathies for a new "liberal-conservative" politics.

Begun at Coxhorne in 1850, continued in the Alps in the summer of 1851, and finished at Amberley Hill, Dobell's cottage in the Cotswolds, *Balder* appeared in the last week of 1853 before a shocked Victorian audience. The forty-two scene, 7,500-verse dramatic poem is a psychological study of Balder; Dobell's chief concern is the exposure of his antihero's mind:

> The cavernous and windy mysteries;
> Yea, all the creeping secrets of her maw,
> The busy rot within her, and the worm
> That preys upon her vitals.

Balder makes other Romantic protagonists look pale by comparison. The omens of his greatness have always been clear; he put his "question to the universe,/And overhead the beech-trees murmured 'Yes.'" He has enjoyed all of the supernatural experiences of Bailey's *Festus*, without need of Mephistophelean aid. Like Faust, he has tried all philosophies and sciences in vain: his pride has climbed above earth, yet Heaven is no nearer. Still, his insatiability surpasses that of all of his predecessors; only Balder could speak of

> mine hunger, unappeased
> That sucks Creation down, and o'er the void
> Still gapes for more.

Balder is also a poet. He has been chosen by Nature and "attains in solitude." Like other Romantic poets he writes about his own heart's woe; but to fulfill his destined mission, Balder goes far beyond his fellow poets. He feels that he must experience everything before he can complete his greatest work. Since death, the ultimate experience, has always eluded him, he seeks it by sacrificing his daughter. He seemingly recovers from the shock of her death, but his wife, Amy, grows increasingly mad; and as the poem ends, Balder is about to kill her. The plot may sound absurd, but its function is to allow for the examination of abnormal states of mind; and as Balder exposes his unconscious through a series of reveries, the whole situation becomes fearfully believable.

Victorian readers were so outraged that when the second edition came out in 1854, Dobell added a preface defending himself. He claimed that the public's description of Balder as "egoistic, self-contained, and sophistical, imperfect in morality, and destitute of recognized religion" was "precisely the impression which I wished the readers of this volume to receive." He explained that he intended to portray, in three parts, the progress "of a doubtful mind to a faithful mind." The first part, now before the public, presented merely "the egoistic hero of isolation and doubt." Balder's progress, however, was never to be completed.

In his preface, Dobell pointed out that although many reviewers mistook his moral purpose, nobody criticized the poetry of the book. *Balder* is a mine of rich ore. By following Bailey's advice to work all things into his poem, Dobell spoiled the artistic unity of *Balder*; almost half of the work is composed of extraneous "beauties." But in Balder's reveries, Dobell exhibits a mastery of sustained blank verse; in Amy's interspersed lyrics, he exhibits a mastery of song. Swinburne believed that the prolific Dobell "never wrote a bad verse." His imagery is original and vivid: Balder describes, for example,

> the man-fruit on the gallows-tree;
> It hung up like a fruit and like a fruit
> Shook in the wind, like a fruit was plucked down
> And the dark wintry branch stood bare.

The only sure thing in *Balder* is the unusual.

During the next twenty years Dobell made plans to fulfill his artistic and moral purpose by finishing *Balder*, but he never did. Part of the reason is attributable to the sheer enormity of the task, part to Dobell's later health problems, and part to one of the finest parodies in English literature. In 1854 William Edmondstoune Aytoun's *Firmilian; or, The Student of Badajoz. A Spasmodic Tragedy*, a brilliant satire on the "Spasmodic School of Poetry," was published. By following the plot of *Balder* and consequently directing most of his parody against that extreme example of spasmody, Aytoun made Dobell the leading member of the "school" and ridiculed his egoistic antihero, emotional extravagance, and lengthy digressions. As Alexander Smith, another member of the school, said, Dobell was "by far" the most important poet among the Spasmodics and so was hurt the most by the ridicule. His poetic reputation has never recovered.

In 1854 the Dobells went to Edinburgh to seek medical advice for Mrs. Dobell. They remained in Scotland for three years, spending the cold months in Corstorphine, just outside the metropolis, and the summers in the Highlands. Dobell became acquainted with a new intellectual and literary circle, including his old nemesis Aytoun and his fellow Spasmodic Smith. Dobell and Smith collaborated on a small volume, *Sonnets on the War* (1855). The thirty-nine poems treat conventional war themes in an undistinguished manner. It is evident that what Wordsworth called "the sonnet's scanty plot of ground" inhibited Dobell's powers of psychological analysis and his command of sustained blank verse. The little brochure was generally ignored by the reviewers, although the anti-Spasmodic *Blackwood's* kept kicking its fallen opponents.

Dobell's more significant companion volume, *England in Time of War,* was published the following year. The most famous poem in the book is undoubtedly "A Nuptial Eve"—popularly known as "Keith of Ravelston"—which Dante Gabriel Rossetti thought "one of the finest, of its length, in any modern poet—ranking with Keats's La Belle Dame sans Merci." Several of the finest poems again display Dobell's remarkable ability to portray a mind under strong emotional stress. Nevertheless, the characters here contrast vividly with Balder, the isolated genius brooding over his forbidden desires. These are ordinary people in recognizable situations: a mother dreaming of her boy's heroics, a Christian lamenting the bloodshed, a widow crying over her husband. The author of the long, digressive, blank-verse dramas *The Roman* and *Balder* here tells his story in forty-four condensed lyrics.

But if Dobell was trying to shake off the epithet "Spasmodic," he was unsuccessful: the critics stressed that this was another publication of that Spasmodic, Dobell. Gilfillan argued against this guilt by association, claiming that "the critics have so lavishly poured out the vials of their wrath" on this excellent poetry simply because "Mr. Dobell has written 'Balder.'" His complaint was futile. The critical strategy was not to examine Dobell's individual works on their own merits but to summarize his Spasmodic reputation and use his new poems as illustrations. Even the favorable reviews must have been as wormwood to Dobell, for they praised him only insofar as he had moved away from *Balder;* but *Balder*, Dobell always maintained, was his best work—the lyrics were a "mere filler" before the completion of his major epic. Now that the minor

Sydney Dobell

poems were being condemned because they resembled his best work or praised because they differed from it, Dobell became discouraged; he never took up *Balder* again, and wrote only occasional poems during the last eighteen years of his life. A touching note is his refusal to allow a friend's book to be dedicated to him, for fear that "Sydney Dobell" on the dedication page would insure the failure of the volume.

It is ironic that Dobell, whom many identified with the egoistic Balder, was actually one of the most generous of men. He helped several struggling artists with advice, encouragement, and money. The poet Robert Buchanan, for example, said of himself and David Gray that Dobell had helped them "as no other living man could or would." Dobell also instituted a profit-sharing plan in his wine business and took a leading role in the charitable enterprises of Gloucestershire.

Otherwise, the story of the last years of his life reads like a medical report. He suffered from various illnesses and accidents. Residing among the Cotswolds most of the year, he and his wife sought warmer climates—Niton in the Isle of Wight, Cannes, Spain, and Italy—during the winters. Serious literary work was forbidden by his doctors, but he continued to write occasional poetry and political tracts. In 1869, as Dobell was trying to tame a horse for a young woman, the animal fell on him, injuring him severely. He was a cheerful invalid for the five years before his death, entertaining many visitors with his brilliant conversation.

Of those labeled "Spasmodics," Dobell was the most unjustly condemned because he was the most original thinker and finest poet in the "school." *Balder* especially deserves reconsideration today. An age more familiar with the antihero and with the psychological analysis of morbid states of mind may discover that it is a significant poetic achievement.

Biography:

E. Jolly, *The Life and Letters of Sydney Dobell*, 2 volumes (London: Smith, Elder, 1878).

Reference:

Mark A. Weinstein, *William Edmondstoune Aytoun and the Spasmodic Controversy* (New Haven: Yale University Press, 1968).

Frederick William Faber
(28 June 1814-26 September 1863)

G. B. Tennyson
University of California, Los Angeles

SELECTED BOOKS: *The Knights of St. John* (London: Vincent, 1836);
The Cherwell Water-lily, and Other Poems (London, 1840);
The Styrian Lake, and Other Poems (London: Rivington, 1842);
Sights and Thoughts in Foreign Churches and among Foreign Peoples (London: Rivington, 1842);
Sir Lancelot: A Legend of the Middle Ages (London: Rivington, 1844);
The Rosary and Other Poems (London: Toovey, 1845);
An Essay on Beatification, Canonisation, and the Processes of the Congregation of Rites (London: Richardson, 1848);
Hymns (London, 1848); enlarged as *Jesus and Mary; or, Catholic Hymns for Singing and Reading* (London, 1849);
Essay on the Interest and Characteristics of the Lives of the Saints (London: Richardson, 1850);
The Spirit and Genius of St. Philip Neri (London: Burns & Lambert, 1850);
All for Jesus; or, The Easy Ways of Divine Love (London: Burns & Oates, 1853);
Growth in Holiness; or, The Progress of the Spiritual Life (London: Burns & Oates, 1854);
The Blessed Sacrament; or, The Works and Ways of God (London: Burns & Oates, 1855);
Poems (London: Burns & Oates, 1856; New York: Benziger, 1856);
The Creator and the Creature; or, The Wonders of Divine Love (London: Burns & Oates, 1857; Baltimore: Murphy, 1857);
The Foot of the Cross; or, The Sorrows of Mary (London: Burns & Oates, 1857);
Ethel's Book; or, Tales of the Angels (London: Derby, 1858; Baltimore: Murphy, 1863);
Spiritual Conferences (Baltimore: Murphy, 1858; London: Burns & Oates, 1859);
Devotion to the Pope (London, 1860; Baltimore: Murphy, 1860);
The Precious Blood; or, The Price of Our Salvation (London: Richardson, 1860; Baltimore: Murphy, 1860?);
Bethlehem (London: Burns & Oates, 1860; Baltimore: Murphy, 1862);

Notes on Doctrinal and Spiritual Subjects, edited by John Edward Bowden, 2 volumes (London: Richardson, 1866; Baltimore: Murphy, 1966);
The First Christmas: "The Infant Jesus" (London: Nister, 1889).

OTHER: Lives of St. Wilfrid, St. Paulinus, St. Oswin, St. Edwin, St. Ebba, St. Ethelburga, St. Adamnan, St. Oswald, and St. Bega, in *Lives of the English Saints,* 16 volumes (London: Toovey, 1844);

Lives of the Canonised Saints and Servants of God, edited by Faber, 42 volumes (London: Derby, 1847-1856);

Jacques Nouet, *The Octave of Corpus Christi,* translated by Faber (London: Derby, 1847);

Giuseppe Crispino, *The School of St. Philip Neri,* translated by Faber (London: Burns & Lambert, 1850);

The Spiritual Doctrine of Father Louis Lallemant, translated by Faber (London, 1855);

L. M. Grignon de Montfort, *A Treatise on the True Devotion to the Blessed Virgin,* translated by Faber (London, 1863).

In his day Frederick William Faber was widely known as a convert from Anglicanism to Roman Catholicism, as a compelling preacher, as the celebrated superior of the Oratory of St. Philip Neri in London (the Brompton Oratory), and as a prolific author of Catholic hymns. An effective spokesman for the Roman church, Faber for a considerable period outshone John Henry Newman, whose disciple he had originally been; but he survives today chiefly as a hymnodist whose work has found its way into hymnbooks of all denominations.

Born to an ecclesiastical family in the West Riding of Yorkshire, Faber was educated at Harrow and at Balliol College and University College, Oxford. During his first year at Oxford, 1833, he wrote "The Cherwell Water-lily," which was published with other poems in 1840.

As an Oxford undergraduate commencing his university career in 1833 Faber came under the spell of John Henry Newman and the Tractarian Movement, which Newman liked to date as having begun in that year with John Keble's Assize Sermon. Faber eagerly joined in various Tractarian projects, most notably in work on the *Library of the Fathers,* for which he translated St. Optatus's work on the Donatist schism. His poem *The Knights of St. John* won the Newdigate Prize in 1836, the year he graduated with a B.A. from Oxford. He went on to write *The Styrian Lake, and Other Poems* (1842), *Sir Lancelot* (1844), and *The Rosary* (1845). "The Cherwell Water-lily" and "The Styrian Lake" gained Wordsworth's approval and were presumably the poems that prompted Wordsworth to remark in 1842, when Faber accepted an ecclesiastical appointment, that "England loses a poet." Faber was destined to make religion his primary profession and to subordinate his poetical instincts to that calling.

His religious convictions had moved steadily Romeward in the late 1830s and early 1840s, stimulated not only by Tractarianism but also by historical study and by several visits to the Continent, where he closely observed Catholic religious life. He fostered various High Church and Catholic practices in his own church at Elton, Huntingdonshire, and in 1844 his *Life of St. Wilfrid,* which was thought by many to be excessively pro-Roman, was published. In November of the following year, only two weeks after Newman's submission to Rome, Faber renounced Anglicanism and was received into the Roman Catholic church.

As a Catholic Faber pursued a vigorous career, at first as the superior of a group he formed in honor of St. Wilfrid called "Brothers of the Will of God"; later, after his ordination as a Roman priest in 1847, as a member of the Oratory of St. Philip Neri, the religious order introduced into England by Newman. Faber prospered as an Oratorian, and eventually his group was established in London with Faber as superior. The London Oratory, which finally settled into impressive quarters in the Brompton Road in the fashionable Knightsbridge section, attained greater celebrity and popularity than Newman's group in the industrial city of Birmingham. Much of this celebrity was due to Faber's personal influence and to his writings.

Faber wrote various devotional treatises, but his chief fame came from the steady stream of hymns that he produced for Roman Catholics. Although Faber had begun as a poet of the Romantic and Tractarian schools, he felt that his talents should be turned to more practical account than allowed by the private devotional style of Tractarian poetry. He was especially conscious of the fact that hymn-singing, originally associated with Methodism, had by the mid-nineteenth century become established and popular even in the most traditional Anglican parishes, whereas Catholic parishes lacked a body of hymns consonant with Roman theology and devotional practices. Faber set himself to remedy this lack and to provide the Roman church with popular hymns in the Wesleyan poetic and musical style. He succeeded so well that many of the 150 hymns from his pen have gained general currency among all Christians, the most notable examples being "My God, How Wonderful Thou Art" and "Sweet Saviour, Bless Us ere We Go." Even some of his most intensely Catholic hymns have proved adaptable for Protestant purposes, such as his well-known "Faith of Our Fathers," which, with the change of a few words, has become a popular Evangelical hymn. (Faber wrote "Faith of our

Fathers! Mary's prayers/Shall win our country back to thee"; the Protestant version reads "Faith of our Fathers! Good men's prayers/Shall win our country all to thee.")

Faber, then, beginning as a Romantic nature poet and developing as a Tractarian devotional one, finally made his mark as the most notable Roman Catholic hymnodist of the nineteenth century.

Biographies:
J. E. Bowden, ed., *Life and Letters of F. W. Faber* (London: Richardson, 1869; revised, London: Burns & Oates, 1888);

Ronald Chapman, *Father Faber* (London: Burns & Oates, 1961);

Raleigh Addington, ed., *Faber: Poet and Priest* (Cowbridge, Wales: Brown, 1974).

Reference:
G. B. Tennyson, *Victorian Devotional Poetry: The Tractarian Mode* (Cambridge: Harvard University Press, 1981), pp. 181-183.

Sir Samuel Ferguson
(10 March 1810-9 August 1886)

Tirthankar Bose
University of British Columbia

BOOKS: *The Cromlech on Howth: A Poem* (London: Day, 1841);

Lays of the Western Gael, and Other Poems (London: Bell & Daldy, 1864);

Father Tom and the Pope; or A Night in the Vatican (New York: Simpson, 1867);

Congal: A Poem in Five Books (Dublin: Ponsonby, 1872; London: Bell, 1872);

Deirdre: A One-Act Drama of Old Irish Story (Dublin: Privately printed, 1880);

Poems (Dublin: McGee, 1880; London: Bell, 1880);

The Forging of the Anchor: A Poem (London & New York: Cassell, 1883);

Hibernian Nights' Entertainments, edited by Lady Mary Ferguson, 3 volumes (Dublin: Sealy, Bryers & Walker, 1887);

Lays of the Red Branch (Dublin: Sealy, Bryers & Walker, 1897; London: Unwin, 1897);

Poems of Sir Samuel Ferguson, edited by A. P. Graves (Dublin: Talbot/London: Unwin, 1918; New York: Stokes, 1918?);

Poems, edited by Padraic Colum (Dublin: Hodges, Figgis, 1963).

OTHER: "Our Architecture," in *Afternoon Lectures on English Literature, Delivered in Dublin* (London: Bell & Daldy, 1864), pp. 27-65;

Leabhar Breac, preface by Ferguson (Dublin: Royal Irish Academy, 1876);

Ogham Inscriptions in Ireland, Wales and Scotland, compiled by Ferguson (Edinburgh: David Douglas, 1887);

The Remains of St. Patrick: The Confessio and Epistle to Coroticus Translated into English Blank Verse (Dublin: Sealy, Bryers & Walker, 1888).

PERIODICAL PUBLICATIONS: "The Forging of the Anchor," *Blackwood's Edinburgh Magazine* (February 1832): 281-283;

"The Fairy Thorn," *Dublin University Magazine* (March 1834): 331-332;

"Father Tom and the Pope," *Blackwood's Edinburgh Magazine* (May 1838): 607-619;

"The Vengeance of the Welshmen of Tirawley," *Dublin University Magazine* (September 1845): 308-314;

"Lament for Thomas Davis," *Dublin University Magazine* (February 1847): 190-199.

Sir Samuel Ferguson, a minor poet of substantial literary influence, was one of the modern makers of the Irish identity. His love for the indigenous literary tradition of Ireland was as compelling as his interest in its archaeology, to the advancement of both of which he committed his life. It was through his pioneering efforts that the bardic heritage became a vitalizing force in modern Irish poetry, especially in the work of William Butler Yeats.

Born in Belfast, Ferguson was the third son of

Sir Samuel Ferguson

John Ferguson of County Antrim, a gentleman of Scottish descent. His schooling began in the Academical Institution in Belfast; he went on to Trinity College, Dublin, where he graduated B.A. in 1826 and received the M.A. in 1832. Oddly, though, his wife quotes him in her biography as saying, "I . . . never graduated, and held no academic rank till the honorary degree of Doctor of Laws was conferred on me." While Ferguson was preparing for a legal career in Dublin he simultaneously launched himself as a poet in the February 1832 issue of *Blackwood's Edinburgh Magazine* with "The Forging of the Anchor," which celebrates in long iambic lines man's heroic spirit as seen in the labors of "merry craftsmen" and "brave mariners." Its publication was an accolade for the young poet, for it was introduced by the editors as "a model of vigorous inspiration." A more sinewy piece, "The Fairy Thorn," appeared in March 1834 in the *Dublin University Magazine*, which he had helped to found in 1833. This poem offers ample evidence of Ferguson's dramatic energy:

> Thus clasped and prostrate all, with their heads together bowed,
> Soft o'er their bosoms beating—the only human sound—
> They hear the silky footsteps of the silent fairy crowd,
> Like a river in the air gliding round.

The interest in folklore evidenced in the poem expressed itself more forcefully in the same magazine from April to November of that year in Ferguson's series of strongly critical reviews of James Hardiman's *Irish Minstrelsy* (1831). He knew little Gaelic himself, but through painstaking consultations with those who did he successfully challenged Hardiman's views on Irish cultural history and his renderings of Irish poetry; he underscored his points by providing his own, far more sensitive, translations. His growing interest in antiquity also led to a series of historical tales, somewhat in the manner of Sir Walter Scott but interspersed with verse, entitled "Hibernian Nights' Entertainments" and published in the *Dublin University Magazine* from 1834 to 1836.

Through this period Ferguson's idea of Ireland was taking political as well as literary turns. During the 1830s all Ireland was looking with fervid hope at the Irish Ordnance Survey that, by mapping in the most ambitious possible way all of Ireland's resources, was promising an imminent economic and cultural boom. The survey stimulated Ferguson's antiquarian interests while it reinforced his inherited belief in the Protestant ascendancy's tutelary role in Ireland's regeneration. Having been raised as a Tory and an Anglican, Ferguson viewed Catholic emancipation with apprehension, to which he gave vent in verse distinguished only by an immoderate sectarianism. The first of these poems was "An Irish Garland," published in *Blackwood's Edinburgh Magazine* in January 1833, which consisted of exhortations, printed side by side, from the Protestant "Gentlemen of Ireland" and the Catholic "Jackasses of Ireland." A more temperate though no less shallow declaration of Anglo-Irish supremacy was the "Inaugural Ode for the New Year" in the first issue of the *Dublin University Magazine.*

Despite this bigotry Ferguson was aware of the ambivalent status of the Anglo-Irish gentry. He recorded this in an essay entitled "A Dialogue between the Head and Heart of an Irish Protestant" in the *Dublin University Magazine* for November 1833, in which he bemoans the betrayal of the Anglo-Irish by an ungrateful Britain. Yet his solution for Ireland remains that of bringing Anglican enlightenment to the Catholics. The same conviction of the need for correcting Papist ignorance through Anglican education shows in the witty satire "Father Tom and the Pope" in *Blackwood's Edinburgh Magazine* in May 1838.

In that year Ferguson's blind sectarianism—at least the literary expression of it—received a fortunate check. He was called to the Irish bar and for several years found the demands of the legal profession too pressing to admit the political muse, or indeed any other. This restraint was evidently salutary, for the next poem to appear in print was one of Ferguson's best. "The Vengeance of the Welshmen of Tirawley" (1845) is a long ballad of considerable metrical flexibility and sustained narrative tension. Ferguson by no means abandoned his social concerns, but political events began to wean him away from partisanship. The termination of the Ordnance Survey in 1841 once again proved British indifference and made even Ferguson and his Protestant peers regard with some sympathy Daniel O'Connell's agitation for the repeal of the union with England.

A greater political influence on Ferguson was Thomas Davis, the charismatic leader of the Young Ireland party and editor of the *Nation,* whose platform called for Irish independence coupled with antisectarianism. Davis's sudden death in 1845 and the resultant crisis of leadership caused Ferguson such anguish that he had to withdraw from chaotic Dublin to go on a year of travel on the Continent. One of Ferguson's finest poems, an elegy on Davis, appeared with an essay on the leader in *Blackwood's Edinburgh Magazine* in February 1847. These related pieces unambiguously show that even though Ferguson retained his belief in Protestant noble-mindedness, his faith in the benevolence of the British was gone.

The disastrous famine of 1846 to 1850, unrelieved by government action, further convinced Ferguson of the need for Irish unity and self-determination. In 1848 he took the significant step of defending in court Dalton Williams, a Catholic charged with treason. A far more decisive gesture, and a dramatic one, was Ferguson's public renunciation of Unionist sympathies at a meeting of the Protestant Repeal Association later in 1848. On the personal side, too, this year proved to be a landmark, for on 16 August Ferguson married Mary Catherine Guinness. She helped him become the host of Dublin's most distinguished cultural circle, and after his death she wrote the fullest biography of Ferguson that has appeared to date.

From the time of his marriage Ferguson's life seems to have followed an even course. He won sufficient success in his profession to be called to the Inner Bar in 1859. Equal if not greater efforts went into his literary and antiquarian studies, and his pioneering exploration led to the modern interest in old Irish legends. His purposeful compilation of the bardic material as well as his own poems on themes taken from them, especially from the Ulster or Red Branch cycle, found many admirers, though they were not published for some years. His declared ambition was "to raise the native elements of Irish History to a dignified level," and this ambition was "the key to all the literary work" of his mature life.

This ambition led to the publication of *Lays of the Western Gael* (1864). In these poems Ferguson resurrects the legendary heroes and their deeds vividly enough but tames their passions into lengthy reflection on life. His narrative flows well and he creates the topographical background in sharp outlines, as in "The Burial of King Cormac" or "Aideen's Grave." His recreation of a heroic age is, however, somewhat spoiled by his insistent interpolation of "the leavening word of Jesus" ("The Healing of Conall Carnach").

The *Lays of the Western Gael* reinforced Ferguson's already high reputation, formal recognition of which came in the form of an LL.D. (honoris causa) from Dublin University in 1864. He began to devote more and more of his energies to the reconstruction of the Irish past, which required a widening of his impressive familiarity with bardic and archaeological materials. In 1867 he gave up the law and accepted the position of deputy keeper of the records of Ireland.

Congal, Ferguson's most ambitious work, appeared in 1872. Conceived as an epic, the poem is crowded with both incidents and characters, some of them supernatural. It tells of the rebellion of the young King Congal against the powerful King Domnal, whose daughter Lafinda is Congal's betrothed. Despite predictions of disaster Congal marches into battle; he proves his valor but, ironically, is killed in an accidental encounter with an idiot boy. The verse movement is uninspired, but the narrative has considerable nervous energy and the moral reflections define with some success the tragic aspects of heroism as a cultural mode. The poem meanders frequently but succeeds in creating atmosphere, as in Congal's eerie midnight encounter with a shadowy giant whose silent refusal to reply to Congal foretells the hero's doom:

"But he who speaks him," Congal said,
    "and gains no answer—he?"
"Within the year, the Seers agree,"

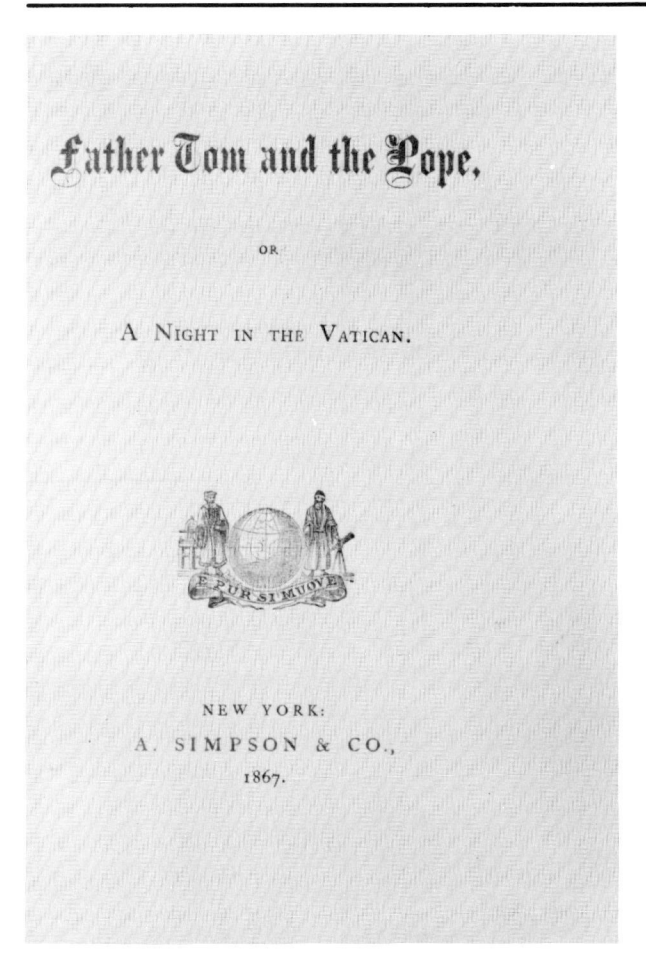

Title page for Ferguson's anti-Catholic satire, which was first published in Blackwood's Edinburgh Magazine *in May 1838 (Thomas Cooper Library, University of South Carolina)*

    said Ardan, "he must die;
For death and silence, we may see,
    bear constant company."

The success of *Congal* as an epic poem is debatable, for it fails to go beyond the central figure to his world, but it remains an important evocation of the Irish bardic tradition both in its subject matter and its form.

Honors came regularly to Ferguson in his later life. In 1874 he was elected a member of the Society of Antiquarians of Scotland. In 1876, at the Royal Irish Academy's invitation, he wrote a preface to the academy's lithographic reproduction of *Leabhar Breac*, an anonymous fourteenth-century collection of Latin and Irish compositions in manuscript. His work in the records office earned him a knighthood in 1878 and his election in 1881 as president of the Royal Irish Academy was applauded on all sides.

Another accolade was one more LL.D. (honoris causa), this one from the University of Edinburgh in 1884.

Ferguson wrote little in the last years of his life, collecting much of his important earlier work in *Poems* (1880), but he worked at his antiquarian studies with undiminished vigor. Early in 1886 a heart ailment forced him to recuperate at Strand Lodge, a friend's house in Howth, where he died on 9 August. A public funeral was held in St. Patrick's Cathedral, Dublin, but by his own wishes he was buried in his family's burial ground at Donegore in County Antrim. An important antiquarian work, *Ogham Inscriptions* (1887), and a verse translation, *The Remains of St. Patrick* (1888), were posthumously published.

Ferguson's distinction as a poet lies in his ability to recreate a bygone age by depicting its social customs and verbal mannerisms. But his lack of concrete imagination, evidenced by a thin and scant imagery, seriously impedes his poetic expression. He undoubtedly had a sense of the dramatic, as is demonstrated in "The Vengeance of the Welshmen of Tirawley," "The Abdication of Fergus Mac Roy," and *Congal;* but his predilection for moralizing diffuses the drama. In his satirical writings he was able to draw sharper figures, of which one of the best examples is "The Loyal Orangeman" (published in Lady Ferguson's biography); but his unresolved political position made satire a dead end for him.

Ferguson's life, full though it was of social success and moral certitude, was nevertheless shaken by the ambiguities of the Anglo-Irish identity. His increased awareness of those ambiguities coincided with a decisive turning away from contemporary issues in favor of legendary themes; yet in all of his endeavors the idea of a richer Ireland remained the shaping force. While few would agree with Yeats that Ferguson was "the greatest poet Ireland has produced," Ferguson brought credibility to the Irish literary persona of modern times by the weight of his scholarship and the strength of his dedication to the Irishness of Ireland's literature.

Biographies:

Lady Mary Ferguson, *Sir Samuel Ferguson in the Ireland of His Day,* 2 volumes (Edinburgh & London: Blackwood, 1896);

A. Deering, *Sir Samuel Ferguson: Poet and Antiquarian* (Philadelphia: University of Pennsylvania Press, 1931).

References:

Malcolm Brown, *Sir Samuel Ferguson* (Lewisburg,

Edward FitzGerald

Joseph Sendry
Catholic University of America

BIRTH: Near Woodbridge, Suffolk, England, 31 March 1809, to John Purcell and Mary Frances FitzGerald.

EDUCATION: B.A., Trinity College, Cambridge University, 1830.

MARRIAGE: 4 November 1856 to Lucy Barton.

DEATH: Merton, Norfolk, England, 14 June 1883.

BOOKS: *Euphranor, a Dialogue on Youth,* anonymous (London: Pickering, 1851; revised, London: Parker, 1855); revised as *Euphranor: A May-Day Conversation at Cambridge, "Tis Forty Years Since"* (London: Privately printed, 1882; New York: Dutton, 1905);
Polonius: A Collection of Wise Saws and Modern Instances, anonymous (London: Pickering, 1852; Portland, Maine: Mosher, 1901);
Six Dramas of Calderón, Freely Translated (London: Pickering, 1853);
Salámán and Absál. An Allegory. Translated from the Persian of Jámí, anonymous (London: Parker, 1856; revised, London: Privately printed, 1871; Boston: Page, 1899);
Rubáiyát of Omar Khayyám, the Astronomer-Poet of Persia. Translated into English Verse, anonymous (London: Quaritch, 1859; revised, 1868; revised, 1872; Boston: Osgood, 1878); revised, combined with *Salámán and Absál* (London: Quaritch, 1879);
The Mighty Magician and Such Stuff as Dreams Are Made Of: Two Plays Translated from Calderón, anonymous (London: Privately printed, 1865);
Agamemnon: A Tragedy Taken from Aeschylus, anonymous (London: Privately printed, 1865; London: Quaritch, 1876; Woodstock, Vt.: Elm Tree Press, 1906);
Readings in Crabbe: Tales of the Hall, anonymous (London: Privately printed, 1879; London: Quaritch, 1882);

The Downfall and Death of King Oedipus: A Drama in Two Parts, Chiefly Taken from the Oedipus Tyrannus and Colonaeus of Sophocles, anonymous, 2 volumes (London: Privately printed, 1880-1881);

Occasional Verses, anonymous (London: Privately printed, 1891);

The Variorum and Definitive Edition of the Poetical and Prose Writings of Edward FitzGerald, edited by George Bentham, 7 volumes (New York: Doubleday, Page, 1902-1903);

Dictionary of Madame de Sévigné, edited by M. E. FitzGerald Kerrich, 2 volumes (London: Macmillan, 1914);

The Two Generals: I, Lucius Aemilius Paullus; II, Sir Charles Napier, anonymous (London: Privately printed, n.d.).

OTHER: "Memoir of Bernard Barton," in *Selections from the Poems and Letters of Bernard Barton,* edited by Lucy Barton (London: Hall, Virtue, 1849).

PERIODICAL PUBLICATION: "The Meadows in Spring," *Hone's Year Book* (30 April 1831): 510-511.

Almost despite himself Edward FitzGerald, country gentleman and amateur man of letters, has secured a permanent place in the history of English poetry as—for want of a better word—the translator of stanzas known as *rubáiyát* by the twelfth-century Persian Omar Khayyám; and as a master of the art of letter writing, several of whose correspondents were major literary figures in their own right.

Born 31 March 1809 at Bredfield House near Woodbridge in Suffolk, Edward Purcell was the sixth of eight children (three sons, five daughters) in the well-to-do family of John Purcell and Mary Frances FitzGerald Purcell. Though the poet's father did not practice the law in which he was educated, he took on several other careers simultaneously or in turn: country squire, militiaman, high sheriff, member of Parliament, and mining speculator. Both parents had aristocratic Irish antecedents, through which they were related to each other; but since Mary FitzGerald's carried more wealth and prestige, Purcell took his wife's name when her father died in 1818. The event brought the newly surnamed FitzGeralds home from a two-year sojourn in France; on their return, Edward began studies at King Edward VI Grammar School in Bury St. Edmunds. In October 1826 he went up to Trinity College, Cambridge, where he took his degree without distinction in February 1830.

More than for most people—because he had the money and the personal freedom to make choices—where he lived reflected the kind of man FitzGerald was. A conservative in most things, he would always center his life in Suffolk, the county where he was born. During his early years, he lived with his parents in fine country houses: at Bredfield House, seven miles northeast of Ipswich, until a year or two before going up to Cambridge and after that at Wherstead Lodge, two miles south of the town. In 1835 the family returned to the neighborhood of Bredfield to occupy Boulge Hall. Instead of sinking roots of his own, in 1837 the light-traveling bachelor of twenty-eight moved into a thatched cottage on the estate.

The year after he left Cambridge FitzGerald's "The Meadows in Spring," a slight poem jaunty enough to be mistaken for one of Charles Lamb's, was published anonymously. He then kept virtual silence as a published writer for almost two decades. When he left the university, FitzGerald asked a friend to fetch some articles from the student lodgings he had vacated; this was the occasion for the first surviving letter, dated 29 January 1830, in the copious correspondence for which FitzGerald has become known.

"He had the gift of creating himself fully in his letters," Elizabeth Drew has observed of FitzGerald in her study of nine preeminent British practitioners of the epistolary art. FitzGerald was modest about his talent in this vein: "I count myself a good correspondent," he once said, "but then I am an idle man." The basic appeal of FitzGerald's letters is that of the familiar essay: a leisurely, literate, and discriminating personal response to whatever interested him. His interests were catholic indeed: besides the music, painting, theater, opera, and omnivorous reading that would predictably draw the attention of a literary man, FitzGerald commented on politics, history, religion, vegetarianism (which he sometimes practiced), and sailing (a favorite hobby in his later life).

FitzGerald tried to make vivid for his correspondents what he had lately seen and done; but the main beneficiary of his lively descriptions is the modern reader, who can gather from the letters what it was like for a contemporary to discover a Constable painting of Salisbury Cathedral or to attend an 1842 performance of Handel's *Acis and Galatea.* The bonus in FitzGerald's letters is their style. Though he is typically candid, even confiding, his prose maintains a structure and cadence that

A page from one of the letters in FitzGerald's copious correspondence

give it an interest in its own right. Here—as in the verse of the *Rubáiyát*—it is a delight to watch his seemingly uncontrolled discursiveness regularly crystallize itself into veritable epigrams before resuming its onward fluency.

FitzGerald's standards in judging art—including his own—were rigorous, but in his personal relations he was usually tolerant. The major theme of the letters is friendship, for which FitzGerald, temperamentally if not technically a lifelong bachelor, had a special need and a distinctive flair. Though given during much of his life to visits in London and in various other parts of England and Ireland, as a country dweller FitzGerald depended a good deal on letters to sustain friendships over the long run. Among his friends were three major British authors: William Makepeace Thackeray, Alfred Tennyson, and Thomas Carlyle. He met Thackeray at Cambridge, where they shared a tutor and a love of fun—at the expense of more serious pursuits—that expressed itself in exuberant marathon letters; unfortunately, only one of FitzGerald's has survived. Tennyson was at Cambridge at the same time and was remembered by "Fitz" as a "sort of Hyperion." Yet their friendship probably did not begin until 1835, when both stayed with their fellow Cantabrigian James Spedding in the Lake District.

For both Thackeray and Tennyson the 1830s and early 1840s were troubled times. Neither had yet achieved fame. Both had lost legacies through imprudent speculation, a small fortune in Thackeray's case. Tennyson had to break off a two-year engagement in 1840, and the same year Thackeray's wife suffered a mental breakdown. In times of distress FitzGerald was the kind of person on whom friends could depend for both financial and emotional help. Mrs. Thackeray once remarked that he would give her husband his last shilling, and Tennyson gratefully praised him to Carlyle as "a man from whom one could take money." Unobtrusive generosity characterized FitzGerald throughout his life: when the second edition of the *Rubáiyát* began to sell, the modest profits were sent anonymously to the Persian Relief Fund in memory of Omar Khayyám.

The third of FitzGerald's famous correspondents, Thomas Carlyle, was fifteen years older than he and was well known as an essayist and historian when the painter Samuel Laurence introduced them in 1842. They were quite unlike: Carlyle was an eccentric, poor-born Scot, who preached in flaring cadences a gospel of work and heroism; FitzGerald was a man privileged from birth, who enunciated in measured prose an attitude of detachment and skepticism. Their friendship and correspondence began with a common interest in the battlefield at Naseby, on which Carlyle wished information for his biography of Cromwell, and which FitzGerald's family owned.

Though FitzGerald associated with steady and prolific writers such as Thackeray and Carlyle and badgered a reluctant Tennyson into bringing out his *Poems* of 1842 after a ten-year silence, he was almost indifferent about making his own appearance in print. When at length he did so, the product was, like his letters, an extension of one of his numerous friendships. In 1849 his Suffolk friend and neighbor Bernard Barton died. At the request of Barton's daughter Lucy, FitzGerald "edited" the work of the Quaker poet—that is, he selected, rearranged, condensed, and even rewrote nine volumes of verse to make 200 pages. If FitzGerald's introductory memoir was as decorous as such nineteenth-century portraits were supposed to be, it still left in a few blemishes, such as Barton's inclination to have everything he wrote published, regardless of quality, and his stubborn refusal to care for his health.

A more ambitious effort was a philosophical dialogue set on a day stolen from study at Cambridge and published in 1851 under the title *Euphranor*. The narrator is an unnamed doctor modeled on FitzGerald's friend William Kenworthy Browne, who was a farmer, magistrate, sportsman, and officer of the militia in real life. Though the subtitle of the piece is "A Dialogue on Youth," its subject more precisely is education. Three undergraduates, minor participants in the proceedings, personify deviations from the norm. At one extreme Lexilogus, a bookworm, buries himself in past learning. At the other, the cynical Lycion and the genial Phidippus shun both the past and learning for cigars and billiards in one case, horses and rowing in the other. The major interlocutor, Euphranor, is an intelligent product of traditional learning who gives the doctor the right openings to expound his reformist view that education should comprise development of the body as much as the mind, and should be directed to acting in present society rather than to knowing the best that was said and thought in the past. Ironically, the dialogue succeeds best as a specimen of the literary education it seems to impugn.

Euphranor cites the call to national regeneration through a "chivalry of labour" that Carlyle had recently issued in *Past and Present* (1843), in which an idealized picture of medieval England was used

FitzGerald's friend William Kenworthy Browne, who served as the model for the narrator in Euphranor *(unfinished oil painting by Samuel Lawrence)*

to expose the evils of modern industrial society. Amid the urbanity of FitzGerald's dialogue (which he later referred to as "odious smart writing") mention of Carlyle, the nineteenth-century Jeremiah, suggests by contrast how little the establishment had to fear from this modest scheme to channel the idealism of youth, which is the age of chivalry in an individual's life as the Middle Ages were in the history of Europe.

FitzGerald often considered Carlyle a crank, but he paid his friend a high compliment by making him the only modern author to be extensively excerpted in his next literary production, *Polonius: A Collection of Wise Saws and Modern Instances* (1852). In the preface FitzGerald declared his intention to break with past compilers of such sayings, who customarily relied on Dr. Johnson and the essayists of the eighteenth century to fill their pages. For FitzGerald eighteenth-century English had lost its energy and "native character," qualities that had vitalized the language in the age of Elizabeth and her successors, and which he sensed reemerging in Carlyle. The preface diagnoses the weakness of FitzGerald's collection along with that of others in the genre: namely, that when writings meant to combine wisdom and wit are excerpted and aggregated (as has been done here on over a hundred topics from "Action" to "Writing Well"), they can easily slip over the line into prolixity and dullness.

Around Christmas 1844 FitzGerald had been introduced to Edward Byles Cowell, a scholarly young man seventeen years his junior and extraordinarily gifted in languages. They may have met at the house of the Reverend John Charlesworth, to whose daughter, Elizabeth, FitzGerald had once thought of proposing and whom Cowell himself married in 1847. FitzGerald and Cowell, the latter the more accomplished classicist, read Latin and Greek together, and by 1850 the younger was teaching Spanish to the older. FitzGerald was especially taken with the dramas of Calderón. By fall of 1852 his letters were full of the Spanish dramatist, whose plays he was not only reading but translating. *Six Dramas of Calderón,* including *The Painter of His Own Dishonour; Keep Your Own Secret; Gil Perez, the Gallician; Three Judgments at a Blow; The Mayor of Zalamea;* and *Beware of Smooth Water,* was published in July 1853. Because another translation of Calderón's plays had just come out, FitzGerald, the chronic self-depreciator, for the only time in his career allowed his name to appear on the title page of a book.

For this translation FitzGerald chose plays he considered to be among the dramatist's lesser achievements, pieces in which plot and incident could carry the day without having to rely on lofty or accomplished verse. As he had done in editing Barton's work, and as he admitted in his preface, FitzGerald took liberties with his material, which he "sunk, reduced, altered . . . replaced . . . simplified" and added to, so as to make the complexities of seventeenth-century Spanish drama accessible to nineteenth-century English readers. FitzGerald suspected that this candor about his methods of composition would give the critics the handle they needed to sound knowing at his expense. He was especially annoyed by the review in the *Athenaeum* of 10 September 1853 that referred to his renderings as English imitations rather than translations of Calderón. Though FitzGerald was probably right in thinking his critic uninformed, the reviewer nevertheless focused on the major point of contention about FitzGerald's work as a translator and—since translations account for a large portion of his output—as an author.

Edward Byles Cowell, who helped FitzGerald learn Persian and introduced him to the writings of Omar Khayyám

In November 1850 Cowell, at his wife's urging and over FitzGerald's objections, had left the management of his father's business in Suffolk to matriculate at Oxford. Far from signaling the end of their tutorial relationship, Cowell's move from FitzGerald's neighborhood initiated its most fruitful phase. When the mature pupil paid one of his occasional visits to Oxford in December 1852, Cowell started him on the study of Persian. By the next October FitzGerald had finished Sir William Jones's book on Persian grammar (1771). From there he went on to Persian poetry, consulting Cowell and translations as needed, and for a brief time comparing notes with Tennyson. The first fruit of this new venture was an English version of *Salámán and Absál,* an allegory by the fifteenth-century poet Jámí that FitzGerald had discovered by May 1854 and had translated by the next winter; it was published in 1856. The love between the Shah's son Salámán and his nurse Absál and its paradoxical outcome, in which the two lovers leap into a funeral pyre—she is destroyed, he survives by virtue of his father's tran-scendent powers—represents the soul's becoming entangled by bodily lusts, then freeing itself through the ordeal of asceticism. In FitzGerald's version Jámí's allegory has a delicate charm and something of the same exoticism that lends his translation of the *Rubáiyát* so much of its appeal. FitzGerald considered *Salámán and Absál* his best job of translation, in part because he was able to give Jámí's diffuse fable a relatively compact form. But even in FitzGerald's drastically shortened version the allegory meanders toward a conclusion for which the reader unfamiliar with the premises of Islamic mysticism is not prepared.

Salámán and Absál was a timely parting gift to Cowell, who left with his wife for India on 1 August 1856 to assume a professorship at Presidency College in Calcutta, where he hoped to improve his knowledge of Oriental languages. The Cowells' leave-taking was only one in a series of personal shocks that FitzGerald suffered in a crucial period of several years. After the failure of a mining venture his father had declared bankruptcy in 1848, had separated from his mother the following year, and had died in 1852. In 1855, the year before the Cowells left, his mother had died. His share of her estate, however, insured FitzGerald's comfort for life.

When he felt constrained to vacate Boulge Cottage on the family estate in 1853, the year after his father's death, he assumed a less settled way of life, taking rooms—when he was not journeying outside of Suffolk—on Job Smith's farm at nearby Farlingay or, for shorter periods, staying with his friend George Crabbe, the vicar of Bredfield and son of the poet of the same name.

Another major setback came from an unlikely quarter three months after Cowell left England, when on 4 November 1856 FitzGerald married Lucy Barton, the daughter of his late friend, the Quaker poet. For most men marriage would have been a sustaining force, but for this congenital bachelor turned reluctant—*unwilling* is not too strong a word—bridegroom, it was a personal debacle. FitzGerald, aged forty-seven, seems to have entered this unhappy union to fulfill a misguided promise to Lucy's father. Though the same age, the couple were mismatched in almost every other way. She was assertive and eager to take her part in society as the wife of a gentleman; he was retiring and repelled by the world of fashion. They separated the following August after eight months of wedlock, during much of which they lived apart. The distaste that he felt for his erstwhile spouse ("The woman has no Delicacy," he remarked after their separation) did not prevent him from feeling compassion toward her and, in his customary way, providing generously for her throughout his life.

Though the year following Cowell's departure marked defeat and the beginning of a long withdrawal in FitzGerald's emotional life, it also saw the start of his advance toward literary triumph. Cowell's going-away present to FitzGerald was a transcript he had made from a manuscript at the Bodleian Library of 158 quatrains by the twelfth-century Persian Omar Khayyám, then all but unknown in England. At first FitzGerald appears not to have given much time to Cowell's discovery. When he returned to his Persian studies during the winter of 1857, it was rather to "Bird-Parliament," the title that he gave to Faríd al-Dín Attár's thirteenth-century allegory. As with *Salámán and Absál*, FitzGerald made a "metrical abstract" of the poem, less than 1,450 English verses, in couplets after the original, from 9,000 lines of Persian. And as in the earlier translation, a seemingly naive fairy-tale charm conceals the serious mystical theme. Various species of birds, each resembling some type of human character, gather to debate the choice of a leader and decide to go in search of Sýmurgh (God). The thirty who succeed in the arduous quest find that the Truth they have sought actually lies in themselves.

FitzGerald not only put aside Attár's allegory but left it unpublished during his lifetime; in late May he took up Khayyám's quatrains "as a sort of Consolation." The next month another transcript arrived from Cowell, this one comprising 516 stanzas by Khayyám that he had found in the library of the Royal Asiatic Society at Calcutta. If the new acquisition made new work for FitzGerald—the Calcutta manuscript was in much worse condition than the manuscript that Cowell had copied at the Bodleian—its arrival also brought him new momentum. In January 1858 he sent *Fraser's* magazine thirty-five quatrains that he had rendered into English. Having received no reply from the editors, he withdrew these a year later, added forty more, had 250 copies printed, and placed most of them on sale at Bernard Quaritch's bookshop in London on 9 April. The title page read: *Rubáiyát of Omar Khayyám, the Astronomer-Poet of Persia. Translated into English Verse.*

As always with FitzGerald, the term "translated" must be carefully qualified. In the first place *Rubáiyát* is not the name of a single poem but the plural of *rubái*, a short verse form in Persian. FitzGerald usually referred to these rubáiyát as "quatrains," a rough English equivalent, sometimes as tetrastichs, and once as "the common form of Epigram in Persia." He was dealing, then, not with a single long work, but with a large number of short pieces, from which he made a selection. Nor did he feel constrained to transmit the exact sense of any given rubái. Edward Heron-Allen, a specialist in Persian who studied this aspect of FitzGerald's translation, judged that of the 101 quatrains in the final version, only forty-nine are faithful paraphrases of specific rubáiyát by Khayyám. Forty-four are composites of two or more of Khayyám's quatrains. The origins of the remaining few are miscellaneous: two are based on a French translation, two on the general spirit of Khayyám's works, and two were translated from other Persian poets, Attár and Hafiz. FitzGerald was quite conscious of the liberties that he had taken: "Many Quatrains are mashed together," he admitted. But he insisted that the English verses had to have life, even if it was his own rather than Khayyám's. As he wrote to Cowell, "Better a live Sparrow than a stuffed Eagle."

FitzGerald's method for bringing Khayyám's verses to life involved not only careful selection but also conscious arrangement, in order to create a continuous poem rather than an anthology of aphorisms such as his own *Polonius*. He gave the rubáiyát shape by having them follow the speaker's moods from sunrise to moonrise on a late spring day. Dawn releases a stream of reflections on the transience of all days, all seasons, all lives, all human endeavors, and on the helplessness of man to influence his destiny or even dimly to comprehend it:

> For in and out, above, about, below,
> 'Tis nothing but a Magic Shadow-show,
>   Play'd in a Box whose Candle is the Sun,
> Round which we Phantom Figures come and go.

Pleasure, especially the grape, is repeatedly prescribed as the remedy for all human ills:

> The Grape that can with Logic absolute
> The Two-and-Seventy jarring Sects confute:
>   The subtle Alchemist that in a Trice
> Life's leaden Metal into Gold transmute.

How much of his own life FitzGerald breathed into this material can be gauged by the fact that he spoke in the same terms of Khayyám, whose "Epicurean Pathos" moved him, as of himself, "a sad Epicurean." In his preface FitzGerald described the Persian's quatrains as a "strange Farrago of Grave and Gay." For his own mixture FitzGerald admitted using a smaller measure of the "drink and

A verse copied by FitzGerald and used by him as the model for the meter of the Rubáiyát of Omar Khayyám *(Anderson Galleries, 15 February 1926)*

make-merry" stanzas than his predecessor. When FitzGerald called Khayyám and himself Epicureans, besides the hedonism of that philosophical school he had in mind its most articulate spokesman, the Roman poet Lucretius, who repudiated the popular religion of his day and ridiculed the abuses perpetrated in its name. The favor that FitzGerald showed to the serious side of Omar Khayyám was quite Victorian; his highlighting of Khayyám's Lucretian sentiments was Victorian with a difference, a difference that defines the place of his masterpiece in the literary history of that epoch.

When the *Rubáiyát* was published in 1859, Tennyson and Robert Browning were the leading poets of the day. Nearly the same age as FitzGerald, they represented a literary status quo that linked poetry with social, moral, and religious concerns. *In Memoriam* (1850) had expressed perplexities similar to Khayyám's concerning Providence, immortality, and the limits of human knowing, and was also made up of discrete sections and written entirely in quatrains. But where Tennyson maintained a reverent attitude as he struggled to validate these threatened values for himself and his contemporaries, FitzGerald's Khayyám treats such questions with a sustained, if usually mild, blasphemy and ridicules the professional sages who try, as Tennyson did, to propound answers to them.

A witty passage of eight stanzas in the first edition (nine in later editions) of the *Rubáiyát* that FitzGerald named "Kúza Náma" or "Book of Pots" recapitulates these themes in parody. Animated pots speculate vainly on who made them and why, but that discussion quickly comes to an end as all eagerly await the wine that will fill them as the new moon ends Ramazán, the Moslem month of fasting:

> So while the Vessels one by one were speaking,
> One spied the little Crescent all were seeking:
>   And then they jogg'd each other, "Brother!
>   Brother!"
> "Hark to the Porter's Shoulder-Knot a-creaking!"

In 1864, five years after the first edition and possi-

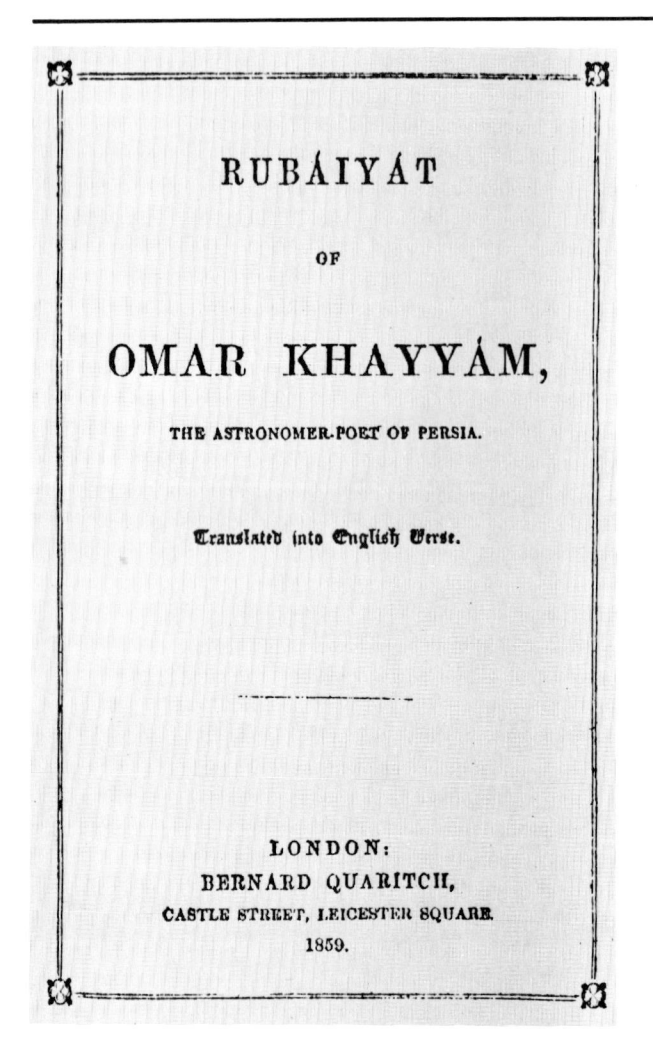

> RUBÁIYÁT
>
> OF
>
> OMAR KHAYYÁM,
>
> THE ASTRONOMER-POET OF PERSIA.
>
> Translated into English Verse.
>
> LONDON:
> BERNARD QUARITCH,
> CASTLE STREET, LEICESTER SQUARE.
> 1859.

Title page for the first publication of FitzGerald's masterpiece (Anderson Galleries, 22 April 1937)

bly in answer to it, Browning used another twelfth-century philosopher-astronomer-poet, the Spanish Jew Ibn Ezra, as his spokesman in "Rabbi Ben Ezra." In that poem Browning also adumbrated the metaphor of God as potter, but to illustrate his conviction that man's struggles on earth shape him into a finished vessel for God's heavenly use.

FitzGerald expected resistance to Khayyám's iconoclasm. He was not yet aware of a group of young poets who belonged to a new generation and who, with Dante Gabriel Rossetti as their leader, would not only find Khayyám a kindred spirit but would play a crucial role in making the *Rubáiyát* known to the world. Their bellwether in print was William Morris, whose *Defence of Guenevere and Other Poems* had appeared in 1858. Accused of adultery, Morris's title character justifies herself, as he and his colleagues were justifying their poetry, on grounds of beauty, apart from religious or moral considerations.

When the *Rubáiyát* was published in 1859, Quaritch priced it at a shilling; but it went unnoticed and by 1861 was relegated to the remainder bin, on sale for a penny. Rossetti learned of it by word of mouth and told A. C. Swinburne. Each bought several copies to distribute among friends. When they returned for more the next day, the price had doubled. Swinburne took a copy to the young novelist George Meredith, and they took turns reading it to each other. That evening Swinburne began his own "Laus Veneris" in the distinctive quatrain that FitzGerald had invented for the *Rubáiyát,* echoing its profanation by paying homage to the lingering power of Venus, the pagan love goddess, who had been driven underground, so to speak, by medieval Christianity. Two years later, in 1863, another disciple of Rossetti's, the painter Edward Burne-Jones, showed a copy of the *Rubáiyát* to John Ruskin. The art critic was so impressed that he left a letter with Burne-Jones to be delivered to Khayyám's anonymous translator if his identity should ever become known.

Crabbe's death in 1857, followed by W. K. Browne's in 1859, left the familiar Suffolk landscape "a Cemetery to me," FitzGerald complained to Elizabeth Cowell in a letter of 21 August 1860, adding that even London was spoiled because "W. Browne is too much connected with my old Taverns and Streets." In December 1860 the semi-itinerant estranged husband abandoned the countryside near Woodbridge and settled in two-room lodgings on Market Hill within the town.

Unlike London and the Suffolk countryside, the sea remained unspoiled by painful memories after the deaths of his parents and friends. "None I have loved have been drown'd," FitzGerald wrote to Mrs. Cowell. He had spent the previous winter at Lowestoft on the Suffolk coast, and for the next decade he would divide his time between there and Woodbridge, which lies inland thirty-three miles to the southwest. At Lowestoft FitzGerald advanced quickly in seamanship. A small hired craft that he used on the River Deben was replaced by the *Waveney,* a sailboat that was built for him in 1861. The next year he tried the open sea in two vessels—one purchased, one rented—that failed to meet his standards. In the *Scandal,* made to his specifications in 1863, he had at last a seagoing yacht that pleased him, and it became his summer home for the next eight years.

FitzGerald relished the blunt, easygoing ways of those who made their living by the sea, and in

FitzGerald's yacht, the Scandal, *which served as his summer home from 1863 to 1871*

1864 he became friendly with a herring fisherman named Joseph ("Posh") Fletcher, in whom he found (as he had earlier in the landsman Browne) an ideal of active manhood that complemented his own retiring nature. They entered a business partnership in 1867, when FitzGerald bought a herring lugger, the *Meum and Tuum,* and Posh became its captain. Squabbles over Posh's drinking and failure to keep accurate records, on one side, and over FitzGerald's interference on the other, made it a strained association. After three years, in which losses were more the rule than profits, the partnership ended. The *Meum and Tuum* and the *Henrietta* (another herring boat, acquired in 1869) were sold. Though the two inevitably parted ways, FitzGerald continued to regard Fletcher as one of the greatest men he had ever known.

Interest in the *Rubáiyát* had grown sufficiently by 1867 for Quaritch to suggest a second edition. The same year a translation of Khayyám by J. B. Nicolas, comprising 464 quatrains, was published in France. The new translation troubled FitzGerald, for Nicolas held that Khayyám belonged to the sect of Moslem mystics known as Súfis. Accordingly, the Frenchman gave the *Rubáiyát* a sacred interpretation in which wine symbolized love of God and intoxication symbolized mystical transport. FitzGerald was familiar with Súfic doctrine from his

Joseph "Posh" Fletcher, FitzGerald's partner in an unsuccessful commercial fishing enterprise

work with the allegories of Jámí and Attár, but to counter the view that Khayyám was a Súfi he called on the more knowledgeable Cowell in India. Cowell, whom FitzGerald once described as "a very religious man," had been "alarmed" at the first edition of the *Rubáiyát* and now backed off from supporting his pupil's literal, secular reading, where wine is indeed wine and is used in defiance of Islamic law.

In the second edition, published in 1868, FitzGerald added thirty-five more stanzas, making this, with 110 quatrains, the longest of the poem's four editions. FitzGerald explained the changes, which included some minor rearranging, by saying that the extra length gave him more room to suggest the passing of time and shifts in the speaker's moods as he imbibes throughout the day. In the revised preface he faced directly the challenge of the French translation, using material from Nicolas's own introduction to argue that Khayyám had opposed the Súfis, and that he came off as more of an iconoclast in Nicolas's translation than in his own version.

The question of the Persian's Súfism and consequently of a mystical versus materialist interpretation of his *Rubáiyát* has not yet been settled. It was aired with some brio in 1967, a century after Nicolas's translation, with the publication of a new translation by the poet Robert Graves comprising 111 quatrains. This version was translated from an "authentic" manuscript supplied by Omar Ali-Shah, described by Graves as "a Súfi poet and classical Persian scholar." In their introductory essays Graves and Ali-Shah claim Khayyám for the Súfis and castigate FitzGerald for what they consider a total distortion of his meaning.

Finally, however, the significance of FitzGerald's *Rubáiyát* in English poetry derives not from the degree of its fidelity to its Persian original but from its impact on generations of readers as a poem in its own right. Charles Eliot Norton anticipated this fact in the first major review of the poem, published across the Atlantic in the *North American Review* for October 1869. "It has all the merit of an original production," he declared, rejecting the word *translation* because that term did not suggest the fresh inspiration that he found in FitzGerald's verses. Thanks to Norton's review, the *Rubáiyát* began its wide popularity in America, prompting Quaritch to approach FitzGerald about a new edition. FitzGerald eventually gave his consent and a third edition was brought out in 1872, shortened to 101 quatrains and with some changes in wording, but still with no indication of authorship.

The American soon reentered the history of the *Rubáiyát* to play a key role in the discovery of FitzGerald as its translator. When Norton arrived from the United States in the autumn of 1872, Burne-Jones, who had introduced him to the poem on a previous visit, passed on a rumor that its author was the "Reverend Edward FitzGerald, who lived somewhere in Norfolk and was fond of boating." When Norton repeated the rumor to Carlyle the next April, the latter quickly made the connection with his old friend from Suffolk, who—though no Reverend—was indeed fond of boats. Now that the secret was out, the letter that Ruskin had left with Burne-Jones was forwarded to FitzGerald through Norton, then Carlyle. FitzGerald's letter of thanks to Norton marked the beginning of their friendship.

In Britain major critical notice of the *Rubáiyát* had first been carried in 1870—ironically, by *Fraser's*, where FitzGerald had first submitted the poem. Not until 1875 was he publicly identified as its author in the February issue of *Lippincott's* magazine. In 1878 James Osgood brought out the first American edition in Boston, and by then demand at home had grown to the point where Quaritch was urging a fourth English edition. But before he would allow a new printing, FitzGerald made, as usual, minor demands for changes in wording, along with a major one that the religious allegory *Salámán and Absál* be bound in the same volume to serve as respectable company for the "Old Reprobate" Omar. The wisdom of that decision was doubtful, and FitzGerald later admitted that *Salámán and Absál*, though a favorite of his, was "dead weight" with the reading public. For once FitzGerald was paid for a publication, a modest sum of twenty-five pounds. The size of the run, 1,000 copies, was also modest, giving no hint of the deluge of print that would follow his death. By the turn of the century the *Rubáiyát* would become one of the most popular poems in the English language, read by people of all tastes throughout the English-speaking world and beyond. When Carl J. Weber produced his Centennial Edition in 1959, he listed 215 earlier editions, most of them American. Many more have appeared since.

The popularity of the poem is not difficult to explain. It appeals to some of the same instincts as the travelogue, offering ready access to a remote world by means of a judicious selection of vivid impressions. Part of the pleasure in the *Rubáiyát* lies in the paradox that much of Omar Khayyám's world is already familiar, or as FitzGerald put it, he "sang . . . of what all men feel in their hearts." If the statement is amended to include the phrase "in their

Little Grange, FitzGerald's home for the last ten years of his life

unguarded moments," it perhaps comes closer to the truth. As FitzGerald recognized, it is easier to confront one's own inclinations to sadness, giddiness, and defiance if one imagines these emotions being played out by an eccentric actor in an exotic setting.

Yet in a sense the *Rubáiyát* has been a victim of its own power to please. Regarding the current reputation of the work, Daniel Schenker has observed that "few poems are so widely circulated . . . and so little talked about." Popularity, however, does not rule out artistic merit, and the fact that the tastemakers have lately been silent about it does not mean that the *Rubáiyát* has forfeited all claim to serious critical study. It is useful to recall that the poem was in the first instance discovered and promoted by some of the most advanced and discriminating readers of its day. The taste of that day was of course different from modern taste, and so besides being a popular poem the *Rubáiyát* has had to bear the additional handicap of being a popular *Victorian* poem. The clouds of anti-Victorian bias that covered much twentieth-century criticism have been dispersing more and more since about 1960, but they have yet to lift from FitzGerald's work. If and when they do, there will be discovered in the trenchant, sometimes disjunct utterances of his mercurial persona a modern spirit who can view his own boasts with grim amusement as he deflates the conventional pieties of others.

Even though FitzGerald had bought a cottage on Pytches Road at the edge of Woodbridge in 1864, had added two rooms the next year, and two more in 1871, he continued to occupy the rented Market Hill lodgings. Only an eviction notice in 1873 impelled him to leave. When he moved into Little Grange, as he called the Pytches Road property, in January 1874, FitzGerald was living in his own house for the first time in his life. The house was unpretentious, for he always despised ostentation. And if he saw less of friends such as Thackeray and Tennyson in later life, it was partly because the grander life-styles they adopted with their success made him feel ill at ease.

Through the 1850s FitzGerald had still seen the members of his old circle from time to time, most commonly in London, though in 1854 he had visited the Tennysons on the Isle of Wight, and in 1855 Carlyle had spent ten days with him in Suffolk. In the 1860s, however, his sailing, his avoidance of the metropolis, and the advancing age of all concerned had meant basic changes in the pattern of his friendships generally. Death had taken Thackeray on Christmas Eve 1863; FitzGerald had not seen him, Tennyson, or Carlyle at all during that decade. Though the effort tended to be one-sided, he had developed a practice of writing to old friends on something like a yearly schedule, oftener if an occasion, such as publication of a book, presented itself. Tennyson in particular could expect, along with assurances of continued affection, candid opinions of the work that he never stopped producing, work that in FitzGerald's view had lost its "champagne flavour" after 1842. Even with his decreased social activity FitzGerald welcomed to his yacht or to Woodbridge anyone who would venture to those parts of the world. The Cowells did so several times after their return from India in 1864. (With FitzGerald's help Cowell was appointed professor of Sanskrit at Cambridge in 1867.) At length Tennyson himself visited, with his son Hallam, in 1876. When the two old friends met for this last time, they got on, as FitzGerald put it, as if they "had only been parted twenty Days instead of so many Years."

As old friendships receded, FitzGerald entered upon new ones, especially in the 1870s, when he had given up the herring business, curtailed his yachting, and settled into Little Grange. Despite deteriorating vision he wrote more letters than before. Among the new correspondents, those who drew out his best were Fanny Kemble, who lived part of the time in the United States; Norton; and James Russell Lowell. FitzGerald had known Fanny Kemble, the sister of his school and college friend John Mitchell Kemble and the daughter of the actor Charles Kemble, since his youth. Fanny herself enjoyed some success as a young actress, but her stage career was a thing of the past when FitzGerald renewed their dormant friendship in the late 1860s through his delightfully informative letters that for some years were dispatched at each full moon. He had begun writing to Norton when the American helped deliver Ruskin's letter about the *Rubáiyát* in 1873. Through Norton he became acquainted — entirely through letters, though they tried several times to arrange a meeting — with the poet and critic Lowell, who became ambassador from the United States to Spain in 1877 and to Great Britain in 1880.

These American connections had an important bearing on FitzGerald's literary career, an impact that had begun with Norton's review of the *Rubáiyát* in 1869 and his discovery of FitzGerald as its author in 1873. The American demand that prompted Quaritch to press for a third edition of the *Rubáiyát* in 1872 and a fourth in 1879 was duplicated with a translation of Aeschylus's *Agamemnon* that FitzGerald had circulated through a private printing in 1865. Fanny Kemble made the existence of the translation known among some of Omar Khayyám's American devotees, and as a result Quaritch began getting requests for copies. In November 1876 FitzGerald sent him several, to be forwarded gratis to inquiring Americans. FitzGerald was shocked to find the play listed in Quaritch's next catalog at 7s. 6d., and he took the bookseller severely to task in a letter dated 7 December 1875. The episode reveals a great deal about FitzGerald's sense of himself as author. He was angry with Quaritch on several counts: because the book had been put on public sale, when he had had it printed only to be given to sympathetic friends; because it was priced well above his own estimate of its monetary value; because his name (absent, as usual, from the title page) appeared in the catalogue, when he diligently sought anonymity; and because a laudatory description was included, which he thought would only invite ridicule. It is easy to see why Edmund Gosse said of FitzGerald that "no one who has left sterling work behind him . . . had less of the professional writer about him." If unprofessional, FitzGerald was still human, and he consented to Quaritch's request that he acknowledge public demand and allow the *Agamemnon* to be published—but not until he made some revisions. The drama, described in his preface as a "Per-version" rather than a version of Aeschylus because of the liberties he took with the original, was published in July 1876.

Precisely because FitzGerald approached his writing as an amateur, one who wrote and was published—or merely printed—mostly for his own satisfaction and more often than not at his own expense, the development of his canon defies neat chronological summary. Just as he could, to a great extent, choose where he lived because he had the means to do so, he could print, withhold, revise, or have his work published or republished as and when he pleased. Thus, having held back from Calderón's best work when he translated the *Six Dramas* in 1853, he returned to the playwright with more confidence a decade later to deal with two plays, *The Mighty Magician* and *Such Stuff as Dreams Are Made Of*, that had daunted him earlier. Even then, he hedged: when printed in 1865, the plays were circulated only among friends. And, just as he brought out four *Rubáiyát*s and two *Agamemnon*s in his lifetime, he also did three slightly different versions of *Euphranor*, the first two published in 1851 and 1855 respectively, and the third privately printed in 1882. Similarly, a second, privately printed edition of *Salámán and Absál* intervened in 1871 between its publication in 1856 and the shortened version that shared a volume with the *Rubáiyát* in 1879.

The habit of tinkering freely with his own writings gave FitzGerald a precedent for doing the same with the work of others. Such tinkering was notable in his two last works of significance, versions of George Crabbe's poetry and of Sophocles' plays. Feeling that Crabbe's *Tales of the Hall* was excessively wordy, FitzGerald cut passages and omitted tales from the original in what turned out to be a vain effort to win a reading audience for the father of his late friend, the vicar of Bredfield. *Readings in Crabbe*, privately printed in 1879, was distributed in

1882 by Quaritch, who published a new edition with an added preface the following year. FitzGerald's boldest reworking, however, was the one he performed on the Oedipus plays, a production that he himself characterized as "neither a Translation, nor a Paraphrase of Sophocles, but 'chiefly taken' from him . . . intended for those who do not read the Greek." Still, his innovations, which included not only omissions (among them the removal of Ismene, Oedipus's daughter) but also substantive changes (such as Oedipus's age in *Oedipus at Colonus*), were not capricious. As he explained to Norton—who became increasingly his sounding board for literary ideas during these last years—he wished by clearing away inconsistencies, redundancies, and difficulties in the Greek text to help the modern reader see what is dramatically essential in Sophocles. The privately printed copies of his *Downfall and Death of King Oedipus*—issued in two parts, *Oedipus in Thebes* (1880) and *Oedipus at Athens* (1881)—were distributed almost without exception to friends in America, where acceptance of his work remained warm.

Settled at Little Grange, FitzGerald spent the last years of his life quietly. His sight deteriorated so far that he had to hire boys from Woodbridge to read to him. He kept aloof from the townspeople otherwise and was regarded, with some justification, as an eccentric. He continued to entertain his favorite nieces and some stalwart friends in Woodbridge or on the seacoast at Lowestoft, and during the last five years of his life he even managed six visits to London. With the deaths of his oldest brother, John, and his youngest sister, Andalusia, both in 1879, he and his sister Jane remained the only survivors among the eight children of John Purcell and Mary Frances FitzGerald. In 1880 Carlyle died, then James Spedding. In the spring of 1883 Tennyson was planning for the publication of "Tiresias," a poem he had written not long before the beginning of his friendship with FitzGerald at Spedding's home in the Lake District, a time when he was doing the kind of poetry of which FitzGerald approved. As a preface to "Tiresias" the laureate composed a dedication in the form of a verse epistle, "To. E. FitzGerald," a masterpiece of its kind. This mellow expression of private feeling controlled by the public occasion never reached "old Fitz," for he died in his sleep on 14 June while visiting George Crabbe, grandson of the poet whose verses he had recently taken it upon himself to improve.

By conducting his career with the same resolute independence as he lived his life, Edward

FitzGerald's grave (flat, to the right of cross) in the Boulge Churchyard, Suffolk

FitzGerald assured that his place in the history of English literature would not be at its center. He shunned public recognition, confined his verse writing mainly to translation, and translated chiefly from works outside the dominant streams of influence. Yet by dint of the same independence, FitzGerald staked out the limited but secure ground of his own fame. His position outside the mainstream afforded a superior vantage point from which he could view his times. FitzGerald's canny observations, combined with his delight in recording impressions and his affection for the friends who sometimes played major roles in contemporary life, enabled him to produce a body of correspondence that ranks him among the great letter writers in English. His poet's sense of word and form, founded on an exacting taste, nurtured by a wide acquaintance with literature and the other arts, and refined by an extensive study of languages—including slang and dialects within his own—came to fruition in that extraordinary achievement, *The Rubáiyát of Omar Khayyám*. In reviving a forgotten

Persian poet of the twelfth century, FitzGerald's quatrains have gained a classic immortality of their own.

Letters:

Letters and Literary Remains of Edward FitzGerald, edited by Aldis Wright, 7 volumes (London & New York: Macmillan, 1902-1903);

Letters of Edward FitzGerald, edited by Alfred McKinley Terhune and Annabelle Burdick Terhune, 4 volumes (Princeton, N.J.: Princeton University Press, 1980).

Bibliography:

Theodore G. Ehrsam, Robert H. Diely, and Robert M. Smith, "Edward FitzGerald," *Bibliographies of Twelve Victorian Authors* (New York: H. W. Wilson, 1936), pp. 77-90.

Biography:

Alfred McKinley Terhune, *The Life of Edward FitzGerald* (New Haven: Yale University Press, 1947).

References:

Arthur J. Arberry, *The Romance of the Rubáiyát* (London: Allen & Unwin, 1959);

William Cadbury, "FitzGerald's Rubáiyát as a Poem," *English Literary History,* 34 (1967): 541-563;

Elizabeth Drew, *The Literature of Gossip: Nine English Letterwriters* (New York: Norton, 1964);

Robert Graves and Omar Ali-Shah, *The Rubáiyát of Omar Khayyám: A New Translation with Critical Commentaries* (London: Cassell, 1967);

Edward Heron-Allen, *Edward FitzGerald's Rubáiyát of Omar Khayyám* (London: Quaritch, 1899);

Robert Bernard Martin, *Tennyson: The Unquiet Heart* (New York: Oxford University Press, 1980);

Daniel Schenker, "Fugitive Articulation: An Introduction to the Rubáiyát of Omar Khayyám," *Victorian Poetry,* 19 (Spring 1981): 49-64;

Michael Timko, "Edward FitzGerald," in *The Victorian Poets: A Guide to Research,* 2nd edition, edited by Frederic E. Faverty (Cambridge: Harvard University Press, 1968), pp. 138-148.

Papers:

Edward FitzGerald's papers are collected principally at Cambridge University in the university library and the library of Trinity College.

David Gray
(29 January 1838-3 December 1861)

Christopher Murray
University of Regina

BOOKS: *The Luggie and Other Poems* (Cambridge: Macmillan, 1862);

Poems, by David Gray. With Memoirs of His Life (Boston: Roberts, 1864);

The Poetical Works (Glasgow: Maclehose/London: Macmillan, 1874).

Dying unpublished and in obscurity, David Gray never reached the audience that he was convinced would rank him high among English poets. He did, however, catch the attention of some influential men of letters, principally Richard Monckton Milnes and Sydney Dobell; and Robert Buchanan's sensitive and self-effacing biography of his friend, appearing in the same issue of the *Cornhill* magazine that contained obituaries of Thackeray by Dickens and Trollope, helped widen that small circle of admirers. Gray scarcely achieved an authentic individual note in the brief time allotted him; his diction is too often artificial, as it is in the worst of his models, and his tone is too often maudlin. Yet his language can be extraordinarily deft and his observation of natural beauty remarkably acute, and his work continues to find readers.

Gray's career was brief and pathetic. The oldest of eight children of a hand-loom weaver living at Merkland, Kirkintilloch, near Glasgow, he showed sufficient promise at school that, with much financial hardship, he managed to attend the University of Glasgow. His parents hoped he would become a minister; though he wanted to be a poet, he resigned himself to a teaching career. Meeting Bu-

David Gray

chanan, who also wished to write, at the university, Gray soon reverted to his original ambition. He wrote to Milnes and Dobell, seeking advice and encouragement; each counseled patience and perseverance. But Gray was impetuous and convinced of his destiny; and in early 1860, when his stint as a student-teacher ended, he resolved to seek his literary fortune in London. He and Buchanan together agreed to go and arranged to meet on 4 May at the railway terminus; but both men neglected to specify at which of the two stations they would meet, and Gray went to one, Buchanan the other. Each believed that the other had decided against the venture, yet each resolutely boarded his train. They did not meet until they had been in London for several weeks, by which time Gray had contracted a severe cold from sleeping out in Hyde Park. Milnes soon befriended Gray and gave him clerical employment. Milnes later submitted Gray's long poem "The Luggie," a celebration of the stream flowing near Gray's home, to Thackeray for publication in the *Cornhill*. Though in parts clearly derivative of James Thomson, the poem contains memorable vignettes of Scottish rural life and passages of rare beauty. Thackeray's rejection of "The Luggie" depressed Gray deeply.

By late August Gray's cold had deteriorated into tuberculosis; he returned to Glasgow but was told by his physician that he might not survive a Scots winter. Desperate and destitute, he wrote to editors, to Dobell, and to Milnes asking for money and medical help, and even briefly considered applying to Robert Browning for sanctuary in Florence. In November 1860 he returned to London. At a sanatorium outside the City he felt very ill at ease among mildly afflicted gentlefolk, and on Milnes's advice he went to another at Torquay. There he saw patients in the last stages of his disease; he fled back to London and returned to Scotland in January 1861.

Facing death and having no hope of a cure, Gray wrote a sequence of poignant sonnets, "In the Shadows," which have been widely anthologized and admired. These, too, are derivative at times and often marred by self-consciously poetical language and a sense of strain, but, though not without cliches, this one (addressing Buchanan) does have a maturity and ease that justify Gray's ambition:

Now, while the long-delaying ash assumes

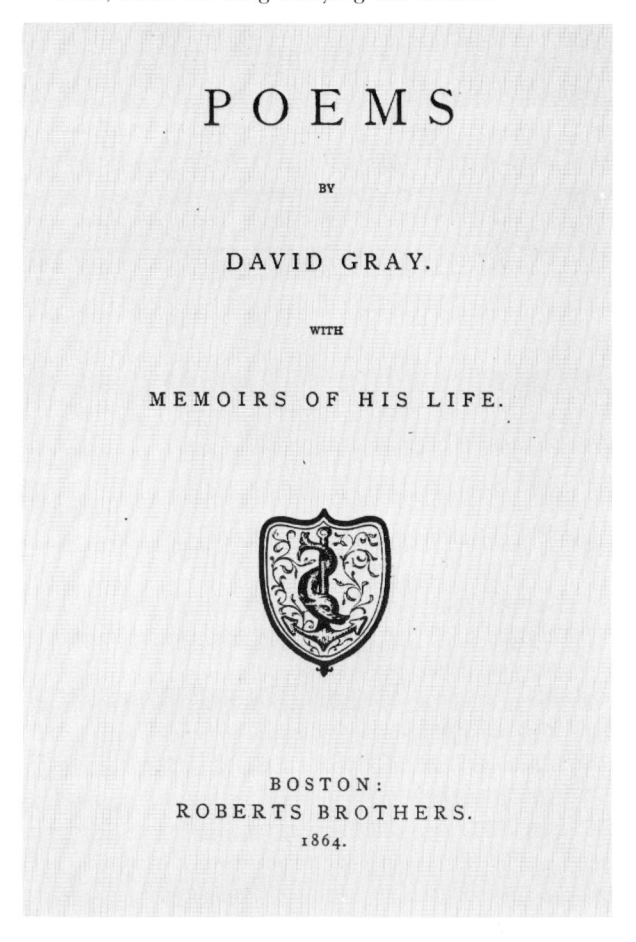

Title page for Gray's posthumously published book of poems

The delicate April green, and, loud and clear,
Through the cool, yellow, mellow twilight glooms,
　The thrush's song enchants the captive ear;
Now, while a shower is pleasant in the falling,
　Stirring the still perfume that wakes around;
Now, that doves mourn, and from the distance
　calling,
　The cuckoo answers, with a sovereign sound,—
Come, with thy native heart, O true and tried!
　But leave all books; for what with converse high,
Flavoured with Attic wit, the time shall glide
　On smoothly, as a river floweth by,
Or as on stately pinion, through the grey
　Evening, the culver cuts his liquid way.

His friends arranged for his work to be published, and Gray saw a proof sheet of *The Luggie and Other Poems* on 2 December 1861, the day before he died. Undoubtedly, as Milnes wrote in the preface, knowledge of Gray's life heightens interest in his work; and few of his readers can have been ignorant of that life, especially as his last work is intensely autobiographical. Several of the sonnets maintain a harmony of image and music that amply justifies Gray's confidence in his talents.

A. C. Swinburne, however, found Gray's assertion of poetic power not to be supported by a reading of his verse, and his gratuitous expression of that opinion in a review of Matthew Arnold's *New Poems* (1867) provided Buchanan, ever Gray's champion, with much of the animus for his subsequent assaults on the Fleshly School of Poetry.

Buchanan's memoir of Gray, republished in 1868, awakened further interest in him and led to the publication of a superior edition of his verse in 1874. Gray has continued to find readers through several excellent anthologies, such as volume six of A. H. Miles's *The Poets and The Poetry of the Century* (1892); scholarly interest in him during the twentieth century, however, has been remarkably scant.

References:
Robert Buchanan, "David Gray," *Cornhill Magazine*, 9 (February 1864): 164-177; republished in his *David Gray, and Other Essays, Chiefly on Poetry* (London: Low, Son & Marston, 1868), pp. 61-174;

"David Gray: Born 1838," *Times Literary Supplement*, 29 January 1938, p. 73;

B. Ifor Evans, *English Poetry in the Later Nineteenth Century* (London: Methuen, 1933), pp. 341-343;

James A. Noble, "David Gray," in *The Poets and The Poetry of the Century*, edited by A. H. Miles, volume 6 (London: Hutchinson, 1892), pp. 355-370;

Alice V. Stuart, "David Gray, 1838-1861: A Study of MS. Material," *Poetry Review*, 54 (1963): 10-16;

Algernon C. Swinburne, "Mr. Arnold's *New Poems*," *Fortnightly Review*, 8 (1867): 414-445.

Thomas Gordon Hake
(10 March 1809-11 January 1895)

John R. Reed
Wayne State University

BOOKS: *Poetic Lucubrations: Containing The Misanthrope and Other Effusions* (London: Lower, Lewes, 1828);

The Piromides: A Tragedy (London: Saunders & Otley, 1839);

A Treatise on Varicose Capillaries (London: Taylor & Walton, 1839);

Vates; or, The Philosophy of Madness: Being an Account of the Life, Actions, Passions and Principles of a Tragic Writer..., 4 parts (London: Southgate, 1840);

The World's Epitaph: A Poem (London: Privately printed, 1866);

On Vital Force: Its Pulmonic Origin, and the General Laws of Its Metamorphosis (London: Renshaw, 1867);

Madeline, with Other Poems and Parables (London: Chapman & Hall, 1871);

Parables and Tales (London: Chapman & Hall, 1872);

New Symbols (London: Chatto & Windus, 1876);

Thomas Gordon Hake

Legends of the Morrow (London: Chatto & Windus, 1879);

Maiden Ecstasy (London: Chatto & Windus, 1880);

The Serpent Play: A Divine Pastoral, in 5 Acts and in Verse (London: Chatto & Windus, 1883);

On the Powers of the Alphabet, I (London: Kegan Paul, Trench, 1883);

The New Day: Sonnets, edited by W. G. Hodgson (London: Remington, 1890);

Memoirs of Eighty Years (London: Bentley, 1892).

PERIODICAL PUBLICATIONS: "Valdarno; or, The Ordeal of Art-Worship," 10 installments, *Ainsworth's,* 17-18 (January-October 1850);

"St. Veronica, or the Ordeal of Fire—A Biography," 11 installments, *Ainsworth's,* 18-20 (November 1850-October 1851);

"Velthinas; or the Ordeal of Sacrifice—a Biography," 12 installments, *Ainsworth's,* 20-23 (November 1851-January 1853);

"Her Winning Ways," 20 installments, *New Monthly,* 143-147 (1868-1870).

Thomas Gordon Hake is remembered more for his associations with other writers than for his own creative work, though his poetry was admired by W. M. and Dante Gabriel Rossetti and other contemporary writers. He became a valued friend of the Rossettis, Theodore Watts-Dunton, and George Borrow.

Hake was born at Leeds on 10 March 1809. His father died when Hake was three. At the age of seven he was admitted to Christ's Hospital in London, a school for poor children. He studied medicine in London, Edinburgh, and Glasgow and graduated from the University of Glasgow in 1831. While engaged in these studies, Hake developed an interest in poetry; a collection of his poems entitled *Poetic Lucubrations: Containing The Misanthrope and Other Effusions* was published in 1828. The volume achieved no notice, and no more of Hake's poetry was published for some time.

During 1831-1832, Hake traveled on the Continent to improve his knowledge of foreign languages and to visit the medical schools of Florence and Paris. Upon his return to England he settled in Brighton to practice as a physician. Five years later he visited Paris, mainly to study anatomy. For a short time after returning to England he took up residence in London, but moved to Bury St. Edmunds in 1839 and became a physician at the County Hospital of Suffolk. Hake became acquainted with the novelist and translator George Borrow at Bury St. Edmunds, and they remained friends thereafter. During this time, Hake did not neglect his creative talent. *The Piromides,* a tragedy based on the mysteries of the Egyptian goddess Isis and her priesthood, was published in 1839. Part of a romance entitled *Vates; or, The Philosophy of Madness* appeared in 1840; the entire work was serialized in ten installments in *Ainsworth's* magazine as "Valdarno; or, The Ordeal of Art-Worship" from January to October 1850. The story recounts the hectic adventures of a tragedian who gives himself up to sinful and criminal experiences as a means of supplying himself with subjects for his art. Two other narratives followed in the same magazine, constituting a loose trilogy. After a visit to Canada and the United States, Hake became a physician at the West London Hospital, a position he held for five years. Hake was professionally active in medicine, writing many scientific articles for medical journals as well as monographs such as *A Treatise on Varicose Capillaries* (1839) and *On Vital Force* (1867).

Hake was inspired to resume the writing of poetry by the lovely woods he enjoyed on visits to

Three of Hake's closest friends: Dante Gabriel Rossetti, George Borrow, and Theodore Watts-Dunton (Watts-Dunton photo by Elliott & Fry)

the estate of his friend and patient Lady Ripon. In 1866 *The World's Epitaph* was published, and attracted the attention of Dante Gabriel Rossetti. Rossetti especially admired the poem "Old Souls," which, through its story of Christ's assuming the role of a lowly tinker to travel through the world mending souls like old pots and pans, criticizes religious sects as well as the fashionable churchgoers who, according to Hake, had put the idea of the poem into his mind. Rossetti and Hake met in 1869.

In 1868, Hake contributed a novel of character called "Her Winning Ways" to the *New Monthly* magazine, a small literary journal; thereafter he dedicated himself to poetry. Encouraged by Rossetti, he brought out *Madeline, with Other Poems and Parables* (1871), which reproduced much of *The World's Epitaph,* adding the long and difficult title poem in which Hake conducts his character through sleep, dreams, sleepwalking, sleep-talking, and the mesmeric state, all of which were subjects of his professional medical interest. Rossetti favorably reviewed this collection as well as *Parables and Tales,* which appeared the next year.

About this time, Hake settled in St. John's Wood in London to devote himself to his poetry,

Cover, designed by Dante Gabriel Rossetti, for Hake's 1872 collection

which improved steadily. He spent a good part of his time traveling in Italy and Germany. In June 1872 Hake took Rossetti, who was suffering from depression and the effects of drugs, into his home. Hake's son George acted as Rossetti's companion and secretary for some time afterward. (In his memoirs, Hake never mentions his marriage or his wife, and scarcely ever refers to his children. He seems to have had at least four sons and two daughters.)

A new collection of his poems was published every few years for the next decade; among these, *New Symbols* (1876) and *Maiden Ecstasy* (1880) are considered his best. In 1890 *The New Day,* a collection of sonnets, some of them inspired by his friendships with Rossetti and Borrow, was published. Hake was by now an old man, yet his creative powers did not flag. In fact, much of his finest poetry was written in his later years. An example is the opening of "The Birth of Venus" from *New Symbols*:

The waters of the warm, surf-laden sea,
   Couched 'neath a heaven of love that o'er them
     bends,
Lie trance-bound in a dream of ecstasy,
   Prophetic of a rapture that impends.

Now they swell up as if love's underflow
   Lifted their bosom, the sun's shredded fires,
Glinting each tremor now, with pulses low
   They lapse into a deluge of desires.

An abiding theme of Hake's poetry is the spiritual quest that must discover its purpose through a proper understanding of nature. Though always interested in the mysteries of nature, as he matured Hake became more mystical in his treatment of man's relationship to the natural world. His subjects ranged from Wordsworthian pastorals to the horrors of slum life. Many of his poems are psychological portraits dealing with historical, legendary, and fictional characters. Hake favored narrative poetry but strove for a lyrical or musical quality in all of his verse. For Rossetti, Hake's poems manifested a combination of homeliness and formality. In a different vein, Arthur Symons called Hake's "a new kind of poetry, in which science becomes an instrument in the creation of a new, curious kind of beauty, the poetry, one might almost say, of pathology."

In 1892 Hake's *Memoirs of Eighty Years* was published. The book concludes with the assertion that all is for the best in this world, where evil can ultimately do nothing but generate more good. For the last four years of his life, he was confined to his couch after fracturing his hip. He died on 11 January 1895.

Although Hake was associated with the Pre-Raphaelites, his poetry is considerably different from theirs, though it shares their strong interest in nature. His poetry belongs to no school, but exhibits what his friend Theodore Watts-Dunton described as "the renascence of wonder" in English poetry. Though his poetry reveals a keen sensibility and moral intelligence, it is not memorable enough to secure Hake a firm place in the history of English poetry.

References:

Thomas Bayne, "Thomas Gordon Hake," in *The Poets and the Poetry of the Century: Frederick Tennyson to Arthur Hugh Clough,* edited by Alfred H. Miles, volume 4 (London: Hutchinson, 1892), pp. 153-160;

Lionel Stevenson, *The Pre-Raphaelite Poets* (Chapel Hill: University of North Carolina Press, 1972), pp. 283-286;

Arthur Symons, *Studies in Two Literatures* (London: Smithers, 1897), pp. 40-43;

Theodore Watts-Dunton, *Old Familiar Faces* (New York: Dutton, 1916), pp. 207-218.

Arthur Henry Hallam
(1 February 1811-15 September 1833)

Jack Kolb
University of California, Los Angeles

BOOKS: *Timbuctoo* (Cambridge: Privately printed, 1829);

Poems by A. H. Hallam Esq. (London: Privately printed, 1830);

Essay on the Philosophical Writings of Cicero (Cambridge: W. Metcalf, 1832);

Oration, on the Influence of Italian Works of the Imagination on the Same Class of Compositions in England (Cambridge: Metcalf, 1832);

Remarks on Professor Rossetti's "Disquisizioni Sullo Spirito Antipapale" (London: Moxon, 1832);

Remains, in Verse and Prose, of Arthur Henry Hallam, edited by Henry Hallam (London: Privately printed, 1834);

The Writings of Arthur Henry Hallam, edited by T. H. Vail Motter (New York: Modern Language Association, 1943; London: Oxford University Press, 1943).

OTHER: "Some Unpublished Poems by Arthur Henry Hallam," edited by Sir Charles Tennyson and F. T. Baker, *Victorian Poetry,* 3, supplement (1965).

PERIODICAL PUBLICATION: "On Some of the Characteristics of Modern Poetry, and on the Lyrical Poems of Alfred Tennyson," *Englishman's Magazine* (August 1831): 616-628.

Arthur Henry Hallam is remembered chiefly as the youthful friend of Alfred Tennyson, whose companionship with Hallam is celebrated in the laureate's elegy *In Memoriam* (1850). But during his brief life, Hallam numbered among his other friends such Victorian luminaries as William Ewart Gladstone, Richard Monckton Milnes, Fanny Kemble, and Richard Chenevix Trench, all of whom testified to his considerable promise and enormous personal appeal. A recent commentator has argued that following the departure of Frederick Denison Maurice, Hallam became the ruling spirit of the Cambridge Apostles Society, and thus exerted a decisive influence upon an important group of his contemporaries. Moreover, a volume of Hallam's poems and several of his influential essays had been published before his death at twenty-two; his 1831 review of Tennyson's *Poems, Chiefly Lyrical* became a sort of manifesto for some of the English aesthetes. Yeats, for example, by his own admission, sought to embody Hallam's precepts in his early writings.

Hallam was the eldest child of Henry Hallam and Julia Maria Elton Hallam; his mother was a scion of the Eltons of Clevedon Court. His early life, at least, was dominated by his strong-willed but apparently adoring father, one of the eminent circle of Whig politicians, journalists, and philosophers associated with the *Edinburgh Review*. With the publi-

Arthur Henry Hallam (by permission of Macmillan and Co., Ltd.)

cation in 1827 of his *Constitutional History of England from the Accession of Henry VII to the Death of George II,* Henry Hallam was acknowledged to be the preeminent Whig historian of the age. It is no surprise, then, that Arthur's first interest at Eton, his father's school, should have been politics. Accounts of the Eton Debating Society, to which he was elected in November 1825, constitute the chief topic of his letters from the time he entered the school in 1822 to his graduation in 1827. Moreover, Hallam's participation in the society—and in private debates and impassioned correspondence on such contemporary issues as Catholic emancipation, Parliamentary reform, and George Canning's brief ministry—formed the basis of lifelong friendships with Francis Hastings Doyle, James Milnes Gaskell, and Gladstone.

At this stage of his life, however, Hallam's literary interests vied with his political pursuits. In his Eton Society speech on Milton's political conduct, he invoked passages from *Paradise Lost;* in another speech, he defended Shakespeare's dramas against the criticism of violating classical rules; and his oration on the superior literary achievements of the age of Leo X over that of Augustus won the votes of all but the most confirmed classicists in the society. Known as "the best poet in Eton," Hallam was one of the originators of the short-lived *Eton Miscellany,* though he contributed little to the journal. Even his father, who clearly envisioned a different career for his son, later admitted that these youthful efforts offered unmistakable evidence that Hallam "was a poet by nature."

The restless, cosmopolitan, and wealthy Henry Hallam conducted his family upon European tours in 1818 and 1822, but it was the Hallams' 1827-1828 winter in Italy that affected Arthur most strongly. Coming after concentrated study at Eton and at the beginning of his adolescence, it led, perhaps inevitably, to an outburst of romantic sentiment. Like so many other Englishmen before and after him, Arthur Hallam was entranced by the landscape and art of Italy: he cherished their beauty throughout his life. Far more important, however, was his first love. An attractive and flirtatious Englishwoman, also residing in Rome, became for him "La bella Stagione" (the season's beauty), the embodiment of his Italian ideal. Anna Wintour was nearly eight years older than Hallam and had a wide circle of admirers. His friend Gaskell's infatuation with Anna preceded, and possibly provoked, Hallam's adoration, which reached full intensity only after he had left Rome and parted from her forever. But the effects were wide-ranging. Gaskell's and Hallam's joint admiration of Anna cemented a lifelong friendship between the two men; Hallam would later rank it second only to that with Tennyson. A year before his death, Hallam recalled in a letter to Gaskell the "inexpressible charm . . . in the recollection of our Italian dreams." Hallam's eleven surviving poems to or about Anna celebrate Italy and Italian literature as much as they celebrate his first love. His particular esteem for Dante—at his death, Hallam had translated twenty-five sonnets from the *Vita Nuova*—seems to have had its origin in his casting of Anna as his personal Beatrice. His parting gift to her was an edition of Dante's works.

Hallam's return to England in 1828 would have been an emotional letdown under any circumstances; it was made traumatic by his father's determination that he attend Trinity College, Cambridge. Though Arthur had achieved a sufficient mastery of the classics to be put into the sixth form before leaving Eton, Henry Hallam felt that he had not been "formed to obtain great academical reputation." Henry also believed that his own college, Christ Church, Oxford, offered inferior training in the exact sciences to that provided at its Cambridge rival, and doubtless hoped that the discipline of mathematics and physical science might improve his son's overall study habits. But for Arthur, Trinity proved a double bane. The separation from Doyle, Gaskell, and Gladstone, all of whom went to Oxford, led to a sense of disruption and alienation that persisted throughout his life. "It is my destiny, it would seem, in this world to form no friendship," he wrote Gladstone, "which when I begin to appreciate it, & hold it dear, is not torn from me by the iron hand of circumstance." Nor did Trinity at first seem to hold compensatory attractions. Hallam's inability, after intense preparation, to achieve any distinction in the 1829 scholarship competition only confirmed for him the futility of studying mathematics. (He barely passed that section of his B.A. exam three years later.) The Cambridge Debating Union, a potential forum for Hallam's considerable rhetorical skills, was dominated by a group of utilitarian political radicals, whose predominant literary interest—seemingly antithetical to Hallam's Etonian sensibilities—was modern poetry, with Shelley as their current hero. The isolation and depression that Hallam felt during his early months at Cambridge may have contributed to his first serious illness in April 1829, a "disorder in the head" that necessitated returning to London more than a month before the end of the term in July.

Yet even during this period, Hallam had begun to respond to some of the intellectual currents at Cambridge and to the stimulus of his new acquaintances. As early as December 1828 he had admitted that his tastes in poetry—his primary source of comfort and solace—were not so different from those of the people he had met at the university. Soon thereafter, he had rejected his father's attack on Coleridge's philosophy and defended Wordsworth's poetry against Henry's charge of "misty metaphysics." By May 1829, an admittedly conservative acquaintance from his Eton days had described Hallam as "a furious Shelleyist"; in the same month, he was elected to the Cambridge Apostles Society. Before returning to London, he had even begun to speak in the Cambridge Union, siding on some subjects with the radicals.

Hallam's friendship with Richard Monckton Milnes developed during this year of transition, and it is easy to believe that Milnes, an experienced speaker in the union and a supporter of many of the Apostles' leading causes, encouraged Hallam's interest in metaphysics and contemporary poetry. Like Gladstone, Milnes stood in youthful awe of his friend, calling him "reserved" and "deep" after their first meeting. Like many of his colleagues, Hallam responded eagerly to the wit, humor, and easygoing nature of Gaskell's cousin. But Milnes's lighthearted, ebullient, playful sensibility offered little comfort to Hallam during a painful period of self-reflection on a trip to Scotland in the summer of 1829. The intensity of Hallam's feelings—which had their origins in his spring illness, his general unhappiness at Cambridge, and his toyings with metaphysics—emerges clearly in his letters to Milnes. "I really am afraid of insanity," he wrote in August. "My own thoughts are more than a match for me; my brain has been fevering with speculations most fathomless, abysmal, ever since I set foot in Scotland." Like those of Thomas Carlyle (in *Sartor Resartus*) and John Stuart Mill, this "spiritual crisis" produced no dramatic change in character or philosophical orientation: Hallam eventually reaffirmed his commitment to poetry and metaphysics within a broadly Christian orientation. The principal facet of this commitment—a resignation to God's will and a trust that his own life fulfilled some larger destiny—was a constant theme in his letters and poetry of the time. More important was its influence on Tennyson, who later alluded to his mentor's successful resolution in section 96 of *In Memoriam:*

> one indeed I knew
> In many a subtle question versed,
> Who touched a jarring lyre at first,
> But ever strove to make it true:
>
> Perplext in faith, but pure in deeds,
> At last he beat his music out.
> There lives more faith in honest doubt,
> Believe me, than in half the creeds.

Though Hallam seems to have been slightly acquainted at Eton with Tennyson's brother Frederick, he undoubtedly met his greatest friend and elegist during their competition for the Cambridge Chancellor's English Verse Prize early in the spring of 1829. Appropriately, each friend belittled his own effort and proclaimed the superiority of his rival's contribution; most critics agree that their poems, on the recherché subject of Timbuctoo, are equal in merit. But Hallam's immediate attraction to Tennyson and his poetry was tempered. In July 1829, Hallam complained that Tennyson had not written to him; this would be an irritating constant throughout their friendship. Moreover, though Hallam described the Cambridge medal winner as "promising fair to be the greatest poet of our generation, perhaps of our century," he argued that Tennyson's "Timbuctoo" was hardly "a specimen of his best manner." Indeed, though Hallam would devote much of the remainder of his life to his friend's work—chiding Tennyson to set pen to paper, coaxing manuscripts from him, pressing for revisions and publication, acting as his literary agent, seeking out favorable reviewers, and writing reviews—he never ceased to maintain a critical objectivity, not merely toward Tennyson's work but also toward the poet's frequent lethargy and melancholy.

That Tennyson valued his friend's personal support and advice is made abundantly clear in *In Memoriam*. That he seldom—during Hallam's lifetime—heeded his friend's literary admonitions is a testimony to the stable independence which cemented their relationship. For Hallam's character seems to have encouraged closer and more dependent friendships than he desired or felt he could handle. With Milnes and Gladstone, Hallam was forced to state, clearly though gently, the exact limits of their intimacy. There was no such problem between Hallam and Tennyson: despite the contrasting backgrounds of the London cosmopolitan and the Lincolnshire recluse, they shared significant characteristics. Both had an essentially elegiac, sometimes melancholy temperament, yearning for things past and times lost. But both also felt that "life must be fought out to the end" (this was how Tennyson described the "message" of "Ulysses," which was written a few weeks after he learned of Hallam's death), and each ultimately proved equal to the struggle.

During the 1829 Christmas break, Hallam brought Tennyson and Tennyson's brother Charles to London and introduced them to some of his Etonian friends. "Alfred Tennyson I like," Doyle wrote to Gladstone, "but to use their own cant or Kant (either will do as the man said of the flea) he is a strange form of Being." This was the time of Fanny Kemble's spectacular success on the London stage, and Hallam readily succumbed to the general contagious enthusiasm, dashing off two sonnets after seeing her performance in *Venice Preserved*. His admiration for the "divine Fanny" did not wane during the next few years: he praised her playwriting as well as her acting. (Indeed, his friendship with her brother John Mitchell Kemble, his Cambridge colleague, seems to have developed after their graduation from college, largely as a result of frequent visits to the Kembles' London household.) Fanny's unflinching and intelligent praise of Tennyson's poetry endeared her to Hallam. But whatever romantic involvement might have developed between them was soon preempted.

By the end of the first Cambridge term of 1830, Tennyson felt secure enough of Hallam's friendship to invite him to Somersby to visit his rather eccentric Lincolnshire family. The friends stayed for the full three weeks of the vacation, returning to Cambridge barely in time for the beginning of classes. Hallam's enthusiasm for the lively Somersby household was unbounded. "If I die," he wrote to a close Cambridge friend, "I hope to be buried here: for never in my life, I think, have I loved a place more. I feel a new element of being within me.... I have floated along a delicious dream of music and poetry and riding and dancing and greenwood-dinners and ladies' conversation till I have been simply exhaled into Paradise." Only in the privacy of his poetry, however, did Hallam reveal the specific source of his joy:

> Lo, in my life a semblance of new morn!
>   A mighty dream has caught me in the sweep
>   Of its regardless course, and I am borne
>   Far, far into the realm where Agonies keep
> Their state terrific round Joy's lightning throne.
>   Oh Emily, my life, my love, my rest,
>   Thy look is on me, and my soul is blest.
>   Oh Emily, I have been all alone—
> How strange it seems but a few weeks agone
>   I knew no glance of thine, and thought of thee
>   Dim in the distance with no hope or fear,
> Now I have seen and may not chuse but see:
>   For ever in my eyes, for ever here
>   In the aching heart thou dwellest, Emily.

Emily Tennyson was only slightly younger than her admirer, was considered a beauty even in a family of striking good looks, and was, of course, Alfred's sister. For Hallam, it was a match made in heaven, and, as he later admitted to Emily, any residual feelings he might have had for Anna Wintour were banished. It was apparently during this three-week period that Alfred first met his future wife, also named Emily. Whether he imitated his friend in falling in love is unknown, but their simultaneous attractions to others seem to have deepened their own attraction to each other.

Hallam's meeting with, and response to, Emily probably helped to overcome the disappointment he must have felt in May, when his father, troubled by the sentiments—and perhaps the Wordsworthian, "metaphysical" style—of his son's poems, vetoed the plan for Tennyson and Hallam to have their poems published together. Hallam's volume,

Emily Tennyson, Hallam's one-time fiancée, in later life. Ten years after Hallam's death she married Capt. Richard Jesse (The Tennyson Research Centre, Lincoln, by permission of Lord Tennyson and the Lincolnshire Library Service).

privately printed, was circulated among a generally admiring group of his Eton and Cambridge friends toward the end of the month; Tennyson's *Poems, Chiefly Lyrical* was published in June.

Since the fall of 1829, Hallam had participated in a number of Cambridge activities: Cambridge Union debates on Wordsworth vs. Byron and on the merits of oratory; a collegiate production of *Much Ado About Nothing* (Hallam played Verges); a trip with Milnes and Thomas Sunderland, a fellow Apostle, to the Oxford Debating Society to defend the poetry of Shelley against the claims of Byron, which were successfully supported by Henry (later Cardinal) Manning and others. Hallam had served twice as essayist in the Apostles' meetings, arguing that the existence of a first cause was not deducible from natural phenomena and that repose was a necessary condition of art. His most ambitious venture, however, was neither academic nor polemic: a journey to the south of France with Tennyson in the summer of 1830 to help support the Spanish Constitutionalist rebels. This abortive undertaking, with elements of both farce and tragedy, marked the limits of Apostolic radicalism; like the majority of their comrades, Hallam and Tennyson returned with a healthy skepticism about revolutionary causes and most revolutionaries. "There is no hope for Spain," Hallam wrote to a Cambridge friend, "the nation being . . . 'willingly and exultingly enslaved.'" Yet as Robert Martin has suggested in his biography of Tennyson, this trip to the Pyrenees had lasting significance for both Hallam and Tennyson: their shared experiences intensified their friendship and provided for Tennyson a continuing source of poetic inspiration, from "Oenone" to the elegiac recollection "In the Valley of Cauteretz."

Hallam and Tennyson had not told their fathers the full details about the trip before they departed, and both parents were less than pleased with their sons' waste of time and money on what Henry Hallam called an "unadvised and unauthorised expedition." Arthur's apparent irresponsibility in the company of Alfred could hardly have given his father a favorable first impression of the Tennyson family. As a result, Hallam agreed to remain in the bosom of his own family during the next two years and apply himself more diligently to schoolwork. He managed to regain at least some of his father's favor in December 1830 by winning the Trinity College declamation prize with a speech defending the conduct of the Independent party during the English Civil War. Not only was the declamation grounded in historical fact, it tactfully drew upon Henry Hallam's *Constitutional History* for both its general position and detailed evidence. On the strength of this triumph, Arthur left for a few days at Somersby, using the excuse that the Tennyson family would soon be forced to leave their Lincolnshire dwelling. His real purpose was to see Emily, and during this visit he declared his love and proposed to her. At this time, he had spent less than four weeks with his fiancée.

During the last three years of his life, Hallam was absorbed with two chief concerns: his engagement to Emily, and her brother's poetry. Though Tennyson's *Poems, Chiefly Lyrical* had been reviewed in the *Westminster Review* and received a few brief local newspaper notices by the beginning of 1831, Hallam was not content. In January he wrote to Leigh Hunt, then editor of the *Tatler,* sending him both Alfred's and Charles Tennyson's volumes and strongly urging Hunt, in appropriately hyperbolical language, to consider the brothers the poetic heirs of Keats. The result was Hunt's laudatory, though somewhat eccentric, discussion in four separate numbers of his paper, which, like

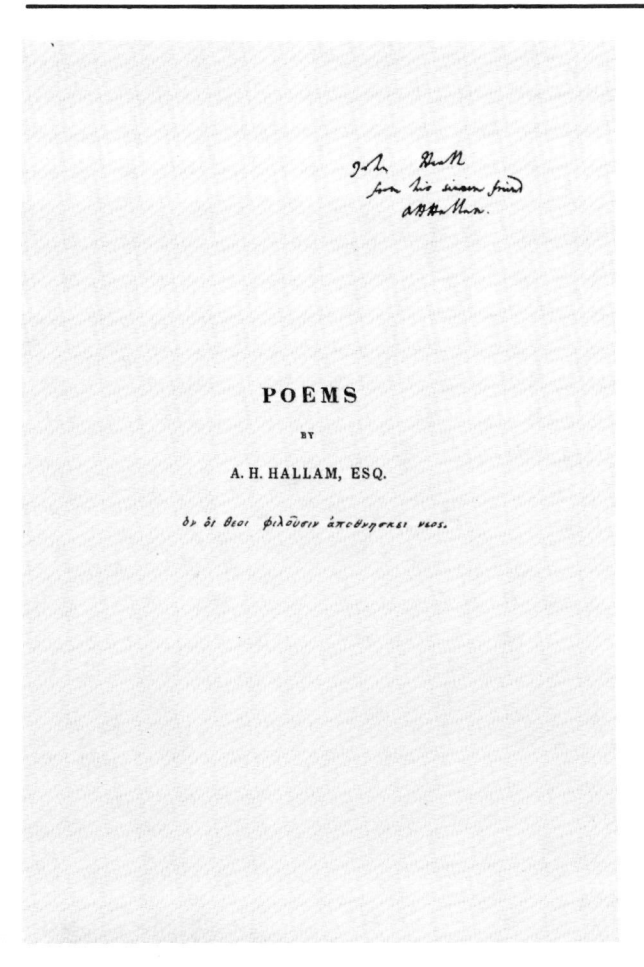

Title page for Hallam's privately published volume of poems, with an inscription by Hallam to his friend John Heath. The Greek characters, probably written by Heath after Hallam's death, say: "Those whom the Gods love die young" (Anderson Galleries, 22 April 1937).

the *Westminster Review,* professed liberal—even radical—politics. Later that summer Hallam learned from Milnes that Edward Moxon, the new editor of another liberal journal, the *Englishman's Magazine,* was soliciting contributions; he immediately sent Moxon a sonnet by Tennyson and suggested that Tennyson could be a regular contributor—all without notifying the poet himself—and offered an article on Tennyson's poetry. Moxon printed not only Tennyson's sonnet and Hallam's review but also a short poem by Hallam on Emily Tennyson. This marked the beginning of Moxon's lifelong position as Tennyson's publisher.

Hallam's review, though written in two weeks in what he described as a "Magazine humour," was a substantial piece of theoretical criticism. Hallam looked back to Tennyson's predecessors, the Romantics, and distinguished between the earlier—Wordsworth and Coleridge—whom he labeled "poets of reflection," and the later—Keats and Shelley—whom he called "poets of sensation." In acknowledging Tennyson's debt to the latter pair, Hallam established an aesthetic tradition which would run through the early pre-Raphaelites and the decadents to Yeats: "Other poets *seek* for images to illustrate their conceptions; these men had no need to seek; they lived in a world of images; for the most important and extensive portion of their life consisted in those emotions, which are immediately conversant with sensation. . . . Hence they are not descriptive; they are picturesque." Hallam also delineated some of the key attributes of Tennyson's poetic achievement: "his luxuriance of imagination, and at the same time his control over it . . . his power of embodying himself in ideal characters, or rather moods of character, with such extreme accuracy of adjustment, that the circumstances of the narration seem to have a natural correspondence with the predominant feeling, and, as it were, to be evolved from it by assimilative force . . . his vivid, picturesque delineation of objects . . . the variety of his lyrical measures, and exquisite modulation of harmonious words and cadences to the swell and fall of the feelings expressed . . . the elevated habits of thought . . . imparting a mellow soberness of tone." The review, however, though praised by members of the Apostles and pleasing to the poet himself, attracted little attention outside their circle; John Wilson, in his 1832 *Blackwood's* magazine review of Tennyson, only half-humorously accused Hallam's article of killing the short-lived *Englishman's Magazine.* Yet even an unfavorable notice in *Blackwood's* served its purpose, and after some castigation of Tennyson's faults and eccentricities, Wilson went on to praise several of his poems considerably. As Hallam himself acknowledged, "He means well, I take it, and as he has extracted nearly your whole book, and has in his soberer mood spoken in terms as high as I could have used myself of some of your best poems, I think the Review will assist rather than hinder the march of your reputation."

Shortly before he undertook his review, Hallam had finished an essay on the philosophical writings of Cicero, which won the Trinity College essay competition in 1831. That December, as one of his last acts before leaving Cambridge, he delivered his "prize" declamation—required of those who had won the previous year's competition—in the Trinity chapel. For his topic, he returned to the land and culture of his first romance, discussing the influence of Italian literature upon English in the medieval and Renaissance periods. Both of these works show his substantial growth and development as a literary and cultural critic. In the essay, Hallam takes a balanced view of Cicero, citing defects as well as virtues, and concluding, much as Matthew Arnold would later argue, that if the nineteenth century failed to appreciate the writings of this ancient, it was the fault of the age rather than of the man. Still his father's son, Hallam traces in the latter work the historical origins of Romance (not merely Italian) literature, showing how it developed out of a combination of social and religious influences. The declamation is notable for its tolerant view of the impact of foreign cultures, including Islam, upon the western world. Though Henry Hallam, determined that Arthur undertake a legal career, insisted that he enroll at the Inner Temple after his graduation, he admitted to a friend that he was "not perhaps quite misled as a father in thinking [Arthur's] performances a little out of the common." Arthur, who felt the declamation represented less than his best effort, nevertheless believed that "if I mistake not, I can write better things than that Essay."

His father was less pleased about Arthur's other chief pursuit. Early in 1831, Alfred and Charles Tennyson had been summoned home from Trinity: their father, long beset by physical and emotional demons, was dying. Hallam, realizing that this crisis would disrupt the Lincolnshire family and could threaten his engagement to Emily, was probably forced to reveal his involvement to his parents sooner than he wished. He may in fact have been arguing with them on 16 March, the day of George Tennyson's death. Henry Hallam was strongly opposed to what he believed was his son's latest infatuation, and may earlier have received Emily's father's consent to try to break the engagement. Arthur, however, remained adamant and

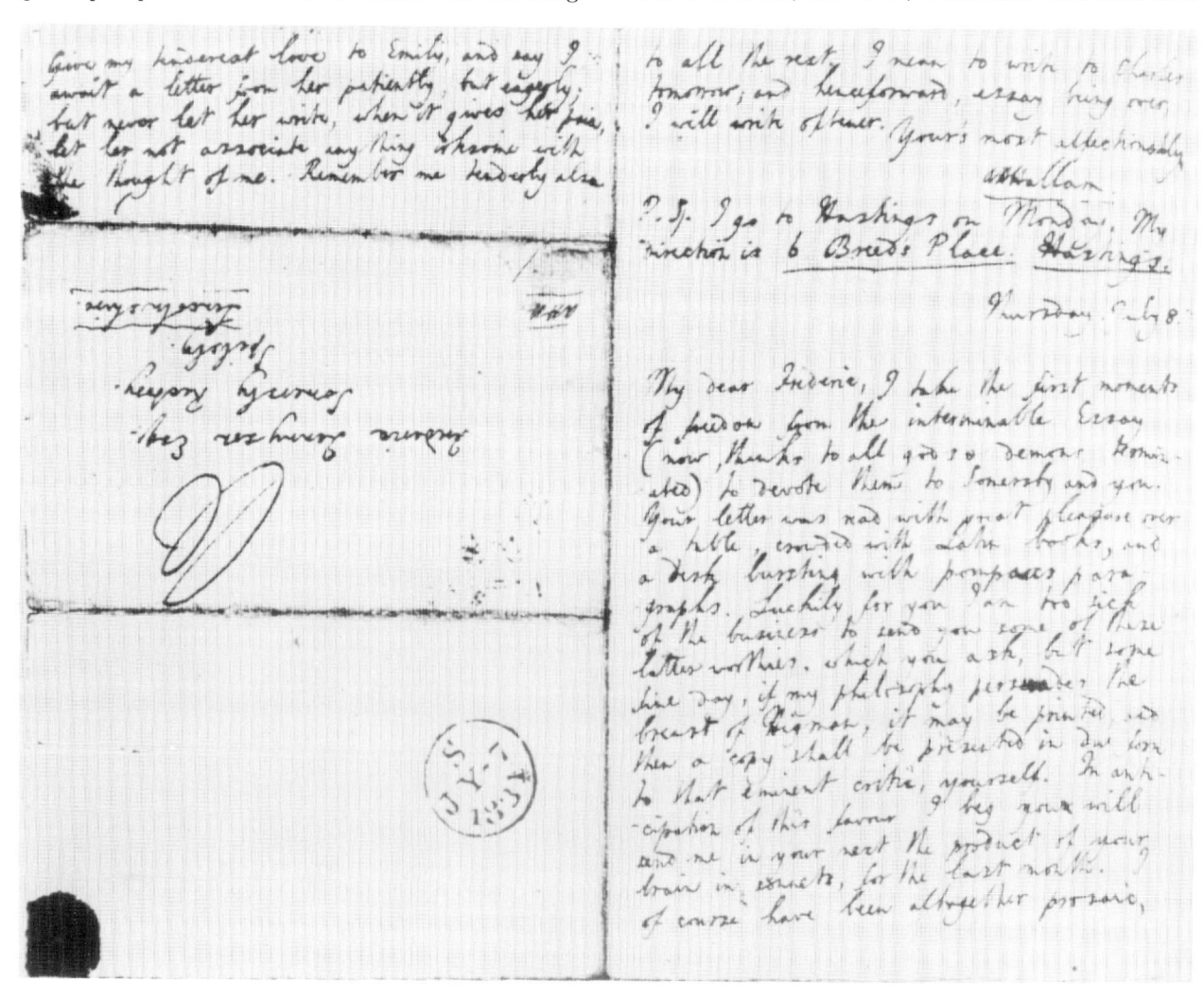

A letter from Hallam to Alfred Tennyson's brother Frederick

would only agree not to see his fiancée again until after his twenty-first birthday on 1 February 1832. Henry intended that the two should not even correspond, but Arthur, deliberately or accidentally, misconstrued his father's words, and during the rest of that year he wrote to Emily and she to him on the average of once a week. Hallam's letters provide the best, although admittedly an indirect, portrait of the Tennyson family during the crucial period between George Tennyson's death in 1831 and Hallam's own death two years later.

There is no question that Hallam deliberately disobeyed his father in arranging to meet surreptitiously with Emily and Alfred at Cheltenham in September 1831—ironically, after traveling for a few weeks with Henry Hallam. Since Tennyson had now left Cambridge permanently, the encounter was all the more delightful—and frustrating. Emily had managed to persuade her family that the trip would be good for her apparently chronic state of ill health, and Alfred too had complained about various ailments since last seeing his friend. Hallam was relieved to find both in reasonably good condition, but the physical and emotional well-being of his fiancée (and, to a lesser degree, of her brother) would become an increasingly troublesome, aggravating concern for him.

After a period of intensive study, during which he yearned to escape to Somersby, Hallam finally received his B.A. on 21 January 1832, and left to join his parents at Tunbridge Wells. A month before, he had resigned from the Apostles and, as was customary, had become an honorary member. His last paper, delivered on 29 October, argued that there was sufficient "ground for believing that the existence of moral evil is absolutely necessary to the fulfillment of God's essential love for Christ." This was later published, at Tennyson's specific request, as "Theodicaea Novissima" in the collection of Hallam's *Remains, in Verse and Prose* (1834); its parallels to, and likely impact on, the philosophical position of *In Memoriam* have been noted by a number of critics.

Hallam's trip to Somersby in the spring of 1832 fulfilled all his expectations. For the first time he could openly declare his love for Emily and announce his engagement. His father had not been pleased to learn how his intentions had been frustrated, and wrongly blamed the Tennyson family for his son's deception. But Henry Hallam acknowledged his son's commitment, and that fall entered into negotiations with Emily's grandfather about a financial settlement. For the moment, however, such issues were forgotten; as Arthur wrote to William Henry Brookfield, "Every shadow of—not doubt, but uneasiness, or what else may be a truer name for the feeling—that Alfred's language [has] sometimes cast over my hope is destroyed in the full blaze of conscious delight with which I perceive that she loves me." Hallam also was pleased to find Tennyson "fully wound up to publication," and in better physical and mental health than he had been led to believe. In truth, Hallam was becoming aware of the chronic state of melancholy, the "black blood," which seemed to affect all the Tennysons and which led them to exaggerate their complaints.

Upon returning to his family's home in London, Hallam threw himself into his legal work with renewed determination and hope for the future, though pained by his separation from his fiancée. Letters became more important than ever, and he eagerly awaited the arrival of the post every week. Fearful when Emily did not write, when she did he chided her gently for not filling up every bit of space on the folded sheet. His irritation at her brother's silence was partly mollified when Alfred arrived in town in June, intending to travel abroad. Hallam played literary agent—introducing him to Moxon, who offered to publish his next volume of poems—and took him to see Fanny Kemble perform. Tennyson, displeased with the prospect of traveling alone, at the last moment persuaded his friend to accompany him to the Continent. Hallam, having finished his term at the Inner Temple, managed to get his father's permission for a short trip. The companions departed at the end of June for Holland. Much to their disgust, they were quarantined off the coast, seemingly condemned to a "double-damned Dutch dreary dull desolate ditch-death." After arriving a week behind schedule in Rotterdam, they quickly moved on to Cologne, "the paradise of painted glass." Both were overwhelmed by the Gothic cathedral and the art; Hallam, Italophile though he was, preferred the old German pictures to Tennyson's favorites, Titian and Raphael. After a trip down the Rhine to Nonnenwerth and Bingen, they returned to England by way of France and Belgium. Unlike their journey to southern France, this trip was hectic, but it renewed and strengthened the ties of friendship between them.

Upon his return, Hallam went directly to Somersby for about a week without telling his parents, for he knew that they would insist that he stay with them throughout the fall. This further deception unfortunately came as the two families were entering into negotiations about the marriage, and can only have increased Henry Hallam's suspicions about the motives of the Tennysons. Were they merely a family of opportunists seizing upon Arthur's infatuation with Emily in order to gain a rich settlement? Nevertheless, Henry's offer to settle £600 per annum on his son was generous, and since Emily's grandfather was known to be wealthy, Henry apparently resigned himself to the marriage. But Emily's grandfather was never on good terms with the Somersby branch of the family, and he made what Henry considered an inadequate offer of settlement from an affluent Lincolnshire landowner. In vain throughout the next months Arthur solicited Emily's uncle, aunts, cousins, even her brother Frederick (who had an independent income) for additional financial support. His hopes for a quick resolution and wedding turned to despair, and he could only feel a sense of frustration in congratulating Gaskell and Richard Chenevix Trench upon their own marriages that year.

Hallam was apprenticed at a conveyancer's office throughout the fall of 1832, but he found time to continue his journalistic efforts, including a brief review of an Italian translation of Milton and sketches of Voltaire, Petrarch, and Burke for an encyclopedia of famous men. His last major essay—*Remarks on Professor Rossetti's "Disquisizioni Sullo Spirito Antipapale"* (1832)—was a skeptical appraisal of Gabriel Rossetti's rather bizzare theories about the hidden, antipapal meaning of Dante's works. Published as a pamphlet by Moxon, Hallam's work is tolerant rather than severe; Rossetti himself found it fair, and its erudition and common sense were recognized and praised by a number of critics who did not know its author. Though he had long ceded the role of poet to Tennyson, choosing "the humbler station" of critic, Hallam continued to write poetry, successfully placing a sonnet on Stefan Lochner's altarpiece in the Cologne Cathedral in the February 1833 number of *Fraser's* magazine, and promising to submit other poems. None of these efforts brought him much money (he got five pounds apiece for his character portraits), but they served to advance his reputation as a promising young writer.

A more pleasurable task was that of preparing Tennyson's manuscripts for publication. Though as usual the poet needed much prodding—indeed, finally an ultimatum that Hallam would undertake the editing himself if he did not hear from Tennyson—he finally began late in September to send Hallam revisions of such works as "Oenone," "The Palace of Art," "The Lotos-Eaters," and "The Lady of Shalott," which would distinguish the 1832 volume. Hallam showed the manuscripts to a number of his relatives, friends, and acquaintances, with mixed results: Henry Hallam seemed to like Juno's speech in "Oenone," though he did not listen to the whole poem, while the lawyer father of Douglas and John Heath argued vehemently against the description "cloud-white" in "The Lady of Shalott," on the grounds that clouds have the most variable colors in nature. Hallam himself offered a number of minor suggestions and revisions, few of which were accepted; he voiced some doubt about Tennyson's inclusion of the fatuous "O Darling Room" and the rather silly attack on John Wilson's *Blackwood's* review, "To Christopher North." Both poems were savaged by the critics and proved embarrassing to the poet. Hallam implored Tennyson—"By all that is dear to thee—by our friendship—by sun moon & stars—by narwhales and seahorses"—not to withdraw "The Lover's Tale" from the volume. Again—and here perhaps the poet was right—the entreaty went unheeded. But all of Tennyson's friends found reason to rejoice in the December publication of his *Poems*. As usual, Hallam busied himself promoting it, contributing a review (unfortunately never printed and apparently lost) to the *Edinburgh Review*, arranging for Gaskell to buy the book and hoping to convert Gaskell's mother to appreciation, forwarding a copy to Leigh Hunt, belittling a negative notice in the *Literary Gazette*, sending Tennyson an annotated favorable review in the *Monthly Repository*, even suggesting that John Mitchell Kemble use Tennyson as an illustration in his philological writings. After John Wilson Croker's infamous attack on the book in the April 1833 *Quarterly Review*, a review which strongly influenced Tennyson's refusal to have anything published for the next ten years and which certainly did considerable damage to his budding reputation, Hallam tried to reassure the poet: "Your book continues to sell tolerably & Moxon says the Quarterly has done good." Ironically, Tennyson's associations with politically radical publications and reviewers, associations which Hallam unwittingly initiated and fostered, accounted for a portion of Croker's vitriol.

Though Hallam had grown largely indifferent to politics, reluctantly accepting the 1832 Reform Bill with only occasional predictions of turmoil and revolution, he welcomed the chance to renew his acquaintance with Gaskell and Gladstone, both of whom were elected to Parliament in the winter of 1832. An increasing interest in Christianity—which helped sustain him as the frustrations over his engagement grew—drew Hallam closer to Trench, who returned that winter to England from Ireland;

Sketch of Hallam by James Spedding, about the year of Hallam's death (The Tennyson Research Centre, Lincoln, by permission of Lord Tennyson and the Lincolnshire Library Service)

in the spring of 1833 Hallam tried without success to obtain a clerical post for the recently ordained Trench, who would later become archbishop of Dublin. Kept apart from Emily, Hallam turned to other distractions, including a series of mild flirtations with various eligible socialites, flirtations which he did not hesitate to mention in his letters to his fiancée. None posed any serious threat to the engagement, but the delay in his wedding, the resentment against Emily's grandfather and other members of the family for not providing the means of settlement, and his own concern about the effect Emily's health might have upon their future life together, all led to an occasional sharpness in his letters to her, and then to a quarrel, quickly resolved, in the spring of 1833. Hallam's Christmas visit to Somersby in 1832, though clouded by the renewed prospect that the Tennysons would have to move, was an idyllic interlude, during which Arthur and Emily practiced their Italian by writing notes to each other in that language.

Hallam's hopes for marriage received a considerable boost in the spring of 1833. Alfred and his sister Mary (Emily was still too weak to travel) visited London, and Hallam was able to arrange for them to spend time with his parents. The results were encouraging: "Mary is a decided favourite with all of us," he wrote to Emily. "Alfred too has got up in my father's good graces.... I feel as if a great barrier was broken down between my own family & that of my adoption. I have tasted a rich foretaste of future union." A report of the imminent death of Emily's eighty-three-year-old grandfather inspired even greater hope, but the report proved premature. (He was to outlive Hallam by two years.) Inevitably, perhaps, such excitement preceded an emotional letdown. Following at least two of his departures from Somersby, Hallam had noted that the "horror of sudden loneliness" took a physical form: headaches, blood rushing to his temples, shortness of breath. Now, whether as cause or effect, Hallam's depression in bidding farewell to Alfred and Mary led quickly to a serious attack of influenza, or "ague," accompanied by severe fever. This debilitating illness lasted nearly a month and infected the entire Hallam family. Arthur was not spared the debut of his socially conscious cousin, Caroline Elton, and by June he was eager to escape London. As it happened, Henry Hallam had proposed another European trip—to Switzerland, Austria, and Hungary—and Arthur readily agreed. His father might not be the ideal traveling companion, but their time together would allow Arthur to advance the cause of his engagement. He spent the last week of June at Cambridge with Tennyson and Kemble; then he spent three weeks at Somersby, for the first time without Alfred, who had gone on to Scotland. Shortly before leaving for France on 3 August, Hallam wrote to Tennyson, and the two may have met in London for a last dinner together.

Europe quickly evoked memories of the past and hopes for the future. On the road to Ath, the Hallams were driven by the same coachman who had taken Arthur and Tennyson on their way to meet the Spanish rebels in 1830; three years later, the coachman assured him, Arthur was in decidedly better health. Although Arthur's spirits rose as he ascended into his old favorites, the Alps, his thoughts were upon more recent objects of affection as they descended into Salzburg, "a jewel of a place," to which he hoped some day to return with Emily. Perhaps they might even settle there, where his £600 per annum would allow them to live in comfort, if not luxury. Certainly Alfred and his music-loving brother Frederick should consider moving there. Yet not all the associations were pleasant. A local wedding at Werfen was a painful reminder of the obstacles to his own marriage, and upon second viewing the charming Italianate character of Salzburg only made him yearn for the real South—the Italy forever associated with his first love and romantic awakening.

However, Arthur found Budapest, a river city like Florence, more attractive than he had expected. Toasting Mary Tennyson's birthday with a glass of tokay, he wrote to her sister of the remaining itinerary—north to Prague and then, turning westward, home to England. First, however, they would stop again at Vienna, where they had spent a few days on the way to Hungary. Arthur had found the Viennese parks and society all too reminiscent of the London he sought to escape, although he was impressed by the city's theater and art galleries. At the Imperial Gallery he recalled his 1832 trip to Germany and his preference for German pictures to those of Titian. In Vienna, however, his praise for the Venetian master was unbounded—Alfred should *write* "as perfect a Danae."

Henry Hallam and his son returned to Vienna on 13 September, with Arthur complaining of fever and chills. It was apparently a recurrence of the ague he had suffered earlier that year, and, though it would delay their departure for Prague, there seemed to be little cause for alarm. Quinine and a few days' rest were prescribed. By the fifteenth, Arthur felt better; and in the evening, after a short walk with his father, he ordered some sack and lay down. Leaving his son reading, Henry went out again. He returned to find Arthur still on the sofa, apparently asleep; but after a short time Henry noticed the odd position of Arthur's head. He called to his son. There was no response. All efforts to rouse him were in vain: Arthur Henry Hallam was dead at age twenty-two.

In the disposition of his son's earthly remains Henry Hallam's usual methodical care was equal to the calamity. The death certificate listed "Schlagfluss"—stroke—as cause. But an autopsy was also required, and it was performed by one of the greatest pathologists of the age, Karl von Rokitansky. It seemed to indicate an aneurism leading to hemorrhage in the brain, apparently related to Arthur's weakened condition, his alternating periods of depression and gaiety accompanied by severe headaches, and the intense flushing of his face following study. It was, as Henry wrote in the biographical preface to his son's *Remains, in Verse and Prose,* only "poor consolation . . . that a few more years would, in the usual chances of humanity, have severed the frail union of his graceful and manly form with the pure spirit that it inshrined." The coffin was quickly sealed and sent via Trieste to England for burial. Even Arthur's final journey was not without its perils: winter storms swept across the Mediterranean, delaying the ship's arrival until late December. The coffin was carried across England in a three-coach procession and interred on 3 January 1834 among the Eltons, Arthur's maternal ancestors, at Clevedon Church, overlooking the river Severn.

The news of the death had reached the Hallam family in England on 28 September, and Arthur's uncle, Henry Elton, had written to the Tennyson family on 1 October. The death, as Hallam's Cambridge friend Henry Alford wrote, came as "a loud and terrible stroke from the reality of things upon the fairy building of our youth." Gladstone noted the anniversary in his diaries for a number of years after, and, together with some of Arthur's other Eton and Cambridge acquaintances, persuaded Henry Hallam to have a portion of his son's writings published as *Remains, in Verse and Prose* in

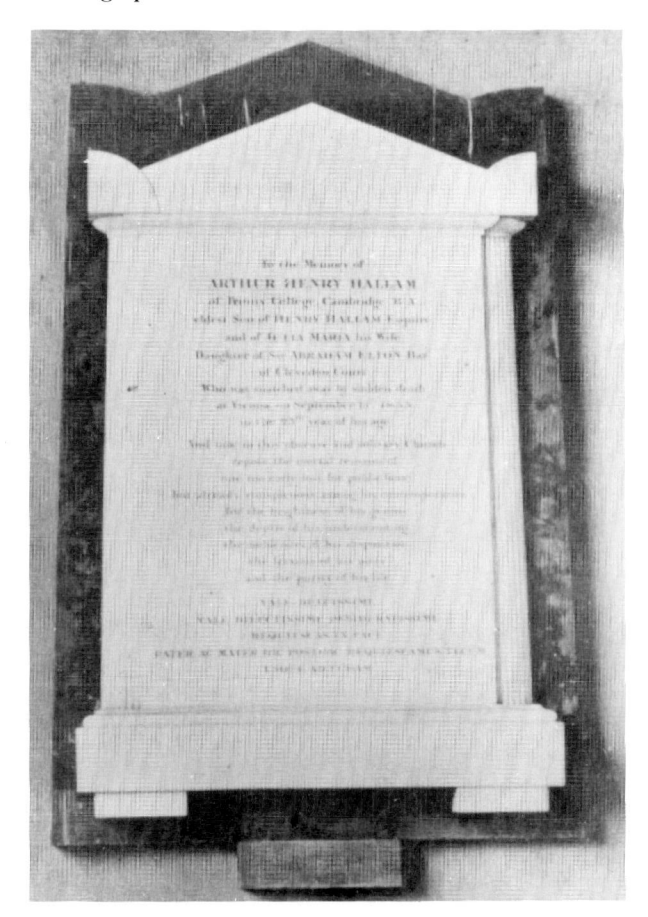

Hallam's memorial plaque in the church at Clevedon

1834. Tennyson, who proved unable to contribute a preface, had already written the early stanzas of the elegy which, seventeen years later, would make the initials *A.H.H.* perhaps the most famous in English literature.

No author, Keats perhaps excepted, should be judged on the basis of his work at the age of twenty-two. Arthur Henry Hallam's significance is additionally complicated: to suggest what role he might have had in literature without *In Memoriam* is only slightly less difficult than to hypothesize what Tennyson and *In Memoriam* might have been without A.H.H. Inevitably, the apotheosized figure of the elegy overshadows the real man, and critics have been suspicious of Tennyson's homage. Inevitably, too, the body of Hallam's writings offers only a promise—though a substantial promise—of what he might have achieved. T. H. Vail Motter has suggested that Hallam's knowledge of Romance languages and literature could have countered, or at least balanced, the Teutonic strain introduced into English literature by such powerful minds as Coleridge and Carlyle. Certainly he might have equaled the achievements of a poet-critic like Arnold. Even his letters offer a somewhat elusive glimpse of the man, though they were cherished by his friends for their outpouring of thought and sentiment, and, for Tennyson at least, were endued with a remarkable evocative power (as he indicates in the climactic ninety-fifth stanza of *In Memoriam*). As Hallam himself wrote to Tennyson, "Poems are good things but flesh & blood is better." It is finally as a man, as the friend and mentor of so many eminent Victorians, that he commands attention. In his brief life and early death he offered a model of someone, as Gladstone said of *In Memoriam*, "for whom no monument could be too noble," an inspiration for those who cherished his memory and believed in his potential.

Letters:
The Letters of Arthur Henry Hallam, edited by Jack Kolb (Columbus: Ohio State University Press, 1981).

Bibliographies:
T. H. Vail Motter, "Arthur Hallam's Centenary: A Bibliographical Note," *Yale University Library Gazette,* 8 (1934): 104-109;

Motter, "Hallam's 'Poems' of 1830: A Census of Copies," *Papers of the Bibliographical Society of America,* 35 (1941): 277-280.

References:
Peter Allen, *The Cambridge Apostles: The Early Years* (Cambridge: Cambridge University Press, 1978);

Norman Friedman, "Hallam on Tennyson: An Early Aesthetic Doctrine and Modernism," *Studies in the Literary Imagination,* 8 (1975): 37-62;

William Ewart Gladstone, *Diaries,* volumes 1 and 2, edited by M. R. D. Foot (New York: Oxford University Press, 1968);

Gladstone, "Personal Recollections of Hallam," *Daily Telegraph* (London), 5 January 1898;

Gladstone, *The Prime Ministers' Papers: W. E. Gladstone. I: Autobiographica,* edited by John Brooke and Mary Sorensen (London: Her Majesty's Stationery Office, 1971);

Gerhard Joseph, *Tennysonian Love: The Strange Diagonal* (Minneapolis: University of Minnesota Press, 1969);

Jack Kolb, "Arthur Hallam and Emily Tennyson," *Review of English Studies,* 28 (1977): 32-48;

Kolb, "The Hero and his Worshippers: The History of Arthur Henry Hallam's Letters," *John Rylands University Library Bulletin,* 56 (1973): 150-173;

Robert Bernard Martin, *Tennyson: The Unquiet Heart* (New York: Oxford University Press, 1980);

Helen Pearce, "Homage to Arthur Henry Hallam," in *The Image of the Work: Essays in Criticism,* edited by B. H. Lehman (Berkeley: University of California Press, 1955), pp. 113-133.

Papers:
Arthur Henry Hallam's letters and manuscripts are held in many locations, including: the British Library; Christ Church Library, Oxford University; Trinity College Library, Cambridge University; Eton College Library; the Lincolnshire Archives Office; the Tennyson Research Center, Lincoln; John Rylands University Library of Manchester; the New York Public Library; the Pierpont Morgan Library; Henry C. Huntington Library and Art Gallery; Houghton Library, Harvard University; Yale University Library; Princeton University Library; University of Iowa Library; Wellesley College Library; and the Miriam Lutcher Stark Library, University of Texas.

Robert Stephen Hawker

(3 December 1803-15 August 1875)

John R. Reed
Wayne State University

SELECTED BOOKS: *Tendrils,* as Reuben (Cheltenham: Bettison, Williams & Roberts/ London: Hatchard, Whittaker, 1821);

Pompeii: A Prize Poem (Oxford: Talboys, 1827);

Records of the Western Shore (Oxford: Talboys, 1832);

Poems: Containing the Second Series of Records of the Western Shore (Stratton, U.K.: Roberts, 1836);

Minster Church, and the Confirmation Day, August XVII, MDCCCXXXVI (Stratton, U.K.: J. Roberts, 1836);

A Welcome to Prince Albert (Oxford: Combe, 1840);

Ecclesia: A Volume of Poems (Oxford: Combe, 1840);

Reeds Shaken with the Wind (London: Burns, 1843);

Rural Synods (London: Edwards & Hughes, 1844);

Reeds Shaken with the Wind; the Second Cluster (Derby: Mozley/London: Burns, 1844);

The Field of Rephidim: A Visitation Sermon (London: Edwards & Hughes, 1845);

Echoes from Old Cornwall (London: Masters, 1846);

A Voice from the Place of S. Morwenna (London: Masters, 1849);

A Letter to a Friend, Containing Some Matters Relating to the Church (London: Royston & Brown, 1857);

The Quest of the Sangraal, Chant the First (Exeter, U.K.: Privately printed, 1864);

The Cornish Ballads, and Other Poems (Oxford & London: Parker, 1869);

Footprints of Former Men in Far Cornwall (London: Smith, 1870);

The Poetical Works of Robert Stephen Hawker, edited by J. G. Godwin (London: Kegan Paul, 1879);

The Prose Works of Rev. R. S. Hawker, Including Footprints of Former Men in Far Cornwall, edited by Godwin (Edinburgh: Blackwood, 1893).

Robert S. Hawker

Robert Stephen Hawker is known more as a notable eccentric than as an important writer, despite the power of his ballads and of his masterpiece, *The Quest of the Sangraal* (1864). Perhaps this is because his early sensational biographers, S. Baring-Gould and F. G. Lee, preferred vivid and bizarre depiction to an accurate account of Hawker's behavior and accomplishments.

Hawker was born at Stoke Damerel, Devonshire, on 3 December 1803, to Jacob Stephen Hawker, a doctor who later became a minister, and Jane Elizabeth Drewitt Hawker. Hawker was influenced by his grandfather and namesake, Robert Hawker, a well-known Calvinist divine and preacher. Throughout his youth, Hawker had a reputation for rebelliousness, mischief, and practical jokes. One of his least harmful hoaxes was an impersonation of a mermaid; he sat on a breakwater for a few nights combing his hair and singing. Hawker resented school. He boarded for a time at Liskeard Grammar School but left at sixteen to work for a solicitor in Plymouth. Deciding against the law as a profession, he entered Cheltenham Grammar School to continue his education. From an early age he had read eagerly, and it was not long before he attempted to write poetry. In 1821, still in his teens, a collection of his poems entitled *Tendrils* was published under the pseudonym Reuben. Although these poems are unremarkable exercises in conventional themes, they are not negligible achievements for a youngster.

In 1823, at the age of nineteen, Hawker earned a place at Pembroke College, Oxford. On 6 November he married Charlotte I'ans, who was then forty-one. Although legend charges Hawker with mercenary motives, the facts suggest that the marriage was one of strong affection; Hawker was desolated when Charlotte died forty years later.

Hawker transferred to Magdalen College; in 1827 he won the Newdigate Prize with a poem entitled *Pompeii*. He received his B.A. degree in 1828 and was ordained a deacon in 1829 and a priest in 1831. After a brief curacy at North Tamerton, Cornwall, he was instituted vicar of Morwenstow on 31 December 1834. He received his M.A. from Magdalen College in 1836. He remained at Morwenstow for the rest of his life, adding to his duties the nearby parish of Wellcombe in 1851.

As vicar of this remote and impoverished dis-

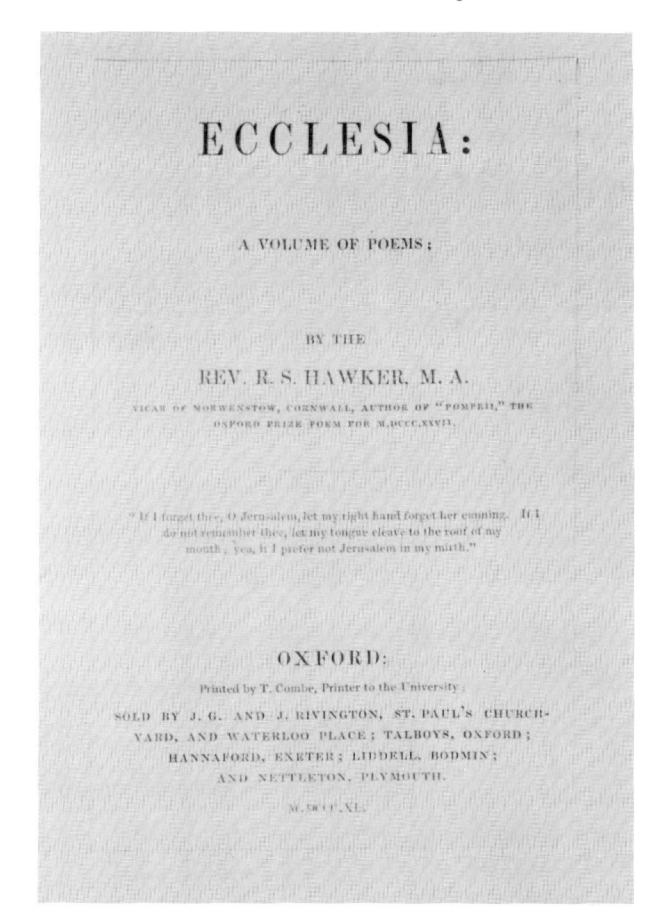

Title page for Hawker's 1840 collection of poems (Thomas Cooper Library, University of South Carolina)

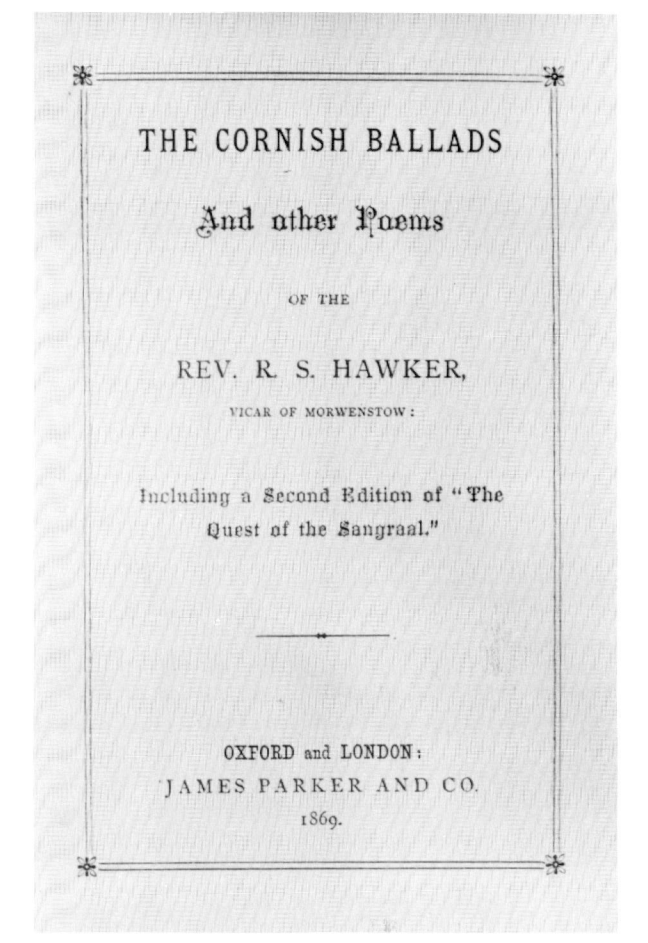

Title page for Hawker's 1869 collection of poems (Thomas Cooper Library, University of South Carolina)

trict, Hawker devoted himself to the construction of a vicarage, the restoration of the church, and the improvement of the local school. At the same time, he operated a substantial farm on old-fashioned principles. He was conspicuously charitable to the poor in his charge. The most harrowing of his self-imposed duties was attending to victims of the shipwrecks that were common on the stormy Cornish coast. He sought, as well, to mitigate the local inhabitants' practice of scavenging the remnants of these wrecks—a practice that was traditional with Cornishmen but was a violation of the law, since the property still belonged to the original owners.

Hawker's religious and social views were conservative but scarcely typical. While he followed the Tractarians in their concern for ritual and their belief in the Eucharistic presence, many of his opinions seem to have been based more on superstition than on reasoned faith. In his behavior as in his convictions, Hawker was a genuine eccentric. He

Publisher's advertisement for a later edition of Hawker's Cornish Ballads

wore outlandish clothing and was inordinately fond of animals. His cats were known to follow him into the pulpit during church services, and Baring-Gould asserts that Hawker once excommunicated a cat for catching a mouse on Sunday. Although Hawker was an eccentric, it must also be remembered that he was a witty and playful man who purposely exploited his eccentricity. If many of his opinions were antiquated and bizarre, Hawker was nonetheless a learned man, well furnished with traditional and exotic lore and knowledgeable about the history of Cornwall, as Alfred Tennyson discovered when he spent some pleasurable hours with him on a visit in 1848.

From the first years of his curacy, Hawker wrote poetry strongly identified with the locales he knew so well. His *Records of the Western Shore* (1832) were legends of the district "done in verse," as he expressed it. Most of the poems published during these years were in the form of ballads. One of the best known was also one of his earliest, "The Song of the Western Men," also known as "Trelawny," which opens:

> A good sword and a trusty hand!
>   A merry heart and true!
> King James's men shall understand
>   What Cornish lads can do.
>
> And have they fixed the where and when?
>   And shall Trelawny die?
> Here's twenty thousand Cornish men
>   Will know the reason why!

When the poem first appeared in print anonymously in the *Royal Devonport Telegraph and Plymouth Chronicle* in 1826 and in *The Gentleman's Magazine* in 1827, it was taken for an authentic ancient ballad. Charles Dickens also published the poem as a genuine old song in *Household Words* in 1852.

Hawker's poems are characterized by a genuine if sometimes rude strength, reflecting his forceful emotions and beliefs, but he was also capable of tasteful occasional verses; for example, "To Alfred Tennyson," his fine acknowledgment of Tennyson's accomplishment in *Idylls of the King* (1859), the last two stanzas of which read:

> I read the Rune with deeper ken,
>   And thus the myth I trace:—
> A bard should rise, mid future men,
>   The mightiest of his race.
>
> He!—would great Arthur's deeds rehearse,
>   On grey Dundagel's shore;

> And so, the King! in laurelled verse,
>   Shall live, and die no more!

Charlotte Hawker died on 2 February 1863 at the age of eighty-one. The following year Hawker met and married twenty-year-old Pauline Anne Kuczynski, the daughter of a Polish exile; they were married on 21 December. Three daughters were born to the couple. In the same year, Hawker's most impressive poem, the incomplete blank verse narrative *The Quest of the Sangraal*, was published. The poem is mystical and has perhaps acquired an additional aura of spirituality from the story that Hawker composed much of it in a rude hut that he had constructed overlooking the sea. In fact, Hawker had long used the hut as a retreat for writing and undisturbed thought. It was in 1864 also that Hawker began to compose the vigorous antiquarian essays collected as *Footprints of Former Men in Far Cornwall* (1870), mainly in an attempt to earn money, for he was regularly in need of funds.

Before his second marriage, Hawker had freed himself from opium, to which he had been addicted for many years, but half a dozen years later he resumed the habit. His health began to fail in 1873. He died at Plymouth on 15 August 1875, being received into the Roman Catholic church in his last hours.

Hawker's poetry has been obscured by his reputation as an eccentric, but his verse, though not subtle in its craftsmanship, has an appealing vigor. Some of his historical narratives and several of his poems set in Cornwall are well worth reading and remembering. His religious poems, like his ballads, are refreshing in their directness and sincerity. What he hoped his children would say of him when they read his poems may honestly be said: "He had good images once in his mind."

Biographies:
Sabine Baring-Gould, *The Vicar of Morwenstow, Being a Life of Robert Stephen Hawker, M.A.* (London: King, 1875; revised, 1876);

F. G. Lee, *Memorials of the Late Rev. Robert Stephen Hawker* (London: Chatto & Windus, 1876);

Charles Edward Byles, *The Life and Letters of R. S. Hawker* (London & New York: Lane, 1905);

Piers Brendon, *Hawker of Morwenstow: Portrait of a Victorian Eccentric* (London: Cape, 1975).

Reference:
Margaret Florence Burrows, *Robert Stephen Hawker: A Study of His Thought and Poetry* (Oxford: Blackwell, 1926).

Papers:
Manuscripts and letters of Robert Stephen Hawker are housed at the Bodleian Library, Oxford; Pembroke College, Oxford; the British Museum; the Cornwall County Record Office; the Exeter Public Library Record Office; the Humanities Research Center at the University of Texas; and in several private collections.

Richard Henry (Hengist) Horne
(31 December 1802 or 1 January 1803-13 March 1884)

Robert G. Laird
Carleton University

BOOKS: *The Exposition of the False Medium and Barriers Excluding Men of Genius from the Public,* anonymous (London: Effingham Wilson, 1833);

Spirit of Peers and People: A National Tragi-Comedy (London: Effingham Wilson, 1834);

Cosmo de' Medici: An Historical Tragedy (London: Templeman, 1837);

The Death of Marlowe: A Tragedy in One Act (London: Saunders & Otley, 1837);

The Russian Catechism (N.p., 1837);

The Life of Van Amburgh the Brute Tamer, with Anecdotes of His Extraordinary Pupils, as Ephraim Watts (London: Tyas, 1838);

Gregory VII: A Tragedy in One Act (London: Saunders & Otley, 1840);

The History of Napoleon, 2 volumes (London: Tyas, 1841);

Orion: An Epic Poem in Three Books (London: Miller, 1843);

Dr. Pusey (London, 1844);

A New Spirit of the Age, 2 volumes (London: Smith, Elder, 1844; New York: Harper, 1844);

The Ill-Used Giant (N.p., 1846);

Ballad Romances (London: Ollier, 1846);

The Good-Natured Bear: A Story for Children of All Ages (London: Cundall, 1846; Boston: Ticknor, Reed & Fields, 1852);

Memoirs of a London Doll, Written by Herself, as Mrs. Fairstar (London, 1846; Boston: Ticknor, Reed & Fields, 1852);

Judas Iscariot: A Miracle Play, with Other Poems (London: Mitchell, 1848);

The Golden Calf: or, Prodigality and Speculation in the Nineteenth Century (New York: Stringer & Townsend, 1849);

The Poor Artist; or, Seven Eye-Sights and One Object (London: Van Voorst, 1850; republished with

Richard Henry (Hengist) Horne

introductory essay, 1871);

Memoir of the Emperor Napoleon (London: Orr, 1850);

The Dreamer and the Worker: A Story of the Present Time, 2 volumes (London: Colburn, 1851);

Australian Facts and Prospects, to Which Is Prefixed the Author's Australian Autobiography (London: Smith, Elder, 1859);

Prometheus, the Fire-Bringer: A Drama in Verse (Edinburgh: Edmondstone & Douglas, 1864);

The Two Georges: A Dialogue of the Dead (Melbourne, 1865);

The South-Sea Sisters: A Lyric Masque (Melbourne: Dwight, 1866);

Galatea Secunda: An Odaic Cantata (Melbourne: Robertson, 1867);

Parting Legacy of R. H. Horne to Australia (John Ferncliffe: An Australian Narrative Poem) (Melbourne: Robertson & Dwight, 1868);

The Great Peace-Maker: A Submarine Dialogue (London: Low, Marston, Low & Searle, 1872);

Ode to the Mikado of Japan (London: N.p., 1873);

Psyche Apocalypté: A Lyric Drama, by Horne and Elizabeth Barrett Browning (London: Hazell, Watson & Viney, 1876);

Laura Dibalzo; or, The Patriot Martyrs: A Tragedy (London: Newman, 1880);

King Nihil's Round Table; or, The Regicide's Symposium (London: Newman, 1881);

Bible Tragedies. John the Baptist; or, The Valour of the Soul. Rahman: The Apocryphal Book of Job's Wife. Judas Iscariot: A Mystery (London: Newman, 1881);

Soliloquium Fratris Rogeri Baconis Anno Domini 1292 (London: Dryden Press, 1882);

The Last Words of Cleanthes: A Poem (London: Spottiswoode, 1883);

Sithron the Star-stricken, Translated by Salem ben Uzäir (London: Redway, 1883);

The Doll and Her Friends; or, Memoirs of the Lady Seraphina (New York: Brentano, 1893);

King Penguin: A Legend of the South Sea Isles, edited by Frances Margaret Fox (New York: Macmillan, 1925).

OTHER: W. Hazlitt, *Characteristics: In the Manner of Rochefoucault's Maxims,* introductory remarks by Horne (London: Templeman, 1837);

A. W. Schlegel, *Lectures on Dramatic Art and Literature,* translated by John Black, introduction by Horne, 2 volumes (London: Templeman, 1839);

The Poems of Geoffrey Chaucer Modernised, introduction and three tales by Horne (London: Whittaker, 1841);

The Works of Shakespeare, edited by Horne (London: Tyas, 1843);

The Complete Works of Shakespeare, edited by Horne and others, 2 volumes (London: London Printing & Publishing Co., 1857-1859);

Was Hamlet Mad? Being a Series of Critiques on the Acting of the Late W. Montgomery, edited by Horne (London, 1871);

S. R. T. Mayer, ed., *Letters of Elizabeth Barrett Browning Addressed to R. H. Horne,* connecting narrative by Horne, 2 volumes (London: Bentley, 1877);

Coustard de Massi, *The History of Duelling in All Countries,* translated by Horne, with introduction and concluding chapter by Horne as "Sir L. O'Trigger" (London: Newman, 1880).

Richard Henry Horne was one of many young writers who struggled to find a new aesthetic creed after 1825, when the explosive impetus given to English literature by the Romantics began to die away. Like his confreres, Horne tirelessly experimented with genre, subject matter, and technique, but unlike the best of them he never developed a unique and lasting voice of his own. What stands out about Horne, however, are the number and range of his writings. He was a journalist, editor, poet, dramatist, novelist, and critic, and in the early stages of his career he was considered to be in the van of the new artists.

The eldest of three sons, Horne was born in Edmonton, Middlesex, just outside London. His father, James Horne, having temporarily abandoned his profligate life after marrying Maria Partridge, soon returned to his old ways and by 1807 was forced to enlist in the army to make a living. Sent to the garrison on Guernsey, the Hornes left Richard with his paternal grandmother in Edmonton until 1810 when, after James's death, the family returned.

He first attended the Reverend John Clarke's school at Enfield—where John Keats first learned to love the classics—and in 1819 was sent to the Royal Military Academy at Sandhurst to prepare for a career in the East India Service. Failing to pass the first year, he returned home and began a course of self-directed reading in the arts and philosophy. In 1825 Horne took up the offer of a family friend and accepted the post of midshipman in the Mexican navy, sailing to Cuba and taking part in the Spanish-Mexican War.

After the cessation of hostilities and a serious bout with yellow fever, he returned home through the United States and Canada. He traveled up the Erie Canal; visited Niagara Falls, where he broke two ribs while bathing; moved on to Montreal; stopped in Quebec City, where he claimed to have killed an Iroquois who tried to stab him; and eventually worked his way back to England on a timber ship, experiencing both a fire and a mutiny on the voyage. He finally settled in London in 1829.

Though Horne's works are highly varied, certain basic themes run through them. He supported the struggle of the working classes, had a strong faith in the value of technological change, and foresaw a new age of peace and progress. Most important, it became his mission to present the case (which Shelley stated most clearly) for considering the vision of the artist as more valuable than that of the philosopher, the historian, the politician, or the priest. He was concerned with the declining role of art, and both his critical and imaginative writings often argued the need to preserve the eminence of the artist.

In fact, his first major publication resulted directly from difficulties he faced in finding a publisher for his own work. *The Exposition of the False Medium and Barriers Excluding Men of Genius from the Public* (1833) detailed the ways in which the great publishing houses, through their religious and political affiliations as well as their interconnections with the journals, controlled the materials readers had available to them. To overcome this problem and to allow authors and other men of genius their rightful influence on society, Horne proposed a "Society of English Literature." Writers judged worthy would have their works published by the society and would receive an annual pension for life.

Not finding his idea accepted, Horne had to continue to earn his living. He worked for some time on the *True Sun,* a newspaper whose other writers included Douglas Jerrold, John Forster, Robert Bell, and Charles Dickens. He soon came into contact with one of the most influential coteries of the time: the group of liberal thinkers who met at the home of the famous Unitarian minister W. J. Fox. Its members included Robert Browning, John Stuart Mill, Harriet Taylor, and Southwood Smith; all of them, like Horne, had been influenced by the work of William Godwin. It was here that Horne gave form to his views on the social responsibility of the artist. Social reform, particularly the development of an egalitarian and peaceful society, became for Horne the primary goal of any true artist.

He next turned his hand to the drama. Like many of his fellow dramatists, Horne believed that a return to Elizabethan styles, settings, and sometimes even themes was necessary for a revitalization of this most social of the literary arts. His first play, however, a bald and unactable allegory called *Spirit of Peers and People* (1834)—intended as the first part of a proposed "National Tragi-Comedy"—dealt with many of the characters and events of the passage of the First Reform Bill. Horne castigates the aristocracy and the church, as might be expected, but he also shows how the middle classes tried to prevent the "Egg of Reform" from hatching, and also how the working classes were frightened because they lacked confidence in their ability to effect change. By pointing out the strengths and weaknesses in all contemporary political and philosophical positions, Horne again makes his case for the value of the artist: only he could view all social groups disinterestedly, and by presenting his truth in an imaginative and moving form he could bring about the necessary marriage of theory and practice, of intellect and action.

In his subsequent and more literary dramas, Horne embodied his belief that art had to express the full range of human desires and actions, not simply those acceptable to the morality of the time. It was precisely by awakening the reader to the potential of man's nature that the artist could raise the age above itself. To counteract the simplistic moralizing tendency of his time, Horne chose to write about four historical figures who, in contemporary moral terms, were clearly evil.

In *Cosmo de' Medici* (1837) he deals with the sixteenth-century Florentine whose pious and mechanical belief in the law leads him to execute his younger son, Garcia, for the supposed murder of Garcia's elder brother, Giovanni. Cosmo's rage for order and his love of the abstract concept of justice overrule his common humanity, and he refuses to accept the real, mixed conditions of life. For all his noble aspirations and social concerns, Cosmo fails because of his inability to see and accept things as they are.

Horne develops this theme further in *The Death of Marlowe* (1837). Marlowe, able to intuit and be inspired by the inherent good qualities of the courtesan Cecilia, gives her a belief in herself which ennobles her. This attempt to idealize the real, however, leads directly to Marlowe's death at the hands of Jacconot, Cecilia's pander. He forces Marlowe to recognize that there is still an earthly and negative side to Cecilia's nature, and in the ensuing struggle, Marlowe is slain with his own sword. "Forgetful of all corporal conditions," Marlowe laments, "my passion has destroyed me."

The third drama, *Gregory VII* (1840), follows the rise to the papacy of the once-simple monk Hildebrand, who began life with a lofty ambition—to make God's will prevail on earth. Unwilling to be patient and trust in the power of virtue and wisdom, Gregory comes to believe that only forceful action, even war if necessary, will change the world. And it is his arrogant trampling of the very humanity he intended to foster, as demonstrated in his inhuman treatment of Henry IV, that leads to his destruction.

Horne's desire to investigate the motivations and reasons behind the actions of historical "villains" led him to choose Judas as the subject of his fourth play, *Judas Iscariot* (1848). Like Gregory, Judas could not accept a policy of gradual reform. His betrayal of Christ is presented not as an act of treachery but as an attempt to force the Son of God to manifest his divinity by destroying his enemies. By trying to incorporate an ideal vision of man through brute force, Judas destroys himself.

All four plays deal with characters Robert Langbaum has called "Heroes of Existence," men who have the courage to "live out the implications of their nature, . . . to venture all on what must turn out to have been a noble delusion." They are "mixed" characters, whose major flaw is the belief that they can operate beyond normal morality, that they can achieve noble ends through ignoble means. In showing their failures, Horne demonstrates the impossibility of immediately translating the ideal into the real world by force alone.

Horne had developed by this time a view that he was to hold throughout his career. Direct political action, whether initiated by powerful autocratic figures like Gregory or Cosmo, or by the masses, as in *Spirit of Peers and People,* could never solve the problems of the nineteenth century. The failure of such action derived from the mistaken belief that material change alone, such as change in the state or the church, or a simple reliance on some ideal concept of justice, could solve human problems. Such action, proceeding from one of the two political poles—aristocracy or masses—inevitably led to extremism, which had to fail because it sought the destruction of what Horne came to see as a necessary polarity.

This belief in what has since been described disdainfully as "compromise" was Horne's version of Hegel's doctrine of the reconciliation of opposites. Horne spoke and read German fluently, and he was well versed in the works of Hegel long before most other English intellectuals had become familiar with the work of the idealist philosopher. From Hegel, and in particular his *Phenomenology of Mind* and *Philosophy of History,* Horne received the concept of the "World-Historical Hero." Such heroes, Hegel claimed, were "thinking men, who had an insight into the requirements of the times—what was ripe for development. . . . It was theirs to know this nascent principle . . . to make this their aim, and to expend their energy in promoting it." Such a character Horne presented in his best-known poetic work, *Orion* (1843).

Originally sold for a farthing, the smallest British coin, in order to reach the widest possible audience, *Orion* was a popular success; it went through six editions in a year, the last three of which were offered for a more normal price. In the poem, Horne paints a portrait of the "Worker and . . . Builder for his fellow men." Powerful in both mind and body, Orion struggles to unify these aspects of his being. Horne shows how the new workers of the nineteenth century, the men of brawn and energy, must link their strength to the intellect if they are to realize their dreams of freedom and equality. In showing the mythic Orion's growth from ignorance to knowledge, then through despair to a wiser hope, Horne depicts the forces arrayed against such an individual. These forces are represented by Orion's worker-friends, such as Chronos (Time), Akinetos (the Unmoving), Rhexergon (the Destroyer), and

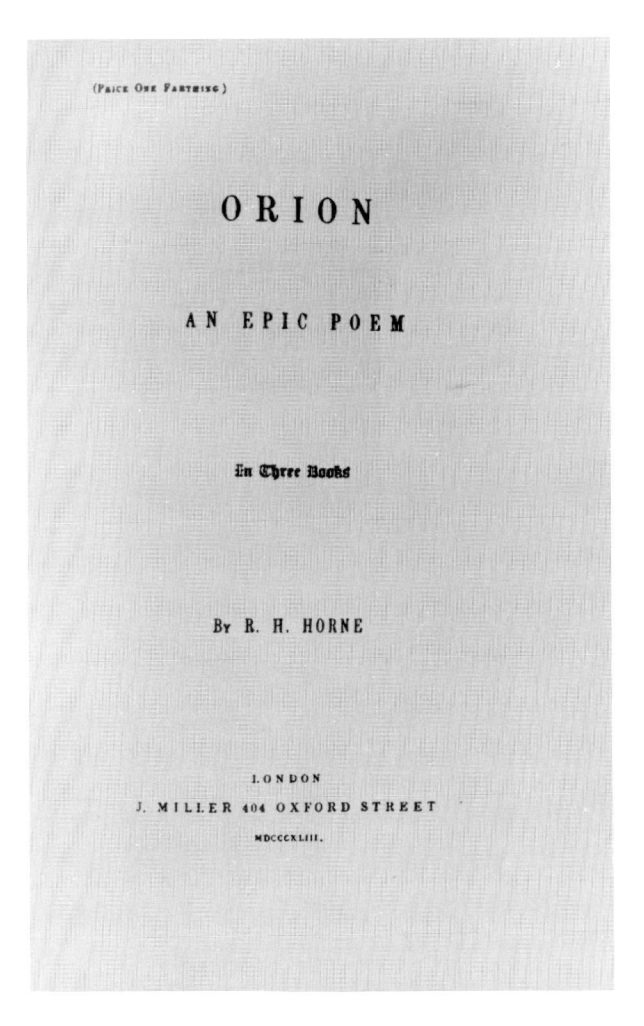

Title page for the one-farthing edition of Horne's best-known work of poetry

Encolyon (the Preventer). Orion moves through Hegel's three stages of thesis, antithesis, and synthesis, each being represented by the women in his life: Artemis, Merope, and Eos.

In his first stage, Orion is a mere dreamer, a "Hunter of shadows." When the goddess Artemis appears to him, however, he realizes that his dreams foreshadow a higher reality:

> Now from a Goddess did he quickly learn
> The mystery of his mood, and saw how vain
> His early life had been, and felt new roots
> Quicken within him....

Unable to live the spiritualized life which Artemis requires of him, he rejects the spiritual and pursues the mortal woman Merope out of animal desire. Having satisfied his lust, Orion falls into the "profound sleep of life's satiety" and is blinded by his enemies. Urged to rise and "seek the source of light," Orion prays for aid from Eos, goddess of the dawn, who represents Hegel's Mediator. She restores his sight, and his new love for her combines the intellectual passion for Artemis with the sensual longing for Merope. Able now to unify the two parts of his life, Orion looks outward and begins to work for others, to make real the dreams he originally had for the betterment of man: he is able to achieve a balance "Of body and soul; each to respect,/And to the other minister, and both/Their one harmonious being to employ/For general happiness, and for their own." In retelling this myth, Horne tries to make his contemporaries aware that only a true blending of thought and action can improve life; he tries also to inspirit those already weary in the long struggle for change by reminding them that hope is ever possible: it is, he notes in the poem's most memorable line, "always morning somewhere in the world."

Having become famous with the publication of *Orion,* Horne continued his attempts to demonstrate the need and value of the artist. Choosing now to write as a critic, he began to gather the essays which would make up his portrait of the artistic world of his time, *A New Spirit of the Age* (1844).

In 1825, when William Hazlitt's collection of articles, *The Spirit of the Age,* was published anonymously, it was clear that Hazlitt had a sense of observing the death of a great spiritual movement: "The present is an age of talkers, and not of doers; and the reason is, that the world is growing old." Five years later, when John Stuart Mill took up the same topic in a series in the *Examiner* also entitled "The Spirit of the Age," he saw beyond this death to a new birth. For one of the first times in history, age was no longer a guarantee of wisdom. "If the old know less than the young," Mill wrote, "it is because it is hard to unlearn...." Agreeing with Mill about the relatively greater importance of young writers and thinkers in this new age, Horne undertook to give critical attention to these rising stars. Although he hoped later to discuss political figures, scientists, and painters, Horne produced only the first two volumes of *A New Spirit of the Age,* both dealing almost entirely with writers. Under the pressure of a publisher's deadline, Horne enlisted the help of Elizabeth Barrett, with whom he had been corresponding since 1841, in writing the twenty-five chapters of critical portraits. Robert Browning selected some of the poetic prefaces to each chapter, and Robert Bell, Thomas Powell, and Mary Gillies may also have contributed work.

Throughout the essays can be seen what Horne held to be the requirements for good art: the exposition of a true, not simply contemporary, morality; the attempt to show how society was responsible for the conditions of the poor and uneducated, and thereby to ameliorate these conditions; and the inspiring of all men and women to continue in the struggle to achieve a world of universal freedom and brotherhood.

To draw attention to the most important modern writers, as well as to give a sense of the diversity of contemporary aesthetic theory, Horne discusses more than forty writers, including novelists, poets, and dramatists. Because of the breadth of treatment there are considerations of many figures, such as Barham, the Howitts, Gore, Banim, and Carleton, who are little known today. At the same time, almost all those writers who are still studied are included, among them Barrett, Browning, Carlyle, Dickens, and Tennyson. It is clear from the placement of the essays on Dickens and Tennyson at the opening of the first and second volumes, respectively, that Horne considered these two men to be the most representative authors of the period. The major difference between them was that Dickens was so popular that readers were in danger of falling into uncritical adulation of him, while Tennyson remained in unwarranted obscurity.

Horne recognized clearly that the novel was emerging as the preeminent genre. No longer a "mere fantasy of the imagination, a dreamy pageant of unintelligible sentiments and impossible incidents," the novel had become the inculcator of "a great deal of useful knowledge, historical, social, and moral." Dickens was the most successful contemporary novelist, Horne says, because he was able to blend the beneficial and destructive qualities of the age, because he was willing to describe and identify with the full range of human possibilities. Dickens was attempting, as had Horne in his earliest work, to "enlarge the bounds of unexclusive sympathy."

Dickens's strength lay in his ability to show the common humanity inherent in the most vicious and brutalized individuals. Tennyson, on the other hand, was valuable because he had a mind which could "force up a vital flower of ideality through the heavy fermenting earth of human experience. . . ." It was this ability which Horne saw as Tennyson's greatest attribute, as well as the quality most required by his contemporaries. The age was one of fact, of political, economic, and social "realities"; what Horne knew to be vitally necessary was a "new spirit."

Like Carlyle, Horne continually made a plea for the union of the spiritual and physical worlds. Unlike Carlyle, however, Horne had a strong belief in the abilities of his audience, a real hope that a democracy of heroes was possible: he also had a stronger and more optimistic view of the potential of the material world and the prospect of its rapid advance. The purpose of *A New Spirit of the Age,* on one level, was to take literary criticism out of the hands of the anonymous and the pseudonymous and to look objectively at living authors. In a deeper sense, though, the volumes were an attempt to show that there was a leavening at work in an age that many thinkers believed was becoming irresistibly utilitarian. Horne never lost his hope that the artist could ensure that spirit, the creative and imaginative vision of what could be, would continue to guide man's progress.

Events in his own life were not of a kind to support such optimism. The response to his works other than *Orion* was lukewarm at best, and Horne returned to journalism in 1845 when he helped Dickens establish the *Daily News.* For the next year he was in Ireland as special correspondent for the paper, and after his return to England he became active in the People's International League, speaking often on behalf of Mazzini and the Italian cause. In 1847 he married Catherine St. George Foggo. In 1850 he briefly edited the *Dramatic Magazine* and *Leigh Hunt's Journal,* and became one of the three full-time staff members of Dickens's *Household Words,* for which he wrote nearly 100 articles over the next few years.

Caricature by George Gordon McCrae of Horne in Australia

In spite of this busyness, he determined that life in England held little hope of success, so on 4 June 1852, leaving his wife behind, he immigrated to the goldfields of Australia. He quickly realized that there was no possibility of his striking it rich; nevertheless, he remained in Australia for seventeen years. During this time he was commander of Melbourne's Private Gold Escort Company, junior assistant gold commissioner, mining registrar and surveyor of the Blue Mountain fields, territorial magistrate, law clerk to one of the leading advocates of the Melbourne bar, and an unsuccessful candidate for Parliament. He wrote occasionally for the Melbourne papers; had another edition of *Orion* published; and wrote several new book-length works, including a guide to would-be immigrants, *Australian Facts and Prospects* (1859). In 1867 he changed his middle name to Hengist, apparently taking the surname of a miner he had met in the fields. By 1869, however, his dreams of success in the new world had failed, and he returned to England in September.

No hero's welcome awaited him. Whatever audience he had once commanded had forgotten him, and many of his friends, including Dickens, avoided him because of his abandonment and supposed mistreatment of his wife. Short of money, he applied for a civil list pension, supported by Browning, Tennyson, Arnold, Rossetti, and others. Gladstone refused him, but Disraeli finally granted him fifty pounds a year in 1874. He still wrote for the magazines, but fitfully, and had one or two longer works published. Browning, out of sympathy, broke the protective silence with which he surrounded the memory of his wife and gave Horne permission in 1877 to have *Letters of Elizabeth Barrett Browning Addressed to R. H. Horne* published.

Horne died quietly and alone in Margate in the spring of 1884 after a life filled with adventure and moderate success. He knew and influenced many of his more famous contemporaries, and it was his eclecticism that gave him whatever prominence he achieved. He adopted various points of view, tried to find ways of synthesizing polar positions, and recognized the strengths and weaknesses of opposing political views. He believed fervently in the possibility of human improvement, and he saw the artist as the necessary catalytic agent in any beneficial change. Through his own creative work, as well as by his assessment and criticism of his fellow authors, Horne attempted to make the case for the primacy of the artistic vision. His efforts on behalf of new writers, and his own steps into the new age, faltering as they were, make him still worthy of study.

Bibliography:

Eri Shumaker, *Concise Bibliography of the Complete Works of Richard Henry Horne* (Granville, Ohio, 1943).

Biographies:

Cyril Pearl, *Always Morning* (Melbourne: Cheshire, 1960);

Ann Blainey, *The Farthing Poet* (London: Longmans, 1968).

Reference:

Robert G. Laird, "The New Spirit of the Age: Richard Henry Horne," Ph.D. dissertation, Yale University, 1972.

Ebenezer Jones
(20 January 1820-14 September 1860)

William B. Thesing
University of South Carolina

BOOKS: *Studies of Sensation and Event: Poems* (London: Fox, 1843);
The Land Monopoly, the Suffering and Demoralization Caused by It; and the Justice and Expediency of Its Abolition (London: Fox, 1849).

Ebenezer Jones—clerk, poet, and political writer—was born in Canonbury Square, Islington, a suburb of London; he was the third child of Robert and Hannah Sumner Jones. His father was of Welsh extraction; his mother came from a long-established Essex family. Material comforts were adequate in the Jones household; spiritually, the family adhered to the strictest form of Calvinism. All books considered to be of a "worldly nature" were excluded from the family's library of mainly religious works: the writings of Shakespeare, Milton, Byron, Shelley, and Carlyle were especially frowned upon by his parents. Rigorous discipline was also enforced upon Ebenezer and his older brother, Sumner, when they attended boarding school in Highgate beginning in 1828. The boys' father died before they graduated.

Most of the biographical information extant on Jones appears in the two memorial notices contributed by Sumner Jones, himself a minor poet, and by W. J. Linton, a famous engraver and literary friend, to the 1879 republication of *Studies of Sensation and Event* (1843). An incident from Jones's early boyhood illustrates both his sensitivity and the stirrings of his later rebellion against his harsh and narrow upbringing. Sumner Jones reports that one afternoon at the boarding school, "a lurcher dog had strayed into the school-room, panting with the heat, his tongue lolling out with thirst. The choleric usher who presided, and was detested by us for his tyranny, seeing this, advanced down the room. Enraged at our attention being distracted from our tasks, he dragged the dog to the top of the stairs, and there lifted him bodily up with the evident

Ebenezer Jones

intention—and we had known him to do similar things—of hurling the poor creature to the bottom. 'YOU SHALL NOT!' rang through the room, as little Ebby, so exclaiming at the top of his voice, rushed with kindling face to the spot...." The dog was dropped, the boy's ears were boxed, and he "burst into an uncontrollable passion of tears." It was an event the young boy never forgot, and soon after his father's death he revolted against his Calvinist upbringing.

In 1837, when Jones was seventeen, he and Sumner were forced to earn a meager living as clerk-accountants in a warehouse associated with the tea trade in central London. Of the long days behind the clerk's desk, Sumner reports: "Our hours of business were twelve daily, from 8 a.m. to 8 p.m., exclusive of getting to and from the premises. They were severe even for those days, nor had the great boon of the Saturday half-holiday then been thought of." At night and on Sundays Ebenezer began to read authors—especially Shelley and Carlyle—that had been excluded from his parents' home. He even had the courage to ask his employer for time off to read, a request that was "met by this rejoinder—that self-culture led to pride of intellect, 'one of Satan's peculiar snares,' and was not wanted in the counting-house." Reading Shelley and Carlyle fostered in Jones a new awakening of political and intellectual consciousness: he began to compose verse which reflected some of the sentiments of these two newly discovered author-heroes.

The forty-five poems collected in Jones's 1843 volume, publication of which was "paid for with his own earnings," can be divided into three categories: lyrics on individual and universal love; poems of social and political protest; and lyrics about the natural world. Most of the love lyrics present memories of past bliss or depict recent disappointment and betrayal. Jones's biographers say that these love poems were "inspired by one who was lost to him by change and estrangement, and who not long after was claimed by death." In "Repose In Love," the speaker's love for an individual woman offers escape from the conflicts and wrongs of society: "I flew to thee, love, I flew to thee, love,/From a world where all's deceit." Clearly, however, it is a remembered bliss—"In former times beside thee glowing,/I've seen all life grow bright." Part of the speaker's regret in "A Happy Sadness" involves the inadequacy of poetry to convey the full force of his feelings: "And song is all too weak, love,/My passion to reveal." Despite its quasi-erotic title, "Dismounting a Mistress" simply captures the symbolic moment of the speaker's assisting a beautiful woman to dismount from a horse. When it touches ground, love becomes constricted to the harsh realities of earth's boundaries and disappointments.

Four or five love poems take a part of the human anatomy—a face, a hand, a limb, a pair of eyes—as a haunting and often unsettling focus of the ravages of tormented passion. In "The Face," the speaker is a woman overcome by "clouds of grief and shame" in the "dreary hours of hopeless gloom." The face of her dead lover cannot be discussed—"It is the face I dare not name;/The face none ever name to me"—even though it reaches the haunting and all-consuming dimensions of a deranged mental obsession: "Although its death-gloom grasps my brain/With crushing unrefused despair." In "The Hand," the speaker flees the falsehood of the world and finds temporary comfort in the assuring hand extended by his younger sister. "Eyeing the Eyes of One's Mistress" sets forth in rather trite fashion the infinite yearnings of focused passion; "A Lady's Hand" also is utterly conventional in its offering of momentary solace in love from the "hurricane" force of the world's misfortunes. The love poem "Whimper of Awakening Passion," however, is refreshingly experimental in its use of the conceit of hands as the lovers' private tent and quite witty in its use of Nonconformist hymn-meter.

A mournful parade of femmes fatales—alluring women without any mercy for their prey—is described in several poems: Lelia in "A Prayer to a Fickle Mistress" and the nymphs Emily and Zingalee in poems named after their central figures. These poems present fantastical "barelimbed" women in situations that involve a blend of the erotic and the morbid that is extraordinary for their time. That "Departed joy leaves dreariest pain" is also the plaint in the more subdued lyric "Remembrance of Feelings." Jones's most extended and sophisticated treatment of the contrast between ideal passion and earthly disappointment is to be found in "A Crisis." Shelleyan echoes surround the progress of the speaker's feelings for the visionary "light-robed maiden." Although the beatific descriptions are sometimes marred by banal diction—"Sleeker than apples show her round young knees"—the erotic encounter with "virgin ignorance unknowing" is subtly presented. The conclusion of "A Crisis" rises to a full-fledged embodiment of the Romantic regret that neither poetry nor the human faculties are capable of capturing or sustaining the power of pure, ideal love.

Several poems call for or demonstrate the advantages of universal love and human brotherhood. More than any other lines in *Sensation and Event*, the second stanza from "Plea for Love of the Universal" captures the faith and hope that Jones invested in the redeeming energy of love:

> Love magnifies existence; love the world,—
> Thy soul shall grow world-great in its sensation;
> And 'neath the blaze of infinite life unfurl'd,
> Pant with the passion of a whole creation.
>   Oh love then! love!

The longest poem in the volume, "Ways of Regard," is a minor redramatization of the action and themes of Shelley's *Prometheus Unbound* (1820). In vivid descriptive language, the poem offers a catalogue of the destructive forces of nature and the evil tendencies at work in human society. Various options of philosophical response are explored objectively. Against the oppressions of tyranny and materialistic smugness, "the seer" offers an extended diatribe of revenge until his followers are aroused to hysterical fury:

> He ceased, o'ercome with passion; his clench'd hands
> Signing the fury that had choked his voice,
> And roll'd his eyeballs backward. In the cave
> Each auditor foams fiercely with his mouth....

The "cave" or "cavern" is a favorite symbol for the poetic imagination in Shelley's poetry. Shelley's influence can also be seen in Jones's restatement of the Romantic proposition that "Man is eternal; tyrants and slavery/Are but the tricks of time." "Ways of Regard" concludes on a triumphant note of celebration as the seer proclaims that "the race of man is culminating!" and that "the superior creatures" will momentarily "displace man." In its call for a transformed world, in its hope for a new age, and in its belief in the expansion of experience through the senses and imaginative powers, the concluding speech delivered by the seer places Jones's poetry squarely in the Romantic tradition:

> "... Sweep, sweep on, companions!
> And glory in our delight. Eternally
> All things intensify; and we must ever
> Intenselier contemplate, intenselier joy.
> Rest we above the cave. Rejoice, companions!
> Brightly speeds on the baptism of the earth."

Five poems in Jones's 1843 volume register indignant social and political protests. In discussing the poet's "Spasmodic affinities," Jerome H. Buckley points out how vicarious the voice of condemnation tends to be with poets of this group, which flourished in the 1840s. Buckley considers it odd that although Jones's "Song of the Gold-Getters" certainly must have been derived from harsh personal experience, in tone it is very close to Elizabeth Barrett Browning's "Cry of the Children"—"a poem strangely intense in its vicarious intuitions." Indeed, in depicting social wrongs and political oppressions, the clerk-poet does not specifically describe scenes of hardship from his own life. Instead, he resorts to a high pitch of emotional rhetoric which often relies on a generalized "us" versus "them" formula to register indirectly his feelings of indignation. The tragic realities of the city pale before the white heat of the poetic impulse. The most direct reference to contemporary abuses is in the epigraph to "Song of the Gold-Getters," wherein the poet quotes very briefly from a speech delivered in the House of Commons: "The essence of trade is to buy cheap, and sell dear." The argument of the poem is developed through an abstract battle between falsehood and virtue. Deceit or lies "best gets the best of the pelf" while "Truth now starves in garrets, or rots in a gaol." A similar juxtaposition appears in "Song of the Kings of Gold": the downtrodden masses—"thousands toiling moan"—are hopeless victims of the arrogant and cynical "Kings of Gold." With their "mighty titles," the superscilious aristocrats assert both their exclusive rights to the fruits of the land and to the labors of "our slaves." In seven choral refrains, the masters tempt fate itself: "We let, we create, we slay./Ha! ha! who are Gods?" "A Slave's Triumph," in which a revolutionary sparks a violent rampage, is the most undisciplined poem of the lot; the unfocused imagery of "beasts" and "tigers" as well as the rhetoric of rage undercut the effectiveness of the poem. In "Opinion's Change" the poet records his lifelong opposition to monarchy because it is "Thoughtless of human needs"; only under a republican form of government could "human rights" and equality be realized. Sumner Jones reports that W. J. Fox gave a "thrilling recital from the platform" of the chant "A Coming Cry." Although this poem again relies on the "they" versus "we" stereotypes, it is Jones's most persuasive protest poem because it details specific abuses, especially those involving the Victorian workhouse system.

For the most part, the nature lyrics in the 1843 volume are conventional celebrations of an idyllic realm of beauty and escape. A note of tranquility is sustained throughout "Inactivity" as the lone stroller records his appreciation of nature's "pleasant languor," its "elysian calm," and its "happy undesiring repose." The secluded meadows cure and uplift the speaker's downcast spirit: "Nor hope, nor grief, found room within my being,/Fill'd with your beautiful presence." The ecstatic effort to capture the full bounty of July in "High Summer" is marred by lines such as "And feel the sunshine throbbing on body and limb/My drowsy brain in pleasant drunkenness swim...." The best nature poems in the volume rely on a sincere or an original description of the poet's emotional responses to natural phenomena: both "Rain" and "Early Spring" succeed admirably for these reasons. Of historical and thematic interest is "The Railroad." To Jones the railroad reproduces nature's awesome powers and binds the people of the kingdom together. It is a poem of celebration which expresses no regret over the disruption of the landscape:

'Tis the railroad!
Like arrowy lightning snatch'd from the sky,
And bound to the earth, the bright rails lie;
And their way is straight driven through mountains high.
And headland to headland o'er valleys they tie;
'Tis the railroad!

The immediate reception of *Studies of Sensation and Event* was almost uniformly negative. Sumner Jones speaks of a public attack in the *Literary Gazette* for 23 December 1843 "that troubled my brother." On 13 April 1844, the *Athenaeum* offered advice to the young poet: "We recommend him to be more humble in his pretensions, and simpler in his address, when next he appears in public." Sumner Jones sent presentation copies of his brother's volume to Thomas Carlyle and Thomas Hood. Carlyle sent a brief reply: "Keep your fire burning, but be careful to consume your own smoke." Hood's private censure was far more devastating: according to Sumner Jones, it was "a very severe, and even 'sav-

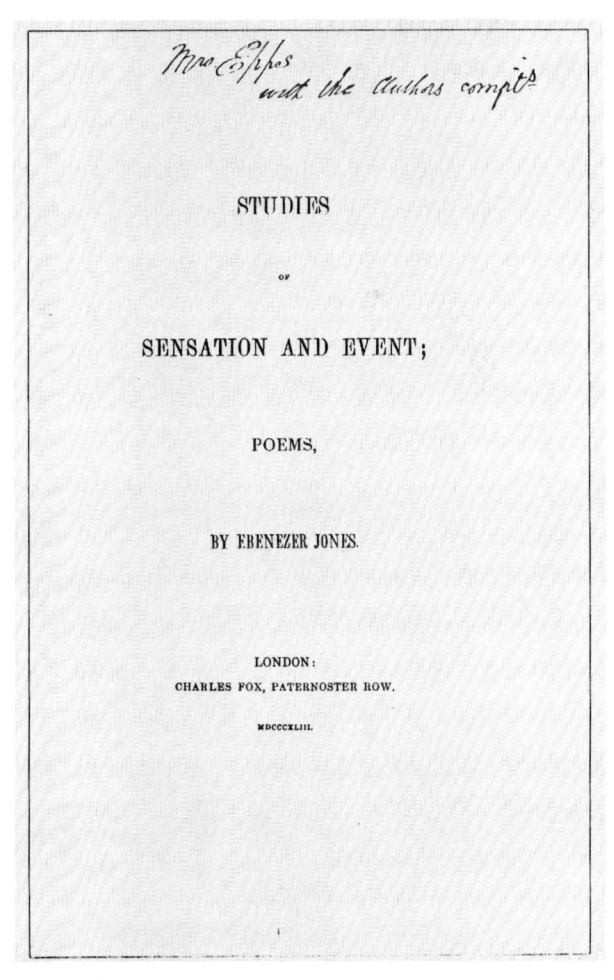

Title page for the only book of Jones's poetry published during his lifetime, with an inscription by him (David Magee/Antiquarian Books Catalogue)

age' letter." Hood condemned the love poems especially; he accused Jones of "impure motive" and of "shamefully prostituting his gift of poetical power." According to Sumner, the reception given to Jones's poems was a "matter of genuine surprise as well as disappointment." In despair over his literary failure, a despair that was heightened by his now certain inability to escape the dull labor of the countinghouse, the young poet "destroyed a mass of poetical composition, which he had in preparation for a second volume—had the first succeeded." He planned to call this sequel "Studies of Resemblance and Consent."

In 1844 Jones married Caroline Atherstone whose uncle, Edwin Atherstone, wrote the thirty-volume poem *The Fall of Ninevah* (1868). For reasons which the two biographers do not elaborate, the marriage was unhappy and ended in a separation. Linton reports meeting the poet's son, whom he describes as "a delicate nervous boy, little able to be of comfort to the life-wearied man." Also in 1844 Jones began to devote more attention to political concerns and schemes for social reform. Although he worked as an accountant until 1858, he also wrote several articles for the radical publishers Cleave and Hetherington, and he became involved in an unfortunate railway scheme in 1846. Three years later Jones's pamphlet on land-ownership reform, in which he anticipated Henry George's proposal to nationalize the land and to adopt a single tax, was published. Throughout the 1840s he was sympathetic to the demands of the Chartists. Dante Gabriel Rossetti met him in 1848 and later recalled that the young man "would hardly talk on any subject but Chartism." However, he did not actively or directly participate in the Chartist movement. During the 1850s he lived in Paultons-square, Chelsea, only a block away from his hero, Thomas Carlyle. Although he never called on the "Sage of Chelsea," he would watch for Carlyle to pass by.

Although Jones's interests turned increasingly to political matters after the failure of his book, he did not abandon poetry completely for politics. Resilience and self-reliance were always traits of his character. Linton reports that "through all unhappiness, even to the last, the poetic spirit had not departed from him." During the 1840s and 1850s journals such as *Ainsworth's* magazine, the *Critic,* the *Illuminated Magazine,* and the *People's Journal* published a half-dozen poems which represent his finest output and most enhance his reputation as a promising minor poet with a clear and impressive voice. A few of these later poems record what one critic views as Jones's "distress at the completeness of his failure." Thus, in "A Warning," the speaker's sensitive, poetic soul is left alone and alienated:

Then took he back his heart from the angels,
And over it long he mourned;
For he either could not or would not offer it
Back to the race he scorn'd.

By 1858 Jones was becoming increasingly weakened by consumption, and his last few years were spent on the Isle of Jersey. A few of his best poems were written there just before his death in 1860. Part of the inscription on his tomb in the rural Shenfield churchyard near Brentwood, Essex, reads: "To live in hearts we leave behind is not to die."

The two best poems of the later years are "When the World Is Burning" and "A Winter Hymn to the Snow." The firmer poem is an intense and impressive celebration of a vital energy which runs through nature and animates men and women to joyful love. The directions under the title read "Stanzas for Music," and the poem demonstrates a more disciplined form and firmer control of rhythm than can be found in most of his earlier compositions. It is the poet's function to paint nature's display of her pyrotechnics: the "Gentle flames" fly across the meadows to be "beholden" by the "bard." The vernal force inspires a joyful and passionate intensity, especially among young maidens:

Where the dance is sweeping,
Through the greensward peeping,
Shall the soft lights start;
Laughing maids, unstaying,
Deeming it trick-playing,
High their robes upswaying . . .

"A Winter Hymn to Snow" also displays remarkable discipline and a new control. In eleven brisk six-line iambic stanzas, the tight *aabccb* rhyme scheme perfectly matches the paralyzed world in winter's cold grip. Although the images are those of death—"the frozen skeleton trees,/Dead to the winds" and "the long interminable frost"—the poem conveys more the impression of winter's awesome, desolate beauty than a morbid preoccupation with gloom or decay. With the most minute description, the poet renders the natural world's humility before the raw power of winter:

The shrunk grass shivers feebly; reed and sedge,
By frozen marsh, by rivulet's iron edge,

Bow, blent into the ice, mix'd stems and blades.

The snow's arrival enhances the "great trance of rest" with the decorative touch of metaphorical "white robes." Yet this final transformation by the snow goes beyond mere decorative significance: it stands for a redemptive force which works upon society. With cautious optimism the dying speaker advances his hope: "How the whole race from out their homes will gaze!/Hard hearts will restless grow, and mean men sigh,/And wish they could be holier...."

In 1870 Dante Gabriel Rossetti aroused a new interest in Jones's life and work which gained momentum throughout the decade. In a letter published in *Notes and Queries*, Rossetti called him "this remarkable poet, who affords nearly the most striking instance of neglected genius in our modern school of poetry.... His poems (the *Studies of Sensation and Event*) ... are full of vivid disorderly power.... For all this, these 'Studies' should be, and one day will be, disinterred from the heaps of verse deservedly buried.... It is fully time that attention should be called to this poet's name, which is a noteworthy one." A trio of articles on Jones appeared during September and October 1878 in the *Athenaeum*. Also, in 1879 Richard Herne Shepherd, who was introduced to Jones's poetry through Rossetti's article, completed the task of republishing the poetry of the forgotten figure, along with extended memorial notices written especially for the volume by Sumner Jones and Linton. Although Shepherd stated his intention of publishing a second volume of some of Jones's unpublished poems, "together with a reprint of the pamphlet on the Land Monopoly, some other prose pieces, and perhaps a few letters," he never completed the project. Two other critics who wrote serious articles seeking to enhance Jones's poetic reputation were T. S. Perry in 1887 and Ramsay Colles in 1904. In 1909, the renewed interest culminated in T. Mardy Rees's revaluative pamphlet, *Ebenezer Jones: The Neglected Poet*. After that, almost no attention was paid to Jones until the 1950s. In 1951 Jerome H. Buckley devoted several pages to him in the chapter on "The Spasmodic School" in *The Victorian Temper*. He concluded that "Of all the forgotten lyrists, the most pathetic may well have been Ebenezer Jones...." In 1957 Hoxie Fairchild complained that his "poems of social indignation are shrill, vague, and trite." Fairchild detected inconsistencies and intellectual incoherence in the verse; with little critical sympathy, he dismissed the poetic efforts of "this confused and desperate man."

Jones's reputation, then, has not been finally settled. Certainly his effort, in his brother's words, to "emancipate himself by his pen from City thraldom, and not himself alone" represents an impressive personal courage that is of some social significance. Although he never attained literary or material success, it is hard not to admire the energy, willpower, and perseverance that he invested in the yearning to be a poet. He composed under very difficult circumstances, and he lacked the refined education to correct his sometimes abrasive poetic lines. Yet in studying his life and his poetry, one senses the authentic, if unfulfilled, promise and recognizes the validity of Linton's tribute: "Sensations of the keenest, whence quick impulses; clear insight as to right and wrong, from which arose his indignation against injustice; fearlessness and fortitude, and with them tenderness for others; rare poetic gifts, and at the same time the practical talent and good sense of a man of the world: all these belonged to Ebenezer Jones."

Biography:
Memorial notices by Sumner Jones and William James Linton, in *Studies of Sensation and Event: Poems by Ebenezer Jones*, edited by Richard Herne Shepherd (London: Pickering, 1879), pp. xvii-lxxxiv.

References:
Jerome H. Buckley, *The Victorian Temper: A Study in Literary Culture* (Cambridge: Harvard University Press, 1951), pp. 48-52, 61;

Ramsay Colles, "Ebenezer Jones," *The Gentleman's Magazine*, 297 (August 1904): 143-155;

Hoxie Neale Fairchild, *Religious Trends in English Poetry*, volume 4 (New York: Columbia University Press, 1957), pp. 409-417;

Jack Lindsay, "Ebenezer Jones, 1820-1860: An English Symbolist," in *Rebels and Their Causes: Essays in Honour of A. L. Morton*, edited by Maurice Cornforth (London: Lawrence & Wishart, 1978; Atlantic Highlands, N.J.: Humanities, 1979), pp. 151-175;

William J. Linton, "Ebenezer Jones," in *The Poets and the Poetry of the Nineteenth Century: Charles Kingsley to James Thomson*, edited by Alfred H. Miles, volume 5 (London: Routledge, 1905), pp. 19-26;

T. S. Perry, "A Poet Redivivus," *Harvard Monthly*, 4 (June 1887): 127-136;

T. Mardy Rees, *Ebenezer Jones: The Neglected Poet, 1820-1860* (London?, 1909).

Ernest Jones

(25 January 1819-26 January 1868)

Nicholas Coles
University of Pittsburgh

BOOKS: *Infantine Effusions* (Hamburg: Nestler, 1830);

The Student of Padua: A Domestic Tragedy in Five Acts (London: Cox, 1836);

The Wood-Spirit: A Novel, 2 volumes (London: Boone, 1841);

My Life; or, Our Social State: A Poem, as Percy de Vere (London: Newby, 1845);

Chartist Songs (London, 1846);

Canterbury versus Rome (London, 1851);

Rhymes on the Times (London: Brettell, 1852);

The Maid of Warsaw; or, The Tyrant Czar: A Tale of the Last Polish Revolution (London, 1855);

The Lass and the Lady; or, Love's Ladder: A Tale of Thrilling Interest, completed by T. Frost (London: McGowan, 1855);

Woman's Wrongs: A Series of Tales (London, 1855);

The Battle-Day, and Other Poems (London & New York: Routledge, 1855);

The Song of the Lower Classes: A Song of Cromwell's Time (London, 1856);

Evenings with the People, 10 parts (London, 1856-1857);

Songs of Democracy (London, 1856);

The Emperor's Vigil, and The Waves and the War (London: Routledge, 1856);

Corayda: A Tale of Faith and Chivalry, and Other Poems (Manchester, U.K., 1856; London: Kent, 1860);

The Revolt of Hindostan; or, The New World: A Poem (London, 1857);

The Trial for Murder, Rex v. Levi Taylor (Manchester, U.K., 1863);

The Slaveholder's War (Ashton-under-Lyme, U.K.: Union and Emancipation Society, 1863);

The Danish War: Non-intervention Meeting at Manchester (Manchester, U.K., 1864);

Oration of Ernest Jones . . . on the American Rebellion (Rochdale, U.K.: Haworth, 1864);

Labour and Capital: A Lecture . . . to Which Are Appended in Full the Leading Articles Thereon from the "Saturday Review," "The Times" and the "Pall Mall Gazette," with Answers Thereto. . . . (London: Simpkin & Marshall, 1867);

Democracy Vindicated . . . in Reply to Professor Blackie's Lecture on Democracy (Edinburgh: Elliot/London: Ridgway/Manchester: Heywood, 1867);

The Politics of the Day (Edinburgh, 1868);

The Right of Public Meeting (Halifax, U.K., 1880).

Ernest Jones

Ernest Jones, "the Chartist Poet," is best known for his leadership in the democratic working-class movement. He came to Chartism late and is credited with having prolonged its life for a decade by virtue of his personal energy and optimism. The failure of the movement for the vote led Jones in the 1850s to advocate socialism; his friends Marx and Engels considered him "the only educated Englishman among the politicians who was... entirely on our side." Jones's political reputation has overshadowed his achievement as a poet and novelist; yet it was in Chartism that he found the audience and the subject matter for his best writing, and his rapid rise to leadership owed much to the popularity of his songs and poems among the Chartist rank and file.

There was little in Ernest Charles Jones's background to suggest his future political path. He was the only child of Major Charles Jones, a distinguished veteran of the Peninsular War, and spent his earliest years at the Prussian royal court in Berlin where his father was equerry to the duke of Cumberland, Queen Victoria's uncle. On the major's retirement the family moved to an estate in Holstein on the borders of the Black Forest. Here Ernest's education became the primary family project. In 1830, "as a reward for his attention to his studies," his father arranged publication of a collection of Ernest's childhood poems. These *Infantine Effusions,* proudly circulated to all the nobles in the major's acquaintance, show appetites for pastoral idyllicism and for military adventure, both of which continued into his mature writing. The volume includes verses on the death of Ernest's godfather, Lord Charles Murray, "who sacrificed his fortune and his life in the cause of the Greeks." At twelve Ernest acted on this martial and libertarian spirit: after having been missing for three days, he was found in the Black Forest on his way to help the Poles in their revolt against the czar.

Jones completed his education at the exclusive military College of St. Michael at Lüneburg, from which he graduated with highest honors. In 1838 his family moved back to England, probably to be in a position to further his intended career as a writer. In London he immersed himself in fashionable society. His diary for these years is largely a record of dinners, dances, and soirees attended by the notables of the day. In 1841 he was presented at court by the duke of Beaufort. Although he was affable by nature and obviously enjoying himself, Jones's careful listing of every new acquaintance—Disraeli, Bulwer-Lytton, John Forster—suggests that he was also cultivating connections that would help him in his literary ventures. He had an early success with his novel *The Wood-Spirit* (1841), which was modestly acclaimed by contemporary critics, though it is now generally judged unreadable. Its subject and setting are typical of Jones's literary preoccupations in the early 1840s: a romance between Altren, an itinerant knight, and Valdine, queen of the fairies, is set in medieval Jutland amid the swirling warfare of the German principalities. "The plot is mysteriously deep," writes George Howell, whose biography of Jones was serialized in the *Newcastle Weekly Chronicle* in 1898. "There is a weirdness in some of its scenes which will be best appreciated by the Jutlanders."

Jones was unable to find publishers for two long poems, "Corayda" and "Lord Lindsay," both also "tales of faith and chivalry." Nor did he fare much better as a dramatist. Although he offered numerous plays to all the London theaters and to his actor friends Kean, Kemble, and Macready, none were ever staged. They did not fail for lack of enticing titles: "King Death," "Love and the Monkey," and "The Libertine" were typical. In November 1842 he complained to his diary of "numberless refusals of work and minor pieces by almost all the magazines and publishers."

In June 1841 Jones married Jane Atherley in a "dashing wedding" in St. George's, Hanover Square. Perhaps because of the tenuousness of his literary prospects he entered the Middle Temple to train as a barrister. He was called to the bar in 1844 but did not practice until 1860, after the last of his Chartist journals folded. In 1844 he bought a large house and estate in Kent for the enormous sum of £57,000. It is not clear why he wanted to take up the life of a country gentleman on such a grand scale, but the result was that he overreached himself financially, could not complete the purchase, and went bankrupt. His house in Kensington was sold; his wife's jewelry was pawned; and the family, which by then included two sons, retreated to a cottage in Hampstead.

It seems likely that it was this cracking of the shell of the affluent life to which he was accustomed that precipitated Jones's dramatic political conversion in the winter of 1845-1846. He was confronted for the first time with the need to earn a living, which he did as secretary to a railway company. *My Life; or, Our Social State,* published in 1845 under the pseudonym Percy de Vere, marks the turning from the medievalism of his earlier writing to a critical evaluation of his own life and times. The poem is about an aristocratic family; the narrative perspective is that of its disaffected younger son. It combines a critique of the aristocrats' betrayal of their responsibilities toward the poor with satirical pity for their shrunken lives:

'Tis wearisome to vegetate,
Still going downwards, slow and late.
. . . .

Their great dim Future overcast
With shadows from their weary Past;
And these proud men with secret pain
Longed—how they longed—to live again!

In January 1846, "having accidentally seen a copy of the *Northern Star,* and finding the political principles advocated harmonized with my own," Jones took a copy of *My Life* to the *Star*'s editorial office and presumably offered to write for the Chartist newspaper. He quickly got to know Feargus O'Connor, the foremost leader of Chartism and its other important recruit from the gentry. Jones's background was, oddly, an asset in his new career; as a fellow Chartist recalled, "The young sprig of Aristocracy, promoted, as O'Connor would have said, to the ranks of the Democracy, was received with enthusiasm." Jones quickly established himself as a superb orator and tireless organizer. He was elected a delegate to the Chartist convention in Leeds; in August he made his first speaking tour of the North, where he was already famous as the "poet of Chartism." His poems in the *Northern Star* had been reprinted as broadsides; and twelve, including "O'Connorville" and "Onward and Upward," were collected into a penny booklet of *Chartist Songs* (1846). Jones here achieves the passionate directness that made his poems favorite recitation pieces among the Chartists. Unlike other Chartist poets who used complex metrics as a way of separating themselves from the disreputable street literature, Jones favored popular verse forms. Many of his political poems were literally songs, usually set to well-known folk tunes, although the popular "Song of the Low" (1852) had music composed for it by John Lowry. Jones's simple melodramatic images focused present wrongs and provided a vision of future liberation. In "The Factory Town,"

Women, children, men were toiling,
    Locked in dungeons close and black,
Life's fast-failing thread uncoiling
    Round the wheel, the *modern rack.*

E'en the very stars seemed troubled
    With the mingled fume and roar;
The city like a cauldron bubbled,
    With its poison boiling o'er.

But after the coming great change,

Then, how many a happy village
    Shall be smiling o'er the plain,
Amid the cornfield's pleasant tillage,
    And the orchard's rich domain!

While, the rotting roof and rafter,
    Drops the factory, stone by stone,
Echoing loud with childhood's laughter,
    Where it rung with manhood's groan.

Even the Tory *Quarterly Review* found the *Chartist Songs* "replete with fire of genius . . . ; for eloquence and destructive power they appear to us almost unrivalled. We say destructive for their tendency is worse than democratic." Jones was exhilarated by the response to his verse. He confided his new sense of mission to his diary: "I am pouring the tide of my songs over England, forming the tone of the mighty mind of the people."

In addition to his nightly lecturing around London, Jones in January 1847 became a subeditor of the *Northern Star* and in the same month launched his first literary-political journal, *The Labourer,* with O'Connor as coeditor. He also found time to stand for Halifax in the 1847 parliamentary elections, the first of five unsuccessful electoral attempts. Chartism was reviving from a decline in activity during the relatively prosperous mid-1840s, inspired in part by the revolutionary movements on the Continent; and the talk turned to "ulterior measures" to be taken if the third petition for the National Charter met the same rejection as those of 1839 and 1842. Jones declared in favor of the use of physical force, "if we must." At the demonstration for the presentation of their "monster" petition on 10 April 1848 at Kennington Common, the Chartists were outnumbered by the police and dispersed peacefully. However, the government began a roundup of the leaders, and on 6 June Jones was arrested for making a seditious speech on 30 May. After a trial in which the prosecution made much of his "turning traitor" to his own class, Jones was sentenced to two years' solitary confinement.

Jones's treatment in prison was severe in the extreme—a deliberate attempt was made to break his health and spirit. At one point he was put on bread and water for three days for refusing to pick oakum; O'Connor was able to purchase his exemption from this duty, and he also paid Jones's legal fees. Two Chartists imprisoned with Jones died from cold and hunger within six months. Appeals by sympathetic M.P.s for Jones's early release were denied by the home secretary, who demanded political recantation as a condition of relief. Jones was held in Tothill Fields, the "model prison" damned for its leniency by Carlyle in his *Latter-Day*

Pamphlets (1850). Jones was, in fact, the "philosophical or literary Chartist" peered at by the visiting Sage and envied for his freedom from the cares of the world—freedom in which Carlyle felt that he would have been able to write the Ultimate Book. Jones was allowed no books or writing materials, but he did manage to compose a number of poems. The best known of these, "The New World," was written "with the aid of blood [he was allowed a razor] and memory," with quills gathered in the prison yard, in the margins of the cell's prayer book. Published in the first issue (May 1851) of *Notes to the People,* the journal Jones started after his release, "The New World" is a historical overview of the progress of liberty, culminating in a utopian prophecy of a unified world freed from oppression. Although its heroic couplets become tiresomely declamatory, it represents a remarkable synthesis of historical knowledge and socialist theory. (The poem was republished as *The Revolt of Hindostan* in 1857, when Jones was defending the Indian mutiny as a nationalist uprising against the empire on which "the sun never sets, but the blood never dries.")

On his release Jones toured the country to revive the movement for the Charter. But the Chartist faithful were divided, this time over the issue of collaboration with middle-class radicals for a limited electoral reform. Jones joined those who were for "the Charter and something more"—the something more being a program of social rights that would be attainable only under socialism—and in doing so he broke politically with O'Connor. In May 1851, with advice and political tutoring from Karl Marx, Jones launched his weekly *Notes to the People,* which a year later became the *People's Paper,* the central Chartist organ of the 1850s. Both papers were committed to literature and the cultural elevation it represented to the Chartists, as well as to economic analysis and political persuasion. Alongside his own verse Jones published his translations of French and German radical poets, an annotated series on "The Poets of England" (particularly Crabbe, Wordsworth, and the Brownings), and another on the American poets. The *People's Paper* also featured Jones's prose political fables, a series of tales entitled *Woman's Wrongs* (republished in a single volume in 1855), and his serialized Chartist novel "De Brassier: a Democratic Romance" (May 1851-March 1852).

The *People's Paper* was never a paying proposition, but Jones was now able to support himself on the fruits of his literary output. His poetry finally gained acceptance among the audience he had cultivated in the early 1840s. His greatest successes came with *The Battle-Day, and Other Poems* (1855), *Corayda: A Tale of Faith and Chivalry, and Other Poems* (1856), and *The Emperor's Vigil, and The Waves and the War* (1856). Jones's political notoriety may have drawn reviewers to his work, but they were relieved by what they found there. *Tait's Magazine* wrote of *The Battle-Day:* "A genuine poet! . . . In these poems he is not more democratic than Tennyson, and not more Socialistic than Lord John Manners." Most of the poems in the first two books were indeed written before the onset of Jones's political enthusiasm: the title poem of *The Battle-Day* is the former "Lord Lindsay"; "Corayda" hails from 1841; "My Life," retitled "Percy Vere," is split between *The Battle-Day* and *Corayda.* Some Chartist poems are reprinted, including "The Better Hope," a moving account of his own political conversion. "The Factory Town," however, appears in amended form, lacking some of its "destructive power." Jones was at pains, as he put it, to "separate the poet from the politician." In dedicating *Corayda* to Bulwer-Lytton, he tactfully expressed his belief that "the Republic of Letters is beyond and above the political differences of the passing day."

The Emperor's Vigil was Jones's contribution to the popular Crimean war fever and, as such, became his surest success with the critics. "Every patriot should possess a copy of this spirited effusion," declared the *Observer.* In the war cause, too, Jones was a master at catching the spirit of the time and translating it into powerful images: he depicts the dying Czar Nicholas pacing the night in his "granite palace," while the ghosts of those he has trampled arise and cry for revenge.

The *People's Paper* folded in 1858 as the last of the Chartist organizations disbanded. In the bitterness which accompanied this collapse G. W. M. Reynolds, the novelist and a rival Chartist leader, accused Jones in *Reynolds's Newspaper* of financial dishonesty in running the *People's Paper.* The charges hurt Jones personally and damaged his campaign for election to Parliament from Nottingham; he had received 614 votes when he stood in 1857, but the total fell to only 151 in 1859. Attributing the difference to Reynolds's attacks, Jones brought a libel action against Reynolds; Jones won handily, drawing tributes from the judge and jury to his "honesty and integrity." As proof of Jones's self-sacrifice in the cause, it was disclosed at the trial that on his release from prison his uncle had offered to leave him an estate worth £2,000 a year if he would abandon his activism. Jones had, of course, refused and the estate went to his uncle's gardener.

With the exception of some fine political pamphlets, Jones did no more substantial writing. His time was filled with his practice as a successful barrister on the Northern circuit and with his lectures for the Reform League. In early 1868 he contested Manchester in his fifth try for Parliament. He ran a strong second to the Conservative, who, however, was petitioned against for corruption. Jones would almost certainly have won the second ballot, but the realization of this ambition was prevented by his sudden death, one day after his forty-ninth birthday. (Some reference works erroneously give the year of his death as 1869.) Deputations from all over England attended the funeral, and he was followed to his grave by a procession of thousands.

In his preface to the *Infantine Effusions* Jones's father had boasted that they were written "without the least apparent labour of the mind and with a rapidity that is truly surprising." Jones always had a certain fatal facility for versification. At its best, however, and particularly under the forced economy of his years in prison or on the road for the Charter, his verse powerfully communicates his anger at oppression and his persistent hope for humanity. It deserves to be studied both for its intrinsic satisfactions and for its part in the political culture of the working class.

Biographies:

George Howell, "Life of Ernest Jones," *Newcastle Weekly Chronicle,* January-August 1898;

John Saville, *Ernest Jones: Chartist* (London: Lawrence & Wishart, 1952).

References:

G. D. H. Cole, *Chartist Portraits* (London: Macmillan, 1965), pp. 337-357;

Martha Vicinus, *The Industrial Muse* (New York: Barnes & Noble, 1974), pp. 94-139.

Papers:

Ernest Jones's papers are housed at the Manchester Reference Library.

John Keble
(25 April 1792-29 March 1866)

G. B. Tennyson
University of California, Los Angeles

BOOKS: *On Translation from Dead Languages: A Prize Essay* (Oxford: Privately printed, 1812);
The Christian Year: Thoughts in Verse for the Sundays and Holydays throughout the Year, anonymous, 2 volumes (Oxford: Parker/London: Rivington, 1827; New York: Dutton, 1827);
National Apostasy Considered in a Sermon (Oxford: Parker/London: Rivington, 1833);
Ode for the Encaenia at Oxford, anonymous (Oxford, 1834);
Tracts for the Times by Members of the University of Oxford, numbers 4, 13, 40, 52, 54, 57, 60, 89 by Keble, 6 volumes (Oxford: Parker/London: Rivington, 1833-1841);
Lyra Apostolica, anonymous, by Keble and John William Bowden, Richard Hurrell Froude, John Henry Newman, Robert Isaac Wilberforce, and Isaac Williams (Derby, U.K.: Mozley, 1836);
Primitive Tradition Recognized in Holy Scripture: A Sermon (London: Rivington, 1836);
The Psalter or Psalms of David in English Verse, anonymous (Oxford: Parker, 1839);
The Case of Catholic Subscription to the Thirty-nine Articles Considered (London: Privately printed, 1841);
De Poeticae vi Medica: Praelectiones Academicae (Oxford: Parker, 1844); translated by Edward Kershaw Francis as Keble's *Lectures on Poetry 1832-1841,* 2 volumes (Oxford: Clarendon Press, 1912);
Lyra Innocentium: Thoughts in Verse on Christian Children, Their Ways, and Their Privileges, anonymous (Oxford & London: Parker, 1846; New York: Wiley & Putnam, 1846);
Sermons, Academical and Occasional (Oxford & London: Parker, 1847);
On Eucharistical Adoration (Oxford & London: Parker, 1857);
The Life of the Right Reverend Father in God, Thomas

John Keble

Wilson, 8 volumes (Oxford: Parker, 1863);

Sermons, Occasional and Parochial (Oxford & London: Parker, 1868);

Village Sermons on the Baptismal Service, edited by E. B. Pusey (Oxford: Parker, 1868);

Miscellaneous Poems, edited by G. Moberly (Oxford & London: Parker, 1869; New York: Polt & Amery, 1869);

Letters of Spiritual Counsel and Guidance, edited by R. F. Wilson (Oxford & London: Parker, 1870);

Sermons for the Christian Year, 11 volumes (Oxford: Parker, 1875-1880);

Occasional Papers and Reviews, edited by Pusey (Oxford & London: Parker, 1877);

Studia Sacra, edited by J. P. Norris (Oxford & London: Parker, 1877).

OTHER: *Works of Richard Hooker,* edited by Keble, 3 volumes (Oxford: Oxford University Press, 1836);

Five Books of St. Irenaeus against Heresies, translated by Keble, in *A Library of the Fathers of the Holy Catholic Church,* edited by E. B. Pusey, 51 volumes (Oxford: Parker, 1838-1885);

Remains of the Late Reverend Richard Hurrell Froude, edited by Keble and John Henry Newman, 4 volumes (London: Rivington, 1838-1839).

Called by John Henry Newman the "true and primary author" of the Oxford or Tractarian Movement, John Keble was also the author of the single most popular volume of verse in the nineteenth century, *The Christian Year* (1827). Though little known today, Keble's poetry was highly enough regarded in the Victorian age to prompt critics and readers to compare him favorably with the greatest devotional poets of the English language, and Keble must still be regarded as an innovative and influential force in English religious poetry.

Keble came from an old, established family in Gloucestershire with longtime ecclesiastical connections. He was the eldest of five children, two boys and three girls, of Sarah Maule Keble and John Keble, Sr. Keble's father was the vicar of Coln St. Aldwyn's and resided at Fairford. The senior John Keble was a Tory churchman of the traditional Catholic-minded school, and Keble the Tractarian always claimed that he preached no doctrine or practice that he had not learned at his father's knee. The senior Keble sent John and his younger brother Thomas to Corpus Christi College, Oxford, where John distinguished himself by taking double first-class honors in 1811; he was only the second person in history to do so. Keble was elected a fellow of Oriel College and was ordained deacon in 1815 and priest in 1816. Legendary at Oxford for his piety and learning (years later Newman recalled being in profound awe when he first gazed upon Keble in the street), Keble served as fellow, tutor, and public examiner until 1823. Upon the death of his mother in that year, he returned to Fairford to care for his father and to serve as a priest at Coln St. Aldwyn's and in adjacent parishes. For the next twelve years he declined all ecclesiastical offers in order to remain near his father. He continued to maintain Oxford contacts, numbering Newman and Richard Hurrell Froude among his disciples, and in 1827 he yielded to the entreaties of his father and Oxford friends that he have his private devotional verse published in book form. The result was *The Christian Year.* It immediately established Keble in the forefront of the serious religious poets of the

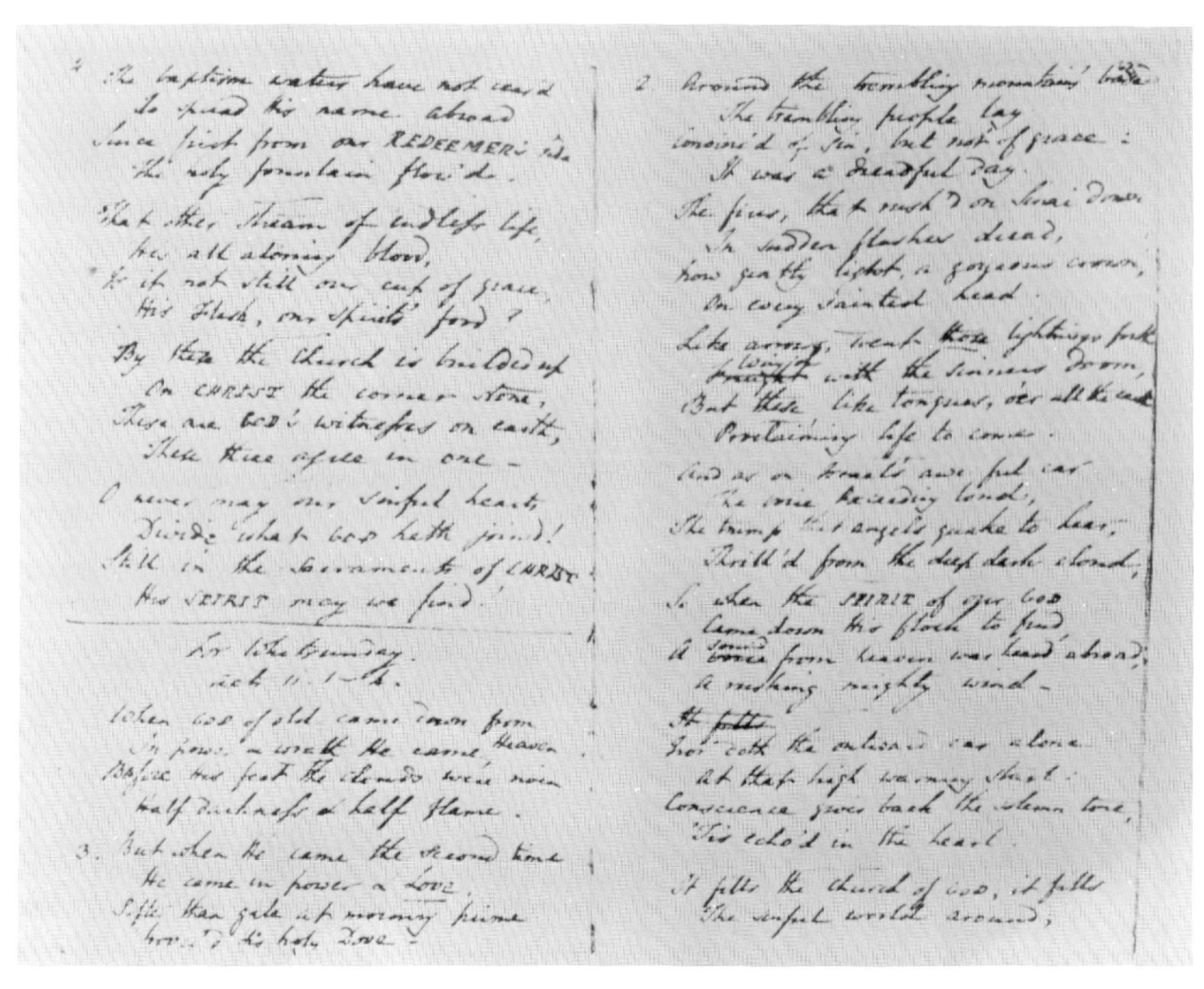

Manuscript pages for an early draft of The Christian Year

age, and it ensured him national celebrity for the rest of his life.

Partly because of the success of *The Christian Year* and partly because of his critical writings and deep theological learning, in 1831 Keble was appointed professor of poetry at Oxford, a post he held for ten years. His lectures, published in their original Latin in 1844 but not translated into English until 1912, exercised an important theoretical influence on the Oxford Movement. In Newman's view that movement had been inaugurated by Keble himself with the delivery of his sermon *National Apostasy* on 14 July 1833. The sermon was an attack on the presumption of the national government in determining to eliminate ten episcopal sees in Ireland, a decision Keble felt should be left entirely to ecclesiastical authorities. It marked the first notable public assertion of the divine status of the Church as commissioned by Christ and as sustained by the apostolic succession, and hence as above state interference. Such a conviction of the Church as a divine institution, coupled with an emphasis on Christian theology, traditional forms of worship, Catholic sacramentalism, and a priestly hierarchy, characterized the beliefs of the Oxford Movement, also known as the Tractarian Movement from the *Tracts for the Times* published between 1833 and 1841.

After 1833 Keble was esteemed as the senior spiritual force behind the Tractarian Movement; and, although not resident in Oxford, he participated in all the major literary and theological undertakings of the movement. He contributed forty-six poems to the Tractarian collection *Lyra Apostolica* (1836), he wrote eight of the most important *Tracts for the Times,* and he edited the works of the great Elizabethan theologian Richard Hooker (1836). He

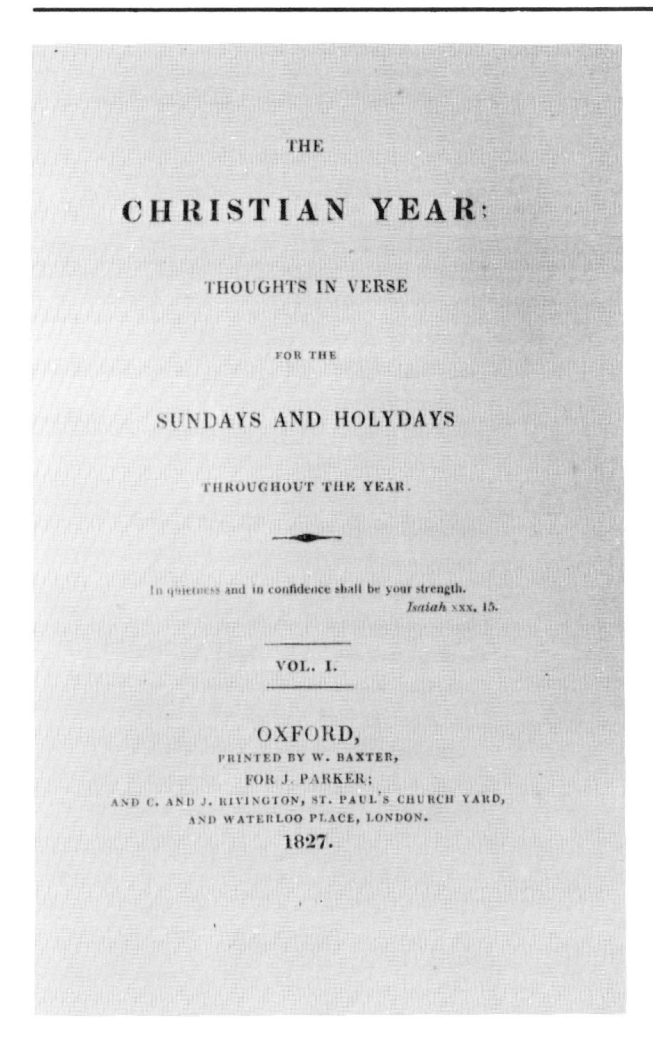

Title page for Keble's most popular work (Thomas Cooper Library, University of South Carolina)

joined in the Tractarian project the *Library of the Fathers* (1838-1885) by contributing a translation of the writings of St. Irenaeus.

Keble's father died in 1835. Later the same year Keble married Charlotte Clarke, a friend from childhood and sister of his brother's wife, and accepted the living of Hursley in Hampshire; he was installed as vicar in January 1836, and remained there until his death in 1866. He continued to write both poetry and theological works and to exercise his irenic and stabilizing influence on the course of the Oxford Movement, especially during the distresses of 1845 when Newman converted to the Roman church. Keble's subsequent written work—the poetry in *Lyra Innocentium* (1846), an eight-volume *Life of the Right Reverend Father in God, Thomas Wilson* (1863) in the Library of Anglo-Catholic Theology, and many volumes of sermons (most published posthumously)—though highly regarded, never attained the extraordinary popularity of *The Christian Year;* but his personal example of self-effacing piety and unswerving pastoral care became so greatly admired that he was widely spoken of as an Anglican saint. Among his local parishioners Keble made an especially deep impression on Charlotte Mary Yonge, who went on to enshrine Keble's attitudes and standards of churchmanship in a series of domestic novels that enjoyed enormous popularity in the Victorian age. She also wrote biographical and critical works on Keble himself.

Keble's health and that of his wife both deteriorated in the mid-1860s, and they sought a milder climate along the southern coast of England. It was at Bournemouth in March 1866 that Keble died, followed in a few weeks by his wife. He was buried at Hursley Churchyard and memorialized with plaques and busts at Salisbury Cathedral and Westminster Abbey. But the most imposing memorial to Keble was the opening in 1869, in buildings designed by the Tractarian architect William Butterfield, of a new Oxford college bearing Keble's

Keble's wife, Charlotte, in the year of their marriage

Keble's favorite corner in the Hursley vicarage

name and dedicated to education in conformity with the principles of the Church of England.

As a poet Keble's claim to attention resides in *The Christian Year,* which is important both as a historical phenomenon and as poetry. Keble's poetry, in this and in later volumes, exhibits a Wordsworthian response to nature as beautiful and moving in its own right, infused at the same time with an intense awareness of nature as a manifestation of God's design and power, and an awareness of nature as a sacrament, a vehicle of divine grace. Keble and the Tractarians called the idea that all of nature is an analogue of God's works and ways and is thus an avenue to Him the doctrine of analogy. At the same time Keble's poetry is intentionally subdued in accordance with another Tractarian doctrine, that of reserve, which holds that sacred matters must be veiled and approached with reverence. These qualities are well illustrated in the first two stanzas of Keble's poem for Septuagesima Sunday:

There is a Book, who runs may read,
    Which heavenly Truth imparts,
And all the lore its scholars need,
    Pure eyes and Christian hearts.

The works of God above, below,

Within us and around,
Are pages in that Book to shew
    How God Himself is found.

What gives Keble's collection a special quality is its organization around the order of the Anglican Book of Common Prayer, with poems for every Sunday and holy day and all other services and provisions of the prayer book. The consonance of *The Christian Year* with the prayer book accounts in some measure for the unparalleled popularity of the volume, for it became a spiritual companion to the prayer book and was widely used in family worship and devotional reading. It was common in middle- and upper-middle-class homes for the appropriate Keble poem from *The Christian Year* to be read aloud at family prayers on Sundays and holy days in conjunction with the appointed prayer book readings. This practice continued in many Anglican homes through the end of the century; and few homes of any shade of religious view were without a copy of Keble's volume, for it had gone through 95 editions by the time of Keble's death in 1866 and more than 200 by the end of the century, a record unmatched by any other single work of the period. Many Victorians came to know Keble poems, or portions of them, by heart. In one celebrated case Newman found himself moved by a scene in nature to utter lines of verse he thought were his own—"Chanting with a solemn voice/Minds us of our better choice"—only later to discover that he had been reciting a passage from *The Christian Year*.

In addition to paving the way for the Tractarian revival and to providing a devotional outlet in verse for High-Church Anglican sensibilities, Keble also enunciated a theoretical basis for the relation of religion and poetry that may prove to be his most enduring contribution to literature. The lectures Keble delivered in his capacity as professor of poetry at Oxford from 1831 to 1841 are still only slightly known, but they constitute the most sustained argument on behalf of the kinship and interaction of religion and poetry undertaken in the nineteenth century. Keble conceives of poetry as religious emotion, discusses the principles of analogy and reserve that guided the literary efforts of the Tractarians, and distinguishes primary from secondary poets. Because the lectures were available only in Latin in Keble's own lifetime they never reached beyond the learned audience, but they have come in for increased attention in recent critical writings about nineteenth-century poetic theory.

Besides holding a secure place in ecclesiastical history, Keble also commands attention both as a poet whose sensibility appealed to a vast body of Victorian readers and as a theorist of poetry whose critical writings well repay study by critics and scholars of the Victorian age.

Charlotte and John Keble in later life

Keble as drawn by George Richmond in 1863

Biographies:
J. T. Coleridge, *A Memoir of the Rev. John Keble* (Oxford & London: Parker, 1869);

John Frewen Moor, *The Birth-Place, Home, Churches and Other Places Connected with the Author of "The Christian Year"* (London: Savage & Parker, 1877);

Walter Lock, *John Keble: A Biography* (London: Methuen, 1893);

Charlotte Mary Yonge, *John Keble's Parishes: A History of Hursley and Otterbourne* (London: Macmillan, 1898);

Georgina Battiscombe, *John Keble* (London: Constable, 1963);

Brian W. Martin, *John Keble, Priest, Professor and Poet* (London: Croom Helm, 1976).

References:

Willem Joseph Antoine Marie Beek, *John Keble's Literary and Religious Contributions to the Oxford Movement* (Nijmegen, Netherlands, 1959);

J. C. Shairp, *John Keble* (Edinburgh: Edmonston & Douglas, 1866);

G. B. Tennyson, *Victorian Devotional Poetry: The Tractarian Mode* (Cambridge: Harvard University Press, 1981), pp. 1-113, 215-232;

Charlotte Mary Yonge, *Musings over "The Christian Year," with Gleanings from Thirty Years' Intercourse with the Late Rev. J. Keble* (Oxford & London: Parker, 1871).

Papers:

Most of John Keble's papers are at Keble College, Oxford; additional holdings are at Pusey House, Oxford, and the Bodleian Library, Oxford.

Fanny Kemble
(27 November 1809-15 January 1893)

Lionel Adey
University of Victoria

BOOKS: *Francis the First: An Historical Drama* (London: Murray, 1832; New York: Peabody, 1833);

Journal of F. A. Butler, 2 volumes (London: Murray, 1835; Philadelphia: Carey, Lea & Blanchard, 1835);

The Star of Seville, a Drama. In Five Acts (London & New York: Saunders & Otley, 1837);

Poems (Philadelphia: Penington, 1844; republished, with poems in a different order, London: Washbourne, 1844);

A Year of Consolation, 2 volumes (London: Moxon, 1847; New York: Wiley, 1849);

Journal of a Residence on a Georgian Plantation in 1838-1839 (London: Longman, Green, Longman, Roberts & Green, 1863; New York: Harper, 1863);

Plays: An English Tragedy, Mary Stuart (Translated from the German of Schiller), Mademoiselle de Belle Isle (Translated from the French of Dumas) (London: Longman, Green, Longman, Roberts & Green, 1863);

Poems (London: Moxon, 1866);

Record of a Girlhood: An Autobiography (3 volumes, London: Bentley, 1878-1879; 1 volume, New York: Holt, 1879);

Notes upon Some of Shakespeare's Plays (London: Bentley, 1882);

Records of Later Life (3 volumes, London: Bentley,

Fanny Kemble as sketched by Sir Thomas Lawrence (courtesy of Edward H. Gooch, Limited)

1882; 1 volume, New York: Holt, 1882);
Adventures of John Timothy Homespun in Switzerland: A Play Stolen from the French of Tartarin de Tareascon (London: Bentley, 1889);
Far Away and Long Ago (London: Bentley, 1889; New York: Holt, 1889);
Further Records 1848-1883, 2 volumes (London: Bentley, 1890; New York: Holt, 1891).

Frances Anne Kemble was born into a theatrical family: she was the niece of John Philip Kemble, the actor-manager of Drury Lane, and the actress Mrs. Sarah Kemble Siddons and the daughter of Charles Kemble, actor-proprietor of Covent Garden. Her mother, the actress Marie Theresa De Camp Kemble, wishing to fit her for a higher milieu than the stage, had her educated in France. From childhood Fanny wrote compulsively, and at sixteen she completed *Francis the First* (1832), a verse-tragedy the actor William Charles Macready found "full of power, poetry and pathos." Its reception by audiences, however, was lukewarm. In 1829 her mother persuaded her to play in *Romeo and Juliet* in a bid to stave off the impending bankruptcy of her father's theater. Stubby figure, pock-marked countenance, and stage fright notwithstanding, her Juliet became the talk of London. Her admirers included Sir Walter Scott, Samuel Rogers, and the painter Sir Thomas Lawrence, whose sketch of her became well known.

Her father took her to America for the 1832-1833 season; Harvard students idolized her and girls wore Fanny Kemble curls. At Philadelphia she and Pierce Butler, heir to a Georgia plantation, fell in love; they were married early in 1834. They had two daughters: Sarah, born in 1835, and Frances, born in 1838. Although she retired thankfully from the stage, her marriage soon proved to have been a tragic error. An unwilling immigrant, she yearned for the social and intellectual life she had known in London. Against her husband's wishes she had a journal published in 1835 that gave widespread offense by its criticism of American life and manners. A devout Evangelical, she openly sympathized with the abolitionist cause. Hoping that experience might change her views, her husband took her to Butler Island, Georgia, for the winter of 1838-1839. This time her journal remained unpublished until 1863, but her horror at the conditions and treatment of the slaves and her energetic but tactless efforts on their behalf infuriated her husband, who was a relatively humane slaveholder. They became more estranged after they returned to England in

Pierce Butler, Kemble's American husband (courtesy of Dr. Owen Wister and Miss Florence B. Kane)

1840 to be with her father, who was gravely ill. She and her sister Adelaide ("Totty"), a prima donna, were feted in London and in country mansions while her mediocre husband passed unnoticed. After their return to the United States in 1843 she refused Butler's demand that she abandon her closest American friends and finally left him for good, after thrice being persuaded by him to return during 1842 and 1843. The separation took place in 1844 but the deed was not signed until March 1845. Butler's conditions were so harsh that Fanny had to borrow her fare to England in the fall. A friend remarked that "Whichever side of the ocean she sojourned, she was homesick for the other." In December 1845 she and her father had their passages booked for America. When he changed his mind, she traveled to Rome to join her sister. Though her idyllic visions of Italian life were soon dispelled by the squalid living conditions of the people, she remained there until December 1846, when she resumed her acting career in the hope of saving up her fare to America to see her children. Her husband decided in 1847 to sue for divorce, citing her

Playbill for Kemble's first appearance on the stage

Slave quarters on Butler's plantation, Butler Island, Georgia (courtesy of Mrs. Margaret Davis Cate)

Kemble during her residence in America (The Historical Society of Pennsylvania)

acting as ground. The real reasons, however, were her refusal to subordinate herself to him and tolerate his extramarital love affairs. The uncontested suit dragged on until November 1849, when a Philadelphia court granted the divorce. Even more painful than the much-publicized lawsuit was Fanny's separation from her daughters until they came of age.

In 1844, to buy back her horse, which her husband had sold, Kemble had a book published containing about 100 of her lyrics and sonnets. Several of these voice an earlier unrequited passion for a fellow actor; a number express her love for Butler; rather more of them indicate her religious love of nature. The most numerous and most powerful reveal her bitter disappointment at the failure of her marriage. While "Prayer of a Lonely Heart" best expresses her frustrated longing for love, "To--" ("The fountain of my life") develops most completely her recurrent image of life as a spring or river. Her favorite and most self-revealing motifs are the tempestuous sea and the storm-clouded landscape. In her weltschmerz she follows her beloved Byron, but her intonation recalls that of Mrs. Browning, who thought her "inelastic . . . unpliant to her age." One of the sonnets from her 1844 volume is representative of her work:

There's not a fibre in my trembling frame
That does not vibrate when thy step draws near,
There's not a pulse that throbs not when I hear
Thy voice, thy breathing, nay, thy very name.
When thou art with me, every sense seems dull,
And all I am, or know, or feel, is thee;
My soul grows faint, my veins run liquid flame,
And my bewildered spirit seems to swim
In eddying whirls of passion, dizzily.
When thou art gone, there creeps into my heart
A cold and bitter consciousness of pain:
The light, the warmth of life, with thee depart,
And I sit dreaming o'er and o'er again
Thy greeting clasp, thy parting look, and tone;
And suddenly I wake—and am alone.

Though she dismissed her poems as "trumpery," they attracted reviews in the *Athenaeum* and *Quarterly Review*. Henry James, who became a friend in her old age, thought them underrated, being "all passionate and melancholy . . . perfectly individual and . . . lyrical."

For the two years before her divorce, Kemble had supported herself by acting in major English cities. Her acting career came to an end in 1848 following continual disagreements with Macready, who favored a naturalistic style of playing Shakespeare as against her concentration on bringing out the sounds and rhythms of the verse. By this time she had come to despise the theater, and turned to those solo readings of the entire Shakespeare corpus that earned her lasting prosperity and esteem. At first these readings were given in British cities to patrons still too dominated by Evangelicalism to approve of acting, but from the fall of 1848 they were mainly presented in America. Although her readings earned her a fortune during the next twenty years, she gave many performances for charity and never allowed her managers to overcharge for admission. Her lifelong admirer and obituarist Henry Lee attributed the success of her readings to her range and quality of voice, grace of gesture, "mobility and eloquence" of face, and, above all, her "comprehensive intelligence and deep feeling" for Shakespeare, "whose priestess she was." Longfellow wrote a sonnet about her readings. Her earnings enabled her to purchase York Farm near Lenox, Massachusetts, and to spend her summers in the Swiss Alps.

Before her final return to England in 1877, her reminiscences were published in the *Atlantic Monthly*. Even in her seventies she wrote a comedy and a historical novel and enjoyed the admiring friendship of Robert Browning, Edward FitzGerald, and Henry James.

In 1859 she had her poems republished, adding a further sixty-eight, many of which had been written during the year in Italy (1845-1846), described in *A Year of Consolation* (1847). Her publisher brought out a revised edition in 1883, replacing many of the 1844 poems with twenty-five new ones. Most of the new poems were on her old theme of disappointed love, now viewed less darkly. Three poetic expressions of her ardor for the Northern cause in the Civil War were much admired at that time. For all its intense and genuine feeling, her verse suffers from a lack of dedication, rather than of talent, evident in her refusal to undertake revisions or corrections for the 1883 edition. Their prolixity and pseudoromantic jargon stamp most, though not all, of her poems as "minor-Victorian."

In her latter years, she depended increasingly upon her servants for the leisure that made possible her incessant writing and other activities. Most of all

Title page for the book Kemble had published in order to buy back a horse her husband had sold

Kemble in old age (New York Public Library)

she treasured her English maid Ellen, who was with her from 1870 and who married Kemble's Italian manservant, Luigi Brianzone, in 1877. Kemble's generosity to her servants caused even the good-natured Sarah to wonder whether her mother was being exploited in her declining years. Any suspicions of this kind should surely be laid to rest by the tenderness and pathos with which Ellen described the death of the "dear mistress" who "passed away peacefully" in her arms while being put to bed. She was buried at Kensal Green cemetery near London.

Fanny Kemble deserves best to be remembered for the freshness and candor of her journal-writing; for her generous, independent, and humane spirit; and supremely for her interpretations of Shakespeare. It is a great misfortune that she lived too early for the latter to be recorded.

Biographies:

Dorothie Bobbe, *Fanny Kemble* (New York: Minton, Balch, 1931);

Leota S. Driver, *Fanny Kemble* (New York: Negro Universities Press, 1933);

Margaret Armstrong, *Fanny Kemble: A Passionate Victorian* (London: Macmillan, 1936; New York: Macmillan, 1938);

Constance C. Wright, *Fanny Kemble and the Lovely Land* (New York: Dodd, Mead, 1972);

Dorothy Marshall, *Fanny Kemble* (London: Weidenfeld & Nicholson, 1977);

J. C. Furnas, *Fanny Kemble: Leading Lady of the Nineteenth-Century Stage* (New York: Dial, 1982).

References:

Henry James, "Frances Anne Kemble," in his *Essays in London and Elsewhere* (New York: Harper, 1893), pp. 81-120;

Henry Lee, "Frances Anne Kemble," *Atlantic Monthly*, 71 (May 1893): 662-675;

Ella McMahon, "Fanny Kemble," *Living Age*, 197 (June 1983): 692-697;

Una Pope-Hennessy, "Fanny Kemble," in her *Three English Women in America* (London: Benn, 1929), pp. 113-210.

Papers:

Fanny Kemble's manuscripts are held by the Library of Congress; the New York Public Library; the Harvard College Library; the Columbia University Library; the Boston Public Library; the British Library, London; and the Victoria and Albert Museum, London.

Charles Kingsley
(12 June 1819-23 January 1875)

Nicholas Coles
University of Pittsburgh

See also the Kingsley entry in *DLB 21, Victorian Novelists Before 1885.*

SELECTED BOOKS: *The Saint's Tragedy: or, The True Story of Elizabeth of Hungary* (London: Parker, 1848; New York: International Book Co., 1855);

Twenty-five Village Sermons (London: Parker, 1849; Philadelphia: Hooker, 1855);

Introductory Lectures, Delivered at Queen's College, London (London: Parker, 1849);

Cheap Clothes and Nasty, as Parson Lot (Cambridge: Macmillan, 1850);

Alton Locke, Tailor and Poet: An Autobiography (2 volumes, London: Chapman & Hall, 1850; 1 volume, New York: Harper, 1850);

The Application of Associative Principles and Methods to Agriculture (London: Bezer, 1851);

Yeast: A Problem (London: Parker, 1851; New York: Harper, 1851);

The Message of the Church to Labouring Men: A Sermon (London: Parker, 1851);

Who Are the Friends of Order? (London: Lumley, 1852);

Phaeton; or, Loose Thoughts for Loose Thinkers (Cambridge: Macmillan, 1852; Philadelphia: Hooker, 1854);

Sermons on National Subjects (London: Griffin, 1852); republished as *The King of the Earth, and Other Sermons Preached in a Village Church* (London: Macmillan, 1872);

Hypatia; or, New Foes with an Old Face (2 volumes, London: Parker, 1853; 1 volume, New York: Lowell, 1853);

Alexandria and Her Schools (Cambridge: Macmillan, 1854);

Sermons on National Subjects: Second Series (London & Glasgow: Griffin, 1854);

Who Causes Pestilence? (London & Glasgow: Griffin, 1854);

Brave Words for Brave Soldiers and Sailors, anonymous (Cambridge, Macmillan, 1855); republished as *True Words for Brave Men* (London: Kegan Paul, 1878);

Westward Ho! or, The Voyages and Adventures of Sir Amyas Leigh, Knight, of Burrough, in the County of Devon, in the Reign of Her Most Glorious Majesty Queen Elizabeth (3 volumes, Cambridge: Macmillan, 1855; 1 volume, Boston: Ticknor & Fields, 1855);

(from a photograph in the possession of Rev. Maurice Godfrey)

Glaucus; or, The Wonders of the Shore (Cambridge: Macmillan, 1855; Boston: Ticknor & Fields, 1855);

Sermons for the Times (London: Parker, 1855; New York: Dana, 1856);

Sermons for Sailors (London, 1855?); republished as *Sea Sermons* (London: Kegan Paul, 1885);

The Heroes; or, Greek Fairy Tales for My Children (Cambridge: Macmillan, 1856; Boston: Ticknor & Fields, 1856);

Two Years Ago: A Novel (3 volumes, Cambridge: Macmillan, 1857; 1 volume, Boston: Ticknor & Fields, 1857);

Andromeda and Other Poems (London: J. W. Parker, 1858; Boston: Ticknor & Fields, 1858);

Miscellanies, 2 volumes (London: Parker, 1859);

The Good News of God: Sermons (London: Parker, 1859; New York: Burt, Hutchinson & Abbey, 1859);

The Massacre of the Innocents: An Address (London: Jarrold, 1859?);

The Limits of Exact Science as Applied to History: An Inaugural Lecture (Cambridge: Macmillan, 1860);

The Example of the Early Navigators: A Sermon (London: Parker, 1860);

Why Should We Pray for Fair Weather? A Sermon (London: Parker, 1860);

New Miscellanies (Boston: Ticknor & Fields, 1860);

Ode Performed in the Senate-House Cambridge, Composed for the Installation of His Grace the Duke of Devonshire, Chancellor of the University (Cambridge & London: Macmillan, 1862);

Speech of Lord Dundreary in Section D on Friday Last. On the Great Hippocampus Question, anonymous (Cambridge: Macmillan, 1862);

A Sermon on the Death of His Royal Highness the Prince Consort (London: Parker, 1862);

The Water-Babies: A Fairy Tale for a Land-Baby (London & Cambridge: Macmillan, 1863; Boston: Burnham, 1864);

The Gospel of the Pentateuch: A Set of Parish Sermons (London: Parker, Son & Bourn, 1863);

Mr. Kingsley and Dr. Newman: A Correspondence on the Question Whether Dr. Newman Teaches that Truth Is No Virtue (London: Longman, Green, Longman, Roberts & Green, 1864);

"What, Then, Does Dr. Newman Mean?": A Reply (London & Cambridge: Macmillan, 1864);

The Roman and the Teuton (Cambridge & London: Macmillan, 1864);

The Irrationale of Speech, by a Minute Philosopher (London: Longmans, 1864); also published as *Hints to Stammerers, by a Minute Philosopher* (London: Longmans, 1864);

David: Four Sermons Preached before the University of Cambridge (London: Macmillan, 1865);

Hereward the Wake: "Last of the English" (2 volumes, London: Macmillan, 1866; 1 volume, Boston: Ticknor & Fields, 1866);

The Temple of Wisdom: A Sermon (London: Macmillan, 1866);

Three Lectures Delivered at the Royal Institution on the Ancien Régime before the French Revolution (London: Macmillan, 1867);

The Water of Life and Other Sermons (London: Macmillan, 1867; Philadelphia: Lippincott, 1868);

The Hermits (London: Macmillan, 1868; Philadelphia: Lippincott, 1868);

Discipline and Other Sermons (London: Macmillan, 1868; Philadelphia: Lippincott, 1868);

Women and Politics (London: National Society for Women's Suffrage, 1869);

God's Feast: A Sermon (London & Cambridge: Macmillan, 1869);

The Address on Education, Read before the National Association for the Promotion of Social Science (London: Head, 1869);

Madam How and Lady Why; or, First Lessons in Earth Lore for Children (London: Bell & Daldy, 1870; New York: Macmillan, 1885);

At Last: A Christmas in the West Indies, 2 volumes (London: Macmillan, 1871; New York: Harper, 1871);

Letter to a Public School Boy, on Betting and Gambling (London: Society for Promoting Christian Knowledge, 1871?);

Town Geology (London: Strahan, 1872; New York: Appleton, 1873);

Poems: Collected Edition (London: Macmillan, 1872; expanded, 1873; New York: Hurst, 1880);

Plays and Puritans, and Other Historical Essays (London: Macmillan, 1873);

Prose Idylls, New and Old (London: Macmillan, 1873);

Frederick Denison Maurice: A Sermon (London: Macmillan, 1873);

Health and Education (London: Isbister, 1874; New York: Appleton, 1874);

Westminster Sermons (London: Macmillan, 1874);

Lectures Delivered in America in 1874 (London: Longmans, Green, 1875; Philadelphia: Coates, 1875);

Letters to Young Men on Betting and Gambling (London: King, 1877);

True Words for Brave Men (London: Kegan Paul, 1878; New York: Whittaker, 1886);

All Saints' Day and Other Sermons, edited by W. Harrison (London: Kegan Paul, 1878; New York: Scribner, Armstrong, 1878);

Out of the Deep: Words for the Sorrowful from the Writings of C. K., edited by Fanny Kingsley (London & New York: Macmillan, 1880);

From Death to Life: Fragments of Teaching to a Village Congregation, with Letters on the Life after Death, edited by His Wife (London & New York: Macmillan, 1887);

Words of Advice to Schoolboys, Collected from Hitherto Unpublished Notes and Letters, edited by E. F. Johns (London: Simpkin, 1912; Winchester, U.K.: Warren, 1912);

The Tutor's Story: An Unpublished Novel, revised and completed by Kingsley's daughter, Lucas Malet (Mrs. Mary St. Leger Harrison) (London: Smith, Elder, 1916; New York: Dodd, Mead, 1916).

Collection: *The Works of Charles Kingsley,* 28 volumes (London & New York: Macmillan, 1885-1902).

OTHER: *Most Glorious Majesty Queen Elizabeth,* rendered into modern English by Kingsley, 3 volumes (Cambridge: Macmillan, 1855);

Charles Blackford Mansfield, *Paraguay, Brazil and the Plate, Letters Written in 1852-1853,* biographical sketch by Kingsley (Cambridge: Macmillan, 1856);

The History and Life of J. Tauler with 25 of His Sermons, preface by Kingsley (London: Smith, Elder, 1857);

H. Brooke, *The Fool of Quality; or, The History of Henry, Earl of Moreland,* preface by Kingsley (London: Smith, Elder, 1859);

John Bunyan, *The Pilgrim's Progress,* preface by Kingsley (London: Longman, 1860).

PERIODICAL PUBLICATION: "Why Should We Fear Romish Priests?," *Fraser's,* 37 (April 1848): 467-474.

Country parson, Christian Socialist, sanitary reformer, naturalist and outdoorsman, novelist and historian, battler with Roman Catholicism: Charles Kingsley was one of those eminent Victorian all-rounders whose restless activity over a broad range of endeavor makes it unfair to categorize him. The phrase "Muscular Christianity"—which, despite his distaste for it, is inevitably linked with his name—expresses only part of his legacy: that blend of physical exertion, patriotism, and public service embodied in the heroes of his novels as well as in his own career. Kingsley was also tender and deeply affectionate, and he was rare among Victorian moral improvers in that his preaching did not rest upon denial of the life of the body. He was, in fact, as controversial as an "apostle of the flesh" as he was for his unorthodox politics.

As a writer Kingsley is best known for his novels and children's books, but he was also prolific as a reviewer and essayist on subjects ranging from socialism in the Bible to cures for stammering (from which he suffered). Several volumes of his sermons popularizing the principles of his mentor F. D. Maurice were published. His writings on geology and marine biology earned him a fellowship in the Geological Society. As a poet he was undoubtedly minor, but several of his songs were immensely popular in their day and remained so into this century.

Born in 1819, Charles Kingsley was the first child of the Reverend Charles Kingsley of Holne Vicarage in Devon and his wife Mary, who came from a line of sugar plantation owners in the West Indies. He was followed by four brothers; two of them died young, while Henry, the third son, also made his mark as a novelist.

Kingsley's childhood was spent in the Fen country and in Devon as his family moved from one country parish to another following the fortunes of his father, who, despite his ancient lineage and the habits of a country gentleman, had been obliged to enter the church to make a living. From 1832 to 1836 Charles attended a school in Helston, Cornwall, run by Derwent Coleridge, son of the poet, where he showed more interest in the local flora and fauna than in Latin or mathematics. There he wrote his first worthwhile poems, including "Trehill Well" and "Hypothesis Hypochondriachae" (1835), which were saved for posterity by his school friend Cowley Powles. They show a Wordsworthian feeling for nature, tinged with adolescent fantasies and sexual longing.

In 1838 he entered Cambridge, where he indulged his social and sporting propensities to the full. He underwent a crisis of religious doubt in revulsion both from his own dissipation and from the worldliness and lethargy of the Anglican church. In 1839 he met Fanny Grenfell, beginning a process that resulted in his conversion to a religious vocation during his last year at Cambridge. When they met, Fanny was under the spell of the Tractarian leader Dr. Pusey and contemplated joining his religious sisterhood and dedicating herself to a life of celibacy. It was through the exchanges with Fanny which averted this outcome that Kingsley

Kingsley's wife, Fanny Grenfell Kingsley (Angela Covey-Crump)

arrived at the conception of the primacy and divinity of human (married) love which distinguished his religious teaching.

Charles and Fanny were alike in being both strongly sexed and instinctively devout; the resulting conflict was depicted by Kingsley in his verse drama *The Saint's Tragedy* (1848), which he began in 1842, the year of his ordination. The central "struggle" is "between healthy human affection, and the Manichean contempt with which a celibate clergy would have all men regard the names of husband, wife, and parent." The play is adapted from chronicles of the life of the thirteenth-century Saint Elizabeth of Hungary. It opens with the heroine, the orphan daughter of the king of Hungary, praying ouside the closed doors of a convent: "Jesus, let me enter in, / Wrap me safe from noise and sin." She is initially saved from retreat to a nunnery by her marriage to Lewis, the Landgrave of Thuringia. The young couple find that marriage is a "life-long miracle"; the earth seems "one vast bride-bed." But Elizabeth is troubled by doubts as to the sinfulness of their pleasure, and on her wedding night she scourges herself and sleeps naked on the floor. She consigns herself to the spiritual guidance of the monk Conrad, a papal heretic-hunter, who weans her from her husband and children and, through a process of torturous asceticism, brings on her death and her canonization.

The project had begun as a prose life of Elizabeth intended as a wedding present to Fanny, but it was not completed in time for the wedding in 1844. Kingsley later transformed it into a Shakespearian blank-verse drama in five acts. The play, however, shows no awareness of stagecraft. Indeed, one critic suggests that Kingsley had a puritan distrust of the theater and, furthermore, confused drama with dialogue. The blank verse is awkwardly handled and suffers from an abundance of double-barreled constructions—"This fog-bred mushroom-spawn of brain-sick wits"—and other "Shakespearian" trappings. Two of the play's themes, however, inspired some fine writing: its celebration of married love and its urging of responsibility toward the poor. Returning from a visit to the slums around her palace, Elizabeth moralizes:

> We sit in a cloud, and sing, like pictured angels,
> And say, the world runs smooth—while right below
> Welters the black fermenting heap of life
> On which our state is built. . . .

Kingsley had difficulty getting his play into print. It was eventually published by John Parker, who was to be the publisher of Kingsley's journal, the *Christian Socialist,* in 1848. High Church reviewers naturally found that it "overstated the ascetic aberration," while the anti-Puseyites at Oxford were its greatest admirers. There was universal admiration for the lyrics with which Kingsley relieved his blank verse. One in particular, "Oh! that we two were Maying," set to music by John Hullah, became a standard recital piece in Victorian drawing rooms.

In 1843 Kingsley accepted the living of Eversley in Hampshire. He was disturbed by the poverty and illiteracy of his flock, and with characteristic vigor undertook in the parish the kinds of reforms he was later to preach to the nation. Besides visiting his parishioners and instructing them in hygiene (a personal obsession), he taught adult evening classes in the rectory, set up a Sunday school for the children, and instituted a coal club, a shoe club, a maternal society, a loan fund, and a lending library, as well as a singing class to improve the church music. He sympathized with the griev-

A drawing by Kingsley of himself and Fanny making love on a cross

ances of the Chartists and, after witnessing their last demonstration in 1848, he joined Maurice in founding the Christian Socialist movement, which attempted to divert the Chartists from political activism into establishing workers' cooperatives. He was outraged by Henry Mayhew's revelations of conditions in the London slums and lobbied for a system of water supply and sewerage which would alleviate the toll of disease. He and his friends carted water to one of the worst areas, Jacob's Island, whose unique filth is described in Chapter 25 of *Alton Locke* (1850).

Alton Locke, an "autobiography" of a Chartist tailor-poet, was one of Kingsley's two "social-problem" novels of these years. The other was *Yeast* (1851), which contained "A Rough Rhyme on a Rough Matter" (republished in 1858 as "The Bad Squire"), a bitter protest against the treatment of the rural poor. It uses the simple ballad form in which Kingsley excelled and speaks in the voice of the widow of a murdered poacher:

"There's blood on your new foreign shrubs, squire,
    There's blood on your pointer's feet;
There's blood on the game you sell, squire,
    And there's blood on the game you eat.

"You have sold the labouring-man, squire,
    Body and soul to shame,
To pay for your seat in the House, squire,
    And to pay for the feed of your game.

"You made him a poacher yourself, squire,
    When you'd give neither work nor meat,
And your barley-fed hares robbed the garden
    At our starving children's feet...."

Such criticism, and the graphic portraits of the conditions of the poor which accompanied it, gave offense to many of his readers, especially coming from a parson of the Church of England. *Yeast* had to be brought to a hasty conclusion as it was ruining *Fraser's* magazine, which was serializing it.

Although he always enjoyed a good controversy, it was painful to Kingsley to criticize his own class and church. His notoriety drew constant fire from the establishment and cost him opportunities for advancement. On 22 June 1851 he gave a sermon in London on "The Message of the Church to Labouring Men," in the course of which he hinted at the iniquity of large landholdings. The vicar of the church cut Kingsley off before he could give the blessing and repudiated his sermon as dangerous and untrue. Although the working-class audience was with Kingsley, the papers pilloried him as the "Apostle of Socialism," and the bishop of London barred him from the city's pulpits. (The prohibition was withdrawn after the bishop read the offending sermon.) Kingsley's depression over the incident kept him up the following night, during which he relieved his mind by writing the famous poem "The Three Fishers," which has been called "an almost perfect distillation of his own anguish into sympathy for others." The poem is based on his childhood memory of shipwrecks off the Devon coast and contains the proverbial line "For men must work and women must weep."

In 1852 Kingsley vowed that he would write no more novels: "I can write poetry better than any Englishman living. I don't say I have written it, but I know I can write it." The proof was to be in his two longer poems of 1852, "Andromeda" and "Saint Maura, A.D. 304." Fresh from a study of classical metrics, Kingsley wrote "Andromeda" with the intention of reinstating the hexameter, "that king of metres," into English literature. He claimed that he could rattle off hexameters while dressing or breakfasting. The result of this facility is that although the story—the Greek legend of Perseus's rescue of Andromeda from the rock to which she was chained as a sacrifice to the sea monster—is vividly told, the cantering dactylic meter and the adjectival diction required by the long lines make for wearisome reading. Nevertheless, Lafcadio Hearn felt that the poem contained "the best examples of the hexameter in English."

"Saint Maura," like *The Saint's Tragedy* and the later *Hypatia* (1853), features the gruesome martyrdom of a young woman. Maura is a country girl, three months pregnant and newly married to a Christian deacon who is being crucified by the pagans. She, too, accepts crucifixion rather than deny her faith in God or her love for her husband. The poem comprises her monologue as the naked couple hang from their crosses at night after the jeering crowds have left. Kingsley wrote it in a "poetic fervour," and called it "the deepest and clearest thing I have ever done." Most readers, although granting its power, found the subject too painfully morbid. Kingsley was drawn to the story because Maura, like Elizabeth, could "exhibit the martyr element . . . brought out and brightened by marriage love." Although the poem is cast as a dramatic monologue in the manner of Robert Browning, it has little of Browning's liveliness. Kingsley wrote his meters largely to rule and came to see eventually that "unrhymed blank verse is very bald in my hands."

The two new poems, along with those published earlier in *Fraser's* and the *Christian Socialist,* were offered to Parker in 1852 for publication in a single volume. Parker declined to publish until 1858, when a pirated American edition forced his hand. *Andromeda and Other Poems* received largely favorable reviews: apart from the "unhealthy" "Saint Maura," they were the work of "a good man and a good sportsman." "Tell Mr. Kingsley to leave novels and write nothing but lyrics," instructed *Chambers's Journal.*

However, between the writing and the publication of his most deliberate poetic efforts Kingsley

Kingsley's mentor and fellow Christian Socialist, F. D. Maurice

Kingsley in the grounds of Eversley Rectory (Rev. Maurice Godfrey)

reversed himself as to his literary vocation. "I have deserted poetry as rats do a sinking ship," he wrote in 1855. "I can tell more truths in prose than I can in verse, and earn ten times as much money...." He began his trilogy of historical novels with *Hypatia* (1853), set in fifth-century Alexandria; it was followed by *Westward Ho!* (1855), a tale of the Spanish Armada; his last novel, *Hereward the Wake* (1866), is about a "half-savage" guerrilla fighter against the Normans. The last two of these were best-sellers and became established school texts on the strength of their patriotic "manliness" and their bloodthirsty battle scenes.

Also a best-seller was the nonhistorical novel *Two Years Ago* (1857), in which Kingsley's fire is concentrated on the character of Elsley Vavasour, the effete and over-dressed poet whom Tennyson paranoically took for himself, causing a temporary rupture in his friendship with Kingsley. Elsley is a vehicle for Kingsley's attitudes—or, rather, prejudices—about the proper role of the poet. Instead of writing, as he ought, about "needlewomen and ragged schools," Elsley's verses, entitled *The Soul's Agonies,* are devoted to introspection or "mere sensuous beauty." As an implied result of this selfish aestheticism Elsley takes to opium, abandons his wife, and goes mad on a Welsh mountaintop. What is required of a poet, according to Kingsley's literary essays (collected in *Miscellanies,* 1859), is (again) manliness, social commitment, and sound religious faith. "Without faith there can be no real art, for art is the outward expression of firm, coherent belief," he wrote in "Alexander Smith and Alexander Pope" (1853). "The 'Poetry of doubt,' however pretty, would stand us in little stead if we were threatened with a second Armada." Most poets naturally failed this rather martial test of poetic quality. Shelley was Kingsley's anathema, and he thought it infinitely preferable to have written "The Song of the Shirt" or "Rule Brittania" than "all of which John Keats has left behind him."

Writing novels, often in serial form and always for the money, was a constant strain on Kingsley, and each novel would be followed by a nervous collapse from which he would recover by secluding himself in the country and engaging in vigorous exercise. Writing poetry was part of the therapy, and many of his songs were composed as he rode through the New Forest or hiked over Dartmoor. He described to Fanny the origin on a fishing trip of the lovely nature-poem "Dartside" (1849): "Yesterday was the most charming *solitary* day I have ever spent in my life—scenery more lovely than tongue can tell. It brought out of me the following bit of poetry with many tears."

Kingsley's verse, then, was not entirely constrained by his ethic of manliness. "Ode to the North-East Wind" (1854)—"the hard grey weather [that] Breeds hard English men"—is indeed dedicated to the muscular virtues, and "The Invitation" (1856) is a comically philistine celebration of perpetual boyhood. But more often his verse is marked by a strain of sensitivity that was absent from his public stance. Most appealing are those tales of lost love such as "The New Forest Ballad" (1847) in which he uses the traditional rollicking meter and narrative economy of the ballad. His lyrics, too, many of which became popular songs, rely on regular rhyme and rhythm. The best of them combine what Susan Chitty calls "an innocent freshness of expression" with a nostalgic melancholy reminiscent of A. E. Housman. "Young and Old" from *The Water-Babies* (1863) is a fine example:

> When all the world is young, lad,
>   And all the trees are green,
> And every goose a swan, lad,
>   And every lass a queen;
> Then hey for boat and horse, lad,
>   And round the world away;
> Young blood must have its course, lad,
>   And every dog his day.
>
> When all the world is old, lad,
>   And all the trees are brown,
> And all the sport is stale, lad,
>   And all the wheels run down;
> Creep home, and take your place there,
>   The spent and maimed among;
> God grant you find one face there
>   You loved when all was young.

Kingsley came to acknowledge where his strength lay as a poet: although "I shall never be a great poet," he wrote in 1858, "I know I can put into singing words the plain things I see and feel."

After the Christian Socialist years Kingsley's career took an upward turn. Prince Albert had long admired his work and in 1859 he was invited to preach before Queen Victoria, becoming her chaplain and, in 1861, tutor to the Prince of Wales. Royal patronage secured him the professorship of modern history at Cambridge, which he held from 1860 until 1867. In the meantime he produced his most famous book, *The Water-Babies*, the tale of little Tom the chimney sweep which inspired an act of Parliament forbidding the use of children in cleaning chimneys. In 1864 Kingsley wrote a review charging the Catholic convert J. H. Newman with intellectual dishonesty, initiating a controversy which, insofar as it called out the cardinal's admirable *Apologia pro Vita Sua* (1865), did the Anglican cause more harm than good.

In 1869 Kingsley became canon of Chester, where he started a botanical club for unemployed youths; the club became the Chester Natural History Society. By the time he received the honor of a stall in Westminster Abbey in 1873 his health was failing. Nevertheless, driven by financial necessity, he set sail in 1874 for a lecture tour of America. He returned exhausted to Eversley and died there early the following year, survived by Fanny and their four children.

Kingsley's literary career was marked by oscillation among genres rather than by steady development; his dominant themes, however, remained constant. He was only occasionally a poet and, after a bout of experimentation, worked most successfully in simple, established forms. His longest-lasting pieces were the lyrics which John Hullah set to music. The popularity of the novels, especially *Westward Ho!*, remained high for a time, but their overly enthusiastic spirit and lengthy sermonizing have eroded their appeal, and Kingsley's literary reputation has declined steadily. Interest in his writings, however, has been superseded by interest in his complex and endearing personality and its expression of the enthusiasms and conflicts of his age.

Letters:

Charles Kingsley: Letters and Memories of His Life, edited by Frances Kingsley, 2 volumes (London: King, 1877);

American Notes: Letters from a Lecture Tour, 1874, edited by R. B. Martin (Princeton, N.J.: Princeton University Library, 1958).

Bibliographies:

Robert A. Campbell, "Charles Kingsley: A Bibliography of Secondary Studies," *Bulletin of Bibliography*, 33 (1976): 78-91, 104, 127-130;

Styron Harris, *Charles Kingsley: A Reference Guide* (Boston: Hall, 1981).

Biographies:

Stanley E. Baldwin, *Charles Kingsley* (Ithaca, N.Y.:

Cornell University Press, 1934; London: Humphry Milford, 1934);
Margaret F. Thorp, *Charles Kingsley, 1819-1875* (Princeton, N.J.: Princeton University Press, 1937; London: Humphry Milford, 1937);
Una Pope-Hennessy, *Canon Charles Kingsley: A Biography* (London: Chatto & Windus, 1948; New York: Macmillan, 1949);
Robert B. Martin, *The Dust of Combat: A Life of Charles Kingsley* (London: Faber & Faber, 1959; New York: Norton, 1960);
Susan Chitty, *The Beast and the Monk: A Life of Charles Kingsley* (London: Hodder & Stoughton, 1975; New York: Mason, Charter, 1975);
Brenda Colloms, *Charles Kingsley* (London: Constable, 1975; New York: Barnes & Noble, 1975).

References:
Gillian Beer, "Charles Kingsley and the Literary Image of the Countryside," *Victorian Studies,* 8 (1965): 243-254;
Owen Chadwick, "Charles Kingsley at Cambridge," *Historical Journal,* 18 (1975): 303-325;
Susan Chitty, *Charles Kingsley's Landscape* (Newton Abbott & North Pomfret, Vt.: David & Charles, 1976);
Lafcadio Hearn, *Appreciations of Poetry* (New York: Dodd, Mead, 1916), pp. 280-297;
Guy Kendall, *Charles Kingsley and His Ideas* (London & New York: Hutchinson, 1947);
Larry K. Uffelman, *Charles Kingsley* (Boston: Twayne, 1979);
Uffelman, "Kingsley, the Poet and the Press," *Kansas Quarterly,* 7 (1975): 79-84.

Papers:
Charles Kingsley's papers are collected at the British Museum; at Princeton University Library; and at Dormy House, Pine Valley, New Jersey.

Edward Lear
(12 May 1812-29 January 1888)

Ina Rae Hark
University of South Carolina

BOOKS: *Illustrations of the Family of Psittacidae, or Parrots* (London: Privately printed, 1832);
Views in Rome and Its Environs: Drawn from Nature and on Stone (London: McLean, 1841);
Gleanings from the Menagerie and Aviary at Knowsley Hall (Knowsley, U.K.: Privately printed, 1846);
Illustrated Excursions in Italy, 2 volumes (London: McLean, 1846);
A Book of Nonsense, as Derry down Derry (2 volumes, London: McLean, 1846; enlarged, as Lear, 1 volume, London: Routledge, Warne & Routledge, 1861; Philadelphia: Hazard, 1863);
Journals of a Landscape Painter in Albania,&c. (London: Bentley, 1851);
Journals of a Landscape Painter in Southern Calabria, &c. (London: Bentley, 1852);
Views in the Seven Ionian Islands (London: Privately printed, 1863);
Journal of a Landscape Painter in Corsica (London: Bush, 1870);
Nonsense Songs, Stories, Botany and Alphabets (London: Bush, 1870; Boston: Osgood, 1871);
More Nonsense, Pictures, Rhymes, Botany Etc. (London: Bush, 1872);
Tortoises, Terrapins and Turtles Drawn from Life, by Lear and James de Carle Sowerby (London: Sotheran, Baer, 1872);
Laughable Lyrics: A Fourth Book of Nonsense Poems, Songs, Botany, Music Etc. (London: Bush, 1877);
Queery Leary Nonsense: A Lear Nonsense Book, edited by Constance, Lady Strachey (London: Mills & Boon, 1911);
The Lear Coloured Bird Book for Children (London: Mills & Boon, 1912);
Lear in Sicily May-July 1847, edited by G. Proby (London: Duckworth, 1938);
The Complete Nonsense of Edward Lear, edited by Holbrook Jackson (London: Faber & Faber, 1947; New York: Dover, 1951);
Indian Journal: Watercolours and Extracts from the Diary of Edward Lear (1873-1875), edited by Ray Murphy (London: Jarrolds, 1953; New

Edward Lear (The Tennyson Research Centre)

York: Coward-McCann, 1955);
Teapots and Quails, and Other New Nonsenses, edited by Angus Davidson and Philip Hofer (London: Murray, 1953; Cambridge: Harvard University Press, 1953).

Vivien Noakes fittingly subtitled her biography of Edward Lear *The Life of a Wanderer.* On a literal level the phrase refers to Lear's constant traveling as a self-proclaimed "dirty landscape painter" from 1837 until he finally settled at his Villa Tennyson on the San Remo coast of Italy in 1880. But *wandering,* in that it suggests rootlessness, aimlessness, loneliness, and uncertainty, is also a metaphor for Lear's emotional life and for the sense of melancholy that so often peeps through the playfully absurd surface of his nonsense verse.

The uncertainty began with his birth. Born 12 May 1812 in the London suburb of Holloway, Lear was the twentieth of twenty-one children (and youngest to survive) of Ann Skerrett Lear and Jeremiah Lear, a stockbroker. Many of the Lear offspring did not live beyond infancy, so Edward's very survival had something of the fortuitous about it. Even though he lived to be seventy-five, his health was always delicate; he had poor eyesight and suffered from chronic respiratory problems. At the age of five he experienced his first epileptic seizure. For Lear this "Demon," as he dubbed his affliction, was a mark of shame. Much of his self-imposed isolation from those he loved derived from his need to hide his condition from them.

The year before the onset of the disease had brought trauma of another sort. Jeremiah Lear underwent severe financial reverses—in later years Lear repeatedly told friends his father had gone to debtors' prison, but no evidence substantiates this claim—and the family had to rent out their home, Bowman's Lodge, for a time. Mrs. Lear entrusted Edward to the care of his eldest sister, twenty-five-year-old Ann, and when financial stability returned, she did not resume her maternal duties. Ann never married and devotedly acted the mother's part to Lear as long as she lived; yet he never recovered from the hurt of his real mother's rejection, as the ambivalence about mother figures in many of his poems indicates.

Lear received little, if any, formal education. Ann tutored him at home and encouraged a talent for drawing and painting that he had early exhibited. When Jeremiah Lear retired and moved south of London in 1828, Edward and Ann remained in the city, taking up lodgings off the Gray's Inn Road. The sixteen-year-old Lear supported them by selling miscellaneous sketches; he soon moved on to anatomical drawings and then to illustrations for natural history books. His skill in this latter capacity led to the publication in 1832 of a volume of twelve folio lithographic prints of parrots, *Illustrations of the Family of Psittacidae.* This volume brought him to the attention of Edward Stanley, later thirteenth earl of Derby, who wanted an artist to draw the animals in his menagerie at Knowsley, the Derby estate in Lancashire. Lear accepted Stanley's offer of residency at Knowsley Hall while the work was in progress; he stayed there off and on from 1832 to 1837.

The Knowsley days shaped the course of Lear's entire subsequent career. In addition to gaining the unflagging patronage of the earl of Derby, he met and charmed many aristocrats who would later buy his paintings and provide entrée to a level of society usually unbreachable by a man of Lear's impecunious middle-class origins. In 1837, when failing eyesight and lungs forced Lear to abandon the detailed work of natural history draftsmanship and the English winters, the earl provided funds and introductions to establish him in Rome to pursue a vocation as a painter of topo-

Lear in Rome in 1840, as drawn by William Marstrand (National Portrait Gallery, London)

graphical landscapes. He remained in Rome for ten years, during which time he first established himself as a nonsense poet and formed several of the deepest of his many intimate friendships.

Lear had initially produced poems, drawings, alphabets, and menus for the entertainment of the children at Knowsley; these "nonsenses"—and Lear's charming conversation and piano improvisations—had soon ingratiated him with the adults as well. In 1846 he gathered together some of his limericks, a verse form he had first encountered in the joke book *Anecdotes and Adventures of Fifteen Gentlemen* (circa 1822), and had them published with his own illustrations in *A Book of Nonsense* under the pseudonym Derry down Derry.

The Learian limerick focuses on the singular individual, an old or young "Person," "Man," or "Lady," who is distinguished by unusual appearance, behavior, talents, diet, or dress. In its most typical form it announces the existence of the eccentric, notes his dwelling place, and describes his distinctive features; then it explains the consequences of his peculiarity and concludes with an apostrophe:

> There was a Young Lady of Norway,
> Who casually sat in a doorway;
> When the door squeezed her flat, she exclaimed "What of that?"
> This courageous Young Lady of Norway.

The limerick generally has a closed structure, repeating the final word of the first line at the end of the last rather than utilizing the unexpected, punch-line rhyme that characterizes the successful modern limerick.

A great number of Lear's limericks set the eccentric in conflict with "they," the faceless, conformist, officious members of society at large. Many times "they" unfairly persecute the individual; at other times he provokes and deserves their hostility. But the primary theme of the limericks remains the problems anyone with the slightest idiosyncrasy has in feeling comfortable among the mass of men. Since these eccentrics often have the oversized noses and long legs Lear gave himself in deprecatory self-caricatures, as well as his affinity for all animals except dogs, the poet probably saw himself as a sharer of their misfit status.

On a less subjective level, the limerick protagonists provided for the didactically surfeited Victorian child examples of bizarre, misbehaving adults, with no blatant moralizing attached. What intrinsic morality the verses contain is conveyed largely in terms of eating habits. Food is often a symbol in Lear's poetry: the sharing of food indicates affection and selflessness, while gluttony denotes egotism and lack of concern for others. Gluttony also receives harsh punishment:

> There was an Old Man of the South,
> Who had an immoderate mouth;
> But in swallowing a dish, that was quite full of fish,
> He was choked, that Old Man of the South.

The year before the publication of the *Book of Nonsense*, Lear formed with Chichester Fortescue, later to become Lord Carlingford, one of the firmest of his many lifelong friendships. Their delightful correspondence, compiled in two volumes by Lady Strachey, is the largest collection of Lear letters published to date. Also in Italy, in 1848, Lear was befriended by another future peer, Thomas

There was an Old Derry down Derry, who loved to see little folks merry;
So he made them a Book, and with laughter they shook
At the fun of that Derry down Derry.

Frontispiece, with illustration by Lear, for A Book of Nonsense

Baring, later Lord Northbrook. (Later, in 1873 and 1874, Lear journeyed to India and Ceylon as Northbrook's guest.) Returning to England in 1849, Lear met Alfred and Emily Tennyson. Lear admired Tennyson's poetry, setting several pieces to music and leaving a projected volume of illustrations of the laureate's works unfinished at his death; Tennyson addressed an admiring poem "To E. L., on His Travels in Greece." Their personal relations were nevertheless rarely more than cordial. Lear, however, adored Emily, and she gradually superseded Ann (who died in 1861) as his confidante and surrogate mother. He also formed a close friendship in 1852 with Holman Hunt, the Pre-Raphaelite painter.

Lear's most fervent and most painful friendship involved Franklin Lushington. He met the young barrister in Malta in 1849 and then toured southern Greece with him. Lear developed an undoubtedly homosexual passion for him that Lushington did not reciprocate. Although they re-mained friends for almost forty years, until Lear's death, the disparity of their feelings for one another constantly tormented Lear.

In 1850 Lear decided to remain in England to take the ten-year painting course at the Royal Academy Schools in order to improve his untrained technique in oils and figure drawing. He also had the first two of three illustrated journals of his travels published. But his low resistance to the English climate curtailed his stay. After three and a half years he abandoned England for the sunny Mediterranean, and in 1855 he resolved that he would never return to Britain permanently. In October of that year he established a home on Corfu, where Lushington's government position had stationed him.

The next years were the most hectic and unsettled of Lear's life. He traveled incessantly throughout the Mediterranean and Near East, moved from Corfu to Rome to Corfu again and then to Cannes, and visited England eight times. He

Manuscript limerick and drawing by Lear for A Book of Nonsense, *indicating Lear's dislike of dogs (from the folio album in the collection of Mr. and Mrs. Hans P. Kraus)*

came close to marrying the one eligible woman with whom he ever maintained a long-term friendship, the Honorable Augusta "Gussie" Bethell of London, whom he had met in the early 1840s, when she was a child. But in 1866 he unwisely consulted her sister Emma about the advisability of a proposal. Emma firmly discouraged him, and he never approached Gussie, who by all accounts would have accepted. Despite his many long-distance friendships, Lear was doomed to a solitary life. His only constant companions were his manservant Giorgio Kokali from 1856 to 1883, and his cat Foss from 1871 to 1887.

Lear did not have any new nonsense published for fifteen years following the appearance of *A Book of Nonsense*. In 1861, however, a new, expanded edition was brought out under his own name. Its enthusiastic reception gratified but also perplexed Lear, who always hoped to gain fame as a painter and regarded nonsense only as a source of fun and money. His success as a poet did encourage him to compose more complex nonsenses, which appeared in three volumes during the 1870s after he had settled in San Remo, Italy.

The first, *Nonsense Songs* (1870), contained longer poems in which characterization is more

Lear as portrayed by William Holman Hunt in 1857

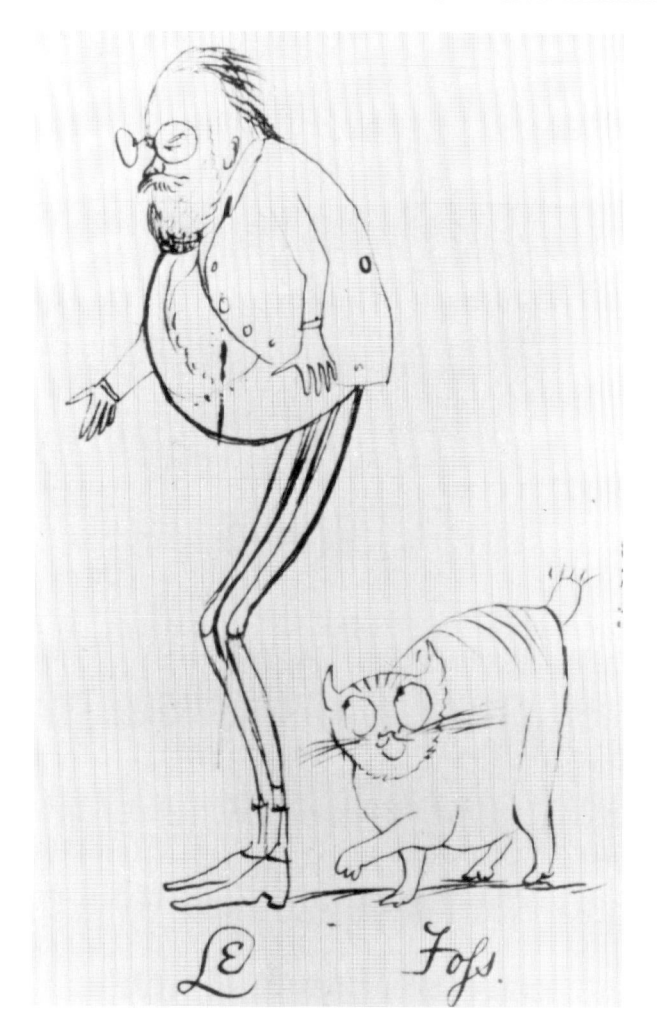

(left) A sketch by Lear of himself—with exaggeratedly long legs—and his cat Foss; (right) Lear's gravestone for Foss, who died less than a year before Lear did

realistic and emotions are less distanced than in the limericks. The characters are nonhuman, and the central actions frequently involve a pair or group taking off on a journey. The Owl and the Pussy-cat go to sea in a beautiful pea-green boat; the Jumblies depart in a sieve; the Duck and Kangaroo hop around the world; and even a nutcracker and some tongs, a table and a chair, go out to take the air. These first lyrics seem clearly to constitute Lear's reflections on his own life as a wanderer. At their happiest they also describe a joyful togetherness that he never attained. The elements of this Learian epiphany—song, dance, food, the shore in the moonlight—are established in "The Owl and the Pussy-cat" and recur frequently in later poems:

> They dined on mince, and slices of quince,
> Which they ate with a runcible spoon;
> And hand in hand, on the edge of the sand,
> They danced by the light of the moon.

More Nonsense (1872) contained additional limericks of the earlier kind but no new songs. Several songs did appear in his last volume of verse, *Laughable Lyrics* (1877). The volume is misnamed, for the tone is melancholy; a majority of the poems deal with some sort of loss. The Pobble loses his toes; the pelicans lose their daughter. Most poignant are those lyrics dealing with the loss of love: "The Dong with a Luminous Nose" and "The Courtship of the Yonghy-Bonghy-Bò." *Laughable Lyrics* also contains the bulk of Lear's invented nonsense creatures such as the Dong, the Bò, the Pobble, the octopod Discobboloses, and the Quangle Wangle. Lear frequently sets these poems in his nonsense landscapes on the Hills of the Chankly Bore or the Great

Drawing by Lear showing him displaying his hat – with his name and address stamped inside – his calling card, and his monogrammed handkerchief to a fellow railway passenger in 1866. Lear had overheard the man claiming that Edward, Earl of Derby, was the real author of A Book of Nonsense, *and that "Edward Lear" was an anagram for "Edward, Earl."*

Gromboolian Plain. It was only by creating such unreal beings and settings that Lear could write with unrepressed emotion about his own unhappiness and sense of isolation.

In 1886 Lear contracted a severe case of bronchitis, from which he never fully recovered. In that same year he wrote his last nonsense poem, "Incidents in the Life of My Uncle Arly." Transparently autobiographical, it sums up in a few brief lines the essence of his life:

> Close beside a leafy thicket: —
> On his nose there was a Cricket, —
> In his hat a Railway-Ticket, —
>   (But his shoes were far too tight.)

Lear was a wandering nonsense minstrel, never completely free of physical and emotional pain. His health steadily deteriorated until he died, alone except for a servant, on 29 January 1888. His last words expressed gratitude for the kindnesses of all his absent friends.

Lear's poetry shares many elements with the nonsense verse of Lewis Carroll, Thomas Hood, W. S. Gilbert, and other Victorians, particularly in the use of verbal play and other distancing devices to derive humor from cruelty, pain, and death. Like nonsense verse as a whole, it influenced such twentieth-century aesthetic movements as surrealism and the theater of the absurd. It also, however, contains themes unique to Lear's personal experience. It is above all an expression of the inmost longings, frustrations, and wish-fulfillment dreams of a lovable and intensely loving man who, despite the fond affection of numerous relatives, friends, and readers—children and adults—was never beloved in the intimate, exclusive, constant manner he so fervently desired.

Letters:

Letters of Edward Lear, edited by Constance, Lady Strachey (London: Unwin, 1907);

Later Letters of Edward Lear, edited by Constance, Lady Strachey (London: Unwin, 1911).

Biographies:

Angus Davidson, *Edward Lear: Landscape Painter and Nonsense Poet* (London: Murray, 1938);

Vivien Noakes, *Edward Lear: The Life of a Wanderer* (London: Collins, 1968).

References:

Thomas Byrom, *Nonsense and Wonder* (New York: Dutton, 1977);

William B. Osgood Field, *Edward Lear on My Shelves* (New York: Privately printed, 1933);

Ina Rae Hark, *Edward Lear* (New York: Twayne, 1982);

Philip Hofer, *Edward Lear as Landscape Draughtsman* (London: Oxford University Press, 1968);

John Lehmann, *Edward Lear and his World* (London: Thames & Hudson, 1977);

Joanna Richardson, *Edward Lear,* in the Writers and Their Work Series (London: Longmans, Green, 1965);

Elizabeth Sewell, *The Field of Nonsense* (London: Chatto & Windus, 1952).

Papers:

The largest collection of Edward Lear's manuscripts and papers plus his manuscript diaries are in the Houghton Library of Harvard University. Lear's correspondence with the Tennyson family, along with some sketches and miscellaneous nonsenses, are at the Tennyson Research Centre, Lincoln, England.

William James Linton
(7 December 1812-29 December 1897)

Tirthankar Bose
University of British Columbia

BOOKS: *The Life of Thomas Paine,* anonymous (London: Watson, 1839; New York: Eckler, 1892);

The Jubilee of Trade: A Vision of the Nineteenth Century after Christ (N.p., 1843);

Bob Thin; or, The Poorhouse Fugitive (London: Privately printed, 1845);

To the Future: The Dirge of the Nations (N.p., 1848);

The People's Land and an Easy Way to Recover It (London: Watson, 1850);

The Plaint of Freedom (Newcastle-on-Tyne: Privately printed, 1852);

Help for Poland (London: Privately printed, 1854);

The Ferns of the English Lake Country (London: Hamilton, Adams, 1865);

Claribel, and Other Poems (London: Simpkin, Marshall, 1865);

Ireland for the Irish: Rhymes and Reasons against Landlordism (New York: American News Co., 1867);

The Flower and the Star, and Other Stories for Children (Boston: Ticknor & Fields, 1868; London: Lawrence & Bullen, 1892);

The House That Tweed Built: Dedicated to Every True Reformer (Republican or Democrat), anonymous (Cambridge, Mass.: Privately printed, 1871);

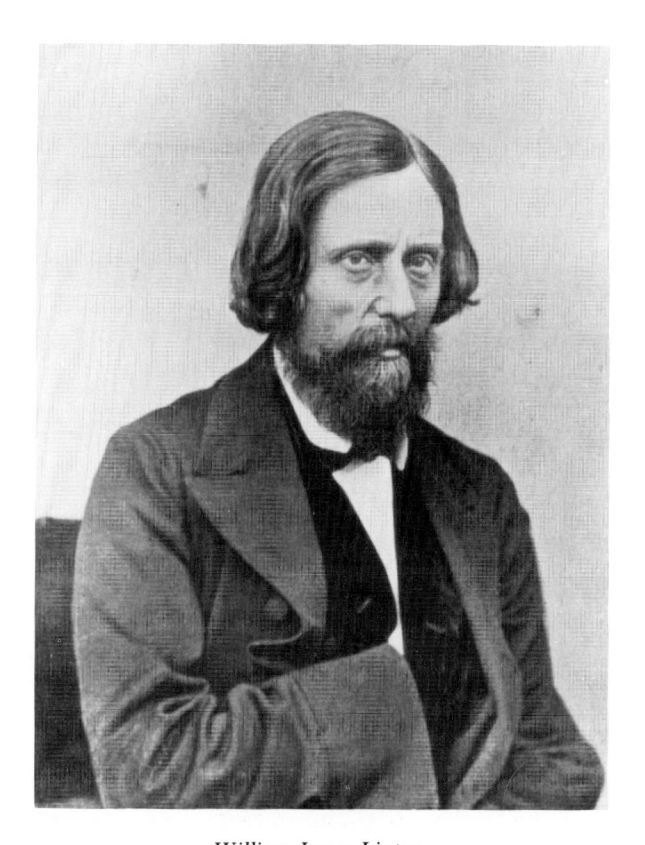

William James Linton

The Paris Commune (Boston: Privately printed, 1871);

Pot-Pourri, as Abel Reid (New York: Green, 1875);

Famine: A Masque (Hamden, Conn.: Appledore, 1875);

England to America, 1876: A New-Year's Greeting (Cambridge, Mass.: Welch, Bigelow, 1876);

The American Odyssey: Adventures of Ulysses (So Much as May Interest the Present Time) Exposed in a Modest Hudibrastic Measure, as Reid and A. N. Broome (Washington, D.C., 1876);

James Watson: A Memoir of the Days of the Fight for a Free Press in England and of the Agitation for the People's Charter (Hamden, Conn.: Appledore, 1879; Manchester, U.K.: Heywood, 1880);

Some Practical Hints on Wood Engraving for the Instruction of Reviewers and the Public (Boston: Lee & Shepard/New York: Dillingham, 1879);

Voices of the Dead: Charlotte Corday and Marat, Mazzini and the Countess Ossoli, Delescluze on the Barricade (Hamden, Conn.: Appledore, 1879);

Cetewayo and Dean Stanley (Hamden, Conn.: Appledore, 1880; London, 1880);

The History of Wood-Engraving in America (Boston: Estes & Lauriat, 1882);

Wood-Engraving: A Manual of Instruction (London: Bell, 1884);

The Masters of Wood-Engraving (New Haven, Conn.: Appledore, 1886; London: Stevens, 1889);

Love-Lore (Hamden, Conn.: Appledore, 1887; enlarged, 1895);

Poems and Translations (London: Nimmo, 1889);

Catoninetales: A Domestic Epic, as Hattie Brown, "edited" by Linton (London: Lawrence & Bullen, 1891);

Change (Hamden, Conn.: Appledore, 1891);

The English Republic (London: Sonnenschein, 1891);

The Religion of Organization (New Haven, Conn.: Appledore, 1892);

Heliconundrums (Hamden, Conn.: Appledore, 1892);

European Republicans: Recollections of Mazzini and His Friends (London: Lawrence & Bullen, 1893);

Broadway Ballads Collected for the Centennial Commemoration of the Republic 1876, as Reid (Hamden, Conn.: Appledore, 1893);

Life of John Greenleaf Whittier (London: Scott, 1893);

A Christmas Carol (N.p., 1893);

Threescore and Ten Years, 1820 to 1890: Recollections (New York: Scribners, 1894); republished as *Memories* (London: Lawrence & Bullen, 1895);

Ultima Verba (London: Privately printed, 1895);

Darwin's Probabilities (Hamden, Conn.: Appledore, 1896).

OTHER: F. R. de Lamennais, *Modern Slavery*, translated from *De l'Esclavage moderne* by Linton (London: Watson, 1840);

Poetry of America: Selections from One Hundred American Poets from 1776 to 1876, edited by Linton (London: Bell, 1878);

"Reminiscences of Eben Jones," in *Studies of Sensation and Event: Poems by Ebenezer Jones*, edited by Richard Herne Shepherd (London: Pickering, 1879);

Wind-Falls, Two Hundred and Odd, edited by Linton (Hamden, Conn.: Appledore, 1882);

Golden Apples of Hesperus: Poems Not in the Collections, edited by Linton (Hamden, Conn.: Appledore, 1882);

Rare Poems of the Sixteenth and Seventeenth Centuries, edited by Linton (New Haven, Conn.: Appledore, 1882; London: Kegan Paul, Trench, 1883; Boston: Roberts, 1883);

English Verse, edited by Linton and R. H. Stoddard, 5 volumes (New York: Scribners, 1883; London: Kegan Paul, Trench, 1884);

Lyrics of the Nineteenth Century, edited by Linton and Stoddard (London: Kegan Paul, Trench, 1884);

Chaucer to Burns, edited by Linton and Stoddard (London: Kegan Paul, Trench, 1884);

In Dispraise of a Woman: Catullus with Variations, translated from "Nulli se dicit mulier mea nubere malle" by Linton (Hamden, Conn.: Appledore, 1886);

C. J. Wells, *Stories after Nature*, preface by Linton (London: Lawrence & Bullen, 1891).

William James Linton was one of those late-Victorians who achieved success in more than one art. The finest wood engraver of his time, Linton won critical acclaim from his contemporaries for his poetry and translations. His imaginative vigor saved him from sentimentality while his sense of melody, economy of phrasing, and gentle epigrammatic irony gave his poems dramatic and lyrical coherence.

Linton was born on 7 December 1812 at Ireland's Row off Mile End Road, London, in comfortable circumstances. He had a younger brother, Henry Duff Linton, who also became a wood engraver. His mother, with a little money of her own, had strong pretensions to a genteel upbringing; she was also rigid in her religious and social beliefs, which eventually alienated Linton from her. On the other hand, his father, William Linton, who made his living at the Stepney riverside as a broker, had a taste for radical politics; this proved to be a power-

"Sleeping Girl," drawn and engraved by Linton

ful influence on Linton. In 1818 the family moved to Stratford, where Linton's education started at Chigwell School. He studied commercial subjects, Latin, and French, and developed a taste for literature and the arts. He did not seem suited for a commercial career, but he was so good at drawing that in 1828 he was apprenticed to the wood engraver George Wilmot Bonner. He went to live with Bonner's family in Kennington and worked under him until 1834. His skill brought him regular employment, first with W. H. Powis between 1834 and 1836, then with John Thompson until the end of 1838. He also began in 1836 to work for John Orrin Smith, with whom he went into partnership in 1842; this partnership, however, was dissolved by Smith's death in 1843.

Meanwhile, from about 1832 Linton's interest in radical politics had begun to take shape; his devotion to poetry, especially to Shelley, was nurtured by his association with the radical circle of Thomas Wade, Richard Henry Horne, and W. J. Fox. He fell deeply in love with Wade's sister Laura and married her in 1837. Her death six months after the marriage was a blow from which he never fully recovered, though he did take her sister Emily as his common-law wife later. He could not marry Emily because of legal restrictions but had several children by her.

Linton's sense of outrage at social conditions, heightened by his bitterness following Laura's death, began to find an outlet in political writing. He founded a short-lived political weekly, the *National*, in 1839. He also translated *De l'Esclavage moderne* by de Lamennais, whom he regarded as his political preceptor. The translation, *Modern Slavery*, was published in 1840 by James Watson, a radical bookseller whose friendship Linton prized and who was Linton's close associate in political activities, many of which were against the law. Another influential friend was the Italian patriot and revolutionist, Giuseppe Mazzini.

Linton's ideological commitment did not, however, destroy his literary interests. He not only leavened the *National* with excerpts from Shakespeare, Wordsworth, Coleridge, Keats, and Tennyson, but as editor of the *Illuminated Magazine* between November 1844 and April 1845 he actively promoted little-known authors such as Sarah Flower Adams and Charles Jeremiah Wells. One of Wells's stories was "Claribel," which Linton subsequently rewrote in dramatic verse. Most of his writings at this time were, however, political. He was contributing copiously under the pseudonym of "Spartacus" to Sir Charles Gavan Duffy's Dublin paper, the *Nation,* where he exhorted the Irish to rise against landlordism. The clumsiness of his doggerel epic *Bob Thin* (1845), a heavily sarcastic denunciation of private property and feudalism, is only partly mitigated by the evocation of nature's beauty in the pastoral scene in the concluding section.

Linton moved his family to Miteside in Northumberland in 1848, a year that saw him visiting Paris with Mazzini to felicitate the people for their uprising. Professional and political interests brought him back from the Lake Country to London in 1849, but he loved the lakes so much that he soon moved to Brantwood at Coniston, the house later occupied by Ruskin. In 1849 he founded the republican weekly the *Leader* with G. H. Lewes and Thornton Hunt. But this paper was not radical enough for Linton, so he left it to start the *English Republic* in 1851.

Linton's political creed kept him busy. He helped to found the International League of patriots and actively worked for the Friends of Italy. On the literary and artistic side, he was a close friend of William Bell Scott's and was well acquainted with the Rossettis. Typically, his first collection of verse, an anonymous publication in 1852, was *The Plaint of Freedom,* a fervent homage to liberty and equality. Dedicated to Milton, this series of poems, written in the meter of Tennyson's *In Memoriam* (1850), celebrates English heroes such as Caractacus, Robin Hood, Wat Tyler, and Cromwell, all warriors for "God and right."

The year 1855 proved to be a year of losses: the *English Republic* had to cease publication, and Emily died of consumption. Her place as mistress of the household was taken by Eliza Lynn, the novelist. Her account of Emily's deathbed plea to her to take care of Linton and the children is, however, purely fictitious. Linton married her in 1858 but they soon proved to be hopelessly mismatched. Linton was offended by Eliza's genteel way of life, while Eliza felt humiliated by Linton's absorption in national politics. By 1860 they were effectively separated, although they never broke off their financial and family connections nor sought a divorce.

The early 1860s brought other disappoint-

Linton's second (legal) wife, the novelist Eliza Lynn Linton

ments. Linton's political activism led to bickerings among his fellow radicals. He launched two magazines in 1882, the *Farthing Times and Advertiser* and the *Illustrated Magazine,* but each died after the first issue. Worse, his engraving proved to be too delicate for commercial publishing. His son Lancelot died in 1863; another son, Edmund, was slow and unemployable; and his eldest daughter, Emily ("Gypsy"), was retarded and paralyzed. His brother Henry was out of work and depended on an allowance from Linton.

The one comforting event of this period of Linton's life was the publication of *Claribel, and Other Poems* (1865), which presents his first major poetic statement. Here the emphasis shifts from struggling for freedom to struggling for love, but Linton's concern with heroic endeavor remains constant. One of the best-known poems in the volume is "Grenville's Last Fight," a narrative in blank verse, in which Linton's pride in England's heroic past quickens the otherwise tedious account. The title poem is about Claribel, princess of Bohemia, who secretly marries Albert, the royal page. When Prince Casimir of Poland, her longtime suitor and

Albert's dearest friend, wins her father's consent to a match, Albert finds himself in the tragic predicament of having to fight a duel to the death with Casimir for the sake of his love. Casimir is killed and the lovers flee, but Albert dies of his wounds and Claribel of a broken heart.

The theme of an ennobling love is carried on in most of the other poems in the volume, especially in "Eurydice," "Iphigenia at Aulis," and "Love." A distinctive note of epigrammatic irony is, however, struck in some of the shorter poems, such as "Valentine's Day" and "To His Love." That Linton also found a creative delight in nature is indicated by the longer "Song of the Streams"; but that delight hardly touches his love poetry, which he sets exclusively in the world of man rather than in that of nature. With these themes of love and nobility Linton continued to mingle his republican concerns, as in "Rich and Poor" and "God's Martyrs."

Satisfying though it was, the publication of his poems drained Linton's resources. By 1866 his financial situation was so desperate that he decided to seek a new life in America. He made arrangements for his children to stay in England, borrowed the fare from friends, and sailed to America in November 1866. After spending some time in New York he took up residence at Appledore, a farmhouse in Hamden, Connecticut, near New Haven, which was to be his home until his death. Here he set up a press, both for wood engraving and for literary publications of his own. Less involved in politics by this time, he began to turn out anthologies and original verse. In *Wind-Falls* (1882) he presented extracts from British dramas, while *Golden Apples of Hesperus* (1882) was a collection of sixteenth- and seventeenth-century poetry. Busy as he was with wood engraving, Linton still found time to translate from Latin and French, write children's stories, and edit anthologies such as *Poetry of America* (1878), *Chaucer to Burns* (1884), and *Lyrics of the Nineteenth Century* (1884)—the latter two jointly with R. H. Stoddard—while keeping the Appledore press running. One of his happiest efforts and a rare prize today for bibliophiles is *In Dispraise of a Woman: Catullus with Variations* (1886), in which he gives thirty-two renderings of an epigram by Catullus. In 1887 he published his *Love-Lore,* a collection of short lyrical poems on love. Their playful tenderness is saved from plunging into sheer affectation by a sense of irony in the Elizabethan vein.

A final outburst of his political feelings appeared in *Famine: A Masque* (1875), which denounces tyranny and plutocracy. But in the latter half of his life, love lyrics formed the staple of his writings. As a translator he was outstandingly successful in reproducing not only the tone but the meters of his originals. His renderings of Ronsard, Hugo, and Béranger—especially the last—are particularly supple. These, as much as his own poetry, won him the esteem of such leading literary figures of his day as Walter Savage Landor, A. H. Bullen, Austin Dobson, H. B. Forman, and W. M. Rossetti. *Catoninetales* (1891) is a mock epic on the death of a cat; Linton displays an impish sense of humor by adding a wealth of deliberately nonsensical annotations.

Between 1883 and 1886 Linton was engaged in his great work, *The Masters of Wood-Engraving*. With painstaking research in London and loving attention to technique at Appledore he put together this massive illustrated history of the art, which was printed in London from his own hand-printed originals in 1889. In 1891 Yale University presented him with an honorary M.A. for his services to literature and art, especially for *The Masters of Wood-Engraving*. With this major work behind him, Linton finished a biography of Whittier (1893) and recollections of Mazzini (1893). His autobiography

Linton as an old man

was published in 1894. He assembled his manuscripts and pamphlets into twenty volumes, which he presented to the British Museum in 1895. Old and infirm, he caught pneumonia late in 1896 but struggled on through the next year. On 29 December 1897 Linton died at New Haven.

Linton's poetic powers were inhibited by pulls in too many directions. His politics made his early poems emotionally fervid and intellectually diffuse, although his strong metrical control lent them form. It is his later work that establishes his identity as a romantic poet. Strangely enough for a graphic artist, his visual imagination does not inspire his poetry, which, though tightly designed, is wholly lacking in metaphoric precision. He was, moreover, too ready to accept sentimental responses to experience as profound philosophical insights. But in the many poems in which he dropped the mantle of the thinker to grasp the immediate moment of experience, especially that of love, he achieved an urbanity that adds more than one dimension to his poetic statements. It is possible that this "wit" was a fruit of his long and deep cultivation of sixteenth- and seventeenth-century English poetry, but his success in the mode suggests more than a merely imitative faculty and calls for serious critical studies of his poetry.

Biography:
F. B. Smith, *Radical Artisan: William James Linton, 1812-97* (Manchester, U.K.: Manchester University Press, 1973; Totowa, N.J.: Rowman & Littlefield, 1973).

References:
A. H. Bullen, "William James Linton," in A. H. Miles, ed., *The Poets and the Poetry of the Century*, volume 4 (London: Hutchinson, 1892), pp. 377-382;

W. F. Hopson, "Sidelights on Linton 1812-97," *PBSA*, 27 (1933): 74-82;

F. G. Kitton, "William James Linton," *English Illustrated Magazine* (April 1891): 491-500;

R. Malcolm Sills, "W. J. Linton at Yale—The Appledore Private Press," *Yale University Library Gazette*, 12 (1938): 43-52.

Papers:
The British Library has twenty volumes of materials collected and presented by Linton under the title "Prose and Verse Written and Published in the Course of Fifty Years 1836-1886." The Beinecke Library at Yale University holds many letters and manuscripts relating mainly to Linton's life in the United States, and partly to earlier periods. The Harvard Library and the New York Public Library have some of Linton's letters. The National Library of Australia in Canberra holds a large collection of Linton's domestic letters and several rare printed works of his. The Istituto Giangiacomo Feltrinelli in Milan holds most of Linton's political correspondence until the 1850s, as well as some domestic letters.

Edward Robert Bulwer Lytton
(Owen Meredith)

(8 November 1831-24 November 1891)

Michael Darling
Vanier College

SELECTED BOOKS: *Clytemnestra, The Earl's Return, The Artist, and Other Poems*, as Owen Meredith (London: Chapman & Hall, 1855);

The Wanderer, as Meredith (London: Chapman & Hall, 1859);

Poems (Boston: Ticknor & Fields, 1859);

Lucile, as Meredith (London: Chapman & Hall, 1860; Boston: Ticknor & Fields, 1860);

Tannhäuser; or, The Battle of the Bards, by Julian Fane and Lytton as Neville Temple and Edward Trevor (London: Chapman & Hall, 1861);

Serbski Pesme; or, National Songs of Servia, as Meredith (London: Chapman & Hall, 1861; Boston: Osgood, 1877);

Edward Robert Bulwer Lytton (Owen Meredith)

The Ring of Amasis, as Meredith (2 volumes, London: Chapman & Hall, 1863; 1 volume, New York: Harper, 1863);

The Apple of Life, as Meredith (Boston: Ticknor & Fields, 1865);

The Poetical Works of Owen Meredith, as Meredith, 2 volumes (London: Chapman & Hall, 1867);

Chronicles and Characters, 2 volumes (London: Chapman & Hall, 1868); republished as *New Poems* (Boston: Ticknor & Fields, 1868);

Orval; or, The Fool of Time (London: Chapman & Hall, 1869);

Julian Fane: A Memoir (London: Murray, 1871);

Fables in Song, 2 volumes (Edinburgh & London: Blackwood, 1874; Boston: Osgood, 1874);

King Poppy: A Story without End (London: Privately printed, 1875; revised, London & New York: Longmans, Green, 1892);

The Imperial Bouquet of Pretty Flowers from the Poetical Parterre of Robert, Lord Lytton . . . with a Collection of His Excellency's Public Speeches in India, edited by N. A. Chick (Calcutta: Newman, 1876);

The Life, Letters and Literary Remains of Edward Bulwer, Lord Lytton, 2 volumes (London: Kegan Paul, Trench, 1883; New York: Harper, 1883);

Glenaveril; or, The Metamorphoses, 2 volumes (London: Murray, 1885; New York: Appleton, 1885);

After Paradise; or, Legends of Exile with Other Poems (London: Stott, 1887; Boston: Estes & Lauriat, 1887);

Marah (New York & London: Longmans, Green, 1892).

In his own lifetime, Edward Robert Bulwer Lytton, better known by his pseudonym Owen Meredith, was much more highly regarded as a poet than he is today. His lyrics were praised by discriminating critics, and he was especially well received in America, where his verse novel *Lucile* (1860) was published in more than 100 editions. However, Lytton never succeeded in establishing a style of his own, and was more than once accused of plagiarism. His works are now read mainly as documents in the history of Victorian taste rather than for any intrinsic merit they might possess, yet his talents as a writer of fables and vers de société are not inconsiderable.

Lytton was born in London on 8 November 1831 to the famous novelist Edward Bulwer-Lytton (later Lord Lytton) and the brilliant but erratic Rosina Wheeler Bulwer-Lytton. His parents, preoccupied with a time-consuming social life complicated by marital discord, showed little interest in their children, and Robert was raised by a sympathetic nurse, Mary Greene. He was educated at home and at a school near Twickenham; at the age of fourteen he was sent to Harrow, where he began to compose poetry. He was encouraged in his literary efforts by his father's friend John Forster, the influential critic and literary advisor to Dickens, Browning, Leigh Hunt, and others. Forster was to act not only as Lytton's editor but also as his guardian and confidant, and as a mediator between Robert and his aloof, sometimes tyrannical father.

In 1849 Lytton was sent to Bonn to study with an English tutor, but illness, debt, and his attempted suicide prompted his father to call him home. The next year he took up a post in Washington, D.C., as unpaid attaché to his uncle, Sir Henry Bulwer, the ambassador to the United States. It was his father's wish that Robert adopt a profession which would

Lytton's father, the novelist Edward Bulwer-Lytton (by permission of Mr. Robert Lutyens)

enable him to support himself and the vast family estate of Knebworth which he would someday inherit, but the demands of diplomacy were inimical to his aesthetic sensibility.

In February 1852 Lytton was transferred to Florence, where he mingled with the Anglo-American expatriate colony which included William Wetmore Story, Frederick Tennyson, George Seymour Kirkup, the Trollopes, and the Brownings. The influence of both Robert and Elizabeth Barrett Browning is evident in Lytton's early poetry, but it was with Mrs. Browning that he was most intimate, sharing her interest in spiritualism. He began at this time to seriously consider himself a poet, but his aspirations in that field brought upon him the wrath of his father, who told him to give up any ideas he might have of a literary career. A compromise was reached by which Robert agreed to forgo his attempts at poetry for two years following the publication of his first book. It was also agreed that, to avoid confusion between father and son, Robert would adopt the pseudonym Owen Meredith, derived from the wife of a Lytton ancestor, Ann Meredith, who was related to Owen Tudor. Lytton kept the pseudonym until 1868, by which time George Meredith had registered his objections to the similarity.

His first book, *Clytemnestra, The Earl's Return, The Artist, and Other Poems,* was published by Chapman and Hall in 1855. "Clytemnestra," a long verse drama with many echoes of Tennyson, Browning, Marlowe, and Shakespeare, not to mention Aeschylus, was easily the most ambitious work in the volume; it found favor with Matthew Arnold, Mrs. Browning, Leigh Hunt, and Bulwer-Lytton, who wrote to his son that he was now "a real poet, and of a genus too that will be practical, and sooner or later popular." A different sort of popularity was gained by "The Earl's Return," a poem whose Pre-Raphaelite medievalism earned it the admiration of William Morris and others at Oxford. Some of the better lyrics in the book also employ medieval materials—specifically, the Arthurian legends so popular in the mid-nineteenth century. Indeed, the success of the volume as a whole may be largely attributed to its author's ability to mirror the tastes of his time.

In the next few years, Lytton's diplomatic career took him from Florence to Paris to The Hague, where he again began to write poetry. His next book, *The Wanderer,* was published in 1859. Its 101 poems have been described by his biographer as "romanticized autobiography" in which he records his response to an unhappy love affair as he wanders through Europe. As confessional poetry, the volume is unremarkable for the profundity of its psychological insights; but Lytton may well have felt that he had revealed too much of himself, for in later editions he omitted many of the poems, while those that remained were completely revised. Besides exploring the theme of unrequited love with a prevailing streak of misogyny (" 'Tis a woman that reigns in Hell"), Lytton touches on other popular Victorian motifs in the book—the Gothic, the grotesque, and the Oriental—but he seems most at ease with the sort of vers de société associated with Winthrop Mackworth Praed. This element of his writing is best observed in "The Portrait," with its ironic wit pointing the direction his work was to take in *Lucile*.

In 1859 Lytton was employed as second secretary in the British embassy at Vienna, and was hard at work on his next book. After a tortuous genesis in which Bulwer-Lytton and Forster took turns in revising each section of the manuscript, *Lucile* appeared in April 1860 and was an immediate success. Its treatment of serious themes such as self-sacrifice, moral regeneration, and the emergence of the "buried self" endeared the poem to the guardians of Victorian moral standards, while its sparkling description in anapestic couplets of aristocratic life made it popular with a younger, predominantly female, audience. It is this latter quality of the poem that makes its prolixity bearable, and the lines from it that are remembered today—"We may live without friends; we may live without books;/But civilized man cannot live without cooks"—are those that reflect its author's wit and self-assured understanding of high society. Lytton later denounced the work as "trashy," but only Mrs. Browning's *Aurora Leigh* (1857) rivaled the popularity of *Lucile* among nineteenth-century readers of the novel in verse.

Lytton's next work was a narrative poem based on the libretto of Wagner's *Tannhäuser,* written jointly with his friend Julian Fane, and published pseudonymously in a limited edition in 1861. In the same year, Lytton brought out a collection of translations and paraphrases of Serbian folk poetry entitled *Serbski Pesme; or, National Songs of Servia.* The book would have been quickly forgotten had it not prompted a charge of plagiarism by the *Saturday Review,* which noted that Lytton's translations relied rather heavily on those of Auguste Dozon in *Poésies populaires serbes* (1859). Lytton's poems were indeed translations from the French of Dozon, whose work he had acknowledged in his preface; but he had also unwisely hinted that he himself had collected the songs "on their native soil." It was neither the first nor the last time that Lytton was to be pained by such an accusation. The *Literary Gazette* had recently pointed to some obvious borrowings in *Lucile* from George Sand's *Lavinia.* Gifted with a prodigious memory and a love of fine phrases, Lytton was repeatedly to prove vulnerable to the charge of plagiarism.

Lytton attempted the drama without success, and then prose with scarcely better results. Both his father and Forster tried desperately to suppress his novel *The Ring of Amasis* (1863). A long-winded and highly implausible romance, *The Ring of Amasis* enjoyed a measure of popularity in America but was almost totally ignored in England. Discouraged, Lytton temporarily abandoned literature to concentrate on his diplomatic career. He was made first secretary of the legation at Copenhagen in February 1863, and a few months later was transferred to the legation at Athens. On a visit to England in

Lytton's wife, Edith Villiers Lytton

the summer of 1864 he met twenty-two-year-old Edith Villiers, whom he married on 4 October 1864. The following year, he was posted to the legation at Lisbon; disliking the city, the Lyttons took up residence in the village of Cintra, about fifteen miles from the capital. Edith returned to England in June for her confinement and the delivery in September of their first child, a son they named Rowland.

A stable home life and the encouragement of his new friend and attaché Wilfrid Scawen Blunt inspired Lytton to set about revising his poems for a collected edition, which appeared in two volumes in 1867, the same year his daughter Elizabeth was born. Lytton was also working on a new book, which he called *Chronicles and Characters.* Published in 1868, this work was intended to be "a poetic history of the *education* of man" in nine books, tracing important cultural developments from ancient Greece to contemporary Europe. It was Lytton's most ambitious work to date, and the first to appear under his own name. He was proud of his efforts, but his father judged the book immature and the critics ignored it. Lytton was again despondent, and resolved to submerge what he considered to be his

Letter from Lytton, at Lisbon, to his wife in England, expressing his joy at the birth of their son, Rowland, in 1865

Wilfred Scawen Blunt, who was Lytton's attaché at Lisbon

true self—the artistic side of his character—and live a double life, thus reflecting in his own psyche the theme of the "buried self" which he had explored in *Lucile*. Though daily called upon to exhibit tact and orthodoxy in the exercise of his duties as a diplomat, Lytton was nonetheless a bit eccentric in his notions and in his personal habits. Poetry became for him a necessary outlet for everything that he was required to suppress in the course of his public life. In *Orval; or, The Fool of Time* (1869), he adopted the pessimistic tone of his source, *The Undivine Comedy* of Count Sigismund Krasinski, and indulged some of his radical opinions on education, politics, and the class system.

A second daughter, Constance, was born in 1869. In April of that year Lytton was transferred to Madrid; he was sent to Vienna in 1870, where he remained for the next three years. In the summer of 1871 all three of the children became ill with whooping cough; the girls survived, but Rowland developed a lung infection and died on 19 July.

The early 1870s were marked by the appearance of Lytton's "Lyrical Fables" in the *Fortnightly Review*, and by his elevation to Baron Lytton on the death of Bulwer-Lytton on 18 January 1873. Lytton was forty-two at the time and had a secure position in the foreign service of his country. He took his seat in the House of Lords, but continued to serve as secretary of legation at Paris, where he had been sent in 1872. In 1874 his *Fables in Song* was published; it was a collection of the *Fortnightly Review* poems with the addition of others in the same vein. These are some of his best works; the beast fables, especially, reveal a sense of humor that was lacking in his early lyrics. He was fond of the ironic anticlimax, as in "Valour" and "The Mountains of Time." Though not particularly profound, the fables are quietly satisfactory in their fluid wit and assured tone, and they do show evidence, for once, of originality, if not of startling innovation. They are among the few works that he was able in later life to look on with approval.

Lytton was looking forward to retirement and relaxation at his ancestral estate, Knebworth; but when Disraeli offered him the position of viceroy of India in 1876, he was unable to refuse. His task was physically and mentally exhausting; his responsibilities included preparing for the pageant at which Queen Victoria was proclaimed empress of India on 1 January 1877, organizing famine relief after crop failures in southern India, abolishing the internal trade barriers in the country, reforming the civil

Lytton at his home in the village of Cintra, Portugal, while he was first secretary to the British legation at Lisbon

service, and overseeing the conduct of the Afghan War. Lytton was generally successful in these endeavors, but he was subjected to harsh criticism in the British press and in Parliament. Some of this criticism was merely partisan, as Disraeli's opponents used Lytton as a scapegoat to attack the prime minister; but Lytton also aroused resentment at home because of his advocacy of the rights of the natives. He was glad to relinquish the post after four years when Disraeli's government was defeated at the polls in March 1880. He was created the first Earl Lytton the following month.

Lytton hoped to devote the rest of his life to literature. He did find time to write a two-volume biography of his father (1883); a long, semiautobiographical poem, *Glenaveril* (1885); and a book of lyrics and fables entitled *After Paradise; or, Legends of Exile* (1887); but his country called him again in 1887, and he agreed—though with great reluctance—to serve as ambassador to France.

In contrast to the criticism that had been heaped upon him as viceroy of India, Lytton was highly praised for his performance as ambassador, and was credited with improving relations between Britain and France during a difficult period in international affairs. His accomplishments were actually due not to any diplomatic initiatives on his part but to his popularity among the French political leaders. Lytton recognized the irony of the situation, saying: "I devoted my life to India and everybody abused me. I come here, do nothing, and am praised to the skies."

Lytton's health was beginning to fail; after a difficult channel crossing in the fall of 1891 he weakened rapidly, dying in Paris on 24 November. He was at work on a new poem up to the moment of his death. In the spring of 1892 Longmans, Green brought out *Marah,* an undistinguished collection of lyrics, and a revised version of *King Poppy* (which Lytton had had privately printed in 1875), a critique of contemporary political and social thought. Some have felt this poem to be Lytton's best work, but it suffers from his habitual diffuseness and the obscurity of its allegorical structure.

The lack of an individual style and a chronic inability to compress his ideas or curb his wordiness have doomed Lytton to second-rate status among his contemporaries. Yet in a few of his fables and in parts of *Lucile* there are flashes of brilliance that rival the work of Robert Browning and Tennyson. But no matter how his work is finally assessed, the study of his poetry is of great value to the historian of Victorian literature. Every shift in popular taste in the last half of the nineteenth century is reflected in the poems of Owen Meredith. He is unquestionably, as one critic put it, "the best of mirrors."

Letters:

Personal and Literary Letters of Robert First Earl of Lytton, edited by Lady Betty Balfour, 2 volumes (London: Longmans, Green, 1906);

Letters from Owen Meredith (Robert, First Earl of Lytton) to Robert and Elizabeth Barrett Browning, edited by Aurelia Brooks Harlan and J. Lee Harlan, Jr. (Waco, Texas: Baylor University Press, 1936);

The Birth of Rowland: An Exchange of Letters in 1865 Between Robert Lytton and His Wife, edited by Lady Emily Lutyens (London: Hart-Davis, 1956).

References:

Wilfrid Scawen Blunt, "Lord Lytton's Rank in Literature," *Nineteenth Century,* 31 (1892): 566-576;

Aurelia Brooks Harlan, *Owen Meredith: A Critical Biography of Robert, First Earl of Lytton* (New York: Columbia University Press, 1946);

The [second] Earl of Lytton, "The Poetry of Owen Meredith," in *The Eighteen-Eighties,* edited by Walter de la Mare (Cambridge: Cambridge University Press, 1930), pp. 16-43;

George Saintsbury, *A History of Nineteenth Century Literature* (London: Macmillan, 1929), pp. 318-320;

Hugh Walker, *The Literature of the Victorian Era* (Cambridge: Cambridge University Press, 1921), pp. 601-603;

Wilfred War, "Robert Earl of Lytton, Statesman and Poet," in his *Ten Personal Studies* (London: Longmans, Green, 1908), pp. 97-116.

Thomas Babington Macaulay

(25 October 1800-28 December 1859)

Richard Tobias
University of Pittsburgh

SELECTED BOOKS: *Pompeii: A Poem Which Obtained the Chancellor's Medal at the Cambridge Commencement, July 1819* (Cambridge, 1819);

Evening: A Poem Which Obtained the Chancellor's Medal at the Cambridge Commencement, July 1821 (Cambridge, 1821);

A Speech in the House of Commons, March 2 1831, on a Bill to Amend the Representation of the People in England and Wales (London: Ridgway, 1831);

The Speech of T. B. Macaulay on the Second Reading of the Third Reform Bill, 16 December 1831 (London: Hansard, 1831);

A Speech . . . on the Second Reading of the East India Bill, in the House of Commons, 10th July, 1833 (London: Hansard, 1833);

Lays of Ancient Rome (London: Longman, Brown, Green & Longmans, 1842; Philadelphia: Carey & Hart, 1843);

Critical and Miscellaneous Essays, 5 volumes (Philadelphia: Carey & Hart, 1842-1844);

Critical and Historical Essays Contributed to the Edinburgh Review (3 volumes, London: Longman, Brown, Green & Longmans, 1843; 5 volumes, New York: White, Stokes & Allen, 1843);

Speech in the House of Commons, February 26 1845, on the Proposed Discriminating Duties on Sugar (Edinburgh: Dalyrymple, 1845);

Speech in the House of Commons, July 9 1845, on the Bill for the Abolition of Scottish University Tests (Edinburgh, 1845);

Government Plan of Education: Speech in the House of Commons, April 19 1847 (London, 1847);

The History of England from the Accession of James II, 5 volumes; volume 5 edited by Lady Hannah Trevelyan (London: Longman, Brown, Green & Longmans, 1849-1861; New York: Harper, 1849-1861);

Inaugural Address Delivered on His Installation as Lord Rector of the University of Glasgow 21st March 1849 (Edinburgh: Stillie, 1849);

The Life and Writings of Addison (London: Longman, Brown, Green & Longmans, 1852; New York: Harper, 1878);

Speeches Corrected by Himself (New York: Redfield, 1853; London: Longman, Brown, Green & Longmans, 1854);

Biographical and Historical Sketches (New York: Appleton, 1857);

Biographies of Lord Macaulay (Edinburgh: Black, 1860; New York: Macmillan, 1894);

The Indian Education Minutes of Lord Macaulay, edited by H. Woodrow (Calcutta, 1862);

Hymn by Lord Macaulay: An Effort of His Early Childhood, edited by L. Horton-Smith (Cambridge: Metcalf, 1902);

Marginal Notes, edited by G. O. Trevelyan (London:

Longmans, Green, 1907);
Essay and Speech on Jewish Disabilities, edited by I. Abrahams and S. Levy (Edinburgh: Ballantyne, Hanson, 1910);
Lord Macaulay's Legislative Minutes, edited by C. D. Dharker (London & New York: Oxford University Press, 1946);
Napoleon and the Restoration of the Bourbons: The Completed Portion of Macaulay's Projected "History of France, from the Restoration of the Bourbons to the Accession of Louis Philippe," edited by Joseph Hamburger (London: Longman, 1977);
Utilitarian Logic and Politics: James Mill's "Essay on Government," Macaulay's Critique and the Ensuing Debate, edited by Jack Lively and John Rees (Oxford: Clarendon Press, 1978).

Collections: *The Works of Lord Macaulay, Complete,* edited by Lady Trevelyan, 8 volumes (London: Longmans, Green, 1866);
The Complete Works of Lord Macaulay, Bibliophile Edition, 20 volumes (Philadelphia: University Library Association, 1910).

Thomas Babington Macaulay was a critic, member of Parliament, cabinet minister, member of the Supreme Council of India, author of the third most popular book of poems in the nineteenth century after John Keble's *The Christian Year* (1827) and Tennyson's *Poems* (1842), and the most successful historian of his age, but his position in cultural history is equivocal. At the age of twenty-five, he astonished all of Britain with an essay on Milton. In his early thirties, he helped achieve parliamentary reform; during his four years in India he codified the Indian penal code and his "Minute on Education" changed Indian history by making English the language of education in that country. After returning from India to London, he served in British governments and planned his monumental history of England from the Great Rebellion of 1688 to the Great Reform of 1832. He spent the last twenty years of his life writing the history but only reached the year 1700 before his death. Now, however, his Milton essay seems merely an attempt to create and justify a Whig literary history; his service in Parliament and cabinet yielded no original reform; his history is a brilliant exposition of party propaganda; his book of poems is described by Jane Millgate as a "paradox, a Philistine work of art." In both history and verse, he tells stories rapidly and dramatically; his sentences move with skill and command, and his diction is a marvel; he recreates historical characters with economy and persuasiveness. Macaulay wrote like an efficient machine, producing volumes of clear, glittering words. He feared sentiment and preferred distance, objectivity, dispassionate vision. Yet withal, he was a brilliant writer who attracted readers and admirers in his own time and is still capable of moving a reader by sheer verbal excitement. His *The History of England from the Accession of James II* (1849-1861) has been overtaken by newly discovered facts, but it still can be read as a statement of *the* liberal view of his time.

Although he was born in Leicestershire, Macaulay grew up in London, where his father, Zachary Macaulay, was a leader in the Clapham Sect. Zachary Macaulay made a fortune in Africa, returned home to marry Selina Mills, the daughter of a Bristol Quaker, and set about doing good deeds. The Clapham Sect was a branch of the Evangelical movement, the movement whose moral intensity and public sense of duty created what is popularly known as Victorianism. Almost singlehandedly, members of the sect ended the slave trade in 1807 and abolished slavery in the British Empire in 1833; they also stayed away from theaters, took a dim view of pleasure, and read edifying books. Their passion was for reform and renewal. From his Evangelical background, Thomas Macaulay learned to concentrate on worthy causes, and he also learned that passionate reform may create as much difficulty as it cures. Macaulay modified his Evangelical fervor to obtain more immediate goals than the complete reconstitution of society. His own career was more meteoric than his father's, but it was also more planned, controlled, and consistent.

Macaulay attended Trinity College, Cambridge. He was called to the bar in 1826 but, gaining little business, he left after two years. He wrote essays for the *Edinburgh Review,* the most successful journal of its day. It was also the organ of the more intelligent men of the Whig oligarchy. His brilliant conversation and oratory attracted the attention of leading political figures who secured his election to Parliament in 1830 from a "pocket borough" (an electoral district in the control of a wealthy landowner). Macaulay spoke in support of the Great Reform of 1832, even though it eliminated his own seat. He was quickly reelected from a new district in Leeds. As a result of his political work, Macaulay received appointment as secretary of the Board of Control of India, and served on the Supreme Council. He served in India from 1834 until 1838 and earned £40,000; he was able to live on the income for the rest of his life from investing this sum and to speak his mind without fear of political debts. When he returned from India, Leeds and Edinburgh sent him back to Parliament; Edinburgh elected him in 1851 even though he did not campaign. He retired from Parliament in 1855 to devote full time to his *History.* He was raised to the peerage in 1857 as Lord Macaulay, Baron Macaulay of Rothley. He died of heart disease in the hard winter of 1859, the same age as the century and one of its most representative men.

Macaulay first attracted widespread attention with his essay on Milton in the *Edinburgh Review* in 1825. Ostensibly a review of a newly discovered Latin text by Milton, the essay gave Macaulay the opportunity to compare Milton favorably with Dante, who was then little known in England, and to praise Milton for expressing a childlike, almost primitive wonder and joy in a rational, controlled, and mechanical time. Although to Macaulay poetry is impossible in the modern age, Milton triumphed over his obstacles and, in *Paradise Lost,* wrote a poem comparable to Dante's *Divine Comedy.* Because Macaulay attempted to balance enthusiasm with social objectivity in the essay, many critics cite it as the first Victorian document, even though it was published twelve years before the queen came to the throne.

Macaulay wrote poetry for entertainment, utility, and escape. His earliest surviving verse is an Evangelical hymn he wrote when he was eight. As an adolescent he exchanged ballad stanzas with the great Hannah More. At Cambridge he wrote love songs, ballads, and parodies. He started *Lays of Ancient Rome* (1842) in India when he was homesick for England and heartbroken because he had lost one sister through death and another through marriage; but he wrote about Rome, not about his own loss or pain. The poems are healthy, athletic, and intelligent, fit for every schoolboy in Britain who would grow up to become a counselor to a new empire formed on Whig principles.

Lays of Ancient Rome, four poems about early Roman history, still enchant readers with their vigor, clarity, and certainty. The heroes and villains are clear. As Jane Millgate says, the verses are "not just easy to remember but virtually impossible to forget." Macaulay knew what his audience wanted—the assertion of true principles of civic action—and he had the language to supply it. He draws sharp, clear pictures; he connects past with present without overt moralizing or pointing. He exploits the ballad tradition, but his ballads are rollicking and patriotic. The Romantic impulse that Macaulay learned from Sir Walter Scott gave him new and striking scenes rather than ambiguity, mysticism, or paradox. Macaulay's poems are as bright as a June day and as emphatic as a military band.

Lays of Ancient Rome purports to be a collection of lost folk poems upon which the early Roman historians based their narratives. For each poem, Macaulay wrote a prose introduction explaining his source and his poetic decisions. By a process of back-formation Macaulay imagined what the long-lost ballads would have been, but he wrote them in English in the style of Scott. Macaulay's narrators are Roman citizens, lost in the anonymity of their citizenship, who express Roman communal virtues. Each poem is spoken at a public gathering to rouse civic pride. "The Battle of the Lake Regillus," for example, is spoken at the installation of a new order of knights.

In the first poem, "Horatius," a brave Roman and two friends hold off an invading Etruscan army while the citizens destroy the last bridge over the Tiber. Thus Rome is saved by common effort. "The Battle of the Lake Regillus" tells of Romans repulsing a Tarquin attack with the help of the god-twins Castor and Pollux. The dictator Aulus in this poem organizes the virtuous, but divergent, powers of society to destroy the common enemy. The third poem, "Virginia," tells Chaucer's Physician's Tale from the *Canterbury Tales.* In both versions, a

The poet Hannah More, with whom the young Macaulay exchanged verses

Portrait of Macaulay by J. Partridge (National Portrait Gallery)

Roman judge, Appius, of an old patrician family, sees and desires the plebeian maiden Virginia. He arranges for the child to be declared a stolen slave, whom the judge will then possess. Her father, rather than see his daughter in sexual bondage, kills her. In Chaucer, the poem says to its audience, in effect, "You too may sin as the judge sinned." In Macaulay, however, the simple schoolgirl and her father are victims of upper-class insolence. Although the preface says that the judge died at the hands of the plebeians, in the poem the guilty judge escapes from the mob and moralizes over the experience to convince himself never to insult the people again. The patricians and plebeians (like good Tories and Whigs) join forces and begin the great period of Roman rule and prosperity. In "The Prophecy of Capys" the twins Romulus and Remus march out to the countryside, where a seer foretells the rise of Rome. In this poem, history is a patriotic parade on a summer's day, with flags flying and boys shouting; four of the last six stanzas begin with "Hurrah!" The final stanza depicts a child's map of the Roman Empire with the promise that "Far o'er the western foam/Shall be great fear on all who hear/The mighty name of Rome." The virtues in these poems are the simple, obvious virtues of patrician and plebeian citizens who rationally cooperate for the common good of a new empire.

English settlers in nineteenth-century Australia possessed three books: the Bible, the works of Shakespeare, and *The History of England from the Accession of James II*. The *History* reads, as Macaulay intended, like a novel. Although it is prose, it is his best piece of poetry, for Macaulay invests his story with high glee, popular romance, and the narrative skill of a master. He had first conceived the project on his return from India in 1838. In India he read prodigiously in Greek and Latin texts. British history, until Macaulay's book, was the province of Tory historians. Macaulay writes of the triumphant rise of Whig and Liberal principles when upper and lower classes would cooperate in trade, manufacturing, and banking. History, to Macaulay, is the progressive, liberal expansion of a society recognizing its common good. The first two volumes sold 22,000 copies in 1849, the year they were published, and in 1855 the third and fourth volumes sold 26,500 copies in less than ten weeks. Only a novelist such as Dickens could equal such a sale. Macaulay had made every effort to read original sources, but the overriding interest of readers, then as now, was in Macaulay's management of his material. The *History* is fiction, the fiction of the Whig party viewing the English past and justifying itself, but it is so innocent in its revision and so energetic in its telling that readers submit willingly to the great, colorful panorama.

In his last decade, Macaulay wrote for the *Encyclopaedia Britannica* striking biographical essays on Francis Atterbury, John Bunyan, Oliver Goldsmith, Samuel Johnson, and William Pitt. These were published separately as *Biographies of Lord Macaulay* (1860). In these essays Macaulay is at the height of his certainty and power. He has arrived at truth, and he uses every tool of a vast rhetorical training to convince his reader. Macaulay's other essays usually began life as reviews, but in the fashion of the time, Macaulay disposes of the book under review in a paragraph or two and goes on to discuss a topic of his own choosing. His 1843 review of Lucy Aiken's biography of the essayist Joseph Addison was published as a book (1878) and has gone into many editions; poor Miss Aiken's volumes were never reprinted.

In addition to *Lays of Ancient Rome,* Macaulay wrote valentines, epitaphs, inscriptions, ballads, translations, and Biblical paraphrases; he could compose vivid, correct, and stirring words on any occasion. "The Cavalier's March to London" (1824)

Macaulay in later life

anticipates Robert Browning's later Cavalier song "Boot, Saddle, to Horse and Away." Macaulay pairs his Cavalier song with a Puritan sergeant's song about the Battle of Nasby and gives equal energy to both sides. These are civilized poems by a man busy governing, appearing at fashionable Whig routs, and writing history.

Serious cultural critics have been hard on Macaulay for his obvious intention to please and instruct the rising middle classes. He seems too consciously the apologist and defender of his own political views, which now seem circumscribed and parochial. Macaulay requires little of his reader but attention to his vivid scenes and moving action. His soldiers never die and his old men speak honorably. In his *History* Macaulay is fond of referring to what "every schoolboy in England knows." Every middle-class schoolboy in the second half of the nineteenth century knew Macaulay's poems and his history, and they inspired that schoolboy when he went to India, Africa, or the other places printed pink on the globes to mark the British Empire. In his poems Macaulay translated Roman virtues into the language of his empire builders; in his *History* he showed the arrival and triumph of the Whig principles which the empire would spread. If the virtues seem not so innocent and untarnished today, one can still admire the skill and charm with which Macaulay presented his "social ideal" and recorded two lost civilizations—ancient Rome and nineteenth-century England.

Letters:
The Letters of Thomas Babington Macaulay, edited by Thomas Pinney, 6 volumes (London: Cambridge University Press, 1974-1981).

Bibliographies:
Donald Cunningham, "Thomas Babington Macaulay: A Bibliography of Twentieth-Century Periodical Articles and Speeches," *Bulletin of Bibliography,* 28 (1971): 19-21;

Thomas Pinney, "Notes on Macaulay's Unacknowledged and Uncollected Writings," *Papers of the Bibliographical Society of America,* 67 (1973): 17-31;

John Clive and Thomas Pinney, "Thomas Babington Macaulay," in *Victorian Prose: A Guide to Research,* edited by David J. DeLaura (New York: Modern Language Association, 1973), pp. 19-30.

Biography:
G. O. Trevelyan, *The Life and Letters of Lord Macaulay,* 2 volumes (London: Longman, 1876).

References:
John Clive, *Macaulay: The Shaping of the Historian* (New York: Knopf, 1973);

Margaret Cruikshank, *Thomas Babington Macaulay* (Boston: Twayne, 1978);

Joseph Hamburger, *Macaulay and the Whig Tradition* (Chicago: University of Chicago Press, 1976);

Jane Millgate, *Macaulay* (London & Boston: Routledge & Kegan Paul, 1973).

Papers:
Trinity College, Cambridge, has Macaulay's diaries, annotated editions of the classics, and corrected proofs of the life of Pitt. Family papers are at the Huntington Library, San Marino, California.

Gerald Massey

(29 May 1828-29 October 1907)

Tirthankar Bose
University of British Columbia

BOOKS: *Poems and Chansons* (Tring, U.K.: Privately printed, 1848);
Voices of Freedom and Lyrics of Love (London: Watson, 1851);
The Ballad of Babe Christabel, with Other Lyrical Poems (London: Bogue, 1854);
War Waits (London: Bogue, 1855);
Craigcrook Castle (London: Bogue, 1856);
The Poetical Works of Gerald Massey: Complete in One Volume (Boston: Ticknor & Fields, 1857);
Robert Burns: A Centenary Song and Other Lyrics (London: Kent, 1859);
Havelock's March and Other Poems (London: Trubner, 1861);
The Poetical Works of Gerald Massey (London: Routledge, Warne & Routledge, 1861);
Shakspeare's Sonnets Never Before Interpreted (London: Longmans, Green, 1866); republished and enlarged as *The Secret Drama of Shakspeare's Sonnets Unfolded, with the Characters Identified* (London: Clay & Taylor, 1872);
In Memory of John William Spencer, Earl Brownlow (London: Privately printed, 1867);
Carmen Nuptiale (London: Privately printed, 1868);
A Tale of Eternity and Other Poems (Boston: Fields, Osgood, 1870; London: Strahan, 1870);
Concerning Spiritualism (London: Burns, 1871);
A Book of the Beginnings, 2 volumes (London: Williams & Newgate, 1881);
The Natural Genesis, 2 volumes (London: Williams & Newgate, 1883);
My Lyrical Life: Poems Old and New (Boston: Colby & Rich, 1889; London: Clay, 1889);
Ancient Egypt, the Light of the World, 2 volumes (London: Unwin, 1907).

Gerald Massey's life and works exemplify the Victorian faith that industry and idealism are sure to win the favors of the Muse. He was one of a number of late Victorians who struggled through the most dispiriting poverty toward a life of letters and gained popularity and critical approbation both in England and in America. Self-taught and naive, Massey was nevertheless capable of presenting to his readers an idealized England possessed of a life

Gerald Massey

at once heroic, aesthetic, and simple.

Massey was born at Gamble's Wharf near Tring in Hertfordshire, England, on 29 May 1828. His father was William Massey, a canal boatman who had to support a large family on ten shillings a week; Gerald was able to go to a national school for only a few terms before he had to start earning a living, at the age of eight, in a silk factory at Tring. Then he worked at straw-plaiting in a marshy part of Buckinghamshire. The unhealthy climate drove him at the age of fifteen to London, where he worked as an errand boy. Through these hard years he used the little leisure he had in studying, writing poetry, and learning French. As he later put it, "Poverty is a cold place to write Poetry in," but it could not quench his fire.

In 1848 Massey privately published his first book of verse, *Poems and Chansons,* of which he sold 250 copies to the townspeople of Tring. His reading of Paine, Volney, and Howitt led him into radical circles. In 1849 he coedited the Chartist paper, the *Spirit of Freedom,* with the painter John Bedford Leno. He also contributed poems to *Cooper's Journal,* a paper run by another Chartist, Thomas Cooper.

Through these interests Massey soon became acquainted with Charles Kingsley and F. D. Maurice; Maurice converted him to Christian Socialism. Massey became a secretary of the Christian Socialist Board and wrote for the board's journal, the *Christian Socialist.* In 1850 he married Rosina Jane Knowles; they had three daughters and a son. In 1851, his second volume of poetry, *Voices of Freedom and Lyrics of Love,* appeared. These poems are marked by Massey's large but undiscerning sympathy for the poor and by a melting adoration of innocent womanhood. The strains of hortatory militancy and romantic rapture heard here were to continue to sound through all of Massey's poetry.

Massey's best-known work appeared in 1854: *The Ballad of Babe Christabel* went through four editions within the year, followed by a fifth in 1855. Besides popular success, it brought him the praise, sometimes wildly adulatory, of major literary figures of the day. Walter Savage Landor wrote to the *Morning Advertiser* comparing Massey with Keats and Shakespeare and calling him a "Hafiz, but chastened and controlled." Ruskin and Tennyson expressed approval. George Eliot, who was a coworker of Massey's at John Chapman's publishing house, modeled her *Felix Holt, The Radical* (1866) partly on him; Sydney Dobell became a close friend, after whom Massey named his first son. Most importantly of all, *The Ballad of Babe Christabel* brought an invitation from Hepworth Dixon to join the staff of the *Athenaeum* as a regular reviewer, which gave Massey a measure of financial security. *Babe Christabel* also won him popularity in America, when an edition of his verses prominently featuring the poem appeared immediately after its London publication.

The Ballad of Babe Christabel describes the birth of a child and her death in infancy. In the main, the poem extols the beauty of suffering motherhood and angelic infancy. Into these outpourings, however, Massey injects a strain of mystery by blurring the distinction between life and death, perceiving these as separate but related planes of existence. The poem gains force as it proceeds from its initial stock responses to a perception of nature as an intuitive sense of immutable human bonds. This perception does not follow the religious meliorism of the fourteenth-century Pearl Poet, but resembles rather the vision of Dante Gabriel Rossetti in "The Blessed Damozel." While it lacks the suggestive ambiguities of the trancelike state created in Rossetti's poem, it does try to articulate a reaching-out into the unknown, especially in the middle section. Massey's poem is virtually contemporaneous with Rossetti's and makes similar use of such key phrases as "A spirit-look was in her face" and "Such mystic love was in her eyes"; the most Rossettian of these parallels is "All last night-tide she seemed near me, like a lost beloved Bird." It is perhaps legitimate to identify in this poem the beginning of an addictive spiritualism that eventually turned Massey away from poetry.

Among other notable poems in the volume is the well-known ballad "Sir Richard Grenville's Last Fight." Its description of a desperate encounter moves briskly from one high point of concrete action to another, gaining a dramatic directness from its economy of detail. Massey firmly reins in his tendency to philosophize, relying rather on the physical event and the ringing tones of the dying commander to build an image of the "second Richard Lion-Heart" and his "grim Sea-Lions." Widely praised by contemporaries, it is best known now as having been used by Tennyson as a suggestion for "The Revenge" (1878).

In 1854 Massey moved with his family to Edinburgh, where he wrote for *Chambers's Journal* and the *Witness* and lectured on politics, poetry, and Pre-Raphaelite art. His engagement with history in the making brought forth *War Waits* (1855), a volume of poetry fired by the Crimean War. Sentimental rather than sensitive, this volume met a need for a national myth—as evidenced by the popular success of the work, which went through two editions within the year. The following year a more lyrical work appeared: *Craigcrook Castle* is a sequence of seven poems related not by subject but by Massey's admiration for a pastoral life and domestic emotions. The nature-painting in the title poem lacks originality but serves to underscore Massey's yearning for an idealized world. A more interesting piece is "The Mother's Idol Broken"; like *The Ballad of Babe Christabel,* this poem mourns the loss of a child, suggesting that the theme was a product of some actual experience.

Massey moved again in 1857, first to Monk's Green, Hertfordshire, and then to Brantwood, Coniston, the property of his friend, William James Linton (who later sold it to Ruskin). Moving closer to London the next year, he came to live at

tional poetry were rewarded by a civil list pension of seventy pounds a year on Lord Palmerston's recommendation in 1863. Of his many prose essays written at Ward's Hurst the most considerable is that on Shakespeare's sonnets. Originally published in the *Quarterly Review* in April 1864, the essay was amplified in 1866 into a monograph called *Shakspeare's Sonnets Never Before Interpreted,* and rewritten and published in 1872 as *The Secret Drama of Shakspeare's Sonnets Unfolded.* Diffuse in treatment and hasty in judgment though it is, the essay does summarize much of the scholarly work available to support the identification of Southampton as the "onlie begetter" of the sonnets.

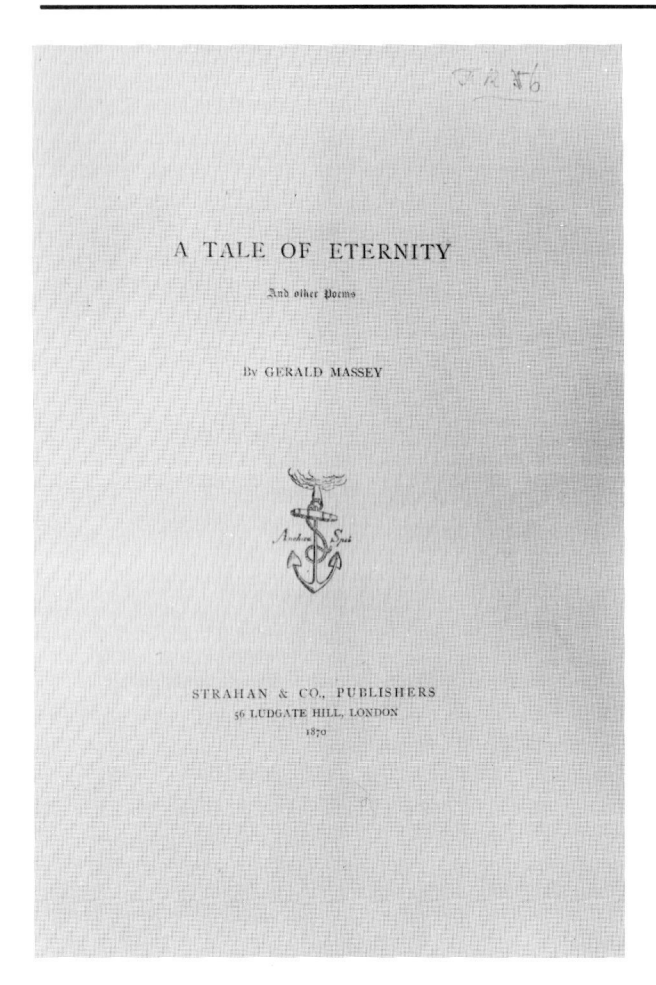

Massey's first wife died in March 1866; in January 1868 he married Eva Byron, by whom he had four daughters and a son. Massey wrote poems to commemorate the death of the second Earl Brownlow in 1867 and the marriage of the earl's

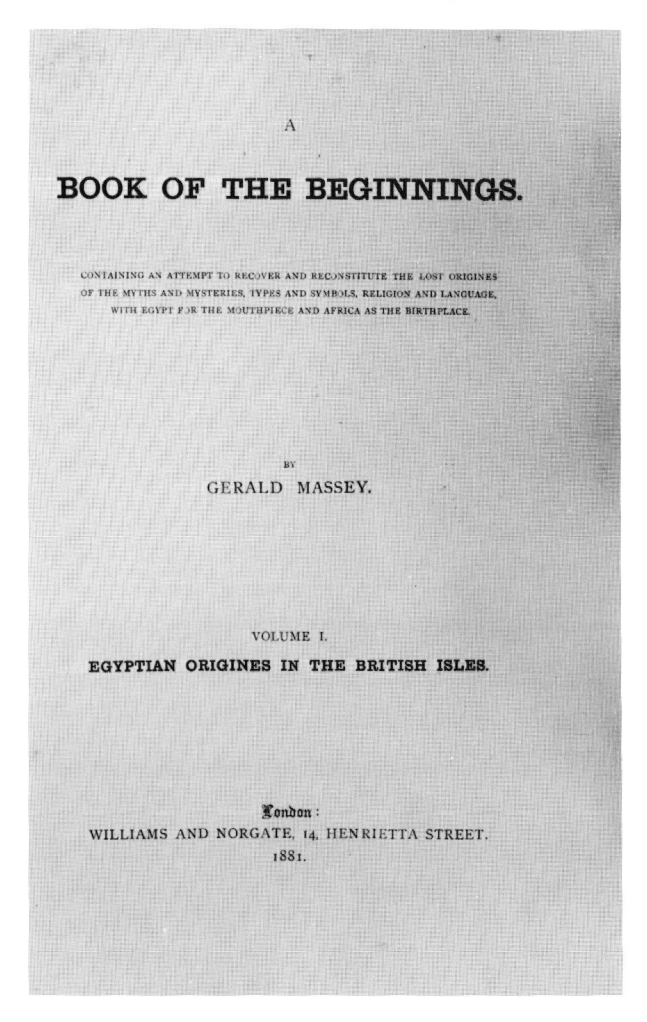

Title page for Massey's last important book of poetry (Thomas Cooper Library, University of South Carolina)

Rickmansworth in Hertfordshire. There he won the friendship of Lady Marian Alford and her son, the second Earl Brownlow, who lived some miles away at Ashridge Park, Berkhamstead. In 1862 Lord Brownlow provided Massey with a house, Ward's Hurst, on his estate. Churton Collins suggests that Massey attributed preternatural qualities to Ward's Hurst; this may explain why Massey's interest in spiritualism developed into an obsessive preoccupation during his residence there.

Meanwhile, he continued to write industriously, though more in a journalistic than a poetic vein. A poem on Burns submitted for the Burns centenary competition at the Crystal Palace in 1859 was placed among the first six, though it was not awarded the prize. A more substantial work, *Havelock's March* (1861), was inspired by the Sepoy mutiny in India. Like his other patriotic poems, the poems in this volume are full of martial ardor and idealized portraiture. His endeavors to create a na-

Title page for one of Massey's books on the occult philosophy of ancient Egypt (Thomas Cooper Library, University of South Carolina)

brother and successor in 1868; neither poem is of any distinction. His life as a poet was, in any case, drawing to a close. In 1870 his last important work, *A Tale of Eternity and Other Poems,* was published. This long narrative of sin and its consequences in this world and the next shows a skill in creating eerie situations that justifies the regret Massey's contemporaries felt at his giving up poetry. Even here, however, the pull of philosophy—especially its spiritualist offshoot—proved too much for Massey's poetic imagination, and much of the poem is given over to moralizings on spirit communication.

Massey's popularity as a writer and speaker remained high throughout his life. From September 1873 to May 1874 he went on an extensive lecture tour of the United States and Canada. Between October 1883 and November 1885 he toured Australia, New Zealand, and, again, the United States. In 1887 Lord Salisbury increased his pension to £100. Yet another American tour began in September 1888 but was cut short by his return to be with a dying daughter.

After leaving Ward's Hurst in 1877, Massey lived at New Southgate until 1890, at Dulwich from 1890 until 1893, and finally moved to a house called Redcot in South Norwood, a London suburb. Through these years he lectured and wrote indefatigably on psychic and spiritualist phenomena, especially on the occult philosophy of ancient Egypt. His principal works on these subjects are *A Book of the Beginnings* (1881), *The Natural Genesis* (1883), and *Ancient Egypt, the Light of the World* (1907). His only poetic venture was to bring out in 1889 a collection of his poems, *My Lyrical Life.*

On 29 October 1907 Massey died at Redcot. He was buried in the Old Southgate cemetery.

Massey's reputation among his contemporaries was mainly built upon his ability to present humble, everyday life lyrically; his liberal sympathies; and his pride and faith in England. Known best as a poet of the people, Massey dealt exclusively in solemn commonplaces of thought and feeling even during his period of social radicalism. But he did so with such facility—not originality—of movement and phrasing that even his untutored perceptions appear charged with vigor. Later generations of readers have not responded to any of these qualities with sympathy, seeing rather an undiscriminating pursuit of sensibility and philosophy in Massey's poetry. Yet, Massey's popularity among his contemporaries ensures his place in literary history, if only as a representative of that part of the Victorian consciousness which encouraged the belief that although, to quote Massey, "The powers of hell are strong today,/The Christ shall rise tomorrow!"

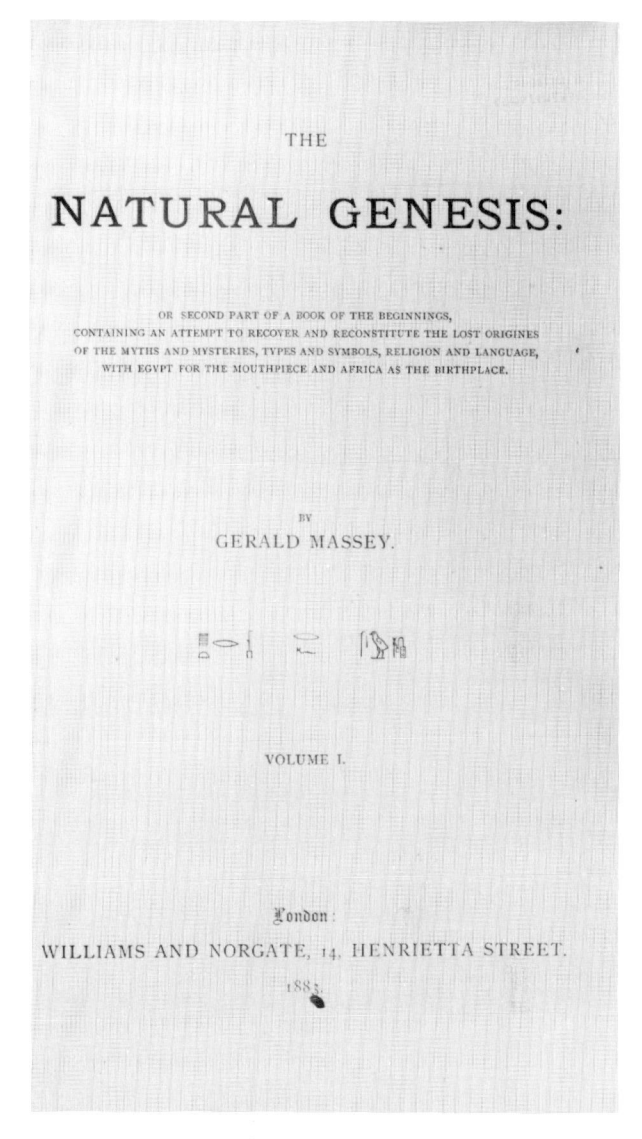

Title page for the sequel to Massey's Book of the Beginnings *(Thomas Cooper Library, University of South Carolina)*

References:

A. Bose, *Chroniclers of Life* (Calcutta: Orient Longmans, 1962), pp. 166-167;

J. Churton Collins, *Studies in Poetry and Criticism* (London: Bell, 1905), pp. 142-166;

H. Dixon, Review of *Babe Christabel, Athenaeum,* No. 1371 (4 February 1854): 139-141;

B. Ifor Evans, in his *English Poetry in the Later Nineteenth Century,* 2nd edition (London: Methuen, 1966), pp. 318-320;

B. O. Flower, *Gerald Massey: Poet, Prophet and Mystic* (Boston: Arena, 1895).

Richard Monckton Milnes
(Lord Houghton)
(19 June 1809-11 August 1885)

David Latham
University of Lethbridge

BOOKS: *The Influence of Homer* (Cambridge: Hodson, 1829);

Memorials of a Tour in Some Parts of Greece, Chiefly Poetical (London: Moxon, 1834);

Memorials of a Residence on the Continent, and Historical Poems (London: Moxon, 1838);

Poems of Many Years (London: Privately printed, 1838; London: Moxon, 1838; Boston: Ticknor, 1846);

A Speech on the Ballot, Delivered in the House of Commons (London: Moxon, 1839);

Poetry for the People, and Other Poems (London: Moxon, 1840);

One Tract More, by a Layman (London: Rivington, 1841);

Thoughts on Purity of Election (London: Privately printed, 1842);

Palm Leaves (London: Moxon, 1844);

The Real Union of England and Ireland (London: Ollivier, 1845);

Speech of R. Monckton Milnes, esq. in the House of Commons, March 11, 1847, on Mr. Hume's Motion Respecting the Suppression of the Free State of Cracow and the Payment of the Russian-Dutch Loan (London: Ollivier, 1847);

Life, Letters, and Literary Remains of John Keats, 2 volumes (London: Moxon, 1848; New York: Putnam's, 1848);

The Events of 1848, Especially in Their Relation to Great Britain. A Letter to the Marquis of Lansdowne (London: Ollivier, 1849);

Answer to R. Baxter on the South Yorkshire Isle of Axholme Bill (Pontefract, U.K.: Privately printed, 1852);

Speech of Richard Monckton Milnes in the House of Commons, April 1, 1852. Extracted from Hansard's Parliamentary Debates (London: Woodfall, 1852);

Another Version of Keats's Hyperion (London: Philobiblon Society, 1856);

A Discourse of Witchcraft (London: Philobiblon Society, 1858);

Good Night and Good Morning: A Ballad (London:

Richard Monckton Milnes

Day, 1859; Philadelphia: American Sunday School Union, 1866);

Address on Social Economy (London: Privately printed, 1862);

Selections from the Poetical Works (London: Murray, 1863);

Monographs: Personal and Social (London: Murray, 1873; New York: Holt & Williams, 1873);

The Poetical Works of (Richard Monckton Milnes) Lord Houghton, Collected Edition, 2 volumes (London: Murray, 1876; Boston: Roberts, 1876);

Some Writings and Speeches of Richard Monckton Milnes in the Last Year of His Life (London: Chiswick, 1888).

OTHER: *Miscellanies of the Philobiblon Society,* edited by Milnes, 15 volumes (London: Philobiblon Society, 1853-1884);

The Poetical Works of John Keats, memoir by Milnes (London: Moxon, 1854);

David Gray, *The Luggie and Other Poems,* preface by Milnes (Cambridge: Macmillan, 1862);

"On the Present Social Results of Classical Education," in *Essays on a Liberal Education,* edited by Frederic William Farrar (London: Macmillan, 1867), pp. 365-384;

The Poetical Works of Thomas Hood, memoir by Milnes, 3 volumes (New York: Miller, 1867);

The Works of Thomas Love Peacock, edited by Henry Cole, preface by Milnes, 3 volumes (London: Bentley, 1875).

Poet, politician, and social dilettante, Richard Monckton Milnes is better known for his ability to recognize literary genius in others than for his own literary work. The stanzas that Milnes cajoled Alfred Tennyson into contributing to an 1836 Christmas annual were published in 1855 as part of "Maud"; in 1848 Milnes wrote the first biography of John Keats; in 1861 he let Algernon Swinburne loose in his library of erotica, and he arranged for the publication of Swinburne's early poems and reviews. As for his own poetry, Milnes will be remembered less for the contemporary popularity of a few verses set to music than as the author of the first English treatment of the Tannhäuser legend.

Milnes was born on Bolton Street in Mayfair, London, to Robert Pemberton Milnes, an eloquent member of Parliament for Pontefract, and Henrietta Maria Monckton Milnes. Richard was educated at Hundhill Hall and then privately tutored until he entered Trinity College, Cambridge, in 1827. At Cambridge he was a member of the Apostles, an elite fraternity of twelve students that included Arthur Hallam and Alfred Tennyson. He was honored by the university with the English Essay Prize in 1829 for *The Influence of Homer,* for which he used two lines by Tennyson as his epigraph. After graduating from Cambridge, he spent three years touring Germany, Italy, and Greece. In 1836 he settled in London, where he made a conscious effort to enter high society—first as a regular guest at Samuel Rogers's breakfast parties in St. James's Place and then as a popular host after he moved to Pall Mall in 1837. Milnes is the model for the satirical portrait of a social bore in Benjamin Disraeli's novel *Tancred* (1847): Mr. Vavasour is the perpetual host of celebrity parties at evening and breakfast. "He liked to know everybody who was

Milnes's father, Robert Pemberton Milnes

known, and to see everything which ought to be seen.... His life was a gyration of energetic curiosity, an insatiable whirl of social celebrity.... His universal sympathies seemed omnipotent. Mr. Vavasour saw something good in everybody and everything, which is certainly amiable, and perhaps just, but disqualified a man in some degree for the business of life which requires for its conduct a certain degree of prejudice."

Disraeli knew the object of his satire well. Milnes was elected Conservative M.P. for his father's old riding, Pontefract, in 1837. Though he was instrumental in securing the Copyright Act and establishing reformatories for convicted juveniles, his work as a politician was not distinguished enough for him to be selected for an office in the ministry. This may be attributed to his enthusiasm for Parliament as "the best club in town," though a contemporary observed that Milnes lost his customary aplomb in Parliament: "One of the best after-dinner speakers in the kingdom, Milnes's natural ease failed him when he addressed the House of Commons, and he gave his audience an impression of affectation." The number of pamphlets he had published based on his speeches suggests that he took politics as seriously as his poetry.

Milnes later described the poems of his first

collection—*Memorials of a Tour in Some Parts of Greece* (1834)—as conventional subjects for a young cultivated Englishman whose experience is "touched and coloured by the studies and memories of the classical world." His next collection—*Memorials of a Residence on the Continent, and Historical Poems* (1838)—commemorates his travels in Germany and Italy. In these companion volumes, he too often makes the predictable comparison of the glories of the ancient civilization with the surviving ruins or merely juxtaposes the pleasant day he had during his trip with the pleasure the memory now gives him. The material in Milnes's two volumes is on a level with the commentary a twentieth-century tourist might write for an evening's slide show.

While *Poems of Many Years* (1838) presents such forgettable verse as the elegy on the loss of Arthur Hallam ("part of myself has lapsed away/ From time to Eternity"), *Poetry for the People* (1840) ranges from the memorably naive to the offensively shallow. Milnes writes in one poem of "the sacred patience of the Poor"; in another he writes of "Alms-Giving" from the perspective of the wealthy aristocrat:

> Let but the rich man do his part,
> And whatsoe'er the issue be
> To those who ask, his answering heart
> Will gain and grow in sympathy.

From this class perspective he ventures forth with conventional inversions:

> What paupers are the ambitious Rich
> How wealthy the contented Poor!

This is not the social consciousness of William Morris, whose *Chants for Socialists* (1885) begins to look like serious poetry in comparison to Milnes's shallow piety.

Included in *Poetry for the People*, however, are two narrative poems noteworthy for their subject matter: "Venus and the Christian Knight" and "The Northern Knight in Italy" first introduced the Tannhäuser legend to an English audience. The first poem is a ballad with a tragic ending and a moral warning. The second poem presents a narrator recounting in a variation of rhyme royals "the record, true as his word," of the Teuton knight; this time the knight eventually is able to return home, "pious, innocent, and brave,/ . . . His dear true wife beside him."

Milnes's tour of Egypt and the Levant provided the subjects for his next volume of verse, *Palm Leaves* (1844): "My object has been . . . to fuse together my own natural and national modes of thought and those of the Oriental province of the human mind." Claiming Goethe's "Oest-Westliche Divan" as his model, he has striven to think "as an educated Frank would think, taking the East as a basis of reflection." He is confident that his poems delineate the true character of the Eastern "sanctuaries of family and faith," the Oriental home, church, and society.

Milnes's newly adopted enthusiasm for Islamic culture reveals his complex and contradictory nature. He complained that his father "was always trying to give me two educations at once, one an education of ambition, vanity, emulation and progress . . . the other of independence, self-abnegation and the highest repose. He thus failed in making me either a successful politician or a contented philosopher." Milnes's sympathies ranged from Oxford Tractarianism to Oriental Mohammedanism, from the Conservative party to the Liberal, from the revolutionaries of 1848 to the House of Lords. His book in support of the Oxford Movement, *One Tract More, by a Layman* (1841), earned praise from John Henry Newman. His defense of harems as the privilege of the rich was mocked by the reviewers of *Palm Leaves*: A. W. Kinglake assumed Milnes to be "the first Englishman—or at least the first publishing Englishman—who ever gained access to the sacred hareems of the Orientals." In 1846 Milnes joined the Liberals, deserting Peel, who had adopted a free trade policy. In 1849 his *Letter to the Marquis of Lansdowne*, in which he supported the revolutionaries in their effort to liberate Italy from the Austrian Empire, elicited such controversy that Milnes challenged the foreign affairs secretary, George Smythe, to a duel for his denunciation of Milnes's argument; violence was averted by Smythe's apology. Two years later, during Milnes's honeymoon with Annabel Crewe, Austria forbade him to enter Hungary because of the Lansdowne pamphlet.

No such controversy surrounds Milnes's poetry: as a poet, he has failed to attract any serious attention. Walter Savage Landor once "rattled on" about Milnes being "the greatest poet now living in England." Elizabeth Barrett more cautiously praised Milnes as a poet whose temperament was "rather elegiac than lyric. . . . He perceives and responds rather than creates." In the preface to his *Poetical Works* (1876), Milnes admitted that he would enjoy reviewing his own poems, "conscious that the distances of time and the alterations of temperament qualify me to do so with perfect impartiality."

Annabel Crewe, whom Milnes married in 1851

Milnes is indeed his own best critic, but only by default: no one since Landor has deemed him a worthy subject. The prefaces to his various collections are an adequate introduction to his conventional concerns. His preferences remained consistently Johnsonian:

> The language of poetry delights in the universal, and ... rejects the minute and transitory. (Preface to *Palm Leaves*)

> The personal inclinations of the moment are no fit themes for verse. (Preface to *Poetical Works*)

> Whatever little hold [these poems] may have taken on their time, is owing to their sincerity of thought and simplicity of expression. (Preface to *Poetical Works*)

Milnes cited as his best poems "The Long Ago," "The Men of Old," "The Worth of Hours," "Happiness," "Domestic Fame," "Never Return," "Requiescat in Pace," and "Strangers Yet." He regarded these poems as "standing on a firm, ethical basis, and aiming at an apt and melodious representation of conditions of thought and emotion which men do not willingly surrender or forget." He vastly inflated their worth: each of these poems presents the conventional declarations common to inspirational verse. They deliver moral platitudes about mankind rather than dramatizing individual experiences:

> A man's best things are nearest him,
>   Lie close about his feet.
> It is the distant and the dim
>   That we are sick to greet.

"The Long Ago" is typically predictable in its contrast of hope's anticipation with nostalgia's peace, of the world of present pain with the refuge of past memories, and of the future's Heaven with the past's Long Ago. However, the juxtaposition of tombs with shrines is, for Milnes, an unusual departure from vague abstractions toward concrete imagery. More successful is "The Brookside," a simple lyric about a woman waiting for her lover for an evening rendezvous. Her anticipation builds as each stanza except the last ends with the refrain "But the beating of my own heart/Was all the sound I heard." Milnes was surprised that this poem, which he dismissed as one written during "a moonlight drive to visit a Miss Edgeworth, in 1830, and thought unworthy of print by myself and others, should within ten years after, have been heard by a traveller parodied in a chorus of slaves singing in the cotton-fields of Western America." George Saintsbury and Lafcadio Hearn praised "Strangers Yet" as his "best poem," which "nobody could write more hauntingly":

> Strangers yet!
> After years of life together,
> After fair and stormy weather,
> After travel in far lands,
> After touch of wedded hands,—
> Why thus joined? Why ever met,
> If they must be strangers yet?

Such praise is unwarranted. Milnes is at his best when he strains the least. "The Brookside," the two Tannhäuser poems, and two nursery rhymes—"Lady Moon, Lady Moon" and "Good Night and Good Morning"—are the extent of his lasting contribution to literature.

Milnes will be remembered for his associations with more accomplished people. One of his friends was Charles Armitage Brown, who had known John Keats. Given Brown's manuscript of an incomplete memoir of Keats, Milnes gathered letters and more information to complete the first biography of the poet whom he had admired since his years with the Apostles at Cambridge: *Life, Letters, and Literary Remains of John Keats* (1848). In Rome, Milnes commissioned another of Keats's friends, the artist Joseph Severn, to draw the portrait of Keats for the book's now oft-reprinted frontispiece. Milnes's biography marked the turning point for Keats's reputation. J. G. Lockhart was mistaken when he warned Milnes that he would "regret few sins more bitterly than the homage he has now rendered at the fantastic shrines of such baby idols as Mr. John Keats and Mr. Alfred Tennyson."

Milnes's friendship with Algernon Swinburne suggests, again, a complex personality that is nowhere evident in Milnes's poetry. Milnes included in his large library at Fryston Hall the most extensive collection in England of Continental erotic literature, as well as accounts of school punishments and flagellation. Swinburne called Milnes "*the* Sadique collector of European fame.... His erotic collection of books, engravings, etc. is unrivalled upon earth—unequalled I should imagine in heaven. Nothing low, nothing that is not good and genuine in the way of art and literature is admitted. There is every edition of every work of our dear and honoured Marquis." Commenting on Milnes's influence on Swinburne, Georges Lafourcade has said that Milnes "would have no more Border Ballads or translations from Boccaccio, and the result was that Swinburne wrote 'Faustine.'" Lafourcade might just as well have cited Swinburne's treatment of the Tannhäuser legend, "Laus Veneris," as the kind of poem which must be attributed to Milnes's influence.

Milnes was a collector of more than erotica. In 1853, he cofounded the Philobiblon Society for those interested in the history and collection of rare books and manuscripts. As the editor of its annual papers, he contributed works ranging from *Another Version of Keats's Hyperion* (1856) to *A Discourse of Witchcraft* (1858). In 1863, when he entered the House of Lords after Palmerston made him Baron Houghton of Great Houghton in the West Riding of Yorkshire, Milnes became the object of affectionate fun. James Robinson Planché, a playwright and an authority on heraldry, commemorated Milnes's peerage with a verse entitled "A Literary Squabble":

The Alphabet rejoiced to hear
That Monckton Milnes was made a Peer;

Milnes about 1868

Algernon Swinburne, who was influenced by Milnes

Milnes and his relatives outside his home, Fryston Hall, about 1873. Left to right: Milnes's daughters Amicia and Florence (in phaeton); Milnes's brother-in-law, Lord Crewe; Milnes; Lord Galway, husband of Milnes's sister Hariette; Annabel Milnes (Lady Houghton); Lady Galway. An unidentified servant holds the horse's head.

> For in this present world of letters
> But few, if any, are his betters.

The letters of the alphabet then squabble over the pronunciation of his title: Hoo-ton (as "through"), Hawt-on (as "nought"), Hof-ton (as "trough"), Huff-ton (as "rough"), Ho-ton (as "though"), or How-ton (as "plow").

> PLOUGH was plow,
> Even "enough" was called "enow"
> And no one who preferred "enough"
> Would dream of saying "Speed the Pluff!"
> So they considered it more wise
> With T to make a compromise,
> And leave no loop to hang a doubt on
> By giving three cheers for "Lord [Hough/How] ton!"

Milnes went on to assume many honorary positions associated with an éminence grise: he represented the Royal Geographical Society at the opening of the Suez Canal in 1869; he was appointed secretary for the Royal Academy's foreign correspondence in 1878 and a trustee of the British Museum in 1881; he succeeded Thomas Carlyle as president of the London Library in 1882. He was constantly busy delivering addresses, entertaining statesmen, and nurturing young talent. During the last three months of his life he enjoyed addressing the Wordsworth Society and conducting the ceremonies for unveiling the busts of Coleridge at Westminster Abbey and Gray at Cambridge. The famous after-dinner speaker and host of breakfast and dinner parties once quipped that his "exit will be the result of too many entrées." But he died in Vichy while conducting a religious argument through the mail with an Anglican churchman, to whom he wrote: "I will not contradict anything you say except the *general usefulness* of suffering. I admit that it is so to the higher natures—but it is my decided experience that the mass of mankind are better for being happier. I am sure I am." Anthony West concludes that those who knew Milnes might have speculated that he died while "indulging in

Florence Nightingale, to whom Milnes proposed marriage in his youth

one of his favorite pastimes—totting up in one of the little reporter's notebooks he always had with him the names of the distinguished, really distinguished, men and women he had shaken by the hand." Milnes's lifelong friend Thomas Carlyle meant to be more kind when he joked that "if Christ was again on earth, Milnes would ask Him to breakfast, and the clubs would all be talking of the 'good things' that Christ had said."

The last word on Milnes should go to Florence Nightingale, to whom Milnes proposed marriage before he married Annabel Crewe. The qualities she found praiseworthy in Milnes are the same as those with which Disraeli found fault in Mr. Vavasour. She describes the public persona which Milnes so proudly cultivated, a persona which was charming among his social circles but destructive to his poetry: "His brilliancy and talents in tongue or pen—whether political, social, or literary—were inspired chiefly by goodwill towards man; but he had the same voice and manners for the dirty brat as he had for a duchess, . . . treating *all* his fellow mortals as if they were his brothers and sisters. In conversation he never allowed his unique power of humour to say an unkind thing."

Biographies:

T. Wemyss Reid, *The Life, Letters, and Friendships of Richard Monckton Milnes, First Lord Houghton* (London: Cassell, 1890);

James Pope-Hennessy, *Monckton Milnes:* volume 1, *The Years of Promise: 1809-1851* (London: Constable, 1949); volume 2, *The Flight of Youth: 1851-1885* (London: Constable, 1951).

References:

John Clive, "More or Less Eminent Victorians: Some Recent Trends in Recent Victorian Biography," *Victorian Studies,* 2 (September 1958): 5-28;

Benjamin Disraeli, *Tancred; or, The New Crusade,* 3 volumes (London: Colburn, 1847);

J. A. Froude, *Thomas Carlyle: A History of His Life in London 1834-81* (London: Longmans, Green, 1884), volume 1, p. 166;

Lafcadio Hearn, "A Poem by Lord Houghton," in his *Interpretations of Literature* (New York: Dodd, Mead, 1915), pp. 300-303;

A. W. Kinglake, "Milnes on the Hareem—the Rights of Women," *Quarterly Review,* 75 (December 1844): 94-125;

Georges Lafourcade, *Swinburne: A Literary Biography* (Oxford: Oxford University Press, 1932);

J. G. Lockhart, review of *Memorials of a Residence on the Continent, Quarterly Review,* 64 (June 1839): 59-64;

J. R. McGillivray, *Keats: A Bibliography and Reference Guide* (Toronto: University of Toronto Press, 1949);

John Henry Newman, *Apologia pro Vita Sua* (London: Longman, Green, Longman, Roberts & Green, 1864);

James Robinson Planché, "A Literary Squabble," in *A Century of Humourous Verse 1850-1950,* edited by Roger Lancelyn Green (London: Dent, 1959), pp. 3-4;

Mario Praz, *The Romantic Agony* (New York: Meridian, 1956);

Henry Crabb Robinson, *Henry Crabb Robinson on Books and Their Writers* (London: Dent, 1938);

John F. Rolph, "Reid's Houghton," *The Academy,* 39 (January 1891): 6;

George Saintsbury, *A History of Nineteenth Century Literature (1780-1895)* (New York & London: Macmillan, 1896);

Lionel Trilling, "Profession: Man of the World," in his *A Gathering of Fugitives* (London: Secker & Warburg, 1957), pp. 107-116;

Anthony West, "Monckton Milnes," in his *Principles and Persuasions* (New York: Harcourt, Brace, 1957), pp. 77-85.

John Henry Newman
(21 February 1801-11 August 1890)

Lionel Adey
University of Victoria

See also the Newman entry in *DLB 18, Victorian Novelists After 1885.*

SELECTED BOOKS: *St. Bartholomew's Eve; A Tale of the Sixteenth Century: in Two Cantos,* anonymous, by Newman and J. W. Bowden (Oxford: Munday & Slatter, 1818);

Suggestions Respectfully Offered to Certain Resident Clergymen of the University in Behalf of the Church Missionary Society, by a Master of Arts (Oxford: Cooke, 1830);

Memorials of the Past (Oxford: King, 1832);

The Arians of the Fourth Century: Their Doctrine, Temper and Conduct, Chiefly as Exhibited in the Councils of The Church, between AD 325 and AD 381 (London: Rivington, 1833; New York: Catholic Publication Society, 1882);

Tracts for the Times, by Members of the University of Oxford, anonymous, nos. 1-3, 6-8 by Newman and R. H. Froude; nos. 10, 11, 15 by Newman and Sir W. Palmer; nos. 19-21, 31, 33, 34, 38, 41, 45, 47, 71, 73, 74 by Newman and B. Harrison; nos. 75, 76, 79, 82, 83, 85, 88, 90 by Newman, 6 volumes (London: Rivington/Oxford: Parker, 1833-1841);

Parochial Sermons (6 volumes, London: Rivington/Oxford: Parker, 1834-1836; 2 volumes, New York: D. Appleton/Philadelphia: G. S. Appleton, 1843);

The Restoration of Suffragan Bishops Recommended, as a Means of Effecting a More Equal Distribution of Episcopal Duties, as Contemplated by His Majesty's Recent Ecclesiastical Commission (London: Rivington/Oxford: Parker, 1835);

Elucidations of Dr. Hampden's Theological Statements (Oxford: Baxter, 1836);

John Henry Newman

Lyra Apostolica, anonymous, by Newman, John William Bowden, Richard Hurrell Froude, John Keble, Robert Isaac Wilberforce, and Isaac Williams (Derby, U.K.: Mozley/London: Rivington, 1836; New York: D. Appleton/Philadelphia: G. S. Appleton, 1844);

Make Ventures for Christ's Sake: A Sermon, anonymous (Oxford: Parker/London: Rivington, 1836; New York: Doolittle & Vermilye, 1837);

Lectures on the Prophetical Office of the Church, Viewed Relatively to Romanism and Popular Protestantism (London: Rivington/Oxford: Parker, 1837);

A Letter to the Rev. Godfrey Faussett D.D., Margaret Professor of Divinity, on Certain Points of Faith and Practice (Oxford: Parker/London: Rivington, 1838);

Lectures on Justification (London: Rivington, 1838);

The Church of the Fathers, anonymous (London: Rivington, 1840);

The Tamworth Reading Room: Letters on an Address Delivered by Sir Robert Peel Bart. M.P. on the Establishment of a Reading Room at Tamworth, by Catholicus, Originally Published in the Times, *and Since Revised and Corrected by the Author* (London: Mortimer, 1841);

A Letter Addressed to the Rev. R. W. Jelf D.D., Canon of Christ Church, in Explanation of No. 90 in the Series Called the Tracts for the Times, by the Author (Oxford: Parker/London: Rivington, 1841);

A Letter to the Right Reverend Father in God, Richard, Lord Bishop of Oxford, on Occasion of No. 90 in the Series Called the Tracts for the Times (Oxford: Parker/London: Rivington, 1841);

"Mr. Vice-Chancellor, I Write This Respectfully to Inform You. . . ." (N.p., 1841);

An Essay on the Miracles Recorded in the Ecclesiastical History of the Early Ages (Oxford: Parker/London: Rivington, 1843);

Sermons Bearing on Subjects of the Day (London: Rivington/Oxford: Parker, 1843; New York: D. Appleton/Philadelphia: G. S. Appleton, 1844);

Sermons, Chiefly on the Theory of Religious Belief, Preached before the University of Oxford (London: Rivington/Oxford: Parker, 1843);

Plain Sermons by Contributors to the "Tracts for the Times," volume 5, anonymous (London: Rivington, 1843);

An Essay on the Development of Christian Doctrine (London: Toovey, 1845; New York: D. Appleton/Philadelphia: G. S. Appleton/Cincinnati: Derby, Bradley, N.d.);

Loss and Gain, anonymous (London: Burns, 1848); republished as *Loss and Gain; or, the Story of a Convert* (Boston: Donahoe, 1854);

Discourses Addressed to Mixed Congregations (London: Longman, Brown, Green & Longmans, 1849; Boston: Donahoe, 1853);

Lectures on Certain Difficulties Felt by Anglicans in Submitting to the Catholic Church (12 parts, London: Burns & Lambert, 1850; 1 volume, New York: Office of New York's Freeman's Journal, 1851);

Christ upon the Waters: A Sermon Preached on Occasion of the Establishment of the Catholic Hierarchy in this Country (Birmingham, U. K.: Maher/London: Burns & Lambert, 1850);

Lectures on the Present Position of Catholics in England, Addressed to the Brothers of the Oratory (London: Burns & Lambert, 1851);

A Correspondence between the Rev. J. H. Newman, D.D., and the Bishop of Norwich on the Credibility of Miracles, Extracted from the Morning Chronicle (Birmingham, U. K.: Freeman, 1851);

Discourses on the Scope and Nature of University Education, Addressed to the Catholics of Dublin, 11 parts (Dublin: Duffy, 1852); revised and republished as *The Idea of a University Defined and Illustrated* (London: Pickering, 1873);

The Second Spring: A Sermon Preached in the Synod of Oscott, on Tuesday July 13th 1852 (London, Dublin & Derby: Richardson, 1852);

Verses on Religious Subjects, anonymous (Dublin: Duffy, 1853);

Lectures on the History of the Turks in Its Relation to Christianity, by the Author of Loss and Gain, anonymous (Dublin: Duffy/London: Dolman, 1854);

Catholic University. The Rector's Report to Their Lordships the Archbishops and Bishops of Ireland. For the Year 1855-1856 (Dublin: Fowler, 1856);

Callista: A Sketch of the Third Century, anonymous (London: Burns & Lambert, 1856; New York & Boston: Sadlier, 1856);

The Office and Work of Universities (London: Longman, Green, Longman & Roberts, 1856);

The Mission of St. Philip Neri: An Instruction, Delivered in Substance in the Birmingham Oratory, January, 1850, and at Subsequent Times (N.p., 1857);

Sermons Preached on Various Occasions (London: Burns & Lambert, 1857; New York: Catholic Publication Society, 1887);

Catholic University. The Rector's Report to Their Lordships the Archbishops and Bishops of Ireland. For the Year 1856-1857 (Dublin: Fowler, 1858);

Lectures and Essays on University Subjects (London: Longman, Brown, Green, Longman & Roberts, 1859);

The Tree beside the Waters: A Sermon Preached in the Chapel of St. Mary's College Oscott on Friday November 11 1859, at the Funeral of the Right Rev. Henry Weedall, D.D. (London: Burns & Lambert, 1859?);

Mr. Kingsley and Dr. Newman: A Correspondence on the

Question Whether Dr. Newman Teaches that Truth Is No Virtue? (London: Longman, Green, Longman, Roberts & Green, 1864);

Apologia pro Vita Sua: Being a Reply to a Pamphlet Entitled "What, Then, Does Dr. Newman Mean?" (8 parts, London: Longman, Green, Longman, Roberts & Green, 1864; 1 volume, New York: Appleton, 1865); republished as *History of My Religious Opinions* (London: Longman, Green, Longman, Roberts & Green, 1865);

The Dream of Gerontius (London: Burns & Oates, 1865; New York: Catholic Publication Society, 1885);

A Letter to the Rev. E. B. Pusey, D.D., on His Recent Eirenicon (London: Longmans, Green, Reader & Dyer, 1866; New York: Kehoe, 1866);

The Pope and the Revolution: A Sermon Preached in the Oratory Church Birmingham on Sunday October 7 1866 (London: Longmans, Green, Reader & Dyer, 1866);

Verses on Various Occasions (London: Burns & Oates, 1868; Boston: Donahoe, 1868);

An Essay in Aid of a Grammar of Assent (London: Burns & Oates, 1870; New York: Catholic Publication Society, 1870);

Miscellanies from the Oxford Sermons and Other Writings of John Henry Newman, D.D. (London: Strahan, 1870);

Two Essays on Scripture Miracles and on Ecclesiastical (London: Pickering, 1870);

Essays Critical and Historical, 2 volumes (London: Pickering, 1871);

Historical Sketches, 3 volumes (London: Pickering, 1872-1873);

Discussions and Arguments on Various Subjects (London: Pickering, 1872);

Prologue to the Andria of Terence (London: Privately printed, 1872);

Orate pro Anima Jacobi Roberti Hope Scott (N.p., 1873); republished as *Sermon Preached in the London Church of the Jesuit Fathers at the Requiem Mass for the Repose of the Soul of James Robert Hope Scott* (London: Burns & Oates, 1873);

Tracts Theological and Ecclesiastical (London: Pickering, 1874);

Characteristics from the Writings of John Henry Newman, Being Selections Personal, Historical, Philosophical, and Religious, from His Various Works, arranged by William Samuel Lilly (London: King, 1874; New York: Scribner, Welford & Armstrong, 1875);

A Letter Addressed to His Grace the Duke of Norfolk on Occasion of Mr. Gladstone's Recent Expostulation (London: Pickering, 1875; New York: Catholic Publication Society, 1875);

Postscript to A Letter Addressed to His Grace the Duke of Norfolk on the Occasion of Mr. Gladstone's Recent Expostulation (London: Pickering, 1875; New York: Catholic Publication Society, 1875);

The Via Media of the Anglican Church, Illustrated in Lectures, Letters, and Tracts Written between 1830 and 1841; with a Preface and Notes, 2 volumes (London: Pickering, 1877);

Selection Adapted to the Seasons of the Ecclesiastical Year from the Parochial and Plain Sermons of John Henry Newman, B.D., Sometime Vicar of St. Mary's Oxford (London, Oxford & Cambridge: Rivington, 1878);

Two Sermons Preached in the Church of St. Aloysius, Oxford on Trinity Sunday 1880 (Oxford: Privately printed, 1880);

Lead, Kindly Light. Illustrated (Boston: Roberts, 1884);

What Is of Obligation for a Catholic to Believe Concerning the Inspiration of the Canonical Scriptures: Being a Postscript to an Article in the February No. of the Nineteenth Century Review in Answer to Professor Healy (London: Burns & Oates, 1884);

The Development of Religious Error (London: Burns & Oates, 1886);

On a Criticism Urged against a Catholic Doctrine (Birmingham: Billing, 1889);

Stray Essays on Controversial Points Variously Illustrated (Birmingham: Privately printed, 1890);

Meditations and Devotions of the Late Cardinal Newman, edited by William P. Neville (London & New York: Longmans, Green, 1893);

My Campaign in Ireland, Part I: Catholic University Reports and Other Papers, edited by Neville (Aberdeen: Privately printed, 1896);

Sermon Notes of John Henry Cardinal Newman, 1849-1878, edited by Fathers of the Birmingham Oratory (London: Longmans, Green, 1913);

John Henry Newman: Autobiographical Writings, edited by Henry Tristam (London & New York: Sheed & Ward, 1956);

Faith and Prejudice and Other Unpublished Sermons of Cardinal Newman, edited by Charles Stephen Dessain (New York: Sheed & Ward, 1956); republished as *Catholic Sermons of Cardinal Newman* (London: Burns & Oates, 1957);

On Consulting the Faithful in Matters of Doctrine, edited by John Coulson (London: Chapman, 1961);

Criticisms Urged against Certain Catholic Doctrines, as J. H. N. (N.p, N.d).

Collections: *Works of John Henry Newman,* Uniform

Grey Court House at Ham, Richmond, where Newman spent much of his youth and which he later recalled as a lost paradise

Edition, 41 volumes (London: Longmans, Green, 1908-1918);

Newman: Prose and Poetry, edited by Geoffrey Tillotson (London: Hart-Davis, 1957; Cambridge: Harvard University Press, 1957).

John Henry Newman is known today primarily for his *Discourses on the Scope and Nature of University Education* (1852) and his spiritual autobiography *Apologia pro Vita Sua* (1864). In his own time his fame rested on his hymns, sermons, and theological works, and his leading role in the Oxford Movement and the subsequent Catholic revival in England. His marvelously clear and supple prose, rather than his poetry, entitles him to a place in the English literary canon.

The eldest child of John Newman, a London banker, and Jemima Fourdrinier Newman, of Huguenot descent, Newman spent most of his early years at Ham, Richmond; in old age he dreamed of this home as a lost paradise. He was educated at Dr. Nicholas's private school in Ealing, where he developed a lifelong love of Scott's novels. During 1816 his father's bank failed; he suffered his first serious illness; and, influenced by a schoolmaster, he became a Calvinistic Evangelical, feeling called to a celibate life. In June 1817 he entered Trinity College, Oxford, where he won a scholarship in 1818. Although in 1820 he nearly failed his degree examinations because of exhaustion, in 1822 he won a fellowship at Oriel College, which was then dominated by the "Noetics," a group of liberal theologians. One of these, Richard Whately, drew him out of his congenital shyness; but between 1826, when Hurrell Froude arrived at Oriel, and 1833, when John Keble's *National Apostasy* sermon launched the Oxford Movement, Newman passed from liberal to High Church convictions. A second serious illness in 1827 and his beloved sister Mary's death in 1828 intensified the otherworldliness that was responsible for his power to inspire both the poor of St. Clement's, whom he served as curate from 1824, and the university congregation of St. Mary's, of which he became vicar in 1828.

In that year Newman wrote, among other poems, his moving "Consolations in Bereavement." He composed four-fifths of the 124 lyrics in *Verses on Various Occasions* (1868) between November 1832

in his famous "Lead, Kindly Light." Although "The Elements: A Tragic Chorus" has a Sophoclean grandeur, the numerous meditations on St. Paul and other biblical heroes now sound stiff and dated. With one further exception, even Newman's most lucid and graceful lyrics are worth reading only as revealing his preoccupations at that time.

The exception is "Lead, Kindly Light," originally entitled "The Pillar of the Cloud" after the fiery pillar that led the Israelites out of Egypt. After being set to J. B. Dykes's sentimental tune in 1864, this exquisite lyric became one of the favorite Victorian hymns—though Newman never regarded it as a hymn, nor is it often sung now. In April, after Froude had gone home with his father, Newman hastened to revisit Sicily, "the nearest approach to Paradise of which sinful man is capable." There,

Richard Whately, one of the liberal theologians at Oriel College, Oxford, who influenced Newman; Newman later switched from a liberal to a High Church position

and July 1833, while accompanying Froude on a Mediterranean cruise prescribed by Froude's doctor. Newman, who rarely wrote without "a definite call," composed short lyrics almost daily to occupy his unaccustomed leisure and to distract himself when feeling seasick. Most of the poems appeared in his friend Hugh Rose's *British Magazine* and subsequently in *Lyra Apostolica* (1836), an anonymous collection by members of the movement including Keble, Froude, and Isaac Williams. "In the *Lyra*," Newman wrote, "my object was *not* poetry *but* to bring out *ideas*." In his little-known essay "Poetry, with Reference to Aristotle's Poetics" (1829) he finds "poetry" not in a poem's words but in its originating idea, which is best conveyed in "simple and colourless terms." Among these Mediterranean lyrics, "England" and "Progress of Unbelief" best express his apprehensions, "Liberalism" and "The Patient Church" his dogmatic Anglo-Catholicism, "Rome" his divided feelings about the Roman church, "Our Future" (written where St. Paul was martyred) and "Desolation" that sense of being guided toward some great work or vision so evident

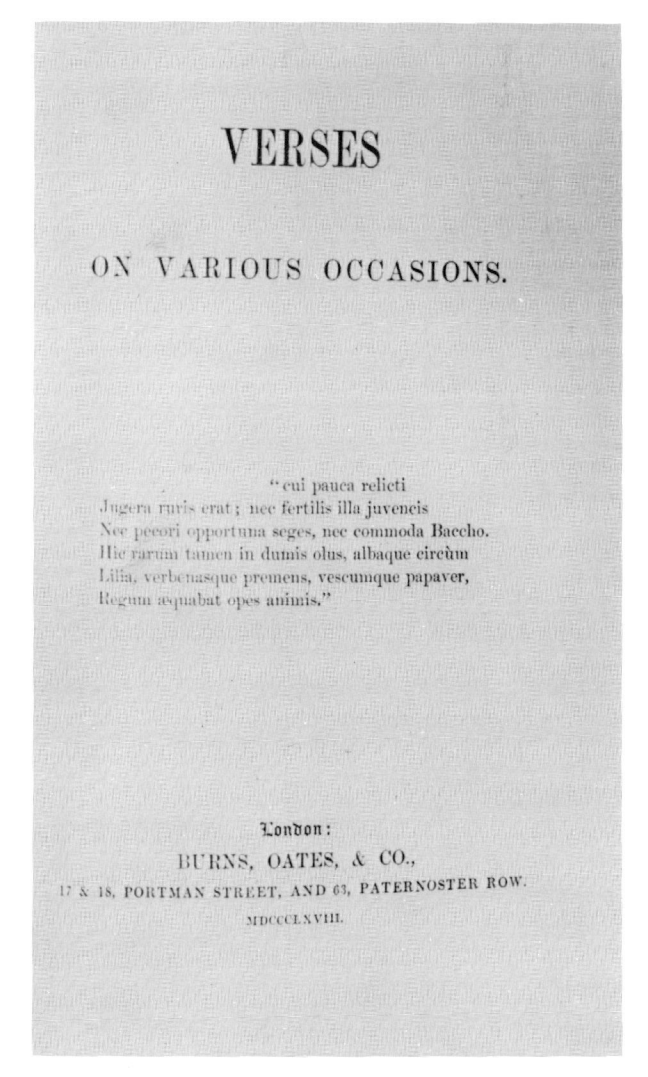

Title page for Newman's book of lyrics, most of which were composed on a Mediterranean cruise in 1832-1833 (Thomas Cooper Library, University of South Carolina)

Stable cottages in the village of Littlemore, where Newman lived from 1842 until 1846

Newman in 1844, the year before he became a Catholic, as portrayed by George Richmond

during his third and most dangerous illness, he muttered in delirium, "I shall not die. . . . I have not sinned against the light. . . . I have a work to do." In June, while returning home after his recovery, he wrote the poem one night as his ship lay becalmed in the strait between Corsica and Sardinia. "Lead, Kindly Light" touched the hearts of Victorian and later readers by its image of divine light; its English sense of the spiritual life as a coming home; its simple avowal "I do not ask to see/The distant scene—one step enough for me"; and its nostalgia for the "angel faces" seen in childhood, to be found again hereafter. Though Newman later ascribed his Mediterranean poems to his vision of Anglican renewal, the finest of them achieves its universality of meaning because he transforms his homesickness and wistful retrospect into a metaphor for his own spiritual voyage.

Between 1833 and 1839, Newman's editing of *Tracts for the Times* (of which he wrote or coauthored thirty) and his Sunday afternoon sermons at St. Mary's—memorably described by Matthew Arnold; J. A. Froude, the historian; and many others—gave him an unparalleled influence over Oxford undergraduates. In 1839 his study of the Donatist heresy made him doubt the catholicity of the Anglican church. After his Catholic interpretation of the Thirty-Nine Articles in Tract 90 was censured by the assembled heads of colleges in 1841, the bishop of Oxford advised him to discontinue the Tracts. In 1843 he retracted his criticisms of Rome, resigned as vicar of St. Mary's, and withdrew to the nearby village of Littlemore. In 1845 he joined the Catholic church.

While at Littlemore, Newman and his friends daily recited the Offices of the Breviary, from which he translated a number of hymns from Latin into English. These translations never came into use as hymns as did those of the Catholic Edward Caswall, who joined the Birmingham Oratory of St. Philip Neri, which Newman founded in 1849, or those of the Anglican J. M. Neale.

In the next fifteen years Newman suffered many setbacks, notably his unfair conviction in a libel suit brought by the renegade ex-monk Achilli and the failure of his attempts to found a Catholic university at Dublin and to inaugurate a new translation of the Bible. During this time he wrote a mere handful of occasional poems, mostly in honor of St. Philip and of departed Oratorians. Two poems on early Christian martyrdom, a subject also dealt with in his novel *Callista* (1856), pursue the major theme of his imaginative writing, the spiritual journey. This received its finest expression in his *Apologia,* written to rebut Charles Kingsley's charge of intellectual dishonesty. During the controversy, he felt a presentiment of impending death. Since the failures of his middle years, moreover, the onset of old age had become almost an obsession. On 17 January 1865, as he wrote in a letter, "it came into my head.... I really cannot tell how" to write his only long poem, *The Dream of Gerontius.* He finished this in three weeks, put it away, and forgot it until the rejection of an article by the Jesuit magazine the *Month* caused him to search his desk. The poem occupied two numbers of the magazine; when it was published in book form in 1865, it won even more acclaim than the *Apologia.* The *Times* and lesser papers printed long, enthusiastic reviews, and as late as 1888 Gladstone hoped it would "take its position in the literature of the world." By 1900, when Edward Elgar composed his oratorio, *The Dream of Gerontius* had been reprinted some thirty times and translated into French and German. Now only choral performances of Elgar's masterpiece keep the complete poem before non-Catholics.

Newman especially feared death from a stroke, such as had afflicted Keble, Scott, and others of his favorite authors. Significantly, Gerontius experiences in his dream a "strange inmost abandonment ... shapeless, scopeless, blank abyss" and "utter nothingness of which I came." He hears his

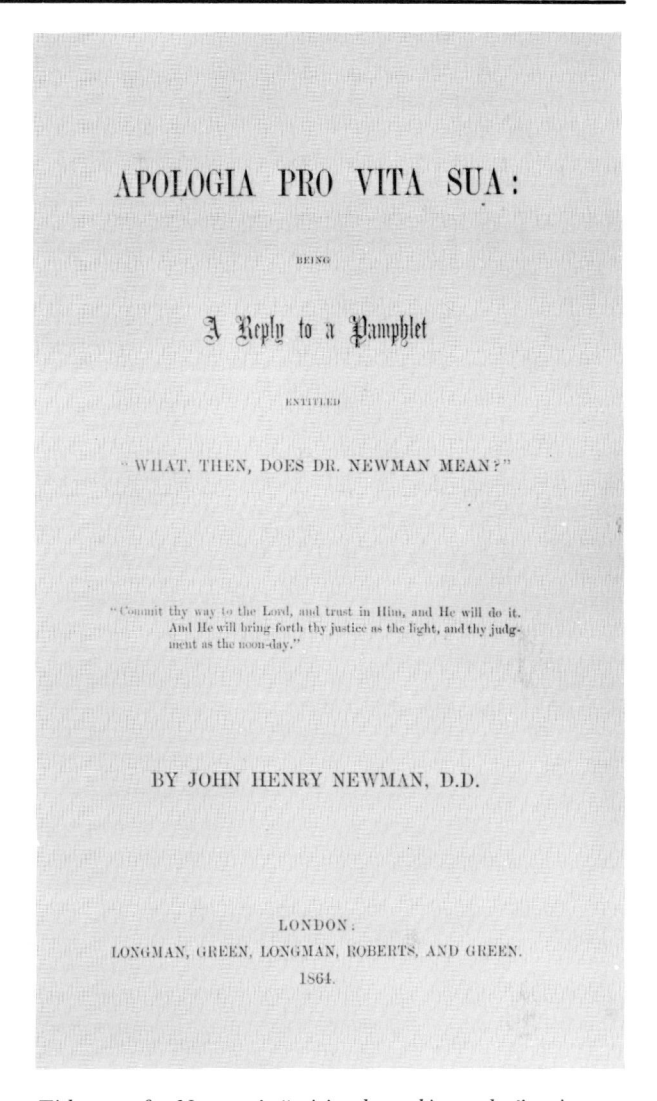

Title page for Newman's "spiritual autobiography," written as part of a controversy between him and Charles Kingsley (Thomas Cooper Library, University of South Carolina)

own last rites before his guardian angel conducts his soul safely past the Chorus of Demons into the divine presence. After judgment, his soul is finally bathed in the cleansing waters of Purgatory.

Despite its severely splendid rhetoric, *The Dream of Gerontius* only occasionally rises to the unforgettable incantation characteristic of great poetry. Its finest moment is the climax, when the Fifth Choir of Angelicals sings "Praise to the Holiest in the Height," a recital of the Fall, Incarnation, and Redemption that epitomizes, in phrases redolent of St. Paul and St. Augustine, two millennia of Christian belief. In this great hymn, now sung wherever Christians worship in English, Newman transcends the self-preoccupation that constitutes both his ground and his limitation as a poet. As many critics have remarked, it was in prose that he regularly attained poetic greatness.

Created cardinal in 1879, Newman, by then a national institution, lived in retirement until his death in 1890. His pervading metaphor of the spiritual journey finds its last expression in his epitaph at the Oratorian cemetery in Rednal: *Ex umbris et imaginibus in veritatem* ("Out of shadows and images into truth").

Letters:
Letters and Diaries of John Henry Newman, edited by Charles Stephen Dessain, Ian Ker, and Thomas Gornal, 31 volumes (Oxford: Clarendon Press, 1961-1980).

Bibliography:
J. Rickaby, *Index to All Works of John Henry Cardinal Newman* (London: Longmans, Green, 1914).

Biographies:
Wilfrid Ward, *The Life of John Henry Cardinal Newman, Based on His Private Journals and Correspondence,* 2 volumes (London: Longmans, Green, 1921);

Meriol Trevor, *Newman,* 2 volumes (London: Macmillan, 1962);

Charles Stephen Dessain, *John Henry Newman* (London: Nelson, 1966).

References:
Charles Frederick Harrold, *John Henry Newman: An Expository and Critical Study of His Mind, Thought and Art* (London: Longmans, Green, 1945);

Americo D. Lapati, *John Henry Newman* (New York: Twayne, 1972);

J. Lewis May, *Cardinal Newman* (Westminster, Maryland: Newman Press, 1951).

Papers:
The archives of the Birmingham Oratory, Birmingham, England, contain manuscripts, correspondence, and diaries of John Henry Newman.

Adelaide Anne Procter
(30 October 1825-2 February 1864)

Susan Drain
Mount Saint Vincent University

BOOKS: *Legends and Lyrics: A Book of Verses,* first series (London: Bell & Daldy, 1858; New York: Appleton, 1858);
Legends and Lyrics: A Book of Verses, second series (London: Bell & Daldy, 1861);
A Chaplet of Verses (London: Longman, Green, Longman & Roberts, 1862);
Complete Works, with an introduction by Charles Dickens (London: Bell, 1905).

OTHER: *Victoria Regia: A Volume of Original Contributions in Poetry and Prose,* edited by Procter (London: Faithfull, 1861).

If Adelaide Anne Procter still holds a place in popular memory, it is because of Arthur Sullivan's setting of her poem "A Lost Chord." Yet a little over a hundred years ago her books of verse outsold those of all living poets except Tennyson, and her popularity was crowned by royal approbation. To modern eyes, Procter's verse is a curiosity of Victorian taste; but it is also a memorial to a woman's determination to make her life her own.

Procter was the eldest child of the three daughters and three sons of Bryan Waller Procter, who as "Barry Cornwall" was known for his poetry, his drama, and his circle of literary friends. Her childhood was privileged; friends and relations filled the Procter house with brilliant company and conversation. Her mother, Anne Skepper Procter, stitched a little volume of Adelaide's favorite poems for her, and her talents for music and languages were encouraged.

The golden child became an adult whose emotional intensity was masked by the poetic conventions and parental protections with which she was surrounded. Nevertheless, the intensity can be felt in all the main concerns of her life—her religious pilgrimage, her feminism, and her poetry, and indirectly in the ill health with which she paid, perhaps, for her intensity and her measure of independence.

The family was affectionate and protective: breaking out required careful hoarding of energy before each step. It took courage to avow her conversion to Roman Catholicism in 1851, when religious tensions were running high in England. There is some evidence that she had adopted her new faith two years earlier but did not profess it until two of her sisters joined her.

Procter's next initiative was to arrange for publication of her poems. As an eighteen-year-old she had had a poem included in Heath's *Book of Beauty* for 1843, edited by the countess of Blessington. Nearly ten years later, she was determined to test her poetic effect in another kind of publication. She chose Dickens's *Household Words* and submitted her verses under the pseudonym of "Mary Berwick," fearing a kind rather than a candid response from the editor, who was an old friend of Barry Cornwall's. Dickens approved, and Mary Berwick's first contribution appeared in February 1853. For two years her poems appeared frequently, and Dickens wove a romantic tale around the mysterious poetess. She was, he was sure, a governess who hid a broken heart beneath a brisk and businesslike manner. When the secret was finally out, both friend and family exclaimed at the modest deception and rejoiced at the literary success.

Dickens had been an excellent choice for Procter's attempt. He was unfailingly encouraging, and his standards were not excessively high. Dickens was not a good judge of poetry, but he could almost infallibly choose what would stir the popular heart—though even his gorge sometimes rose at

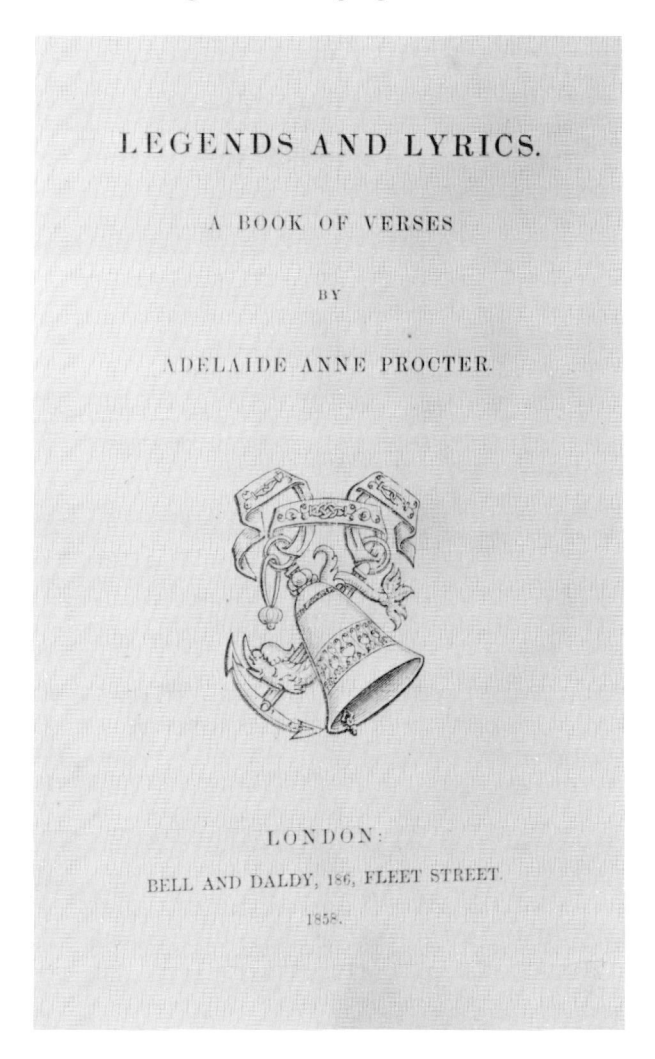

Title page for Procter's first collection of poems (Thomas Cooper Library, University of South Carolina)

the more sentimental of Procter's offerings. She was a faithful contributor to Dickens's periodicals; very few of her poems appeared elsewhere.

Five years after Mary Berwick's first poem appeared in *Household Words,* a collection of her poems entitled *Legends and Lyrics* (1858) was published. A second series appeared in 1861. These two volumes contain the best of her work. Both include longish narratives, either retellings of legends or rearrangements of stock characters and situations, with frequent supernatural interventions. One narrative from the 1858 volume, "Homeward Bound," has the same subject as Tennyson's "Enoch Arden" (1864). Although there was a copy of Procter's volume in the Tennyson library, Hallam Tennyson claimed in his memoir of his father that Tennyson did not know of Procter's poem until after "Enoch Arden" had been published. Since, however, Tennyson had taken the outline and many details from Thomas Woolner's "The Fisherman's Story," it is not surprising that there should be more than one reworking of the tale in verse.

The shorter poems in these volumes are limited in variety of form. They are also narrow in range of theme: nostalgia, spiritual exhortation, social conscience, love won (rarely) and lost (frequently), and earthly resignation and/or heavenly consolation are her usual fare. Procter's lyrical verse is like a cambric handkerchief: it is fine stuff, delicately embroidered, sometimes limp and sometimes starched—but that occasional firmness is not inherent in the fabric. The exhortation, resignation/consolation, and social conscience poems are generally the weakest, though three or four of them were employed as meditative hymns. Sometimes in the poems of love or nostalgia, true feeling and direct expression achieve real lyricism.

Her status as a published poet freed Procter to pursue her other interests more actively. She began to associate with Barbara Smith and Bessie Parkes and their group of friends, who were dedicated to literary projects and such social questions as employment for women. As evidence of their sincerity and seriousness, she and her friends produced *Victoria Regia* (1861), a collection of verse and prose edited by Procter, typeset by female compositors, and printed on Bessie Parkes's press. Its more distinguished contributors (Tennyson, Thackeray and Matthew Arnold among them) were, however, mostly males, though Harriet Martineau and Procter herself were also included.

In his memoir of her, written in 1866 at her parents' request and published as an introduction to subsequent editions of her poems, Dickens de-

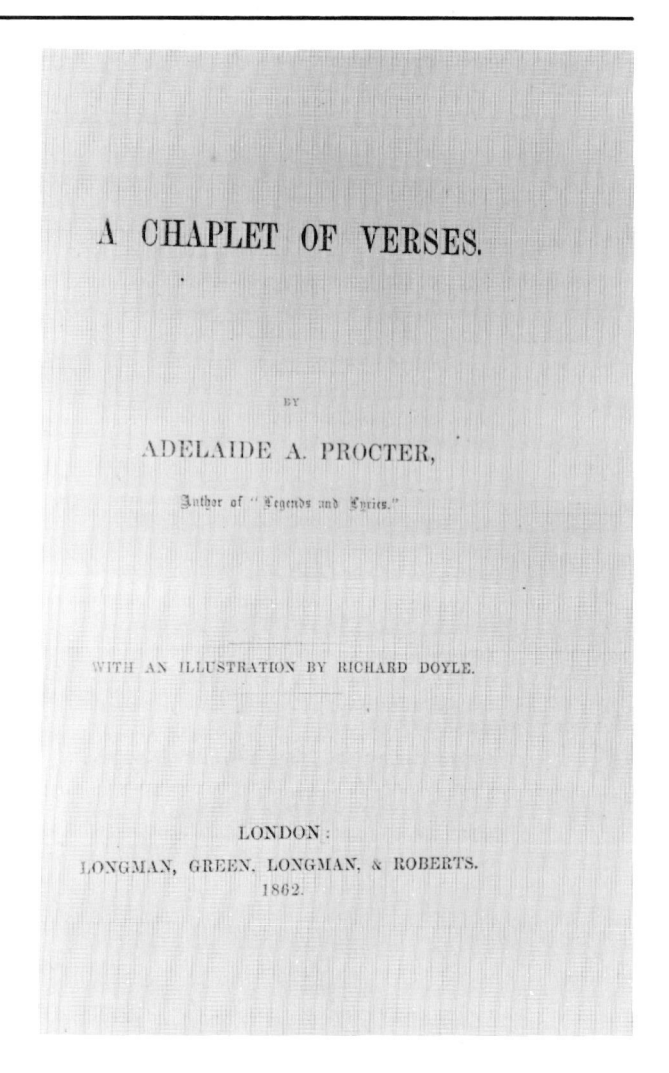

Title page for the book of poems Procter had published to raise money for a shelter for homeless women. The volume contains her worst verse (Thomas Cooper Library, University of South Carolina).

scribes a range of philanthropic activities befitting a Mrs. Jellyby. One of her charities was the Providence Row Night Refuge, a temporary shelter for homeless women, and it was to support this project that she had *A Chaplet of Verses* published in 1862. This volume is the repository of her worst verse, showing all the sentimental excesses of the Roman Catholic convert.

Procter's health would not sustain the demands she made upon her energies, and she died of consumption at the age of thirty-eight. Dickens described a calm and confident deathbed.

Procter preferred that no ambitious claims be made for her poetry: "Papa is a poet," she said. "I only write verses." The speaker of her poem "True Honours" describes—perhaps with more coyness than would indicate true contentment—the modest satisfactions such a versifier may know (the ambiguity of the word *them* in the fourth line of the first stanza is noteworthy):

> Then I strung my rhymes together
>   Only for the poor and low.
> And, it pleases me to know it
>   (For I love them well indeed),
> They care for my humble verses,
>   Fitted for their humble need.
>
> And, it cheers my heart to hear it,
>   Where the far-off settlers roam,
> My poor words are sung and cherished,
>   Just because they speak of Home.
> And the little children sing them
>   (That, I think, has pleased me best),
> Often, too, the dying love them,
>   For they tell of Heaven and rest.

References:

Edith Duméril, "Un poète catholique anglais au XIXe siècle: A. A. Procter," *Nouvelle revue des jeunes*, 2 (25 May 1930): 724-738;

F. Janku, *Adelaide Anne Procter: Ihr Leben und Ihre Werke* (Vienna: Wiener Beiträge zur englischen Philologie, 38, 1912);

John Julian, "Adelaide Anne Procter," in *A Dictionary of Hymnology*, edited by John Julian (London: Murray, 1892), p. 913;

Anne Lohrli, *Household Words, A Weekly Journal 1850-1859 Conducted by Charles Dickens. Table of Contents, List of Contributors and Their Contributions Based on the Household Words Office Book in the Morris L. Parrish Collection of Victorian Novelists, Princeton University Library* (Toronto: University of Toronto Press, 1973), pp. 404-406;

Margaret Maison, "Queen Victoria's Favorite Poet," *Listener* (29 April 1965): 636-637;

"The Poems of Adelaide Anne Procter," *The Month*, 4 (January 1866): 79-88;

Eric S. Robertson, *English Poetesses: A Series of Critical Biographies with Illustrative Extracts* (London: Cassell, 1883), pp. 226-239;

Hallam Tennyson, *Tennyson: A Memoir*, volume 2 (London: Macmillan, 1897), p. 1.

William Bell Scott
(12 September 1811-22 November 1890)

William E. Fredeman
University of British Columbia

BOOKS: *Hades; or, The Transit: and The Progress of Mind. Two Poems* (London: Renshaw, 1838);

Ornamental Designs for Furniture and House Decoration, Being a Series of Designs in Lithography, Selected from the Works of the Best French and German Ornamentalists. With a Treatise on Perspective, and an Introductory Essay on Ornamental Art (Edinburgh, London & Dublin: Fullarton, 1845);

The Year of the World: A Philosophical Poem on "Redemption from the Fall" (Edinburgh: Tait/London: Simpkin & Marshall, 1846);

Memoir of David Scott, R.S.A., Containing His Journal in Italy, Notes on Art and Other Papers (Edinburgh: Black, 1850);

Chorea Sancti Viti; or, Steps in the Journey of Prince Legion. Twelve Designs (London: Bell, 1851);

Antiquarian Gleanings in the North of England, Being Examples of Antique Furniture, Plate, Church Decorations, Objects of Historical Interest, Etc. (London: Bell, 1851);

Poems (London: Smith, Elder, 1854);

Half-hour Lectures on the History and Practice of the Fine and Ornamental Arts (London: Longman, Green, Longman & Roberts, 1861);

Mural Decorations at the Mansion of Sir Walter Trevelyan, Bart., at Wallington (N.p., 1867?);

Albert Durer: His Life and Works (London: Longmans, Green, 1869);

Report on Miscellaneous Art (London: Johnson, 1871?);

Gems of French Art: A Series of Carbon-Photographs from the Pictures of Eminent Modern Artists, with Remarks on the Works Selected, and an Essay on the French School (London: Routledge, 1871);

Our British Landscape Painters, from Samuel Scott to

David Cox (London: Virtue, 1872);
The British School of Sculpture, Illustrated by Twenty Engravings from the Finest Works of Deceased Masters of the Art, and Fifty Woodcuts. With a Preliminary Essay and Notices of the Artists (London: Routledge, 1872);
Gems of Modern Belgian Art: A Series of Carbon-Photographs from the Pictures of Eminent Living Artists. With Remarks on the Works Selected, and an Essay on the Schools of Belgium and Holland (London: Routledge, 1872);
Gems of Modern German Art: A Series of Carbon-Photographs from the Pictures of Eminent Modern Artists, with Remarks on the Works Selected, and an Essay on the Schools of Germany (London & New York: Routledge, 1873);
Murillo and the Spanish School of Painting: Fifteen Engravings on Steel and Nineteen on Wood. With an Account of the School and Its Great Masters (London & New York: Routledge, 1873);
Pictures by Italian Masters, Greater and Lesser, with an Introductory Essay and Notices of the Painters and Subjects Engraved (London & New York: Routledge, 1874);
Pictures by Venetian Painters. With Notices of the Artists and Subjects Engraved (London & New York: Routledge, 1875);
Poems: Ballads, Studies from Nature, Sonnets, Etc. (London: Longmans, Green, 1875);
William Blake: Etchings from His Works (London: Chatto & Windus, 1878);
The Little Masters (London: Low, Marston, Searle & Rivington, 1879; New York: Scribner & Welford, 1879);
A Poet's Harvest Home: Being One Hundred Short Poems (London: Stock, 1882); expanded as *A Poet's Harvest Home: Being One Hundred Short Poems, with an Aftermath of Twenty Short Poems* (London: Mathews & Lane, 1893);
Illustrations of Robert Burns' Works (Edinburgh: Jack, 1885);
Illustrations to the King's Quair, of King James I of Scotland, Painted on the Staircase of Penkill Castle, Ayrshire, by William Bell Scott, June 1865 to August 1868. Etched by Him 1885 (Edinburgh: Privately printed, 1887);
Autobiographical Notes of the Life of William Bell Scott and Notices of His Artistic and Poetic Circle of Friends, 1830 to 1882, edited by William Minto, 2 volumes (London: Osgood, 1892; New York: Harper, 1892);
*A Descriptive Catalogue of Engravings, Brought Together with a View to Illustrate the Art of Engraving on Copper and Wood from the Time of the Floren-

William Bell Scott

tine Niello Workers in the XVth Century to That of William Blake* (N.p., n.d.).

OTHER: *The Poetical Works of John Keats,* edited by Scott (London: Routledge, 1873);
The Poetical Works of Percy Bysshe Shelley, edited by Scott (London: Routledge, 1874);
Albrecht Altdorfer, *The Fall of Man,* edited by Alfred Aspulad, introduction by Scott (Manchester, U.K.: Brothers, 1876);
The Complete Poetical and Dramatic Works of Sir Walter Scott, introductory memoir by Scott (London & New York: Routledge, 1883).

William Bell Scott had attained midlife anonymity when, in 1847, he received an unsolicited communication from an aspiring "Student of the Academy" signing himself "Gabriel Chas. Rossetti" and expressing in the warmest terms his unbridled enthusiasm for the poetic effusions of the older man—his poems "Rosabell" and "A Dream of Love" (published in the *Monthly Repository* in 1838) and his volume of quasi-philosophic musings, *The Year of the World* (1846). Having seen a notice of the latter work, the young poet-painter wrote: "I rushed from my friend's house where I had seen the announcement, . . . and having got the book, fell upon it like a vulture. You may be pretty certain that you had in me one of those readers who 'read the volume at a single sitting.' A finer, a more dignitous, a more deeply thoughtful production—a work that is more truly a *work*—has seldom indeed shed its light upon me. To me at least I can say most truly that it seemed to reveal [quoting the opening line of *The Year of the World*] 'Some depth unknown, some inner life unlived.' The execution, moreover, is as admirable as the conception; and would not the Illustration to the fourth part make a most delightful picture? This was a rich feast...."

Critical recognition having eluded Scott during the first half of his life, such acclaim must have been sweet indeed, even from an unknown source. But there was more: for Rossetti had come across a reference to Scott's first book of poems, *Hades* (1838), which—perhaps because he had been unable to locate it—had, he said, "once more thrown [him] into a state of uneasy excitement. I assure you," he continued, "these perplexities are real misfortunes to me; they set my mind puzzling and conjecturing . . . so . . . as to interfere with my studies and occupations," and he earnestly requested details of publication, concluding with the hope that "bearing in mind the interest which your works cannot but excite, you may be induced to excuse, at least in some degree, this otherwise unwarrantable intrusion."

Scott had no way of knowing at the time, any more than did Rossetti, that this praise was genius paying obeisance to mediocrity; but even in the retrospective glow of memory, as he recorded the episode in his *Autobiographical Notes* (1892), his innate immodesty was temporarily (if only partially) overwhelmed: "This generously enthusiastic letter took me by surprise. I was, it seemed, not destined to be wholly unknown at a significant distance.... These my early poems he had mentioned have each a distinct specific character, which from time to time attracts people given to research, and makes them fancy they have discovered a new man. I have had other similar letters, the writers of which have disappeared again in the ebb and flow of life; but Rossetti . . . and William, his brother, from that day to this . . . have often been to me like brothers.... What I wrote in reply I cannot now say [Scott's early letters to Rossetti are not extant] . . . but in a few days the post brought me a bundle of MSS. for perusal, which I opened with something of his own avidity. I thought his letter showed no common boy; but what was my wonder and perplexity when I found the 'Blessed Damozel,' 'My Sister's Sleep,' and other admirable poems, marshalled under the title 'Songs of the Art Catholic,' still making sunshine in the shady place of memory. It may easily be allowed that I must now have written with extraordinary delight." However slight the direct influence of Rossetti and the Pre-Raphaelites on Scott's poetry, his friendship with the Rossettis, by widening appreciably his circle of contacts, marked a clear demarcation in the course of his life. Only his meeting with Alice Boyd a dozen years later had a comparable significance for his personal and artistic development.

Scott's total output was both eclectic and enormous, but the capstone of his career, his *Autobiographical Notes,* did not appear until two years after his death. These volumes of his reminiscences, more than any of his other publications or artistic achievements—along with an inept attempt over seventy years later to link him romantically with Christina Rossetti—have insured his remembrance by posterity. The *Autobiographical Notes* are not only one of the principal primary sources for biographical information on Scott; they also provide the background for his poetic and philosophic thought and a thorough record of his critical assessments of his literary and artistic contemporaries. Like many other volumes of Victorian recollections, they often lack precision in matters of dates and details (which unfortunately laid them open to controversy and attack), but they possess an honesty and candor, sometimes naively advanced, that is missing from most of the memoirs of the period. Most important, they provide a wonderfully focused portrait of Scott himself, who emerges in a somewhat contradictory light. On the one hand warm, generous, and outgoing, he was also capable of vainglory, petulance, and spite. Possessing a tetchy personality and an acerbic wit, Scott was nevertheless the most sociable of men, whose network of friends and acquaintances, as his correspondence testifies—and Scott was one of the better letter-writers of the century—was vast. Swinburne and others, including his lifelong friend William Michael Rossetti, took great exception to his plain dealing, but the new biographical materials which surfaced in the 1960s have served in great measure to exculpate him from the charges leveled against him in "The New Terror," in which Swinburne castigated him as the "Parasite of the North."

Scott was born in Edinburgh in 1811, the seventh child of Robert and Ross Bell Scott. The Scotts' four eldest sons had died during an epidemic in 1807, a tragedy which reinforced the Calvinistic gloom of the household. Scott spent his first quarter-century in Edinburgh under the shadows of a father whom he feared and of his brother David, five years his senior, whom he admired and held in awe. He felt trapped by his father's ill health and diminished finances and destined to become the "family victim" in sustaining his father's engraving business. Educated in the local high school, he aspired to a career in art and poetry; but under pressure from his father, "who cared little for painting," he learned engraving. Before he was twenty a collection of eight of his engravings, *Views of Loch Katrine and Adjacent Scenery,* was published. Encouraged in his writings by such luminaries of the Edinburgh literati as Professor John Wilson ("Christopher North") and Sir Walter Scott, Scott had his first poem, "In Memory of P. B. Shelley," published in *Tait's Edinburgh Magazine* in 1831. He exhibited two small works at the Trustees Academy, where he studied in the Antique School, at about the same time; and he also had a brief excursion in London, drawing at the British Museum. In 1834 he exhibited his first picture at the Royal Scottish Academy, a landscape subject from Coleridge's "Rime of the Ancient Mariner," *Ave Maria of a Hermit.* Sponsored by Wilson, Scott became the only nonuniversity member of the St. Luke's Club. At the club's annual dinner of the 1832-1833 school year, he met William A. C. Shand, the center of a coterie of theology students who shared common literary interests. Shand was to become one of Scott's best friends and the most influential force of his formative years.

Virtually nothing is known of William Shand beyond the information supplied in the *Autobiographical Notes,* in which he is portrayed by Scott as a kind of Hallam figure—Scott entitled his 1882 poem on Shand "A Genius?"—who abandoned his friend not by dying but through dissipation and disappearance. Like Tennyson and Hallam, Scott and Shand planned a joint future: "To be free and to live always together." They "made frantic plans of revolt against family ties and the ways of middle life" and thought of "each demanding his portion of life like the prodigal son, and going off together to a Norwegian fiord," where they "would make all the sagas and northern stories and poetry known to the English people." Like Hallam's, Shand's was regarded as the greater talent, but all that survives of his work is six poems contained in the *Edinburgh University Souvenir,* the Christmas annual he edited and dedicated to Scott in October 1834, and to which both Scott and his brother David also contributed. A man of unusual linguistic ability, Shand ultimately made his way to St. Petersburg, where he was engaged as a tutor. In 1846 he suddenly appeared in Newcastle, where he and Scott had a bittersweet reunion, Shand being then in trouble with the law and unable to get a renewal of his passport to return to Russia. The poignancy of his final departure from Scott after his passport finally arrived is recorded in *Autobiographical Notes:* " 'Oh, what it is to guide myself!' he said, in a low voice; 'if I could always have you with me—but I should have been born a woman!' With that," Scott, who accompanied him to the ship, laments, "he mounted out of my sights forever." Shand's role in Scott's life, like Hallam's in Tennyson's, was catalytic; soon after Shand's departure from Edinburgh, Scott broke with his family and sought his fortunes in London.

All the contributors to the *Edinburgh University Souvenir* were anonymous; even Shand's name does not appear as editor. At some point, however, Scott presented Rossetti with a copy of the volume with his own, David Scott's, and Shand's names penciled in next to their contributions on the contents page. William Scott is represented by three poems; a prose prologue to "Traditions of St. Columba"; and two verse paraphrases of the Norwegian sagas *Regnor Lodbrog* and the *Hervarer Saga,* which anticipate William Morris's interest in Northern legends

Portrait of Scott at age twenty-one by his brother David (The National Galleries of Scotland)

by more than thirty years.

His three poems are typical of his poetry written at this time. "The Progress of Mind" is a longer version of the second poem in his *Hades,* which was to be published three years later. Beginning with an invocation suggested by Shelley's *Alastor* (1816), the poem is a tiresome imitation, almost to the point of plagiarism, of themes that recur throughout Shelley's poetry. "To the Memory of Keats" is interesting for its tribute to another of Scott's youthful passions—in later life he edited the works of both poets—but the poem becomes a kind of stilted version of Shelley's *Adonais* (1821), blending images from both Shelley and Keats to celebrate the poet for whom "I would some thought inurn,/Worthy the poet's name to whom I bow."

"The Dance of Death" is probably the best of Scott's early poems; it is sustained by its narrative thread, which tends to hide the weaknesses of its meter and imagery. The poem is a Gothic tale in which Clerk Hubert awakens from a dream of death to find himself confronted by the reality of "the ancient One." After inviting Hubert to accompany him to survey his "vast realm," Death subjects him to a rhetorical, pseudophilosophic harangue, which Swinburne—as hyperbolic in praising Scott as in damning him—called "about his noblest piece of verse, and one of the finest in the language." Returned to his bed, Hubert, trembling in fear, awakens his wife, who tells him "it was his love alone/ That caused his dream"; but Hubert is so obsessed with death that the morning breaks on his "sheeted corse." Scott's fascination with the macabre is evident in several poems in his later volumes—notably "A Ghost" and "Love in Death" in *Poems* (1854)— and it may be related generally to his wider attraction to the mystical and occult. His portrait of Death in "The Dance" is closer to the grotesque imitation of Hans Holbein that proliferated from the sixteenth century onward than to Thomas Beddoes's more subtle depictions in *Death's Jest Book* (1850), but the poem does show more facility in the handling of his subject than many of his early poems. The *Edinburgh University Souvenir* provided Scott with his first public forum for his poetry; it did not have a wide circulation—it is now extremely scarce—or win him much in the way of recognition, but it is at least a unique relic of his early association with his first and perhaps his closest friend, William A. C. Shand.

Arriving in London in the spring of 1837, "a shy youth with poetry in his pockets, and little knowledge of the world and himself," Scott found a totally different literary scene. Lacking money and social or professional training, Scott spent several years familiarizing himself with the London scene and making new literary and artistic friends. Among his artistic acquaintances, including William P. Frith, Augustus Egg, Henry Nelson O'Neil, Richard Dadd (all members of the "Clique"), Ralph Nicholson Wornum, Kenny Meadows, W. J. Linton, and Thomas Sibson (Sibson, who died young, was his closest friend), he found a common bond for rebelling against the monopolistic control of the Royal Academy. Initially, Scott sought to make a name as an illustrator; but while his illustrations for a volume of poetry called *Landscape Lyrics* (1839), employing the "painter's etching" process, attracted much attention, his timing was not conducive to success. He eventually abandoned engraving for historical painting, exhibiting several pictures at various London galleries between 1839 and 1842, when his first picture, *Chaucer, John of Gaunt, and Their Wives* was accepted by the Royal Academy.

While Scott depended on his artistic work to support himself during his London period, he was not wholly divorced from literature. Through his meeting with Leigh Hunt, the editor of the *Monthly Repository,* he placed an article on art appreciation and two poems in that journal. "A Dream of Love" (the first of the poems addressed to "Mignon" in his 1854 *Poems*) appeared in January 1838; "Rosabell" appeared the following month. Through Hunt he also made the acquaintance of G. H. Lewes, the future "husband" of George Eliot, who was to remain a lifelong friend. Of his single volume of poems published at this time, *Hades; or, The Transit: and The Progress of Mind. Two Poems,* Scott is singularly silent in the *Autobiographical Notes;* he observes only that of the second poem in the volume, which was revised from the *Edinburgh University Souvenir,* "the less said the better."

It was in London that Scott took what he termed "the most imprudent step in my life"—his marriage on 31 October 1839 to Letitia Margery Norquoy, the daughter of a seafaring man. She was, he says, his "fate," but he confessed in another context that "she was the most difficult human creature to understand" that he had known. Neither the *Autobiographical Notes* nor the letters illuminates their enigmatic relationship. Letitia is omnipresent but never is she allowed to step from the shadowy background onto the lighted stage of Scott's life. However productive Scott was during his free-lance years in London, he had not achieved the financial security adequate to the needs of a married man. For this reason, when his unsuccessful entry of a northern subject in the competition for decorations

Etching by Scott of his brother David on his deathbed in 1849

for the new Houses of Parliament in 1843 brought him to the attention of the Board of Trade, he readily accepted their offer of a founding headmastership in the government school of design at Newcastle.

Within three years of Scott's arrival in Newcastle, the volume which had been incubating in his mind since adolescence, *The Year of the World: A Philosophical Poem on "Redemption from the Fall"* (1846), was published. The publication of the book, he announced in the preface, "possesses to the Author something of the interest attaching to the promulgation of a creed, as well as that of a work of art." Scott had aspired since boyhood to write a "sublime . . . religious-didactic" poem that "would be the grandest ever written." (If the prose program for a work called "The Pillars of Seth" is indicative of his ambitious juvenile poetic efforts, it is perhaps fortunate that no remnant survives of the hundreds of lines he composed for that blank verse epic.) From the outset, Scott viewed poetry as an exercise in grandiloquence; and because neither Professor Wilson nor Sir Walter Scott could woo him from his resolve to write on lofty themes in Miltonic blank verse, his poetry, as he said in later life, "for some years produced no adequate results."

Byron's amusing stricture on Wordsworth, "Who both by precept and example shows/That prose is verse and verse is merely prose," is literally true when applied to Scott's first two volumes. His poetry in these books is derivative almost to the point of parody, particularly of his mentor Shelley. Both "Hades" and "The Progress of Mind" were versified tracts emulating the master, but lacking any trace of the splendor of Shelley's language and imagery. By the time he wrote *The Year of the World*, Scott had added to his Shelleyan excesses the "lunatic infection" of the Spasmodics, which made his work even more pedantic, pompous, dull, rhetorical, stilted, and prosaic—in a word unreadable—than the poems in his first volume.

One of the recurring themes in Scott's writing is his sense of frustration at not winning the recognition he felt was his due. Fame seemed always to elude him; even as late as 1878, he refers to *The Year of the World* in his "Chronological Memoir" as "an exceedingly erudite and allegorical production which the world at large took little notice of." That the book was ignored was probably fortunate for Scott. The three central books of his canon—*Poems* (1854), *Poems: Ballads, Studies from Nature, Sonnets, Etc.* (1875), and *A Poet's Harvest Home* (1882)—while not totally free of the high speculation and philosophical musings of his early verse, do explore a wider range of poetic topics and themes. While he does not fully abandon the metaphysical predilections that characterize "Hades," "The Progress of Mind," and *The Year of the World,* he at least in the main restricts his discourse to the confines of the sonnet, the form which dominates his later volumes.

It is a misrepresentation, however, to say, as B. Ifor Evans does, that "after 1846, the religious and philosophical poems ended," or to attribute the shift in Scott's poetry exclusively to the influence of Rossetti. His introduction to Rossetti and the Pre-Raphaelites certainly had a rejuvenating effect on Scott's life, poetry, and thought; and his association with them doubtless accounts in part for the new diversity in his verse from 1854 onward. That Scott himself recognized the impact of the Pre-Raphaelites on his views of art and poetry is evident

Scott (left) with Dante Gabriel Rossetti and John Ruskin

in his sonnet "To the Artists Called P.R.B."; but most of the change was due simply to his own maturation and to a growing awareness, best articulated in a late poem entitled "Remonstrance," that "Philosophy is not poesy."

Throughout his life, however, Scott was preoccupied with a poetry of ideas in which he explored, as William Michael Rossetti said, "the deepest mysteries of life, death, and immortality, of matter and spirit, of revelation, and religion, of ethnic and Christian dogma"—topics reflected in the titles of sonnets and short poems in his last three volumes: "On Praying for Courage," "Life without Faith," and "Restoration of Belief" among the "Ten Sonnets Embodying Religious Ideals" in the 1854 *Poems;* "Contentment in the Dark," "The Universe Void," and "Spiritual Longings Unanswered," from "Outside the Temple" in the 1875 *Poems;* and "Left Alone," "Hortus Paradisi," and "Continuity of Life"

Scott's wife, Letitia Margery Norquoy Scott, in later years

in *A Poet's Harvest Home*. Scott was obsessed all his life by a vague sense of a personal mission "to solve the great Perhaps" (a phrase reiterated in at least two poems, "Rabelais" and the "Michael Angelo" sonnet of "Hortus Paradisi") that he never quite understood. He says in "Birthday, Aet. 70,"

> This wonder was my constant guest,
> Wonder at our environing,
> And at myself within the ring:
> Still that abides with me, some quest
> Before my footsteps seems to lie,
> But quest of what I scarcely know,
> Life itself makes no reply:
> A quest for nought that earth supplies,
> This is our life's last compromise.

More interesting than his speculative poetry in the later volumes are his love poems, such as those "Occasionally Addressed to 'Mignon'" in *Poems* (1854); poems based on legendary and historical subjects, such as "Woodstock Maze" in *Poems* (1854) and "Lady Janet, May Jean" in *Poems* (1875), which bear a balladlike resemblance to Rossetti's "Sister Helen," "Eden Bower," and "Troy Town"; poems such as "The Duke's Funeral" and "Bede in the Nineteenth Century" that treat contemporary subjects in a realistic fashion in the manner of the Pre-Raphaelite formula in the *Germ* concerning the "poetry of things around us." Although in his later poems Scott would adopt a kind of Edenic view of Penkill Castle and its environs, in 1854 he rejects purely naturalistic and descriptive lyrics and attacks Wordsworth in a sonnet: "Cumberland was the world to him and art/Was landscape gardening." In one of the best poems in the book, "Green Cherries," he predicts that nature will be exposed by "the poet of the future," who will not "prate/With vague loose phrase of Nature: he shall see/The inexorable step-dame as she is,/A teacher blind, whose task-work and closed door,/Body and soul we strive against."

Many of Scott's poems sound minor variations on themes expounded by the major Victorian poets, especially Tennyson and Arnold. His single most important original work, however, is a blank verse narrative on his meeting with an Edinburgh prostitute, an episode recounted in his *Autobiographical Notes*:

> She was dressed out in the manner of her class, but she was evidently new to the street and harmless. She looked at me in fact with an honest, ingenuous expression which perplexed and fascinated me. I addressed her, and we walked along, talking of I know not what; only she talked like any other woman, and not, as I expected or feared, like one abandoned by society, till she asked if I would give her some supper.
>
> . . . I was astonished to find this young woman, who was my own age, but who had already played out at least the first act of her drama, was not transformed, but was still a woman with a little of the child. I tried to learn her history, but . . . she had none to tell. . . . She had a pretty name, Rosabell Bonally, and she came from the little village of that name in the vicinity of the city. . . . She was wholly uneducated, and had no faith but in a sort of fatalism. She had fallen into bad hands. "What could I do?" she asked; "what maun be, maun" (what must be, must). . . .
>
> I did meet her again and again, but I saw I could do her no good. So instead of seeing her, I made a history for her as one of the doomed. . . .

The bibliographical history of the poem is complicated. It was first printed in Leigh Hunt's *Monthly Repository* for February and March 1838; it was revised substantially and retitled "Maryanne" for publication in *Poems* (1854); a final revised—indeed almost rewritten—version intended for a volume which never appeared is included in the first volume of *Autobiographical Notes*. The first version is the most striking, perhaps because it was more immediate to the episode depicted.

The *Monthly Repository* version of the poem consists of fourteen sections describing Rosabell at ten points in her life from the age of eight until her premature death. The narrative is broken by occasional exchanges of dialogue, and is interspersed with four lyrics climaxing four stages of her career from rural innocence to her tragic demise. Because the narrator manages to distance himself from the antiheroine of the story, the poem transcends the traps of sentimentalism and eroticism that might easily have swamped it. The moral tone of the poem is one of stark and simple contrasts between the good and evil social forces that have brought Rosabell to this pass. Rosabell is a country girl who is sent to the city to become a sempstress. Corrupted by the false sophistication of city values, she loses the virtues of her rural upbringing and returns home, where she rejects her mother, jilts her country lover for a wag appropriately named Lizard, then abandons him for his friend Thorn. Thorn eventually leaves her debt-ridden. Rosabell goes quickly downhill, losing everything from her self-respect to her beauty, until finally she is no more than "a spot

Penkill Castle, which became a second home for Scott

upon the sun,/A foul thing on the street,/A blight on the fields, a festering sore/Unto her sister woman." Inevitably, as in William Hogarth's series of paintings, *The Harlot's Progress* (1731), and other models on which Scott drew, she dies too soon, her life a total waste.

But "Rosabell" is more than a story, and Scott is concerned with the problem of responsibility. Rosabell's case poses genuine social issues that were only beginning to be taken seriously when he wrote the poem. Scott divides the blame among Rosabell herself, her seducer, her family, and the respective environments of the country and the city. He shows that country life neither prepares the rustic to cope with the realities of urban temptation nor offers sufficiently attractive values to counter the lures of the city. The poem also considers the social attitudes that condemn Rosabell as a prostitute while offering her no realistic opportunity to improve her lot.

Whether or not Scott's poem was a direct influence on Rossetti's "Jenny" (1869), it was the poem that first attracted Rossetti to Scott; and Holman Hunt has recorded how at Pre-Raphaelite Brotherhood meetings Rossetti would declaim its "pathetic strains" to his associates. Certainly the poem introduced the theme of the fallen woman to the Pre-Raphaelites, inspiring a series of poems on the subject, as well as paintings such as Rossetti's unfinished *Found* and P. H. Calderon's *Broken Vows* (1857). On a personal level, the friendships he formed with the Rossettis and the Pre-Raphaelites in the late 1840s, which led to Newcastle visits by the Rossetti brothers and an invitation to contribute to the Pre-Raphaelite journal the *Germ,* provided Scott with a welcome social alternative to the isolation and cultural sterility of his northern retreat. How welcome is made clear by his own account in the *Autobiographical Notes* of a visit with Rossetti and Holman Hunt on a trip to London: "Although I saw no more of these two men for nearly a year, this meeting was the beginning of a new interest of life to me: from them sprang a knowledge of many men, and of other fields. My having left London was really the result of disappointment, not so much in my chances of coming to the front and making a good position, but disappointment in the art and poetry of the day: I had become indifferent to working my brain in any perfunctory struggle for popularity.

My social circle was not sufficiently interesting. Poetry seemed to be going extinct.... Hunt and Rossetti and all their circle made me almost regret having left London."

In the early years after 1843, the administrative problems involved in organizing the Newcastle School of Design—establishing a curriculum, recruiting faculty and students, teaching—offset to some degree the absence of intellectual and social stimulation; but within three years of taking on his position Scott ran into difficulties with the London Council which jeopardized the grant on which the operation of the school and his own salary depended. Whether these conflicts centered on complaints about the time Scott spent in the school or on pedogogical differences between him and the council over artistic priorities is not clear, but the issue was not finally resolved until the establishment of the Department of Practical Art under the direction of Sir Henry Cole in 1851. These complications must have added even more strain to the professional burdens of his first decade in Newcastle.

It was only after he made the acquaintance of the Trevelyans at Wallington Hall in 1854—a dozen years after his arrival in Newcastle—that he found anything like a compatible environment in the north. At the center of the Wallington coterie was the brilliant and sensitive first wife of Sir Walter Calverley Trevelyan, Pauline Jermyn Trevelyan, whose social gatherings included some of the most prominent scientists, poets, and artists of the time. Scott exhibited widely during this period both in the local North of England Exhibitions and in the more important exhibitions at the Portland Gallery, the National Institute of the Arts, and the Royal Scottish Academy. He made frequent forays to London in these years and exhibited at the Royal Academy in 1851 and 1852; but it was through his contact with the Trevelyans that he received his first major artistic commissions: to do eight historical pictures of border scenes, of which the most important is *Iron and Coal* (1861); and to do the spandrel decorations for the newly enclosed gallery at Wallington, undertaken on Ruskin's suggestion and designed by the architect John Dobson. To this decorative scheme, involving both pictures and sculpture, a number of the Pre-Raphaelites contributed, including Arthur Hughes, Alexander Munro, and Thomas Woolner. (Even Ruskin embarked on a picture, which was left unfinished when it was criticized by the forthright Lady Trevelyan.) Scott delivered two lectures on the decorations before the Institute of British Architects in the winter of 1867-1868, after his return to London.

The Newcastle years were devoted almost exclusively to art rather than literature. The publication of his *Memoir of David Scott* in 1850, a year after his brother's death, won him wider recognition and, indeed, was what first brought him to the attention of the Trevelyans—Pauline reviewed the book for the *Scotsman*—but there is a twenty-one-year hiatus between the publication of *Poems* (1854), many of which were written earlier, and the appearance of his next collection in 1875. It may have been his virtually total commitment to art that led him to call his 1854 work on the illustrated title page "Poems by a Painter," a title usurped by Noel Paton in 1861. (Thomas Carlyle misread the title as "Poems by a Printer" in acknowledging receipt of a complimentary copy of Scott's book.)

If his introduction to the Trevelyans revitalized his artistic interests at Newcastle, it was his meeting with Alice Boyd in 1859 that altered the whole course of his domestic life. Scott was nearly fifty when Boyd, then in her mid-thirties, came on

Alice Boyd, who lived in an open ménage à trois with William and Letitia Scott for twenty-six years

Boyd and Scott at Penkill Castle

the scene; he was disappointed in both his career and his marriage, and what began as a teacher-pupil relationship quickly blossomed into a fervid friendship. Scott describes their relationship, which lasted more than thirty years, as "the perfect friendship, the ambition of my life," but this statement discreetly understates the depth of feeling, the strength of the bond that existed between them: in every sense save the legal one they were married. Even Scott's wife, Letitia, seems to have acquiesced in the intimacy of their friendship—perhaps because she had no choice.

In July 1860 Scott made his first visit to Penkill Castle in Ayrshire, Alice's family seat which she then shared with her brother Spencer, the incumbent laird. Alice became a regular guest of the Scotts at St. Thomas' Crescent in Newcastle, where she met Swinburne, Dante Gabriel and William Rossetti, and Scott's two principal patrons, Lady Trevelyan and James Leathart. In 1861 she accompanied Scott to London to attend the opening of Gambart's exhibition of Scott's English Border pictures at the French Gallery. Penkill Castle became for Scott a second home, which he found almost as companionable as its mistress. By 1863 Scott was thinking of moving to London; and in February 1864, after a triumphant leave-taking from Newcastle, he settled with Alice and Letitia in an open ménage à trois at 33 Elgin Road, Kensington Park Gardens, Notting Hill.

From this point, Scott's life to 1885 assumed a routine pattern broken only occasionally by trips to the Continent. He spent his summers—often accompanied by Letitia—at Penkill, which Alice inherited on her brother's death in 1865. That year, Scott embarked on the painting of the staircase at Penkill, for which he prepared a series of designs based on *The King's Quair*. Scott and Alice entertained a number of Pre-Raphaelite and family guests at Penkill, including Christina Rossetti in 1866 and William Rossetti in 1867. In the summers of 1868 and 1869 Dante Gabriel found at Penkill the inspiration to take up the poetry he had abandoned on the death of his wife, Elizabeth Siddal. Alice normally stayed on at Penkill until late fall, tending to the business of the castle. Their life in London, as recorded in Alice's diaries, was a full one compounded of work and a constant round of social activities. Scott became increasingly close to Rossetti, moving in 1870 to Bellevue House in Cheyne Walk, where propinquity enhanced their friendship. Scott supported himself in these years mainly through investments and through commissioned monographs on artistic subjects. Though he continued to paint and exhibit, he was not able to rely on his art for a living; and in 1873 he reluctantly agreed to become one of the examiners at South Kensington, a post he retained for over a decade.

Two years later his *Poems* were published, with designs by himself and Alma Tadem; a "Dedicatio Postica" in which he acknowledged his indebtedness to Rossetti, Morris, and Swinburne; and a six-page preface explaining that his intention in bringing out the volume, on the advice of friends "whose judgment in matters poetic is not mere opinion," was to fulfill the "pleasant task of putting his poetical house in order." *Poems* contains some new compositions—principally those in the section entitled "The Old Scotch House" which focus on Penkill Castle, and the amatory poems that owe their inspiration to Alice Boyd—but is mainly a collection of earlier poems, most of them severely revised. The book is divided into eight sections, including "Sonnets on Literary Subjects," "Occasional Sonnets," and "Juvenile Poems." Scott's preface suggests that he was in this volume gathering his verse for posterity; but the penultimate paragraph, which he says concerns the author rather than the reader, is a sad credo for an unheralded poet: "No external or adventitious merits, nor even purely intellectual qualities, can altogether determine the value of poetry. It must affect us like music or wine, but it must certainly have Wisdom, like an instinct, directing it from within. Every excellent poetic work has a physiognomy of its own, an organic character of its own, the possession or non-possession of which the world will sooner or later sympathetically determine."

Scott's final volume, *A Poet's Harvest Home: Being One Hundred Short Poems* (1882) departs radically from his earlier books. All but eight of the poems are new compositions, and only one, "The Norns Watering Yggdrasill," written for one of his own pictures, appears to have been previously printed. While in quality none of the short poems in *A Poet's Harvest Home* compares with "Rosabell" and a handful of poems in previous volumes, the book is interesting from a biographical standpoint. Not only are many of the poems descriptive reveries recalling past scenes, persons, and experiences, including episodes from Scott's childhood, but they are consciously written in a plain style dramatically different from most of Scott's other compositions. Many are still marred by infelicities of diction, rhyme, and meter, but they have a directness and clarity often missing from his earlier verse. *A Poet's*

Self-portrait of Scott in 1868 (The National Galleries of Scotland)

Harvest Home is clearly an old man's book, and many of the titles have a definitive final ring about them, as in "To the Dead," "Love and Death," "A Garland for Advancing Years," "The Falling Leaf," "Left Alone," "End of Harvest," "Memory," "Age," "Birthday, Aet. 70," and "A-dieu." Though many of the pieces are occasional poems, the overall impression one takes away from the book is a sense of retrospectivity. But it is also a would-be poet's book, and more than a quarter of the poems either treat poetry in the abstract or address directly those poets who have been Scott's inspiration: Shakespeare, Dante, Wordsworth, Byron, Chatterton, and, of course, Shelley. Only the two poems entitled "The Sphinx" contain any hint of his old religious and philosophical preoccupations, but as reflections on Homer they bear no resemblance to the poem "To the Sphinx" in *Poems* (1875), subtitled "(Considered as the Symbol of Religious Mystery)." The hundred poems of *A Poet's Harvest Home* range widely over a number of lesser themes and subjects, including several dealing with Celtic folk legends. The poem that best epitomizes both the message and the source of inspiration for this last of Scott's volumes is "The Garden Bower," which is probably Scott's finest poetic tribute to Penkill Castle and to Alice Boyd:

> But what have wars or kings to do
>   With our quiet country ways,
> Or with poetry now-a-days?
> The foxglove by the gate that grew
> Brought them to mind, and made me lose
> Myself in that past stream of news:
> And there it still remains to-day;
> The Mistress of our Garden Bower
> Caring for each wild blossoming
> The summer months successive bring.
>
> Each morning here, in sun or shower,
> Awhile we sit while I rehearse
> As matin service, some new lay,
>   Some little verse,
> Various as this sea-tide weather,
> Or that hill-side rough with heather,
> Rhyme children of the transient hour,
> Records perchance of yesterday,
>   Or tales from twilights far away.

Scenes from The King's Quair *painted on the staircase at Penkill by Scott*

Within three years of publishing his last volume, Scott suffered an attack of angina pectoris that forced him to retire permanently to Penkill under the care of Alice, whom he called his "life preserver." In the years remaining to him, he composed the twenty poems in the "Aftermath" to the second edition of *A Poet's Harvest Home* (posthumously published in 1893), completed the engravings for *The King's Quair,* maintained a running correspondence with his friends in London, and made his final revisions for the *Autobiographical Notes.* In his twilight years he was made an honorary member of the Royal Scottish Academy and awarded an honorary degree by Aberdeen University. When he died on 22 November 1890, all the letters of condolence were sent to Alice Boyd, a testament that belies the generalizations normally made about Victorian propriety.

A self-taught man, Scott was probably more erudite than talented, as either poet or painter. He was grotesquely overpraised as a poet by critics such as Buxton Forman, Joseph Knight, and Swinburne. At the other extreme, he was belittled mercilessly after his death by Swinburne for daring to speak his mind in his *Autobiographical Notes.* "Here . . . is a man," Swinburne wrote, "whose name would never have been heard, whose verse would never have been read, whose daubs would never have been seen, outside some aesthetic Lilliput of the North, but for his casual and parasitical association with the Trevelyans, the Rossettis, and Myself." The words are both untrue and ungenerous. In any final critical reckoning of Victorian poets (or painters), Scott can only be ranked in the lower echelons—he referred to himself as a "Pictor Ignotis"—but he deserves better than Swinburne allows him. Taking into account his complete life's output—as poet, painter, engraver, editor, autobiographer, art and literary critic, letter writer, and all-around friend—he achieved some degree of distinction, if not prominence, in the pantheon of eminent Victorians.

Letters:

A Pre-Raphaelite Gazette: The Penkill Letters of Arthur Hughes to William Bell Scott and Alice Boyd, 1886-97, edited by William E. Fredeman (Manchester, U.K.: John Rylands Library, 1967);

The Letters of Pictor Ignotis: William Bell Scott's Correspondence with Alice Boyd, 1859-1884, edited by

Fredeman (Manchester, U.K.: John Rylands Library, 1976).

References:

David J. Black, *Hermits and Termits . . . Together with Biographical Notices on Robert Scott . . . David Scott, and William Bell Scott* (Edinburgh: Seventh Horizon Press, 1972);

Bernarda C. Broers, "William Bell Scott," in *Mysticism in the Neo-Romanticists* (Amsterdam: Paris, 1913);

Van Akin Burd, "Ruskin, Rossetti, and William Bell Scott: A Selected Arrangement," *Philological Quarterly*, 48 (January 1969): 102-107;

Austin Chester, "The Art of William Bell Scott," *Windsor Magazine*, 40 (September 1914): 413-428;

M. D. E. Clayton-Stamm, "William Bell Scott: Observer of the Industrial Revolution," *Apollo*, 89 (May 1969): 386-390;

B. Ifor Evans, "Minor Pre-Raphaelite Poets," in *English Poetry in the Later Nineteenth Century*, second edition (London: Methuen, 1966);

H. Buxton Forman, "William Bell Scott," in *Our Living Poets: An Essay in Criticism* (London: Tinsley, 1871);

William E. Fredeman, *Prelude to the Last Decade: Dante Gabriel Rossetti in the Summer of 1872* (Manchester: John Rylands Library, 1971);

Fredeman, "William Bell Scott," in his *Pre-Raphaelitism: A Bibliocritical Study* (Cambridge, Mass.: Harvard University Press, 1965);

Herbert P. Horne, "William Bell Scott, Poet, Painter, and Critic," *Century Guild Hobby Horse*, new series 6 (January 1891): 16-27;

Robin Ironside, "Pre-Raphaelite Paintings at Wallington: A Note on William Bell Scott and Ruskin," *Architectural Review*, 92 (December 1942): 147-149;

Joseph Knight, "William Bell Scott," in *The Poets and the Poetry of the Century*, edited by A. H. Miles, volume 8 (London: Hutchinson, 1891-1897);

Lona Mosk Packer, *Christina Rossetti* (Berkeley: University of California Press, 1963);

William Michael Rossetti, "William Bell Scott and Modern British Poetry," *Macmillan's*, 33 (March 1876): 418-429;

Scenes from Northumbrian History: The Mural Paintings at Wallington Hall, by William Bell Scott (Newcastle on Tyne: Graham, 1972);

[John Skelton], "Dante Rossetti and Mr. William Bell Scott," *Blackwood's Magazine*, 153 (February 1893): 229-235;

Raleigh Trevelyan, "Enter Scotus," in *A Pre-Raphaelite Circle* (London: Chatto & Windus, 1978);

Vera Walker [K. H. Smith], "A Biographical and Critical Study of William Bell Scott," Ph.D. dissertation, University of Durham, 1952;

Lyall Wilkes, "William Bell Scott," in *Tyneside Portraits* (Newcastle on Tyne: Frank Graham, 1971);

"William Bell Scott, Poet and Painter," *London Quarterly Review*, 45 (October 1875): 149-167.

Papers:

The Special Collections Division of the University of British Columbia contains the most extensive collection of materials relating to Scott, including the mutilated manuscript "Journal," the abortive prolegomenon for the *Autobiographical Notes* (ca. 1847-1853); the manuscript of a "Chronological Memoir" (ca. 1878); the manuscripts of "Anthony" (in the Colbeck Collection); a scrapbook of periodical and newspaper clippings (from 1832 onward); and virtually his complete correspondence with Alice Boyd.

Alexander Smith
(31 December 1830-5 January 1867)

Mark A. Weinstein
University of Nevada, Las Vegas

BOOKS: *Poems* (London: Bogue, 1853; Philadelphia: Moss, 1853);

Sonnets on the War, by Smith and Sydney Dobell (London: Bogue, 1855);

City Poems (Cambridge: Macmillan, 1857; Boston: Ticknor & Fields, 1857);

Edwin of Deira (Cambridge: Macmillan, 1861; Boston: Ticknor & Fields, 1861);

Dreamthorpe: A Book of Essays Written in the Country (London: Strahan, 1863; Boston: Tilton, 1864);

A Summer in Skye (2 volumes, London: Strahan, 1865; 1 volume, Boston: Ticknor & Fields, 1865);

Alfred Hagart's Household (Boston: Ticknor & Fields, 1865; 2 volumes, London & New York: Strahan, 1866);

Miss Oona McQuarrie: A Sequel to Alfred Hagart's Household (Boston: Ticknor & Fields, 1866);

Last Leaves: Sketches and Criticisms, edited by Patrick Proctor Alexander (Edinburgh: Nimmo, 1868);

A Life-Drama, City Poems, Etc., edited by R. E. D. Sketchley (London: Scott, 1901);

The Poetical Works of Alexander Smith, edited by W. Sinclair (Edinburgh: Nimmo, Hay & Mitchell, 1909).

OTHER: John Bunyan, *Divine Emblems; or, Temporal Things Spiritualised,* preface by Smith (London: Bickers, 1864);

The Poetical Works of Robert Burns, edited by Smith, 2 volumes (London: Macmillan, 1865; Philadelphia: Lippincott, 1865);

J. W. S. Howe, *Golden Leaves from the American Poets,* introduction by Smith (London & Edinburgh, 1866).

PERIODICAL PUBLICATION: "Wardie—Spring Time," *Good Words,* 3 (1862): 272-273.

Alexander Smith is a remarkable example of the young poet who meets with great initial success but then fades into obscurity. His first major poem, "A Life-Drama," was overrated by its earliest critics and readers, then condemned as "Spasmodic." Smith spent the rest of his career trying to shake off the derogatory label but never succeeded, and he is largely and undeservedly forgotten today.

Alexander was born in Kilmarnock, in the Scottish Lowlands southwest of Glasgow. His father, Peter Smith, a Lowlander, was a designer of calico printing and sewed muslins. His mother, Helen Murray Smith, a Highlander, was a woman of considerable mental endowment and tenderest maternal feeling. The deep love between mother and son was "the real sunshine of his youth," according to Smith's biographer, Thomas Brisbane. She and a Highland servant girl first introduced the boy to Gaelic songs and Ossianic legends. It was perhaps inevitable that the poet would win out over the laborer in the young man.

Because of the vicissitudes of trade during the 1830s, the family moved back and forth between Kilmarnock and Paisley before settling in Glasgow. Here Smith attended primary school, his only formal education. Although there had been some thought of training Smith to be a minister, "Daft Sandie"—as the poetic youth was affectionately called—was apprenticed to his father's occupation of pattern designer at about the age of twelve.

Outwardly, Smith's circumstances were unpromising: he had no friends at first and was working long hours at an uncongenial job. But his real life was internal. He was becoming a self-taught man, delighting especially in literature. Although Wordsworth, Byron, and Shelley seem to have been his earliest favorites, he developed a more lasting affinity for Keats and Tennyson. He read early in the morning and late at night; in his mid-teens, he began writing his own verses. He had found his true ambition. As he later told a friend, "[Poetry] has been the seventh heaven of my aspirations for years; a passion running as deep as the aboriginal waters of my being."

External horizons also began to enlarge. Smith became a leader of the Addisonian Society, a working-class literary group for essay writing and debating. He became a close friend of Thomas Brisbane, his future biographer, with whom he took weekend excursions along the Clyde and summer expeditions to the Highlands. These rambles through the rich scenery of Scotland inspired much of Smith's best poetry. He also became friends with John Nichol, a future professor at Glasgow University; Hugh Macdonald, a naturalist and Scots poet; and James Hedderwick, the proprietor and editor of the Glasgow *Evening Citizen*, where Smith's first poems were published in 1850 and 1851 under the pseudonym "Smith Murray."

The publication of these poems emboldened Smith, after nearly a decade as a pattern designer, to try to realize his heart's desire. In April 1851 he submitted a selection of his poems to the Reverend George Gilfillan of Dundee, an influential critic and encourager of aspiring poets. Gilfillan sent Smith so eulogistic a response that, according to Brisbane, "Smith was filled with unwonted joy, incited to increase [*sic*] hopefulness, and stirred to greater activity in composition." Additional poems were sent to Gilfillan for his inspection, and a friendly correspondence developed between the poet and the critic.

At the same time, Gilfillan introduced Smith to the public in the *Eclectic Review*. He lavished the highest praise upon him and, to illustrate Smith's "exquisite thoughts and imagery," included selections from "Life Fragment," the major poem of the manuscript volume. Additional encomiums and selections were soon sent forth by Gilfillan in the *Critic* and *Hogg's Instructor,* so the reading public grew eager to see the poems themselves. The author, too, became restless and impatient. When Gilfillan suggested that the literary world would be best satisfied with a longer poem than any he had yet written, Smith attempted to fuse the independent pieces he had composed into one extensive work, based on the plan of "Life Fragment." Thus his most famous poem, "A Life-Drama," was the product of much "detaching, transposing, piecing, uniting, and supplementing," in Brisbane's words. It was published, along with some shorter pieces, in *Poems* (1853).

"A Life-Drama" has the fitful structure that one would expect from its method of composition. The joints frequently stick out, and isolated purple passages result. The concept of digression reaches its reductio ad absurdum with the inclusion of long digressive poems within long digressive poems. The plot is too thin and incoherent to bring the originally separate poems together into a meaningful unity. Walter, the hero, hopes passionately to realize his ambition through poetry: "O Fame! Fame! next grandest word to God!/I seek the look of Fame!" He violates a girl named Violet, rushes "through Pleasure and through Devil-world," writes a great poem, rejoins Violet, and accepts the world of social responsibility and domestic togetherness.

But the plot is actually little more than a peg upon which Smith hangs his poetic beauties. "A Life-Drama" gained its initial success because of its sensuousness and spectacular imagery; Smith seemed to be a new Keats at a time when Keats was becoming extremely popular. Walter describes Smith's practice as well as his own when he reports that

> our chief joy
> Was to draw images from everything
> And images lay thick upon our talk,
> As shells on ocean sands.

It is undeniable that Smith had a remarkable ability for image making, but his very felicity seems detrimental in a long, dramatic poem. Each image is rich—yet, when together, they are too opulent and,

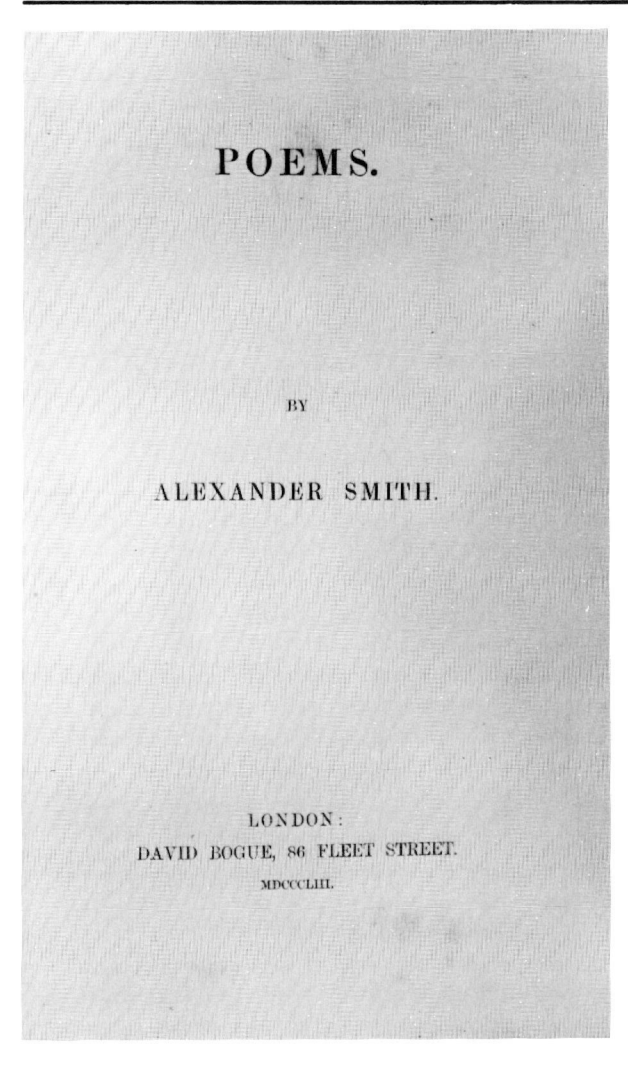

Title page for Smith's first volume of poems, which included "A Life-Drama" (Thomas Cooper Library, University of South Carolina)

in juxtaposition, often incongruous. Smith's sensuousness generally takes the form of reveling in color. Walter describes his own technique as a limning, "with words like colours," on the canvas of the senses. Thus there is frequent scene painting. At this point in his career, Smith's talent is lyrical rather than dramatic. As Elizabeth Barrett Browning wrote, "he has more imagery than verity, more colour than form."

Nevertheless, "A Life-Drama" attained a remarkable success at first; Smith, like Byron before him, awoke and found himself famous. George Meredith wrote a sonnet hailing "The mighty warning of a poet's birth," and Herbert Spencer was "strongly inclined to rank him as the greatest poet since Shakespeare." Although the first edition was double the usual number of copies, the volume was reprinted within the year and reached a fourth edition in 1856.

The early success of "A Life-Drama" caused a considerable change in Smith's life. He finally gave up pattern designing and traveled to London. In England he met people of culture and influence, including Spencer and G. H. Lewes, two admirers of his poetry, and the poets Philip James Bailey and Sydney Dobell. Upon his return to Glasgow, he edited the *Glasgow Miscellany*, a literary magazine, for a short while but was looking for a more secure and remunerative position. In early 1854 he was appointed secretary of Edinburgh University and afterwards took on the additional duties of registrar and secretary to the university council, at an annual salary of £200.

But the praise soon turned to laughter. In July 1854, William Edmondstoune Aytoun's *Firmilian; or, The Student of Badajoz. A Spasmodic Tragedy*, a brilliant parody of the "Spasmodic School of Poetry," was published. Aytoun made Smith a leading member of the school, along with Bailey and Dobell, and ridiculed his sensuous imagery, emotional extravagances, and lengthy digressions. The critical tide shifted. Classical standards of unity and coherence appeared more frequently; heroes of dubious morality were examined more strictly. Although Smith himself admitted the justice of Aytoun's criticism and was determined to learn from it, his future career in poetry was largely an unsuccessful attempt to escape the epithet *Spasmodic*.

Nevertheless, Smith found life in Edinburgh congenial. He was a member of a sophisticated intellectual and artistic community for the first time. He joined—and perhaps helped to found—the Raleigh Club. One of his closer friends was Dobell, who was living in Corstorphine because of his wife's illness. The two "Spasmodic poets" collaborated on a small volume, *Sonnets on the War* (1855). The thirty-nine sonnets treat conventional war themes in an undistinguished manner. It is evident that what Wordsworth called "the Sonnet's scanty plot of ground" constrained Smith's ability to elaborate images. The little book was generally ignored.

In the spring of 1857 Smith married Flora Macdonald, a descendant of the Jacobite heroine of that name. In 1858 they moved to Wardie, near Granton, where they lived until Smith's death; they spent the summer holidays in Skye, his wife's home. Smith, an excessively romantic young man just a few years before, was becoming the paterfamilias of a relatively happy Victorian family.

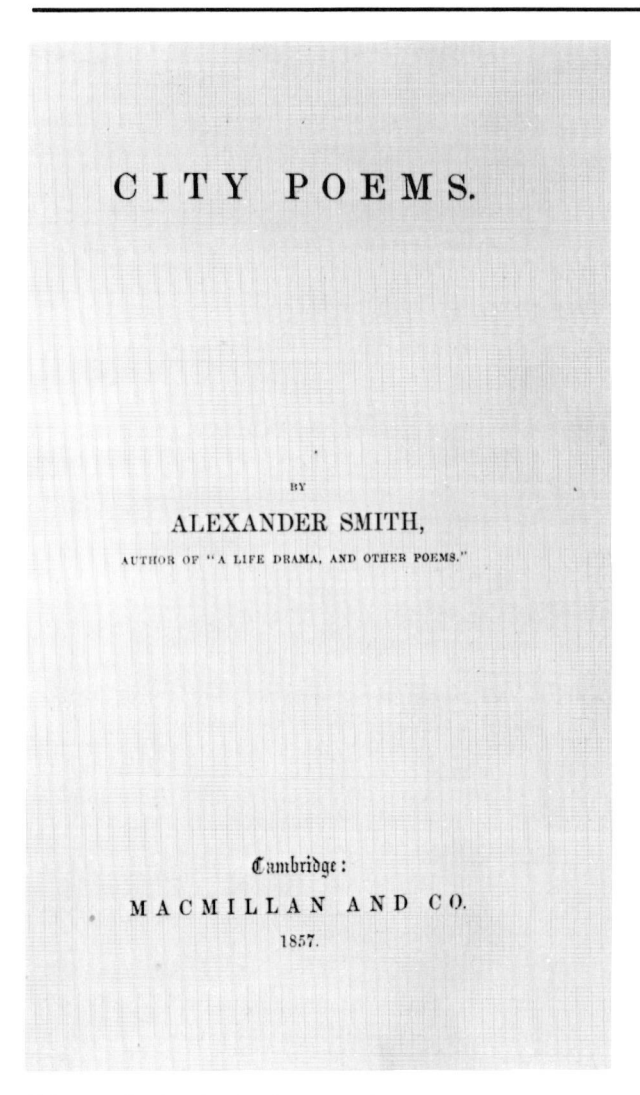

Title page for Smith's third volume of poetry, which gave rise to charges of plagiarism (Thomas Cooper Library, University of South Carolina)

His poetic career was less successful. In his attempt to rid himself of the *Spasmodic* label, Smith toned down his distinctive voice. *City Poems* (1857), a volume equal in length to "A Life-Drama," contains six poems about more realistic characters than Walter. Smith selects simple themes, chastens his diction, and varies his imagery more frequently; in the three longest poems, he adds an arbitrary narrator to strengthen the impression of objectivity. In "Horton," for example, the hero is another romantic poet heading "for the coast of Fame"; he, too, experiences a crucial love for a "lily-woman." But this time the career of the dead poet is filtered through the judgments of realistic men of the world. When one of them begins to glorify poetry, another shouts him down. Likewise, "A Boy's Poem," more realistically autobiographical than "A Life-Drama," distances its material by having a forty-year-old Englishman send his friend in India "a forgotten poem of my youth." "Glasgow," perhaps the finest of the poems, presents the narrator's honestly ambivalent attitude toward the city of Smith's youth. Throughout the volume, Smith is struggling to keep his romantic bias under control. Because he partially succeeded, *City Poems* met with a mixed critical reception. Those who saw the volume as a movement away from "A Life-Drama" praised it, while those whose glance fixed on the lingering elements of the earlier work censured it. All concurred that another "Life-Drama" had to be avoided. Another reason for the relative failure of *City Poems* was the charge of plagiarism, mainly of Keats and Tennyson, which was advanced by the *Athenaeum* and picked up by others. Today, however, Smith's indebtedness seems no more than a legitimate tribute to his literary fathers.

Sensitive to critical opinion and anxious for popular support, Smith determined to eliminate Spasmody from his work altogether. For his final volume of poetry, *Edwin of Deira* (1861), he went to history for his subject matter. He later explained that he "chose the subject thoughtfully, as knowing that his besetting sin was a certain unstrictness and vagrancy—so call it—a want of severity in the outline of substantial forms—and seeking without in the defined Historic framework some supplement of the deficiency within." He kept the main story, the career of Edwin, "the earliest Christian King/That England knew," clearly before the reader and maintained a simple and direct style of blank verse. The reviewers were pleased to the extent that they saw the poem, correctly, as an abandonment of Spasmody. But Smith had become respectable with a vengeance, eliminating also his individual poetic voice. The charge of plagiarism was renewed because the early narratives of Tennyson's *Idylls of the King* had been published two years before. Nevertheless, *Edwin of Deira* was "acceptable," as Smith put it later, and a second edition was called for after "a reasonable time." But Smith was just another poet, by this time earning slightly more than fifteen pounds for the four years of labor. "He became," his biographer says, "a little disheartened." He turned to prose; his poetic career was essentially over.

Aytoun, his old nemesis and current colleague at Edinburgh University, introduced Smith's prose into the pages of *Blackwood's*. Smith also wrote for other magazines, various newspapers, and encyclopedias. In 1863 his most famous book of essays,

EDWIN OF DEIRA

BY

ALEXANDER SMITH

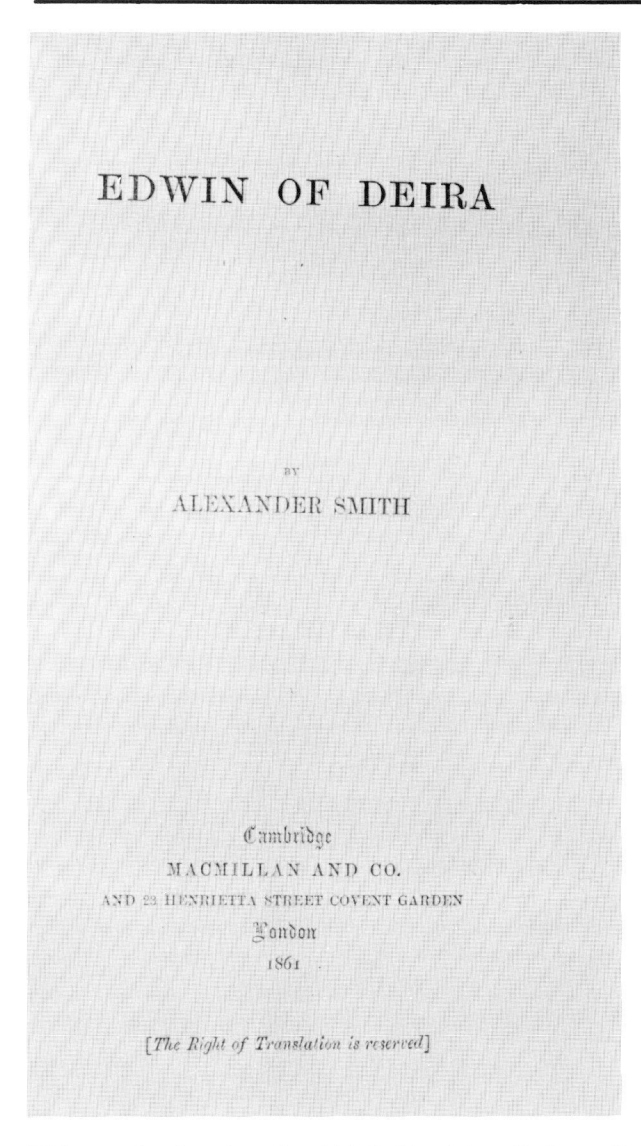

Cambridge
MACMILLAN AND CO.
AND 23 HENRIETTA STREET COVENT GARDEN
London
1861

[The Right of Translation is reserved]

Title page for the volume in which Smith tried to eliminate all traces of "Spasmody" from his poetry (Thomas Cooper Library, University of South Carolina)

Hagart's Household (1865). All of these writings provided a valuable supplement to his salary at the university. His growing family owed more to his prose than to his poetry; but for Smith himself, it must have been a melancholy triumph. Poetry had always been his greatest love.

The essays do, however, reflect the even, quiet tenor of his final years. Gesto Villa, his home at Wardie, allowed him to indulge his love of natural beauty on a daily basis. Many friends visited him there. He wrote small poetic pieces for magazines and the more ambitious "Edinburgh," which remained unfinished at his death. On 20 November 1866 he was forced into bed by gastric fever, complicated with diphtheria. The illness developed into typhoid fever. Smith died in his house at Wardie at 9:00 A.M. on 5 January 1867, just a few days after his thirty-sixth birthday.

Thus, the poetic career of Alexander Smith suffered a radical decline: at first, he was hailed as a great Romantic poet; soon, he was condemned as a Spasmodic poet; now, he is largely forgotten. Aware of his own youthful excesses, Smith had tried to move from a poetry of image building and sensuousness to a poetry of firm structure, realistic sub-

Smith in his last years

Dreamthorpe, was published. But in a sense, the poet had merely assumed another guise, for many of his essays are poetical in rhythm and temperament. His ideal essayist, according to William Sinclair, who edited a collection of his poetry, was "a kind of poet in prose, one who plays with his subject, now in whimsical, now in grave, now in melancholy mood." The poet-essayist is evident again in *A Summer in Skye* (1865) and *Last Leaves* (1868). In the latter, posthumous collection, Smith shows that he had developed into a thoughtful critic of poetry. Most notable among his other works are his insightful preface to his two-volume edition of Burns (1865) and his largely autobiographical novel, *Alfred*

ject matter, and chastened diction, but in the process, he lost his distinctive poetic voice. Nevertheless, just as he was overrated at the start of his career, he is underrated today. "A Life-Drama" contains remarkable passages, and *City Poems* has some fine poems.

Biography:
Thomas Brisbane, *The Early Years of Alexander Smith, Poet and Essayist* (London: Hodder & Stoughton, 1869).

Reference:
Mark A. Weinstein, *William Edmondstoune Aytoun and the Spasmodic Controversy* (New Haven: Yale University Press, 1968).

Charles Swain
(4 January 1801-22 September 1874)

Dorothy W. Collin
University of Western Australia

SELECTED BOOKS: *Metrical Essays on Subjects of History and Imagination* (London: Andover, 1827);
Beauties of the Mind: A Poetical Sketch, with Lays Historical and Romantic (London: Simpkin & Marshall, 1831); revised as *The Mind and Other Poems* (London: Simpkin & Marshall, 1832);
Dryburgh Abbey: A Poem on the Death of Sir Walter Scott (London: Simpkin & Marshall/Manchester: Dewhurst, 1832; Boston: Munroe & Francis, 1833);
Cabinet of Poetry and Romance: Female Portraits from the Writings of Byron and Scott. With Poetical Illustrations (London: Bogue, 1845);
Dramatic Chapters, Poems and Songs (London: Bogue, 1847);
English Melodies (London: Longman, Brown, Green & Longmans, 1849);
Letters of Laura d'Auverne (London: Longman, Brown, Green & Longmans, 1853);
Poems, edited by C. C. Smith (Boston: Roberts, 1854);
Art and Fashion: With other Sketches, Songs and Poems (London: Virtue, 1863);
Songs and Ballads (London: Simpkin & Marshall/Manchester, U.K.: Ireland, 1867);
Selections from Charles Swain, Compiled by His Third Daughter [Clara Swain Dickins] (London: Fifield, 1906).

OTHER: *Engravings from the Works of Henry Liverseege*, verse dedication to Robert Southey and memoir of Henry Liverseege by Swain (London: Hodgson, Boys & Graves, 1835);
"I Cannot Mind My Wheel, Mother," words by Swain, music by George Linley, *Australian Music Magazine*, 33 (1894): 6;
"When the Heart Is Young," words by Swain, music by Dudley Buck (London: Pitman, Hart, n.d.).

Charles Swain wrote a substantial body of poetry, which "received the unanimous eulogiums of the press, both English and American," according to a contemporary reviewer. Southey, then poet laureate, saluted his first volume: "If ever man were born to be a poet, you were." Swain's sensibility was especially alert to musical and visual stimuli, but it was responsive rather than creative. His strength was deemed to lie in "lucid enunciation of healthy truths"; his was "poetry for the million," reflecting the aesthetic norms of his age.

He was born in Manchester, the "Cottonopolis" of England's industrial north. His father, John Swain, was a northerner; his mother, Caroline Nünes de Tavarez Swain, was Dutch. When they died Swain turned to his maternal uncle, Charles Tavaré, a scholarly Manchester dyer, as his "friend in every adversity." He attended school in Manchester under William Johns, the author of a paper on figurative language. John Dalton, the founder of the atomic theory, to whom Swain alludes in "The Mind," lived with Johns's family while Swain was a pupil. At fifteen Swain went to work as a clerk in Tavaré's dye house. By 1821 his letters tell of his life as an actor and dancer in a traveling theatrical company; about this activity nineteenth-century memoirs of Swain are strangely silent. The young man found life outside Manchester stimulating; he admired the gay clothes and fell violently in and out of love—and into debt. In 1826 he returned to Manchester to take up bookselling; on 8 January 1827 he married Ann Glover.

Swain's early poems were published in journals, the first in 1822. His volumes usually included several poems already published in another form; some contained a "principal" poem as well as shorter verses.

"The Mind" was greeted as his chef d'oeuvre; it appeared first in *Beauties of the Mind* (1831), was substantially revised in *The Mind and Other Poems* (1832), and went through three more editions in his lifetime. Swain depicts Mind as "mystery" and as "majesty," capable of sublimity and transcendence yet limited by God. Mind is the holy impulse of the artist; it has seen the "primal wonders," and seems to share in continuing acts of creation:

The fine associations of the Mind,
With their own loveliness, invest each hue
And form of Nature: . . . .

The same "creative spirit" moves through Literature and Science (Swain insisted upon his capitals):

The first conception Dalton's mind made known
Of the Atomic Theory was *then*
A vision beautiful as Fancy's own!
A fine poetic thought worth Milton's pen!

The last of many apostrophes are addressed to the "Cross of Christ" and the "Bethlehem star," beseeching Salvation for "man's majestic faculties"; for "without Redemption, Mind were like the night/Which finds no morn." The Spenserian stanzas are controlled with modest skill; they express a sequence of illustrations which are not wholly discrete but are not interlocked with the complexity and tautness appropriate to such a subject. Except in his dramatic verse, Swain usually wrote in loosely linked stanzas which touch lightly upon an image, leaving connection and implication to the reader. In some of his ballads this understatement works well; in "The Mind" the argument is frail and disjointed. In affirming a comprehensive field for "The Mind" Swain undertook, by implication, to resolve contemporary perceptions of disturbed relationships between man and nature ("Spirit of Science") and within the social order ("Spirit of Commerce"). He fails to solve the dilemma that if the natural elements have been enrolled as "servants" of science, then they can no longer be divinely ordered; hence the appeal to religion echoes rhetorically, not convincingly. That which most pleases in the poem is to be perceived in the imagery rather than in the argument for "mental freedom" and "new worlds"; but the images of water, sun, and Alpine grandeur are in unwittingly ironic contrast with the loss of freedom imposed by expanding technology.

Dryburgh Abbey (1832) is a memorial tribute to Sir Walter Scott, based upon the invention that characters from Scott's novels form his funeral train. It is written in fourteeners; that easily fractured meter holds together remarkably well, and the poem stimulated W. H. C. Hosmer to compose a similar tribute to Fenimore Cooper.

In 1832, apparently, nefarious dealings by a partner caused Swain to seek a new occupation in engraving, in which he worked with illustrators of the quality of George du Maurier. His next volume, *Cabinet of Poetry and Romance* (1845), is a slight collection of "costume poetry": ten poems, each on a female figure in the work of Scott or Byron, and each illustrated by a full-page engraving which emphasizes the remoteness of strong passions from the Victorian reader. *Dramatic Chapters* (1847) opens with a blank verse melodrama in twenty-one chapters, a tale of intrigue, honor besmirched, and vengeance, set in India and England. The blank verse invites recitation in a high declamatory style, and the witches speak in the rhythms of *Macbeth*. The action progresses by chance, and the drama offers no insight into the nature of evil. The title poem of *Letters of Laura d'Auverne* (1853) consists of eight letters from the proud and rebellious Laura, who is reclaimed from mania into proper wifely submission by the soothing ministrations of a saintly mother figure. It is written in stanzas of four rambling fifteen-syllabled lines. Post-Freudian curiosity is aroused by the occasion of Laura's rebellion against her husband's orders: "If I have a passion, Bertha, 'tis to mount the graceful steed,/ Curb his haughty pace elastic, check his hot and dashing speed." Swain prefaced this volume with a motto from the fourteenth-century poet John Gower, "Although I sickness have, and pain . . . ," which alarmed his friends in London.

Swain's fellow citizens admired him for being an amateur, writing within a shelter of domestic felicity; his literary fame seemed to deliver Manchester from the opprobrium of indifference to the arts. In 1852 they presented him with a house, and in 1856 he was awarded a civil list pension of fifty pounds. These favors may have been assistance during a period of ill health as well as tokens of esteem. Swain resented the poet's empty purse, but he enjoyed some literary power: other writers sought favorable reviews from him, and he was proposed for membership in the Royal Society of Literature by his "literary father," William Jerdan of the *Literary Gazette*. Southey accepted the dedication of *The Mind and Other Poems,* and invited him to Greta Hall; in turn Swain sent presents of a patent lamp and engraved cards. Hawthorne met Swain in 1856 and found him shy but amiable, "with much feeling," a man "of pleasant aspect, with black hair, black eyebrows, and bright, dark eyes, . . . limping a little."

Art and Fashion (1863) is named for six dramatic sketches in which painters such as Reynolds and Leonardo da Vinci debate the value the world places on their art. The imagery of "vats" and "actors" in the dialogue between the young Gainsborough and his mother, in which Gainsborough pleads for release from his father's business to "carve out fortune with [his] pallette knife," may be a clue to the circumstances in which Swain left his uncle's dye house.

Swain died at Prestwich Park, his home near Manchester, in 1874. One of his daughters, Clara Swain Dickins, became a poet in her own right; she also edited a volume of selections from her father's poetry after his death.

Swain's poems reflected the taste of his time. He wrote felicitously in a variety of meters, and several lyrics became popular as songs for parlor pianoforte and a female voice of limited range. Violence and evil were distanced in history or myth; immediate human feelings were recreated within the restraints of tranquil domesticity. An undertone of pessimism, possibly associated with his feeling that his early life had been unhappy, is heard in much of his work, which values passive suffering and the reformatory benefits of goodness ("Be kind to each other"). Frequent Wordsworthian echoes in diction and rhythm indicate a nostalgic attraction to a romantic view of nature; his poems are peopled by solitaries, not factory crowds. But the artist needing bread must subdue his art to Fashion:

> She keeps the "World" in busy agitation;
> Shore, quay and bustling wharf, warehouse and shop,
> Teem with her queenly orders. . . .
> . . . .
> . . . let her but speak
> And she will turn thy palette into gold,
> Transmute thy colours into costly gems;
> Patrons, in throngs, shall lounge about thy doors.

Cynicism roughens the sweetness of tone only on the mean bread-and-cheese question. The decline of Swain's reputation at the end of his life may be attributed to his inability to enter into the tensions of his age, as well as to his diffuseness and lack of a crystallizing imagination. A few poems, such as "Perseverance" and "Human Progress," urge a Benthamite resolution of the human dilemma posed by the new technology:

> Glorious thoughts of Education,
>   Holding universal sway!
> . . . .
> Hasten then the People's progress,
>   Ere their last faint hope be gone;
> Teach the Nations, that their interest
>   And the People's good, ARE ONE!

In spite of religious exhortation and moral exemplar his tone falls short of absolute faith. A seam of "*granite* Fate" lies in the way of man's progress. "The prizes in the wheel of chance/Are thrown

Title page for Swain's volume in which great artists of the past discuss the value of art

by some blind elf," and man can only "Work on" in defiance and perseverance.

References:

William E. A. Axon, *The Annals of Manchester: A Chronological Record from the Earliest Times to 1885* (Manchester, U.K.: Heywood, 1886), pp. 193-194, 344-345;

James Dawson, Jr., "Lancashire Poets II: Charles Swain," Manchester *Weekly Times Supplement*, 4 February 1871, pp. 33-34;

John Evans, *Lancashire Authors and Orators: A Series of Literary Sketches of Some of the Principal Authors, Divines, Members of Parliament &c Connected with the County of Lancaster* (London: Houlston & Stoneman, 1850), pp. 260-267;

Nathaniel Hawthorne, *Our Old Home and English Notebooks*, 2 volumes (Boston & New York: Houghton Mifflin, 1912), volume 2, pp. 285-286;

Manchester City News, Notes and Queries (1879): 285, 291-292, 296, 304, 309;

J. H. Nodal and George Milner, "Charles Swain," reviews of *The Mind, Manchester Literary Club Transactions*, 1 (1875): 96-101;

Richard Wright Proctor, *Memorials of Bygone Manchester with Glimpses of the Environs* (Manchester, U.K.: Palmer & Howe/London: Simpkin & Marshall, 1880), pp. 148-231;

Michael A. Smith, "The Charles Swain Collection," *Manchester Review*, 9 (Fall 1962): 323-332;

John Randal Swann, *Lancashire Authors: A Series of Biographical Sketches* (St. Anne's-on-the-Sea, U.K.: Robertson, 1924), pp. 202-203;

J. Cuming Walters, *The Life and Times of Charles Swain, Manchester Quarterly* (January 1922): 29-49.

Papers:
Some of Charles Swain's manuscripts and letters are in the Manchester Central Library.

Sir Henry Taylor
(18 October 1800-27 March 1886)

Lawrence Poston
University of Illinois at Chicago

BOOKS: *Isaac Comnenus: A Play* (London: Murray, 1827);

Philip van Artevelde: A Dramatic Romance. In Two Parts (2 volumes, London: Moxon, 1834; 1 volume, Cambridge & Boston: Munroe, 1835);

The Statesman (London: Longman, Rees, Orme, Brown, Green & Longman, 1836);

Edwin the Fair: An Historical Drama (London: Murray, 1842);

The Eve of the Conquest, and Other Poems (London: Moxon, 1847);

Notes from Life, in Six Essays (London: Murray, 1847); republished as *Notes from Life in Seven Essays* (Boston: Ticknor, Reed & Fields, 1853);

Notes from Books, in Four Essays (London: Murray, 1849);

The Virgin Widow: A Play (London: Longman, Brown, Green & Longmans, 1850);

St. Clement's Eve: A Play (London: Chapman & Hall, 1862);

Crime Considered, in a Letter to the Rt. Hon. W. E. Gladstone (London: Hamilton & Adams, 1868);

Autobiography 1800-75 (London: Privately printed, 1877); republished as *Autobiography of Henry Taylor, 1800-1875*, 2 volumes (London: Longmans, Green, 1885; New York: Harper, 1885);

The Works of Sir Henry Taylor (volumes 1 and 2, London: King, 1877; volumes 3, 4, and 5, London: Kegan Paul, 1878).

Throughout his life Sir Henry Taylor was known as "the Author of *Philip van Artevelde*," a "dramatic romance" in verse first published in 1834 and frequently revised and reprinted in the author's lifetime. Today the play is less read than its preface, an important document in the early Victorian reaction against Byron and Shelley, while *The Statesman* (1836), a gently ironic treatise which owes more to Bacon than to Machiavelli, still enjoys some attention from students of the history of political theory.

Taylor grew up in the vicinity of Durham; he was the third son of George Taylor, whose wife, Eleanor Ashworth Taylor, died in Henry's infancy. George Taylor managed a farm and led his life in bookish solitude, educating his sons himself. Entered as a midshipman in the navy in 1814, Henry was discharged for reasons of health a few months afterward. His father and two brothers, who died within a fortnight of each other shortly after taking up residence in London in 1817, all appear to have been poetically inclined; fragments of their poetry appear in Taylor's *Autobiography* (1877), where he also records writing a now-lost juvenile poem influenced by Byron. In 1822 he sent William Gifford a short article on Moore's Irish Melodies; the article was published in the *Quarterly Review* that October, followed by articles on Lord John Russell and Walter Savage Landor in the same periodical and on "Recent Poetical Plagiarisms and Imitations" in the *London Magazine*. The latter article, drawing on Byron for some of its illustrations, doubtless reflects the gradual diminution of Taylor's earlier "enthusiastic admiration" for the older poet, an admiration which in later years Taylor dismissed as "morally stultifying." Over the next few years Wordsworth and Southey, both of whom he met and with whom he corresponded, replaced Byron altogether in his pantheon of literary heroes.

Partly because of Gifford's friendship, in 1824 Taylor received a clerkship in the Colonial Office, where he rapidly acquired influence as a moderate on the abolition of the slave laws. He was to remain in the position until 1872, although, following a severe asthma attack in 1859, he was permitted to do his work at home. The effect of his government job on his career as a poet is manifested primarily in the political themes of his dramas. The first of these, *Isaac Comnenus*, attracted little attention upon its publication in 1827, save for a flattering notice by Southey in the *Quarterly Review*. The play shows Taylor's fondness for a historical period remote in time and turbulent in its factionalism; his dislike of religious fanaticism; and his interest in protagonists capable of decisive action but too contemplative and solitary to endure for long the burdens of political power—thus Isaac gives the crown to his brother Alexis and is subsequently killed by Theodora, the daughter of the emperor he has deposed. In his *Autobiography*, Taylor commented that the neglect of the play on its first appearance left him in no hurry to have another work published. Soon after, at Southey's suggestion, he turned to the subject of Philip van Artevelde, "with little reference to success in publication, with hardly any anticipation of it, and with a disposition, therefore, to work only in favourable moods and when it gave me present pleasure." Seven years elapsed before the appearance of *Philip van Artevelde* in 1834.

The character of Philip is the ideal combination of energy and equanimity which Taylor drew from Bacon's *De Negotis* (1597) and which he described in 1836 in *The Statesman*, his own treatise on statecraft. The play also reflects the attitude toward the study of history which Taylor outlined in *The Statesman*, namely that "a knowledge of particular epochs, connected with peculiarity and revolution in the state of societies, and especially with modern revolutions," was to be preferred over the summary histories of Hume and Gibbon. Too long to be acted (although Macready essayed a staging of a condensed version which ran for six nights in 1847), the play is divided into two parts. The first part traces Philip's rise to power in Bruges, where he leads a rebellion of oppressed citizens against the despotic earl of Flanders; the second part describes his decline and defeat at the hands of the French. Drawn from the historians Froissart and Barante, the figure of Philip is alternately commanding and touching; he retains a dignity to the end of the play, despite some erosion of his moral character, and in two or three of his soliloquies there is genuine poetic power. Taylor never again equaled this performance, and the play, like his other historical dramas, suffers from an uncertain wedding of the political and domestic spheres. *Philip van Artevelde* enjoyed continuing respect in the nineteenth century, but has attracted only a few admirers in the twentieth—the most notable being Sir Winston Churchill.

The preface to *Philip van Artevelde,* however, has been justly seen as an important document in early Victorian poetic criticism. Taylor discusses Byron's lack of philosophical intellect and Shelley's more powerful but essentially irrational imagination, and asserts that "I would have no man depress his imagination, but I would have him raise his reason to be its equipoise." Taylor's insistence on careful dramatic construction, though dismissed by some contemporaries as pedantic, attracted approbation at home and abroad; discussing the preface in the *Revue des deux mondes* in 1847, E.-D. Forgues described Taylor as a poet who occupied a prominent rank among his British contemporaries.

Over the next several years, Taylor considered writing dramas on Becket, Charles of Anjou, and (at Macaulay's suggestion) Mary, Queen of Scots, before settling on an obscure chapter of Anglo-Saxon history. In the meantime he married Theodosia Spring-Rice, the daughter of a Colonial Office colleague, on 17 October 1839, after an engagement which had been briefly broken off on grounds of alleged religious unorthodoxy; Taylor did keep a private journal during this period in which he described his inability to arrive fully and confidently at a belief in the central doctrines of Christianity. His marriage brought him in touch with his bride's cousin, Aubrey de Vere, whose poetic career was closely entwined with Taylor's during the remainder of the latter's long life.

Edwin the Fair (1842), Taylor's third play, is prefaced by the statement that the poet's intention is to show how "the spirit of religious enthusiasm," however laudable in its initial impulse, "commonly passes into a spirit of ecclesiastic discord." Taylor, at work on the play by 1839, had told Southey that the

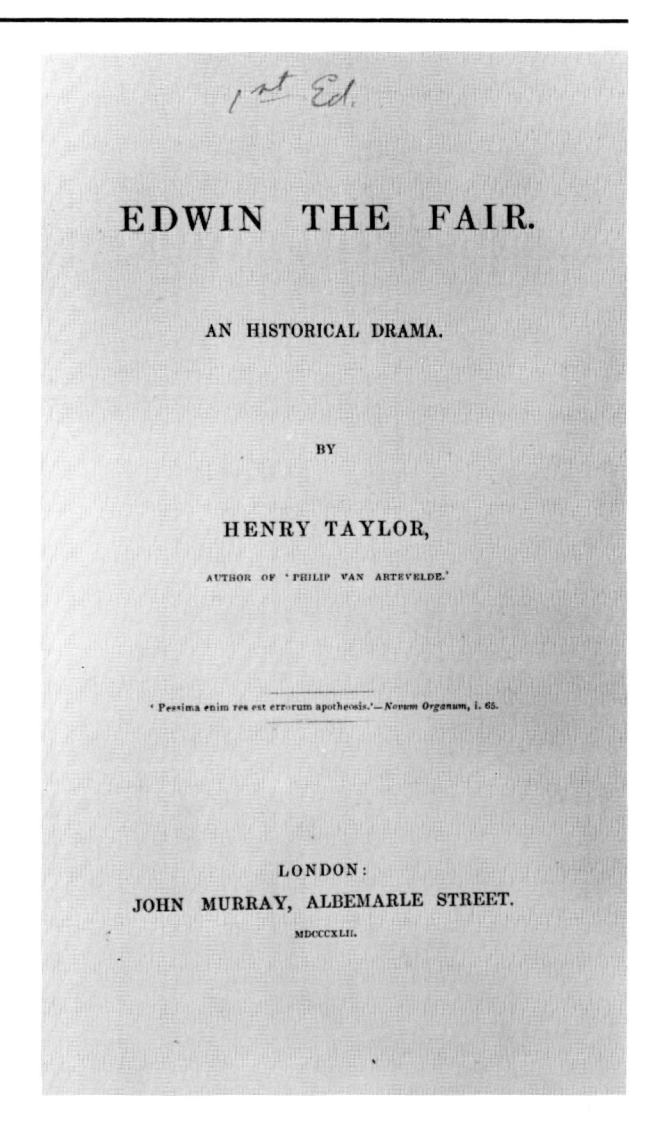

Title page for Taylor's third play in verse (Thomas Cooper Library, University of South Carolina)

work would "want a predominating *persona*" and would depend for its interest on unity of action; lacking such a persona, however, it fails. The play is dominated by the fanatical Dunstan to the extent that it is dominated by anyone; Edwin is too passive, too tenuously rendered, to serve as the focal point of interest. There is little reason to challenge Wordsworth's complaint that "the subject is most unfortunately chosen, and still more unfortunately treated," and in later years Taylor himself was an equally harsh critic.

Soon after the publication of *Edwin the Fair,* Taylor's health broke down; after a winter in Italy with de Vere, he settled at Mortlake in 1844. He emulated his hesitant heroes by declining an offer to succeed his good friend Sir James Stephen as undersecretary at the Colonial Office, partly because of scruples at having encouraged Stephen's retirement. The following December he began his next play, *The Virgin Widow,* a neo-Elizabethan romantic comedy which owes something to Beaumont and Fletcher; it was not published until 1850. Of more interest is the collection of shorter poems, *The Eve of the Conquest, and Other Poems* (1847), which suggests that Taylor could have made more of his genuine, if modest, lyrical gifts. The lines entitled "In Remembrance of the Honorable Edward Ernest Villiers" and "Heroism in the Shade" achieve a measured dignity which is at once reminiscent of Wordsworth's "Character of the Happy Warrior" and anticipatory of Tennyson's Wellington ode. "Lago Varese" is a graceful, if derivative, reworking of the basic situation in Wordsworth's "The Solitary Reaper," and "The Lynnburn" is an autobiographical meditation—perhaps the most personally revealing of Taylor's poems—which still repays perusal. Throughout the volume the poet exhibits a practiced ear and a gift for throwing out an occasional arresting line or phrase; lacking the philosophical complexity of Wordsworth's major poems, the shorter pieces perhaps more often recall some of the domestic idylls of Southey.

In 1853 Taylor moved to a house at Sheen built from his wife's plans, and in 1861 he purchased a summer residence at Bournemouth, where he later settled. In 1862 he was awarded a D.C.L. from Oxford, and he was knighted in 1869. An uneventful home life was broken by the death of his eldest son in 1870, an event to which Taylor devotes a single pained sentence in his *Autobiography*. Taylor's last verse drama, *St. Clement's Eve* (1862), to some extent recaptures the ground lost in the preceding two. As in *Edwin the Fair,* the focal point of interest is a divided kingdom under a weak monarch. The portraits of Charles VI, Louis Duke of Orleans, and Jean Duke of Burgundy are well drawn; but once again the play suffers from an imperfect fusion of political and domestic interests. In his preface, Taylor describes his intention as a historical dramatist in terms which aptly summarize his entire career in that genre: "The fidelity of a historian is not to be expected of a dramatist. Some transposition of events and compression of time have been necessary . . . and without some variation of detail truth to art must have been sacrificed to historic truth in a larger measure than is demanded for the chief ends which historic truth is designed to subserve. . . . But under these conditions . . . my endeavour has been to represent faithfully the characters of the principal persons and the temper of the times." Like *Philip van Artevelde,* the drama draws heavily on Barante, to whom Taylor had returned during a sequence of nocturnal asthmatic attacks in 1859, in the course of which he read some thirty volumes of the historian's works.

Taylor's renunciation of poetry in his later years seems to have been due to a recognition that his poetic power was ebbing. In his *Autobiography* he wrote that Wordsworth "had continued the exercise of his poetic faculty beyond the age at which it is often desirable either for a poet or for his fame that it should still strive to be active and productive." Elsewhere he described his own mind as "slow" and "brooding," and he regarded old age as preeminently the time of revision rather than original composition—a time when, as he had written in an earlier essay, "The Life Poetic," the poet's house might be put in order. He spent his declining years with frequent recourse to the company of Charles

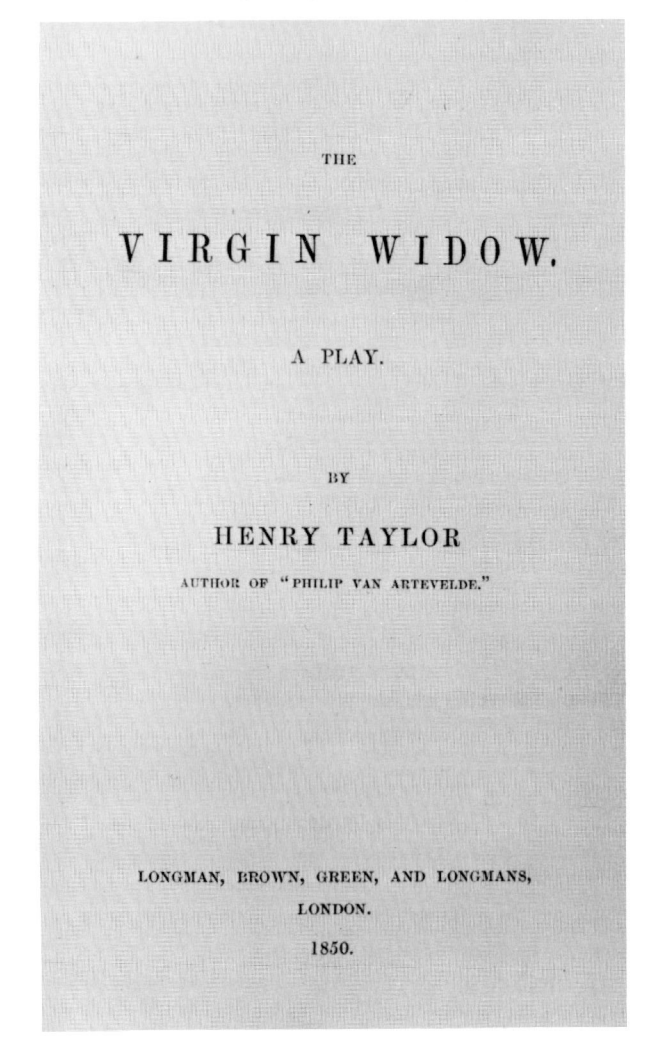

Title page for Taylor's neo-Elizabethan romantic comedy (Thomas Cooper Library, University of South Carolina)

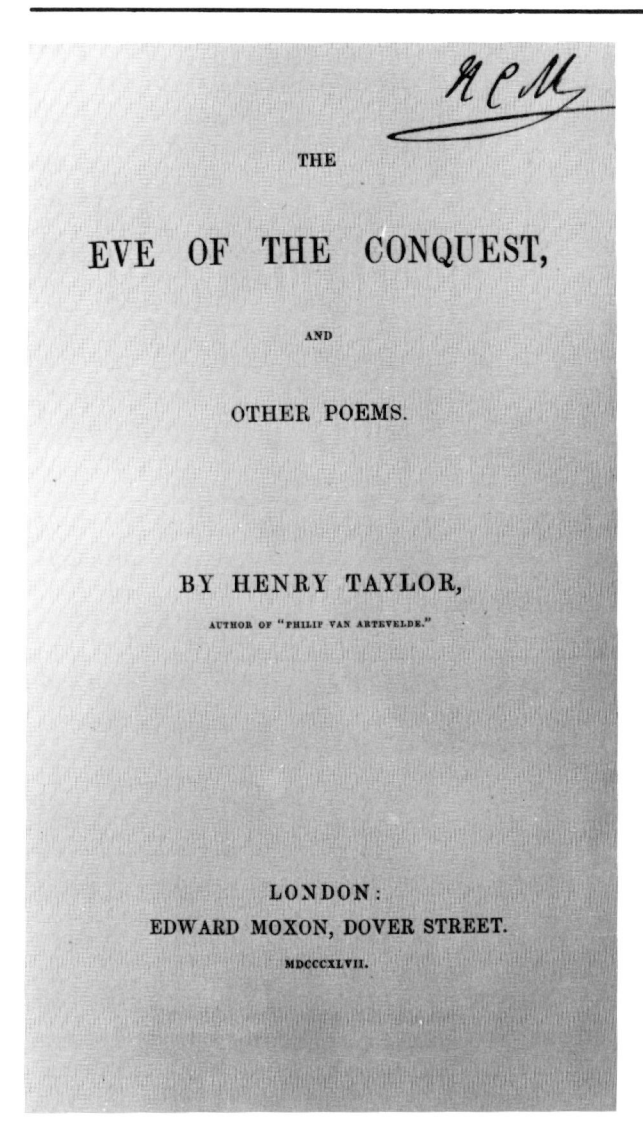

Title page for Taylor's only volume of short, lyrical poems (Thomas Cooper Library, University of South Carolina)

and Julia Cameron and Alfred and Emily Tennyson. He died in Bournemouth on 27 March 1886.

Una Taylor described her father's mind as "clear, just, and tolerant, wholly indifferent in its calm anchorage to the veering winds of popular opinion," and his friend Sir Francis Hastings Doyle wrote in his *Reminiscences and Opinions* (1886) that "jealousy and vanity were unknown to him." Although the Taylor who emerges through the memoirs of Doyle and de Vere is a trifle chilly and forbidding, he seems to have enjoyed a singularly tranquil family life and an affectionate relationship with his children. His significance in the history of nineteenth-century English poetry, diminished by time, is now primarily that of a critic, due to the preface to *Philip van Artevelde* and to two essays in the *Quarterly Review* in 1834 and 1841 (subsequently collected) which are among the ablest defenses of Wordsworth to appear during the latter's lifetime. Of the dramas, only *Philip van Artevelde*, a consistently competent work, deserves rereading. Both persistent ill health and a scrupulous concern for detail seem to have precluded greater productivity. In "The Life Poetic," Taylor wrote that any poet who wished "to take the highest rank in his art" ought, to a moderate degree, to be "mixed up with the affairs of life.... His speculations should emanate from facts and events, and his poetry should have its roots in the common earth." Though such a mixture does not place Taylor himself among poets of the highest rank, it does describe the dominant effect of his work.

Letters:
Correspondence of Sir Henry Taylor, edited by Edward Dowden (London: Longmans, Green, 1888).

References:
Lascelles Abercrombie, "Sir Henry Taylor," in *The Eighteen-Sixties*, edited by John Drinkwater (Cambridge: Cambridge University Press, 1932), pp. 1-19;

Aubrey de Vere, *Recollections* (London & New York: Arnold, 1897), pp. 145-180;

de Vere, "Sir Henry Taylor's Poetry," *Essays, Chiefly on Poetry*, 2 volumes (London & New York: Macmillan, 1887), volume 1, pp. 265-314; volume 2, pp. 1-99;

Sir Francis Hastings Doyle, *Reminiscences and Opinions, 1813-1885* (London: Longmans, Green, 1886), pp. 408-409;

Walter E. Houghton and G. Robert Stange, *Victorian Poetry and Poetics*, 2nd edition (Boston: Houghton Mifflin, 1968), pp. 861-865;

Robert E. Lovelace, "Wordsworth and the Early Victorians: A Study of His Influence and Reputation, 1830-1860," Ph.D. Dissertation, University of Wisconsin, 1951, pp. 184-210;

Lawrence Poston, "*Philip van Artevelde*: The Poetry and Politics of Equipoise," *Victorian Poetry*, 18 (1980): 383-391;

Poston, "Wordsworth among the Victorians: The Case of Sir Henry Taylor," *Studies in Romanticism*, 17 (1978): 293-305;

Leo Silberman, introduction to *The Statesman* (Cambridge: Heffer, 1927), pp. xi-lii;

Una Taylor, *Guests and Memories: Annals of a Seaside Villa* (Oxford: Humphrey Milford, Oxford University Press, 1924).

Alfred Tennyson

BIRTH: Somersby, Lincolnshire, 6 August 1809, to the Reverend George Clayton Tennyson and Elizabeth Fytche Tennyson.

EDUCATION: Trinity College, Cambridge, 1827-1831.

MARRIAGE: 13 June 1850 to Emily Sellwood; children: Hallam and Lionel.

DEATH: Blackdown, Sussex, 6 October 1892.

BOOKS: *Poems by Two Brothers,* anonymous, by Tennyson and Frederick and Charles Tennyson (London: Simpkin & Marshall/Louth, U.K.: Jackson, 1827);
Timbuctoo: A Poem (in Blank Verse) Which Obtained the Chancellor's Gold Medal at the Cambridge Commencement (Cambridge: Smith, 1829);
Poems, Chiefly Lyrical (London: Effingham Wilson, 1830);
Poems (London: Moxon, 1832);
Poems, 2 volumes (London: Moxon, 1842; Boston: Ticknor, 1842);
The Princess: A Medley (London: Moxon, 1847; Boston: Ticknor, 1848);
In Memoriam, anonymous (London: Moxon, 1850; Boston: Ticknor, Reed & Fields, 1850);
Ode on the Death of the Duke of Wellington (London: Moxon, 1852);
Maud, and Other Poems (London: Moxon, 1855; Boston: Ticknor & Fields, 1855);
Idylls of the King (London: Moxon, 1859; Boston: Ticknor & Fields, 1859);
Enoch Arden, etc. (London: Moxon, 1864; Boston: Ticknor & Fields, 1865);
The Holy Grail and Other Poems (London: Moxon, 1869; Boston: Fields, Osgood, 1870);
Gareth and Lynette Etc. (London: Strahan, 1872; Boston: Osgood, 1872);
Queen Mary: A Drama (London: King, 1875; Boston: Osgood, 1875);
Harold: A Drama (London: King, 1876; Boston: Osgood, 1877);
Ballads and Other Poems (London: Kegan Paul, 1880; Boston: Osgood, 1880);

Alfred Tennyson (Tennyson Research Centre)

Becket (London: Macmillan, 1884; New York: Dodd, Mead, 1894);
The Cup and The Falcon (London: Macmillan, 1884; New York: Macmillan, 1884);
Tiresias and Other Poems (London: Macmillan, 1885);
Locksley Hall Sixty Years After, Etc. (London & New York: Macmillan, 1886);
Demeter and Other Poems (London & New York: Macmillan, 1889);
The Foresters, Robin Hood and Maid Marian (New York & London: Macmillan, 1892);
The Death of Oenone, Akbar's Dream, and Other Poems (London: Macmillan, 1892; New York: Macmillan, 1892);
The Poems of Tennyson, edited by Christopher Ricks (London: Longmans, Green, 1969).

More than any other Victorian writer, Tennyson has seemed the embodiment of his age, both to his contemporaries and to modern readers. In his own day he was said to be—with Queen Victoria and Gladstone—one of the three most famous living persons, a reputation no other poet writing in English has ever had. As official poetic spokesman for the reign of Victoria, he felt called upon to celebrate a quickly changing industrial and mercantile world with which he felt little in common, for his deepest sympathies were called forth by an unaltered rural England; the conflict between what he thought of as his duty to society and his allegiance to the eternal beauty of nature seems peculiarly Victorian. Even his most severe critics have always recognized his lyric gift for sound and cadence, a gift probably unequaled in the history of English poetry, but one so absolute that it has sometimes been mistaken for mere facility.

The lurid history of Tennyson's family is interesting in itself, but some knowledge of it is also essential for understanding the recurrence in his poetry of themes of madness, murder, avarice, miserliness, social climbing, marriages arranged for profit instead of love, and estrangements between families and friends.

Alfred Tennyson was born in the depths of Lincolnshire, the fourth son of the twelve children of the rector of Somersby, George Clayton Tennyson, a cultivated but embittered clergyman who took out his disappointment on his wife Elizabeth and his brood of children—on at least one occasion threatening to kill Alfred's elder brother Frederick. The rector had been pushed into the church by his own father, also named George, a rich and ambitious country solicitor intent on founding a great family dynasty that would rise above their modest origins into a place among the English aristocracy. Old Mr. Tennyson, aware that his eldest son, the rector, was unpromising material for the family struggle upward, made his second son, his favorite child, his chief heir. Tennyson's father, who had a strong streak of mental instability, reacted to his virtual disinheritance by taking to drink and drugs, making the home atmosphere so sour that the family spoke of the "black blood" of the Tennysons.

Part of the family heritage was a strain of epilepsy, a disease then thought to be brought on by sexual excess and therefore shameful. One of Tennyson's brothers was confined to an insane asylum most of his life, another had recurrent bouts of addiction to drugs, a third had to be put into a mental home because of his alcoholism, another was intermittently confined and died relatively young. Of the rest of the eleven children who reached maturity, all had at least one severe mental break-

Tennyson's parents, the Reverend George Clayton Tennyson and Elizabeth Fytche Tennyson (Tennyson Research Centre)

Somersby rectory, home of the Tennysons (Tennyson Research Centre)

down. During the first half of his life Alfred thought that he had inherited epilepsy from his father and that it was responsible for the trances into which he occasionally fell until he was well over forty years old.

It was in part to escape from the unhappy environment of Somersby rectory that Alfred began writing poetry long before he was sent to school, as did most of his talented brothers and sisters. All his life he used writing as a way of taking his mind from his troubles. One peculiar aspect of his method of composition was set, too, while he was still a boy: he would make up phrases or discrete lines as he walked, and store them in his memory until he had a proper setting for them. As this practice suggests, his primary consideration was more often rhythm and language than discursive meaning.

When he was not quite eighteen his first volume of poetry, *Poems by Two Brothers* (1827), was published. Alfred Tennyson wrote the major part of the volume, although it also contained poems by his two elder brothers, Frederick and Charles. It is a remarkable book for so young a poet, displaying great virtuosity of versification and the prodigality of imagery that was to mark his later works; but it is also derivative in its ideas, many of which came from his reading in his father's library. Few copies were sold, and there were only two brief reviews, but its publication confirmed Tennyson's determination to devote his life to poetry.

Most of Tennyson's early education was under the direction of his father, although he spent nearly four unhappy years at a nearby grammar school. His departure in 1827 to join his elder brothers at Trinity College, Cambridge, was due more to a desire to escape from Somersby than to a desire to undertake serious academic work. At Trinity he was living for the first time among young men of his own age who knew little of the problems that had beset him for so long; he was delighted to make new friends; he was extraordinarily handsome, intelligent, humorous, and gifted at impersonation; and soon he was at the center of an admiring group of young men interested in poetry and conversation. It was probably the happiest period of his life.

In part it was the urging of his friends, in part the insistence of his father that led the normally indolent Tennyson to retailor an old poem on the subject of Armageddon and submit it in the coming skepticism of the twentieth century about such matters, it is almost certain that there was nothing homosexual about the friendship: definitely not on a conscious level and probably not on any other. Indeed, it was surely the very absence of such overtones that made the warmth of their feelings acceptable to both men, and allowed them to express those feelings so freely.

Also in 1829 both Hallam and Tennyson became members of the secret society known as the Apostles, a group of roughly a dozen undergraduates who were usually regarded as the elite of the entire university. Tennyson's name has ever since been linked with the society, but the truth is that he dropped out of it after only a few meetings, although he retained his closeness with the other members and might even be said to have remained the poetic center of the group. The affection and acceptance he felt from his friends brought both a new warmth to Tennyson's personality and an increasing sensuousness to the poetry he was con-

A sketch of Alfred (left) and Charles Tennyson by their younger brother Arthur, indicating the gloomy atmosphere at the rectory brought on by their father's mental instability (Tennyson Research Centre)

petition for the chancellor's gold medal for poetry; the announced subject was Timbuctoo. Tennyson's *Timbuctoo* is a strange poem, as the process of its creation would suggest. He uses the legendary city for a consideration of the relative validity of imagination and objective reality; Timbuctoo takes its magic from the mind of man, but it can turn to dust at the touch of the mundane. It is far from a successful poem, but it shows how deeply engaged its author was with the Romantic conception of poetry. Whatever its shortcomings, it won the chancellor's prize in the summer of 1829.

Probably more important than its success in the competition was the fact that the submission of the poem brought Tennyson into contact with the Trinity undergraduate usually regarded as the most brilliant man of his Cambridge generation, Arthur Henry Hallam. This was the beginning of four years of warm friendship between the two men, in some ways the most intense emotional experience of Tennyson's life. Despite the too know-

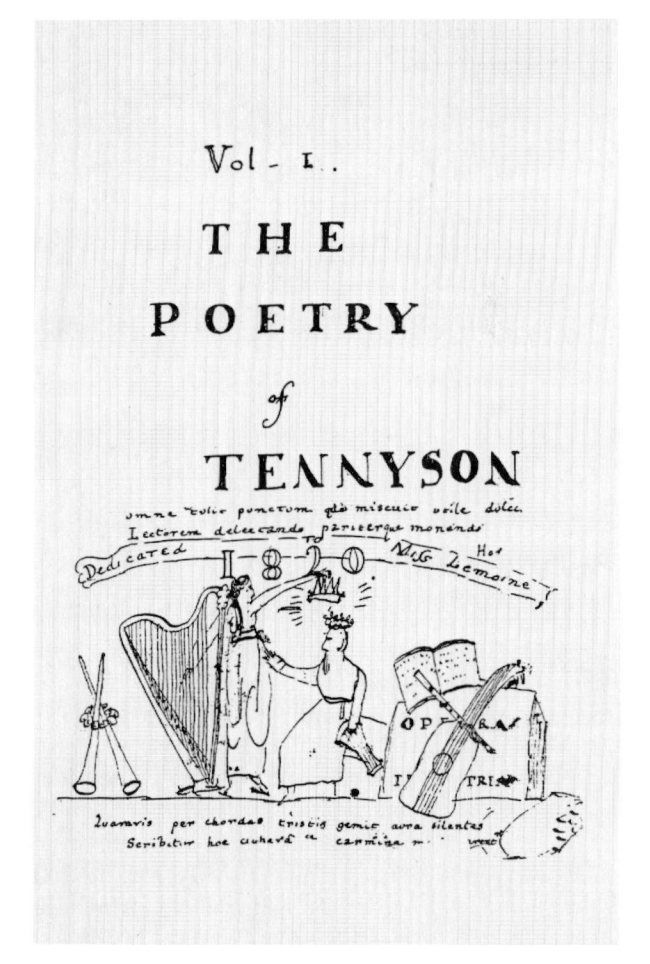

Title page for a notebook volume of Latin poetry, composed and illustrated by Tennyson at about age twelve (Anderson Galleries, 10 December 1936)

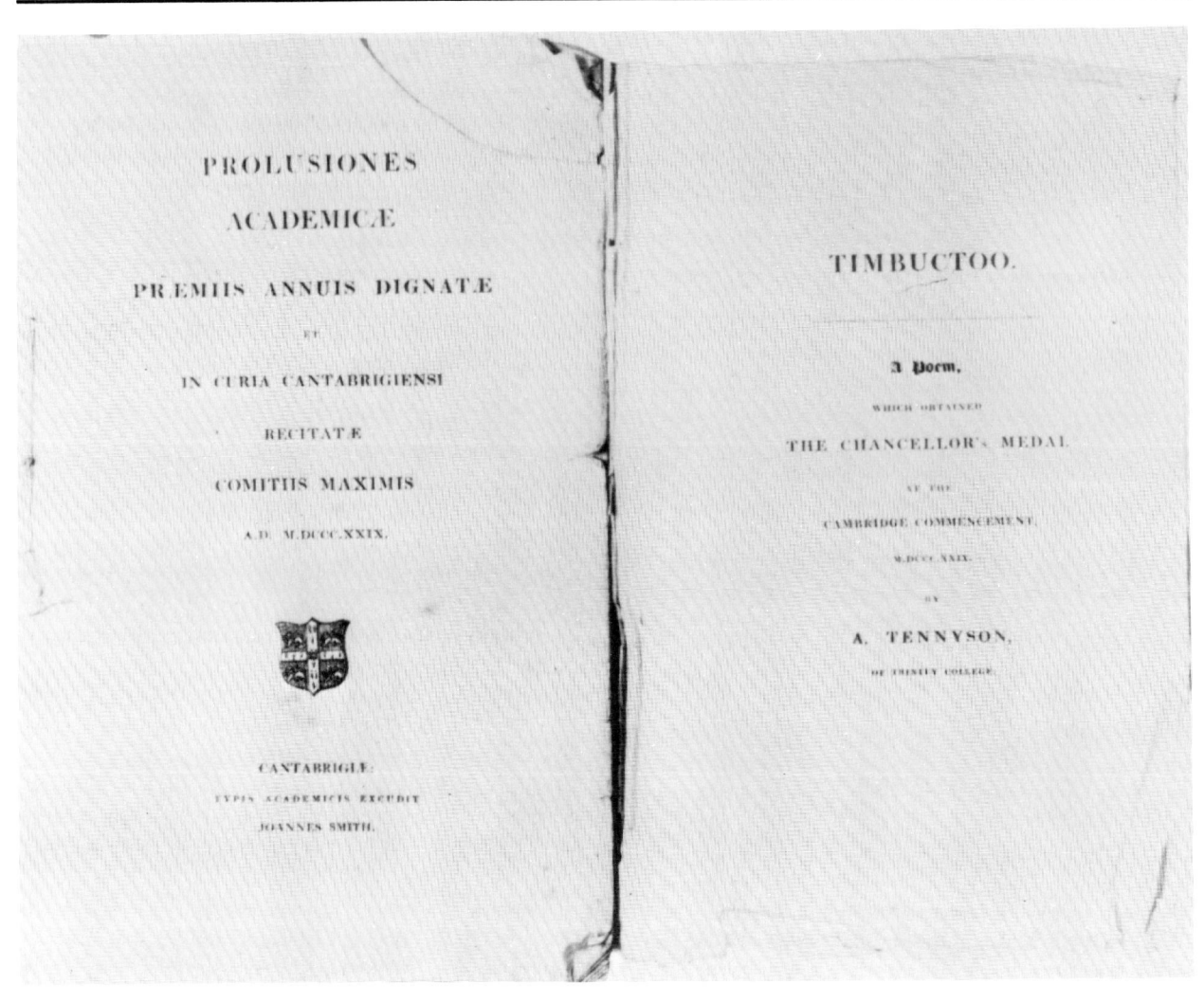

Title pages for 1829 book of Cambridge University prize poems and for Tennyson's poem which won the chancellor's gold medal (Tennyson Research Centre)

stantly writing when he was supposed to be devoting his time to his studies.

Hallam, too, wrote poetry, and the two friends planned on having their work published together; but at the last moment Hallam's father, perhaps worried by some lyrics Arthur had written to a young lady with whom he had been in love, forbade him to include his poems. *Poems, Chiefly Lyrical* appeared in June 1830. The standard of the poems in the volume is uneven, and it has the self-centered, introspective quality that one might expect of the work of a twenty-year-old; but scattered among the other poems that would be forgotten if they had been written by someone else are several fine ones such as "The Kraken," "Ode to Memory," and—above all—"Mariana," which is the first of Tennyson's works to demonstrate fully his brilliant use of objects and landscapes to convey a state of strong emotion. That poem alone would be enough to justify the entire volume.

The reviews appeared slowly, but they were generally favorable. Both Tennyson and Hallam thought they should have come out more quickly, however, and Hallam reviewed the volume himself in the *Englishman's Magazine,* making up in his critical enthusiasm for having dropped out of being published with his friend.

The friendship between the young men was knotted even more tightly when Hallam fell in love with Tennyson's younger sister, Emily, while on a visit to Somersby. Since they were both so young, there was no chance of their marrying for some time, and meanwhile Hallam had to finish his undergraduate years at Trinity. All the Tennyson

Title page for the volume of poems on which Tennyson and Arthur Henry Hallam were to have collaborated; Hallam was forced to withdraw by his father.

brothers and sisters, as well as their mother, seem to have taken instantly to Hallam, but he and Emily prudently said nothing of their love to either of their fathers. Dr. Tennyson was absent on the Continent most of the time, sent there by his father and his brother in the hope that he might get over his drinking and manage Somersby parish sensibly. Arthur's father, the distinguished historian Henry Hallam, had plans for his son that did not include marriage to the daughter of an obscure and alcoholic country clergyman.

In the summer of 1830 Tennyson and Hallam were involved in a harebrained scheme to take money and secret messages to revolutionaries plotting the overthrow of the Spanish king. Tennyson's political enthusiasm was considerably cooler than Hallam's, but he was glad to make his first trip abroad. They went through France to the Pyrenees, meeting the revolutionaries at the Spanish border. Even Hallam's idealistic fervor scarcely survived the disillusionment of realizing that the men they met were animated by motives as selfish as those of the royalist party against whom they were rebelling. Nonetheless, in the Pyrenees Tennyson marked out a new dimension of the metaphorical landscape that had already shown itself in "Mariana," and for the rest of his life the mountains remained as a model for the classical scenery that so often formed the backdrop of his poetry. The Pyrenees generated such marvelous poems as "Oenone," which he began writing there; "The Lotos-Eaters," which was inspired by a waterfall in the mountains; and "The Eagle," which was born from the sight of the great birds circling above them as they climbed in the rocks. Above all, the little village of Cauteretz and the valley in which it lay remained more emotionally charged for Tennyson than any other place on earth. He came again and again to walk in the valley, and it provided him with imagery until his death more than sixty years later.

Early the following year Tennyson had to leave Cambridge because of the death of his father. Dr. Tennyson had totally deteriorated mentally and physically, and he left little but debts to his family, although he had enjoyed a good income and a large allowance from his father. Tennyson's grandfather naturally felt that it was hardly worth his while to keep Alfred and his two elder brothers at Cambridge when it was only too apparent that they were profiting little from their studies and showed no promise of ever being able to support themselves. The allowance he gave the family was generous enough, but it was not intended to support three idle grandsons at the university. Worse still, neither he nor Dr. Tennyson's brother Charles, who was now clearly marked out as the heir to his fortune, attended the rector's funeral, making the division in the family even more apparent. The widow and her eleven children were so improvident that they seemed incapable of living on the allowance, and they were certainly not able to support themselves otherwise.

This began a very bitter period of Tennyson's life. An annual gift of £100 from an aunt allowed him to live in a modest manner, but he refused his grandfather's offer to help him find a place in the church if he would be ordained. Tennyson said then, as he said all his life, that poetry was to be his career, however bleak the prospect of his ever earning a living. His third volume of poetry was published at the end of 1832, although the title page was dated 1833.

The 1832 *Poems* was a great step forward poetically and included the first versions of some of Tennyson's greatest works, such as "The Lady of Shalott," "The Palace of Art," "A Dream of Fair Women," "The Hesperides," and three wonderful poems conceived in the Pyrenees, "Oenone," "The Lotos-Eaters," and "Mariana in the South." The volume is notable for its consideration of the opposed attractions of isolated poetic creativity and social involvement; the former usually turns out to be the more attractive course, since it reflected Tennyson's own concerns, but the poems demonstrate as well his feeling of estrangement in being cut off from his contemporaries by the demands of his art.

The reviews of the volume were almost universally damning. One of the worst was written by Edward Bulwer (later Bulwer-Lytton), who was a friend of Tennyson's uncle Charles. The most vicious review, however, was written for the *Quarterly Review* by John Wilson Croker, who was proud that his brutal notice of *Endymion* years before was said to have been one of the chief causes of the death of Keats. Croker numbered Tennyson among the Cockney poets who imitated Keats, and he made veiled insinuations about the lack of masculinity of both Tennyson and his poems. Tennyson, who was abnormally thin-skinned about criticism, found some comfort in the steady affection and support of Hallam and the other Apostles.

Hallam and Emily Tennyson had by then made their engagement public knowledge, but they saw no way of marrying for a long time: the senior Hallam refused to increase his son's allowance sufficiently to support both of them; and when Arthur wrote to Emily's grandfather, he was answered in the third person with the indication that old Mr. Tennyson had no intention of giving them any more money. By the summer of 1833, Hallam's father had somewhat grudgingly accepted the engagement, but still without offering further financial help. The protracted unhappiness of both Arthur and Emily rubbed off on the whole Tennyson family.

That autumn, in what was meant as a gesture of gratitude and reconciliation to his father, Arthur Hallam accompanied him to the Continent. In Vienna Arthur died suddenly of apoplexy resulting from a congenital malformation of the brain. Emily Tennyson fell ill for nearly a year; the effects of Hallam's death were less apparent externally in Alfred but were perhaps even more catastrophic than for his sister.

The combination of the deaths of his father and his best friend, the brutal reviews of his poems, his conviction that both he and his family were in desperate poverty, his feelings of isolation in the depths of the country, and his ill-concealed fears that he might become a victim of epilepsy, madness, alcohol, and drugs, as others in his family had, or even that he might die like Hallam, was more than enough to upset the always fragile balance of Tennyson's emotions. "I suffered what seemed to me to shatter all my life so that I desired to die rather than to live," he said of that period. For a time he determined to leave England, and for ten years he refused to have any of his poetry published, since he was convinced that the world had no place for it.

Although he was adamant about not having it published, Tennyson continued to write poetry; and he did so even more single-mindedly than before. Hallam's death nearly crushed him, but it also provided the stimulus for a great outburst of some of the finest poems he ever wrote, many of them con-

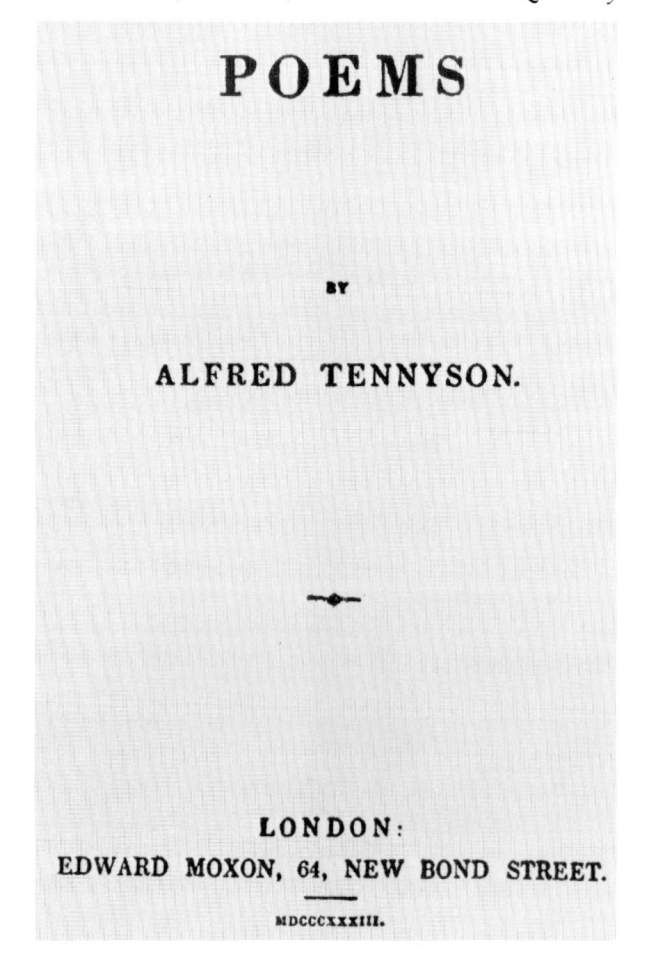

Title page for Tennyson's third volume of poetry

nected overtly or implicitly with the loss of his friend. "Ulysses," "Morte d'Arthur," "Tithonus," "Tiresias," "Break, break, break," and "Oh! that 'twere possible" all owe their inception to the passion of grief he felt but carefully hid from his intimates. Most important was the group of random individual poems he began writing about Hallam's death and his own feeling of loneliness in the universe as a result of it; the first of these "elegies," written in four-line stanzas of iambic tetrameter, was begun within two or three days of his hearing the news of Hallam's death. He continued to write them for seventeen years before collecting them to form what is perhaps the greatest of Victorian poems, *In Memoriam* (1850).

The death of his grandfather in 1835 confirmed Tennyson's fear of poverty, for the larger part of Mr. Tennyson's fortune went to Alfred's uncle Charles, who promptly changed his name to Tennyson d'Eyncourt and set about rebuilding his father's house into a grand Romantic castle, with the expectation of receiving a peerage to cap the family's climb to eminence. His hopes were never realized, but his great house, Bayons Manor, became a model for the home of the vulgar, nouveau-riche characters in many of Tennyson's narrative poems, such as *Maud* (1855). Charles Tennyson d'Eyncourt's inheritance was the final wedge driving the two branches of the family apart; he and his nephew were never reconciled, but Alfred's dislike of him was probably even more influential than admiration would have been in keeping Charles as an immediate influence in so much of Alfred's poetry.

The details of Tennyson's romantic attachments in the years after Hallam's death are unclear, but he apparently had at least a flirtation with Rosa Baring, the pretty young daughter of a great banking family, some of whose members had rented Harrington Hall, a large house near Somersby. Tennyson wrote a dozen or so poems to her, but it is improbable that his affections were deeply involved. The poems suggest that her position made it impossible for him to be a serious suitor to her, but she may have been more important to him as a symbol of wealth and unavailability than as a flesh-and-blood young woman. Certainly, he seems not to have been crushed when she married another man.

In 1836, however, at the age of twenty-seven, Tennyson became seriously involved with Emily Sellwood, who was four years younger than he. By the following year they considered themselves engaged. Emily had been a friend of Tennyson's sisters, and one of her own sisters married his next

Rosa Baring, the wealthy young woman with whom Tennyson was romantically involved in the early 1830s (Tennyson Research Centre)

older (and favorite) brother, Charles. Most of the correspondence between Tennyson and Emily has been destroyed, but from what remains it is clear that she was very much in love with him, although he apparently withheld himself somewhat in spite of his affection for her. He was worried about not having enough money to marry, but he seems also to have been much concerned with the trances into which he was still falling, which he thought were connected with the epilepsy from which other members of the family suffered. To marry, he thought, would mean passing on the disease to any children he might father.

In the summer of 1840 Tennyson broke off all relations with Emily. She continued to think of herself as engaged to him, but he abandoned any hope of marriage, either then or in the future. To spare her further embarrassment, the story was put out that her father had forbidden their marriage because of Tennyson's poverty; this legend has been perpetuated in the present century.

Through the second half of the 1830s and most of the 1840s Tennyson lived an unsettled, nomadic life. Nominally he made his home with his mother and his unmarried brothers and sisters, who continued to rent Somersby rectory until 1837, then moved successively to Essex and to Kent; but he was as often to be found in London, staying in cheap hotels or cadging a bed from friends who lived there. He was lonely and despondent, and he drank and smoked far too much. Many of those who had known him for years believed that his poetic inspiration had failed him and that his great early promise would remain unfulfilled; but this was to neglect the fact that when all else went wrong, he clung to the composition of poetry. He was steadily accumulating a backlog of unpublished poems, and he continued adding to his "elegies" to Hallam's memory.

One of the friends who worried away at Tennyson to have his work published was Edward FitzGerald, who loved both the poems and their author, although he was too stubborn to hide his feelings when a particular poem failed to win his approval. "Old Fitz" nagged at Tennyson, who in the spring of 1842 agreed to break his ten long years of silence.

The two volumes of *Poems* (1842) were destined to be the best-loved books Tennyson ever wrote. The first volume was made up of radically revised versions of the best poems from the 1832 volume, most of them in the form in which they are now known. The second volume contained new poems, among them some of those inspired by Hallam's death, as well as poems of widely varying styles, including the dramatic monologue "St. Simeon Stylites"; a group of Authurian poems; his first attempt to deal with rampant sexuality, "The Vision of Sin"; and the implicitly autobiographical narrative "Locksley Hall," dealing with the evils of worldly marriages, which was to become one of his most popular poems during his lifetime.

After the reception of the 1832 *Poems* and after being unpublished for so long, Tennyson was naturally apprehensive about the reviews of the new poems; but nearly all were enthusiastic, making it clear that he was now the foremost poet of his generation. Edgar Allan Poe wrote guardedly, "I am not sure that Tennyson is not the greatest of poets."

But the bad luck that Tennyson seemed to invite struck again just as the favorable reviews were appearing. Two years earlier, expecting to make a fortune, he had invested his patrimony in a scheme to manufacture cheap wood carvings by steam-driven machines. In 1842 the scheme crashed, taking with it nearly everything that Tennyson owned, some £4,000. The shock set back any progress he had made in his emotional state over the past ten years, and in 1843 he had to go into a "hydropathic" establishment for seven months of treatment in the hope of curing his deep melancholia.

This was the first of several stays in "hydros" during the next five years. Copious applications of water inside and out, constant wrappings in cold, wet sheets, and enforced abstinence from tobacco and alcohol seemed to help him during each stay; but he would soon ruin any beneficial effects by his careless life once he had left the establishment, resuming his drinking and smoking to the despair of his friends. A rather more effective form of treatment was the £2,000 he received from an insurance policy at the death of the organizer of the wood-carving scheme. In 1845 he was granted a government civil list pension of £200 a year in recognition of both his poetic achievements and his apparent financial need. Tennyson was in reality released from having to worry about money, but the habit of years was too much for him; for the rest of his life he complained constantly of his poverty, although his poetry had made him a rich man by the time of his death. In 1845 the betterment of his fortunes brought with it no effort to resume his engagement to Emily Sellwood, showing that it was not financial want that kept them apart.

The Princess, which was published on Christmas 1847, was Tennyson's first attempt at a long narrative poem, a form that tempted him most of his life although it was less congenial to him temperamentally than the lyric. The ostensible theme is the education of women and the establishment of female colleges, but it is clear that Tennyson's interest in the subject runs out before the poem does, so that it gradually shifts to the consideration of what he thought of as the unnatural attempt of men and women to fulfill identical roles in society; only as the hero becomes more overtly masculine and the heroine takes on the traditional attributes of women is there a chance for their happiness. Considerably more successful than the main narrative are the thematic lyrics that Tennyson inserted into the action to show the growth of passion and between the cantos to indicate that the natural end of the sexes is to be parents of another generation in a thoroughly traditional manner. The subtitle, *A Medley,* was his way of anticipating charges of inconsistency in the structure of the poem. As always, the blank verse in which the main part of the poem is written is superb, and the interpolated lyrics include some of his most splendid short poems, such as "Come down, O maid," "Now sleeps the crimson petal," "Sweet and low," "The splendour falls on castle walls," and

Manuscript for three stanzas of "The Princess," written by Tennyson for presentation to a friend, and containing variations from the published version (Anderson Galleries, 5 April 1934)

"Tears, idle tears." The emotion of these lyrics does more than the straight narrative to convey the forward movement of the entire poem, and their brief perfection indicates well enough that his genius lay there rather than in the descriptions of persons and their actions; this was not, however, a lesson that Tennyson himself was capable of learning. The seriousness with which the reviewers wrote of the poem was adequate recognition of his importance, but many of them found the central question of feminine education to be insufficiently considered. The first edition was quickly sold out, and subsequent editions appeared almost every year for several decades.

Tennyson's last stay in a hydropathic hospital was in the summer of 1848, and though he was not completely cured of his illness, he was reassured about its nature. The doctor in charge apparently made a new diagnosis of his troubles, telling him that what he suffered from was not epilepsy but merely a form of gout that prefaced its attacks by a stimulation of the imagination that is very like the "aura" that often warns epileptics of the onset of a seizure. The trances that he had thought were mild epileptic fits were in fact only flashes of illumination over which he had no reason to worry. Had it been in Tennyson's nature to rejoice, he could have done so at this time, for there was no longer any reason for him to fear marriage, paternity, or the transmission of disease to his offspring. The habits of a lifetime, however, were too ingrained for him to shake them off at once. The real measure of his relief at being rid of his old fear of epilepsy is that he soon set about writing further sections to be inserted into new editions of *The Princess,* in which the hero is said to be the victim of "weird seizures" inherited from his family; at first he is terrified when he falls into trances, but he is at last released from the malady when he falls in love with Princess Ida. Not only this poem, but his three other major long works, *In Memoriam, Maud,* and *Idylls of the King* (1859), all deal in part with the meaning of trances, which are at first frightening but then are revealed to be pathways to the extrasensory, to be rejoiced over rather than feared. After his death Tennyson's wife and son burned many of his most personal letters, and in what remains there is little reference to his trances or his recovery from them; but the poems bear quiet testimony to the immense weight he must have felt lifted from his shoulders when he needed no longer worry about epilepsy.

Tennyson's luck at last seemed to be on the upturn. At the beginning of 1849 he received a large advance from his publisher with the idea that he would assemble and polish his "elegies" on Hallam, to be published as a whole poem. Before the year was over he had resumed communication with Emily Sellwood, and by the beginning of 1850 he was speaking confidently of marrying. On 1 June *In Memoriam* was published, and less than two weeks later he and Emily were married quietly at Shiplake Church. Improbable as it might seem for a man to whom little but bad fortune had come, both events were total successes.

The new Mrs. Tennyson was thirty-seven years old and in delicate health, but she was a woman of iron determination; she took over the running of the externals of her husband's life, freeing him from the practical details at which he was so inept. Her taste was conventional, and she may have curbed his religious questioning, his mild bohemianism, and the exuberance and experimentation of his poetry, but she also brought a kind of peace to his life without which he would not have been able to write at all. There is some evidence that Tennyson occasionally chafed at the responsibilities of marriage and paternity and at the loss of the vagrant freedom he had known, but there is nothing to indicate that he ever regretted

Tennyson's wife, Emily Sellwood Tennyson, with their sons Hallam (left) and Lionel (Tennyson Research Centre)

his choice. It was probably not a particularly passionate marriage, but it was full of tenderness and affection. Three sons were born, of whom two, Hallam and Lionel, survived.

After a protracted honeymoon of some four months in the Lake Country, Tennyson returned to the south of England to find that the publication of *In Memoriam* had made him, without question, the major living poet. It had appeared anonymously, but his authorship was an open secret.

This vast poem (nearly 3,000 lines) is divided into 131 sections, with prologue and epilogue; the size is appropriate for what it undertakes, since in coming to terms with loss, grief, and the growth of consolation, it touches on most of the intellectual issues at the center of the Victorian consciousness: religion, immortality, geology, evolution, the relation of the intellect to the unconscious, the place of art in a workaday world, the individual versus society, the relation of man to nature, and as many others. The poem grew out of Tennyson's personal grief, but it attempts to speak for all men rather than for one. The structure often seems wayward, for in T. S. Eliot's famous phrase, it has "only the unity and continuity of a diary" instead of the clear direction of a philosophical statement. It was bound to be somewhat irregular since it was composed with no regard for either chronology or continuity and was for years not intended to be published. The vacillation in mood of the finished poem, however, is neither haphazard nor capricious, for it is put together to show the wild swoops between depression and elation that grief brings, the hesitant gropings toward philosophical justification of bereavement, the tentative little darts of conviction that may precede a settled belief in a beneficent world. It is intensely personal, but one must also believe Tennyson in his reiterated assertions that it was a poem, not the record of his own grief about Hallam; in short, that his own feelings had prompted the poem but were not necessarily accurately recorded in it.

To the most perceptive of the Victorians (and to modern readers) the poem was moving for its dramatic recreation of a mind indisposed to deal with the problems of contemporary life, and for the sheer beauty of so many of its sections. To a more naive, and far larger, group of readers it was a work of real utility, to be read like the Bible as a manual of consolation, and it is surely to that group that the poem owed its almost unbelievable popularity. Edition followed edition, and each brought Tennyson more fame and greater fortune.

Wordsworth, who had been poet laureate for

Title page for the anonymously published tribute to Arthur Hallam that made Tennyson famous

seven years, had died in the spring of 1850. By the time Tennyson returned from his honeymoon, it must have seemed to many a foregone conclusion that he would be nominated as Wordsworth's successor. Tennyson knew that the prince consort, who advised the queen on such matters, was an admirer of his, and the night before receiving the letter offering the post, he dreamed that the prince kissed him on the cheek, and that he responded, "Very kind but very German." Early the following year he was presented to the queen as her poet laureate and kissed her hand, wearing the borrowed and too-tight court clothes that Wordsworth had worn for the same purpose on the occasion of his own presentation. The straining court suit was emblematic of the passing of the office from the greatest of

Romantic poets to the greatest of the Victorians.

At the end of November 1853 Alfred and Emily Tennyson moved into the secluded big house on the Isle of Wight known as Farringford, which has ever since been associated with his name. Emily loved the remoteness and the fact that their clocks were not even synchronized with those elsewhere, but her husband sometimes had a recurrence of his old longing to be rattling around London. Most of the time, however, he was content to walk on the great chalk cliffs overlooking the sea, composing his poems as he tramped, their rhythm often deriving from his heavy tread.

It was perhaps his very isolation that made him so interested in the Crimean War, for he read the newspapers voraciously in order to keep current with world affairs. "The Charge of the Light Brigade" was one result in 1854 of his fascination with the heroism of that unpopular war. *Maud,* in which the hero redeems his misspent life by volunteering for service in the Crimea, was published the following year. In spite of that somewhat conventional-sounding conclusion, the poem is Tennyson's most experimental, for it tells a thoroughly dramatic narrative in self-contained lyrics; the reader must fill in the interstices of the story by inference. The lyrics are not even like one another in scansion, length, or style. The narrator of the poem is an unnamed young man whose father has committed suicide after being swindled by his partner. The son then falls in love with Maud, the daughter of the peccant partner; but since he is poor and she is rich, there is no possibility of their marrying. When he is bullied by her brother, he kills him in a duel. After Maud also dies the narrator goes temporarily insane; he finally realizes that he has been as selfish and evil as the society on which he has blamed his bad fortune. In an attempt to make up for his wasted life, he goes to the Crimea, with his subsequent death hinted at in the last section of the poem.

As always, Tennyson is not at his best in narrative, but the melodramatic content of the plot finally matters little in comparison with the startling originality of his attempt to extend the limits of lyricism in order to make it do the work of narrative and drama, to capitalize on his own apparently circumscribed gift in order to include social criticism, contemporary history, and moral comment in the lyric. In part it must have been a deliberate answer to those who complained that his art was too self-absorbed and negligent of the world around him.

The experimental quality of *Maud* has made it

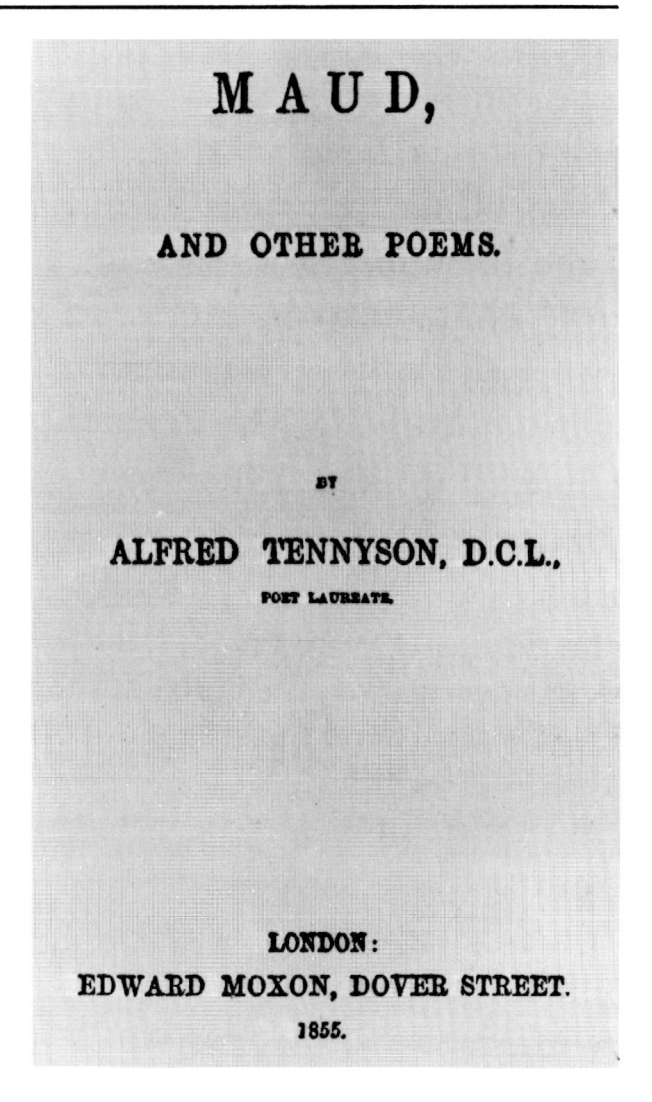

Title page for the volume whose title poem is Tennyson's most experimental work

one of the most interesting of his poems to modern critics, but to Tennyson's contemporaries it seemed so unlike what they expected from the author of *In Memoriam* that they could neither understand nor love it. An age that was not accustomed to distinguishing between narrator and poet found it almost impossible not to believe that Tennyson was directly portraying his own thoughts and personal history in those of the central figure. The result was the worst critical abuse that Tennyson received after that directed at the 1832 *Poems.* One reviewer went so far as to say that *Maud* had one extra vowel in the title, and that it made no difference which was to be deleted. Tennyson's predictable response was to become defensive about the poem and to read it aloud at every opportunity in order to show how badly misunderstood both poem and poet were. Since it was a performance that took between two and three hours, the capitulation to its beauty that he often won thereby was probably due as much to weariness on the part of the hearer as to intellectual or aesthetic persuasion.

Ever since the publication of the 1842 *Poems* Tennyson had been something of a lion in literary circles, but after he became poet laureate he was equally in demand with society hostesses, who were more interested in his fame than in his poetic genius. For the rest of his life Tennyson was to be caught awkwardly between being unable to resist the flattery implied by their attentions and the knowledge that their admiration of him usually sprang from the wrong reasons. It was difficult for him to refuse invitations, but he felt subconsciously impelled when he accepted them to behave gruffly, even rudely, in order to demonstrate his independence. His wife's bad health usually made it impossible for her to accompany him, which probably increased his awkwardness. It all brought out the least attractive side of a fundamentally shy man, whose paroxysms of inability to deal with social situations made him seem selfish, bad-mannered, and assertive. In order to smooth his ruffled feathers, his hostesses and his friends would resort to heavy flattery, which only made him appear more arrogant. One of the saddest aspects of Tennyson's life is that his growing fame was almost in inverse ratio to his ability to maintain intimacy with others, so that by the end of his life he was a basically lonely man. All the innate charm, humor, intelligence, and liveliness were still there, but it took great understanding and patience on the part of his friends to bring them into the open.

Idylls of the King was published in 1859; it contained only four ("Enid," "Vivien," "Elaine," and "Guinevere") of the eventual twelve idylls. The matter of Arthur and Camelot had obsessed Tennyson since boyhood, and over the years it became a receptacle into which he poured his deepening feelings of the desecration of decency and of ancient English ideals by the gradual corruption of accepted morality. The decay of the Round Table came increasingly to seem to him an apt symbol of the decay of nineteenth-century England. It was no accident that the first full-length idyll had been "Morte d'Arthur," which ultimately became—with small additions—the final idyll in the completed cycle. It had been written at the time of the death of Arthur Hallam, who seemed to Tennyson "Ideal manhood closed in real man," as he wrote of King Arthur; no doubt both Hallam's character and Tennyson's grief at his death lent color to the entire poem.

Like *The Princess, In Memoriam,* and *Maud,* the idylls were an assembly of poetry composed over a long time—in this case nearly half a century in all, for they were not finished until 1874 and were not all published until 1885. Taken collectively, they certainly constitute Tennyson's most ambitious poem, but not all critics would agree that the poem's success is equal to its intentions.

For a modern reader, long accustomed to the Arthurian legend by plays, musicals, films, and popular books, it is hard to realize that the story was relatively unfamiliar when Tennyson wrote. He worked hard at his preparation, reading most of the available sources, going to Wales and the west country of England to see the actual places connected with Arthur, and even learning sufficient Welsh to read some of the original documents. "There is no grander subject in the world," he wrote, and he meant his state of readiness to be equal to the loftiness of his themes, which explains in part why it took him so long to write the entire poem.

Although Tennyson always thought of the idylls as allegorical (his word was "parabolic"), he refused to make literal identifications between incidents, characters, or situations in the poems and what they stood for, except to indicate generally that by King Arthur he meant the soul and that the disintegration of the court and the Round Table showed the disruptive effect of the passions.

In all the time that he worked on the idylls Tennyson constantly refined their structure—by framing the main action between the coming of Arthur and his death, by repetition of verbal motifs, by making the incidents of the plot follow the course of the year from spring to winter, by making different idylls act as parallels or contrasts to each other, by trying to integrate the whole poem as closely as an extended musical composition. Considering how long he worked on the poem, the result is amazingly successful, although perhaps more so when the poem is represented schematically than in the actual experience of reading it.

As always, the imagery of the poem is superb. It is less successful in characterization and speech, which are often stilted and finally seem more Victorian than Arthurian. Even Arthur, who is meant to be the firm, heroic center of the poem, occasionally seems merely weak at the loss of his wife and the decay of the court rather than nobly forgiving. Individual idylls such as "The Last Tournament" and "Gareth and Lynette" have considerable narrative force, but there is an almost fatal lack of forward movement in the poem as a whole.

The reviewers were divided between those who thought it a worthy companion of Malory and those who found it more playacting than drama, with the costumes failing to disguise Tennyson's contemporaries and their concerns. The division between critics still maintains that split of opinion, although it is probably taken more seriously in the 1980s than it was earlier in the twentieth century. Whether that attitude will last is impossible to predict.

In spite of the adverse reviews and the reservations of many of Tennyson's fellow poets, the sales of *Idylls of the King* in 1859 were enough to gladden the heart of any poet: 40,000 copies were printed initially and within a week or two more than a quarter of these were already sold; it was a pattern that was repeated with each succeeding volume as they appeared during the following decades.

The death of his admirer Prince Albert in 1861 prompted Tennyson to write a dedication to the *Idylls of the King* in his memory. The prince had taken an interest in Tennyson's poetry ever since 1847, when it is believed that he called on Tennyson when the poet was ill. He had written to ask for Tennyson's autograph in his own copy of *Idylls of the King*, and he had come over unannounced from Osborne, the royal residence on the Isle of Wight, to call on Tennyson at Farringford. In spite of the brevity of their acquaintance and its formality, Tennyson had been much moved by the prince's kindness and friendliness, and he had greatly admired the way Albert behaved in the difficult role of consort.

Four months after Albert's death the queen invited Tennyson to Osborne for an informal visit. Tennyson went with considerable trepidation, fearful that he might in some way transgress court etiquette, but his obvious shyness helped to make the visit a great success. It became the first of many occasions on which he visited the queen, and a genuine affection grew up on both sides. The queen treated Tennyson with what was great informality by her reserved standards, so that the relationship between monarch and laureate was probably more intimate that it has ever been before or since. She had an untutored and naive love of poetry, and he felt deep veneration for the throne; above all, each was a simple and unassuming person beneath a carapace of apparent arrogance, and each recognized the true simplicity of the other. It was almost certainly the queen's feeling for Tennyson that lay behind the unprecedented offer of a baronetcy four times beginning in 1865; Tennyson each time turned it down for himself while asking that if possible it be given to Hallam, his elder son, after his own death.

His extraordinary popularity was obvious in other ways as well. He was given honorary doctorates by Oxford and Edinburgh universities; Cambridge three times invited him to accept an honorary degree, but he modestly declined. The greatest men in the country competed for the honor of meeting and entertaining him. Thomas Carlyle and his wife had been good friends of Tennyson's since the 1840s, and Tennyson felt free to drop in on them unannounced, at last even having his own pipe kept for him in a convenient niche in the garden wall. He had met Robert Browning at about the same time as he had met Carlyle, and though the two greatest of Victorian poets always felt a certain

Title page for the first of Tennyson's volumes based on the Arthurian legends

Photograph of Tennyson taken by his Isle of Wight neighbor Julia Margaret Cameron in 1865. Tennyson called it the "Dirty Monk" portrait (Tennyson Research Centre).

reserve about each other's works, their mutual generosity in acknowledging genius was exemplary; Browning, like most of the friends Tennyson made in his maturity, was never an intimate, but their respect for each other never faltered. Tennyson was somewhat lukewarm in his response to the overtures of friendship made by Charles Dickens, even after he had stood as godfather for one of Dickens's sons. It is tempting to think that some of his reserve stemmed from an uneasy recognition of the similarity of their features that occasionally led to their being confused, particularly in photographs or portraits, which can hardly have been welcome to Tennyson's self-esteem.

Tennyson maintained a reluctant closeness with William Gladstone for nearly sixty years. It was generally accepted in London society that if a dinner was given for one of them, the other ought to be invited. Yet the truth was that they were never on an easy footing, and though they worked hard at being polite to each other, their edginess occasionally flared into unpleasantness before others. It is probable that some of their difficulties came from their friendship with Arthur Hallam when they were young men; Gladstone had been Hallam's best friend at Eton and felt left out after Hallam met Tennyson. To the end of their days the prime minister and the poet laureate were mildly jealous of their respective places in Hallam's affections so many years before. The feeling certainly colored Gladstone's reactions to Tennyson's poetry (which he occasionally reviewed), and nothing he could do ever made Tennyson trust Gladstone as a politician. The relationship hardly reflects well on either man.

Almost as if he felt that his position as laureate and the most popular serious poet in the English-speaking world were not enough, Tennyson deliberately tried to widen his appeal by speaking more directly to the common people of the country about the primary emotions and affections that he felt he shared with them. The most immediate result of his wish to be "the people's poet" was the 1864 volume whose title poem was "Enoch Arden" and which also contained another long narrative poem, "Aylmer's Field." These are full of the kinds of magnificent language and imagery that no other Victorian poet could have hoped to produce, but the sentiments occasionally seem easy and secondhand. The volume also contained a number of much more experimental translations and metrical innovations, as well as such wonderful lyrics as "In the Valley of

William Ewart Gladstone, with whom Tennyson maintained an uneasy relationship for many years (Tennyson Research Centre)

Cauteretz," which was written thirty-one years after he and Hallam had wandered through that beautiful countryside, and "Tithonus." There was no question that Tennyson was still a very great poet, but his ambition to be more than a lyricist often blinded him to his own limitations. His hope of becoming "the people's poet" was triumphantly realized; the volume had the largest sales of any during his lifetime. More than 40,000 copies were sold immediately after publication, and in the first year he made more than £8,000 from it, a sum equal to the income of many of the richest men in England.

Popularity of the kind he had earned had its innate disadvantages, and Tennyson was beginning to discover them as he was followed in the streets of London by admirers; at Farringford he complained of the total lack of privacy when the park walls were lined with craning tourists who sometimes even came up to the house and peered into the windows to watch the family at their meals. In 1867 he built a second house, Aldworth, on the southern slopes of Blackdown, a high hill near Haslemere, where the house was not visible except from miles away. Curiously, the house resembles a smaller version of Bayons Manor, the much-hated sham castle his uncle Charles Tennyson d'Eyncourt had built in the Lincolnshire wolds. To his contemporaries it appeared unnecessarily grand for a second house, even slightly pretentious; today it seems emblematic of the seriousness with which Tennyson had come to regard his own public position in Victorian England, which was not his most attractive aspect. For the rest of his life he was to divide his time between Farringford and Aldworth, just as he divided his work between the essentially private, intimate lyricism at which he had always excelled and the poetry in which he felt obliged to speak to his countrymen on more public matters.

In the years between 1874 and 1882 Tennyson made yet another attempt to widen his poetic horizons. As the premier poet of England, he had been compared—probably inevitably—to Shakespeare, and he determined to write for the stage as his great predecessor had done. At the age of sixty-five he wrote his first play as a kind of continuation of Shakespeare's historical dramas. *Queen Mary* (1875) was produced in 1876 by Henry Irving, the foremost actor on the English stage; Irving himself played the main male role. It had been necessary to hack the play to a fraction of its original inordinate length in order to play it in one evening, and the result was hardly more dramatic than the original long version had been. In spite of the initial curios-

Aldworth, Tennyson's home on a high hill near Haslemere (National Monument Record)

ity about Tennyson's first play, the audiences soon dwindled, and it was withdrawn after twenty-three performances; that was, however, a more respectable run than it would be today.

His next play, *Harold* (1876), about the early English king of that name, failed to find a producer during Tennyson's lifetime, although he had conscientiously worked at making it less sprawling than its predecessor. *Becket* (1884), finished in 1879, was a study of the martyred archbishop of Canterbury; Tennyson found the subject so fascinating that he once more wrote at length, in this case making a play considerably longer than an uncut *Hamlet*. *Becket* was, not surprisingly, not produced until 1893, the year after Tennyson's death. Following *Becket* in quick succession came *The Falcon* and *The Cup* (published together in 1884), *The Foresters* (1892), and *The Promise of May* (published in *Locksley Hall Sixty Years After, Etc.* in 1886), all of which abandoned the attempt to follow Shakespeare. On the stage only *The Cup* had any success, and that was in part due to the lavish settings and the acting of Irving and Ellen Terry. After the failure of *The Promise of May* (a rustic melodrama and the only prose work in his long career), Tennyson at last accepted the fact that

> Crossing the Bar.
>
> Sunset & evening star,
>   And one clear call for me.
> And may there be no moaning of the bar,
>   When I put out to sea,
>
> But such a tide as moving seems asleep,
>   Too full for sound & foam,
> When that which drew from out the boundless deep
>   Turns again home.
>
> Twilight & evening bell,
>   And after that the dark!
> And may there be no sadness of farewell,
>   When I embark!
>
> For tho' from out our bourne of Time & Place
>   The flood may bear me far,
> I hope to see my Pilot face to face,
>   When I have crost the bar.

Manuscript for the poem which Tennyson asked to be placed at the end of all editions of his poetry (Tennyson Research Centre)

nearly a decade of his life had been wasted in an experiment that had totally gone amiss. Today no one would read even the best of the plays, *Queen Mary* and *Becket,* if they were not the work of Tennyson. They betray the fact that he was not profound at understanding the characters of other persons or in writing speech that had the sound of conversation. Even the flashes of metaphor fail to redeem this reckless, admirable, but totally failed attempt to fit Tennyson's genius to another medium.

The climax of public recognition of Tennyson's achievement came in 1883 when Gladstone offered him a peerage. After a few days of consideration Tennyson accepted. Surprisingly, his first thought was to change his name to Baron Tennyson d'Eyncourt in an echo of his uncle's ambition, but he was discouraged by the College of Arms and finally settled on Baron Tennyson of Aldworth and Freshwater. Since he was nearly seventy-five when he assumed the title, he took little part in the activities of the House of Lords, but the appropriateness of his being ennobled was generally acknowledged. It was the first time in history that a man had been given a title for his services to poetry. Tennyson claimed that he took the peerage on behalf of all literature, not as personal recognition.

The rest of his life was spent in the glow of love that the public occasionally gives to a distinguished man who has reached a great age. He continued to write poetry nearly as assiduously as he had when young, and though some of it lacked the freshness of youth, there were occasional masterpieces that mocked the passing years. He had always felt what he once described as the "passion of the past," a longing for the days that had gone, either the great ages of earlier history or the more immediate past of his own life, and his poetic genius always had something nostalgic, even elegiac, at its heart. Many of the finest poems of his old age were written in memory of his friends as they died off, leaving him increasingly alone.

Of all the blows of mortality, the cruelest was the death from "jungle fever" of his younger son, Lionel, who had fallen ill in India and was returning by ship to England. Lionel died in the Red Sea, and his body was put into the waves "Beneath a hard Arabian moon/And alien stars." It took Tennyson two years to recover his equanimity sufficiently to write the poem from which those lines are taken: the magnificent elegy dedicated "To the Marquis of Dufferin and Ava," who had been Lionel's host in India. Hauntingly, the poem is written in the same meter as *In Memoriam,* that masterpiece of his youth celebrating the death of another beloved young man, Arthur Hallam. There were also fine elegies to his brother Charles, to FitzGerald, and to several others, indicating the love he had felt for old friends even when he was frequently unable to express it adequately in person.

Lionel's death was the climax of Tennyson's sense of loss, and from that time until his own death he became increasingly troubled in his search for the proofs of immortality, even experimenting with spiritualism. His poetry of this period is saturated with the desperation of the search, sometimes in questioning, sometimes in dogmatic assertion that scarcely hides the fear underlying it. Yet there were moments of serenity, reflected in such beautiful poems as "Demeter and Persephone," in which he uses the classical legend as a herald of the truth of Christianity. And there was, of course, "Crossing the Bar," written in a few minutes as he sailed across the narrow band of water separating the Isle of Wight from the mainland. At his request, this grave little prayer of simple faith has ever since been placed at the end of editions of his poetry.

Tennyson continued to compose poetry during the last two years of his life; when he was too weak to write it down, his son or his wife would copy it for him. When he had a good day, he was still able to take long walks or even to venture to London. The year before his death he wrote a simple and delicate little poem, "June Heather and Bracken," as an offering of love to his faithful wife; to her he dedicated his last volume of poetry, which was not published until a fortnight after his death. His friends noticed that he was gentler than he had been for years, and he made quiet reparation to some of those whom he had offended by thoughtless brusquerie.

On 6 October 1892, an hour or so after midnight, he died at Aldworth with the moon streaming in at the window overlooking the Sussex Weald, his finger holding open a volume of Shakespeare, his family surrounding the bed. A week later he was buried in the Poets' Corner of Westminster Abbey, near the graves of Browning and Chaucer. To most of England it seemed as if an era in poetry had passed, a divide as great as that a decade later when Queen Victoria died.

One of the most levelheaded summations of what he had meant to his contemporaries was made by Edmund Gosse on the occasion of Tennyson's eightieth birthday: "He is wise and full of intelligence; but in mere intellectual capacity or attainment it is probable that there are many who excel him. This, then, is not the direction in which his greatness asserts itself. He has not headed a single

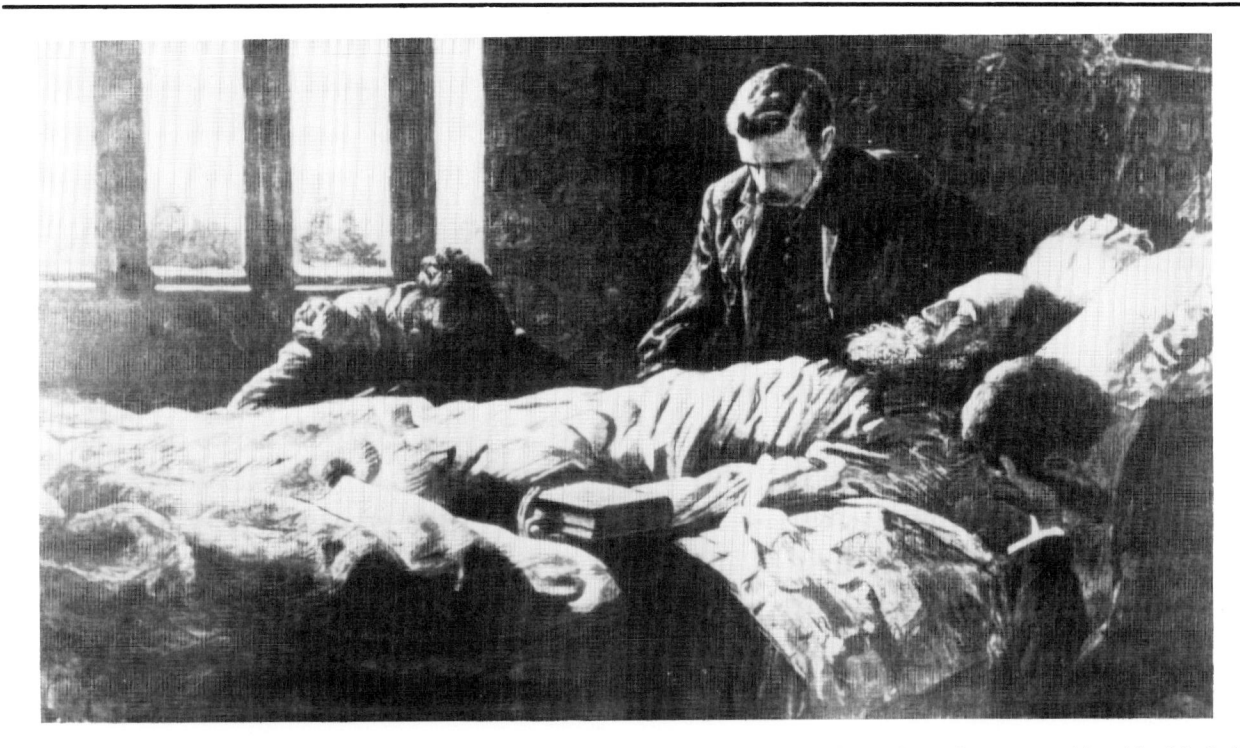

Illustration from a contemporary periodical of the death of Tennyson. Hallam Tennyson and his wife, Audrey, are on either side of the bed; Tennyson's physician, Dr. Dabbs, is beside Audrey Tennyson (Tennyson Research Centre).

moral reform nor inaugurated a single revolution of opinion; he has never pointed the way to undiscovered regions of thought; he has never stood on tip-toe to describe new worlds that his fellows were not tall enough to discover ahead. In all these directions he has been prompt to follow, quick to apprehend, but never himself a pioneer. Where then has his greatness lain? It has lain in the various perfections of his writing. He has written, on the whole, with more constant, unwearied, and unwearying excellence than any of his contemporaries.... He has expended the treasures of his native talent on broadening and deepening his own hold upon the English language, until that has become an instrument upon which he is able to play a greater variety of melodies to perfection than any other man."

But this is a kind of perfection that is hard to accept for anyone who is uneasy with poetry and feels that it ought to be the servant of something more utilitarian. Like most things Victorian, Tennyson's reputation suffered an eclipse in the early years of this century. In his case the decline was more severe than that of other Victorians because he had seemed so much the symbol of his age, so that for a time his name was nearly a joke. After two world wars had called into question most of the social values to which he had given only the most reluctant of support, readers were once more able to appreciate that he stood apart from his contemporaries. Now one can again admire without reservation one of the greatest lyric gifts in English literature, although it is unlikely that he will ever again seem quite the equal of Shakespeare.

When the best of his poetry is separated out from the second-rate work of the kind that any writer produces, Tennyson can be seen plainly as one of the half-dozen great poets in the English language, at least the equal of Wordsworth or Keats and probably far above any other Victorian. And that is precisely what his contemporaries thought.

Letters:

The Letters of Alfred Lord Tennyson: 1821-1850, volume 1, edited by Cecil Y. Lang and Edgar F. Shannon, Jr. (Cambridge: Harvard University Press/Oxford: Oxford University Press, 1981).

Bibliographies:

T. J. Wise, *A Bibliography of the Writings of Alfred, Lord Tennyson,* 2 volumes (London: Privately printed, 1908);

Charles Tennyson and Christine Fall, *Alfred Tenny-*

son: An Annotated Bibliography* (Athens: University of Georgia Press, 1967);
Nancie Campbell, *Tennyson in Lincoln: A Catalogue of the Collections in the Research Centre,* 2 volumes (Lincoln, U.K.: Tennyson Research Centre, 1971-1973).

Biographies:
Hallam Tennyson, *Alfred Lord Tennyson: A Memoir,* 2 volumes (New York & London: Macmillan, 1897);
Tennyson, ed., *Tennyson and His Friends* (London: Macmillan, 1911);
Charles Tennyson, *Alfred Tennyson* (New York & London: Macmillan, 1949);
Andrew Wheatcroft, *The Tennyson Album: A Biography in Original Photographs* (London, Boston & Henley, U.K.: Routledge & Kegan Paul, 1980);
Robert Bernard Martin, *Tennyson: The Unquiet Heart* (New York: Oxford University Press/Oxford: Clarendon Press/London: Faber & Faber, 1980).

References:
Jerome H. Buckley, *Tennyson: The Growth of a Poet* (Cambridge: Harvard University Press, 1960);
A. Dwight Culler, *The Poetry of Tennyson* (New Haven & London: Yale University Press, 1977);
John Olin Eidson, *Tennyson in America: His Reputation and Influence from 1827-1858* (Athens: University of Georgia Press, 1943);
James R. Kincaid, *Tennyson's Major Poems: The Comic and Ironic Patterns* (New Haven & London: Yale University Press, 1975);
W. D. Paden, *Tennyson in Egypt: A Study of the Imagery in His Earlier Work* (Lawrence: University of Kansas Press, 1942);
Valerie Pitt, *Tennyson Laureate* (London: Barrie & Rockliff, 1962);
Ralph Wilson Rader, *Tennyson's "Maud": the Biographical Genesis* (Berkeley, Los Angeles & London: University of California Press, 1963);
Christopher Ricks, *Tennyson* (New York & London: Macmillan, 1972);
Edgar F. Shannon, Jr., *Tennyson and the Reviewers: A Study of His Literary Reputation and the Influence of the Critics upon His Poetry, 1827-1851* (Cambridge: Harvard University Press, 1952);
Paul Turner, *Tennyson* (Boston & London: Routledge & Kegan Paul, 1976).

Papers:
Tennyson materials are scattered around the world. The major collection of correspondence and manuscripts is at the Tennyson Research Centre, Lincoln, England. A vast family archive is housed at the Lincolnshire Archives Office, Lincoln. Among other important collections are those at Trinity College, Cambridge; Houghton Library, Harvard; Beinecke Library, Yale; Perkins Library, Duke; and the British Library.

Frederick Tennyson
(5 June 1807-26 February 1898)

Rowland L. Collins
University of Rochester

BOOKS: *Poems by Two Brothers,* anonymous, by Tennyson and Charles and Alfred Tennyson (London: Simpkin & Marshall/Louth, U.K.: Jackson, 1827; second edition, edited by Hallam Tennyson, London: Macmillan, 1893);

Poems (Florence: Privately printed, 1853);

Days and Hours (London: Parker, 1854);

The Isles of Greece; Sappho and Alcaeus (London & New York: Macmillan, 1890);

Daphne and Other Poems (London & New York: Macmillan, 1891);

Poems of the Day and Year (London: Lane, 1895; Chicago: Stone & Kimball, 1895).

OTHER: Henry Melville, *Veritas: Revelations of Mysteries, Biblical, Historical, and Social, by Means of the Median and Persian Laws,* edited by Tennyson and A. Tudor (London: Hall, 1874).

Frederick Tennyson

Frederick Tennyson claims continued interest not only as an older brother of the laureate but as an educated Victorian who was a skilled poet in Greek and English, who accumulated a vast knowledge of ancient Greek literature and history, and who developed a substantial interest in spiritualism. His explorations of Swedenborgianism, astrology, and psychic phenomena are especially interesting, although not wholly unusual for his time. His career is also remarkable for its great efflorescence in his ninth decade.

Frederick Tennyson was born in 1807 in Louth, Lincolnshire, the second child (but the first to live) of the Reverend George Clayton Tennyson and Elizabeth Fytche Tennyson. Early in 1808, the Tennysons moved to Somersby to live in a rectory which had been enlarged for them by Mr. Tennyson's father, also named George Tennyson, who was an ambitious and prosperous attorney and landowner. By the time Frederick was twelve, he had six brothers and four sisters, and the rectory was seriously crowded. The rich grandfather never seems to have had much affection for the Somersby family, and the tension only increased as the family grew up in crowded and financially strained circumstances. The unpleasant relationship between Frederick's father (who suffered from epilepsy, often aggravated by alcohol) and grandfather led to frequent misunderstandings about money; these came to be regarded by the rector's family as threats of disinheritance, a kind of perpetual and open "will rattling" which made for even greater bitterness.

Frederick's first education was at home, under the shadow of his father's substantial library of around 2,500 volumes. The two brothers next in age, Charles and Alfred, probably received some early training with Frederick. The three shared a converted attic where they all slept, studied, and exercised on a structural beam. Frederick was fair and blond, whereas all his siblings were dark in coloring. He grew tall, strikingly handsome, and immensely strong, and was much admired for his wit, brilliance, and musical ability; small wonder, then, that he was sometimes thought to be arrogant. In 1814 Frederick went to live with the Fytches in Louth so that he could be enrolled in the grammar school under the governance of his mother's cousin, the Reverend Dr. J. Waite, who proved to be more tyrant than loving pedagogue. Frederick was sent to Eton in 1818. He had problems there as a country boy amid the urban sophisticates, but his Greek poem received a prize and was published in 1825. Among his acquaintances was Arthur Hallam, the young man who would someday be engaged to his sister, Emily, and who would be so close a friend of Alfred's. In addition to Frederick's scholarly record, he made his mark as an athlete before he moved on to matriculate at St. John's College, Cambridge, in 1825.

In 1827 Frederick joined Charles and Alfred in the publication of *Poems by Two Brothers,* printed for distribution principally in Louth. Of the 104 poems in the book, only three or four are by Frederick; the authorship of the others is not altogether established. (In 1893 Frederick, the only one of the three brothers then alive, reviewed the entire volume and could identify only his own for sure. In a letter to Alfred's son Hallam in that year, Frederick refers to "my four poems"; but in the second edition of *Poems by Two Brothers,* the initials "F. T." appear beside only three poems. It is known that Hallam changed some attributions.) While he was certainly the least important contributor, his ramblingly rhapsodic "The Oak of the North," at 228 lines, is by far the longest single poem in the book.

At Cambridge he won the Browne medal for a Greek ode which was published in *Prolusiones Academicae* in 1828, but he became a disciplinary problem for failure to attend chapel and had to endure rustication. He finally received his degree in 1832, after some brief employment as a tutor.

The death of his father in 1831 after a protracted illness thrust Frederick into a position of leadership of the Somersby Tennysons. This was a position for which he was ill suited, especially since one of the requirements was to work smoothly with his rich grandfather, on whose generosity Elizabeth Tennyson and all eleven of her children were dependent. None of the qualities attributed to Frederick—reticence, violence, ebullient affection, short temper, independence—were attractive to his demanding and unhappy grandfather. Nevertheless, when old George Tennyson died in 1835, Frederick, as the oldest son of his older son, was left a sizable estate at Grimsby; and his inheritance was charged with supporting his mother and one of his brothers for life. While Frederick and all his family were bitter over the disparity between the provisions for the Somersby Tennysons and the provisions for old George Tennyson's second son, Charles, Frederick was able to live the rest of his life without profession or employment.

Not long after Tennyson came into this property, he impulsively proposed marriage to his cousin Julia, the daughter of his father's brother, who now called himself Charles Tennyson d'Eyncourt of Bayons Manor. After Julia refused him, he left for Italy; in 1839 he married Maria Giuliotti, the daughter of the chief magistrate in Siena. Tennyson's failure to register their marriage immediately with the British consulate led to their first son's being considered illegitimate under British law and to many subsequent legal problems. Not long after Frederick and Maria were married, they settled in Florence, where their family grew to three daughters and two sons and where they all lived in considerable affluence. Frederick indulged his delight in music by frequently hiring an orchestra to play for his pleasure. His relaxed existence also left time for new interests, including the writings of the mystic Emanuel Swedenborg and various aspects of spiritualism.

Tennyson rarely returned to England, but in 1843 he went back to try to help his mother and brothers and sisters extricate themselves from disastrous financial investments with Matthew Allen; he could not effect a recovery, however. On 26 July 1848, the Manchester, Sheffield and Lincolnshire Railway settled an agreement with Tennyson for construction on his land at Grimsby. While the proceeds from this arrangement did not come nearly as quickly as he expected, his income from his various

Tennyson's uncle, Charles Tennyson d'Eyncourt, to whose daughter, Julia, Tennyson proposed marriage (Tennyson Research Centre)

holdings did ultimately increase; in 1854 he acknowledged an annual income of £800.

Elizabeth and Robert Browning met Tennyson in the early 1850s, and their friendship developed rapidly; they shared interests in poetry, of course, but also in religious and spiritual experiences. Elizabeth Browning especially shared Tennyson's growing passion for table rapping and automatic writing. Tennyson was always an accomplished letter writer and for many years he also regularly wrote poetry, which he showed only to a few friends. In 1853, he had a substantial volume of lyrics, entitled simply *Poems,* privately printed. The friends who saw this book or heard him read from it encouraged him, and the next year John W. Parker of London published Tennyson's *Days and Hours,* a volume of sixty-six lyrics which was in large part a new edition of major sections of the privately printed volume. His subjects are not unusual: poems about the seasons or months or fixed days of the year, about natural phenomena (such as the rainbow, stars, forests, the swallow), or about abstract qualities (hope, sorrow, ambition) take up most of the volume; two poems on poetry itself are included. Iambic meters predominate; stanzaic forms vary, but are generally four, six, or eight lines.

Days and Hours was enthusiastically received by

Edward FitzGerald and Mary Brotherton, two of Tennyson's friends who had been most eager for the book to appear, and also by Charles Kingsley, who praised the book lavishly and at length in the *Critic* (15 March and 1 April 1854). While not finding Tennyson a "faultless writer," Kingsley thought he had claims "to be classed among the most gifted and deeply feeling poets of our age." He quoted several poems and discussed their individual merits, noting in all an "impression of unity, though suggestive of infinite variety." He concluded by noting that while Frederick Tennyson "has great genius . . . , we shall be disappointed if, in the future, he fails to become a more highly-perfected artist of verse than he appears in this volume." Much less generous was the anonymous reviewer in the *Athenaeum* (15 April 1854) who compared Frederick's poems at length with Alfred's and found nothing to praise. "We have not been able, in most of [his poems] . . . , to detect any subject at all,— finding them to be without organization, beginning and end, or sequence of thought or presentment. All is personification, from the first page to the last. . . . [W]e decline to receive Mr. Frederick Tennyson—artist as he is in the use of melodious words—into the high category of the Poets." Needless to say, Tennyson was not encouraged.

In 1856, Tennyson began to cast about for another place to live. After short residences in Pisa and Genoa, he and his family moved in 1859 to Jersey, where he purchased St. Ewolds, a substantial house with a commanding view, near St. Helier. His interest in spiritualism and Swedenborg increased and diversified and for a time he was a British Israelite. He added to these passions a concern for the origins of freemasonry, principally because of the alleged discoveries of his neighbor, Henry Melville. Melville claimed to have found the origins of Masonic symbolism in the science of astrology. In Tennyson's enthusiasm, he brought Melville to London in 1874 in an attempt to impress people of influence with the importance of these discoveries. With "A. Tudor," Tennyson also edited Melville's *Veritas: Revelations of Mysteries, Biblical, Historical, and Social, by Means of the Median and Persian Laws,* and saw to its publication that same year in London.

The schedule of Tennyson's composition is not known, but the bulk and variety of his surviving papers suggest that he was writing a fair amount throughout these decades. His poetry was not published again, however, until 1890, when a substantial volume, *The Isles of Greece,* was brought out by Macmillan in London. The subtitle, *Sappho and Alcaeus,* indicates correctly that the long (443 pages; over 12,000 lines) blank verse narrative deals with the story of the two principal literary figures of Lesbos. Tennyson added a helpful and learned introduction in which he explained his elaborations on and deviations from historical records as he "drift[ed] before the breeze of Fancy . . . [to] weave them into a whole; a sort of Epic or Rhythmical Romance." Tennyson develops the lives of both poets so that they "intersect." Their final meeting in old age is brought about by the marriage of Sappho's granddaughter to the great-nephew of Alcaeus. The book is divided into three major parts: the first is about Sappho; the second is about Alcaeus; and the third, called "Kleis, or the Return," deals with their reunion. Most sections are introduced by translations from the surviving fragments of the two poets; these headings, Tennyson says, "have contributed more or less to the structure of a story, such as it is, and the unification of the series as an Epical whole." The narrative is leisurely, diffuse, and monotonous, but the verse is almost always competent and intelligent. Tennyson's Sappho is neither a poet of fiery passion nor the lesbian lover she is thought to be by most twentieth-century readers. She is a wise, kindly, meditative woman who meets Alcaeus on an utterly equal footing. Tennyson's narrative provides readers with an interesting but not a gripping portrait of the ancient world.

The next year a second volume, *Daphne and Other Poems,* was also published by Macmillan; it contained another lengthy crop of meditative narratives on classical subjects. This book is clearly a continuation of *The Isles of Greece,* which concentrated on Lesbos, for the large rubrics of the first half of the volume are "Delos" (for the poem "Daphne"), "Cyprus" (for "Pygmalion"), "Crete, Naxos" (for "Ariadne"), "Hesperides" (for "Hesperia"), and "Atlantis." Then follow poems on "Halcyone," "Psyche," "Niobe," "Aeson," and "King Athamas." This volume contains nearly 15,000 lines of poetry based on a vast knowledge of Greek history and literature. It has a readable narrative flow which, however, is not always secure because of its pace and its length. Much of Tennyson's religious philosophy can be read in these poems.

In the early 1890s Frederick's publisher, Macmillan, also published the works of Alfred Tennyson; advertisements for the work of Lord Tennyson were the most prominent of those placed at the end of *The Isles of Greece* and *Daphne.* Nevertheless, Frederick's work was well received and his publishers were able to cite, at the back of *Daphne,* five favorable reviews for *The Isles of Greece.* E. D. A. Morshead's review in the *Academy* was, of course, not so uniformly favorable as the twenty-five-word quotation from it might suggest: although he did recognize the book as "a work of beauty" he also found it "ill put together."

Frederick and Alfred Tennyson remained fairly close throughout their long lives. Alfred and Emily visited Frederick and Maria in the fall of 1851, the year after Alfred had been named poet laureate. In later years Frederick came to dislike his sister-in-law, considering her unattractively ambitious, but the brothers had no problems with each other. They corresponded with some regularity. Frederick was at Alfred's home, Farringford, in 1859 and 1876; when Alfred visited Frederick in Jersey in 1887 he was able to quote an earlier sonnet by Frederick from memory. They had another happy reunion at St. Ewolds in 1892, not long before the laureate's death.

Although Frederick was nearly eighty-five, the relatively favorable reception of his two substantial volumes of blank verse led him to plan on even more publication. Four years after *Daphne* he brought out *Poems of the Day and Year,* a new selection from the lyrics first published in 1853 and 1854. Only thirty-three poems were selected, with the help of his nephew, Walter C. A. Ker; of these, twenty-two had appeared in *Days and Hours* and almost all the others were drawn from the privately printed volume of 1853. Although there are slight revisions in almost every poem, it is hard to say how great a part Tennyson had in these changes. Three sonnets are included; one of them, "The Poet and the Fount of Happiness," is a version of the one that had been committed to memory by Alfred Tennyson. The reviewer in the *Athenaeum* was considerably more favorable than his predecessor had been forty-two years earlier. Tennyson was, for him, "the most interesting figure among living poets." While Tennyson had an "aloofness of attitude toward the human drama," his interest in nature had led to responses which could be shared attractively. He was, nevertheless, prolix: "What he says in a dozen lines, Lord Tennyson would say in two."

Frederick Tennyson was recognized in an important way when four of his poems were included in F. T. Palgrave's *The Golden Treasury: Second Series* (1897). Palgrave's first series (1861), dedicated to Alfred Tennyson, had been limited to writers no longer alive and had set out to include "all the best original Lyrical pieces and Songs in our language." The second series, dedicated to the laureate's memory, included seven living writers out of thirty-eight, and both Frederick and his brother Charles were among them. Frederick's four poems—"The Glory of Nature," "Song of an Angel," "The Skylark," and "A Dream of Autumn"—were from *Days and Hours;* the first and third had also been in *Poems of the Day and Year* (1895). Palgrave seems to have formed his text from the latter volume for those two poems, but his changes in punctuation, spelling and capitalization, and other inconsistencies, make it difficult to be sure. He evidently felt free to modify texts, for he omitted two stanzas from "A Dream of Autumn."

Tennyson's poetical remains include a lengthy blank verse narrative, "Orpheus," which draws heavily upon his interest in spiritualism and the supernatural world. The narrator, with whom Tennyson clearly identified, seeks knowledge of the afterlife from Eurydice, who gratifyingly responds with substantial lectures on the fabric of the spirit world. Maria, to whom Tennyson was devoted, had died in 1884; his attachment to her made the subject of Orpheus and Eurydice particularly congenial.

In 1896, Tennyson left Jersey and went to live with his son Julius in London, where he died in 1898. He was buried at Highgate Cemetery near his

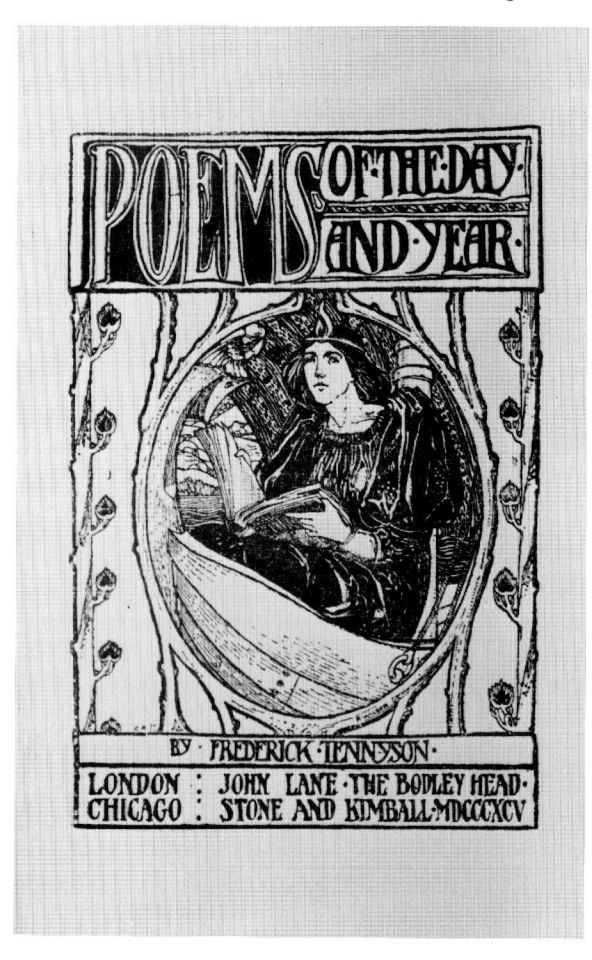

Title page for Tennyson's 1895 collection of lyrics (Thomas Cooper Library, University of South Carolina)

Tennyson in about 1895

mother, who had died in 1865. He was ninety and had outlived six of his younger siblings.

While Tennyson always wrote competent verse, he tended to go on at much too great length. Alfred Tennyson referred to his brother's poems as "organ-tones echoing among the mountains," but now, nearly a hundred years later, Frederick Tennyson's poetry is hardly read at all except as a gloss on the more attractive work of Alfred and Charles. Interest in Frederick's spiritualism and in its literary expression has sparked some small additional attention, however.

References:
Rowland L. Collins, foreword to Sir Charles Tennyson, "The Somersby Tennysons," *Victorian Studies,* 7, Christmas Supplement (1963): 5-6;

Christine Fall, "An Index of the Letters from Papers of Frederick Tennyson," *Texas Studies in English,* 36 (1957): 155-163;

Sir Francis Hill, "The Disinheritance Tradition Reconsidered," *Tennyson Research Bulletin,* 3 (November 1978): 41-54;

Robert Bernard Martin, *Tennyson: The Unquiet Heart* (Oxford: Clarendon Press, 1980);

Harold Nicolson, *Tennyson's Two Brothers* (Cambridge: Cambridge University Press, 1947);

H. D. Rawnsley, *Memories of the Tennysons* (Glasgow: MacLehose, 1912);

Hugh J. Schonfield, ed., *Letters to Frederick Tennyson* (London: Hogarth, 1930);

Charles Tennyson, *Alfred Tennyson* (London: Macmillan, 1950);

Tennyson, "The Somersby Tennysons," *Victorian Studies,* 7, Christmas Supplement (1963): 7-56;

Tennyson, "Tennyson and his Brothers, Frederick and Charles," in *Tennyson and His Friends,* edited by Hallam, Lord Tennyson (London: Macmillan, 1911), pp. 33-68;

Tennyson and Hope Dyson, *The Tennysons: Background to Genius* (London: Macmillan, 1974);

Tennyson, ed., *The Shorter Poems of Frederick Tennyson* (London: Macmillan, 1913);

Hallam, Lord Tennyson, *Alfred Lord Tennyson: A Memoir,* 2 volumes (London: Macmillan, 1897).

Papers:
The Lilly Library of Indiana University, Bloomington, has the Frederick Tennyson archive, including manuscripts of published and unpublished poetry, over 1,000 letters by and to Frederick and other members of his family, photographs, business papers, trial books, and memorabilia. See Rowland L. Collins, "The Frederick Tennyson Collection," *Victorian Studies,* 7, Christmas Supplement (1963): 57-76.

Martin F. Tupper

(17 July 1810-29 November 1889)

Patrick Scott
University of South Carolina

SELECTED BOOKS: *Sacra Poesis* (Oxford: Nisbet, 1832);

A Voice from the Cloister, by a Young Collegian (Oxford: Wheeler, 1835);

Proverbial Philosophy: A Book of Thoughts and Arguments, Originally Treated (London: Rickerby, 1838; Boston: Pierce, 1840; Second Series, London: Hatchard, 1842; Philadelphia: Hooker, 1843; Third Series, London: Moxon, 1867; Fourth Series, London: Moxon, 1869);

An Ode on the Coronation of Her Majesty, Queen Victoria, June 28, 1838 (London: Rickerby, 1838);

Geraldine, A Sequel to Coleridge's Christabel: with Other Poems (London: Rickerby, 1838; Boston: Saxon & Kelt, 1846);

A Modern Pyramid: to Commemorate a Septuagint of Worthies (London: Rickerby, 1839);

St. Martha's: near Guildford, Surrey (Guildford, U.K.: Privately printed, 1841);

An Author's Mind: The Book of Title-Pages (London: Bentley, 1841; Philadelphia: Carey & Hart, 1847);

The Crock of Gold: A Rural Novel (London: Bentley, 1844; New York: Wiley & Putnam, 1845);

The Twins: A Domestic Novel (London: Bentley, 1844; New York: Wiley & Putnam, 1845);

Heart: A Social Novel (London: Bentley, 1844; New York: Colyer, 1844);

A Thousand Lines: Now First Offered to the World We Live In (London: Hatchard, 1845; Philadelphia: Hooker, 1846);

Probabilities: An Aid to Faith (London: Hatchard, 1847; New York: Wiley & Putnam, 1847);

Hactenus: More Droppings from the Pen That Wrote "Proverbial Philosophy," "A Thousand Lines," &c. &c. &c. (London: Hatchard, 1848; Boston: Pierce, 1848);

A Loving Ballad to Brother Jonathan (Burlington, Vt., 1848);

Surrey: A Rapid Review of Its Principal Interests, in Persons and Places (Guildford, U.K.: Andrews, 1849);

Tupper's Poetical Works (Boston: Phillips, Sampson, 1849);

(Elliott & Fry, Photographers)

Farley Heath: A Record of Its Roman Remains and Other Antiquities (Guildford, U.K.: Andrews, 1850);

The Complete Prose Works of Martin Farquhar Tupper, edited by W. C. Armstrong (Hartford, Conn.: Andrus, 1850);

Ballads for the Times, Now First Collected (London:

Virtue, 1850; Philadelphia: Butler, 1852);
A Hymn for All Nations . . . Translated into Thirty Languages, music by S. Sebastian Wesley (London: Hatchard, 1851);
Half-a-dozen No-Popery Ballads, etc. (Guildford, U.K. & London: Privately printed, 1851);
Things to Come: A Prophetic Ode (London: Bosworth, 1852);
A Dirge for Wellington (London: Hatchard, 1852);
Half-a-dozen Ballads for Australian Emigrants (London: Bosworth, 1853);
A Dozen Ballads for the Times, about Church Abuses (London: Bosworth, 1854);
A Dozen Ballads for the Times about White Slavery (London: Bosworth, 1854);
A Batch of War Ballads (London: Bosworth, 1854);
Lyrics of the Heart and Mind (London: Hall, Virtue, 1855);
Paterfamilias's Diary of Everybody's Tour: Belgium and the Rhine, Munich, Switzerland, Milan, Geneva and Paris, anonymous (London: Hatchard, 1856);
Rides and Reveries of the Late Mr. Aesop Smith, as Peter Query (London: Hurst & Blackett, 1858; Philadelphia: Butler, 1858);
Stephan Langton, 2 volumes (London: Hurst & Blackett, 1858);
Alfred: A Patriotic Play, in Five Acts (Westminster, U.K.: Brettell, 1858);
Martin F. Tupper on Rifle-Clubs. Some Verse and Prose (London, 1859);
Three Hundred Sonnets (London: Hall, Virtue, 1860);
Cithara: A Selection from the Lyrics of M. F. Tupper (London: Virtue, 1863);
Shakespeare, an Ode for His Three-Hundredth Birthday (N.p., 1864?);
A Lyric of Congratulation (Guildford, U.K.: Stent, 1864);
A Selection from the Works of Martin F. Tupper (London: Moxon, 1865);
Plan of the Ritualistic Campaign (Middle Hill, U.K.: Privately printed, 1865?); republished as *The Anti-Ritualistic Satire. Tupper's Directorium or Plan of the Ritualistic Campaign, Being Secret Instructions to Our Anglican Clergy* (London: Simpkin, Marshall, 1868);
Raleigh: His Life and His Death (London: Mitchell, 1866);
Our Canadian Dominion: Half-a-dozen Ballads about a King for Canada (London: Algar, 1868);
Twenty-One Protestant Ballads, Published in "The Rock" (London, 1868);
A Creed, etcetera (London: Simpkin, Marshall, 1870);
Fifty of the Protestant Ballads, and "The Anti-Ritualistic Directorium" (London: Ridgway, 1874);
Select Miscellaneous Poems (Edinburgh: Gall & Inglis, 1874);
Washington: A Drama, in Five Acts (London: Privately printed, 1876; New York: Miller, 1876);
Three Five-Act Plays and Twelve Dramatic Scenes, Suitable for Private Theatricals (London: Allen, 1882);
My Life as an Author (London: Low, Marston, Searle & Rivington, 1886);
Jubilate: An Offering for 1887 (London: Low, 1887).

TRANSLATION: *King Alfred's Poems . . . Turned into English Metres* (London: Hall, Virtue, 1850).

Tupper was once famous enough to be included, along with Byron, Wordsworth, Shelley, and others, in the standard Victorian series "Moxon's Popular Poets"; yet even in his lifetime his reputation fell into eclipse, and by the 1860s smart young reviewers were finding "Tupperish" a handy term of critical abuse. His most famous work, *Proverbial Philosophy* (1838), sold much more heavily than the works of any of his more important contemporaries, including Tennyson, at least in the middle decades of the century; but no one since has had a good word to say for it, and its significance now is almost wholly as an index of the intellectual and literary tendencies of Tupper's class and time. That granted, it is worth closer examination than it has usually received.

Martin Farquhar Tupper was born in London in 1810, the eldest son of Dr. Martin Tupper, a successful physician, and Ellin Devis Tupper. He was educated from 1818 to 1821 at Joseph Railton's famous Eagle House; from 1821 to 1826 at Charterhouse, where he was a contemporary of Thackeray's; and from 1828 to 1832 at Christ Church, Oxford, where his religious seriousness brought him the friendship of W. E. Gladstone, the future prime minister. Tupper even won a theological essay prize, for which Gladstone came in second. A severe stutter inhibited his academic advancement (oral examinations were required for honors), and it also ended his successive hopes for careers as a clergyman and a lawyer—though he studied law in London after graduation from Oxford and was called to the bar in 1835. After his marriage that year to his second cousin, Isabelle Devis, he appears to have given up all career ambitions, living first off his father's bounty and then off his own considerable literary earnings. When he came into possession of the small, partly sixteenth-century family home, Albury House in Surrey, in 1839, he reveled in his various roles as country gentleman, Victorian paterfamilias (he had eight children), and literary celebrity.

The early poem "The Stammerer's Complaint" describes the frustration his speech impediment caused him.

> Oh! 'tis a sore affliction to restrain
> From mere necessity, the glowing thought;
> To feel the fluent cataract of speech
> Check'd by some wintry spell, and frozen up.

He made the plight of the stutterer a main topic in his essay "Of Speaking" in *Proverbial Philosophy* and submitted to drastic treatments, such as reading the whole of Milton's *Paradise Lost* aloud with his chin propped on a crutch and his tongue restrained by a gag. No such inhibitions, however, froze up the cataract of Tupper's written utterance, and his first verses, a patriotic account of a Continental tour, appeared in the *Literary Chronicle* when he was only fifteen. He retained throughout his life the strongly Evangelical beliefs with which he had been raised; his first book, *Sacra Poesis* (1832), was wholly religious in character, and his second, *A Voice from the Cloister* (1835), was a long appeal in verse to Oxford undergraduates to abstain from extravagance, gambling, seduction, and drink: "Stop, desperate youth, and dash the wine-cup down!"

It was Tupper's third book that brought him his enormous early Victorian popularity, both English and American, and his subsequent notoriety. From early adolescence he had been in love with his cousin Isabelle; shortly before he went away to the university he had written a number of long, rhythmic verse essays, "in the manner of Solomon's Proverbs," to tell her his notions of friendship, matrimony, love, and so on:

> If the love of the heart is blighted, it buddeth not again;
> If that pleasant song is forgotten, it is to be learnt no more:
> Yet often will thought look back, and weep over early affection;
> And the dim notes of that pleasant song will be heard as a reproachful spirit,
> Moaning in Aeolian strains over the desert of the heart,
> Where the hot siroccos of the world have withered its one oasis.

Thus warned, Isabelle agreed to an immediate engagement; but it was not until after his marriage and the abandonment of other career hopes that he took the advice of his parish clergyman and expanded these "notions" for publication. The expansion, *Proverbial Philosophy: A Book of Thoughts and Arguments, Originally Treated*, appeared on 24 January 1838. Tupper's prefatory verses indicate the fragmentary and miscellaneous nature of the volume:

> Thoughts, that have tarried in my mind, and peopled its inner chambers,
> The sober children of reason, or desultory train of fancy;
> Clear sunny wine of conviction, with the scum and lees of speculation.
> . . . .
> The fruits I have gathered of prudence, the ripened harvest of my musings,
> These I commend unto you, O docile scholar of Wisdom,
> These I give to thy gentle heart, thou lover of the right.

The verse essays that follow cover an extraordinary range of subjects—some primarily moral ("Humility," "Tolerance," "Cruelty to Animals," "Indirect Influences"); some pop-psychological ("Memory," "Estimating Character," "Self-Acquaintance"); some exhorting to self-improvement ("Ambition," "Reading"); some philosophical, reflecting Tupper's optimism ("Of Truth in Things False," "Of Good in Things Evil"); and some directly religious ("Prayer," "Of a Trinity"). None of the sections sticks very closely to its announced topic, nor are the thoughts very original, though a few survive in dictionaries of quotations even today. Where Tupper was distinctive was in his treatment, an extraordinary mixture of commonsense advice and abstract speculation, with dense and often oddly juxtaposed imagery, and an insistent religiosity of tone. The extraordinary effect can only be understood by detailed examination, and the section "Of Thinking" is fairly representative of Tupper's method. It propounds for 150 lines the idea that serious thought takes study, concentration, humility, and faith. Even in the opening lines, however, the imagery seems almost independent of the thought, perhaps because the lines tend to split into two parts, with abstract moral meaning in the first part and imagery alone in the second: "Reflection is a flower of the mind, giving out wholesome fragrance,/But reverie is the same flower, when rank and running to seed." Some of what follows is

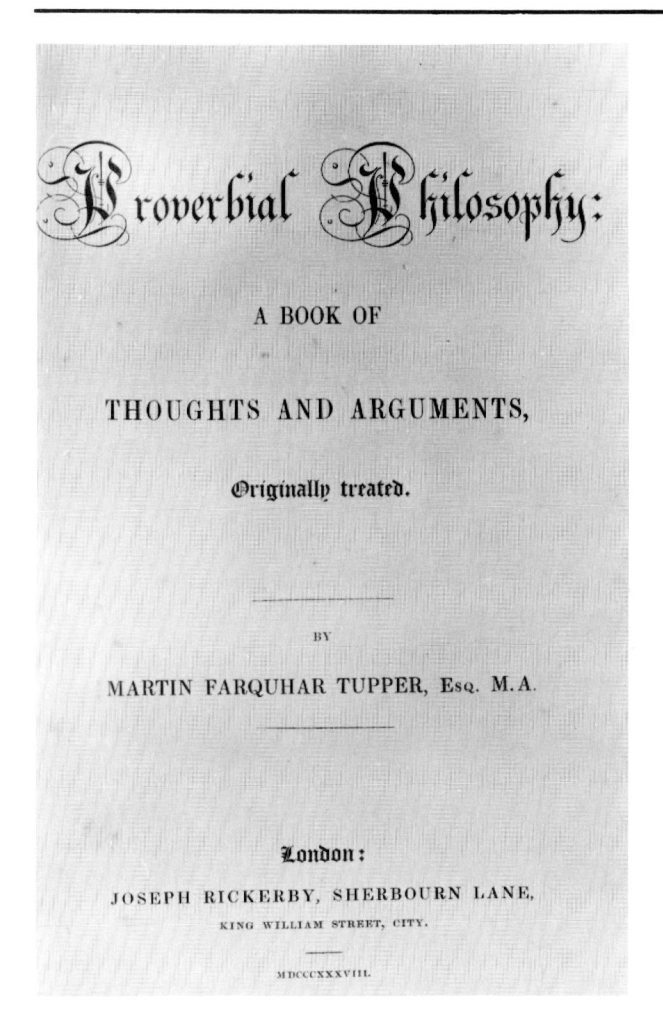

Title page for Tupper's most famous work

composed of simple, rather abstract maxims, seemingly outdated and Augustan in their use of personification: "Memory, the daughter of Attention, is the teeming mother of Wisdom,/And safer is he that storeth knowledge, than he that would make it for himself." Such lines not only illuminate Tupper's attitude to his own derivativeness but also, in their combination of an emphasis on safety in thought with an appeal through imagery to the psychological supports of parenthood and financial security ("storeth"), illustrate his appeal to a middle class seeking assurance amid social and intellectual uncertainties. Sometimes Tupper attempts a more sustainedly poetic flight, but his similes are second-hand and sub-Romantic, and he switches giddily from image to image:

> . . . the wearied spirit lieth as a fainting maiden
> Captive and borne away on the warrior's foam-covered steed,
> And sinketh down wounded as a gladiator on the sand,
> While the keen falchion of Intellect is cutting through the scabbard of the brain.

Surely that dactylic "foam-covered steed" is by Byron out of the Honorable Mrs. Norton, and the sudden shifts of image from captive maiden to wounded gladiator and piercing sword—from female to male imagery—suggest a psychological fever behind the explicit moral argument that the soul loses out to the mind. Tupper is clearly identifying different modes of thinking with different sex roles, though he will not let himself say so. At some points—often the most interesting and least conventional—Tupper simply abandons his ostensible topic altogether:

> In a dream, thou mayst be mad, and feel the fire within thee;
> In a dream thou mayst travel out of self, and see with the eyes of another;
> Or sleep in thine own corpse; or wake in as many bodies:
> Or swell, as expanded to infinity; or shrink, as imprisoned to a point;
> Or among moss-grown ruins may wander with the sullen disembodied,
> Or gaze upon their glassy eyes until thy heart-blood freeze.

Illustration by Tupper for Proverbial Philosophy: *"The Soul Carried Captive by Imagination"*

Such quotations show, of course, the technical weaknesses of Tupper's writing—ametricality, conventionality, and prolixity—but they also show that *Proverbial Philosophy* is less simpleminded than might at first appear; its secret appeal was that, at the subconscious level, it invoked and even indulged the exciting early-Victorian sense of psychic disintegration, while at the conscious level it tamed such thoughts through a traditional religious affirmation. The same duality can be seen in the distinctive meter, which is both a kind of exploratory free verse and a deliberate echo of Old Testament balance.

Proverbial Philosophy sold its way respectably through two editions in Britain, and after the unsold remainder sheets of the third edition were shipped to the United States, it gradually established itself as a standard work for middle-class family reading on both sides of the Atlantic. Tupper wrote a second series of twenty-four additional sections for serialization in *Ainsworth's* magazine in 1842, including some quite effective domestic description in "Of Life" and the longest section of all, the religious speculation "Of Immortality." In book form, and using the relatively new technology of stereotyping, the two parts were constantly reprinted together and were issued with various illustrations and in many different fancy gift bindings. During Tupper's lifetime, over fifty British editions were sold, totaling a quarter of a million copies; and American sales were estimated at over a million. *Proverbial Philosophy* was read as a modern oracle, and it was always the more original sections ("Love," "Friendship," "Marriage") that were most popular. There is a revealing story that the famous Baptist preacher C. H. Spurgeon first intimated his affection for a female member of his congregation by reading to her Tupper's section "Of Marriage" while on a chapel outing to the Crystal Palace at Sydenham in 1854: "Seek a good wife of thy God, for she is the best gift of His providence." She understood this to mean a proposal, and they duly married and lived happily ever after. From the approbation of Queen Victoria and Prince Albert when Tupper was presented at court in 1857 ("I thank you, Mr. Tupper, for your beautiful poetry," said the queen), to the fulsomely inscribed "love-token" sent to him by the *Ladies' Repository* of Cincinnati on behalf of "fifty thousand American" admirers, Tupper's already strong sense of his own achievement received constant reinforcement. When he first visited America in 1851, Millard Fillmore (perhaps the appropriate president to do so) twice received him, "avowing himself a great

Tupper on his first American tour in 1851

lover of my works"; selections from Tupper's rather expansive philosophizing began to appear, not only solo as in *Gems from Tupper, Compiled by a Clergyman* (1848) but also—under the title *The Proverbialist and the Poet* (1851)—teamed up with those earlier great thinkers, Solomon and Shakespeare, with illustrations of Solomon's Temple, Stratford-on-Avon, and Albury House.

Against this acceptability to Victorian readers must be set the strictures of most Victorian critics. Though there were early favorable reviews in middlebrow papers, the serious reviewers soon condemned Tupper as a pompous fool. *Fraser's* magazine, for instance, declared in 1852 that "his success indicates a defect in the public taste" and described *Proverbial Philosophy* as strings of "commonplaces in a sing-song manner," only relieved by "the comic touches of self-satisfaction in the writer." Subsequent comments have been almost uniformly derogatory, from Saintsbury's "incredible rubbish . . . intolerable imbecility" to C. E. Vulliamy's description of the form as "a gluttinously [*sic*] crawling metre, like rivulets of treacle." It was no accident that Tupper became one of the most parodied of all

Tupper's poster advertising the celebration of King Alfred's birthday in the town of Wantage in 1849

Victorian authors, attracting the scornful attention of such masters as Aytoun, Gilbert, Carroll, and Calverley. Though Derek Hudson's splendid modern biography of Tupper enters a plea in mitigation, even for Hudson the significance of *Proverbial Philosophy* is as a historical phenomenon, a symptom of its times. In content, it points to the early nineteenth-century appeal of "wisdom literature," where gnomic fragments yield glimpses of a truth too complex or mystical or intuitive for systematic exposition; one thinks, for instance, of Tennyson's *In Memoriam* (1850), or of the Hare brothers' *Guesses at Truth* (1827). In form, its loose verse structure and metrical freedom—unrhymed with strong midline breaks, more like Latin hexameters than the steady iambic of traditional English verse— suggest the efforts at verse spontaneity of such English "Spasmodics" as Philip James Bailey, and point forward to Whitman (indeed, several of Whitman's early critics, Henry James and Swinburne among them, thought him "the Tupper of the West"). If Tupper's *Proverbial Philosophy* is no longer of much interest in itself, it is at least a valuable pointer to contemporary poetic tendencies.

Tupper followed his most famous work with a constant stream of other publications, and his success as the Proverbial Philosopher seems to have given him the confidence to write directly on contemporary issues, rather than just on timeless truth and universal feelings. He now belonged with those, as he had written in "Of Authorship," "whose sound is gone out into all lands," and he used this new prominence for one of Authorship's other prerogatives, "to embalm as in amber the poor insects of an hour." His works show a shift also in form: he had been writing unrhymed verse, in accordance with his notion that rhyme was a monkish innovation with no adequate scriptural or classical precedent; but for his more occasional verse he used bouncing, regular, rhymed verse, even in his campaign to defeat the new monkish innovation of Ritualist services in the Church of England. His efforts to speak directly to the issues of his day, and his inability to distinguish between the important and unimportant issues, often make his career after *Proverbial Philosophy* seem like a parody of the similar ambitions of his greater contemporary, Tennyson. In 1838 Tupper had produced a coronation ode ("in a spirit of deifying royalty," reported the *Sunday Times,* disapprovingly) and a continuation of Coleridge's unfinished poem *Christabel,* entitled *Geraldine* ("we are surprised by his impertinence, and pained by his stupidity," thundered *Blackwood's,* attempting in vain to silence Tupper as it had earlier silenced Keats and Tennyson). *A Modern Pyramid* (1839) was a sequence of seventy biographical essays, with accompanying sonnets, on great heroes from Abel and Zoroaster to George Washington and Lord Nelson. *An Author's Mind* (1841), subtitled *The Book of Title-Pages,* outlined thirty-four books on everything from the souls of dumb animals to the folly of shaving—books Tupper mercifully felt that he did not have time to write out in full. "I feel Malthusian among my mental nurslings," he admitted engagingly in his preface; "I write these things only to be quit of them." Thereafter he was less Malthusian, and books and pamphlets poured from his pen unceasingly. Was the local church in need of repair? Tupper obliged with a verse appeal for funds, and with verses for its rededication, and with hymns for four successive harvest festivals:

> Gaze round in deep emotion:
>   The rich and ripened grain
> Is like a golden ocean
>   Becalmed upon the plain;
> And we, who late were weepers
>   Lest judgment should destroy,
> Now sing because the reapers
>   Are come again with joy!

Did the dreaded cholera threaten a new epidemic? Tupper was ready with a verse prayer against "this baneful plague." Was it the thousandth anniversary of King Alfred's birth? Tupper got up a public commemoration, wrote suitable celebratory songs, and translated Alfred's own poetry from Anglo-Saxon into modern English. Did the social and moral "condition of England" loom in public concern? Tupper wrote three novels in 1844 to set his contemporaries to rights. Did the French threaten an invasion of the British Isles? Tupper, like Tennyson, poured out verses in support of the volunteer rifle companies. Was the topic of conversation at a dinner party the new Atlantic cable-telegraph? Tupper politely withdrew, soon to reappear with a poem recommending that "Peace upon earth, good will to men" be the first transatlantic message. (His suggestion was put into effect.) Did American admirers make a pilgrimage to Albury? Tupper readily improvised appropriate verses on Anglo-American relations:

> Ho! Brother, I'm a Britisher,
>   A chip of heart of oak
> That wouldn't warp or swerve or stir
>   From what I thought or spoke,—
> And you—a blunt and honest man,

> Straightforward, kind, and true,
> I tell you, Brother Jonathan,
>   That you're a Briton too.

His guests were delighted, and speedily arranged for Tupper's thirteen stanzas to be published in newspapers and pamphlets in the U.S.A. Surveying such well-intentioned productivity, one sympathizes with the remark of a later American visitor to Albury, Nathaniel Hawthorne, who reported that Tupper was "a person for whom I immediately felt a kindness, and instinctively knew to be a bore." The European revolutions of 1848, the commissioning of a missionary ship in Philadelphia, the attempted assassination of the queen, the opening of the Crystal Palace ("Hurrah! for honest Industry, hurrah! for handy Skill"), the need for Liberian independence, the benefits of literary lectures at the Manchester Athenaeum, the death of the Duke of Wellington, the plight of London's seamstresses and prostitutes, Australian emigration, the evils of animal experiments, the devious designs of papists and Puseyites to pervert the Church of England, the Crimean War, every royal birth and every royal wedding—on all these, and on countless other topics of the day, Tupper turned out verses with innocent facility. As the *Athenaeum*

Tupper and his family outside their home, Albury House, in 1864. Tupper and his wife, Isabelle Devis Tupper, are seated at left and right. Standing (from left) are their children, Walter, Ellin, Mary, Martin, Margaret, and William. Lying on the ground is Henry.

Cover of a song by Tupper in praise of volunteer rifle companies in 1859

reviewer commented on his *Batch of War Ballads* (1854), "Mr. Tupper's lyre is always ready. If he has not the talent, he has the readiness of an *improvisatore*."

Nor was he neglectful of social recognition for his efforts. He got himself elected a fellow of the Royal Society, ostensibly for services to Surrey archaeology, proceeded to the doctorate of civil law at Oxford, and proudly put their letters after his name on his title pages. He offered to solve the religious doubts of the age in a prose work, *Probabilities* (1847). He arranged for a particularly dim Oxford professor of poetry, James Garbett, to nominate him for poet laureate in 1850 after Wordsworth's death, and apparently believed himself a serious candidate. (Garbett wrote to the prime minister that "Mr. Tupper is the most vigorous Lyric Poet of the day.") With strengthened confidence, he conquered his stammer and gave readings of his works throughout Britain and the eastern United States in 1851. No other writer can have reveled so happily in the early Victorian poet's presumed duty to speak out on the happenings and crises of his time, and none can have derived so much innocent enjoyment from the fame it brought him. His later volumes, for the most part, are simply collections and reprintings, in varying combinations, of these multifarious ephemera, and no collected edition is anything like complete.

A few poems, however, stand out from the general ruck; significantly, they seem to be ones less specifically tied to particular occasions. Tupper's collection *A Thousand Lines* (1845) includes several poems on the stages of man's life; among them was "The Song of Seventy," which became a standard late-Victorian recitation piece:

> I am not old—I cannot be old
>   Though three-score years and ten
> Have wasted away, like a tale that is told,
>   The lives of other men.
> ....
> The heart, the heart, is a heritage
>   That keeps the old man young!

The same volume also includes the once-famous inspirational poem "Never Give Up!":

> Never give up! or the burthen may sink you,—
>   Providence kindly has mingled the cup,
> And in all trials or troubles, bethink you,
>   The watchword of life must be, Never give up!

(Tupper was naively delighted to find on his visit to the Pennsylvania Hospital for the Insane that printed copies of these lines had been posted in every ward, and that the patients were "grateful for the good hope my verses had helped them to.") His subsequent volume, *Hactenus* (1848), was an attempt to rework the same vein with such poems as "All's for the best" and "Cheer up!," but it also contains an imaginative dramatic monologue, the complaint of an Ancient Briton whose tomb has been disturbed by eager Victorian archaeologists. There is a trio of sonnets about fishing, included in Tupper's autobiography, that are almost eighteenth-century in their self-conscious classicism of language. In general, also, Tupper's hymns are better than his political poems, perhaps because in the hymns he had a more stable traditional language to draw on and was less dependent on his own ear and taste.

By the 1850s, however, Tupper had become slightly ridiculous to educated readers; as early as 1854 the *Athenaeum* remarked that "no man of judgment seriously speaks of Mr. Tupper except as a curiosity." His large and demanding family and his continually rising expenses led him to experiment in other potentially profitable literary genres. He wrote a travel book, *Paterfamilias's Diary* (1856); a historical novel on a Surrey theme, *Stephan Langton* (1858), that stayed in print well into the twentieth century; and a series of historical dramas, *Alfred* (1858), *Raleigh* (1866), and *Washington* (1876), though only *Alfred* ever made it to the commercial stage. Probably the most interesting of these money-making books is *Rides and Reveries* (1858), a Rabelaisian miscellany of essays, fables, and verses. It purports to be the horseback reflections of a hunchback named Aesop Smith, but in fact it gives once again all of Tupper's own pet crotchets, from

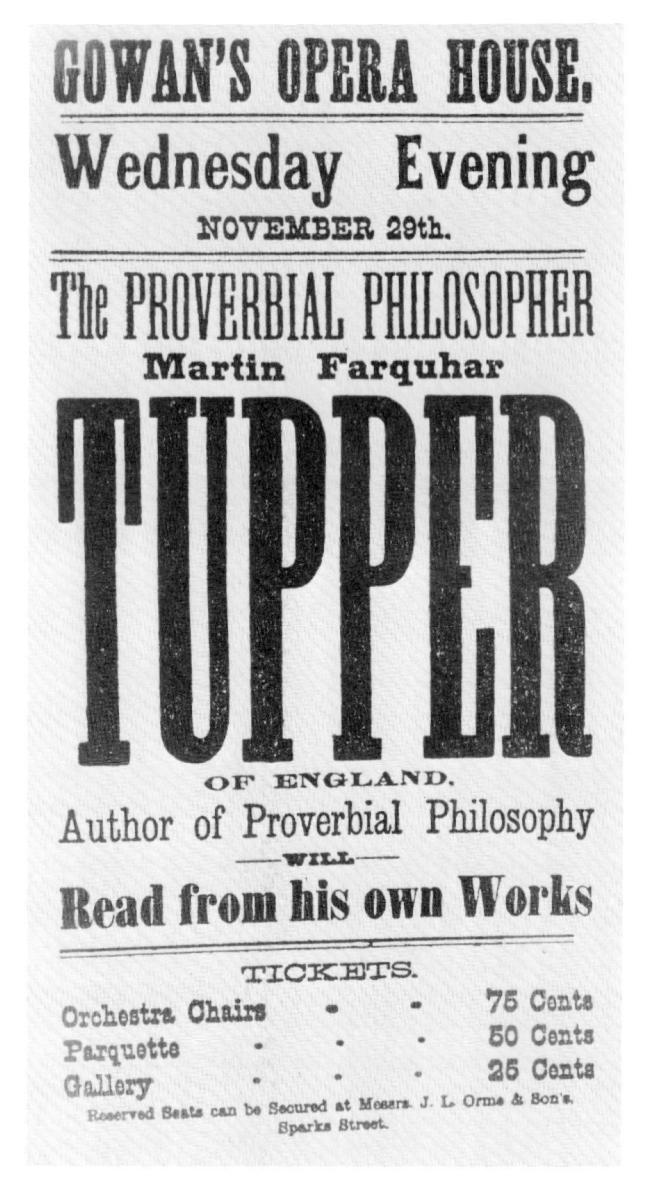

Poster advertising an appearance by Tupper in Ottawa, Canada, in 1876

the value of beards and the malignancy of reviewers to the right way to solve the Irish problem and the tribulations of matrimony (the unkind story is that living with the Proverbial Philosopher had driven Mrs. Tupper to drink). Tupper's attempts to puff the flagging sales of *Proverbial Philosophy* with the addition of third (1867) and fourth series (1869), and his second, barely profitable, reading tour in the United States and Canada in 1876 were further efforts to stave off the unpalatable economic consequences of changing public taste. Though Tupper was ready with an ode for the Shakespeare tercentenary in 1864, ballads for the new Canadian federation in 1868, and a special poem for Queen Victoria's jubilee in 1887, he had long outlived his popularity by the time of his death in 1889. It is one of the charms of his autobiography, *My Life as an Author* (1886), that he takes these reversals in his fortune quite good-humoredly, yet even then he still retained enough self-confidence to close the book with his own translation from Ovid:

My name shall never die; but through all time
....
There, in that people's tongue, shall this my page

Tupper dressed for an appearance at Court in 1885

Martin Tupper's Autobiography

MY LIFE

AS AN AUTHOR

BY

MARTIN FARQUHAR TUPPER
D.C.L. F.R.S.

Vixi, vivo, vivam.

LONDON:
SAMPSON LOW, MARSTON, SEARLE, & RIVINGTON
CROWN BUILDINGS, 188 FLEET STREET, E.C.
1886
[*All rights reserved*]

Title page for Tupper's autobiography

Be read and glorified from age to age:—
Yes, if the bodings of my spirit give
True note of inspiration, I shall live!

Absurd, of course, and even pathetic. Tupper's output was stupendous, and among his works can be found ebullient verses on almost any early Victorian popular concern. The imagery, structure, and verse-form of his most famous work are also worth attention, as they are good illustrations of some general tendencies in early Victorian poetry toward metrical freedom and a more spontaneous, psychologically based verse. Yet Tupper's only real value, as the *Athenaeum* pointed out in 1854, is that his admittedly enormous sales "give us a kind of guide to the taste of certain classes of reader." He is a marvelous source of information about the Victorian middle-class mind, simply because in his ideas and prejudices he was representative rather than original.

Biography:
Derek Hudson, *Martin Tupper: His Rise and Fall* (London: Constable, 1949); republished as *An Unrepentant Victorian* (New York: Macmillan, 1950).

References:
Ralf Buchmann, *Martin F. Tupper and the Victorian Middle-Class Mind* (Bern: Francke, 1941);

John Drinkwater, "Martin Tupper," in *The Eighteen-Eighties*, edited by Walter de la Mare (Cambridge: Cambridge University Press, 1930), pp. 197-217;

Richard Goodchild, "Martin Tupper," *Times Literary Supplement*, 5 March 1938, p. 156;

"Mr. Tupper and the Poets," *Times Literary Supplement*, 26 February 1938, p. 137;

Harold Nicolson, "Marginal Comment," *Spectator*, 182 (18 February 1949): 217;

Robert Preyer, "Victorian Wisdom Literature: Fragments and Maxims," *Victorian Studies*, 6 (1963): 245-262;

George Saintsbury, "Lesser Poets," in *Cambridge History of English Literature*, edited by A. W. Ward and A. R. Waller (Cambridge: Cambridge University Press, 1916), pp. 147-152;

Louis B. Salomon, "He Gave the Victorians What They Wanted," *English Journal* (College Edition), 27 (1938): 648-661;

"Tea-Table Literature," *Fraser's*, 46 (October 1852): 466-475;

C. E. Vulliamy, "Never Give Up," *Spectator*, 182 (18 February 1949): 226;

[John Wilson], "Tupper's *Geraldine*," *Blackwood's Edinburgh Magazine*, 44 (December 1838): 835-852.

Papers:
Tupper's letters to Gladstone and his scrapbooks for the years 1848 to 1853 are in the British Library, London; other manuscript items are at the University of Virginia and Christ Church, Oxford. The main archive, consisting of sixty-two volumes of correspondence, ephemera, press cuttings, and so forth, put together by Tupper himself and used by Hudson for his biography, is at the University of Illinois, Urbana-Champaign.

Charles (Tennyson) Turner
(4 July 1808-25 April 1879)

Rowland L. Collins
University of Rochester

BOOKS: *Poems by Two Brothers*, anonymous, by Tennyson and Alfred and Frederick Tennyson (London: Simpkin & Marshall/Louth, U. K.: Jackson, 1827);

Sonnets and Fugitive Pieces, as Charles Tennyson (Cambridge: Bridges, 1830);

Sonnets, as Charles Turner (London & Cambridge: Macmillan, 1864);

Small Tableaux, as Turner (London: Macmillan, 1868);

Sonnets, Lyrics and Translations, as Turner (London: King, 1873);

Collected Sonnets, Old and New, as Charles Tennyson Turner (London: Kegan Paul, 1880).

OTHER: "To a Lady" and "Sonnet, On Seeing a Bevy of Humming-Birds in a Glass Case," in *The Tribute: A Collection of Miscellaneous Unpublished Poems, by Various Authors*, edited by Lord Northampton [Spencer Joshua Alwyne Compton] (London: Murray & Lindsell, 1837).

PERIODICAL PUBLICATIONS: "Four Sonnets": "Spring," "A Thought for March, 1860," "Sunrise," "Resurrection," *Macmillan's*, 2 (June 1860): 98-99;

"An Eastern Legend Versified, from Alphonse de Lamartine's Travels," *Macmillan's*, 2 (July 1860): 226-227;

"A Myth about The Nightingales" and "The Rainbow," *Macmillan's*, 4 (June 1861): 167-168;

Charles (Tennyson) Turner

"To Mrs. Cameron," in Julia Margaret Cameron, *Illustrations to Tennyson's Idylls of the King, and Other Poems,* 2 volumes (London: King, 1875), volume 1, unnumbered page after dedication.

Charles (Tennyson) Turner is recognized as an accomplished and thoughtful sonneteer in his own right; his work also provides an interesting gloss on that of his younger brother, Alfred Tennyson. Their upbringing was the same; both were serious writers. Charles concentrated on one genre and earned the admiration of a few, while Alfred explored all sorts of poetic forms and became the most famous writer of the Victorian age.

Charles Tennyson was the second son of the Reverend George Clayton Tennyson, rector of Somersby and Bag Enderby, Lincolnshire, and Elizabeth Fytche Tennyson. He was born in Somersby rectory, and within eleven years he had five younger brothers and four younger sisters, as well as an older brother, Frederick. Charles's favorite was Alfred, who was thirteen months younger than he, and they shared an early interest in writing poetry along with all the other activities of a rural childhood. They also shared an attic room with Frederick, Charles's senior by thirteen months, where they studied, slept, and exercised on an exposed wooden beam. They all benefited from their father's desire to see them educated in Latin and Greek as well as in French and German.

Charles's childhood, youth, and young manhood were colored by the pervasively unpleasant relationship between his father and his grandfather Tennyson, also named George. The rector was a neurotic and difficult man who suffered from epilepsy and often was too friendly with alcohol. The friction of his relationship with his father extended also to the rector's younger brother—another Charles—and led to an isolation of the rector and his numerous and crowded family from almost all of their relatives. The financial problems of a large and not very frugal family increased the tension greatly.

By 1815 Charles and Frederick were living in Louth with their mother's family, the Fytches, and were enrolled at the grammar school; Alfred joined them in December 1816. Their instruction, given harshly under the administration of their mother's cousin, the Reverend Dr. J. Waite, was never remembered kindly. The rector removed Alfred in 1820 and Charles in 1821 (Frederick had gone on to Eton in 1818) and began to educate them himself in Somersby. The resources of their father's sizable library meant a good bit to these two eager and acquisitive minds. So did their mother's encouragement of their first efforts to write poetry.

When Charles was eighteen, he and Alfred, with some assistance from Frederick, had their first volume of poetry published. *Poems by Two Brothers* was printed in 1827 primarily for distribution by J. and J. Jackson of Louth. While the 104 poems in this volume are scarcely the most accomplished that any of the brothers ever produced, they show a remarkable range of poetic forms and lyrical attitudes, and the epigraphs and footnotes reveal an unusual range of learning in classical and other literatures. When Alfred's son Hallam brought out a second edition of this book in 1893, he consulted Frederick (the only one of the three then living) about the authorship of the poems. Frederick could identify his own but was not sure which of the others were by Charles and which by Alfred. Various traditions and readings assign about half to each brother, and Charles seems to have had the privilege of writing the prefatory poem. Charles and Alfred were much stimulated by this publication and celebrated its advent with a joyous trip to the shore at Mablethorpe. Perhaps this same ebullience contributed to Charles's abortive attachment to his sister's governess later that year.

Title page for the anonymously published volume of poems by Charles, Alfred, and Frederick Tennyson

Charles began work at Trinity College, Cambridge, in October 1827; he shared rooms with Frederick, who had preceded him to the university. Alfred joined them shortly thereafter and before long Charles and he found new rooms together. Two years later, Charles won a Bell Scholarship for his translations of Greek; by then the three brothers enjoyed a reputation for general distinction and were regarded as young poets of unusual promise. In March 1830, W. Metcalfe in St. Mary's Street, Cambridge, printed for the publisher B. Bridges of Market Hill Charles's first separate volume of poetry, *Sonnets and Fugitive Pieces*. Charles dedicated the volume to his sister Mary and included fifty sonnets and fifteen other poems, at least three of which were translations from Anacreon. The slim volume of eighty-three pages was received with considerable enthusiasm, not only in Trinity but outside as well. While the volume was to some degree overshadowed in student eyes by Alfred's *Poems, Chiefly Lyrical,* published that June, Leigh Hunt's appreciative review of both first books gave the nod to Charles as perhaps the poet of greater promise. Hunt saw them both as able to "take their stand at once among the first poets of the day.... Mr. Wordsworth and Mr. Coleridge may give them the right hand of fellowship; and ... all who love genuine poetry, will read them, and quote them." Indeed, Mr. Coleridge did see Charles's volume and admired his poems greatly; Coleridge noted in his copy of the book that "To the Lark" was "among the best sonnets in our language." While the particular poem selected by Coleridge may not strike modern readers as a great work, it is a graceful, intelligent, and pleasing poem. The subject matter and formal peculiarities are representative of the volume as a whole. Most of the sonnets deal with concentrated perceptions of nature: of larks, nightingales, robins, butterflies, or spiders; of twilight, evening, or autumn; of ocean, lake, or rainbow. Others present aspects of human life: a lover's kiss, a birthday, an early perception of death. Still others treat contemporary Greece or address a particular person, such as Arthur Hallam. Charles's form is flexible, following neither the Petrarchan nor the Shakespearean patterns of rhymes. Usually the first eight lines form two quatrains, but even here the patterns vary. The last six lines cohere in almost as many different ways as possible.

By the fall of 1830 Charles had decided not to return to Cambridge; the cause may have been fear of examinations or may have been a genuine illness, such as asthma, chronic neuralgia, or early dependence on opium. The rector was already taking opium as a misguided remedy for his epilepsy, and Charles could easily have had access to the drug from this source. In November, however, Charles did return to Cambridge with Alfred, and he continued his education until the major disruption occasioned by the collapse of his father in February 1831. After the rector's death on 16 March the financial insecurities of the family increased. Although future prospects for support from grandfather George Tennyson seemed reasonable enough, there was little cash and the debts from Cambridge were formidable. While old George Tennyson paid these bills, he required Frederick, Charles, and Alfred to sign bonds against their father's estate to cover the total required. Nevertheless, Charles returned to Cambridge in the fall of 1831 and took his degree in January of the next year.

Charles's financial future was less bleak than the required bonds might make it seem. For some years he had been recognized openly as the heir of his great-uncle, Samuel Turner, the vicar of Grasby and the brother of his grandmother Tennyson. Because of his grandfather Tennyson's arrangements and because of his own father's will, the inheritance from Samuel Turner, who died 9 March 1835, was joined (after George Tennyson's death on 4 July) with the substantial properties of grandmother Tennyson's bachelor brother, John Turner, which had long been intended for Charles. The combined inheritance amounted to a substantial living. Samuel Turner required that his heir take the name of Turner, which Charles, by royal license, promptly did, using that surname for the rest of his life.

Urgings all around—from his grandfather, from his great-uncle Turner, from his uncle Charles Tennyson, and from general practical necessity—had moved Charles toward taking holy orders. He was ordained in 1832 and served as curate at Tealby until his inheritance allowed him to move to the big Turner house at Caistor. By the next year, however, he had become seriously addicted to opium, a problem which haunted him for decades to come. The habit was sufficiently shaken, however, for Charles to court Louisa Sellwood of Horncastle, and after an engagement of eight months they were married on 24 May 1836. After a honeymoon in Switzerland, they settled into Charles's parish life, to which they both became wholeheartedly dedicated. The problems with opium recurred, however, and Charles's condition became so serious that he and Louisa were separated from 1839 until 1849; their problems led to a rupture of the Tennyson and Sellwood families. Their reunion in the new vicarage at Grasby marked the beginning of an unbroken thirty-year devotion to that parish, its people, and its institutions. They had no children but gave themselves unstintingly to the people around them. Charles's money (some of which he was forced to recover from an unscrupulous agent whom he had trusted during his illness) was used to refurbish the church and the school and also to purchase the village inn. Charles was in no way obsessed with promptitude, and his relaxed and generous, if at times eccentric, concern for his parish derived from the complete Christian confidence and humility which sustained him for the rest of his life.

After a silence of thirty-four years, Turner arranged for Macmillan to publish a second volume of his poetry in 1864. It was entitled simply *Sonnets* and contained 100 of them, with a few notes. Ninety-eight poems were presented for the first time; two were revised from the 1830 volume. The general range of subject matter is little changed except that more sonnets on historical subjects, events in the Christian year, and contemporary theological problems are included. The rhyme schemes vary as they had in *Sonnets and Fugitive Pieces*; but in this volume a few are in a Shakespearean pattern.

Four years later, Turner had *Small Tableaux* published by Macmillan. This volume presented 109 sonnets and two pages of notes; the last twenty-three sonnets were revisions from the 1830 volume. The range of subjects is not greatly changed from the previous two books, except that many more events from the Grasby parish are treated and at least two poems, "Vienna and In Memoriam" and "A Farewell to the Isle of Wight," deal with Alfred. Two others memorialize a visit to Frederick in Jersey.

After only a slightly greater interval, Turner had *Sonnets, Lyrics and Translations* published in 1873 by Henry S. King. He dedicated the volume to his wife's niece, Agnes Grace Weld, who had often been their guest when she was a child. This volume, Turner's fourth, was only his second to include poems which are not sonnets. To the seventy-eight sonnets (fifty-nine new, nineteen revised from earlier volumes) are added nine lyrics on a wide variety of subjects and four translations from Greek poetry; over half of the lyrics and translations had first been published in 1830. Again, the closeness of all these poems to Turner's immediate experience—as pastor, as lover of nature and of people, as devoted Christian, and as sensitive Englishman—tend to keep them honest and attractive works of art. The *Athenaeum* (16 August 1873) gave brief notice to the book, along with ten others, under the heading "Minor Poets." The sonnets are called "gracefully written ... which prove the author to be a man of culture with special gifts of taste, but without the informing power which belongs only to a high and genuine poetic genius." The reviewer goes on to observe that some of Turner's best poems are about the lives of children. The quick condescension of this reviewer, even in a context of general appreciation, is typical of the few public notices which Turner's poetry received in his lifetime.

In 1876 Turner told a visitor, H. D. Rawnsley, an old family friend, a good bit about the relationship of his poetry to the other parts of his life. When Rawnsley asked him why he had stayed so exclusively with the sonnet form, he answered "that Alfred's fame, and name, and great mastery" of so many different forms, lyric and epic, had intimidated him and that he had remained with what he knew best. When Rawnsley asked Turner why he had been silent from 1830 to 1864 (except for a very few periodical publications), Turner at first could not or would not offer a reason. At last he suggested that either his inspiration had been frozen or that "Alfred's perfect work . . . made me feel so ashamed of my own poor attempts that I did not brace myself to the task."

On 25 April 1879, after an illness of about a year, Turner died in Cheltenham, where he had gone for medical attention. Louisa died less than a month later and was buried beside her beloved husband in the Cheltenham cemetery.

Of all the laureate's six brothers, Charles was the closest to him. As children, as students, and as young men they shared almost everything. They married sisters; Alfred Tennyson and Emily Sellwood were witnesses at the wedding of Charles and Louisa in 1836 but, because of a variety of problems, Alfred and Emily did not marry until 1850. On the other hand, Turner was as removed from the public eye as Tennyson was in it. Turner's life was devoted without challenge to his wife and parish; Tennyson's dedication to his family was maintained against constant public pressure. For most of his life, Turner had plenty of money and gave it little thought; Tennyson accumulated a vastly greater fortune than Turner ever had, but he never wholly lost his early feelings of financial insecurity. Charles was the first of the literary Tennyson brothers to die, by thirteen years. Alfred, who had already publicly expressed his particular closeness to Charles in section seventy-nine of *In Memoriam* (written as a gloss to section nine, which had been open to misinterpretation by Charles), urged that a collected edition of his brother's sonnets be published. He wrote a touching elegy of twenty-eight lines for Turner's *Collected Sonnets Old and New*, which was published in 1880 with a preface by Hallam Tennyson and a lengthy essay, reprinted from the *Nineteenth Century*, by James Spedding. This volume gave the author's name as Charles Tennyson Turner, the first volume ever to do so, and presented 50 sonnets not previously published, in addition to the canon of 293 sonnets. After a visit to Catullus's Sirmio in 1880, Tennyson wrote his better-known poem "Frater Ave atque Vale," another reminiscence with a clear reference to Charles.

While Charles Turner, in his quiet life at Grasby, saw relatively little of Alfred Tennyson in the last twenty-five or thirty years of his life, their early closeness formed an important bond of emotional sustenance which each of them was eager to maintain; Turner's modest contributions to poetry pleased Tennyson deeply. Turner was mourned not by a vast public—the obituaries were short and few—but by his family, the parishioners whom he loved and served, and the readers who recognized the importance of his valid, homely perceptions recorded in a disciplined poetic form. Writing sonnets helped sustain Turner as a dedicated pilgrim in the emotionally varied rural world he knew and loved; his poems were an added grace for those who knew him and an unexpected blessing for readers who did not.

References:

Roger Evans, " 'Midnight, June 30, 1879' and the Sonnets of Charles Tennyson Turner," *Tennyson Research Bulletin,* 4 (November 1983): 81-91;

Henry G. Hewlett, "English Sonneteers: Mr. Charles Turner," *Contemporary Review,* 22 (September 1873): 633-642;

Sir Francis Hill, "The Disinheritance Tradition Reconsidered," *Tennyson Research Bulletin,* 3 (November 1978): 41-54;

K. A. Jelinek, *Charles Tennyson-Turner—Leben und Werke* (Leipzig, 1909);

Robert Bernard Martin, *Tennyson: The Unquiet Heart* (Oxford: Clarendon Press, 1980);

Harold Nicolson, *Tennyson's Two Brothers* (Cambridge: Cambridge University Press, 1947);

H. D. Rawnsley, *Memories of the Tennysons* (Glasgow: MacLehose, 1912);

Christopher Ricks, ed., *The Poems of Tennyson* (London: Longmans, Green, 1969);

James Spedding, "Charles Tennyson Turner," *Nineteenth Century* (6 September 1879): 461-480; republished as introductory essay to Charles Tennyson Turner, *Collected Sonnets Old and New* (London: Kegan Paul, 1880), pp. 1-31;

Charles Tennyson, *Alfred Tennyson* (London: Macmillan, 1950);

Tennyson, "Tennyson and His Brothers, Frederick and Charles," in *Tennyson and His Friends,* edited by Hallam, Lord Tennyson (London: Macmillan, 1911), pp. 33-68;

Tennyson, "The Vicar of Grasby," *English,* 8 (1950): 117-120;

Tennyson and John Betjeman, introduction to Charles Tennyson Turner, *A Hundred Sonnets* (London: Hart-Davis, 1960), pp. 7-15;

Tennyson and Hope Dyson, *The Tennysons: Background to Genius* (London: Macmillan, 1974);

Hallam, Lord Tennyson, *Alfred Lord Tennyson: A Memoir,* 2 volumes (London: Macmillan, 1897).

Papers:

The best collection (but by no means a full archive) of Charles Turner's papers is available at the Tennyson Research Centre in Lincoln. At Turner's death much of his library was dispersed, but well over 200 of his books (some originally from the Somersby library) and some of his papers came into the possession of his brother Alfred and subsequently came to the centre. The books are fully catalogued as nos. 2383-2618 in Nancie P. Campbell, *Tennyson in Lincoln: A Catalogue of the Collections in the Research Centre* (Lincoln: Tennyson Society, 1971), volume 1, pp. xv and 109-123.

Charles Jeremiah Wells
(ca. 1800-17 February 1879)

Ira Bruce Nadel
University of British Columbia

BOOKS: *Stories after Nature,* anonymous (London: Allman, 1822);

Joseph and His Brethren, A Scriptural Drama, as H. L. Howard (London: Whittaker, 1823; expanded and revised, as Wells, London: Chatto & Windus, 1876).

OTHER: "Sonnet to Chaucer," in *The Poems of Geoffrey Chaucer Modernised,* edited by R. H. Horne (London: Whittaker, 1841);

"A Dramatic Scene," edited by H. B. Forman, in *Literary Anecdotes of the Nineteenth Century,* edited by W. R. Nicoll and T. J. Wise, volume 1 (London: Hodder & Stoughton, 1895), pp. 291-318.

PERIODICAL PUBLICATIONS: "A Boar-Hunt in Brittany," anonymous, *Fraser's,* 34 (October 1846): 416-427;

"Love Passages in the Life of Perron the Breton, Being a Sequel to the Chasseurs' 'Boar-Hunt in Brittany,' " *Fraser's,* 35 (June 1847): 655-667.

Perhaps the only nineteenth-century poet to know both Keats and Swinburne, Charles Jeremiah Wells was a writer of limited productivity with a small but enthusiastic coterie of readers. The author of only two published books, the first appear-

Charles Jeremiah Wells

ing anonymously, the second under the pseudonym "H. L. Howard," Wells nonetheless received praise from Dante Gabriel Rossetti, Algernon Charles Swinburne, George Meredith, and Edmund Gosse for his major poem, *Joseph and His Brethren* (1823). Keats addressed a sonnet to him in 1816; Rossetti offered to edit his work in 1850; Swinburne praised him in a critical essay in 1875. Although *Joseph and His Brethren* was neglected when it first appeared, the Pre-Raphaelites rediscovered the work and strenuously sought to establish Wells's reputation as a major figure in nineteenth-century poetry.

Wells was born in London of moderately well-to-do parents who pledged him to law early in life, as Keats's parents had prepared him for a career in medicine. A short and sturdy boy with dark red hair and bright blue eyes, Wells called himself "the cub" in reference to his habitually rough manners. At Edmonton, where he was sent to Cowden Clark's school, Wells became friendly with John Keats's younger brother, Thomas, who was apprenticed to an apothecary. Wells gradually developed a friendship with the poet and his circle, which included Leigh Hunt. Keats's sonnet "To a Friend Who Sent Me Some Roses," written in June 1816, is addressed to Wells, although Keats was never sure whether the roses were sent in praise or in jest.

While Wells was articled to a London solicitor following school, his friendship with Keats flourished. Between November 1817 and March 1818, Keats lived with his brothers in the Cheapside section of London, and he and Wells explored the city—attending, for example, William Hazlitt's lectures on the English poets in the early months of 1818. (Wells became an intimate of Hazlitt's, whose epitaph he composed in 1830.) But after Keats left London in March to nurse the ailing Tom, who died on 1 December, their friendship dissolved. Precipitating the break was Keats's belief that a practical joke played by Wells had hastened Tom's death. Wells had sent some false love letters to Tom in a style burlesquing the neo-Spenserian manner of the Keats circle and employing several of Keats's less felicitous poetic expressions. Keats's discovery of this hoax in the spring of 1819 prompted him to write to his brother George that "it was no thoughtless hoax—but a cruel deception on a sanguine Temperament, with every show of friendship. I do not think death too bad for the villain. . . . I will be opium to his vanity—if I cannot injure his interests."

The rupture with Keats prompted Wells to write *Joseph and His Brethren* in six weeks "to compel Keats to esteem me and admit my *power*," as he recalled in an 1875 letter. Probably composed some time between 1818 and 1820—Wells had a tendency to obscure crucial dates, including his birthday—the work was then forgotten while he turned to a translation of Boccaccio's prose narratives. Wells was varying a scheme proposed by Keats and John Hamilton Reynolds to versify the *Decameron*. The result was his first published work, *Stories after Nature* (1822). Edmund Gosse summarized the half-Gothic, half-Keatsian style of the book as "a curious little volume of brocaded prose." Published a year after the death of Keats, the volume used Elizabethan diction, creating what Theodore Watts-Dunton called "a fascinating remoteness not to be found . . . elsewhere, save in metrical composition." Richard Garnett noted that the tales are "the nearest approach to the Italian novelette that our literature can show." However, these prose adventures, with their elaborate style and involved syntax, met with little public interest, although several were illustrated and reprinted in 1845 by W. J. Linton in his *Illuminated Magazine*.

Using the pseudonym "H. L. Howard," Wells had *Joseph and His Brethren* published in December 1823, although the title page read 1824. Hazlitt ungenerously called the work "not only original but aboriginal" and urged Wells to stick to law. Indifferent about the poem's prospects, Wells admitted having forgotten his pseudonym when he met his publisher, and he left the proofing and production of the volume to his friend R. H. Horne, who also lent him the money to finance the publication. Rossetti recalled that "never did a book fall more dead from the press than did *Joseph*," although notices appeared in a variety of periodicals, including the *Literary Chronicle* and the *Gentleman's Magazine*.

Joseph and His Brethren is a dramatic verse narrative in four acts. Elizabethan echoes of language, imagery, and character exist throughout the work, an account of the biblical Joseph and his brothers. Act One relates the decision of the sons of Jacob to sell their brother and the reaction of their father to the news of his son's apparent death. Act Two begins with a stunning descriptive prologue that presents the Egyptian landscape, where "the fiery heat doth beat against the ground/In a reflective waste of golden light;/Nor tree, nor shrub chequers the tedious blank:/Like a dull stain curs'd o'er with barrenness/Sear'd in the angry glances of the sun." From "speckled snakes and adders blue" to "birds of the night" who "wing their slow way across the desert sands," Wells creates a world of Keatsian images and Shakespearean intensity.

Phraxanor, the wife of Potiphar, is Wells's most dramatic creation, and she dominates the second act. Her declarations of love and her concentrated effort to seduce Joseph display a powerful character not unlike that of Cleopatra. Her voice expresses a Shakespearean clarity of purpose as she tells Joseph, "We are most dear/In our affections; in vengeance most resolv'd." Imprisoned in Act Three, Joseph displays his ability to interpret dreams, explaining to Pharaoh that

Like the sea beast, the huge Leviathan,
Truth often swims at bottom of the world,
While dolphins play above his grainèd back:
So men o'erfigure truth.

The climax of Joseph's rise in the court is his confrontation with his brothers in Act Four, which culminates in his reunion with his father. In its prologues and descriptions, *Joseph and His Brethren* parallels the early writing of Keats, notably *Endymion*, as Wells simulates, with technical mastery, the sensuousness of Keats's imagery. The entire poem possesses the aura of Keats, which has caused one recent critic, Priscilla Johnston, to comment that Wells is "the earliest and probably the most overt follower that Keats ever had."

Indifferent to his literary career, Wells practiced law in London between 1820 and the early 1830s. He married Emily Jane Hill, the daughter of a Hertfordshire schoolmaster, in 1827. They had three daughters and a son; the son became an engineer and quite notorious for his various investment scandals, and also inspired the song "The Man Who Broke the Bank at Monte Carlo." In the early 1830s Wells gave up the practice of law for reasons of health. He retired first to Wales and then in 1835 to Hertfordshire to devote himself to shooting, fishing, boating, and horticulture. In 1840 or 1841 he left England for Brittany, where he was professor of English at a college in Quimper for a short time. In 1841 a sonnet he had written on Chaucer in 1823 appeared in a volume entitled *The Poems of Geoffrey Chaucer Modernised*, edited by his friend R. H. Horne.

Learning from Hazlitt's son in 1845 that several of his *Stories after Nature* had been reprinted, he quickly wrote two more. "Claribel" was accepted by the *Illuminated Magazine* in 1845 but the other was refused. That same year Wells made a brief trip to England to visit W. J. Linton, editor of the *Illuminated Magazine*, and to submit a historical romance, "Gaston de Blondeville," to Smith, Elder and Company. It was never published. In 1850 his wife went to London in an attempt to have a new edition of *Joseph and His Brethren* printed, but she succeeded only in enlisting the support of Rossetti, who had come across Wells's writing in 1844 through Horne's *New Spirit of the Age* (1844). Rossetti began a correspondence with Wells which resulted in a revision of the poem, but no action to republish occurred at that time. By 1861 the work was being celebrated by Swinburne, who had been introduced to it by Rossetti. While at Oxford, Swinburne wrote an essay on the poem, using extracts from the 1850 revision, and sent it in October to Richard Monckton Milnes, who tried to place it in *Fraser's* magazine. The essay was returned, only to be revised and published in 1875 in the *Fortnightly Review* and then modified as the introduction to the 1876 edition of the work, published by Chatto and Windus. As early as 1837 Thomas Wade, in his poem *Contention of Love and Death,* had placed Wells in the front rank of nineteenth-century poets, an estimate Swinburne repeated in 1876 when he sought to enhance the reputation of one whom he called "the Patriarch of living poets." Throughout the 1860s and 1870s *Joseph and His Brethren* became, in the words of Gosse, "a kind of Shibboleth—a rite of initiation into the true poetic culture," and no self-respecting follower of Swinburne or Rossetti would enter Rossetti's home in Cheyne Walk or Ford Madox Brown's studio in Fitzroy Square without having first acquainted himself with the poetic drama Rossetti considered "more Shakespearean than anything else out of Shakespeare."

Except for two essays on hunting in *Fraser's* magazine in 1846 and 1847, nothing else by Wells was published in his lifetime, although at his wife's death in 1874 he had burned, in his words, "a novel, three volumes of short stories, poems, one advanced epic, etc." He told Horne in 1877 that he had done this because he had been unsuccessful in finding a publisher for any of the works.

While the Pre-Raphaelites proceeded to reestablish his reputation, Wells moved to Marseilles. After learning of Chatto and Windus's decision to reprint *Joseph and His Brethren*, he prepared a third version, having lost the 1850 version that had recently been returned to him (probably by his supporter Rossetti). But at the age of seventy-five, Wells left the chores of publication to H. Buxton Forman, who also published an unincorporated scene of the third version of the poem in 1895. Since the 1908 reprint in the World's Classics series, however, literary taste has not agreed with Swinburne's estimate that *Joseph and His Brethren* possesses "enough of genius to make it almost the most remarkable poem ever published at that time of life."

References:

H. Buxton Forman, "Concerning the Friend Who Sent Keats Some Roses," in *Twelfth Year Book* (Boston: Bibliophile Society, 1913), pp. 75-116;

Edmund Gosse, "Charles Jeremiah Wells," *Encyclopaedia Britannica,* eleventh edition (Cam-

bridge: Cambridge University Press, 1911), volume 28, pp. 513-514;
Priscilla Johnston, "Charles Jeremiah Wells: An Early Keatsian Poet," *Keats-Shelley Journal*, 26 (1977): 72-87;
W. J. Linton, preface to Charles Jeremiah Wells, *Stories after Nature* (London: Lawrence & Bullen, 1891), pp. vii-xvii;
Donald H. Reiman, introduction to *Joseph and His Brethren*, in Cornelius Webb and Charles Jeremiah Wells, *Sonnets; Summer; Joseph and His Brethren* (New York: Garland, 1978), pp. i-vii;
A. C. Swinburne, "An Unknown Poet," *Fortnightly Review* (23 February 1875): 217-232;
Molly Tatchell, "Charles Jeremiah Wells (1800-1879)," *Keats-Shelley Memorial Bulletin*, 22 (1971): 7-17;
Thomas Wade, *Contention of Love and Death: A Poem* (London: Moxon, 1837);
Theodore Watts-Dunton, "Rossetti and Charles Wells: A Reminiscence of Kelmscott Manor," in Charles Jeremiah Wells, *Joseph and His Brethren* (London: Oxford University Press, 1908), pp. xix-lviii.

Isaac Williams
(12 December 1802-1 May 1865)

G. B. Tennyson
University of California, Los Angeles

BOOKS: *Ars Geologica: Poema Cancellarii Praemio Donatum, et in Theatro Sheldoniano Recitatum Die Jun. XII A.D. MDCCCXXIII* (Oxford: Collingwood, 1823);
Tracts for the Times, by Members of the University of Oxford, nos. 80, 86, and 87 by Williams, 6 volumes (Oxford: Parker/London: Rivington, 1833-1841);
Lyra Apostolica, anonymous, by Williams, John William Bowden, Richard Hurrell Froude, John Keble, John Henry Newman, and Robert Isaac Wilberforce (Derby, U.K.: Mozley/London: Rivington, 1836; New York: D. Appleton/Philadelphia: G. S. Appleton, 1844);
The Cathedral; or, The Catholic and Apostolic Church of England (Oxford: Parker, 1838);
Thoughts in Past Years, anonymous (Oxford: Parker, 1838; New York: Appleton, 1841);
Christian Liberty; or, Why Should We Belong to the Church of England? (London: Rivington, 1840);
On the Church as Viewed by Faith and by the World (London: Rivington, 1840);
A Few Remarks on the Charge of the Lord Bishop of Glocester [sic] and Bristol on the Subject of Reserve in Communicating Religious Knowledge as Taught in the Tracts for the Times, No. 80, and No. 87, anonymous (Oxford: Parker, 1841);
Short Address to His Brethren on the Nature and Constitution of the Church of Christ and of the Branch of It Established in England (London: Rivington, 1841);
The Gospel Narrative of Our Lord's Passion Harmonized: With Reflections (London: Rivington, 1841; New York: Sparks, 1846);
Thoughts on the Study of the Holy Gospels, Intended as an Introduction to a Harmony and Commentary (London: Rivington, 1842);
The Baptistery; or, The Way of Eternal Life, 2 volumes (Oxford: Parker/London: Rivington, 1842-1844);
Hymns on the Catechism, anonymous (London: Burns, 1843; New York: Blake, 1845);
The Gospel Narrative of Our Lord's Resurrection Harmonized: With Reflections (London: Rivington, 1845);
Days and Seasons; or, Church Poetry for the Year (N.p., 1845);
The Altar; or, Meditations in Verse on the Great Christian Sacrifice, anonymous (London: Burns, 1847);
The Gospel Narrative of Our Lord's Ministry Harmonized: With Reflections, 3 volumes (London: Rivington, 1847-1849);
The Christian Scholar, anonymous (Oxford & London: Parker, 1849);
The Seven Days; or, The Old and New Creation (London: Parker, 1850);
Plain Sermons, on the Latter Part of the Catechism (Lon-

don: Rivington, 1851); republished as *Plain Sermons on the Catechism: New Edition* (New York: Pott, 1883);

A Short Memoir of R. A. Suckling, with Correspondence and Sermons (London: Master, 1852);

The Apocalypse, with Notes and Reflections (London: Rivington, 1852);

A Series of Sermons on the Epistle and Gospel, 3 volumes (London: Rivington, 1853-1855);

The Christian Seasons (London: Rivington, 1854);

Sermons on the Characters of the Old Testament (London: Rivington, 1856);

Female Characters of Holy Scripture (London: Rivington, 1859);

The Beginning of the Book of Genesis, with Notes and Reflections (London: Rivington, 1861);

The Psalms, Interpreted of Christ (London & Oxford: Rivington, 1864);

Devotional Commentary on the Gospel Narratives, 8 volumes (London: Rivington, 1869-1870);

The Autobiography of Isaac Williams, B.D., Fellow and Tutor of Trinity College, Oxford, edited by Sir George Prevost (London & New York: Longmans, Green, 1892).

OTHER: *Hymns Translated from the Parisian Breviary* (London: Rivington, 1839);

Antoine Sucquet, *Some Meditations and Prayers Selected from "The Way of Eternal Life," in Order to Illustrate and Explain the Pictures by Boetius a Bolswert for the Same Work*, translated from Latin by Williams (Oxford: Parker, 1845);

Sacred Verses with Pictures, edited by Williams (London: Burns, 1846);

Ancient Hymns for Children, compiled by Williams (London: Masters, 1848).

Isaac Williams was the most innovative and productive of a group of Tractarian devotional poets that flourished in the early and mid-Victorian years and that also included John Keble and John Henry Newman. Williams's several volumes of illustrated verse and verse meditations carried devotional poetry into new regions; however, his fame has faded almost entirely in this century and only recently has he received renewed scholarly and critical attention.

Williams was the third of four sons born to Isaac Lloyd and Anne Davies Williams of Cwmcynfelin, near Aberystwyth, Wales. Williams spent his early years in London, where his father was a barrister, but frequent visits to his birthplace and the strong Welsh associations of his family insured that he always felt an intense attraction for the Welsh countryside. He was educated privately, then at Harrow, and subsequently at Trinity College, Oxford, from which he received his degree in 1826.

As a result of receiving the chancellor's prize for Latin verse at Oxford in 1823 with his poem *Ars Geologica*, Williams gained the favorable attention of John Keble and others of Oriel College who would later lead the Oxford Movement. He studied in the summers with Keble at Fairford, and he spent much time with Richard Hurrell Froude. Williams was ordained deacon in 1829 and priest in 1831 of Windrush-cum-Sherborne in Gloucestershire. In 1831 he won a fellowship at Trinity College, where he was successively tutor, lecturer, dean, and vice-president, until his departure from Oxford in 1842. During his Trinity years he also served as John Henry Newman's curate, both at the university church of St. Mary the Virgin in Oxford and at the affiliated church in nearby Littlemore, where Williams officiated at the funeral of Newman's mother in 1836. Williams was widely known during these years for his high standards of scholarship and his Anglican High Churchmanship. He readily aligned himself with the Oxford or Tractarian Movement when it got under way in the early 1830s.

Williams had long been an avid writer of poetry, having distinguished himself for composition of Latin verse at Harrow well before writing his Oxford prize poem, and he diligently applied his talents to the Tractarian cause. The earliest of Williams's Tractarian devotional poetry to be published appeared in the *British Magazine* in the early 1830s and then in the collection *Lyra Apostolica* (1836). This volume, assembled by Newman, brought together poems, by divers hands, designed to express the theological and ecclesiastical views of the Oxford Movement. Williams's *Thoughts in Past Years*, containing poetry from as early as the 1820s, and the highly original volume of verse titled *The Cathedral* were both published in 1838. The latter was the first of a series of ingenious applications of Tractarian poetic principles to ecclesiastical subjects that would later include *The Baptistery* (1842-1844) and *The Altar* (1847). Williams was also a contributor to the *Tracts for the Times* (1833-1841).

In the contest in 1841-1842 to select a successor to John Keble as the Oxford professor of poetry, Williams was the candidate of the Tractarian party; but he could not gain majority support and withdrew his name from contention. On 22 June 1842 he married Caroline Champernowne of Dartington, Devon (also the seat of the Froude family), and retired from Oxford to serve as curate to John Keble's brother Thomas at Bisley, near Fairford,

Gloucestershire. He thus became a member of the "Bisley School," a group of especially dedicated and uncompromising Tractarians led by Thomas Keble. Six years later Williams removed to Stinchcombe, near Dursley, Gloucestershire, where he remained until his death in 1865. Although he suffered from poor health during much of his adult life, he continued to write poetry and prose, especially sermons. He also fathered six sons and one daughter. His *Autobiography,* published posthumously in 1892, offers an exceptionally attractive account of a Victorian ecclesiastical life and also much interesting information on the course of the Tractarian Movement by one who was intimately involved with it.

As a poet Williams enjoyed considerable esteem in his own day, although even then he stood much in the shadow of the preeminent devotional poet of the age, his friend and mentor John Keble. But Williams's poetry, though it shares Keble's convictions and poetic principles, has a character and quality all its own. His early work, most notably that in *Thoughts in Past Years,* reflects much of the Wordsworthian nature feeling so evident in Tractarian poetry in general, though Williams's verse is suffused with much more explicit theological and religious concerns than are evident in Wordsworth and is colored as well by Williams's interest in scenes from Wales and the west country of England. But Williams's other volumes of verse have a distinctive character that sets them apart from the work of any of his Victorian predecessors in devotional poetry, and these are the works that make a claim upon modern attention. They include above all *The Cathedral, The Baptistery,* and *The Altar.*

Williams's three ecclesiologically titled volumes provide a lengthy series of poems designed to illustrate the architectural features of the structure under consideration. These poems are accompanied by pictures intended to enhance the reader's awareness of the symbolic significance of the buildings and designs being examined. The illustrations were appropriated from Continental books of devotion and other such sources and were intended to help familiarize English readers with European styles of Catholic worship. The effort in each case is ambitious and programmatic—that is, arranged to reinforce a preexisting plan—hence it is sometimes forced but is always striking and individual. When Williams succeeds in these volumes he creates a new form—part verse, part visual enhancement—that intensifies the reader's awareness of the interaction of the verbal and the visual in traditional Catholic worship and devotion.

Williams's concern for the symbolic aspects of Christian worship and their representation in art, architecture, and verse rested in large measure on his interest in Gothic architecture, with its wealth of visual symbolism. He was one of the earliest enthusiasts for Gothic ecclesiastical structures, and his volumes of verse, especially *The Cathedral,* helped

Symbolic illustration, with explanatory text, for Williams's The Baptistery

Illustrated prayer for Williams's The Altar

stimulate the Victorian Gothic Revival. Likewise, Williams found certain Gothic features, such as the rood screen, to be the visual embodiment of the doctrine of reserve, a Tractarian favorite on which Williams discoursed at length in his most notable contribution to the *Tracts for the Times,* No. 80, "On Reserve in Communicating Religious Knowledge." Reserve was the Tractarian belief that sacred matters should be approached reverently and by degrees of gradual unveiling rather than confronted without due preparation of the soul. The rood screen before the altar symbolizes such a veiling. Williams also wrote eloquently in favor of the traditional Catholic approach to biblical and ecclesiastical typology and frequently included typological references in his poetry. These include the belief that persons and events in the Old Testament prefigure corresponding ones in the New Testament. Thus, Moses is a "type" of Christ, and the parting of the Red Sea is a prefigurement of Christian baptism. Williams advocated such interpretations and used them often in his verse.

The taste for Isaac Williams's poetry requires a degree of familiarity with Christian doctrine and with Gothic architecture, but Williams's practice of uniting verse and design helps remove many obstacles to understanding. Williams's range as poet, critic, and theologian is wider and richer than is generally assumed; and the most recent student of these topics to consider Williams has called his "an achievement that is imaginative in conception, vigorous in execution, and catholic in breadth of sympathy."

References:

O. W. Jones, *Isaac Williams and His Circle* (London: Society for Promoting Christian Knowledge, 1971);

G. B. Tennyson, *Victorian Devotional Poetry: The Tractarian Mode* (Cambridge: Harvard University Press, 1981), pp. 138-172.

Appendix

On Some of the Characteristics of Modern Poetry

Thoughts on Poetry and Its Varieties

The Hero as Poet. Dante; Shakspeare.

Essay on Chatterton

Introductory Essay

The Novel in "The Ring and the Book."

Preface to *Poems* (1853)

Editors' Note

The seven essays that form the appendix to *Victorian Poets Before 1850* indicate both the diversity of critical approaches and the range of interests among Victorian writers and critics. Reprinted here are Arthur Henry Hallam's early defense of Tennyson and analysis of Romantic poetry; John Stuart Mill's attempt to define the nature of poetry as "the delineation of states of feeling"; Thomas Carlyle's celebration of the poet's vision—"To the Poet . . . we say first of all, *See*"; Robert Browning's interpretation of the poetic mind and his division of poetry into subjective and objective categories in his essays on Chatterton and Shelley; Henry James's assessment of Browning and his commentary on character as "enveloping consciousness"; and Matthew Arnold's famous 1853 declaration on the nature of poetry and the importance of significant action. These essays reveal the fecundity and probity of the intellectual response to the development of Victorian verse.

Most notably, the essays articulate the role of the poet and his essential place in society. Browning sums up that function in his essay on Shelley when he says that the poet is sent to remedy "the misapprehensiveness of his age." Carlyle characterizes the imagination of the poet as part of the "Power of Insight" which "discloses the inner harmony of things." Mill argues that "the poetry of a poet is feeling itself, employing thought only as the medium of its expression." Hallam distinguishes between a Romantic and a classic school of poets, the first essentially subjective, represented by Shelley, Keats, and the young Tennyson; the second objective, focusing on the political and social issues that concerned poets such as Wordsworth. In the twenty-two years between Hallam's essay and Arnold's preface, Victorian poetry established a distinctive and unique voice, which was representative not only of the age of Victoria but of a lasting poetic and critical tradition.

On Some of the Characteristics of Modern Poetry

AND ON THE LYRICAL POEMS OF ALFRED TENNYSON

Arthur Henry Hallam

First published in the Englishman's Magazine *(August 1831): 616-628.*

When Mr. Wordsworth, in his celebrated Preface to the *Lyrical Ballads,* asserted that immediate or rapid popularity was not the test of poetry, great was the consternation and clamour among those farmers of public favour, the established critics. Never had so audacious an attack been made upon their undoubted privileges and hereditary charter of oppression.

"What! *The Edinburgh Review* not infallible!" shrieked the amiable petulance of Mr. Jeffrey.

"*The Gentleman's Magazine* incapable of decision!" faltered the feeble garrulity of Silvanus Urban.

And straightway the whole sciolist herd, men of rank, men of letters, men of wealth, men of business, all the "mob of gentlemen who think with ease," and a terrible number of old ladies and boarding-school misses began to scream in chorus, and prolonged the notes of execration with which they overwhelmed the new doctrine, until their wits and their voices fairly gave in from exhaustion. Much, no doubt, they did, for much persons will do when they fight for their dear selves; but there was one thing they could not do, and unfortunately it was the only one of any importance. They could not put down Mr. Wordsworth by clamour, or prevent his doctrine, once uttered, and enforced by his example, from awakening the minds of men, and giving a fresh impulse to art. It was the truth, and it prevailed; not only against the exasperation of that hydra, the Reading Public, whose vanity was hurt, and the blustering of its keepers, whose delusion was exposed, but even against the false glosses and narrow apprehensions of the Wordsworthians themselves. It is the madness of all who loosen some great principle, long buried under a snow-heap of custom and superstition, to imagine that they can restrain its operation, or circumscribe it by their purposes. But the right of private judgment was stronger than the will of Luther; and even the genius of Wordsworth cannot expand itself to the full periphery of poetic art.

It is not true, as his exclusive admirers would have it, that the highest species of poetry is the reflective; it is a gross fallacy, that because certain opinions are acute or profound, the expression of them by the imagination must be eminently beautiful. Whenever the mind of the artist suffers itself to be occupied, during its periods of creation, by any other predominant motive than the desire of beauty, the result is false in art.

Now there is undoubtedly no reason why he may not find beauty in those moods of emotion, which arise from the combinations of reflective thought; and it is possible that he may delineate these with fidelity, and not be led astray by any suggestions of an unpoetical mood. But though possible, it is hardly probable; for a man whose reveries take a reasoning turn, and who is accustomed to measure his ideas by their logical relations rather than the congruity of the sentiments to which they refer, will be apt to mistake the pleasure he has in knowing a thing to be true, for the pleasure he would have in knowing it to be beautiful, and so will pile his thoughts in a rhetorical battery, that they may convince, instead of letting them flow in a natural course of contemplation, that they may enrapture.

It would not be difficult to shew, by reference to the most admired poems of Wordsworth, that he is frequently chargeable with this error; and that much has been said by him which is good as philosophy, powerful as rhetoric, but false as poetry. Perhaps this very distortion of the truth did more in the peculiar juncture of our literary affairs to enlarge and liberalize the genius of our age, than could have been effected by a less sectarian temper.

However this may be, a new school of reformers soon began to attract attention, who, professing the same independence of immediate favor, took their stand on a different region of Parnassus from that occupied by the Lakers,[1] and one, in our opinion, much less liable to perturbing currents of air from ungenial climates. We shall not hesitate to express our conviction, that the cockney school (as it was termed in derision from a cursory view of its accidental circumstances) contained more genuine inspiration, and adhered more steadily to that portion of truth which it embraced, than any *form* of art that has existed in this country since the days of Milton. Their *caposetta* was Mr. Leigh Hunt, who did little more than point the way, and was diverted from his aim by a thousand personal predilections and political habits of thought.

But he was followed by two men of very superior make; men who were born poets, lived poets, and went poets to their untimely graves. Shelley and Keats were indeed of opposite genius; that of the one was vast, impetuous, and sublime, the other seemed to be "fed with honeydew," and to have "drunk the milk of Paradise." Even the softness of Shelley comes out in bold, rapid, comprehensive strokes; he has no patience for minute beauties, unless they can be massed into a general effect of grandeur. On the other hand, the tenderness of Keats cannot sustain a lofty flight; he does not generalize or allegorize Nature; his imagination works with few symbols, and reposes willingly on what is given freely.

Yet in this formal opposition of character there is, it seems to us, a groundwork of similarity sufficient for the purposes of classification, and constituting a remarkable point in the progress of literature. They are both poets of sensation rather than reflection. Susceptible of the slightest impulse from external nature, their fine organs trembled into emotion at colors, and sounds, and movements, unperceived or unregarded by duller temperaments. Rich and clear were their perceptions of visible forms; full and deep their feelings of music. So vivid was the delight attending the simple exertions of eye and ear, that it became mingled more and more with their trains of active thought, and tended to absorb their whole being into the energy of sense. Other poets *seek* for images to illustrate their conceptions; these men had no need to seek; they lived in a world of images; for the most important and extensive portion of their life consisted in those emotions which are immediately conversant with the sensation. Like the hero of Goethe's novel, they would hardly have been affected by what is called the pathetic parts of a book; but the *merely beautiful* passages, "those from which the spirit of the author looks clearly and mildly forth," would have melted them to tears. Hence they are not descriptive, they are picturesque. They are not smooth and *negatively* harmonious; they are full of deep and varied melodies.

This powerful tendency of imagination to a life of immediate sympathy with the external universe, is not nearly so liable to false views of art as the opposite disposition of purely intellectual contemplation. For where beauty is constantly passing before "that inward eye, which is the bliss of solitude;" where the soul seeks it as a perpetual and necessary refreshment to the sources of activity and intuition; where all the other sacred ideas of our nature, the idea of good, the idea of perfection, the idea of truth, are habitually contemplated through the medium of this predominant mood, so that they assume its colour, and are subject to its peculiar laws, there is little danger that the ruling passion of the whole mind will cease to direct its creative operations, or the energetic principle of love for the beautiful sink, even for a brief period, to the level of a mere notion in the understanding.

We do not deny that it is, on other accounts, dangerous for frail humanity to linger with fond attachment in the vicinity of sense. Minds of this description are especially liable to moral temptations; and upon them, more than any, it is incumbent to remember, that their mission as men, which they share with their fellow-beings, is of infinitely higher interest than their mission as artists, which they possess by rare and exclusive privilege. But it is obvious that, critically speaking, such temptations are of slight moment. Not the gross and evident passions of our nature, but the elevated and less separable desires, are the dangerous enemies which misguide the poetic spirit in its attempts at self-cultivation. That delicate sense of fitness which grows with the growth of artist feelings, and strengthens with their strength, until it acquires a celerity and weight of decision hardly inferior to the correspondent judgments of conscience, is weakened by every indulgence of heterogeneous aspirations, however pure they may be, however lofty, however suitable to human nature.

We are therefore decidedly of opinion that the heights and depths of art are most within the reach of those who have received from nature the "fearful and wonderful" constitution we have described, whose poetry is a sort of magic, producing a number of impressions, too multiplied, too minute, and too diversified to allow of our tracing them to their causes, because just such was the effect, even so boundless and so bewildering, produced on their imaginations by the real appearance of Nature.

These things being so, our friends of the new school had evidently much reason to recur to the maxim laid down by Mr. Wordsworth, and to appeal from the immediate judgment of lettered or unlettered contemporaries to the decision of a more equitable posterity. How should they be popular, whose senses told them a richer and ampler tale than most men could understand, and who constantly expressed, because they constantly felt, sentiments of exquisite pleasure or pain, which most men were not permitted to experience? The public very naturally derided them as visionaries, and gibbeted *in terrorem* those inaccuracies of diction occasioned sometimes by the speed of their conceptions, sometimes by the inadequacy of language to their peculiar conditions of thought.

But it may be asked, does not this line of argument prove too much? Does it not prove that there is a barrier between these poets and all other persons so strong and immovable, that, as has been said of the Supreme Essence, we must be themselves before we can understand them in the least? Not only are they not liable to sudden and vulgar estimation, but the lapse of ages, it seems, will not consolidate their fame, nor the suffrages of the wise few produce any impression, however remote or slow matured, on the judgment of the incapacitated many.

We answer, this is not the import of our argument. Undoubtedly the true poet addresses himself, in all his conceptions, to the common nature of us all. Art is a lofty tree, and may shoot up far beyond our grasp, but its roots are in daily life and experience. Every bosom contains the elements of those complex emotions which the artist feels, and every head can, to a certain extent, go over in itself the process of their combination, so as to understand his expressions and sympathize with his state. But this requires exertion; more or less, indeed, according to the difference of occasion, but always some degree of exertion. For since the emotions of the poet, during composition, follow a regular law of association, it follows that to accompany their progress up to the harmonious prospect of the whole, and to perceive the proper dependence of every step on that which preceded, it is absolutely necessary *to start from the same point,* i.e. clearly to apprehend that leading sentiment of the poet's mind, by their conformity to which the host of suggestions are arranged.

Now this requisite exertion is not willingly made by the large majority of readers. It is so easy to judge capriciously, and according to indolent impulse! For very many, therefore, it has become *morally* impossible to attain the author's point of vision, on account of their habits, or their prejudices, or their circumstances; but it is never *physically* impossible, because nature has placed in every man the simple elements, of which art is the sublimation. Since then this demand on the reader for activity, when he wants to peruse his author in a luxurious passiveness, is the very thing that moves his bile, it is obvious that those writers will be always most popular who require the least degree of exertion. Hence, whatever is mixed up with art, and appears under its semblance, is always more favorably regarded than art free and unalloyed. Hence, half the fashionable poems in the world are mere rhetoric, and half the remainder are, perhaps, not liked by the generality for their substantial merits. Hence, likewise, of the really pure compositions, those are most universally agreeable which take for their primary subject the *usual* passions of the heart, and deal with them in a simple state, without applying the transforming powers of high imagination. Love, friendship, ambition, religion, &c., are matters of daily experience even amongst unimaginative tempers. The forces of association, therefore, are ready to work in these directions, and little effort of will is necessary to follow the artist.

For the same reason, such subjects often excite a partial power of composition, which is no sign of a truly poetic organization. We are very far from wishing to depreciate this class of poems, whose influence is so extensive, and communicates so refined a pleasure. We contend only that the facility with which its impressions are communicated is no proof of its elevation as a form of art, but rather the contrary.

What, then, some may be ready to exclaim, is the pleasure derived by most men, from Shakespeare, or Dante, or Homer, entirely false and factitious? If these are really masters of their art, must not the energy required of the ordinary intelligences that come in contact with their mighty genius, be the greatest possible? How comes it then, that they are popular? Shall we not say, after all, that the difference is in the power of the author, not in the tenor of his meditations? Those eminent spirits find no difficulty in conveying to common apprehensions their lofty sense and profound observation of Nature. They keep no aristocratic state, apart from the sentiments of society at large; they speak to the hearts of all, and by the magnetic force of their conceptions, elevate inferior intellects into a higher and purer atmosphere.

The truth contained in this observation is undoubtedly important; geniuses of the most universal order, and assigned by destiny to the most propitious era of a nation's literary development, have a clearer and a larger access to the minds of their compatriots than can ever open to those who are circumscribed by less fortunate circumstances. In the youthful periods of any literature there is an expansive and communicative tendency in mind which produces unreservedness of communion, and reciprocity of vigor between different orders of intelligence.

Without abandoning the ground which has always been defended by the partizans of Mr. Wordsworth, who declare with perfect truth, that the number of real admirers of what is really admirable in Shakespeare and Milton is much fewer than the number of apparent admirers might lead one to imagine, we may safely assert that the intense thoughts set in circulation by those "orbs of song" and their noble satellites "in great Eliza's golden time," did not fail to awaken a proportionable intensity of the nature of numberless auditors. Some might feel feebly, some strongly; the effect would vary according to the character of the recipient; but upon none was the stirring influence entirely unimpressive. The knowledge and power thus imbibed became a part of national existence; it was ours as Englishmen; and amid the flux of generations and customs we retain unimpaired this privilege of intercourse with greatness.

But the age in which we live comes late in our national progress. That first raciness and juvenile vigor of literature, when nature "wantoned as in her prime, and played at will her virgin fancies" is gone, never to return. Since that day we have undergone a period of degradation. "Every handicraftsman has worn the mask of Poesy." It would be tedious to repeat the tale so often related of the French contagion and the heresies of the Popian school.

With the close of the last century came an era of reaction, an era of painful struggle to bring our over-civilised condition of thought into union with the fresh productive spirit that brightened the morning of our literature. But repentance is unlike innocence; the laborious endeavor to restore has more complicated methods of action than the freedom of untainted nature. Those different powers of poetic disposition, the energies of Sensitive,[2] of Reflective, of Passionate Emotion, which in former times were intermingled, and derived from mutual support an extensive empire over the feelings of men, were now restrained within separate spheres of agency. The whole system no longer worked harmoniously, and by intrinsic harmony acquired external freedom; but there arose a violent and unusual action in the several component functions, each for itself, all striving to reproduce the regular power which the whole had once enjoyed.

Hence the melancholy which so evidently characterises the spirit of modern poetry; hence that return of the mind upon itself and the habit of seeking relief in idiosyncrasies rather than community of interest. In the old times the poetic impulse went along with the general impulse of the nation; in these it is a reaction against it, a check acting for conservation against a propulsion towards change.

We have indeed seen it urged in some of our fashionable publications, that the diffusion of poetry must be in the direct ratio of the diffusion of machinery, because a highly civilized people must have new objects of interest, and thus a new field will be open to description. But this notable argument forgets that against this *objective* amelioration may be set the decrease of *subjective* power, arising from a prevalence of social activity, and a continual absorption of the higher feelings into the palpable interests of ordinary life. The French Revolution may be a finer theme than the war of Troy; but it does not so evidently follow that Homer is to find his superior.

Our inference, therefore, from this change in the relative position of artists to the rest of the community is, that modern poetry in proportion to its depth and truth is likely to have little immediate authority over public opinion. Admirers it will have; sects consequently it will form; and these strong under-currents will in time sensibly affect the principal stream. Those writers whose genius, though great, is not strictly and essentially poetic, become mediators between the votaries of art and the careless cravers for excitement.[3] Art herself, less manifestly glorious than in her periods of undisputed supremacy, retains her essential prerogatives, and forgets not to raise up chosen spirits who may minister to her state and vindicate her title.

One of the faithful Islám, a poet in the truest and highest sense, we are anxious to present to our readers. He has yet written little and published less; but in these "preludes of a loftier strain" we recognize the inspiring god. Mr. Tennyson belongs decidedly to the class we have already described as Poets of Sensation. He sees all the forms of nature with the "eruditus oculus," and his ear has a fairy fineness. There is a strange earnestness in his worship of beauty which throws a charm over his impassioned song, more easily felt than described, and not to be escaped by those who have once felt it. We think he has more definiteness and roundness of general conception than the late Mr. Keats, and is much more free from blemishes of diction and hasty capriccios of fancy. He has also this advantage over that poet and his friend Shelley, that he comes before the public unconnected with any political party or peculiar system of opinions. Nevertheless, true to the theory we have stated, we believe his participation in their characteristic excellences is sufficient to secure him a share of their unpopularity.

The volume of "Poems, chiefly Lyrical," does not contain above 154 pages; but it shews us much more of the character of its parent mind, than many books we have known of much larger compass and more boastful pretensions. The features of original genius are clearly and strongly marked. The author imitates nobody; we recognise the spirits of his age, but not the individual form of this or that writer. His thoughts bear no more resemblance to Byron or Scott, Shelley or Coleridge, than to Homer or Calderon, Firdúsí or Calidasa.

We have remarked five distinctive excellencies of his own manner. First, his luxuriance of imagination, and at the same time his control over it. Secondly his power of embodying himself in ideal characters, or rather moods of character, with such extreme accuracy of adjustment, that the circumstances of the narration seem to have a natural correspondence with the predominant feeling, and, as it were, to be evolved from it by assimilative force. Thirdly his vivid, picturesque delineation of objects, and the peculiar skill with which he holds all of them *fused,* to borrow a metaphor from science, in a medium of strong emotion. Fourthly, the variety of his lyrical measures, and exquisite modulation of harmonious words and cadences to the swell and fall of the feelings expressed. Fifthly, the elevated habits of thought, implied in these compositions, and imparting a mellow soberness of tone, more impressive, to our minds, than if the author had drawn up a set of opinions in verse, and sought to instruct the understanding rather than to communicate the love of beauty to the heart.

We shall proceed to give our readers some specimens in illustration of these remarks, and, if possible, we will give them entire; for no poet can be fairly judged of by fragments, least of all, a poet like Mr. Tennyson, whose mind conceives nothing isolated, nothing abrupt, but every part with reference to some other part, and in subservience to the idea of the whole.

Recollections of the Arabian Nights!—What a delightful, endearing title! How we pity those to whom it calls up no reminiscence of early enjoyment, no sentiment of kindliness as towards one who sings a song they have loved, or mentions with affection a departed friend! But let nobody expect a multifarious enumeration of Viziers, Barmecides, Fireworshippers, and Cadis; trees that sing, horses that fly, and Goules that eat rice-pudding!

Our author knows what he is about; he has, with great judgment, selected our old acquaintance, "the good Haroun Alraschid," as the most prominent object of our childish interest, and with him has called up one of those luxurious garden scenes, the account of which, in plain prose, used to make our mouth water for sherbet, since luckily we were too young to think much about Zobeide! We think this poem will be the favourite among Mr. Tennyson's admirers; perhaps upon the whole it is our own; at least we find ourselves recurring to it oftener than to any other, and every time we read it, we feel the freshness of its beauty increase, and are inclined to exclaim with Madame de Sevigne "*a force d'etre ancien, il m'est nouveau.*" But let us draw the curtain.

RECOLLECTIONS OF THE ARABIAN NIGHTS

When the breeze of a joyful dawn blew free
In the silken sail of infancy,
The tide of time flow'd back with me,
  The forward-flowing tide of time;
And many a sheeny summer-morn,
Adown the Tigris I was borne,
By Bagdat's shrines of fretted gold,
High-walled gardens green and old;
True Mussulman was I and sworn,
  For it was in the golden prime
    Of good Haroun Alraschid.

Anight my shallop, rustling thro'
The low and bloomed foliage, drove
The fragrant, glistening deeps, and clove
The citron-shadows in the blue;
By garden porches on the brim,
The costly doors flung open wide,
Gold glittering thro' lamplight dim,
And broider'd sofas on each side.
  In sooth it was a goodly time,
  For it was in the golden prime
    Of good Haroun Alraschid.

Often, where clear-stemm'd platans guard
The outlet, did I turn away
The boat-head down a broad canal
From the main river sluiced, where all
The sloping of the moonlit sward
Was damask-work, and deep inlay
Of braided blooms unmown, which crept
Adown to where the water slept.
  A goodly place, a goodly time,
  For it was in the golden prime
    Of good Haroun Alraschid.

A motion from the river won
Ridged the smooth level, bearing on
My shallop thro' the star-strown calm,

Until another night in night
I enter'd, from the clearer light,
Imbower'd vaults of pillar'd palm,
Imprisoning sweets, which, as they clomb
Heavenward, were stay'd beneath the dome
  Of hollow boughs. A goodly time,
    For it was in the golden prime
      Of good Haroun Alraschid.

Still onward; and the clear canal
Is rounded to as clear a lake.
From the green rivage many a fall
Of diamond rillets musical,
Thro' little crystal arches low
Down from the central fountain's flow
Fallen silver-chiming, seemed to shake
The sparkling flints beneath the prow.
  A goodly place, a goodly time,
    For it was in the golden prime
      Of good Haroun Alraschid

Above thro' many a bowery turn
A walk with vari-colored shells
Wander'd engrain'd. On either side
All round about the fragrant marge
From fluted vase, and brazen urn
In order, eastern flowers large,
Some dropping low their crimson bells
Half-closed, and others studded wide
  With disks and tiars, fed the time
    With odor in the golden prime
      Of good Haroun Alraschid.

Far off, and where the lemon grove
In closest coverture upsprung,
The living airs of middle night
Died round the bulbul as he sung;
Not he, but something which possess'd
The darkness of the world, delight,
Life, anguish, death, immortal love,
Ceasing not, mingled, unrepress'd
  Apart from place, withholding time,
    But flattering the golden prime
      Of good Haroun Alraschid.

Black the garden-bowers and grots
Slumber'd; the solemn palms were ranged
Above, unwoo'd of summer wind;
A sudden splendor from behind
Flush'd all the leaves with rich gold-green,
And, flowing rapidly between
Their interspaces, counterchanged
The level lake with diamond-plots
  Of dark and bright. A lovely time,
    For it was in the golden prime
      Of good Haroun Alraschid.

Dark-blue the deep sphere overhead,
Distinct with vivid stars inlaid,
Grew darker from that under-flame;
So, leaping lightly from the boat,
With silver anchor left afloat,
In marvel whence that glory came
Upon me, as in sleep I sank
In cool soft turf upon the bank,
  Entranced with that place and time,
    So worthy of the golden prime
      Of good Haroun Alraschid.

Thence thro' the garden I was drawn—
A realm of pleasance, many a mound,
And many a shadow-chequer'd lawn
Full of the city's stilly sound,
And deep myrrh-thickets blowing round
The stately cedar, tamarisks,
Thick rosaries of scented thorn,
Tall orient shrubs, and obelisks
  Graven with emblems of the time,
    In honor of the golden prime
      Of good Haroun Alraschid.

With dazed vision unawares
From the long alley's latticed shade
Emerged, I came upon the great
Pavilion of the Caliphat.
Right to the carven cedarn doors,
Flung inward over spangled floors,
Broad-based flights of marble stairs
Ran up with golden balustrade,
  After the fashion of the time,
    And humor of the golden prime
      Of good Haroun Alraschid.

The fourscore windows all alight
As with the quintessence of flame,
A million tapers flaring bright
From twisted silvers look'd to shame
The hollow-vaulted dark, and stream'd
Upon the mooned domes aloof
In inmost Bagdat, till there seem'd
Hundreds of crescents on the roof
  Of night new-risen, that marvellous time
    To celebrate the golden prime
      Of good Haroun Alraschid.

Then stole I up, and trancedly
Gazed on the Persian girl alone,
Serene with argent-lidded eyes
Amorous, and lashes like to rays
Of darkness, and a brow of pearl
Tressed with redolent ebony,
In many a dark delicious curl,
Flowing beneath her rose-hued zone;
  The sweetest lady of the time,
    Well worthy of the golden prime
      Of good Haroun Alraschid.

Six columns, three on either side,
Pure silver, underpropt a rich
Throne of the massive ore, from which
Down-droop'd, in many a floating fold,
Engarlanded and diaper'd
With inwrought flowers, a cloth of gold.
Thereon, his deep eye laughter-stirr'd
With merriment of kingly pride,
  Sole star of all that place and time,
  I saw him—in his golden prime,
    THE GOOD HAROUN ALRASCHID

Criticism will sound but poorly after this; yet we cannot give silent votes. The first stanza, we beg leave to observe, places us at once in the position of feeling, which the poem requires. The scene is before us, around us; we cannot mistake its localities, or blind ourselves to its colours. That happy ductility of childhood returns for the moment; "true Mussulmans are we, and sworn," and yet there is a latent knowledge, which heightens the pleasure, that to our change from really childish thought we owe the capacities by which we enjoy the recollection.

As the poem proceeds, all is in perfect keeping. There is a solemn distinctness in every image, a majesty of slow motion in every cadence, that aids the illusion of thought, and steadies its contemplation of the complete picture. Originality of observation seems to cost nothing to our author's liberal genius; he lavishes images of exquisite accuracy and elaborate splendour, as a common writer throws about metaphorical truisms, and exhausted tropes. Amidst all the varied luxuriance of the sensations described, we are never permitted to lose sight of the idea which gives unity to this variety, and by the recurrence of which, as a sort of mysterious influence, at the close of every stanza, the mind is wrought up, with consummate art, to the final disclosure. This poem is a perfect gallery of pictures; and the concise boldness, with which in a few words an object is clearly painted, is sometimes (see the 6th stanza) majestic as Milton, sometimes (see the 12th) sublime as Aeschylus.

We have not, however, so far forgot our vocation as critics, that we would leave without notice the slight faults which adhere to this precious work. In the 8th stanza, we doubt the propriety of using the bold compound "black-green," at least in such close vicinity to "gold-green;" nor is it perfectly clear by the term, although indicated by the context, that "diamond plots" relates to shape rather than colour. We are perhaps very stupid, but "vivid stars unrayed" does not convey to us a very precise notion. "Rosaries of scented thorn," in the 10th stanza is, we believe, an entirely unauthorized use of the world. Would our author translate *"biferique rosaria Paesti"*—"And *rosaries* of Paestum, twice in bloom?"

To the beautiful 13th stanza we are sorry to find any objection; but even the bewitching loveliness of that "Persian girl" shall not prevent our performing the rigid duty we have undertaken, and we must hint to Mr. Tennyson that "redolent" is no synonyme for "fragrant." Bees may be redolent *of* honey; spring may be "redolent *of* youth and love;" but the absolute use of the word has, we fear, neither in Latin nor English any better authority than the monastic epitaph on Fair Rosamond: *"Hic jacet in tombá Rosa Mundi, non Rosa Munda, non redolet, sed olet, quae redolere solet."*

We are disposed to agree with Mr. Coleridge when he says "no adequate compensation can be made for the mischief a writer does by confounding the distinct senses of words." At the same time our feelings in this instance rebel strongly in behalf of "redolent;" for the melody of the passage, as it stands, is beyond the possibility of improvement, and unless he should chance to light upon a word very nearly resembling this in consonants and vowels, we can hardly quarrel with Mr. Tennyson if, in spite of our judgment, he retains the offender in his service.

Our next specimen is of a totally different character, but not less complete, we think, in its kind. Have we among our readers any who delight in the heroic poems of Old England, the inimitable ballads? Any to whom Sir Patrick Spens, and Clym of the Clough, and Glorious Robin are consecrated names? Any who sigh with disgust at the miserable abortions of simpleness mistaken for simplicity, or florid weakness substituted for plain energy which they may often have seen dignified with the title of Modern Ballads?

Let such draw near and read *The Ballad of Oriana*. We know no more happy seizure of the antique spirit in the whole compass of our literature; yet there is no foolish self-desertion, no attempt at obliterating the present, but everywhere a full discrimination of how much ought to be yielded and how much retained. The author is well aware that the art of one generation cannot *become* that of another by any will or skill; but the artist may transfer the spirit of the past, making it a temporary form for his own spirit, and so effect, by idealizing power, a new and legitimate combination. If we were asked to name among the real antiques that which bears greatest resemblance to this gem, we should refer to the ballad of *Fair Helen of Kirkconnel Lea* in the *Minstrelsy of the Scottish Border*. It is a resemblance of mood, not of execution. They are both highly wrought lyrical expressions of pathos; and it is very remarkable with what intuitive art every expression and cadence in *Fair Helen* is accorded to the main feeling.

The characters that distinguish the language of our *lyrical* from that of our *epic* ballads have never yet been examined with the accuracy they deserve. But, beyond question, the class of poems which in point of harmonious combination *Oriana* most resembles, is the Italian. Just thus the meditative tenderness of Dante and Petrarch is embodied in the clear, searching notes of Tuscan song. These mighty masters produce two-thirds of their effect by *sound*. Not that they sacrifice sense to sound, but that sound conveys their meaning where words would not. There are innumerable shades of fine emotion in the human heart, especially when the senses are keen and vigilant, which are too subtle and too rapid to admit of corresponding phrases. The understanding takes no definite note of them; how then can they leave signatures in language? Yet they exist; in plenitude of being and beauty they exist; and in music they find a medium through which they pass from heart to heart. The tone becomes the sign of the feeling; and they reciprocally suggest each other.

Analogous to this suggestive power may be reckoned, perhaps, in a sister art, the effects of Venetian colouring. Titian *explains* by tints, as Petrarch by tones. Words would not have done the business of the one, nor any groupings or *narration by form,* that of the other. But, shame upon us! we are going back to our metaphysics, when that "sweet, meek face" is waiting to be admitted.

The Ballad of Oriana

My heart is wasted with my woe,
    Oriana.
There is no rest for me below,
    Oriana.
When the long dun wolds are ribb'd with snow,
And loud the Norland whirlwinds blow,
    Oriana,
Alone I wander to and fro,
    Oriana.

Ere the light on dark was growing,
    Oriana,
At midnight the cock was crowing,
    Oriana;
Winds were blowing, waters flowing,
We heard the steeds to battle going,
    Oriana,
Aloud the hollow bugle blowing,
    Oriana.

In the yew-wood black as night,
    Oriana,
Ere I rode into the fight,
    Oriana,
While blissful tears blinded my sight
By star-shine and by moonlight,
    Oriana,
I to thee my troth did plight,
    Oriana.

She stood upon the castle wall,
    Oriana;
She watch'd my crest among them all,
    Oriana;
She saw me fight, she heard me call,
When forth there stept a foeman tall,
    Oriana,
Atween me and the castle wall,
    Oriana.

The bitter arrow went aside,
    Oriana;
The false, false arrow went aside,
    Oriana;
The damned arrow glanced aside,
And pierced thy heart, my love, my bride,
    Oriana!
Thy heart, my life, my love, my bride,
    Oriana!

O, narrow, narrow was the space,
    Oriana!
Loud, loud rung out the bugle's brays,
    Oriana.
O, deathful stabs were dealt apace,
The battle deepen'd in its place,
    Oriana;
But I was down upon my face,
    Oriana.

They should have stabb'd me where I lay,
    Oriana!
How could I rise and come away,
    Oriana?
How could I look upon the day?
They should have stabb'd me where I lay,
    Oriana—
They should have trod me into clay,
    Oriana.

O breaking heart that will not break,
    Oriana!
O pale, pale face so sweet and meek,
    Oriana!
Thou smilest, but thou dost not speak,

And then the tears run down my cheek,
    Oriana.
What wantest thou? whom dost thou seek,
    Oriana?

I cry aloud; none hear my cries,
    Oriana.
Thou comest atween me and the skies,
    Oriana.
I feel the tears of blood arise
Up from my heart unto my eyes,
    Oriana.
Within thy heart my arrow lies,
    Oriana.

O cursed hand! O cursed blow!
    Oriana!
O happy thou that liest low,
    Oriana!
All night the silence seems to flow
Beside me in my utter woe,
    Oriana.
A weary, weary way I go,
    Oriana!

When Norland winds pipe down the sea,
    Oriana,
I walk, I dare not think of thee,
    Oriana.
Thou liest beneath the greenwood tree,
I dare not die and come to thee,
    Oriana.
I hear the roaring of the sea,
    Oriana.

We have heard it objected to this poem that the name occurs once too often in every stanza. We have taken the plea into our judicial consideration, and the result is that we overrule it and pronounce that the proportion of the melodious cadences to the pathetic parts of the narration could not be diminished without materially affecting the rich lyrical impression of the ballad.

For what is the author's intention? To gratify our curiosity with a strange adventure? To shake our nerves with a painful story? Very far from it. Tears indeed may "blind our sight" as we read; but they are "blissful tears." The strong musical delight prevails over every painful feeling and mingles them all in its deep swell until they attain a composure of exalted sorrow, a mood in which the latest repose of agitation becomes visible, and the influence of beauty spreads like light over the surface of the mind.

The last line, with its dreamy wildness, reveals the design of the whole. It is transferred, if we mistake not, from an old ballad (a freedom of immemorial usage with ballad-mongers, as our readers doubtless know) but the merit lies in the abrupt application of it to the leading sentiment, so as to flash upon us in a few little words a world of meaning, and to consecrate the passion that was beyond cure or hope by resigning it to the accordance of inanimate Nature, who, like man, has her tempests and occasions of horror, but august in their largeness of operation, awful by their dependence on a fixed and perpetual necessity.

We must give one more extract, and we are almost tempted to choose by lot among many that crowd on our recollection, and solicit our preference with such witchery as it is not easy to withstand. The poems towards the middle of the volume seem to have been written at an earlier period than the rest. They display more unrestrained fancy and are less evidently proportioned to their ruling ideas than those which we think of later date. Yet in the *Ode to Memory*—the only one which we have the poet's authority for referring to early life—there is a majesty of expression, united to a truth of thought, which almost confounds our preconceived distinctions.

The *Confessions of a Second-rate, Sensitive Mind* are full of deep insight into human nature, and into those particular trials which are sure to beset men who think and feel for themselves at this epoch of social development. The title is perhaps ill-chosen. Not only has it an appearance of quaintness which has no sufficient reason, but it seems to us incorrect. The mood portrayed in this poem, unless the admirable skill of delineation has deceived us, is rather the clouded season of a strong mind than the habitual conditions of one feeble and "second-rate." Ordinary tempers build up fortresses of opinion on one side or another; they will see only what they choose to see. The distant glimpse of such an agony as is here brought out to view is sufficient to keep them for ever in illusions, voluntarily raised at first, but soon trusted in with full reliance as inseparable parts of self.

Mr. Tennyson's mode of "rating" is different from ours. He may esteem none worthy of the first order who has not attained a complete universality of thought, and such trustful reliance on a principle of repose which lies beyond the war of conflicting opinions, that the grand ideas, *"qui planent sans cesse au dessus de l'humanité,"* ["which soar forever above humanity"] cease to affect him with bewildering impulses of hope and fear. We have not space to enter further into this topic; but we should not despair of convincing Mr. Tennyson that such a position of intellect would not be the most elevated, nor even the most conducive to perfection of art.

The "How" and the "Why" appears to present the reverse of the same picture. It is the same mind still: the sensitive sceptic, whom we have looked upon in his hour of distress, now scoffing at his own state with an earnest mirth that borders on sorrow. It is exquisitely beautiful to see in this, as in the former portrait, how the feeling of art is kept ascendant in our minds over distressful realities, by constant reference to images of tranquil beauty, whether touched pathetically, as the Ox and the Lamb in the first piece, or with fine humour, as the "great bird" and "little bird" in the second.

The Sea Fairies is another strange title; but those who turn to it with the very natural curiosity of discovering who these new births of mythology may be, will be unpardonable if they do not linger over it with higher feelings. A stretch of lyrical power is here exhibited which we did not think the English language had possessed. The proud swell of verse as the harp tones "run up the ridged sea," and the soft and melancholy lapse as the sounds die along the widening space of water, are instances of that right imitation which is becoming to art, but which in the hands of the unskilful, or the affecters of easy popularity, is often converted into a degrading mimicry, detrimental to the best interests of the imagination.

A considerable portion of this book is taken up with a very singular and very beautiful class of poems on which the author has evidently bestowed much thought and elaboration. We allude to the female characters, every trait of which presumes an uncommon degree of observation and reflection. Mr. Tennyson's way of proceeding seems to be this. He collects the most striking phenomena of individual minds until he arrives at some leading fact, which allows him to lay down an axiom or law; and then, working on the law thus attained, he clearly discerns the tendency of what new particulars his invention suggests, and is enabled to impress an individual freshness and unity on ideal combinations. These expressions of character are brief and coherent; nothing extraneous to the dominant fact is admitted, nothing illustrative of it, and, as it were, growing out of it, is rejected. They are like summaries of mighty dramas. We do not say this method admits of such large luxuriance of power as that of our real dramatists; but we contend that it is a new species of poetry, a graft of the lyric on the dramatic, and Mr. Tennyson deserves the laurel of an inventor, an enlarger of our modes of knowledge and power.

We must hasten to make our election; so, passing by the "airy, fairy Lilian," who "clasps her hands" in vain to retain us; the "stately flower" of matronly fortitude, "revered Isabel"; Madeline, with her voluptuous alternation of smile and frown; Mariana, last, but oh not least—we swear by the memory of Shakespeare, to whom a monument of observant love has here been raised by simply expanding all the latent meanings and beauties contained in one stray thought of his genius—we shall fix on a lovely, albeit somewhat mysterious lady, who has fairly taken our "heart from out our breast."

ADELINE

I

Mystery of mysteries,
   Faintly smiling Adeline,
   Scarce of earth nor all divine,
Nor unhappy, nor at rest,
   But beyond expression fair
   With thy floating flaxen hair;
Thy rose-lips and full blue eyes
   Take the heart from out my breast.
   Wherefore those dim looks of thine,
   Shadowy, dreaming Adeline?

II

Whence that aery bloom of thine,
   Like a lily which the sun
Looks thro' in his sad decline,
   And a rose-bush leans upon,
Thou that faintly smilest still,
   As a Naiad in a well,
   Looking at the set of day,
Or a phantom two hours old
   Of a maiden past away,
Ere the placid lips be cold?
Wherefore those faint smiles of thine,
   Spiritual Adeline?

III

What hope or fear or joy is thine?
Who talketh with thee, Adeline?
   For sure thou art not all alone.
     Do beating hearts of salient springs
   Keep measure with thine own?
     Hast thou heard the butterflies

      What they say betwixt their wings?
        Or in stillest evenings
    With what voice the violet woos
    To his heart the silver dews?
      Or when little airs arise,
        How the merry bluebell rings
      To the mosses underneath?
      Hast thou look'd upon the breath
        Of the lilies at sunrise?
Wherefore that faint smile of thine,
Shadowy, dreaming Adeline?

            IV

Some honey-converse feeds thy mind,
    Some spirit of a crimson rose
    In love with thee forgets to close
    His curtains, wasting odorous sighs
All night long on darkness blind.
What aileth thee? whom waitest thou
With thy soften'd, shadow'd brow,
    And those dew-lit eyes of thine,
    Thou faint smiler, Adeline?

            V

Lovest thou the doleful wind
    When thou gazest at the skies?
Doth the low-tongued Orient
    Wander from the side of the morn,
    Dripping with Sabaean spice
On thy pillow, lowly bent
    With melodious airs lovelorn,
Breathing Light against thy face,
While his locks a-drooping twined
Round thy neck in subtle ring
Make a carcanet of rays,
    And ye talk together still,
In the language wherewith Spring
    Letters cowslips on the hill?
Hence that look and smile of thine,
    Spiritual Adeline.

Is not this beautiful? When this Poet dies, will not the Graces and the Loves mourn over him *"fortunatâque favilla nascentur violae?"* ["Violets will be born from these blest ashes"] How original is the imagery, and how delicate! How wonderful the new world thus created for us, the region between real and unreal! The gardens of Armida were but poorly musical compared with the roses and lilies that bloom around thee, thou faint smiler, Adeline, on whom the glory of imagination reposes, endowing all thou lookest on with sudden and mysterious life. We could expatiate on the deep meaning of this poem, but it is time to twitch our critical mantles; and, as our trade is not that of mere enthusiasm, we shall take our leave with an objection (perhaps a cavil) to the language of cowslips, which we think too ambiguously spoken of for a subject on which nobody, except Mr. Tennyson, can have any information. The "ringing bluebell," too, if it be not a pun, suggests one, and might probably be altered to advantage.

One word more before we have done, and it shall be a word of praise. The language of this book, with one or two rare exceptions, is thorough and sterling English. A little more respect, perhaps, was due to the *"jus et norma loquendi"* ["the right and rule of speech"]; but we are inclined to consider as venial a fault arising from generous enthusiasm for the principles of sound analogy, and for that Saxon element, which constituted the intrinsic freedom and nervousness of our native tongue. We see no signs in what Mr. Tennyson has written of the Quixotic spirit which has led some persons to desire the reduction of English to a single form, by excluding nearly the whole of Latin and Roman derivatives. Ours is necessarily a compound language; as such alone it can flourish and increase; nor will the author of the poems we have extracted be likely to barter for a barren appearance of symmetrical structure that fertility of expression and variety of harmony which "the speech that Shakspeare spoke" derived from the sources of southern phraseology.

In presenting this young poet to the public as one not studious of instant popularity, nor likely to obtain it, we may be thought to play the part of a fashionable lady who deludes her refractory mate into doing what she chooses by pretending to wish the exact contrary; or of a cunning pedagogue who practises a similar manoeuvre on some self-willed Flibbertigibbet of the schoolroom. But the supposition would do us wrong. We have spoken in good faith, commending this volume to feeling hearts and imaginative tempers, not to the stupid readers, or the voracious readers, or the malignant readers, or the readers after dinner!

We confess, indeed, we never knew an instance in which the theoretical abjurers of popularity have shewn themselves very reluctant to admit its actual advances. So much virtue is not, perhaps, in human nature; and if the world should take a fancy to buy up these poems, in order to be revenged on the *Englishman's Magazine*, who knows whether even we might not disappoint its malice by a cheerful adaptation of our theory to "existing circumstances?"

---

1. This cant term was justly ridiculed by Mr. Wordsworth's supporters; but it was not so easy to substitute an inoffensive denomination. We are not at all events the first who have used it without a contemptuous intention, for we remember to have heard a disciple quote Aristophanes in its behalf:—[*Outos ou toiu edadon toud on orau ymeis aei alla AIMNAIOS.*] "This is no common, no barn-door fowl: No, but a Lakist."

2. We are aware that this is not the right word, being appropriated by common use to a different signification. Those who think the caution given by Caesar should not stand in the way of urgent occasion, may substitute "sensuous"; a word in use amongst our elder divines, and revived by a few bold writers in our own time.

3. May we not compare them to the bright but unsubstantial clouds which, in still evenings, girdle the side of lofty mountains, and seem to form a natural connexion between the lowly vallies spread out beneath, and those isolated peaks that hold the "last parley with the setting sun?"

Thoughts on Poetry and Its Varieties

John Stuart Mill

First published in the Monthly Repository, *new series 7 (January 1833): 60-70.*

I

IT HAS OFTEN BEEN ASKED, What is Poetry? And many and various are the answers which have been returned. The vulgarest of all—one with which no person possessed of the faculties to which poetry addresses itself can ever have been satisfied—is that which confounds poetry with metrical composition: yet to this wretched mockery of a definition, many had been led back, by the failure of all their attempts to find any other that would distinguish what they have been accustomed to call poetry, from much which they have known only under other names.

That, however, the word poetry imports something quite peculiar in its nature, something which may exist in what is called prose as well as in verse, something which does not even require the instrument of words, but can speak through the other audible symbols called musical sounds, and even through the visible ones which are the language of sculpture, painting, and architecture; all this, we believe, is and must be felt, though perhaps indistinctly, by all upon whom poetry in any of its shapes produces any impression beyond that of tickling the ear. The distinction between poetry and what is not poetry, whether explained or not, is felt to be fundamental: and where every one feels a difference, a difference there must be. All other appearances may be fallacious, but the appearance of a difference is a real difference. Appearances too, like other things, must have a cause, and that which can cause anything, even an illusion, must be a reality. And hence, while a half-philosophy disdains the classifications and distinctions indicated by popular language, philosophy carried to its highest point frames new ones, but rarely sets aside the old, content with correcting and regularizing them. It cuts fresh channels for thought; but does not fill up such as it finds ready-made; it traces, on the contrary, more deeply, broadly, and distinctly, those into which the current has spontaneously flowed.

Let us then attempt, in the way of modest inquiry, not to coerce and confine nature within the bounds of an arbitrary definition, but rather to find the boundaries which she herself has set, and erect a barrier round them; not calling mankind to account for having misapplied the word poetry, but attempting to clear up the conception which they already attach to it, and to bring forward as a distinct principle that which, as a vague feeling, has really guided them in their employment of the term.

The object of poetry is confessedly to act upon the emotions; and therein is poetry sufficiently distinguished from what Wordsworth affirms to be its logical opposite, namely, not prose, but matter of fact or science. The one addresses itself to the belief, the other to the feelings. The one does its work by convincing or persuading, the other by moving. The one acts by presenting a proposition to the understanding, the other by offering interesting objects of contemplation to the sensibilities.

This, however, leaves us very far from a definition of poetry. This distinguishes it from one thing, but we are bound to distinguish it from everything. To bring thoughts or images before the mind for the purpose of acting upon the emotions, does not belong to poetry alone. It is equally the province (for example) of the novelist: and yet the faculty of the poet and that of the novelist are as distinct as any other two faculties; as the faculties of the novelist and of the orator, or of the poet and the metaphysician. The two characters may be united, as characters the most disparate may; but they have no natural connexion.

Many of the greatest poems are in the form of fictitious narratives, and in almost all good serious fictions there is true poetry. But there is a radical distinction between the interest felt in a story as such, and the interest excited by poetry; for the one is derived from incident, the other from the representation of feeling. In one, the source of the emotion excited is the exhibition of a state or states of human sensibility; in the other, of a series of states of mere outward circumstances. Now, all minds are capable of being affected more or less by representations of the latter kind, and all, or almost all, by those of the former; yet the two sources of interest correspond to two distinct, and (as respects their greatest development) mutually exclusive, characters of mind.

At what age is the passion for a story, for almost any kind of story, merely as a story, the most intense? In childhood. But that also is the age at which poetry, even of the simplest description, is least relished and least understood; because the feelings with which it is especially conversant are yet undeveloped, and not having been even in the slightest degree experienced, cannot be sympathized with. In what stage of the progress of society, again, is story-telling most valued, and the story-teller in greatest request and honour?—In a rude state, like that of the Tartars and Arabs at this day, and of almost all nations in the earliest ages. But in this state of society there is little poetry except ballads, which are mostly narrative, that is, essentially stories, and derive their principal interest from the incidents. Considered as poetry, they are of the lowest and most elementary kind: the feelings depicted, or rather indicated, are the simplest our nature has; such joys and griefs as the immediate pressure of some outward event excites in rude minds, which live wholly immersed in outward things, and have never, either from choice or a force

they could not resist, turned themselves to the contemplation of the world within. Passing now from childhood, and from the childhood of society, to the grown-up men and women of this most grown-up and unchildlike age—the minds and hearts of greatest depth and elevation are commonly those which take greatest delight in poetry; the shallowest and emptiest, on the contrary, are, at all events, not those least addicted to novel-reading. This accords, too, with all analogous experience of human nature. The sort of persons whom not merely in books, but in their lives, we find perpetually engaged in hunting for excitement from without, are invariably those who do not possess, either in the vigour of their intellectual powers or in the depth of their sensibilities, that which would enable them to find ample excitement nearer home. The most idle and frivolous persons take a natural delight in fictitious narrative; the excitement it affords is of the kind which comes from without. Such persons are rarely lovers of poetry, though they may fancy themselves so, because they relish novels in verse. But poetry, which is the delineation of the deeper and more secret workings of human emotion, is interesting only to those to whom it recalls what they have felt, or whose imagination it stirs up to conceive what they could feel, or what they might have been able to feel had their outward circumstances been different.

Poetry, when it is really such, is truth; and fiction also, if it is good for anything, is truth; but they are different truths. The truth of poetry is to paint the human soul truly: the truth of fiction is to give a true picture of life. The two kinds of knowledge are different, and come by different ways, come mostly to different persons. Great poets are often proverbially ignorant of life. What they know has come by observation of themselves; they have found within them one highly delicate and sensitive specimen of human nature, on which the laws of emotion are written in large characters, such as can be read off without much study. Other knowledge of mankind, such as comes to men of the world by outward experience, is not indispensable to them as poets: but to the novelist such knowledge is all in all; he has to describe outward things, not the inward man; actions and events, not feelings; and it will not do for him to be numbered among those who, as Madame Roland said of Brissot, know man but not men.

All this is no bar to the possibility of combining both elements, poetry and narrative or incident, in the same work, and calling it either a novel or a poem; but so may red and white combine on the same human features, or on the same canvas. There is one order of composition which requires the union of poetry and incident, each in its highest kind—the dramatic. Even there the two elements are perfectly distinguishable, and may exist of unequal quality, and in the most various proportion. The incidents of a dramatic poem may be scanty and ineffective, though the delineation of passion and character may be of the highest order; as in Goethe's admirable *Torquato Tasso:* or again, the story as a mere story may be well got up for effect, as is the case with some of the most trashy productions of the Minerva press: it may even be, what those are not, a coherent and probable series of events, though there be scarcely a feeling exhibited which is not represented falsely, or in a manner absolutely commonplace. The combination of the two excellencies is what renders Shakespeare so generally acceptable, each sort of readers finding in him what is suitable to their faculties. To the many he is great as a story-teller, to the few as a poet.

In limiting poetry to the delineation of states of feeling, and denying the name where nothing is delineated but outward objects, we may be thought to have done what we promised to avoid—to have not found, but made a definition, in opposition to the usage of language, since it is established by common consent that there is a poetry called descriptive. We deny the charge. Description is not poetry because there is descriptive poetry, no more than science is poetry because there is such a thing as a didactic poem. But an object which admits of being described, or a truth which may fill a place in a scientific treatise, may also furnish an occasion for the generation of poetry, which we thereupon choose to call descriptive or didactic. The poetry is not in the object itself, nor in the scientific truth itself, but in the state of mind in which the one and the other may be contemplated. The mere delineation of the dimensions and colours of external objects is not poetry, no more than a geometrical ground-plan of St. Peter's or Westminster Abbey is painting. Descriptive poetry consists, no doubt, in description, but in description of things as they appear, not as they are; and it paints them not in their bare and natural lineaments, but seen through the medium and arrayed in the colours of the imagination set in action by the feelings. If a poet describes a lion, he does not describe him as a naturalist would, nor even as a traveller would, who was intent upon stating the truth, the whole truth, and nothing but the truth. He describes him by imagery, that is, by suggesting the most striking likenesses and contrasts which might occur to a mind contemplating the lion, in the state of awe, wonder, or terror, which the spectacle naturally excites, or is, on the occasion, supposed to excite. Now this is describing the lion professedly, but the state of excitement of the spectator really. The lion may be described falsely or with exaggeration, and the poetry be all the better; but if the human emotion be not painted with scrupulous truth, the poetry is bad poetry, *i.e.* is not poetry at all, but a failure.

Thus far our progress towards a clear view of the essentials of poetry has brought us very close to the last two attempts at a definition of poetry which we happen to have seen in print, both of them by poets and men of genius. The one is by Ebenezer Elliott, the author of *Corn-Law Rhymes,* and other poems of still greater merit. "Poetry," says he, "is impassioned truth." The other is by a writer in *Blackwood's Magazine,* and comes, we think, still nearer the mark. He defines poetry, "man's thoughts tinged by his feelings." There is in either definition a near approximation to what we are in search of. Every truth which a human being can enunciate, every thought, even every outward impression, which can enter into his consciousness, may become poetry when shown through any impassioned medium, when invested with the colouring of joy, or grief, or pity, or affection, or admiration, or reverence, or awe, or even hatred or terror: and, unless so coloured, nothing, be it as interesting as it may, is poetry. But both these definitions fail to discriminate between poetry and eloquence. Eloquence, as well as poetry, is impassioned truth; eloquence, as well as poetry, is thoughts coloured by the feelings. Yet common apprehension and philosophic criticism alike recognise a distinction between the two: there is much that every one would call eloquence, which no one would think of classing as poetry. A question will sometimes arise, whether some particular author is a poet; and those who maintain the negative commonly allow, that though not a poet, he is a highly eloquent writer. The distinction between poetry and eloquence appears to us to be equally fundamental with the distinction between poetry and narrative, or between poetry and description, while it is still farther from having been satisfactorily cleared up than either of the others.

Poetry and eloquence are both alike the expression or utterance of feeling. But if we may be excused the antithesis, we should say that eloquence is *heard,* poetry is *over*heard. Eloquence supposes an audience; the peculiarity of poetry appears to us to lie in the poet's utter unconsciousness of a listener. Poetry is feeling, confessing itself to itself in moments of solitude, and embodying itself in symbols, which are the nearest possible representations of the feeling in the exact shape in which it exists in the poet's mind. Eloquence is feeling pouring itself out to other minds, courting their sympathy, or endeavouring to influence their belief, or move them to passion or to action.

All poetry is of the nature of soliloquy. It may be said that poetry which is printed on hot-pressed paper and sold at a bookseller's shop, is a soliloquy in full dress, and on the stage. It is so; but there is nothing absurd in the idea of such a mode of soliloquizing. What we have said to ourselves, we may tell to others afterwards; what we have said or done in solitude, we may voluntarily reproduce when we know that other eyes are upon us. But no trace of consciousness that any eyes are upon us must be visible in the work itself. The actor knows that there is an audience present; but if he act as though he knew it, he acts ill. A poet may write poetry not only with the intention of printing it, but for the express purpose of being paid for it; that it should *be* poetry, being written under such influences, is less probable; not, however, impossible; but no otherwise possible than if he can succeed in excluding from his work every vestige of such lookings-forth into the outward and every-day world, and can express his emotions exactly as he has felt them in solitude, or as he is conscious that he should feel them though they were to remain forever unuttered, or (at the lowest) as he knows that others feel them in similar circumstances of solitude. But when he turns round and addresses himself to another person; when the act of utterance is not itself the end, but a means to an end—viz. by the feelings he himself expresses, to work upon the feelings, or upon the belief, or the will, of another,—when the expression of his emotions, or of his thoughts tinged by his emotions, is tinged also by that purpose, by that desire of making an impression upon another mind, then it ceases to be poetry, and becomes eloquence.

Poetry, accordingly, is the natural fruit of solitude and meditation; eloquence, of intercourse with the world. The persons who have most feeling of their own, if intellectual culture has given them a language in which to express it, have the highest faculty of poetry; those who best understand the feelings of others, are the most eloquent. The persons, and the nations, who commonly excel in poetry, are those whose character and tastes render them least dependent upon the applause, or sympathy, or concurrence of the world in general. Those to whom that applause, that sympathy, that concurrence are most necessary, generally excel most in eloquence. And hence, perhaps, the French, who are the least poetical of all great and intellectual nations, are among the most eloquent: the French, also, being the most sociable, the vainest, and the least self-dependent.

If the above be, as we believe, the true theory of the distinction commonly admitted between eloquence and poetry; or even though it be not so, yet if, as we cannot doubt, the distinction above stated be a real *bona fide* distinction, it will be found to hold, not merely in the language of words, but in all other languages and to intersect the whole domain of art.

Take, for example, music: we shall find in that art, so peculiarly the expression of passion, two perfectly distinct styles; one of which may be called the poetry, the other the oratory of music. This difference, being seized, would put an end to much musical sectarianism. There has been much contention whether the music of the modern Italian school, that of Rossini and his successors, be impassioned or not. Without doubt, the passion it expresses is not the musing, meditative tenderness or pathos, or grief of Mozart or Beethoven. Yet it is passion, but garrulous passion—the passion which pours itself into other ears; and therein the better calculated for dramatic effect, having a natural adaptation for dialogue. Mozart also is great in musical oratory; but his most touching compositions are in the opposite style—that of soliloquy. Who can imagine "Dove sono" *heard?* We imagine it *over*heard.

Purely pathetic music commonly partakes of soliloquy. The soul is absorbed in its distress, and though there may be bystanders, it is not thinking of them. When the mind is looking within, and not without, its state does not often or rapidly vary, and hence the even, uninterrupted flow, approaching almost to monotony, which a good reader, or a good singer, will give to words or music of a pensive or melancholy cast. But grief taking the form of a prayer, or of a complaint, becomes oratorical; no longer low, and even, and subdued, it assumes a more emphatic rhythm, a more rapidly returning accent; instead of a few slow equal notes, following one after another at regular intervals, it crowds note upon note, and often assumes a hurry and bustle like joy. Those who are familiar with some of the best of Rossini's serious compositions, such as the air "Tu che i miseri conforti," in the opera of *Tancredi*, or the duet "Ebben per mia memoria," in *La Gazza Ladra,* will at once understand and feel our meaning. Both are highly tragic and passionate; the passion of both is that of oratory, not poetry. The like may be said of that most moving invocation in Beethoven's *Fidelio*—

> Komm, Hoffnung, lass das letzte Stern
> Der Müde nicht erbleichen;

in which Madame Schröder Devrient exhibited such consummate powers of pathetic expression. How different from Winter's beautiful "Paga fui," the very soul of melancholy exhaling itself in solitude; fuller of meaning, and, therefore, more profoundly poetical than the words for which it was composed—for it seems to express not simple melancholy, but the melancholy of remorse.

If, from vocal music, we now pass to instrumental, we may have a specimen of musical oratory in any fine military symphony or march: while the poetry of music seems to have attained its consummation in Beethoven's Overture to *Egmont,* so wonderful in its mixed expression of grandeur and melancholy.

In the arts which speak to the eye, the same distinctions will be found to hold, not only between poetry and oratory, but between poetry, oratory, narrative, and simple imitation or description.

Pure description is exemplified in a mere portrait or a mere landscape—productions of art, it is true, but of the mechanical rather than of the fine arts, being works of simple imitation, not creation. We say, a mere portrait, or a mere landscape, because it is possible for a portrait or a landscape, without ceasing to be such, to be also a picture; like Turner's landscapes, and the great portraits by Titian or Vandyke.

Whatever in painting or sculpture expresses human feeling—or character, which is only a certain state of feeling grown habitual—may be called, according to circumstances, the poetry, or the eloquence, of the painter's or the sculptor's art: the poetry, if the feeling declares itself by such signs as escape from us when we are unconscious of being seen; the oratory, if the signs are those we use for the purpose of voluntary communication.

The narrative style answers to what is called historical painting, which it is the fashion among connoisseurs to treat as the climax of the pictorial art. That it is the most difficult branch of the art we do not doubt, because, in its perfection, it includes the perfection of all the other branches: as in like manner an epic poem, though in so far as it is epic (*i.e.* narrative) it is not poetry at all, is yet esteemed the greatest effort of poetic genius, because there is no kind whatever of poetry which may not appropriately find a place in it. But an historical picture as such, that is, as the representation of an incident, must necessarily, as it seems to us, be poor and ineffective. The narrative powers of painting are extremely limited. Scarcely any picture, scarcely even any series of pictures, tells its own story without the aid of an interpreter. But it is the single figures, which, to us, are the great charm even of an historical picture. It is in these that the power of the art is really seen. In the attempt to narrate, visible and permanent signs are too far behind the fugitive audible ones, which follow so fast one after another, while the faces and figures in a narrative picture, even though they be Titian's, stand still. Who would not prefer one Virgin and Child of Raphael, to all the pictures which Rubens, with his fat, frouzy Dutch Venuses, ever painted? Though Rubens, besides excelling almost every one in his mastery over the mechanical parts of his art, often shows real genius in grouping his figures, the peculiar problem of historical painting. But then, who, except a mere student of drawing and colouring, ever cared to look twice at any of the figures themselves? The power of painting lies in poetry, of which Rubens had not the slightest tincture—not in narrative, wherein he might have excelled.

The single figures, however, in an historical picture, are rather the eloquence of painting than the poetry: they mostly (unless they are quite out of place in the picture) express the feelings of one person as modified by the presence of others. Accordingly the minds whose bent leads them rather to eloquence than to poetry, rush to historical painting. The French painters, for instance, seldom attempt, because they could make nothing of, single heads, like those glorious ones of the Italian masters, with which they might feed themselves day after day in their own Louvre. They must all be historical; and they are, almost to a man, attitudinizers. If we wished to give any young artist the most impressive warning our imagination could devise against that kind of vice in the pictorial, which corresponds to rant in the histrionic art, we would advise him to walk once up and once down the gallery of the Luxembourg. Every figure in French painting or statuary seems to be showing itself off before spectators: they are not poetical, but in the worst style of corrupted eloquence.

II

NASCITUR POËTA is a maxim of classical antiquity, which has passed to these latter days with less questioning than most of the doctrines of that early age. When it originated, the human faculties were occupied, fortunately for posterity, less in examining how the works of genius are created, than in creating them: and the adage, probably, had no higher source than the tendency common among mankind to consider all power which is not visibly the effect of practice, all skill which is not capable of being reduced to mechanical rules, as the result of a peculiar gift. Yet this aphorism, born in the infancy of psychology, will perhaps be found, now when that science is in its adolescence, to be as true as an epigram ever is, that is, to contain some truth: truth, however, which has been so compressed and bent out of shape, in order to tie it up into so small a knot of only two words, that it requires an almost infinite amount of unrolling and laying straight, before it will resume its just proportions.

We are not now intending to remark upon the grosser misapplications of this ancient maxim, which have engendered so many races of poetasters. The days are gone by, when every raw youth whose borrowed phantasies have set themselves to a borrowed tune, mistaking, as Coleridge says, an ardent desire of poetic reputation for poetic genius, while unable to disguise from himself that he had taken no means whereby he might become a poet, could fancy himself a born one. Those who would reap without sowing, and gain the victory without fighting the battle, are ambitious now of another sort of distinction, and are born novelists, or public speakers, not poets. And the wiser thinkers understand and acknowledge that poetic excellence is subject to the same necessary conditions with any other mental endowment; and that to no one of the spiritual benefactors of mankind is a higher or a more assiduous intellectual culture needful than to the poet. It is true, he possesses this advantage over others who use the "instrument of words," that, of the truths which he utters, a larger proportion are derived from personal consciousness, and a smaller from philosophic investigation. But the power itself of discriminating between what really is consciousness, and what is only a process of inference completed in a single instant—and the capacity of distinguishing whether that of which the mind is conscious be an eternal truth, or but a dream—are among the last results of the most matured and perfect intellect. Not to mention that the poet, no more than any other person who writes, confines himself altogether to intuitive truths, nor has any means of communicating even these but by words, every one of which derives all its power of conveying a meaning, from a whole host of acquired notions, and facts learnt by study and experience.

Nevertheless, it seems undeniable in point of fact, and consistent with the principles of a sound metaphysics, that there are poetic *natures.* There is a mental and physical constitution or temperament, peculiarly fitted for poetry. This temperament will not of itself make a poet, no more than the soil will the fruit; and as good fruit may be raised by culture from indifferent soils, so may good poetry from naturally unpoetical minds. But the poetry of one who is a poet by nature, will be clearly and broadly distinguishable from the poetry of mere culture. It may not be truer; it may not be more useful; but it will be different: fewer will appreciate it, even though many should affect to do so; but in those few it will find a keener sympathy, and will yield them a deeper enjoyment.

One may write genuine poetry, and not be a poet; for whosoever writes out truly any human feeling, writes poetry. All persons, even the most unimaginative, in moments of strong emotion, speak poetry; and hence the drama is poetry, which else were always prose, except when a poet is one of the characters. What is poetry, but the thoughts and words in which emotion spontaneously embodies itself? As there are few who are not, at least for some moments and in some situations, capable of some strong feeling, poetry is natural to most persons at some period of their lives. And any one whose feelings are genuine, though but of the average strength,—if he be not diverted by uncongenial thoughts or occupations from the indulgence of them, and if he acquire by culture, as all persons may, the faculty of delineating them correctly,—has it in his power to be a poet, so far as a life passed in writing unquestionable poetry may be considered to confer that title. But ought it to do so? Yes, perhaps, in a collection of "British Poets." But "poet" is the name also of a variety of man, not solely of the author of a particular variety of book: now, to have written whole volumes of real poetry, is possible to almost all kinds of characters, and implies no greater peculiarity of mental construction than to be the author of a history or a novel.

Whom, then, shall we call poets? Those who are so constituted, that emotions are the links of association by which their ideas, both sensuous and spiritual, are connected together. This constitution belongs (within certain limits) to all in whom poetry is a pervading principle. In all others, poetry is something extraneous and superinduced: something out of themselves, foreign to the habitual course of their every-day lives and characters; a world to which they may make occasional visits, but where they are sojourners, not dwellers, and which, when out of it, or even when in it, they think of, peradventure, but as a phantom-world, a place of *ignes fatui* and spectral illusions. Those only who have the peculiarity of association which we have mentioned, and which is a natural though not an universal consequence of intense sensibility, instead of seeming not themselves when they are uttering poetry, scarcely seem themselves when uttering anything to which poetry is foreign. Whatever be the thing which they are contemplating, if it be capable of connecting itself with their emotions, the aspect under which it first and most naturally paints itself to them, is its poetic aspect. The poet of culture sees his object in prose, and describes it in poetry; the poet of nature actually sees it in poetry.

This point is perhaps worth some little illustration; the rather, as metaphysicians (the ultimate arbiters of all philosophical criticism), while they have busied themselves for two thousand years, more or less, about the few universal laws of human nature, have strangely neglected the analysis of its diversities. Of these, none lie deeper or reach further than the varieties which difference of nature and of education makes in what may be termed the habitual bond of association. In a mind entirely uncultivated, which is also without any strong feelings, objects, whether of sense or of intellect, arrange themselves in the mere casual order in which they have been seen, heard, or otherwise perceived. Persons of this sort may be said to think chronologically. If they remember a fact, it is by reason of a fortuitous coincidence with some trifling incident or circumstance which took place at the very time. If they have a story to tell, or testimony to deliver in a witness-box, their narrative must follow the exact order in which the events took place: *dodge* them, and the thread of association is broken; they cannot go on. Their associations, to use the language of philosophers, are chiefly of the successive, not the synchronous kind, and whether successive or synchronous, are mostly casual.

To the man of science, again, or of business, objects group themselves according to the artificial classifications which the understanding has voluntarily made for the convenience of thought or of practice. But where any of the impressions are vivid and intense, the associations into which these enter are the ruling ones: it being a well-known law of association, that the stronger a feeling is, the more quickly and strongly it associates itself with any other object or feeling. Where, therefore, nature has given strong feelings, and education has not created factitious tendencies stronger than the natural ones, the prevailing associations will be those which connect objects and ideas with emotions, and with each other through the intervention of emotions. Thoughts and images will be linked together, according to the similarity of the feelings which cling to them. A thought will introduce a thought by first introducing a feeling which is allied with it. At the centre of each group of thoughts or images will be found a feeling; and the thoughts or images will be there only because the feeling was there. The combinations which the mind puts together, the pictures which it paints, the wholes which imagination constructs out of the materials supplied by fancy, will be indebted to some dominant feeling, not as in other natures to a dominant thought, for their unity and consistency of character—for what distinguishes them from incoherencies.

The difference, then, between the poetry of a poet, and the poetry of a cultivated but not naturally poetic mind, is, that in the latter, with however bright a halo of feeling the thought may be surrounded and glorified, the thought itself is always the conspicuous object; while the poetry of a poet is feeling itself, employing thought only as the medium of its expression. In the one, feeling waits upon thought; in the other, thought upon feeling. The one writer has a distinct aim, common to him with any other didactic author; he desires to convey the thought, and he conveys it clothed in the feelings which it excites in himself, or which he deems most appropriate to it. The other merely pours forth the overflowing of his feelings; and all the thoughts which those feelings suggest are floated promiscuously along the stream.

It may assist in rendering our meaning intelligible, if we illustrate it by a parallel between the two English authors of our own day who have produced the greatest quantity of true and enduring poetry, Wordsworth and Shelley. Apter instances could not be wished for; the one might be cited as the type, the *exemplar,* of what the poetry of culture may accomplish; the other as perhaps the most striking example ever known of the poetic temperament. How different, accordingly, is the poetry of these two great writers. In Wordsworth, the poetry is almost always the mere setting of a thought. The thought may be more valuable than the setting, or it may be less valuable, but there can be no question as to which was first in his mind: what he is impressed with, and what he is anxious to impress, is some proposition, more or less distinctly conceived; some truth, or something which he deems such. He lets the thought dwell in his mind, till it excites, as is the nature of thought, other thoughts, and also such feelings as the measure of his sensibility is adequate to supply. Among these thoughts and feelings, had he chosen a different walk of authorship (and there are many in which he might equally have excelled), he would probably have made a different selection of media for enforcing the parent thought: his habits, however, being those of poetic composition, he selects in preference the strongest feelings, and the thoughts with which most of feeling is naturally or habitually connected. His poetry, therefore, may be defined to be, his thoughts, coloured by, and impressing themselves by means of, emotions. Such poetry, Wordsworth has occupied a long life in producing. And well and wisely has he so done. Criticisms, no doubt, may be made occasionally both upon the thoughts themselves, and upon the skill he has demonstrated in the choice of his media: for, an affair of skill and study, in the most rigorous sense, it evidently was. But he has not laboured in vain: he has exercised, and continues to exercise, a powerful, and mostly a highly beneficial influence over the formation and growth of not a few of the most cultivated and vigorous of the youthful minds of our time, over whose heads poetry of the opposite description would have flown, for want of an original organization, physical or mental, in sympathy with it.

On the other hand, Wordsworth's poetry is never bounding, never ebullient; has little even of the appearance of spontaneousness: the well is never so full that it overflows. There is an air of calm deliberateness about all he writes, which is not characteristic of the poetic temperament: his poetry seems one thing, himself another; he seems to be poetical because he wills to be so, not because he cannot help it: did he will to dismiss poetry, he need never again, it might almost seem, have a poetical thought. He never seems *possessed* by any feeling; no emotion seems ever so strong as to have entire sway, for the time being, over the current of his thoughts. He never, even for the space of a few stanzas, appears entirely given up to exultation, or grief, or pity, or love, or admiration, or devotion, or even animal spirits. He now and then, though seldom, attempts to write as if he were; and never, we think, without leaving an impression of poverty: as the brook which on nearly level ground quite fills its banks, appears but a thread when running rapidly down a precipitous declivity. He has feeling enough to form a decent, graceful, even beautiful decoration to a thought which is in itself interesting and moving; but not so much as suffices to stir up the soul by mere sympathy with itself in its simplest manifestation, nor enough to summon up that array of "thoughts of power" which in a richly stored mind always attends the call of really intense feeling. It is for this reason, doubtless, that the genius of Wordsworth is essentially unlyrical. Lyric poetry, as it was the earliest kind, is also, if the view we are now taking of poetry be correct, more eminently and peculiarly poetry than any other: it is the poetry most natural to a really poetic temperament, and least capable of being successfully imitated by one not so endowed by nature.

Shelley is the very reverse of all this. Where Wordsworth is strong, he is weak; where Wordsworth is weak, he is strong. Culture, that culture by which Wordsworth has reared from his own inward nature the richest harvest ever brought forth by a soil of so little depth, is precisely what was wanting to Shelley: or let us rather say, he had not, at the period of his deplorably early death, reached sufficiently far in that intellectual progression of which he was capable, and which, if it has done so much for greatly inferior natures, might have made of him the most perfect, as he was already the most gifted, of our poets. For him, voluntary mental discipline had done little: the vividness of his emotions and of his sensations had done all. He seldom follows up an idea; it starts into life, summons from the fairy-land of his inexhaustible fancy some three or four bold images, then vanishes, and straight he is off on the wings of some casual association into quite another sphere. He had scarcely yet acquired the consecutiveness of thought necessary for a long poem; his more ambitious compositions too often resemble the scattered fragments of a mirror; colours brilliant as life, single images without end, but no picture. It is only when under the overruling influence of some one state of feeling, either actually experienced, or summoned up in the vividness of reality by a fervid imagination, that he writes as a great poet; unity of feeling being to him the harmonizing principle which a central idea is to minds of another class, and supplying the coherency and consistency which would else have been wanting. Thus it is in many of his smaller, and especially his lyrical poems. They are obviously written to exhale, perhaps to relieve, a state of feeling, or of conception of feeling, almost oppressive from its vividness. The thoughts and imagery are suggested by the feeling, and are such as it finds unsought. The state of feeling may be either of soul or of sense, or oftener (might we not say invariably?) of both: for the poetic temperament is usually, perhaps always, accompanied by exquisite senses. The exciting cause may be either an object or an idea. But whatever of sensation enters into the feeling, must not be local, or consciously organic; it is a condition of the whole frame, not of a part only. Like the state of sensation produced by a fine climate, or indeed like all strongly pleasurable or painful sensations in an impassioned nature, it pervades the entire nervous system. States of feeling, whether sensuous or spiritual, which thus possess the whole being, are the fountains of that which we have called the poetry of poets; and which is little else than a pouring forth of the thoughts and images that pass across the mind while some permanent state of feeling is occupying it.

To the same original fineness of organization, Shelley was doubtless indebted for another of his rarest gifts, that exuberance of imagery, which when unrepressed, as in many of his poems it is, amounts to a fault. The susceptibility of his nervous system, which made his emotions intense, made also the impressions of his external senses deep and clear: and agreeably to the law of association by which, as already remarked, the strongest impressions are those which associate themselves the most easily and strongly, these vivid sensations were readily recalled to mind by all objects or thoughts which had coexisted with them, and by all feelings which in any degree resembled them. Never did a fancy so teem with sensuous imagery as Shelley's. Wordsworth economizes an image, and detains it until he has distilled all the poetry out of it, and it will not yield a drop more: Shelley lavishes his with a profusion which is unconscious because it is inexhaustible.

If, then, the maxim *Nascitur poëta,* mean, either that the power of producing poetical compositions is a peculiar faculty which the poet brings into the world with him, which grows with his growth like any of his bodily powers, and is as independent of culture as his height, and his complexion; or that any natural peculiarity whatever is implied in producing poetry, real poetry, and in any quantity—such poetry too, as, to the majority of educated and intelligent readers, shall appear quite as good as, or even better than, any other; in either sense the doctrine is false. And nevertheless, there *is* poetry which could not emanate but from a mental and physical constitution peculiar, not in the kind, but in the degree of its susceptibility: a constitution which makes its possessor capable of greater happiness than mankind in general, and also of greater unhappiness; and because greater, so also more various. And such poetry, to all who know enough of nature to own it as being in nature, is much more poetry, is poetry in a far higher sense, than any other; since the common element of all poetry, that which constitutes poetry, human feeling, enters far more largely into this than into the poetry of culture. Not only because the natures which we have called poetical, really feel more, and consequently have more feeling to express; but because, the capacity of feeling being so great, feeling, when excited and not voluntarily resisted, seizes the helm of their thoughts, and the succession of ideas and images becomes the mere utterance of an emotion; not, as in other natures, the emotion a mere ornamental colouring of the thought.

Ordinary education and the ordinary course of life are constantly at work counteracting this quality of mind, and substituting habits more suitable to their own ends: if instead of substituting, they were content to superadd, there would be nothing to complain of. But when will education consist, not in repressing any mental faculty or power, from the uncontrolled action of which danger is apprehended, but in training up to its proper strength the corrective and antagonist power?

In whomsoever the quality which we have described exists, and is not stifled, that person is a poet. Doubtless he is a greater poet in proportion as the fineness of his perceptions, whether of sense or of internal consciousness, furnishes him with an ampler supply of lovely images—the vigour and richness of his intellect with a greater abundance of moving thoughts. For it is through these thoughts and images that the feeling speaks, and through their impressiveness that it impresses itself, and finds response in other hearts; and from these media of transmitting it (contrary to the laws of physical nature) increase of intensity is reflected back upon the feeling itself. But all these it is possible to have, and not be a poet; they are mere materials, which the poet shares in common with other people. What constitutes the poet is not the imagery nor the thoughts, nor even the feelings, but the law according to which they are called up. He is a poet, not because he has ideas of any particular kind, but because the succession of his ideas is subordinate to the course of his emotions.

Many who have never acknowledged this in theory, bear testimony to it in their particular judgments. In listening to an oration, or reading a written discourse not professedly poetical, when do we begin to feel that the speaker or author is putting off the character of the orator or the prose writer, and is passing into the poet? Not when he begins to show strong feeling; then we merely say, he is in earnest, he feels what he says; still less when he expresses himself in imagery; then, unless illustration be manifestly his sole object; we are apt to say, This is affectation. It is when the feeling (instead of passing away, or if it continue, letting the train of thoughts run on exactly as they would have done if there were no influence at work but the mere intellect) becomes itself the originator of another train of association, which expels, or blends, with the former, when (for example) either his words, or the mode of their arrangement, are such as we spontaneously use only when in a state of excitement, proving that the mind is at least as much occupied by a passive state of its own feelings, as by the desire of attaining the premeditated end which the discourse has in view.

Our judgments of authors who lay actual claim to the title of poets, follow the same principle. Whenever, after a writer's meaning is fully understood, it is still matter of reasoning and discussion whether he is a poet or not, he will be found to be wanting in the characteristic peculiarity of association so often adverted to. When, on the contrary, after reading or hearing one or two passages, we instinctively and without hesitation cry out, This is a poet, the probability is, that the passages are strongly marked with this peculiar quality. And we may add that in such case, a critic who, not having sufficient feeling to respond to the poetry, is also without sufficient philosophy to understand it though he feel it not, will be apt to pronounce, not "this is prose," but "this is exaggeration," "this is mysticism," or, "this is nonsense."

Although a philosopher cannot, by culture, make himself, in the peculiar sense in which we now use the term, a poet, unless at least he have that peculiarity of nature which would probably have made poetry his earliest pursuit; a poet may always, by culture, make himself a philosopher. The poetic laws of association are by no means incompatible with the more ordinary laws; are by no means such as must have their course, even though a deliberate purpose require their suspension. If the peculiarities of the poetic temperament were uncontrollable in any poet, they might be supposed so in Shelley; yet how powerfully, in *The Cenci,* does he coerce and restrain all the characteristic qualities of his genius; what severe simplicity, in place of his usual barbaric splendour; how rigidly does he keep the feelings and the imagery in subordination to the thought.

The investigation of nature requires no habits or qualities of mind, but such as may always be acquired by industry and mental activity. Because at one time the mind may be so given up to a state of feeling, that the succession of its ideas is determined by the present enjoyment or suffering which pervades it, this is no reason but that in the calm retirement of study, when under no peculiar excitement either of the outward or of the inward sense, it may form any combinations, or pursue any trains of ideas, which are most conducive to the purposes of philosophic inquiry; and may, while in that state, form deliberate convictions, from which no excitement will afterwards make it swerve. Might we not go even further than this? We shall not pause to ask whether it be not a misunderstanding of the nature of passionate feeling to imagine that it is inconsistent with calmness; whether they who so deem of it, do not mistake passion in the militant or antagonistic state, for the type of passion universally; do not confound passion struggling towards an outward object, with passion brooding over itself. But without entering into this deeper investigation; that capacity of strong feeling, which is supposed necessarily to disturb the judgment, is also the material out of which all *motives* are made; the motives, consequently, which lead human beings to the pursuit of truth. The greater the individual's capability of happiness and of misery, the stronger interest has that individual in arriving at truth; and when once that interest is felt, an impassioned nature is sure to pursue this, as to pursue any other object, with greater ardour; for energy of character is commonly the offspring of strong feeling. If, therefore, the most impassioned natures do not ripen into the most powerful intellects, it is always from defect of culture, or something wrong in the circumstances by which the being has originally or successively been surrounded. Undoubtedly strong feelings require a strong intellect to carry them, as more sail requires more ballast: and when, from neglect, or bad education, that strength is wanting, no wonder if the grandest and swiftest vessels make the most utter wreck.

Where, as in some of our older poets, a poetic nature has been united with logical and scientific culture, the peculiarity of association arising from the finer nature so perpetually alternates with the associations attainable by commoner natures trained to high perfection, that its own particular law is not so conspicuously characteristic of the result produced, as in a poet like Shelley, to whom systematic intellectual culture, in a measure proportioned to the intensity of his own nature, has been wanting. Whether the superiority will naturally be on the side of the philosopher-poet or of the mere poet — whether the writings of the one ought, as a whole, to be truer, and their influence more beneficent, than those of the other — is too obvious in principle to need statement: it would be absurd to doubt whether two endowments are better than one; whether truth is more certainly arrived at by two processes, verifying and correcting each other, than by one alone. Unfortunately, in practice the matter is not quite so simple; there the question often is, which is least prejudicial to the intellect, uncultivation or malcultivation. For, as long as education consists chiefly of the mere inculcation of traditional opinions, many of which, from the mere fact that the human intellect has not yet reached perfection, must necessarily be false; so long as even those who are best taught, are rather taught to know the thoughts of others than to think, it is not always clear that the poet of acquired ideas has the advantage over him whose feeling has been his sole teacher. For, the depth and durability of wrong as well as of right impressions, is proportional to the fineness of the material; and they who have the greatest capacity of natural feeling are generally those whose artificial feelings are the strongest. Hence, doubtless, among other reasons, it is, that in an age of revolutions in opinion, the cotemporary poets, those at least who deserve the name, those who have any individuality of character, if they are not before their age, are almost sure to be behind it. An observation curiously verified all over Europe in the present century. Nor let it be thought disparaging. However urgent may be the necessity for a breaking up of old modes of belief, the most strong-minded and discerning, next to those who head the movement, are generally those who bring up the rear of it.

The Hero as Poet. Dante; Shakspeare.

Thomas Carlyle

First published in On Heroes, Hero-Worship and the Heroic in History *(London: Fraser, 1841).*

The Hero as Divinity, the Hero as Prophet, are productions of old ages; not to be repeated in the new. They presuppose a certain rudeness of conception, which the progress of mere scientific knowledge puts an end to. There needs to be, as it were, a world vacant, or almost vacant of scientific forms, if men in their loving wonder are to fancy their fellow-man either a god or one speaking with the voice of a god. Divinity and Prophet are past. We are now to see our Hero in the less ambitious, but also less questionable, character of Poet; a character which does not pass. The Poet is a heroic figure belonging to all ages; whom all ages possess, when once he is produced, whom the newest age as the oldest may produce;—and will produce, always when Nature pleases. Let Nature send a Hero-soul; in no age is it other than possible that he may be shaped into a Poet.

Hero, Prophet, Poet,—many different names, in different times and places, do we give to Great Men; according to varieties we note in them, according to the sphere in which they have displayed themselves! We might give many more names, on this same principle. I will remark again, however, as a fact not unimportant to be understood, that the different *sphere* constitutes the grand origin of such distinction; that the Hero can be Poet, Prophet, King, Priest or what you will, according to the kind of world he finds himself born into. I confess, I have no notion of a truly great man that could not be *all* sorts of men. The Poet who could merely sit on a chair, and compose stanzas, would never make a stanza worth much. He could not sing the Heroic warrior, unless he himself were at least a Heroic warrior too. I fancy there is in him the Politician, the Thinker, Legislator, Philosopher;—in one or the other degree, he could have been, he is all these. So too I cannot understand how a Mirabeau, with that great glowing heart, with the fire that was in it, with the bursting tears that were in it, could not have written verses, tragedies, poems, and touched all hearts in that way, had his course of life and education led him thitherward. The grand fundamental character is that of Great Man; that the man be great. Napoleon has words in him which are like Austerlitz Battles. Louis Fourteenth's Marshals are a kind of poetical men withal; the things Turenne says are full of sagacity and geniality, like sayings of Samuel Johnson. The great heart, the clear deep-seeing eye: there it lies; no man whatever, in what province soever, can prosper at all without these. Petrarch and Boccaccio did diplomatic messages, it seems, quite well: one can easily believe it; they had done things a little harder than these! Burns, a gifted song-writer, might have made a still better Mirabeau. Shakspeare,—one knows not what *he* could not have made, in the supreme degree.

True, there are aptitudes of Nature too. Nature does not make all great men, more than all other men, in the self-same mould. Varieties of aptitude doubtless; but infinitely more of circumstance; and far oftenest it is the *latter* only that are looked to. But it is as with common men in the learning of trades. You take any man, as yet a vague capability of a man, who could be any kind of craftsman; and make him into a smith, a carpenter, a mason; he is then and thenceforth that and nothing else. And if, as Addison complains, you sometimes see a street-porter staggering under his load on spindle-shanks, and near at hand a tailor with the frame of a Samson handling a bit of cloth and small Whitechapel needle,—it cannot be considered that aptitude of Nature alone has been consulted here either!—The Great Man also, to what shall he be bound apprentice? Given your Hero, is he to become Conqueror, King, Philosopher, Poet? It is an inexplicably complex controversial-calculation between the world and him! He will read the world and its laws; the world with its laws will be there to be read. What the world, on *this* matter, shall permit and bid is, as we said, the most important fact about the world.—

Poet and Prophet differ greatly in our loose modern notions of them. In some old languages, again, the titles are synonymous; *Vates* means both Prophet and Poet: and indeed at all times, Prophet and Poet, well understood, have much kindred of meaning. Fundamentally indeed they are still the same; in this most important respect especially, That they have penetrated both of them into the sacred mystery of the Universe; what Goethe calls 'the open secret.' "Which is the great secret?" asks one.—"The *open* secret,"—open to all, seen by almost none! That divine mystery, which lies everywhere in all Beings, 'the Divine Idea of the World,' that which lies at 'the bottom of Appearance,' as Fichte styles it; of which all Appearance, from the starry sky to the grass of the field, but especially the Appearance of Man and his work, is but the *vesture*, the embodiment that renders it visible. This divine mystery *is* in all times and in all places; veritably is. In most times and places it is greatly overlooked; and the Universe, definable always in one or the other dialect, as the realised Thought of God, is considered a trivial, inert, commonplace matter,—as if, says the Satirist, it were a dead thing, which some upholsterer had put together! It could do no good, at present, to *speak* much about this; but it is a pity for every one of us if we do not know it, live ever in the knowledge of it. Really a most mournful pity;—a failure to live at all, if we live otherwise!

But now, I say, whoever may forget this divine mystery, the *Vates,* whether Prophet or Poet, has penetrated into it; is a man sent hither to make it more impressively known to us. That always is his message; he is to reveal that to us,—that sacred mystery which he more than others lives ever present with. While others forget it, he knows it,—I might say, he has been driven to know it; without consent asked of *him,* he finds himself living in it, bound to live in it. Once more, here is no Hearsay, but a direct Insight and Belief; this man too could not help being a sincere man! Whosoever may live in the shows of things, it is for him a necessity of nature to live in the very fact of things. A man once more, in earnest with the Universe, though all others were but toying with it. He is a *Vates,* first of all, in virtue of being sincere. So far Poet and Prophet, participators in the 'open secret,' are one.

With respect to their distinction again: The *Vates* Prophet, we might say, has seized that sacred mystery rather on the moral side, as Good and Evil, Duty and Prohibition; the *Vates* Poet on what the Germans call the aesthetic side, as Beautiful, and the like. The one we may call a revealer of what we are to do, the other of what we are to love. But indeed these two provinces run into one another, and cannot be disjoined. The Prophet too has his eye on what we are to love: how else shall he know what it is we are to do? The highest Voice ever heard on this earth said withal, "Consider the lilies of the field; they toil not, neither do they spin: yet Solomon in all his glory was not arrayed like one of these." A glance, that, into the deepest deep of Beauty. 'The lilies of the field,'—dressed finer than earthly princes, springing-up there in the humble furrow-field; a beautiful *eye* looking-out on you, from the great inner Sea of Beauty! How could the rude Earth make these, if her Essence, rugged as she looks and is, were not inwardly Beauty? In this point of view, too, a saying of Goethe's, which has staggered several, may have meaning: 'The Beautiful,' he intimates, 'is higher than the Good; the

Beautiful includes in it 'the Good.' The *true* Beautiful; which however, I have said somewhere, 'differs from the *false* as Heaven does from Vauxhall!' So much for the distinction and identity of Poet and Prophet.—

In ancient and also in modern periods, we find a few Poets who are accounted perfect; whom it were a kind of treason to find fault with. This is noteworthy; this is right: yet in strictness it is only an illusion. At bottom, clearly enough, there is no perfect Poet! A vein of Poetry exists in the hearts of all men; no man is made altogether of Poetry. We are all poets when we *read* a poem well. The 'imagination that shudders at the Hell of Dante,' is not that the same faculty, weaker in degree, as Dante's own? No one but Shakspeare can embody, out of *Saxo Grammaticus,* the story of *Hamlet* as Shakspeare did: but every one models some kind of story out of it; every one embodies it better or worse. We need not spend time in defining. Where there is no specific difference, as between round and square, all definition must be more or less arbitrary. A man that has *so* much more of the poetic element developed in him as to have become noticeable, will be called Poet by his neighbours. World-Poets too, those whom we are to take for perfect Poets, are settled by critics in the same way. One who rises *so* far above the general level of Poets will, to such and such critics, seem a Universal Poet; as he ought to do. And yet it is, and must be, an arbitrary distinction. All Poets, all men, have some touches of the Universal; no man is wholly made of that. Most Poets are very soon forgotten: but not the noblest Shakspeare or Homer of them can be remembered *forever;*—a day comes when he too is not!

Nevertheless, you will say, there must be a difference between true Poetry and true Speech not poetical: what is the difference? On this point many things have been written, especially by late German Critics, some of which are not very intelligible at first. They say, for example, that the Poet has an *infinitude* in him; communicates an *Unendlichkeit,* a certain character of 'infinitude,' to whatsoever he delineates. This, though not very precise, yet on so vague a matter is worth remembering: if well meditated, some meaning will gradually be found in it. For my own part, I find considerable meaning in the old vulgar distinction of Poetry being *metrical,* having music in it, being a Song. Truly, if pressed to give a definition, one might say this as soon as anything else: If your delineation be authentically *musical,* musical not in word only, but in heart and substance, in all the thoughts and utterances of it, in the whole conception of it, then it will be poetical; if not, not.—Musical: how much lies in that! A *musical* thought is one spoken by a mind that has penetrated into the inmost heart of the thing; detected the inmost mystery of it, namely the *melody* that lies hidden in it; the inward harmony of coherence which is its soul, whereby it exists, and has a right to be, here in this world. All inmost things, we may say, are melodious; naturally utter themselves in Song. The meaning of Song goes deep. Who is there that, in logical words, can express the effect music has on us? A kind of inarticulate unfathomable speech, which leads us to the edge of the Infinite, and lets us for moments gaze into that!

Nay all speech, even the commonest speech, has something of song in it: not a parish in the world but has its parish-accent;—the rhythm or *tune* to which the people there *sing* what they have to say! Accent is a kind of chanting; all men have accent of their own,—though they only *notice* that of others. Observe too how all passionate language does of itself become musical,—with a finer music than the mere accent; the speech of a man even in zealous anger becomes a chant, a song. All deep things are Song. It seems somehow the very central essence of us, Song; as if all the rest were but wrappages and hulls! The primal element of us; of us, and of all things. The Greeks fabled of Sphere-Harmonies; it was the feeling they had of the inner structure of Nature; that the soul of all her voices and utterances was perfect music. Poetry, therefore, we will call *musical Thought.* The Poet is he who *thinks* in that manner. At bottom, it turns still on power of intellect; it is a man's sincerity and depth of vision that makes him a Poet. See deep enough, and you see musically; the heart of Nature *being* everywhere music, if you can only reach it.

The *Vates* Poet, with his melodious Apocalypse of Nature, seems to hold a poor rank among us, in comparison with the *Vates* Prophet; his function, and our esteem of him for his function, alike slight. The Hero taken as Divinity; the Hero taken as Prophet; then next the Hero taken only as Poet: does it not look as if our estimate of the Great Man, epoch after epoch, were continually diminishing? We take him first for a god, then for one god-inspired; and now in the next stage of it, his most miraculous word gains from us only the recognition that he is a Poet, beautiful verse-maker, man of genius, or suchlike!—It looks so; but I persuade myself that intrinsically it is not so. If we consider well, it will perhaps appear that in man still there is the *same* altogether peculiar admiration for the Heroic Gift, by what name soever called, that there at any time was.

I should say, if we do not now reckon a Great Man literally divine, it is that our notions of God, of the supreme unattainable Fountain of Splendour, Wisdom and Heroism, are ever rising *higher;* not altogether that our reverence for these qualities, as manifested in our like, is getting lower. This is worth taking thought of. Sceptical Dilettantism, the curse of these ages, a curse which will not last forever, does indeed in this the highest province of human things, as in all provinces, make sad work; and our reverence for great men, all crippled, blinded, paralytic as it is, comes out in poor plight, hardly recognisable. Men worship the shows of great men; the most disbelieve that there is any reality of great men to worship. The dreariest, fatalest faith; believing which, one would literally despair of human things. Nevertheless look, for example, at Napoleon! A Corsican lieutenant of artillery; that is the show of *him:* yet is he not obeyed, *worshipped* after his sort, as all the Tiaraed and Diademed of the world put together could not be? High Duchesses, and ostlers of inns, gather round the Scottish rustic, Burns;—a strange feeling dwelling in each that they never heard a man like this; that, on the whole, this is the man! In the secret heart of these people it still dimly reveals itself, though there is no accredited way of uttering it at present, that this rustic, with his black brows and flashing sun-eyes, and strange words moving laughter and tears, is of a dignity far beyond all others, incommensurable with all others. Do not we feel it so? But now, were Dilettantism, Scepticism, Triviality, and all that sorrowful brood, cast-out of us,—as, by God's blessing, they shall one day be; were faith in the shows of things entirely swept-out, replaced by clear faith in the *things,* so that a man acted on the impulse of that only, and counted the other non-extant; what a new livelier feeling towards this Burns were it!

Nay here in these ages, such as they are, have we not two mere Poets, if not deified, yet we may say beatified? Shakspeare and Dante are Saints of Poetry; really, if we will think of it, *canonised,* so that it is impiety to meddle with them. The unguided instinct of the world, working across all these perverse impediments, has arrived at such result. Dante and Shakspeare are a peculiar Two. They dwell apart, in a kind of royal solitude; none equal, none second to them: in the general feeling of the world, a certain transcendentalism, a glory as of complete perfection, invests these two. They *are* canonised, though no Pope or Cardinals took hand in doing it! Such, in spite of every perverting influence, in the most unheroic times, is still our indestructible reverence for heroism.—We will look a little at these Two, the Poet Dante and the Poet Shakspeare: what little it is permitted us to say here of the Hero as Poet will most fitly arrange itself in that fashion.

Many volumes have been written by way of commentary on Dante and his Book; yet, on the whole, with no great result. His Biography is, as it were, irrecoverably lost for us. An unimportant, wandering, sorrowstricken man, not much note was taken of him while he lived; and the most of that has vanished, in the long space that now intervenes. It is five centuries since he ceased writing and living here. After all commentaries, the Book itself is mainly what we know of him. The Book;—and one might add that Portrait commonly attributed to Giotto, which, looking on it, you cannot help inclining to think genuine, whoever did it. To me it is a most touching face; perhaps of all faces that I know, the most so. Lonely there, painted as on vacancy, with the simple laurel wound round it; the deathless sorrow and pain, the known victory which is also deathless;—significant of the whole history of Dante! I think it is the mournfulest face that ever was painted from reality; an altogether tragic, heart-affecting face. There is in it, as foundation of it, the softness, tenderness, gentle affection as of a child; but all this is as if congealed into sharp contradiction, into abnegation, isolation, proud hopeless pain. A soft ethereal soul looking-out so stern, implacable, grim-trenchant, as from imprisonment of thick-ribbed ice! Withal it is a silent pain too, a silent scornful one: the lip is curled in a kind of godlike disdain of the thing that is eating-out his heart,—as if it were withal a mean insignificant thing, as if he whom it had power to torture and strangle were greater than it. The face of one wholly in protest, and life-long unsurrendering battle, against the world. Affection all converted into indignation: an implacable indignation; slow, equable, silent, like that of a god! The eye too, it looks-out as in a kind of *surprise,* a kind of inquiry, Why the world was of such a sort? This is Dante: so he looks, this 'voice of ten silent centuries,' and sings us 'his mystic unfathomable song.'

The little that we know of Dante's Life corresponds well enough with this Portrait and this Book. He was born at Florence, in the upper class of society, in the year 1265. His education was the best then going; much school-divinity, Aristotelean logic, some Latin classics,—no inconsiderable insight into certain provinces of things: and Dante, with his earnest intelligent nature, we need not doubt, learned better than most all that was learnable. He has a clear cultivated understanding, and of great subtlety; this best fruit of education he had contrived to realise from these scholastics. He knows accurately and well what lies close to him; but, in such a time, without printed books or free intercourse, he could not know well what was distant: the small clear light, most luminous for what is near, breaks itself into singular *chiaroscuro* striking on what is far off. This was Dante's learning from the schools. In life, he had gone through the usual destinies; been twice out campaigning as a soldier for the Florentine State, been on embassy; had in his thirty-fifth year, by natural gradation of talent and service, become one of the Chief Magistrates of Florence. He had met in boyhood a certain Beatrice Portinari, a beautiful little girl of his own age and rank, and grown-up thenceforth in partial sight of her, in some distant intercourse with her. All readers know his graceful affecting account of this; and then of their being parted; of her being wedded to another, and of her death soon after. She makes a great figure in Dante's Poem; seems to have made a great figure in his life. Of all beings it might seem as if she, held apart from him, far apart at last in the dim Eternity, were the only one he had ever with his whole strength of affection loved. She died: Dante himself was wedded; but it seems not happily, far from happily. I fancy, the rigorous earnest man, with his keen excitabilities, was not altogether easy to make happy.

We will not complain of Dante's miseries: had all gone right with him as he wished it, he might have been Prior, Podesta, or whatsoever they call it, of Florence, well accepted among neighbours,—and the world had wanted one of the most notable words ever spoken or sung. Florence would have had another prosperous Lord Mayor; and the ten dumb centuries continued voiceless, and the ten other listening centuries (for there will be ten of them and more) had no *Divina Commedia* to hear! We will complain of nothing. A nobler destiny was appointed for this Dante; and he, struggling like a man led towards death and crucifixion, could not help fulfilling it. Give *him* the choice of his happiness! He knew not, more than we do, what was really happy, what was really miserable.

In Dante's Priorship, the Guelf-Ghibelline, Bianchi-Neri, or some other confused disturbances rose to such a height, that Dante, whose party had seemed the stronger, was with his friends cast unexpectedly forth into banishment; doomed thenceforth to a life of woe and wandering. His property was all confiscated and more; he had the fiercest feeling that it was entirely unjust, nefarious in the sight of God and man. He tried what was in him to get reinstated; tried even by warlike surprisal, with arms in his hand: but it would not do; bad only had become worse. There is a record, I believe, still extant in the Florence Archives, dooming this Dante, wheresoever caught, to be burnt alive. Burnt alive; so it stands, they say: a very curious civic document. Another curious document, some considerable number of years later, is a Letter of Dante's to the Florentine Magistrates, written in answer to a milder proposal of theirs, that he should return on condition of apologising and paying a fine. He answers, with fixed stern pride: "If I cannot return without calling myself guilty, I will never return, *nunquam revertar*."

For Dante there was now no home in this world. He wandered from patron to patron, from place to place; proving, in his own bitter words, 'How hard is the path, *Come è duro calle*.' The wretched are not cheerful company. Dante, poor and banished, with his proud earnest nature, with his moody humours, was not a man to conciliate men. Petrarch reports of him that being at Can della Scala's court, and blamed one day for his gloom and taciturnity, he answered in no courtier-like way. Della Scala stood among his courtiers, with mimes and buffoons (*nebulones ac histriones*) making him heartily merry; when turning to Dante, he said: "Is it not strange, now, that this poor fool should make himself so entertaining; while you, a wise man, sit there day after day, and have nothing to amuse us with at all?" Dante answered bitterly: "No, not strange; your Highness is to recollect the Proverb, *Like to Like*;"—given the amuser, the amusee must also be given! Such a man, with his proud silent ways, with his sarcasms and sorrows, was not made to succeed at court. By degrees, it came to be evident to him that he had no longer any resting-place, or hope of benefit, in this earth. The earthly world had cast him forth, to wander, wander; no living heart to love him now; for his sore miseries there was no solace here.

The deeper naturally would the Eternal World impress itself on him; that awful reality over which, after all, this Time-world, with its Florences and banishments, only flutters as an unreal shadow. Florence thou shalt never see: but Hell and Purgatory and Heaven thou shalt surely see! What is Florence, Can della Scala, and the World and Life altogether? ETERNITY: thither, of a truth, not elsewhither, art thou and all things bound! The great soul of Dante, homeless on earth, made its home more and more in that awful other world.

Naturally his thoughts brooded on that, as on the one fact important for him. Bodied or bodiless, it is the one fact important for all men:—but to Dante, in that age, it was bodied in fixed certainty of scientific shape; he no more doubted of that *Malebolge Pool,* that it all lay there with its gloomy circles, with its *alti guai,* and that he himself should see it, than we doubt that we should see Constantinople if we went thither. Dante's heart, long filled with this, brooding over it in speechless thought and awe, bursts forth at length into 'mystic unfathomable song;' and this his *Divine Comedy,* the most remarkable of all modern Books, is the result.

It must have been a great solacement to Dante, and was, as we can see, a proud thought for him at times, That he, here in exile, could do this work; that no Florence, nor no man or men, could hinder him from doing it, or even much help him in doing it. He knew too, partly, that it was great; the greatest a man could do, 'If thou follow thy star, *Se tu segui tua stella,*'—so could the Hero, in his forsakenness, in his extreme need, still say to himself: "Follow thou thy star, thou shalt not fail of a glorious haven!" The labour of writing, we find, and indeed could know otherwise, was great and painful for him; he says, This Book, 'which has made me lean for many years.' Ah yes, it was won, all of it, with pain and sore toil,—not in sport, but in grim earnest. His Book, as indeed most good Books are, has been written, in many senses, with his heart's blood. It is his whole history, this Book. He died after finishing it; not yet very old, at the age of fifty-six;—broken-hearted rather, as is said. He lies buried in his death-city Ravenna: *Hic claudor Dantes patriis extorris ab oris.* The Florentines begged back his body, in a century after; the Ravenna people would not give it. "Here am I Dante laid, shut-out from my native shores."

I said, Dante's Poem was a Song: it is Tieck who calls it 'a mystic unfathomable Song;' and such is literally the character of it. Coleridge remarks very pertinently somewhere, that wherever you find a sentence musically worded, of true rhythm and melody in the words, there is something deep and good in the meaning too. For body and soul, word and idea, go strangely together here as everywhere. Song: we said before, it was the Heroic of Speech! All *old* Poems, Homer's and the rest, are authentically Songs. I would say, in strictness, that all right Poems are; that whatsoever is not *sung* is properly no Poem, but a piece of Prose cramped into jingling lines,—to the great injury of the grammar, to the great grief of the reader, for most part! What we want to get at is the *thought* the man had, if he had any: why should he twist it into jingle, if he *could* speak it out plainly? It is only when the heart of him is rapt into true passion of melody, and the very tones of him, according to Coleridge's remark, become musical by the greatness, depth and music of his thoughts, that we can give him right to rhyme and sing; that we call him a Poet, and listen to him as the Heroic of Speakers,—whose speech *is* Song. Pretenders to this are many; and to an earnest reader, I doubt, it is for most part a very melancholy, not to say an insupportable business, that of reading rhyme! Rhyme that had no inward necessity to be rhymed;—it ought to have told us plainly, without any jingle, what it was aiming at. I would advise all men who *can* speak their thought, not to sing it; to understand that, in a serious time, among serious men, there is no vocation in them for singing it. Precisely as we love the true song, and are charmed by it as by something divine, so shall we hate the false song, and account it a mere wooden noise, a thing hollow, superfluous, altogether an insincere and offensive thing.

I give Dante my highest praise when I say of his *Divine Comedy* that it is, in all sense, genuinely a Song. In the very sound of it there is a *canto fermo;* it proceeds as by a chant. The language, his simple *terza rima,* doubtless helped him in this. One reads along naturally with a sort of *lilt.* But I add, that it could not be otherwise; for the essence and material of the work are themselves rhythmic. Its depth, and rapt passion and sincerity, makes it musical;—go *deep* enough, there is music everywhere. A true inward symmetry, what one calls an architectural harmony, reigns in it, proportionates it all: architectural; which also partakes of the character of music. The three kingdoms, *Inferno, Purgatorio, Paradiso,* look-out on one another like compartments of a great edifice; a great supernatural world-cathedral, piled-up there, stern, solemn, awful; Dante's World of Souls! It is, at bottom, the *sincerest* of all Poems; sincerity, here too, we find to be the measure of worth. It came deep out of the author's heart of hearts; and it goes deep, and through long generations, into ours. The people of Verona, when they saw him on the streets, used to say, "*Eccovi l' uom ch' è stato all' Inferno,* See, there is the man that was in Hell!" Ah yes, he had been in Hell;—in Hell enough, in long severe sorrow and struggle; as the like of him is pretty sure to have been. Commedias that come-out *divine* are not accomplished otherwise. Thought, true labour of any kind, highest virtue itself, is it not the daughter of Pain? Born as out of the black whirlwind;—true *effort,* in fact, as of a captive struggling to free himself: that is Thought. In all ways we are 'to become perfect through *suffering.*'—But, as I say, no work known to me is so elaborated as this of Dante's. It has all been as if molten, in the hottest furnace of his soul. It had made him 'lean' for many years. Not the general whole only; every compartment of it is worked-out, with intense earnestness, into truth, into clear visuality. Each answers to the other; each fits in its place, like a marble stone accurately hewn and polished. It is the soul of Dante, and in this the soul of the middle ages, rendered forever rhythmically visible there. No light task; a right intense one: but a task which is *done.*

Perhaps one would say, *intensity,* with the much that depends on it, is the prevailing character of Dante's genius. Dante does not come before us as a large catholic mind; rather as a narrow, and even sectarian mind: it is partly the fruit of his age and position, but partly too of his own nature. His greatness has, in all senses, concentered itself into fiery emphasis and depth. He is world-great not because he is world-wide, but because he is world-deep. Through all objects he pierces as it were down into the heart of Being. I know nothing so intense as Dante. Consider, for example, to begin with the outermost development of his intensity, consider how he paints. He has a great power of vision; seizes the very type of a thing; presents that and nothing more. You remember that first view he gets of the Hall of Dite; *red* pinnacle, redhot cone of iron glowing through the dim immensity of gloom;—so vivid, so distinct, visible at once and forever! It is an emblem of the whole genius of Dante. There is a brevity, an abrupt precision in him: Tacitus is not briefer, more condensed; and then in Dante it seems a natural condensation, spontaneous to the man. One smiting word; and then there is silence, nothing more said. His silence is more eloquent than words. It is strange with what a sharp decisive grace he snatches the true likeness of a matter: cuts into the matter as with a pen of fire. Plutus, the blustering giant, collapses at Virgil's rebuke; it is 'as the sails sink, the mast being suddenly broken.' Or that poor Brunetto Latini, with the *cotto aspetto,* 'face *baked,*' parched brown and lean; and the 'fiery snow' that falls on them there, a 'fiery snow without wind,' slow, deliberate, never-ending! Or the lids of those Tombs; square sarcophaguses, in that silent dim-burning Hall, each with its Soul in torment; the lids laid open there; they are to be shut at the Day of Judgment, through Eternity. And how Farinata rises; and how Cavalcante falls—at hearing of his Son, and the past tense *'fue'*! The very movements in Dante have something brief; swift, decisive, almost military. It is of the inmost essence of his genius this sort of painting. The fiery, swift Italian nature of the man, so silent, passionate, with its quick abrupt movements, its silent 'pale rages,' speaks itself in these things.

For though this of painting is one of the outermost developments of a man, it comes like all else from the essential faculty of him; it is physiognomical of the whole man. Find a man whose words paint you a likeness, you have found a man worth something; mark his manner of doing it, as very characteristic of him. In the first place, he could not have discerned the object at all, or seen the vital type of it, unless he had, what we may call, *sympathised* with it,—had sympathy in him to bestow on objects. He must have been *sincere* about it too; sincere and sympathetic; a man without worth cannot give you the likeness of any object; he dwells in vague outwardness, fallacy and trivial hearsay, about all objects. And indeed may we not say that intellect altogether expresses itself in this power of discerning what an object is? Whatsoever of faculty a man's mind may have will come out here. Is it even of business, a matter to be done? The gifted man is he who *sees* the essential point, and leaves all the rest aside as surplusage: it is his faculty too, the man of business's faculty, that he discern the true *likeness,* not the false superficial one, of the thing he has got to work in. And how much of *morality* is in the kind of insight we get of anything; 'the eye seeing in all things what it brought with it the faculty of seeing'! To the mean eye all things are trivial, as certainly as to the jaundiced they are yellow. Raphael, the Painters tell us, is the best of all Portrait-painters withal. No most gifted eye can exhaust the significance of any object. In the commonest human face there lies more than Raphael will take-away with him.

Dante's painting is not graphic only, brief, true, and of a vividness as of fire in dark night; taken on the wider scale, it is everyway noble, and the outcome of a great soul. Francesca and her Lover, what qualities in that! A thing woven as out of rainbows, on a ground of eternal black. A small flute-voice of infinite wail speaks there, into our very heart of hearts. A touch of womanhood in it too: *della bella persona, che mi fu tolta;* and how, even in the Pit of woe, it is a solace that *he* will never part from her! Saddest tragedy in these *alti guai.* And the racking winds, in that *aer bruno,* whirl them away again, to wail forever!—Strange to think: Dante was the friend of this poor Francesca's father; Francesca herself may have sat upon the Poet's knee, as a bright innocent little child. Infinite pity, yet also infinite rigour of law: it is so Nature is made; it is so Dante discerned that she was made. What a paltry notion is that of his *Divine Comedy*'s being a poor splenetic impotent terrestrial libel; putting those into Hell whom he could not be avenged-upon on earth! I suppose if ever pity, tender as a mother's, was in the heart of any man, it was in Dante's. But a man who does not know rigour cannot pity either. His very pity will be cowardly, egoistic,— sentimentality, or little better. I know not in the world an affection equal to that of Dante. It is a tenderness, a trembling, longing, pitying love: like the wail of Aeolean harps, soft, soft; like a child's young heart;—and then that stern, sore-saddened heart! These longings of his towards his Beatrice; their meeting together in the *Paradiso;* his gazing in her pure transfigured eyes, her that had been purified by death so long, separated from him so far:—one likens it to the song of angels; it is among the purest utterances of affection, perhaps the very purest, that ever came out of a human soul.

For the *intense* Dante is intense in all things; he has got into the essence of all. His intellectual insight as painter, on occasion too as reasoner, is but the result of all other sorts of intensity. Morally great, above all, we must call him; it is the beginning of all. His scorn, his grief are as transcendent as his love;—as indeed, what are they but the *inverse* or *converse* of his love? '*A Dio spiacenti ed a' nemici sui,* Hateful to God and to the enemies of God:' lofty scorn, unappeasable silent reprobation and aversion; '*Non ragionam di lor,* We will not speak of *them,* look only and pass.' Or think of this; 'They have not the *hope* to die, *Non han speranza di morte.*' One day, it had risen sternly benign on the scathed heart of Dante, that he, wretched, never-resting, worn as he was, would full surely *die;* 'that Destiny itself could not doom him not to die.' Such words are in this man. For rigour, earnestness and depth, he is not to be paralleled in the modern world; to seek his parallel we must go into the Hebrew Bible, and live with the antique Prophets there.

I do not agree with much modern criticism, in greatly preferring the *Inferno* to the two other parts of the Divine *Commedia.* Such preference belongs, I imagine, to our general Byronism of taste, and is like to be a transient feeling. The *Purgatorio* and *Paradiso,* especially the former, one would almost say, is even more excellent than it. It is a noble thing that *Purgatorio,* 'Mountain of Purification;' an emblem of the noblest conception of that age. If Sin is so fatal, and Hell is and must be so rigorous, awful, yet in Repentance too is man purified; Repentance is the grand Christian act. It is beautiful how Dante works it out. The *tremolar dell' onde,* that 'trembling' of the ocean-waves, under the first pure gleam of morning, dawning afar on the wandering Two, is as the type of an altered mood. Hope has now dawned; never-dying Hope, if in company still with heavy sorrow. The obscure sojourn of daemons and reprobate is underfoot; a soft breathing of penitence mounts higher and higher, to the Throne of Mercy itself. "Pray for me," the denizens of that Mount of Pain all say to him. "Tell my Giovanna to pray for me," my daughter Giovanna; "I think her mother loves me no more!" They toil painfully up by that winding steep, 'bent-down like corbels of a building,' some of them,— crushed-together so 'for the sin of pride;' yet nevertheless in years, in ages and aeons, they shall have reached the top, which is Heaven's gate, and by Mercy shall have been admitted in. The joy too of all, when one has prevailed; the whole Mountain shakes with joy, and a psalm of praise rises, when one soul has perfected repentance and got its sin and misery left behind! I call all this a noble embodiment of a true noble thought.

But indeed the Three compartments mutually support one another, are indispensable to one another. The *Paradiso,* a kind of inarticulate music to me, is the redeeming side of the *Inferno;* the *Inferno* without it were untrue. All three make-up the true Unseen World, as figured in the Christianity of the Middle Ages; a thing forever memorable, forever true in the essence of it, to all men. It was perhaps delineated in no human soul with such depth of veracity as in this of Dante's; a man *sent* to sing it, to keep it long memorable. Very notable with what brief simplicity he passes out of the every-day reality, into the Invisible one; and in the second or third stanza, we find ourselves in the World of Spirits; and dwell there, as among things palpable, indubitable! To Dante they *were* so; the real world, as it is called, and its facts, was but the threshold to an infinitely higher Fact of a World. At bottom, the one was as *preter*natural as the other. Has not each man a soul? He will not only be a spirit, but is one. To the earnest Dante it is all one visible Fact; he believes it, sees it; is the Poet of it in virtue of that. Sincerity, I say again, is the saving merit, now as always.

Dante's Hell, Purgatory, Paradise, are a symbol withal, an emblematic representation of his Belief about this Universe:—some Critic in a future age, like those Scandinavian ones the other day, who has ceased altogether to think as Dante did, may find this too all an 'Allegory,' perhaps an idle Allegory! It is a sublime embodiment, or sublimest, of the soul of Christianity. It expresses, as in huge worldwide architectural emblems, how the Christian Dante felt Good and Evil to be the two polar elements of this Creation, on which it all turns; that these two differ not by *preferability* of one to the other, but by incompatibility absolute and infinite; that the one is excellent and high as light and Heaven, the other hideous, black as Gehenna and the Pit of Hell! Everlasting Justice, yet with Penitence, with everlasting Pity,—all Christianism, as Dante and the Middle Ages had it, is emblemed here. Emblemed: and yet, as I urged the other day, with what entire truth of purpose; how unconscious of any embleming! Hell, Purgatory, Paradise: these things were not fashioned as emblems; was there, in our Modern European Mind, any thought at all of their being emblems! Were they not indubitable awful facts; the whole heart of man taking them for practically true, all Nature everywhere confirming them? So is it always in these things. Men do not believe an Allegory. The future Critic, whatever his new thought may be, who considers this of Dante to have been all got-up as an Allegory, will commit one sore mistake!—Paganism we recognised as a veracious expression of the earnest awe-struck feeling of man towards the Universe; veracious, true once, and still not without worth for us. But mark here the difference of Paganism and Christianism; one great difference. Paganism emblemed chiefly the Operations of Nature; the destinies, efforts, combinations, vicissitudes of things and men in this world; Christianism emblemed the Law of Human Duty, the Moral Law of Man. One was for the sensuous nature: a rude helpless utterance of the *first* Thought of men,—the chief recognised virtue, Courage, Superiority to Fear. The other was not for the sensuous nature, but for the moral. What a progress is here, if in that one respect only!—

And so in this Dante, as we said, had ten silent centuries, in a very strange way, found a voice. The *Divina Commedia* is of Dante's writing; yet in truth *it* belongs to ten Christian centuries, only the finishing of it is Dante's. So always. The craftsman there, the smith with that metal of his, with these tools, with these cunning methods,—how little of all he does is properly *his* work! All past inventive men work there with him;—as indeed with all of us, in all things. Dante is the spokesman of the Middle Ages; the Thought they lived by stands here, in everlasting music. These sublime ideas of his, terrible and beautiful, are the fruit of the Christian Meditation of all the good men who had gone before him. Precious they; but also is not he precious? Much, had not he spoken, would have been dumb; not dead, yet living voiceless.

On the whole, is it not an utterance, this mystic Song, at once of one of the greatest human souls, and of the highest thing that Europe had hitherto realised for itself? Christianism, as Dante sings it, is another than Paganism in the rude Norse mind; another than 'Bastard Christianism' half-articulately spoken in the Arab Desert seven-hundred years before!—The noblest *idea* made *real* hitherto among men, is sung, and emblemed-forth abidingly, by one of the noblest men. In the one sense and in the other, are we not right glad to possess it? As I calculate, it may last yet for long thousands of years. For the thing that is uttered from the inmost parts of a man's soul, differs altogether from what is uttered by the outer part. The outer is of the day, under the empire of mode; the outer passes away, in swift endless changes; the inmost is the same yesterday, today and forever. True souls, in all generations of the world, who look on this Dante, will find a brotherhood in him; the deep sincerity of his thoughts, his woes and hopes, will speak likewise to their sincerity; they will feel that this Dante too was a brother. Napoleon in Saint-Helena is charmed with the genial veracity of old Homer. The oldest Hebrew Prophet, under a vesture the most diverse from ours, does yet, because he speaks from the heart of man, speak to all men's hearts. It is the one sole secret of continuing long memorable. Dante, for depth of sincerity, is like an antique Prophet too; his words, like theirs, come from his very heart. One need not wonder if it were predicted that his Poem might be the most enduring thing our Europe has yet made; for nothing so endures as a truly spoken word. All cathedrals, pontificalities, brass and stone, and outer arrangement never so lasting, are brief in comparison to an unfathomable heart-song like this: one feels as if it might survive, still of importance to men, when these had all sunk into new irrecognisable combinations, and had ceased individually to be. Europe has made much; great cities, great empires, encyclopaedias, creeds, bodies of opinion and practice: but it has made little of the class of Dante's Thought. Homer yet *is*, veritably present face to face with every open soul of us; and Greece, where is *it*? Desolate for thousands of years; away, vanished; a bewildered heap of stones and rubbish, the life and existence of it all gone. Like a dream; like the dust of King Agamemnon! Greece was; Greece, except in the *words* it spoke, is not.

The uses of this Dante? We will not say much about his 'uses.' A human soul who has once got into that primal element of *Song,* and sung-forth fitly somewhat therefrom, has worked in the *depths* of our existence; feeding through long times the life-*roots* of all excellent human things whatsoever,—in a way that 'utilities' will not succeed well in calculating! We will not estimate the Sun by the quantity of gas-light it saves us; Dante shall be invaluable, or of no value. One remark I may make: the contrast in this respect between the Hero-Poet and the Hero-Prophet. In a hundred years, Mahomet, as we saw, had his Arabians at Grenada and at Delhi; Dante's Italians seem to be yet very much where they were. Shall we say, then, Dante's effect on the world was small in comparison? Not so: his arena is far more restricted; but also it is far nobler, clearer;—perhaps not less but more important. Mahomet speaks to great masses of men, in the coarse dialect adapted to such; a dialect filled with inconsistencies, crudities, follies: on the great masses alone can he act, and there with good and with evil strangely blended. Dante speaks to the noble, the pure and great, in all times and places. Neither does he grow obsolete, as the other does. Dante burns as a pure star, fixed there in the firmament, at which the great and the high of all ages kindle themselves: he is the possession of all the chosen of the world for uncounted time. Dante, one calculates, may long survive Mahomet. In this way the balance may be made straight again.

But, at any rate, it is not by what is called their effect on the world by what *we* can judge of their effect there, that a man and his work are measured. Effect? Influence? Utility? Let a man *do* his work; the fruit of it is the care of Another than he. It will grow its own fruit; and whether embodied in Caliph Thrones and Arabian Conquests, so that it 'fills all Morning and Evening Newspapers,' and all Histories, which are a kind of distilled Newspapers; or not embodied so at all;—what matters that? That is not the real fruit of it! The Arabian Caliph, in so far only as he did something, was something. If the great Cause of Man, and Man's work in God's Earth, got no furtherance from the Arabian Caliph, then no matter how many scimetars he drew, how many gold piasters pocketed, and what uproar and blaring he made in this world,—*he* was but a loud-sounding inanity and futility; at bottom, he *was* not at all. Let us honour the great empire of *Silence,* once more! The boundless treasury which we do *not* jingle in our pockets, or count up and present before men! It is perhaps, of all things, the usefulest for each of us to do, in these loud times.——

As Dante, the Italian man, was sent into our world to embody musically the Religion of the Middle Ages, the Religion of our Modern Europe, its Inner Life; so Shakspeare, we may say, embodies for us the Outer Life of our Europe as developed then, its chivalries, courtesies, humours, ambitions, what practical way of thinking, acting, looking at the world, men then had. As in Homer we may still construe Old Greece; so in Shakspeare and Dante, after thousands of years, what our modern Europe was, in Faith and in Practice, will still be legible. Dante has given us the Faith or soul; Shakspeare, in a not less noble way, has given us the Practice or body. This latter also we were to have; a man was sent for it, the man Shakspeare. Just when that chivalry way of life had reached its last finish, and was on the point of breaking down into slow or swift dissolution, as we now see it everywhere, this other sovereign Poet, with his seeing eye, with his perennial singing voice, was sent to take note of it, to give long-enduring record of it. Two fit men: Dante, deep, fierce as the central fire of the world; Shakspeare, wide, placid, far-seeing, as the Sun, the upper light of the world. Italy produced the one world-voice; we English had the honour of producing the other.

Curious enough how, as it were by mere accident, this man came to us. I think always, so great, quiet, complete and self-sufficing is this Shakspeare, had the Warwickshire Squire not prosecuted him for deer-stealing, we had perhaps never heard of him as a Poet! The woods and skies, the rustic Life of Man in Stratford there, had been enough for this man! But indeed that strange out-budding of our whole English Existence, which we call the Elizabethan Era, did not it too come as of its own accord? The 'Tree Igdrasil' buds and withers by its own laws,—too deep for our scanning. Yet it does bud and wither, and every bough and leaf of it is there, by fixed eternal laws; not a Sir Thomas Lucy but comes at the hour fit for him. Curious, I say, and not sufficiently considered; how everything does coöperate with all; not a leaf rotting on the highway but is indissoluble portion of solar and stellar systems; no thought, word or act of man but has sprung withal out of all men, and works sooner or later, recognisably or irrecognisably, on all men! It is all a Tree: circulation of sap and influences, mutual communication of every minutest leaf with the lowest talon of a root, with every other greatest and minutest portion of the whole. The Tree Igdrasil, that has its roots down in the Kingdoms of Hela and Death, and whose boughs overspread the highest Heaven!—

In some sense it may be said that this glorious

Elizabethan Era with its Shakspeare, as the outcome and flowerage of all which had preceded it, is itself attributable to the Catholicism of the Middle Ages. The Christian Faith, which was the theme of Dante's Song, had produced this Practical Life which Shakspeare was to sing. For Religion then, as it now and always is, was the soul of Practice; the primary vital fact in men's life. And remark here, as rather curious, that Middle-Age Catholicism was abolished, so far as Acts of Parliament could abolish it, before Shakspeare, the noblest product of it, made his appearance. He did make his appearance nevertheless. Nature at her own time, with Catholicism or what else might be necessary, sent him forth; taking small thought of Acts of Parliament. King-Henrys, Queen-Elizabeths go their way; and Nature too goes hers. Acts of Parliament, on the whole, are small, notwithstanding the noise they make. What Act of Parliament, debate at St. Stephen's, on the hustings or elsewhere, was it that brought this Shakspeare into being? No dining at Freemasons' Tavern, opening subscription-lists, selling of shares, and infinite other jangling and true or false endeavouring! This Elizabethan Era, and all its nobleness and blessedness, came without proclamation, preparation of ours. Priceless Shakspeare was the free gift of Nature; given altogether silently;—received altogether silently, as if it had been a thing of little account. And yet, very literally, it is a priceless thing. One should look at that side of matters too.

Of this Shakspeare of ours, perhaps the opinion one sometimes hears a little idolatrously expressed is, in fact, the right one; I think the best judgment not of this country only, but of Europe at large, is slowly pointing to the conclusion, That Shakspeare is the chief of all Poets hitherto; the greatest intellect who, in our recorded world, has left record of himself in the way of Literature. On the whole, I know not such a power of vision, such a faculty of thought, if we take all the characters of it, in any other man. Such a calmness of depth; placid joyous strength; all things imaged in that great soul of his so true and clear, as in a tranquil unfathomable sea! It has been said, that in the constructing of Shakspeare's Dramas there is, apart from all other 'faculties' as they are called, an understanding manifested, equal to that in Bacon's *Novum Organum*. That is true; and it is not a truth that strikes every one. It would become more apparent if we tried, any of us for himself, how, out of Shakspeare's dramatic materials, *we* could fashion such a result! The built house seems all so fit,—everyway as it should be, as if it came there by its own law and the nature of things,—we forget the rude disorderly quarry it was shaped from. The very perfection of the house, as if Nature herself had made it, hides the builder's merit. Perfect, more perfect than any other man, we may call Shakspeare in this: he discerns, knows as by instinct, what condition he works under, what his materials are, what his own force and its relation to them is. It is not a transitory glance of insight that will suffice; it is deliberate illumination of the whole matter; it is a calmly *seeing* eye; a great intellect, in short. How a man, of some wide thing that he has witnessed, will construct a narrative, what kind of picture and delineation he will give of it,—is the best measure you could get of what intellect is in the man. Which circumstance is vital and shall stand prominent; which unessential, fit to be suppressed; where is the true *beginning*, the true sequence and ending? To find out this, you task the whole force of insight that is in the man. He must *understand* the thing; according to the depth of his understanding, will the fitness of his answer be. You will try him so. Does like join itself to like; does the spirit of method stir in that confusion, so that its embroilment becomes order? Can the man say, *Fiat lux,* Let there be light; and out of chaos make a world? Precisely as there is *light* in himself, will he accomplish this.

Or indeed we may say again, it is in what I called Portrait-painting, delineating of men and things, especially of men, that Shakspeare is great. All the greatness of the man comes out decisively here. It is unexampled, I think, that calm creative perspicacity of Shakspeare. The thing he looks at reveals not this or that face of it, but its inmost heart, and generic secret: it dissolves itself as in light before him, so that he discerns the perfect structure of it. Creative, we said: poetic creation, what is this too but *seeing* the thing sufficiently? The *word* that will describe the thing, follows of itself from such clear intense sight of the thing. And is not Shakspeare's *morality,* his valour, candour, tolerance, truthfulness; his whole victorious strength and greatness, which can triumph over such obstructions, visible there too? Great as the world! No *twisted,* poor convex-concave mirror, reflecting all objects with its own convexities and concavities; a perfectly *level* mirror;—that is to say withal, if we will understand it, a man justly related to all things and men, a good man. It is truly a lordly spectacle how this great soul takes-in all kinds of men and objects, a Falstaff, an Othello, a Juliet, a Coriolanus; sets them all forth to us in their round completeness; loving, just, the equal brother of all. *Novum Organum,* and all the intellect you will find in Bacon, is of a quite secondary order; earthy, material, poor in comparison with this. Among modern men, one finds, in strictness, almost nothing of the same rank. Goethe alone, since the days of Shakspeare, reminds me of it. Of him too you say that he *saw* the object; you may say what he himself says of Shakspeare: 'His characters are like watches with dial-plates of transparent crystal; they show you the hour like others, and the inward mechanism also is all visible.'

The seeing eye! It is this that discloses the inner harmony of things; what Nature meant, what musical idea Nature has wrapped-up in these often rough embodiments. Something she did mean. To the seeing eye that something were discernible. Are they base, miserable things? You can laugh over them, you can weep over them; you can in some way or other genially relate yourself to them;—you can, at lowest, hold your peace about them, turn away your own and others' face from them, till the hour come for practically exterminating and extinguishing them! At bottom, it is the Poet's first gift, as it is all men's, that he have intellect enough. He will be a Poet if he have: a Poet in word; or failing that, perhaps still better, a Poet in act. Whether he write at all; and if so, whether in prose or in verse, will depend on accidents: who knows on what extremely trivial accidents,—perhaps on his having had a singing-master, on his being taught to sing in his boyhood! But the faculty which enables him to discern the inner heart of things, and the harmony that dwells there (for whatsoever exists has a harmony in the heart of it, or it would not hold together and exist), is not the result of habits or accidents, but the gift of Nature herself; the primary outfit for a Heroic Man in what sort soever. To the Poet, as to every other, we say first of all, *See*. If you cannot do that, it is of no use to keep stringing rhymes together, jingling sensibilities against each other, and *name* yourself a Poet; there is no hope for you. If you can, there is, in prose or verse, in action or speculation, all manner of hope. The crabbed old Schoolmaster used to ask, when they brought him a new pupil, "But are ye sure he's *not a dunce?*" Why, really one might ask the same thing, in regard to every man proposed for whatsoever function; and consider it as the one inquiry needful: Are ye sure he's not a dunce? There is, in this world, no other entirely fatal person.

For, in fact, I say the degree of vision that dwells in a man is a correct measure of the man. If called to define Shakspeare's faculty, I should say superiority of Intellect, and think I had included all under that. What indeed are faculties? We talk of faculties as if they were distinct, things separable; as if a man had intellect, imagination, fancy, &c., as he has hands, feet and arms. That is a capital error. Then again, we hear of a man's 'intellectual nature,' and of his 'moral nature,' as if these again were divisible, and existed apart. Necessities of language do perhaps prescribe such forms of utterance; we must speak, I am aware, in that way, if we are to speak at all. But words ought not to harden into things for us. It seems to me, our apprehension of this matter is, for most part, radically falsified thereby. We ought to know withal, and to keep forever in mind, that these divisions are at bottom but *names;* that man's spiritual nature, the vital Force which dwells in him, is essentially one and indivisible; that what we call imagination, fancy, understanding, and so forth, are but different figures of the same Power of Insight, all indissolubly connected with each other, physiognomically related; that if we knew one of them, we might know all of them. Morality itself, what we call the moral quality of a man, what is this but another *side* of the one vital Force whereby he is and works? All that a man does is physiognomical of him. You may see how a man would fight, by the way in which he sings; his courage, or want of courage, is visible in the word he utters, in the opinion he has formed, no less than in the stroke he strikes. He is *one;* and preaches the same Self abroad in all these ways.

Without hands a man might have feet, and could still walk: but, consider it,—without morality, intellect were impossible for him; a thoroughly immoral *man* could not know anything at all! To know a thing, what we can call knowing, a man must first *love* the thing, sympathise with it: that is, be *virtuously* related to it. If he have not the justice to put down his own selfishness at every turn, the courage to stand by the dangerous-true at every turn, how shall he know? His virtues, all of them, will lie recorded in his knowledge. Nature, with her truth, remains to the bad, to the selfish and the pusillanimous forever a sealed book: what such can know of Nature is mean, superficial, small; for the uses of the day merely.—But does not the very Fox know something of Nature? Exactly so: it knows where the geese lodge! The human Reynard, very frequent everywhere in the world, what more does he know but this and the like of this? Nay, it should be considered too, that if the Fox had not a certain vulpine *morality,* he could not even know where the geese were, or get at the geese! If he spent his time in splenetic atrabiliar reflections on his own misery, his ill usage by Nature, Fortune and other Foxes, and so forth; and had not courage, promptitude, practicality, and other suitable vulpine gifts and graces, he would catch no geese. We may say of the Fox too, that his morality and insight are of the same dimensions; different faces of the same internal unity of vulpine life!—These things are worth stating; for the contrary of them acts with manifold very baleful perversion, in this time: what limitations, modifications they require, your own candour will supply.

If I say, therefore, that Shakspeare is the greatest of Intellects, I have said all concerning him. But there is more in Shakspeare's intellect than we have yet seen. It is what I call an unconscious intellect; there is more virtue in it than he himself is aware of. Novalis beautifully remarks of him, that those Dramas of his are Products of Nature too, deep as Nature herself. I find a great truth in this saying. Shakspeare's Art is not Artifice; the noblest worth of it is not there by plan or precontrivance. It grows-up from the deeps of Nature, through this noble sincere soul, who is a voice of Nature. The latest generations of men will find new meanings in Shakspeare, new elucidations of their own human being; 'new harmonies with the infinite structure of the Universe; concurrences with later ideas, affinities with the higher powers and senses of man.' This well deserves meditating. It is Nature's highest reward to a true simple great soul, that he get thus to be *a part of herself*. Such a man's works, whatsoever he with utmost conscious exertion and forethought shall accomplish, grow up withal *unconsciously*, from the unknown deeps in him;—as the oak-tree grows from the Earth's bosom, as the mountains and waters shape themselves; with a symmetry grounded on Nature's own laws, conformable to all Truth whatsoever. How much in Shakspeare lies hid; his sorrows, his silent struggles known to himself; much that was not known at all, not speakable at all: like *roots,* like sap and forces working underground! Speech is great; but Silence is greater.

Withal the joyful tranquillity of this man is notable. I will not blame Dante for his misery: it is as battle without victory; but true battle,—the first, indispensable thing. Yet I call Shakspeare greater than Dante, in that he fought truly, and did conquer. Doubt it not, he had his own sorrows: those *Sonnets* of his will even testify expressly in what deep waters he had waded, and swum struggling for his life;—as what man like him ever failed to have to do? It seems to me a heedless notion, our common one, that he sat like a bird on the bough; and sang forth, free and offhand, never knowing the troubles of other men. Not so; with no man is it so. How could a man travel forward from rustic deer-poaching to such tragedy-writing, and not fall-in with sorrows by the way? Or, still better, how could a man delineate a Hamlet, a Coriolanus, a Macbeth, so many suffering heroic hearts, if his own heroic heart had never suffered?—And now, in contrast with all this, observe his mirthfulness, his genuine overflowing love of laughter! You would say, in no point does he *exaggerate* but only in laughter. Fiery objurgations, words that pierce and burn, are to be found in Shakspeare; yet he is always in measure here; never what Johnson would remark as a specially 'good hater.' But his laughter seems to pour from him in floods; he heaps all manner of ridiculous nicknames on the butt he is bantering, tumbles and tosses him in all sorts of horse-play; you would say, with his whole heart laughs. And then, if not always the finest, it is always a genial laughter. Not at mere weakness, at misery or poverty; never. No man who *can* laugh, what we call laughing, will laugh at these things. It is some poor character only *desiring* to laugh, and have the credit of wit, that does so. Laughter means sympathy; good laughter is not 'the crackling of thorns under the pot.' Even at stupidity and pretension this Shakspeare does not laugh otherwise than genially. Dogberry and Verges tickle our very hearts; and we dismiss them covered with explosions of laughter: but we like the poor fellows only the better for our laughing; and hope they will get on well there, and continue Presidents of the City-watch. Such laughter, like sunshine on the deep sea, is very beautiful to me.

We have no room to speak of Shakspeare's individual works; though perhaps there is much still waiting to be said on that head. Had we, for instance, all his plays reviewed as *Hamlet,* in *Wilhelm Meister,* is! A thing which might, one day, be done. August Wilhelm Schlegel has a remark on his Historical Plays, *Henry Fifth* and the others, which is worth remembering. He calls them a kind of National Epic. Marlborough, you recollect, said, he knew no English History but what he had learned from Shakspeare. There are really, if we look to it, few as memorable Histories. The great salient points are admirably seized; all rounds itself off, into a kind of rhythmic coherence; it is, as Schlegel says, *epic;*—as indeed all delineation by a great thinker will be. There are right beautiful things in those Pieces, which indeed together form one beautiful thing. That battle of Agincourt strikes me as one of the most perfect things, in its sort, we anywhere have of Shakspeare's. The description of the two hosts: the worn-out, jaded English; the dread hour, big with destiny, when the battle shall begin; and then that deathless valour: "Ye good yeomen, whose limbs were made in England!" There is a noble Patriotism in it,—far other than the 'indifference' you sometimes hear ascribed to Shakspeare. A true English heart breathes, calm and strong, through the whole business; not boisterous, protrusive; all the better for that. There is a sound in it like the ring of steel. This man too had a right stroke in him, had it come to that!

But I will say, of Shakspeare's works generally, that we have no full impress of him there; even as full as we have of many men. His works are so many windows, through which we see a glimpse of the world that was in him. All his works seem, comparatively speaking, cursory, imperfect, written under cramping circumstances; giving only here and there a note of the full utterance of the man. Passages there are that come upon you like splendour out of Heaven; bursts of radiance, illuminating the very heart of the thing: you say, "That is *true*, spoken once and forever; wheresoever and whensoever there is an open human soul, that will be recognised as true!" Such bursts, however, make us feel that the surrounding matter is not radiant; that it is, in part, temporary, conventional. Alas, Shakspeare had to write for the Globe Playhouse: his great soul had to crush itself, as it could, into that and no other mould. It was with him, then, as it is with us all. No man works save under conditions. The sculptor cannot set his own free Thought before us; but his Thought as he could translate it into the stone that was given, with the tools that were given. *Disjecta membra* are all that we find of any Poet, or of any man.

Whoever looks intelligently at this Shakspeare may recognise that he too was a *Prophet,* in his way; of an insight analogous to the Prophetic, though he took it up in another strain. Nature seemed to this man also divine; *un*speakable, deep as Tophet, high as Heaven: 'We are such stuff as Dreams are made of!' That scroll in Westminster Abbey, which few read with understanding, is of the depth of any seer. But the man sang; did not preach, except musically. We called Dante the melodious Priest of Middle-Age Catholicism. May we not call Shakspeare the still more melodious Priest of a *true* Catholicism, the 'Universal Church' of the Future and of all times? No narrow superstition, harsh asceticism, intolerance, fanatical fierceness or perversion: a Revelation, so far as it goes, that such a thousandfold hidden beauty and divineness dwells in all Nature; which let all men worship as they can! We may say without offence, that there rises a kind of universal Psalm out of this Shakspeare too; not unfit to make itself heard among the still more sacred Psalms. Not in disharmony with these, if we understood them, but in harmony!—I cannot call this Shakspeare a 'Sceptic,' as some do; his indifference to the creeds and theological quarrels of his time misleading them. No: neither unpatriotic, though he says little about his Patriotism; nor sceptic, though he says little about his Faith. Such 'indifference' was the fruit of his greatness withal: his whole heart was in his own grand sphere of worship (we may call it such); these other controversies, vitally important to other men, were not vital to him.

But call it worship, call it what you will, is it not a right glorious thing, and set of things, this that Shakspeare has brought us? For myself, I feel that there is actually a kind of sacredness in the fact of such a man being sent into this Earth. Is he not an eye to us all; a blessed heaven-sent Bringer of Light?—And, at bottom, was it not perhaps far better that this Shakspeare, everyway an unconscious man, was *conscious* of no Heavenly message? He did not feel, like Mahomet, because he saw into those internal Splendours, that he specially was the 'Prophet of God:' and was he not greater than Mahomet in that? Greater; and also, if we compute strictly, as we did in Dante's case, more successful. It was intrinsically an error that notion of Mahomet's, of his supreme Prophethood; and has come down to us inextricably involved in error to this day; dragging along with it such a coil of fables, impurities, intolerances, as makes it a questionable step for me here and now to say, as I have done, that Mahomet was a true Speaker at all, and not rather an ambitious charlatan, perversity and simulacrum; no Speaker, but a Babbler! Even in Arabia, as I compute, Mahomet will have exhausted himself and become obsolete, while this Shakspeare, this Dante may still be young;—while this Shakspeare may still pretend to be a Priest of Mankind, of Arabia as of other places, for unlimited periods to come!

Compared with any speaker or singer one knows, even with Aeschylus or Homer, why should he not, for veracity and universality, last like them? He is *sincere* as they; reaches deep down like them, to the universal and perennial. But as for Mahomet, I think it had been better for him *not* to be so conscious! Alas, poor Mahomet; all that he was *conscious* of was a mere error; a futility and triviality,—as indeed such ever is. The truly great in him too was the unconscious: that he was a wild Arab lion of the desert, and did speak-out with that great thunder-voice of his, not by words which he *thought* to be great, but by actions, by feelings, by a history which *were* great! His Koran has become a stupid piece of prolix absurdity; we do not believe, like him, that God wrote that! The Great Man here too, as always, is a Force of Nature: whatsoever is truly great in him springs-up from the *in*articulate deeps.

Well: this is our poor Warwickshire Peasant, who rose to be Manager of a Playhouse, so that he could live without begging; whom the Earl of Southampton cast some kind glances on; whom Sir Thomas Lucy, many thanks to him, was for sending to the Treadmill! We did not account him a god, like Odin, while he dwelt with us;—on which point there were much to be said. But I will say rather, or repeat: In spite of the sad state Hero-worship now lies in, consider what this Shakspeare has actually become among us. Which Englishman we ever made, in this land of ours, which million of Englishmen, would we give-up rather than the Stratford Peasant? There is no regiment of highest Dignitaries that we would sell him for. He is the grandest thing we have yet done. For our honour among foreign nations, as an ornament to our English Household, what item is there that we would not surrender rather than him? Consider now, if they asked us, Will you give-up your Indian Empire or your Shakspeare, you English; never have had any Indian Empire, or never have had any Shakspeare? Really it were a grave question. Official persons would answer doubtless in official language; but we, for our part too, should not we be forced to answer: Indian Empire, or no Indian Empire; we cannot do without Shakspeare! Indian Empire will go, at any rate, some day; but this Shakspeare does not go, he lasts forever with us; we cannot give-up our Shakspeare!

Nay, apart from spiritualities; and considering him merely as a real, marketable, tangibly-useful possession. England, before long, this Island of ours, will hold but a small fraction of the English: in America, in New Holland, east and west to the very Antipodes, there will be a Saxondom covering great spaces of the Globe. And now, what is it that can keep all these together into virtually one Nation, so that they do not fall-out and fight, but live at peace, in brotherlike intercourse, helping one another? This is justly regarded as the greatest practical problem, the thing all manner of sovereignties and governments are here to accomplish: what is it that will accomplish this? Acts of Parliament, administrative prime-ministers cannot. America is parted from us, so far as Parliament could part it. Call it not fantastic, for there is much reality in it: Here, I say, is an English King, whom no time or chance, Parliament or combination of Parliaments, can dethrone! This King Shakspeare, does not he shine, in crowned sovereignty, over us all, as the noblest, gentlest, yet strongest of rallying-signs; *in*destructible; really more valuable in that point of view than any other means or appliance whatsoever? We can fancy him as radiant aloft over all the Nations of Englishmen, a thousand years hence. From Paramatta, from New York, wheresoever, under what sort of Parish-Constable soever, English men and women are, they will say to one another: "Yes, this Shakspeare is ours; we produced him, we speak and think by him; we are of one blood and kind with him.' The most common-sense politician, too, if he pleases, may think of that.

Yes, truly, it is a great thing for a Nation that it get an articulate voice; that it produce a man who will speak-forth melodiously what the heart of it means! Italy, for example, poor Italy lies dismembered, scattered asunder, not appearing in any protocol or treaty as a unity at all; yet the noble Italy is actually *one:* Italy produced its Dante; Italy can speak! The Czar of all the Russias, he is strong, with so many bayonets, Cossacks and cannons; and does a great feat in keeping such a tract of Earth politically together; but he cannot yet speak. Something great in him, but it is a dumb greatness. He has had no voice of genius, to be heard of all men and times. He must learn to speak. He is a great dumb monster hitherto. His cannons and Cossacks will all have rusted into nonentity, while that Dante's voice is still audible. The Nation that has a Dante is bound together as no dumb Russia can be.—We must here end what we had to say of the *Hero-Poet.*

Essay on Chatterton

Robert Browning

First published in the Foreign Quarterly Review *(July 1842): 465-483.*

ART. VIII.—*Conjectures and Researches concerning the Love Madness and Imprisonment of Torquato Tasso.* By RICHARD HENRY WILDE. 2 vols. New York. 1842.

Upon the minuteness and obscurity of our attainable evidences with regard to a single important portion of a great poet's history—the Love and Madness of Tasso—great light is thrown by these clever volumes. And further additions to a very meagre stock are not, it seems, to be absolutely despaired of. The Medicean Records may be laid under more liberal contributions, and the Archives of Este cease to remain impenetrable. What even if a ray of light should straggle over the unsunned hoards of sumless wealth in the Vatican? "If windows were in heaven, might this thing be."

But in our days the poorest loophole will have to be broken, we suspect, with far different instruments from those it is the fashion to employ just now in Italy. It is enough at present if the oily instances of this or the other Minister-Residentiary operate so happily upon the ruffled apprehensiveness of this or the other Chamberlain-Omnipotentiary, as to allow a minute's glimpse of the Fortunate Isles through the incessant breakers that girdle them. The rude sea now and then grows civil, indeed; but a positive current setting landwards is the thing wanted, and likely to remain so. Ever and anon we seem on the point of a discovery. A scrap of letter turns up, or a bundle of notices drop out, and the Head Librarian for the time being considers the curiosity of some Dilettante Ambassador for the place being, and, provided the interest of the whole civilized world is kept out of sight with sufficient adroitness, becomes communicative.

"The anger of the Grand Duke arises from his being informed that I had revealed to the Duke of Ferrara . . . . . . ! I cannot write all freely, but this is the gospel." So writes Tasso to "the one friend he now believes in, Scipio Gonzaga." And "this blank," sorrowfully subjoins Mr. Wilde, "is found in the first copy of the letter furnished for publication by the learned and candid Muratori, then librarian to the Duke of Modena." It contained an expression, says he, which it would be indecorous to repeat! Thus at every step, where there is the slightest prospect of a clue to the truth, are we mortified by its destruction through reserve or timidity. And if things were so in the green-tree time of the Muratoris, what shall be done in the dry stump of modern Lombardy or Tuscany?

Of certain important manuscripts recently discovered at Rome, and now in the course of publication, we regret to learn that the authenticity is considered too questionable to allow of their being brought forward to any useful purpose: so that, for the present, this result of Mr. Wilde's labour, now before us, must be regarded as conclusive: and fortunately our last, proves also our best, news. It is pleasant to find that the popular notion (we might say instinct) concerning this particular point of Tasso's career, grown up, uncertain how, from biographical gleanings here and gatherings there,—somewhat shaken, as it was sure to be, by subsequent representations,—seems again confirmed by these latest discoveries.

A couplet in a canzone, a paragraph in an epistle, had thus been sufficient to begin with. "Tasso was punished in a living hell by angels, because he unburthened his bosom to his lyre." "He would fain be released from this prison of Saint Anna without being troubled for those things which from frenzy he has done and written in matters of love." After these, and a few other like notices, Professors might search, and Abbates research; the single Leonora become "three lady-loves at once;" and the dim torture at Ferrara a merciful effect of Duke Alfonso's consideration for "Signor Tasso, the noted poet's, deplorable madness;"—but the world, satisfied with its own suspicion, remained deaf to it all.

"If we suppose," sums up Mr. Wilde, "that his imprisonment was occasioned by the accidental or treacherous disclosure of amatory poetry suspected to be addressed to the princess, every thing becomes intelligible—his mistress's early injunctions of silence—his directions to Rondinelli—the dearer mysteries of his heart half-hinted to Gonzaga—the ref-

349

erence to her who corresponded so little to his love—his heavy sin of temerity—Madalò's more important treasons—the attempt to extort confession—the bitter rigour and unwonted arts—the words and acts that might increase Alfonso's ire—the order to feign insanity—the sacrifice of Abraham—the command that he must aspire to no fame of letters—the prohibition to write—the anger of the princesses—the allusions to his fond faults—to his Proserpine—to Ixion, and to the angels that punished him. By this supposition, also, Leonora's voluntary celibacy, notwithstanding the most advantageous offers of marriage, and Tasso's constant devotion to the duke, in spite of the rigour of his chastisement, are sufficiently accounted for."

How much that establishes old convictions, and how little that is even supplementary to them, have we here!

Such as it is, however, in what Mr. Wilde has done, he has gone the right way to work and done it well. He has steadily restricted himself to the single point in question. It is that point in the poet's history, indeed, from which those to whom sonnets and madrigals, the Rinaldo and the Aminta, are all but unknown, will take warrant for some belief in their reported truth and beauty. It is undoubtedly that to which every student of Italian verse must refer the touching glimmer, as an outbreak through prison-bars, that colours every page of the Giurusalemme. Still it is but a point; and Mr. Wilde has not perhaps done less gracefully and wisely in leaving the rest untouched, than in accomplishing so thoroughly the task he took in hand. He relies upon his subject; is sure of the service he can render by an efficacious treatment of thus much of it; nor entertains any fear lest the bringing in a Before and After, with which he has no immediate concern, should be thought necessary to give interest to the At Present on which he feels he can labour to advantage. We suspect that if we would make any material progress in knowledge of this description, such works must be so undertaken. If, for example, the materials for a complete biography of Tasso are far from exhausted, let some other traveller from the west be now busied in the land of Columbus and Vespucci with the investigation,—say, of the circumstances of the wondrous youth of Tasso; the orations at Naples and the Theses at Padua,—and in the end we should more than probably have two spots of sunshine to find our way by, instead of one such breadth of dubious twilight, as, in a hazy book written on the old principle of doing a little for every part of a subject, and more than a little for none, rarely fails to perplex the more.

Thinking thus, and grieving over what must be admitted to be the scantiness of the piece of sunshine here, and the narrow and not very novel track it would alone serve to lead us into,—a book[1] was sent to us on a subject not very different from Mr. Wilde's, but on which the service he has sought to render to the memory of Tasso has not hitherto been attempted for a memory more foully outraged. We make no apology for a proposed effort to render some such service. It is no very abrupt desertion of the misfortunes of Tasso, to turn to the misfortunes of Chatterton. All these disputed questions in the lives of men of genius—all these so-called calamities of authors—have a common relationship, a connexion so close and inalienable, that they seldom fail to throw important light upon each other.

To the precocity of genius in the Neapolitan boy at seven years old—the verse and prose from the College of the Jesuits—no parallel can be found in modern times, till we arrive at the verses of Chatterton, to whom Campbell has very properly said "Tasso alone may be compared as a juvenile prodigy." But the parallel will, in other respects, admit of application. The book before us, for example, on the love and madness of the Italian, is in itself a direct text from which to speak of what concerns us most in the disputed character of our own countryman. As the whole of Mr. Wilde's argument may be said to include itself in his commentary upon the opening couplet of the first Sonnet of the collection of *Rime*,

"True were the loves and transports which I sung,"

so let us say of the Englishman, that his were far from that untruth, that absence of reality, so constantly charged against them. In a word, poor Chatterton's life was not the Lie it is so universally supposed to have been; nor did he "perish in the pride" of refusing to surrender Falsehood and enter on the ways of Truth. We can show, we think, and by some such process as Mr. Wilde adopts in regard to Tasso, that he had already entered on those ways when he was left, without a helping hand, to sink and starve as he might. And to this single point we shall as far as possible restrict ourselves.

Mr. Wilde remarks of the great Italian, that though there are indeed passages in Tasso's life and letters, scarcely reconcilable with the strick regard for truth which Manso, his friend and contemporary, ascribes to him,

> "yet that to whatever dissimulation he may have been driven, upon some memorable occasions—by a hard and, if you will, a criminal, but still almost irresistible necessity—there is no reason to believe him habitually insincere: and that, avoiding every subtle refinement, it cannot be too much to assume that he was like other men, who in the absence of all inducement, were not supposed deliberately to utter falsehood."

It shall be our endeavour, by extending the application of this text from Tasso to Chatterton, to throw a new light upon a not dissimilar portion of the latter poet's career, and in some degree soften those imputations of habitual insincerity with which the most sympathizing of Chatterton's critics have found themselves compelled to replace the "great veracity" attributed to him by his earliest and most partial biographer.

For Tasso, a few words will say how his first false step was an indiscretion; how, having published love-poetry under a false name, and suffered himself to be suspected its author, he, to avoid the ill-consequences, feigned at the Duke's suggestion, Madness; and how his protracted agony at Saint Anna was but an unremitting attempt to free himself from the effect of this false step without being compelled to reveal the truth, and disavow his whole proceedings since the time of that sad starting-aside from the right way. But before we speak of the corresponding passage in Chatterton's story, something should be premised respecting the characteristic shape his first error took, as induced by the liabilities of that peculiar development of genius of which he was the subject.

Genius almost invariably begins to develop itself by imitation. It has, in the short-sightedness of infancy, faith in the world: and its object is to compete with, or prove superior to, the world's already recognised idols, at their own performances and by their own methods. This done, there grows up a faith in itself: and, no longer taking the performance or method of another for granted, it supersedes these by processes of its own. It creates, and imitates no longer. Seeing cause for faith in something external and better, and having attained to a moral end and aim, it next discovers in itself the only remaining antagonist worthy of its ambition, and in the subduing what at first had seemed its most enviable powers, arrives at the more or less complete fulfilment of its earthly mission. This first instinct of Imitation, which with the mediocre takes the corresponding mediocre form of an implied rather than expressed appropriation of some other man's products, assumed perforce with Chatterton, whose capabilities were of the highest class, a proportionably bolder and broader shape in the direction his genius had chosen to take. And this consideration should have checked the too severe judgment of what followed. For, in simple truth, the startling character of Chatterton's presentment, with all its strange and elaborately got up accompaniments, was in no more than strict keeping with that of the thing he presented. For one whose boy's essay was "Rowley" (a Man, a Time, a Language, all at once) the simultaneous essay of inventing the details of muniment-room treasures and yellow-roll discoveries, by no means exceeded in relative hardihood the mildest possible annexing—whatever the modern author's name may be—to the current poetry or prose of the time. But, alas! for the mere complacent forbearance of the world in the one case, must come sharp and importunate questionings in the other; and, at every advance in such a career, the impossibility of continuing in the spirit of the outset grows more and more apparent. To begin with the step of a giant is one thing, suddenly for another's satisfaction to increase to a colossal stride is a very different. To the falsehood of the mediocre, truth may easily be superinduced, and true works, with them, silently take the place of false works: but before one like Chatterton could extricate himself from the worse than St. Anna dungeon which every hour was building up more surely between him and the common earth and skies, so much was to be dared and done! That the attempt was courageously made in Chatterton's case, there are many reasons for believing. But to understand his true position, we must remove much of the colouring which subsequent occurrences imparted to the dim beginnings of his course of deception. He is to the present day viewed as a kind of Psalmanazar or Macpherson, producing deliberately his fabrications to the world and challenging its attention to them. A view far from the truth. Poor Chatterton never had that chance. Before the world could be appealed to, a few untoward circumstances seem to have effectually determined and given stability to what else had not impossibly proved a mere boy's fancy, destined to go as lightly as it came and leave no trace, save in a fresh exertion of the old means to a new and more commensurate end.

In September, 1768, a New Bridge at Bristol was completed, and early in the next month the principal newspaper of the city contained a prose "description of the Fryar's (Mayor's) first passing over the Old Bridge, taken from an old manuscript." The attention of—what are called in the accounts we have seen—"the literati of Bristol," was excited. Application was made to the publisher for a sight of the surprising and interesting original. No such thing was forthcoming; but the curiosity of Literati must be appeased; and the bearer of the newspaper marvel, one Thomas Chatterton,—a youth of sixteen, educated at Colston's Charity-school where reading, writing and arithmetic only were taught, and, since, a clerk to an attorney of the place,—was recognised on his next appearance at the printing-office with another contribution, and questioned whence he obtained that first-named paper. He was questioned "with threatenings in the first instance, to which he refused any answer, and next with milder usage and promises of patronage,"—which extorted from him at last the confession, that the manuscript was one of many his father (parish clerk, usher, or sexton) had taken from a coffer in the church of St. Mary, Redcliff.

It was his own composition; and being the first of what are called the Rowleian forgeries, suggests a remark upon literary forgery in general, and that of Chatterton in particular.[2]

Is it worth while to mention, that the very notion of obtaining a free way for impulses that can find vent in no other channel (and consequently of a liberty conceded to an individual, and denied to the world at large), is implied in all literary production? By this fact is explained, not only the popular reverence for, and interest in even the personal history of, the acknowledged and indisputable possessors of this power—as so many men who have leave to do what the rest of their fellows cannot—but also the as popular jealousy of allowing this privilege to the first claimant. And so instinctively does the Young Poet feel that his desire for this kind of self-enfranchisement will be resisted as a matter of course, that we will venture to say, in nine cases out of ten his first assumption of the licence will be made in a borrowed name. The first communication, to even the family circle or the trusted associate, is sure to be "the work of a friend;" if not, "something extracted from a magazine," or "Englished from the German." So is the way gracefully facilitated for Reader and Hearer finding themselves in a new position with respect to each other.

Now unluckily, in Chatterton's case, this communication's whole value, in the eyes of the Bristolians, consisted in its antiquity. Apart from that, there was to them no picturesqueness in "Master Mayor, mounted on a white horse, dight with sable trappings wrought about by the nuns of St. Kenna;" no "most goodly show in the priests and freres all in white albs." Give that up, and all was given; and poor Chatterton could not give all up. He could only determine for the future to produce Ellas and Godwyns, and other "beauteous pieces;" wherein "the plot should be clear, the language spirited; and the songs interspersed in it, flowing, poetical, and elegantly simple; the similes judiciously applied; and though written in the reign of Henry VI., not inferior to many of the present age." Had there but been any merit of this kind, palpable even to Bristol Literati, to fall back upon in the first instance, if the true authorship were confessed! But that was otherwise; and so the false course, as we have said, was unforeseeingly entered upon. Yet still, from the first, he was singularly disposed to become communicative of his projects and contrivances for carrying them into effect. There was, after all, no such elaborate deception about any of them. Indeed, had there only happened to be a single individual of ordinary intelligence among his intimates, the event must assuredly have fallen out differently. But as it was, one companion would be present at the whole process of "antiquating," as Chatterton styled it, his productions (the pounding of ochre and crumpling of parchments); another would hear him carelessly avow himself master of a power "to copy, by the help of books he could name, the style of our elder poets so exactly, that they should escape the detection of Mr. Walpole himself;"—and yet both these persons remain utterly incapable of perceiving that such circumstances had in the slightest degree a bearing upon after events at Bristol! It is to be recollected, too, that really in Bristol itself there was not anything like a general interest excited in the matter. And when at last, yielding to the pertinacity of inquirers, these and similar facts came lingeringly forth, as the details of so many natural appearances with which unconscious rustics might furnish the philosopher anxious to report and reason upon them—Chatterton was dead.

Of several of his most characteristic compositions, he confessed, at various times, on the least solicitation, the authorship. He had found and versified the argument of the Bristowe Tragedy—he had written the Lines on our Ladye's Church. But these confidences were only to his mother and sister. Why? Because mother and sister were all who cared for him rather than for Rowley, and would look at his connexion with any verses as a point in their favour. As for his two patrons, Barrett and Catcott, they took great interest in the yellow streaks, and verse written like prose without stops; less interest in the poetry; and in Chatterton least, or none at all! And a prophet's fate in his own country was never more amusingly exemplified than when grave Deans and Doctors, writing to inquire after Chatterton's abilities of his old companions, got the answers on record. "Not having any taste myself for ancient poetry," writes Mr. Cary, "I do not recollect Chatterton's ever having shown such writings to me, *but* he often mentioned them, *when,* great as his capacity was, I am convinced that he was incapable of writing them!" "He had intimated," remarks Mr. Smith, "very frequently both a desire to learn, and a design to teach himself—Latin; but I always dissuaded him from it, *as being in itself impracticable.* But I advised him by all means *to try* at French. As to Latin, *depend upon it you will find it too hard for you.* Try at French, if you please: of *that* you may acquire *some* knowledge *without much difficulty,* and it will be of real service to you." "And, sir," winds up Mr. Clayfield, "*take my word for it,* the poems were no more his composition than *mine!*" With such as these there was no fellowship possible for Chatterton. We soon discover him, therefore, looking beyond. From the time of his communication of the Rowley poems, "his ambition," writes Mrs. Newton, his sister, "increased daily. When in spirits he would enjoy his rising fame; confident of advancement, he would promise that my mother and I should be partakers of his success." As a transcriber, we suppose! We find Sir Herbert Croft, to whom this very letter was addressed, declaring "that he will not be sure that the writer and her mother might not have easily been made to believe that injured justice demanded their lives at Tyburn, for being the relatives of him who forged the poems of Rowley." Thus only, in this sideway at the best, could the truth steal out.

Meanwhile the sorry reception given to the so-called falsehood produced its natural effects. On the one hand there is a kind of ambition on being introduced to Mr. Barrett and Mr. Catcott, which increases daily; but on the other we are told that his spirits became at the same time "rather uneven—sometimes so *gloomed,*[3] that for some days together he would say very little, and that by constraint." No doubt, and no wonder! For there was the sense of his being the author of the transcendent chorus to Freedom, or the delicious roundelay in Ella; ever at fierce variance with the pitiful claim he was entitled to make in the character of their mere transcriber.

We shall not pursue this painful part of the question. Day followed day, and found him only more and more deeply involved. What we have restricted our inquiry to, is the justice or injustice of the common charge that henceforth the whole nature of Chatterton became no other than one headstrong spirit of Falsehood, in the midst of which, and by which, he perished at the last. And we think its injustice will be shown without much difficulty, in showing that he really made the most gallant and manly effort of which his circumstances allowed to break through the sorry meshes that entangled him. We purposely forbear, with any view to this, taking for granted the mere instigation of that Moral Sense which it is the worst want of charity to deny to him, and with direct and strong evidences of which his earliest poetry abounded. We will simply inquire what, in the circumstances referred to, would have been the proper course to pursue, had the writer of the "Bristowe Tragedy" chanced to adopt on a single occasion the practice of its hero, "who summed the actions of the day each night before he slept." Confessions at the market-cross avail nothing, and most injure those to whom they are unavoidably made. Should he not have resolutely left Bristol, at least? and, disengaging himself from the still increasing trammels of his daily life of enforced deceit, begun elsewhere a wiser and happier course? That he did so may in our opinion be shown. It is our firm belief that on this, and no other account, he determined to go to London.

"A few months before he left Bristol," mentions his sister, "he wrote letters to several booksellers in London—I believe to learn if there was any probability of his getting an employment there." He had some time previously applied to Dodsley, the noted publisher, for his assistance in printing the tragedy of *Ella*; on the strength of a submitted specimen, which the great man of the Mall did not vouchsafe, it seems, to glance over. He was led, therefore, to make a final experiment on the taste and apprehensiveness of Horace Walpole: not, as in Dodsley's case, by enclosing the despised poetical samples, but by sending a piece of antiquarian ware in which his presumed patron was understood to especially delight. Of nothing are we so thoroughly persuaded as that these attempts were the predetermined last acts of a course of dissimulation he would fain discard for ever—on their success. The Rowleian compositions were all he could immediately refer to, as a proof of the ability he was desirous of employing in almost any other direction. He grounded no claim on his possession of these MSS.; he was not soliciting an opportunity of putting off to advantage the stock in hand, or increasing it; and when Walpole subsequently avowed his regret at having omitted to transcribe before returning, the manuscript thus received, what has been cited as a singular piece of unprincipled effrontery, appears to us perfectly justifiable. For even after the arrival of a discouraging letter, Chatterton's words are, that "if Mr. Walpole wishes to publish them himself, they are at his service." Nay—Mr. Barrett, or "the Town and Country Magazine, to which copies may be sent," or indeed "the world, which it would be the greatest injustice to deprive of so invaluable a curiosity"—may have them and welcome. And Chatterton's anxiety to recover them afterwards is only intelligible on the supposition that his originals were in jeopardy. To the very conceited question Walpole himself has asked—"Did Chatterton impute to me anything but distrust of his MSS.?"—we should answer, Every thing but that. Let the young poet's own verses, indeed, answer.

> Walpole, I thought not I should ever see
> So mean a heart as thine has proved to be:
> Thou, who in luxury nursed, behold'st with scorn
> The boy who friendless, fatherless, forlorn,
> Asks thy high favour. *Thou mayst call me cheat—*
> *Say didst thou never practise such deceit?*
> *Who wrote Otranto?*—but I will not chide.
> Scorn I'll repay with scorn, and pride with pride.
> Had I the gifts of wealth and luxury shared—
> Not poor and mean—Walpole! thou hadst not dared
> Thus to insult. But I shall live and stand
> By Rowley's side, when thou art dead and damned.

In this unhappy correspondence with Walpole,—it never seems to have been admitted, yet it cannot be said too often,—there is no new "falsehood" discernible: there is nothing but an unavailing and most affecting effort, to get somehow free from the old. He makes no asseveration of the fact of his discoveries; affirms nothing the denial of which hereafter would be essentially disgraceful to him; commits himself by only a few ambiguous words which at any time a little plain speaking (and blushes, if we will) would explain away. Let it be observed, above all, that there is no attempt to forge, and produce, and insist on the genuineness of the MSS.; though this was a step by which he could have lost nothing and might have gained every thing, since Walpole's recognition of their extraordinary merit was before him. In the course the correspondence took, alas! that very recognition was fatal. If Walpole could suspect a boy of sixteen had written thus, and yet see nothing in a scrivener's office and its duties which such an one had any title to withdraw from, all was over with Chatterton's hopes. At this point, accordingly, he simply replied that, "he is not able to dispute with a person of his literary character: he has transcribed Rowley's poems from a transcript in the possession of a gentleman who is assured of their authenticity," (poor Catcott!) "and he will go a little beyond Walpole's advice, by destroying *all his useless lumber of literature and never urging his pen again but in the law.*" Is this any very close or deliberate keeping of Rowley's secret! In a word, he felt that Walpole should have said, "Because I firmly believe you, Chatterton, wrote or forged these verses of Rowley, I will do what you require."[4] And so we all feel now.

And what was it the poor baffled youth required? To ascertain this will in a manner satisfy our whole inquiry—so let us try to ascertain it. His immediate application to Walpole, on his succeeding in forcing his notice, and seemingly engaging his interest, was for some place in a government-office. Did he want to be richer? who had from his earliest boyhood been accustomed to live upon bread and water, and who would refuse to partake of his mother's occasional luxury of a hot meal,—remarking that "he was about a great work, and must make himself no stupider than God had made him." Did he want to obtain leisure, then, for this work—in other words, for the carrying on of his old deceptions? "He had," says his sister, "little of his master's business to do—sometimes not two hours in a day, which gave him an opportunity to pursue his genius." Mr. Palmer states, that "Chatterton was much alone in his office, and much disliked being disturbed in the daytime." We should like to know what kind of government-office would have allowed greater facility for the pursuit of poetical studies and "forgeries" than he was already in possession of; since what advantages, in a literary life, government-office-labour can have over law-business, we are far from guessing. It may be said that the pure disgust and weariness of that law business had formed motive sufficient. But our sympathy with Chatterton's struggles—were nothing to be escaped from worse than this "servitude" as he styles it—would seriously diminish, we confess. Relieve Henry Jones from the bricklayer's hod, and Stephen Duck from the thrasher's flail, if needs must: but Chatterton, from two hours a day's copying precedents!—Ay, but "he was obliged to sleep in the same room with the footboy, and take his meals with the servants—which degradation, to one possessing such pride as Chatterton, must have been mortifying in the highest degree!" Now, Chatterton taking his stand on the inherent qualities of his own mind, shall part company with an Emperor, if he so please, and have our approbation; but let him waive that prerogative, and condescend to the little rules of little men, and we shall not sufficiently understand this right—in a blue-coat charity-boy, apprenticed out with ten pounds of the school-fund, and looking for patronage to pipe-makers and pewterers—to cherish this sensitiveness and contamination. There are more degrading things than eating with footboys, we imagine. "The desire," for example, "of proving oneself worthy the correspondence of Mr. Stephens (leather breeches-maker of Salisbury), by tracing his family from Fitz Stephen, son of Stephen, Earl of Aumerle, in 1095, son of Od, Earl of Bloys, and Lord of Holderness." In a word, Chatterton was very proud, and such crotchets never yet entered the head of a truly proud man. Another motive remains. Had he any dislike to Bristol or its inhabitants generally? "His company pleased universally," he says: "he believed he had promised to write to some hundreds of his acquaintance." And for the place itself,—while at London, nothing out of the Gothic takes his taste, except St. Paul's and Greenwich-hospital: he is never tired of talking in his letters about Bristol, its Cathedral, its street improvements: he even inserts hints to the projectors of these last, in a local paper: nay, he will forestall his mother's intended visit to him at London, and return to Bristol by Christmas: and when somebody suggested, just before his departure, that his professed hatred for the city was connected with ill-treatment received there, he returns, indignantly, "He who without a more sufficient reason than *commonplace scurrility* can look with disgust on his native place, is a villain, and a villain not fit to live. I am obliged to you for supposing *me* such a villain!" Why then, without this hatred or disgust, does he leave Bristol? Whence arises the utmost distress of mind in which the mad "Will," whereby he announced his intention of committing suicide, is written? On being questioned concerning it "he acknowledged that he wanted for nothing, and denied any distress on that account." "The distress was occasioned," says Dr. Gregory, "by the refusal of a gentleman whom he had complimented in his poems, to accommodate him with a supply of money." Here are his own reasons. "In regard to my motives for the supposed rashness, I shall observe that I keep no worse company than myself: I never drink to excess, and have, without vanity, too much sense to be attached to the mercenary retailers of iniquity. No: it is my PRIDE, my damned, native, unconquerable pride, that plunges me into distraction. You must know that nineteen-twentieth of my composition is Pride. I must either live a Slave, a Servant; to have no Will of my own, no Sentiments of my own, which I may freely declare as such; or DIE. Perplexing alternative! But it distracts me to think of it—I will endeavour to learn Humility—but it cannot be HERE."

That is, at Bristol. It is needless for us here to interpose that our whole argument goes, not upon what Chatterton said, but what he did: it is part of our proof to show that all his distress arose out of the impossibility of his saying any thing to the real purpose. But is there no approximation to the truth in what has just been quoted? Had he *not* reduced himself to the alternative of living, as Rowley's transcriber, "a slave, with no sentiment of his own which he might freely declare as such," or "dying?" And did not the proud man—who, when he felt somewhat later that he had failed, would not bring his poverty to accept the offer of a meal to escape "dying"—solicit and receive, while earlier there was yet the hope of succeeding, his old companions' "subscription of a guinea apiece," to enable himself to break through the "slavery?" This, then, is our solution. For this and no other motive—to break through his slavery—at any sacrifice to get back to truth—he came up to London.

It will, of course, be objected, that Chatterton gave the very reasons for his desire to obtain a release from Bristol that we have rejected. But he was forced to say something, and what came more plausibly? To Walpole the cause assigned was, "that he wished to cease from being dependant on his mother;"—while, by a reference to his indenture of apprenticeship, we find him to have been supplied with "meat, drink, clothing, and lodging" by his master. To others the mercantile character of Bristol is made an insuperable objection;—and he straightway leaves it for Holborn. As who, to avoid the smell of hemlock, should sail to Anticyra! It may also yet be urged—as it has been too often—that Chatterton gave to the very last, occasional symptoms that the fabricating, falsifying spirit was far from extinct in him. "He would turn Methodist preacher, found a new sect,"&c. Now no one can suppose, and we are far from asserting, that at word of command, Chatterton wholly put aside the old habit of imposing upon people—if that is to be the phrase. But this "imposing upon people" has not always that basest meaning. It is old as the world itself, the tendency of certain spirits to subdue each man by perceiving what will master him, by straightway supplying it from their own resources, and so obtaining, as tokens of success, his admiration, or fear, or wonder. It has been said even that classes of men are immediately ruled in no other way. Poor Chatterton's freedom from some such tendency we do not claim. He is indeed superior to it when alone, in the lumber-closet on Redcliff Hill, or the lathwalled garret at Shoreditch; but in company with the Thistlethwaites and Burgums, he must often have felt a certain power he had, lying dormant there, of turning their natures to his own account. He, "knowing that a great genius can effect any thing, endeavoured in the foregoing poems to represent an Enthusiastic Methodist, and intended to send it to Romaine, and impose it on the infatuated world as a reality;"—but Now, no sooner is the intellectual effort made than the moral one succeeds, and destroying these poems he determined to kill himself. Every way unsuccessful, every way discouraged, the last scene had come. When he killed himself, his room was found "strewn thick over with torn papers."

To the Rowley forgeries he had recurred but in one instance, the acknowledgment of which by a magazine only appeared after his death. He had come to London to produce works of his own; writings he had hoped to get some hearing for. "At the Walmsleys," says Sir Herbert Croft, "he used frequently to say he had many writings by him, which would produce a great deal of money, if they were printed. To this it was once or twice observed, that they lay in a small compass, for that he had not much luggage. But he said he had them, nevertheless. When he talked of writing something which should procure him money to get some clothes—to paper the room in which he lodged; and to send some more things to his sister, mother, and grandmother—he was asked why he did not enable himself to do all this by means of those writings which were 'worth their weight in gold.' His answer was, that 'they were not written with a design to buy old clothes, or to paper rooms; and that if the world did not behave well, it should never see a line of them.'"

It behaves indifferently, we think, in being so sure these were simply fresh books of the "Battle of Hastings," or remodellings of "the Apostate." Look back a little, and see to what drudgery he had submitted in this London, that he could but get the means at last of going on his own ground. "A History of England"—"a voluminous history of London; to appear in numbers the beginning of next week"—"necessitates him to go to Oxford, Cambridge, Lincoln, Coventry, and every collegiate church near."—*Any thing but Rowley!* And when the hopes he had entertained of engaging in such projects fail him, he cheerfully betakes himself to the lowest of all literary labour. He writes any thing and every thing for the magazines. Projects the Moderator; supports the Town and Country; "writes, for a whim, for the Gospel Magazine;" contributes to the London, Middlesex Freeholders', Court and City;—and Registers and Museums get all they ask from him. Thus, we say, with these ultimate views, was he constantly at work in this London pilgrimage; at work, heart and soul; living on a halfpenny roll, or a penny tart, and a glass of water a day, with now and then a sheep's tongue; writing all the while brave letters about his happiness and success to his grandmother, mother, and sister at Bristol, the only creatures he loved as they loved him; and managing, in as miraculous a way as any of his old exercises of power, to buy them china, and fans, and gowns, and so forth, out of his (we cannot calculate how few) pence a day;—being, as such a genius could not but be, the noblest-hearted of mortals. To be sure he had better have swept a crossing in the streets than adopted such a method of getting bread and water; but he had tried to find another outlet till he was sick to the soul, and in this he had been driven to he resolved to stay. If he could, he would have got, for instance, his livelihood as a surgeon. "Before he left Bristol, Mr. Barrett," says his sister, "lent him many books on surgery, and I believe he bought many more, as I remember to have packed them up to send to him in London;" and almost the only intelligible phrase in a mad letter of gibberish, addressed to a friend about the same time, is to the effect that "he is resolved to forsake the Parnassian mount, and would advise that friend to do so too, and attain the mystery of composing *smegma*"—*ointment* we suppose. But nobody would help him, and this way he was helping himself, though never so little.

Sufficient for the Magazine price and Magazine purpose was the piece contributed. "Maria Friendless" and the "Hunter of Oddities" may be a medley of Johnson and Steele;—the few shillings they brought, fully were they worth, though only meant to give a minute's pleasure. As well expect to find, at this time of day, the sheep's tongues on which he lived unwasted, and the halfpenny loaves no way diminished, as find his poor "Oratorio" (the price of a gown for his sister), or bundle of words for tunes that procured these viands, as pleasant as ever. "Great profligacy and tergiversation in his political writings!" is muttered now, and was solemnly outspoken once, as if he were not in some sort still a scrivener—writing out in plain text-hand the wants of all kinds of men of all kinds of parties. Such sought utterance, and had a right to find it—there was an end. There might be plenty of falsehood in this new course, as he would soon have found; but it seemed as truth itself, compared with the old expedients he had escaped from. The point is, *No more Rowley*. His connexion with the Magazines had commenced with Rowley—they had readily inserted portions of his poems—and we cannot conceive a more favourable field of enterprise than London would have afforded, had he been disposed to go on with the fabrication. No prying intimates, nor familiar townsmen, in Mrs. Angel's quiet lodging! He had the ear, too, of many booksellers. Now would have been indeed the white minute for discoveries and forgeries. He was often pressed for matter; had to solicit all his Bristol acquaintance for contributions (some of such go under his own name now, possibly); but with the one exception we have alluded to (affecting for a passage in which his own destitute condition is too expressly described to admit of mistake)—the Ballad of Charity—*Rowley was done with*.

We shall go no farther—the little we proposed to attempt, having here its completion—though the plastic and co-ordinating spirit which distinguishes Chatterton so remarkably, seems perhaps stronger than ever in these few last days of his existence. We must not stay to speak of it. But ever in Chatterton did his acquisitions, varied and abundant as they were, do duty so as to seem but a little out of more in reserve. If only a foreign word clung to his memory, he was sure to reproduce it as if a whole language lay close behind—setting sometimes to work with the poorest materials; like any painter a fathom below ground in the Inquisition, who in his penury of colour turns the weather-stains on his dungeon wall into effects of light and shade, or outlines of objects, and makes the single sputter of red paint in his possession go far indeed! Not that we consider the mere fabrication of old poetry so difficult a matter. For what *is* poetry, whether old or new, will have its full flow in such a scheme; and any difficulty or uncouthness of phrase that elsewhere would stop its course at once, here not only passes with it, but confers the advantage of authenticity on what, in other circumstances, it deforms: the uncouthness will be set down to our time, and whatever significancy may lurk in it will expand to an original meaning of unlimited magnitude. But there is fine, the finest poetry in Chatterton. And surely, when such an Adventurer so perishes in the Desert, we do not limit his discoveries to the last authenticated spot of ground he pitched tent upon, dug intrenchments round, and wrote good tidings home from—but rather give him the benefit of the very last heap of ashes we can trace him to have kindled, and call by his name the extreme point to which we can track his torn garments and abandoned treasures.

Thus much has been suggested by Mr. Wilde's method with Tasso. As by balancing conflicting statements, interpreting doubtful passages, and reconciling discrepant utterances, he has examined whether Tasso was true or false, loved or did not love the Princess of Este, was or was not beloved by her,—so have we sought, from similar evidences, if Chatterton was towards the end of his life hardening himself in deception or striving to cast it off. Let others apply in like manner our inquiry to other great spirits partially obscured, and they will but use us—we hope more effectually—as we have used these able and interesting volumes.

---

1. "The Poetical Works of Thomas Chatterton, with Notices of his Life, a History of the Rowley Controversy, a Selection of his Letters, and Notes Critical and Explanatory." Cambridge. 1842.
2. That there should have been a controversy for ten minutes about the genuineness of any ten verses of "Rowley" is a real disgrace to the scholarship of the age in which such a thing took place: we shall not touch on it here, certainly. Conceive the entering on such a discussion at all, when the poor charity-boy had himself already furnished samples of Rowley in the different stages of partial completeness, from the rough draught in the English of the day, ungarnished by a single obsolete word, to the finished piece with its strange incrustation of antiquity! There is never theft for theft's sake with Chatterton. One short poem only, *The Romaunt of the Cnyghte,* is in part a tacking together of old lines from old poets, out of rhyme and time, yet at the same time not so utterly unlike an approximation to the genuine ware. And why? Because the Mr. Burgum, to one of whose ancestors it is attributed, and whose taste solely it was intended to suit, happened to be *hopelessly incapable of understanding any composition of the mixed sort which Chatterton had determined upon producing; and which, retaining what he supposed the ancient garb should also include every modern refinement.* The expedient which would alone serve with the good Mr. Burgum, was to ply him with something entirely unintelligible, so begetting a reverence; and after that with another thing perfectly comprehensible, so ministering to his pleasure. Accordingly, Chatterton, for that once, attempted to write thorough old verse, because he could, as he did, accompany it by thorough new verse too: a modern paraphrase to wit.

But though we will not touch the general and most needless question, it happens that, by a curious piece of fortune, we have been enabled, since taking up the subject of this article, to bring home to Chatterton one, and by no means the least ingenious of his "forgeries," which has hitherto escaped detection. Rowley's *Sermon on the Holy Spirit,* with its orthodoxy and scripture citations, its Latin from St. Cyprian, and its Greek from St. Gregory, is triumphantly referred to by the learned and laborious Jacob Bryant (who wrote one folio to disprove the Tale of Troy and another to prove the Tale of Rowley), as a flight clearly above Chatterton's reach. Now this aforesaid Greek quotation was the single paragraph which struck our eye some two or three days since, in looking hastily through a series of sermons on the Nature of the Holy Spirit, by the Rev. John Hurrion, originally printed, it should seem, in 1732; on a reference to which we found Rowley's discourse to be a mere cento from their pages, artfully enough compiled. For example, thus saith ROWLEY: "Seyncte Paulle prayethe the Holye Spryte toe assyste hys flocke ynn these wordes, The Holye Spryte's communyonn bee wythe you. Lette us dhere desyerr of hymm to ayde us . . . lette us saye wythe Seyncte Cyprian, *'Adesto, Sancte Spiritus, et paraclesin tuam expectantibus illabere coelitus; sanctifica templum corporis nostri et consecra inhabitaculum tuum.'* Seyncte Paulle sayethe yee are the temple of Godde; for the Spryte of Godde dwellethe ynn you. Gyff yee are the temple of Godde alleyne bie the dwellynge of the Spryte, wote yee notte that the Spryte ys Godde? . . . The Spryte or dyvyne will of Godde moovedd uponn the waterrs att the Creatyonn of the worlde; thys meaneth the Deeitie . . . . Gyff the Spryte bee notte Godde, howe bee ytt the posessynge of the Spryte dothe make a manne sayedd toe be borne of Godde? Itt requyreth the powerr of Godde toe make a manne a new creatyonn, yette such dothe the Spryte. Thus sayethe Seyncte Gregorie Naz. of the Spryte and hys wurchys: [*Genatai Kristos; protrechei. Baptizetai; marturei. Peira zetai; anagei. Dunameis*]." And now let us listen to HURRION, *Serm.* I. "As therefore the apostle prayed on the behalf of the Corinthians . . . . in these words: 'The communion of the Holy Ghost be with you,' it is very proper to apply to him for his gracious aid and assistance. An example of this we have in Cyprian. 'O Holy Spirit be thou present,' &c.—*Cyp. de Spir. S.* p. 484. [quoted, no doubt, at length, like the other references, in the first edition.] . . . . Now if he that dwells in us as his temple is God, what other conclusion can be drawn from thence but this, that we are the temple of God? &c. &c. [The rest of the verse, with the authority of St. Paul being the text of the Sermon.] . . . . which is also God—as when it is said 'the Spirit of God moved upon the waters, in the creation of the world. *Sermon 4.* Believers are born of the Spirit . . this is a new creation, and requires the same Almighty power to effect as the first creation did . . if the Spirit is not God by nature . . how are they said to be born of God who are regenerated by the Spirit? *'Christ,'* says one of the ancients, *'is born—the Spirit is his forerunner,'* &c." And in a foot-note the Greek text and proper authority are subjoined.

It is, perhaps worth a remark in concluding this note, that Chatterton, a lawyer's clerk, takes care to find no law-papers in Canning's Coffer, of which tradition had declared it to be full. That way detection was to be feared. But the pieces on devotional subjects, to which his earlier taste inclined, came so profusely from the "Godlie preeste Rowlie," that Chatterton thinks it advisable, from the time of his discoveries, to forget his paraphrases of Job and Isaiah, and to disclaim for himself a belief in Christianity on every and no occasion at all!

3. The only word in Chatterton's communication to the genuineness of which Walpole seems to have objected. "The modern gloomy," says Chatterton, in reply to some critical exception taken against poems he had sent, "seems but a refinement of the old word Glomming, in Anglo-Saxon the twilight." And in a note to a line of the Ballad of Charity, "Look in his *glommed* face," &c., he observes, " 'Glommed' clouded, dejected. A person of some note in the literary world is of opinion that 'glum' and 'glom' are modern cant words, and from this circumstance doubts the authenticity of Rowley MSS. 'Glummong,' in the Saxon signifies twilight, a dark or dubious light and the modern word gloomy is derived from the Saxon 'glum.' " It is to be added that Chatterton, throughout, only objects to men's doubting the genuineness of Rowley on the insufficient grounds they give—and is in the right there.

4. Walpole's share in the matter may be told in a few words. Indifferent antiquary as he was, at best—in these matters, at worst, his ignorance was complete. "The admirable reasoning in Bryant's work" could "stagger him," he confesses. On receiving Chatterton's first letter and specimens, as his belief in them was implicit, so his mortification on Gray and Mason's setting him right was proportionable. "They both pronounced the poems to be modern forgeries, and recommended the returning them without any further notice,"—stepping a little out of their province in that, certainly; *but they might have felt Chatterton safer at Bristol than nearer home.* Walpole himself did no more in the refusal he gave, than avail himself of Chatterton's own statement that his communications were "taken from a transcript in the possession of a gentleman who was assured of their authenticity." This unknown personage had clearly the first claim to the good things of the Clerk of the Pipe and Usher of the Receipt, and to the unknown they were left therefore, without more heed. Who can object? Truth to say, he of Strawberry Hill was at all times less disposed to expend his doit on a living beggar than on a dead Indian; and, in his way, cowlsfull of Ellas and Godwyns were nothing to a spurious cardinal's hat, empty enough. Beside, what was there to him in the least pressing in the application of a mere transcriber ("who had not quitted his master, nor was necessitous, nor otherwise poorer than attorney's clerks are"), to "emerge from a dull profession and obtain a place that would enable him to follow his propensities." Therefore is it more a pity that ten years after, when he had partly forgotten the matter (this must be allowed, since, with respect to two points which strengthen his case materially, he professes uncertainty), Walpole should have made, on compulsion, a statement of its main circumstances, and leisurely put himself in what he conceived the handsomest of positions,—which turns out to be not quite so handsome. Never for an instant, forsooth, was he deceived by Rowley. "Chatterton had not commenced their intercourse in a manner to dazzle his judgment, or give him a high idea of Chatterton's own." "Somebody, he at first supposed, desired to laugh at him, not very ingeniously, he thought." Little imagining all this while that his letters were in existence, and forthcoming! and that every piece of encouragement to further forgeries, by the expression of belief in those before him, which he professes would have been the height of baseness in him to make, *he had already made!* Indeed the whole statement is modelled on Benedick's *Old Tale:* "If this were so, so were it uttered—but it is not so, nor 'twas not so—but, indeed, God forbid it should be so!"

One while, he "does not believe there ever existed so masterly a genius as Chatterton." And another while, he has regard to the "sad situation of the world, if every muse-struck lad who is bound to an attorney were to have his fetters struck off." Wanting is the excellent Horace Walpole, in short, through all these unhappy matters, in that good memory which Swift has pronounced indispensable to a certain class of statement-makers.

And here would enough seem to have been said on the subject, did not one vile paragraph in the Walpole Explanations leer at us—the news to wit, that "all of the house of forgery are relations, and that Chatterton's ingenuity in counterfeiting styles, and it is believed, hands, might easily have led him to those more facile imitations of prose, promissory notes." House of forgery!—from one not only enabled by his first preface to Otranto to march in at its hall-door, but qualified, by a trait noted in "Walpoliana," to sneak in through its area-wicket! *Exempli gratiâ.* "The compiler having learned that the celebrated epistle to Sir William Chambers was supposed to be written by Mason, very innocently expressed to Mr. Walpole his surprise that Mason, the general characteristic of whose poesy is feeble delicacy, but united with a pleasing neatness, should be capable of composing so spirited a satire. Mr. Walpole, *with an arch and peculiar smile, answered, that it would indeed be surprising.* An instantaneous and unaccountable impression arose that he was himself the author, but delicacy prevented the direct question," &c. &c.

Introductory Essay

Letters of Percy Bysshe Shelley (London: Moxon, 1852)

Robert Browning

The volume was withdrawn from publication when the letters were discovered to be spurious.

An opportunity having presented itself for the acquisition of a series of unedited letters by Shelley, all more or less directly supplementary to and illustrative of the collection already published by Mr. Moxon, that gentleman has decided on securing them. They will prove an acceptable addition to a body of correspondence, the value of which towards a right understanding of its author's purpose and work, may be said to exceed that of any similar contribution exhibiting the worldly relations of a poet whose genius has operated by a different law.

Doubtless we accept gladly the biography of an objective poet, as the phrase now goes; one whose endeavour has been to reproduce things external (whether the phenomena of the scenic universe, or the manifested action of the human heart and brain) with an immediate reference, in every case, to the common eye and apprehension of his fellow men, assumed capable of receiving and profiting by this reproduction. It has been obtained through the poet's double faculty of seeing external objects more clearly, widely, and deeply, than is possible to the average mind, at the same time that he is so acquainted and in sympathy with its narrow comprehension as to be careful to supply it with no other materials than it can combine into an intelligible whole. The auditory of such a poet will include, not only the intelligences which, save for such assistance, would have missed the deeper meaning and enjoyment of the original objects, but also the spirits of a like endowment with his own, who, by means of his abstract, can forthwith pass to the reality it was made from, and either corroborate their impressions of things known already, or supply themselves with new from whatever shows in the inexhaustible variety of existence may have hitherto escaped their knowledge. Such a poet is properly the [*poietes*], the fashioner; and the thing fashioned, his poetry, will of necessity be substantive, projected from himself and distinct. We are ignorant what the inventor of "Othello" conceived of that fact as he beheld it in completeness, how he accounted for it, under what known law he registered its nature, or to what unknown law he traced its coincidence. We learn only what he intended we should learn by that particular exercise of his power,—the fact itself,—which, with its infinite significances, each of us receives for the first time as a creation, and is hereafter left to deal with, as, in proportion to his own intelligence, he best may. We are ignorant, and would fain be otherwise.

Doubtless, with respect to such a poet, we covet his biography. We desire to look back upon the process of gathering together in a lifetime, the materials of the work we behold entire; of elaborating, perhaps under difficulty and with hindrance, all that is familiar to our admiration in the apparent facility of success. And the inner impulse of this effort and operation, what induced it? Did a soul's delight in its own extended sphere of vision set it, for the gratification of an insuppressible power, on labour, as other men are set on rest? Or did a sense of duty or of love lead it to communicate its own sensations to mankind? Did an irresistible sympathy with men compel it to bring down and suit its own provision of knowledge and beauty to their narrow scope? Did the personality of such an one stand like an open watch-tower in the midst of the territory it is erected to gaze on, and were the storms and calms, the stars and meteors, its watchman was wont to report of, the habitual variegation of his every-day life, as they glanced across its open roof or lay reflected on its four-square parapet? Or did some sunken and darkened chamber of imagery witness, in the artificial illumination of every storied compartment we are permitted to contemplate, how rare and precious were the outlooks through here and there an embrasure upon a world beyond, and how blankly would have pressed on the artificer the boundary of his daily life, except for the amorous diligence with which he had rendered permanent by art whatever came to diversify the gloom? Still, fraught with instruction and interest as such details undoubtedly are, we can, if needs be, dispense with them. The man passes, the work remains. The work speaks for itself, as we say: and the biography of the worker is no more necessary to an understanding or enjoyment of it, than is a model or anatomy of some tropical tree, to the right tasting of the fruit we are familiar with on the marketstall,—or a geologist's map and stratification, to the prompt recognition of the hill-top, our land-mark of every day.

We turn with stronger needs to the genius of an opposite tendency—the subjective poet of modern classification. He, gifted like the objective poet with the fuller perception of nature and man, is impelled to embody the thing he perceives, not so much with reference to the many below, as to the One above him, the supreme Intelligence which apprehends all things in their absolute truth,—an ultimate view ever aspired to, if but partially attained, by the poet's own soul. Not what man sees, but what God sees—the *Ideas* of Plato, seeds of creation lying burningly on the Divine Hand—it is toward these that he struggles. Not with the combination of humanity in action, but with the primal elements of humanity he has to do; and he digs where he stands,—preferring to seek them in his own soul as the nearest reflex of that absolute Mind, according to the intuitions of which he desires to perceive and speak. Such a poet does not deal habitually with the picturesque groupings and tempestuous tossings of the forest-trees, but with their roots and fibres naked to the chalk and stone. He does not paint pictures and hang them on the walls, but rather carries them on the retina of his own eyes: we must look deep into his human eyes, to see those pictures on them. He is rather a seer, accordingly, than a fashioner, and what he produces will be less a work than an effluence. That effluence cannot be easily considered in abstraction from his personality,—being indeed the very radiance and aroma of his personality, projected from it but not separated. Therefore, in our approach to the poetry, we necessarily approach the personality of the poet; in apprehending it we apprehend him, and certainly we cannot love it without loving him. Both for love's and for understanding's sake we desire to know him, and as readers of his poetry must be readers of his biography also.

I shall observe, in passing, that it seems not so much from any essential distinction in the faculty of the two poets or in the nature of the objects contemplated by either, as in the more immediate adaptability of these objects to the distinct purpose of each, that the objective poet, in his appeal to the aggregate human mind, chooses to deal with the doings of men, (the result of which dealing, in its pure form, when even description, as suggesting a describer, is dispensed with, is what we call dramatic poetry), while the subjective poet, whose study has been himself, appealing through himself to the absolute Divine mind, prefers to dwell upon those external scenic appearances which strike out most abundantly and uninterruptedly his inner light and power, selects that silence of the earth and sea in which he can best hear the beating of his individual heart, and leaves the noisy, complex, yet imperfect exhibitions of nature in the manifold experience of man around him, which serve only to distract and suppress the working of his brain. These opposite tendencies of genius will be more readily descried in their artistic effect than in their moral spring and cause. Pushed to an extreme and manifested as a deformity, they will be seen plainest of all in the fault of either artist, when subsidiarily to the human interest of his work his occasional illustrations from scenic nature are introduced as in the earlier works of the originative painters—men and women filling the foreground with consummate mastery, while mountain, grove and rivulet show like an anticipatory revenge on that succeeding race of landscape-painters whose "figures" disturb the perfection of their earth and sky. It would be idle to inquire, of these two kinds of poetic faculty in operation, which is the higher or even rarer endowment. If the subjective might seem to be the ultimate requirement of every age, the objective, in the strictest state, must still retain its original value. For it is with this world, as starting point and basis alike, that we shall always have to concern ourselves: the world is not to be learned and thrown aside, but reverted to and relearned. The spiritual comprehension may be infinitely subtilised, but the raw material it operates upon, must remain. There may be no end of the poets who communicate to us what they see in an object with reference to their own individuality; what it was before they saw it, in reference to the aggregate human mind, will be as desirable to know as ever. Nor is there any reason why these two modes of poetic faculty may not issue hereafter from the same poet in successive perfect works, examples of which, according to what are now considered the exigences of art, we have hitherto possessed in distinct individuals only. A mere running-in of the one faculty upon the other, is, of course, the ordinary circumstance. Far more rarely it happens that either is found so decidedly prominent and superior, as to be pronounced comparatively pure: while of the perfect shield, with the gold and the silver side set up for all comers to challenge, there has yet been no instance. Either faculty in its eminent state is doubtless conceded by Providence as a best gift to men, according to their especial want. There is a time when the general eye has, so to speak, absorbed its fill of the phenomena around it, whether spiritual or material, and desires rather to learn the exacter significance of what it possesses, than to receive any augmentation of what is possessed. Then is the opportunity for the poet of loftier vision, to lift his fellows, with their half-apprehensions, up to his own sphere, by intensifying the import of details and rounding the universal meaning. The influence of such an achievement will not soon die out. A tribe of successors (Homerides) working more or less in the same spirit, dwell on his discoveries and reinforce his doctrine; till, at unawares, the world is found to be subsisting wholly on the shadow of a reality, on sentiments diluted from passions, on the tradition of a fact, the convention of a moral, the straw of last year's harvest. Then is the imperative call for the appearance of another sort of poet, who shall at once replace this intellectual rumination of food swallowed long ago, by a supply of the fresh and living swathe; getting at new substance by breaking up the assumed wholes into parts of independent and unclassed value, careless of the unknown laws for recombining them (it will be the business of yet another poet to suggest those hereafter), prodigal of objects for men's outer and not inner sight, shaping for their uses a new and different creation from the last, which it displaces by the right of life over death,—to endure until, in the inevitable process, its very sufficiency to itself shall require, at length, an exposition of its affinity to something higher,—when the positive yet conflicting facts shall again precipitate themselves under a harmonising law, and one more degree will be apparent for a poet to climb in that mighty ladder, of which, however cloud-involved and undefined may glimmer the topmost step, the world dares no longer doubt that its gradations ascend.

Such being the two kinds of artists, it is naturally, as I have shown, with the biography of the subjective poet that we have the deeper concern. Apart from his recorded life altogether, we might fail to determine with satisfactory precision to what class his productions belong, and what amount of praise is assignable to the producer. Certainly, in the face of any conspicuous achievement of genius, philosophy, no less than sympathetic instinct, warrants our belief in a great moral purpose having mainly inspired even where it does not visibly look out of the same. Greatness in a work suggests an adequate instrumentality; and none of the lower incitements, however they may avail to initiate or even effect many considerable displays of power, simulating the nobler inspiration to which they are mistakenly referred, have been found able, under the ordinary conditions of humanity, to task themselves to the end of so exacting a performance as a poet's complete work. As soon will the galvanism, that provokes to violent action the muscles of a corpse, induce it to cross the chamber steadily: sooner. The love of displaying power for the display's sake, the love of riches, of distinction, of notoriety,—the desire of a triumph over rivals, and the vanity in the applause of friends,—each and all of such whetted appetites grow intenser by exercise and increasingly sagacious as to the best and readiest means of self-appeasement,—while for any of their ends, whether the money or the pointed finger of the crowd, or the flattery and hate to heart's content, there are cheaper prices to pay, they will all find soon enough, than the bestowment of a life upon a labour, hard, slow, and not sure. Also, assuming the proper moral aim to have produced a work, there are many and various states of an aim: it may be more intense than clear-sighted, or too easily satisfied with a lower field of activity than a steadier aspiration would reach. All the bad poetry in the world (accounted poetry, that is, by its affinities) will be found to result from some one of the infinite degrees of discrepancy between the attributes of the poet's soul, occasioning a want of correspondency between his work and the verities of nature,—issuing in poetry, false under whatever form, which shows a thing not as it is to mankind generally, nor as it is to the particular describer, but as it is supposed to be for some unreal neutral mood, midway between both and of value to neither, and living its brief minute simply through the indolence of whoever accepts it, or his incapacity to denounce a cheat. Although of such depths of failure there can be no question here, we must in every case betake ourselves to the review of a poet's life ere we determine some of the nicer questions concerning his poetry,—more especially if the performance we seek to estimate aright, has been obstructed and cut short of completion by circumstances,—a disastrous youth or a premature death. We may learn from the biography whether his spirit invariably saw and spoke from the last height to which it had attained. An absolute vision is not for this world, but we are permitted a continual approximation to it, every degree of which in the individual, provided it exceed the attainment of the masses, must procure him a clear advantage. Did the poet ever attain to a higher platform than where he rested and exhibited a result? Did he know more than he spoke of?

I concede however, in respect to the subject of our study as well as some few other illustrious examples, that the unmistakeable quality of the verse would be evidence enough, under usual circumstances, not only of the kind and degree of the intellectual but of the moral constitution of Shelley: the whole personality of the poet shining forward from the poems, without much need of going further to seek it. The "Remains"—produced within a period of ten years, and at a season of life when other men of at all comparable genius have hardly done more than prepare the eye for future sight and the tongue for speech—present us with the complete enginery of a poet, as signal in the excellence of its several adaptitudes as transcendent in the combination of effects,—examples, in fact, of the whole poet's function of beholding with an understanding keenness the universe, nature and man, in their actual state of perfection in imperfection,—of the whole poet's virtue of being untempted by the manifold partial developments of beauty and good on every side, into leaving them the ultimates he found them,—induced by the facility of the gratification of his own sense of those qualities, or by the pleasure of acquiescence in the short-comings of his predecessors in art, and the pain of disturbing their conventionalisms,—the whole poet's virtue, I repeat, of looking higher than any manifestation yet made of both beauty and good, in order to suggest from the utmost actual realisation of the one a corresponding capability in the other, and out of the calm, purity and energy of nature, to reconstitute and store up for the forthcoming stage of man's being, a gift in repayment of that former gift, in which man's own thought and passion had been lavished by the poet on the else-incompleted magnificence of the sunrise, the else-uninterpreted mystery of the lake,—so drawing out, lifting up, and assimilating this ideal of a future man, thus descried as possible, to the present reality of the poet's soul already arrived at the higher state of development, and still aspirant to elevate and extend itself in conformity with its still-improving perceptions of, no longer the eventual Human, but the actual Divine. In conjunction with which noble and rare powers, came the subordinate power of delivering these attained results to the world in an embodiment of verse more closely answering to and indicative of the process of the informing spirit, (failing as it occasionally does, in art, only to succeed in highest art),—with a diction more adequate to the task in its natural and acquired richness, its material colour and spiritual transparency,—the whole being moved by and suffused with a music at once of the soul and the sense, expressive both of an external might of sincere passion and an internal fitness and consonancy,—than can be attributed to any other writer whose record is among us. Such was the spheric poetical faculty of Shelley, as its own self-sufficing central light, radiating equally through immaturity and accomplishment, through many fragments and occasional completion, reveals it to a competent judgment.

But the acceptance of this truth by the public, has been retarded by certain objections which cast us back on the evidence of biography, even with Shelley's poetry in our hands. Except for the particular character of these objections, indeed, the non-appreciation of his contemporaries would simply class, now that it is over, with a series of experiences which have necessarily happened and needlessly been wondered at, ever since the world began, and concerning which any present anger may well be moderated, no less in justice to our forerunners than in policy to ourselves. For the misapprehensiveness of his age is exactly what a poet is sent to remedy; and the interval between his operation and the generally perceptible effect of it, is no greater, less indeed, than in many other departments of the great human effort. The "E pur si muove" of the astronomer was as bitter a word as any uttered before or since by a poet over his rejected living work, in that depth of conviction which is so like despair.

But in this respect was the experience of Shelley peculiarly unfortunate—that the disbelief in him as a man, even preceded the disbelief in him as a writer; the misconstruction of his moral nature preparing the way for the misappreciation of his intellectual labours. There existed from the beginning,—simultaneous with, indeed anterior to his earliest noticeable works, and not brought forward to counteract any impression they had succeeded in making,—certain charges against his private character and life, which, if substantiated to their whole breadth, would materially disturb, I do not attempt to deny, our reception and enjoyment of his works, however wonderful the artistic qualities of these. For we are not sufficiently supplied with instances of genius of his order, to be able to pronounce certainly how many of its constituent parts have been tasked and strained to the production of a given lie, and how high and pure a mood of the creative mind may be dramatically simulated as the poet's habitual and exclusive one. The doubts, therefore, arising from such a question, required to be set at rest, as they were effectually, by those early authentic notices of Shelley's career and the corroborative accompaniment of his letters, in which not only the main tenor and principal result of his life, but the purity and beauty of many of the processes which had conduced to them, were made apparent enough for the general reader's purpose,—whoever lightly condemned Shelley first, on the evidence of reviews and gossip, as lightly acquitting him now, on that of memoirs and correspondence. Still, it is advisable to lose no opportunity of strengthening and completing the chain of biographical testimony; much more, of course, for the sake of the poet's original lovers, whose volunteered sacrifice of particular principle in favour of absorbing sympathy we might desire to dispense with, than for the sake of his foolish haters, who have long since diverted upon other objects their obtuseness or malignancy. A full life of Shelley should be written at once, while the materials for it continue in reach; not to minister to the curiosity of the public, but to obliterate the last stain of that false life which was forced on the public's attention before it had any curiosity on the matter,—a biography, composed in harmony with the present general disposition to have faith in him, yet not shrinking from a candid statement of all ambiguous passages, through a reasonable confidence that the most doubtful of them will be found consistent with a belief in the eventual perfection of his character, according to the poor limits of our humanity. Nor will men persist in confounding, any more than God confounds, with genuine infidelity and an atheism of the heart, those passionate, impatient struggles of a boy towards distant truth and love, made in the dark, and ended by one sweep of the natural seas before the full moral sunrise could shine out on him. Crude convictions of boyhood, conveyed in imperfect and inapt forms of speech,—for such things all boys have been pardoned. There are growing-pains, accompanied by temporary distortion, of the soul also. And it would be hard indeed upon this young Titan of genius, murmuring in divine music his human ignorances, through his very thirst for knowledge, and his rebellion, in mere aspiration to law, if the melody itself substantiated the error, and the tragic cutting short of life perpetuated into sins, such faults as, under happier circumstances, would have been left behind by the consent of the most arrogant moralist, forgotten on the lowest steps of youth.

The responsibility of presenting to the public a biography of Shelley, does not, however lie with me: I have only to make it a little easier by arranging these few supplementary letters, with a recognition of the value of the whole collection. This value I take to consist in a most truthful conformity of the Correspondence, in its limited degree, with the moral and intellectual character of the writer as displayed in the highest manifestations of his genius. Letters and poems are obviously an act of the same mind, produced by the same law, only differing in the application to the individual or collective understanding. Letters and poems may be used indifferently as the basement of our opinion upon the writer's character; the finished expression of a sentiment in the poems, giving light and significance to the rudiments of the same in the letters, and these, again, in their incipiency and unripeness, authenticating the exalted mood and reattaching it to the personality of the writer. The musician speaks on the note he sings with; there is no change in the scale, as he diminishes the volume into familiar intercourse. There is nothing of that jarring between the man and the author, which has been found so amusing or so melancholy; no dropping of the tragic mask, as the crowd melts away; no mean discovery of the real motives of a life's achievement, often, in other lives, laid bare as pitifully as when, at the close of a holiday, we catch sight of the internal lead-pipes and wood-valves, to which, and not to the ostensible conch and dominant Triton of the fountain, we have owed our admired waterwork. No breaking out, in household privacy, of hatred anger and scorn, incongruous with the higher mood and suppressed artistically in the book: no brutal return to self-delighting, when the audience of philanthropic schemes is out of hearing: no indecent stripping off the grander feeling and rule of life as too costly and cumbrous for every-day wear. Whatever Shelley was, he was with an admirable sincerity. It was not always truth that he thought and spoke; but in the purity of truth he spoke and thought always. Everywhere is apparent his belief in the existence of Good, to which Evil is an accident; his faithful holding by what he assumed to be the former, going everywhere in company with the tenderest pity for those acting or suffering on the opposite hypothesis. For he was tender, though tenderness is not always the characteristic of very sincere natures; he was eminently both tender and sincere. And not only do the same affection and yearning after the well-being of his kind, appear in the letters as in the poems, but they express themselves by the same theories and plans, however crude and unsound. There is no reservation of a subtler, less costly, more serviceable remedy for his own ill, than he has proposed for the general one; nor does he ever comtemplate an object on his own account, from a less elevation than he uses in exhibiting it to the world. How shall we help believing Shelley to have been, in his ultimate attainment, the splendid spirit of his own best poetry, when we find even his carnal speech to agree faithfully, at faintest as at strongest, with the tone and rhythm of his most oracular utterances?

For the rest, these new letters are not offered as presenting any new feature of the poet's character. Regarded in themselves, and as the substantive productions of a man, their importance would be slight. But they possess interest beyond their limits, in confirming the evidence just dwelt on, of the poetical mood of Shelley being only the intensification of his habitual mood; the same tongue only speaking, for want of the special excitement to sing. The very first letter, as one instance for all, strikes the key-note of the predominating sentiment of Shelley throughout his whole life—his sympathy with the oppressed. And when we see him at so early an age, casting out, under the influence of such a sympathy, letters and pamphlets on every side, we accept it as the simple exemplification of the sincerity, with which, at the close of his life, he spoke of himself, as—

"One whose heart a stranger's tear might wear
As water-drops the sandy fountain stone;
Who loved and pitied all things, and could moan
For woes which others hear not, and could see
The absent with the glass of phantasy,
And near the poor and trampled sit and weep,
Following the captive to his dungeon deep—
One who was as a nerve o'er which do creep
The else-unfelt oppressions of this earth."

Such sympathy with his kind was evidently developed in him to an extraordinary and even morbid degree, at a period when the general intellectual powers it was impatient to put in motion, were immature or deficient.

I conjecture, from a review of the various publications of Shelley's youth, that one of the causes of his failure at the outset, was the peculiar *practicalness* of his mind, which was not without a determinate effect on his progress in theorising. An ordinary youth, who turns his attention to similar subjects, discovers falsities, incongruities, and various points for amendment, and, in the natural advance of the purely critical spirit unchecked by considerations of remedy, keeps up before his young eyes so many instances of the same error and wrong, that he finds himself unawares arrived at the startling conclusion, that all must be changed—or nothing: in the face of which plainly impossible achievement, he is apt (looking perhaps a little more serious by the time he touches at the decisive issue), to feel, either carelessly or considerately, that his own attempting a single piece of service would be worse than useless even, and to refer the whole task to another age and person—safe in proportion to his incapacity. Wanting words to speak, he has never made a fool of himself by speaking. But, in Shelley's case, the early fervour and power to *see,* was accompanied by as precocious a fertility to *contrive:* he endeavoured to realise as he went on idealising; every wrong had simultaneously its remedy, and, out of the strength of his hatred for the former, he took the strength of his confidence in the latter—till suddenly he stood pledged to the defence of a set of miserable little expedients, just as if they represented great principles, and to an attack upon various great principles, really so, without leaving himself time to examine whether, because they were antagonistical to the remedy he had suggested, they must therefore be identical or even essentially connected with the wrong he sought to cure,—playing with blind passion into the hands of his enemies, and dashing at whatever red cloak was held forth to him, as the cause of the fireball he had last been stung with—mistaking Churchdom for Christianity, and for marriage, "the sale of love" and the law of sexual oppression.

Gradually, however, he was leaving behind him this low practical dexterity, unable to keep up with his widening intellectual perception; and, in exact proportion as he did so, his true power strengthened and proved itself. Gradually he was raised above the contemplation of spots and the attempt at effacing them, to the great Abstract Light, and, through the discrepancy of the creation, to the sufficiency of the First Cause. Gradually he was learning that the best way of removing abuses is to stand fast by truth. Truth is one, as they are manifold; and innumerable negative effects are produced by the upholding of one positive principle. I shall say what I think,—had Shelley lived he would have finally ranged himself with the Christians; his very instinct for helping the weaker side (if numbers make strength), his very "hate of hate," which at first mistranslated itself into delirious Queen Mab notes and the like, would have got clearer-sighted by exercise. The preliminary step to following Christ, is the leaving the dead to bury their dead—not clamouring on his doctrine for an especial solution of difficulties which are referable to the general problem of the universe. Already he had attained to a profession of "a worship to the Spirit of good within, which requires (before it sends that inspiration forth, which impresses its likeness upon all it creates) devoted and disinterested homage, *as Coleridge says,*"—and Paul likewise. And we find in one of his last exquisite fragments, avowedly a record of one of his own mornings and its experience, as it dawned on him at his soul and body's best in his boat on the Serchio—that as surely as

> "The stars burnt out in the pale blue air,
> And the thin white moon lay withering there—
> Day had kindled the dewy woods,
> And the rocks above, and the stream below,
> And the vapours in their multitudes,
> And the Apennine's shroud of summer snow—
> Day had awakened all things that be;"

just so surely, he tells us (stepping forward from this delicious dance-music, choragus-like, into the grander measure befitting the final enunciation),

> "All rose to do the task He set to each,
> Who shaped us to his ends and not our own;
> The million rose to learn, and One to teach
> What none yet ever knew or can be known."

No more difference than this, from David's pregnant conclusion so long ago!

Meantime, as I call Shelley a moral man, because he was true, simple-hearted, and brave, and because what he acted corresponded to what he knew, so I call him a man of religious mind, because every audacious negative cast up by him against the Divine, was interpenetrated with a mood of reverence and adoration,—and because I find him everywhere taking for granted some of the capital dogmas of Christianity, while most vehemently denying their historical basement. There is such a thing as an efficacious knowledge of and belief in the politics of Junius, or the poetry of Rowley, though a man should at the same time dispute the title of Chatterton to the one, and consider the author of the other, as Byron wittily did, "really, truly, nobody at all."[1] There is even such a thing, we come to learn wonderingly in these very letters, as a profound sensibility and adaptitude for art, while the science of the percipient is so little advanced as to admit of his stronger admiration for Guido (and Carlo Dolce!) than for Michael Angelo. A Divine Being has Himself said, that "a word against the Son of man shall be forgiven to a man," while "a word against the Spirit of God" (implying a general deliberate preference of perceived evil to perceived good) "shall not be forgiven to a man." Also, in religion, one earnest and unextorted assertion of belief should outweigh, as a matter of testimony, many assertions of unbelief. The fact that there is a gold-region is established by the finding of one lump, though you miss the vein never so often.

Shelley died before his youth ended. In taking the measure of him as a man, he must be considered on the whole and at his ultimate spiritual stature, and not be judged of at the immaturity and by the mistakes of ten years before: that, indeed, would be to judge of the author of "Julian and Maddalo" by "Zastrozzi." Let the whole truth be told of his worst mistake. I believe, for my own part, that if anything could now shame or grieve Shelley, it would be an attempt to vindicate him at the expense of another.

In forming a judgment, I would, however, press on the reader the simple justice of considering tenderly his constitution of body as well as mind, and how unfavourable it was to the steady symmetries of conventional life; the body, in the torture of incurable disease, refusing to give repose to the bewildered soul, tossing in its hot fever of the fancy,—and the laudanum-bottle making but a perilous and pitiful truce between these two. He was constantly subject to "that state of mind" (I quote his own note to "Hellas") "in which ideas may be supposed to assume the force of sensation, through the confusion of thought with the objects of thought, and excess of passion animating the creations of the imagination:" in other words, he was liable to remarkable delusions and hallucinations. The nocturnal attack in Wales, for instance, was assuredly a delusion; and I venture to express my own conviction, derived from a little attention to the circumstances of either story, that the idea of the enamoured lady following him to Naples, and of the "man in the cloak" who struck him at the Pisan post-office, were equally illusory,—the mere projection, in fact, from himself, of the image of his own love and hate.

> "To thirst and find no fill—to wail and wander
> With short unsteady steps—to pause and ponder—
> To feel the blood run through the veins and tingle
> What busy thought and blind sensation mingle,—
> To nurse the image of *unfelt caresses*
> Till dim imagination just possesses
> The half-created shadow"—

of unfelt caresses,—and of unfelt blows as well: to such conditions was his genius subject. It was not at Rome only (where he heard a mystic voice exclaiming, "Cenci, Cenci," in reference to the tragic theme which occupied him at the time),—it was not at Rome only that he mistook the cry of "old rags." The habit of somnambulism is said to have extended to the very last days of his life.

Let me conclude with a thought of Shelley as a poet. In the hierarchy of creative minds, it is the presence of the highest faculty that gives first rank, in virtue of its kind, not degree; no pretension of a lower nature, whatever the completeness of development or variety of effect, impeding the precedency of the rarer endowment though only in the germ. The contrary is sometimes maintained; it is attempted to make the lower gifts (which are potentially included in the higher faculty) of independent value, and equal to some exercise of the special function. For instance, should not a poet possess common sense? Then the possession of abundant common sense implies a step towards becoming a poet. Yes; such a step as the lapidary's, when, strong in the fact of carbon entering largely into the composition of the diamond, he heaps up a sack of charcoal in order to compete with the Koh-i-noor. I pass at once, therefore, from Shelley's minor excellencies to his noblest and predominating characteristic.

This I call his simultaneous perception of Power and Love in the absolute, and of Beauty and Good in the concrete, while he throws, from his poet's station between both, swifter, subtler, and more numerous films for the connexion of each with each, than have been thrown by any modern artificer of whom I have knowledge; proving how, as he says,

> "The spirit of the worm within the sod,
> In love and worship blends itself with God."

I would rather consider Shelley's poetry as a sublime fragmentary essay towards a presentment of the correspondency of the universe to Deity, of the natural to the spiritual, and of the actual to the ideal, than I would isolate and separately appraise the worth of many detachable portions which might be acknowledged as utterly perfect in a lower moral point of view, under the mere conditions of art. It would be easy to take my stand on successful instances of objectivity in Shelley: there is the unrivalled "Cenci;" there is the "Julian and Maddalo" too; there is the magnificent "Ode to Naples:" why not regard, it may be said, the less organised matter as the radiant elemental foam and solution, out of which would have been evolved, eventually, creations as perfect even as those? But I prefer to look for the highest attainment, not simply the high,—and, seeing it, I hold by it. There is surely enough of the work "Shelley" to be known enduringly among men, and, I believe, to be accepted of God, as human work may; and around the imperfect proportions of such, the most elaborated productions of ordinary art must arrange themselves as inferior illustrations.

It is because I have long held these opinions in assurance and gratitude, that I catch at the opportunity offered to me of expressing them here; knowing that the alacrity to fulfil an humble office conveys more love than the acceptance of the honour of a higher one, and that better, therefore, than the signal service it was the dream of my boyhood to render to his fame and memory, may be the saying of a few, inadequate words upon these scarcely more important supplementary letters of SHELLEY.

PARIS, *Dec. 4th*, 1851.

---

1. Or, to take our illustrations from the writings of Shelley himself, there is such a thing as admirably appreciating a work by

Andrea Verocchio,—and fancifully characterising the Pisan Torre Guelfa by the Ponte a Mare, black against the sunsets,—and consummately painting the islet of San Clemente with its penitentiary for rebellious priests, to the west between Venice and the Lido—while you believe the first to be a fragment of an antique sarcophagus,—the second, Ugolino's Tower of Famine (the vestiges of which should be sought for in the Piazza de' Cavalieri)—and the third (as I convinced myself last summer at Venice), San Servolo with its madhouse—which, far from being "windowless," is as full of windows as a barrack.

The Novel in "The Ring and the Book."

Henry James

First published in Transactions of the Royal Society of Literature, *2nd series, 31 (1912): 269-298.*

If on such an occasion as this—even with our natural impulse to shake ourselves free of reserves—some sharp choice between the dozen different aspects of one of the most copious of our poets becomes a prime necessity, though remaining at the same time a great difficulty, so in respect to the most voluminous of his works the admirer is promptly held up, as we have come to call it; finds himself almost baffled by alternatives. 'The Ring and the Book' is so vast and so essentially Gothic a structure, spreading and soaring and branching at such a rate, covering such ground, putting forth such pinnacles and towers and brave excrescences, planting its transepts and chapels and porticos, its clustered hugeness or inordinate muchness (to put the effect at once most plainly and most expressively), that with any first approach we but walk vaguely and slowly, rather bewilderedly, round and round it, wondering at what point we had best attempt such entrance as will save our steps and light our uncertainty—most enable us, in a word, to reach our personal chair, our indicated chapel or shrine, when once within. For it is to be granted that to this inner view the likeness of the literary monument to one of the great religious gives way a little, sustains itself less than in the first, the affronting mass; unless we simply figure ourselves, under the great roof, looking about us through a splendid thickness and dimness of air, an accumulation of spiritual presences or unprofaned mysteries, that makes our impression heavily general—general only—and leaves us helpless for reporting on particulars. The particulars for our purpose have thus their identity much rather in certain features of the twenty faces—either of one or of another of these—that the structure turns to the outer day, and that we can, as it were, sit down before and consider at our comparative ease. I say "comparative" advisedly, for I cling to the dear old tradition that Browning is "difficult"—which we were all brought up on, and which I think we should, especially on a rich retrospective day like this, with the atmosphere of his great career settling upon us as much as possible, feel it a shock to see break down in too many places at once. Selecting my ground, by your kind invitation, for sticking in and planting before you, to flourish so far as it shall, my little sprig of bay, I have of course tried to measure the quantity of ease with which our material may on that noted spot allow itself to be treated. There are innumerable things in 'The Ring and the Book'—as the comprehensive image I began with makes it needless I should say; and I have been above all appealed to by the possibility that one of these, pursued for a while through the labyrinth, but at last overtaken and then more or less confessing its identity, might have yielded up its best essence (as a grateful theme, of course I mean) under some fine strong economy of *prose* treatment. So here you have me talking at once of prose and seeking that connection to help out my case.

From far back, from my first reading of these volumes, which took place at the time of their disclosure to the world, when I was a fairly young person, the sense, almost the pang, of the novel they might have constituted, sprang sharply from them; so that I was to go on through the years almost irreverently, all but quite profanely, if you will, thinking of the great loose and uncontrolled composition, the great heavy-hanging cluster of related but unreconciled parts, as a fiction of the so-called historic type, that is as a suggested study of the manners and conditions from which our own have more or less traceably issued, just tragically spoiled—or as a work of art, in other words, smothered in the producing. To which I hasten to add my consciousness of the scant degree in which such a fresh start from our author's documents, such a re-projection of them, wonderful documents as they can only have been, may claim a critical basis. Conceive me as simply astride of my different fancy, my other dream, of the matter—which bolted with me, as I have said, at the first alarm. Browning worked, in this connection, literally *upon* documents; no page of his long story is more vivid and splendid than that of his find of the Book in the litter of a market-stall in Florence, and the swoop of practised perception with which he caught up in it a treasure. Here was a subject stated to the last ounce of its weight, a living and breathing record of facts pitiful and terrible, a mass of matter bristling with revelations, and yet at the same time wrapped over with layer upon layer of contemporary appreciation; which appreciation, in its turn, was a part of the wealth to be appreciated. What our great master saw was his situation founded, seated there in positively packed and congested significance, though by just so much as it was charged with meanings and values were those things undeveloped and unexpressed. They looked up at him, even at that first flush and from their market-stall, and said to him, in their compressed compass, as with the muffled rumble of a slow-coming earthquake, "Express us, express us, immortalise us as we'll immortalise *you*!"—so that the terms of the understanding were so far cogent and clear. It was an understanding, on their side, with the Poet; and, since that Poet had produced "Men and Women," "Dramatic Lyrics," "Dramatis Personae" and sundry plays—we needn't even foist on him "Sordello"—he could but understand in his own way. That way would have had to be quite some other, we fully see, had he been by habit and profession not just the lyric, epic, dramatic commentator, the extractor, to whatever essential potency and redundancy, of the moral of the fable, but the very fabulist himself, the inventor and projector, layer down of the postulate and digger of the foundation. I doubt if we have a precedent for this energy of appropriation of a deposit of *stated* matter, a block of sense already in position and requiring not to be shaped and squared and caused any further to solidify, but rather to suffer disintegration, be pulled apart, melted down, hammered, by the most characteristic of the poet's processes, to powder—dust of gold and silver let us say. He was to apply to it his favourite system—that of looking at his subject from the point of view of a sort of sublime curiosity, and of smuggling as many more points of view together into that one as the fancy might take him to smuggle—on a scale on which even he had never before applied it; this with a courage and confidence that, in presence of all the conditions, conditions many of them arduous and arid and thankless even to defiance, we can only pronounce splendid, and of which the issue was to be of a proportioned monstrous magnificence.

The one definite forecast for this product would have been that it should figure for its producer as a poem—as if he had simply said, "I embark at any rate for the Golden Isles"; everything else was of the pure incalculable, the frank voyage of adventure. To what extent the Golden Isles were in fact to be reached is a matter we needn't pretend, I think, absolutely to determine; let us feel for ourselves and as we will about it—either see our adventurer, disembarked bag and baggage and in possession, plant his flag on the highest eminence within his ring of sea, or, on the other hand, but watch him approach and beat back a little, tack and circle and stand off, always fairly in sight of land, catching rare glimpses and meeting strange airs, but not quite achieving the final *coup* that annexes the group. He returns to us under either view all scented and salted with his measure of contact, and that for the moment is enough for us; more than enough for me, at any rate, engaged, for your beguilement, in this practical relation of snuffing up what he brings. He brings, anyhow one puts it, a detailed report, which is but another word for a story; and it is with his story, his offered, not his borrowed one—a very different matter—that I am concerned. We are probably most of us so aware of its general content that if I sum this up I may do so briefly. The book of the Florentine rubbish-heap is the full account (as full accounts were conceived in those days) of the trial before the Roman courts, with inquiries and judgments by the Tuscan authorities intermixed, of a certain Count Guido Franceschini of Arezzo—decapitated, in company with four confederates, these latter hanged, on the 22nd of February, 1698, for the murder of his young wife, Pompilia Comparini, and her adopted parents, Pietro and Violante of that ilk. The circumstances leading to this climax had been primarily his marriage to Pompilia, some years before, in Rome, she being then but in her thirteenth year, under the impression, fostered in him by the elder pair, that she was their own child and on this head heiress to moneys settled on them from of old in the event of their having a child. They had in fact had none, and had, in substitution, invented, so to speak, Pompilia, the luckless base-born baby of a woman of lamentable character easily induced to part with her for cash. They bring up the hapless creature as their daughter, and as their daughter they marry her, in Rome, to the middle-aged and impecunious Count Guido, a rapacious and unscrupulous fortune-seeker, by whose superior social position, as we say, dreadfully *decaduto* though he be, they are dazzled out of all circumspection. The girl, innocent, ignorant, bewildered and scared, is purely passive, is taken home by her husband to Arezzo, where she is at first attended by Pietro and Violante, and where the direst disappointments await the three. Count Guido proves the basest of men and his home a place of terror and of torture, from which, at the age of seventeen, and shortly prior to her giving birth to an heir to the house, such as it is, she is rescued by a pitying witness of her misery, Canon Caponsacchi, a man of the world and adorning it, yet in holy orders, as men of the world in Italy might then be, who clandestinely helps her, at peril of both their lives, back to Rome, and of whom it is attested that he has had no other relation with her but this of distinguished and all-disinterested friend in need. The pretended parents have at an early stage thrown up their benighted game, fleeing from the rigour of their dupe's domestic rule, disclosing to him vindictively the part they have played and the consequent failure of any profit to him through his wife, and leaving him in turn to wreak his spite, which has become infernal, on the wretched Pompilia. He pursues her to Rome on her eventual flight, and overtakes her, with her companion, just outside the gates; but having, by the aid of the authorities, re-achieved possession of her, he contents himself for the time with procuring her sequestration in a convent, from which, however, she is presently allowed to emerge in view of the near birth of her child. She rejoins Pietro and Violante, devoted to her, oddly enough, through all their folly and fatuity, and under their roof, in a lonely Roman suburb, her child comes into the world. Her husband meanwhile, hearing of her release, gives way afresh to the fury that had not at the climax of his former pursuit taken full effect; he recruits a band of four of his young tenants or farm-labourers, and makes his way, armed, like his companions, with knives, to the door behind which three of the parties to all the wrong done him, as he holds, then lurk. He pronounces, after knocking and waiting, the name of Caponsacchi, upon which, as the door opens, Violante presents herself. He stabs her to death, on the spot, with repeated blows; like her companions she is off her guard, and he throws himself on each of these with equally murderous effect. Pietro, crying for mercy, falls second beneath him; after which he attacks his wife, whom he literally hacks to death. She survives, by a miracle, long enough, in spite of all her wounds, to testify; which testimony, as may be imagined, is not the least precious part of the case. Justice is on the whole, though deprecated and delayed, what we call satisfactory: the last word is for the Pope in person, Innocent XII, Pignatelli, at whose deliberation, lone and supreme, on Browning's page, we splendidly assist, and Count Guido and his accomplices, bloodless as to the act though these appear to have been, meet their discriminated doom.

That is the bundle of facts, accompanied with the bundle of proceedings, legal, ecclesiastical, diplomatic and other, *on* the facts, that our author, of a summer's day, made prize of; but our general temptation, as I say—out of which springs this question of the other values of character and effect, the other completeness of picture and drama, that the confused whole might have had for us—is a distinctly different thing. The difference consists, you see, to begin with, in the very breath of our Poet's genius, already, and so inordinately, at play on them from the first of our knowing them. And it consists in the second place of such an extracted sense of the whole, which becomes, after the most extraordinary fashion, bigger by the extraction, immeasurably bigger than even the most cumulative weight of the mere crude evidence, that our choice of how to take it all is in a manner determined for us. We can only take it as tremendously interesting, interesting not only in itself but with the great added interest, the dignity and authority and beauty, of Browning's general perception of it. We cannot accept this—and little enough, on the whole, do we want to: it sees us, with its prodigious push, that of its poetic, aesthetic, historic, psychologic (one scarce knows what to call it) shoulder, so far on our way. Yet all the while we are in presence not at all of an achieved form, but of a mere preparation for one, though on the hugest scale; so that you see, we are no more than decently attentive with our question: "Which of them all, of the various methods of casting the wondrously mixed metal, is he, as he goes, preparing?" Well, as he keeps giving and giving, in immeasurable plenty, it is in our selection from it all and our picking it over that we seek and to whatever various and unequal effect we find our account. He works over his vast material and we then work *him* over—though not availing ourselves, to this end, of a grain he himself doesn't somehow give us—and there we are.

The first thing we do then is to cast about for some centre in our field; seeing that, for such a purpose as ours, the subject might very nearly go a-begging with none more definite than the author has provided for it. I find that centre in the embracing consciousness of Caponsacchi, which, coming to the rescue of our question of treatment, of our search for a point of control, practically saves everything, and shows, itself, moreover, the only thing that *can* save. The more we ask of any other part of our picture that it shall exercise a comprehensive function, the more we see that particular part inadequate; as inadequate even in the extraordinarily magnified range of spirit and reach of intelligence of the infernal Franceschini as in the sublime passivity and plasticity of the childish Pompilia, educated to the last point though she be indeed by suffering, but otherwise so untaught that she can neither read nor write. The magnified state is in this work still more than elsewhere the note of the intelligence, of any and every faculty of thought, imputed by our poet to his creatures—and it takes a great mind, one of the greatest, we may at once say, to make these persons express and confess themselves to such an effect of intellectual splendour. He resorts primarily to their sense, their sense of themselves and of everything else they know, to exhibit them, and has for this purpose to keep them, and to keep them persistently and inexhaustibly, under the huge lens of his own prodigious vision. He thus makes out in them boundless treasures of truth—truth even when it happens to be, as in the case of Count Guido, but the shining wealth of constitutional falsity. Of the extent to which he may after this fashion unlimitedly draw upon them his exposure of Count Guido, which goes on and on, though partly, I admit, by repeating itself, is a wondrous example. It is not too much to say of Pompilia, Pompilia pierced with twenty wounds, Pompilia on her death-bed, Pompilia but seventeen years old and but a fortnight a mother, that she acquires an intellectual splendour just by the fact of the vast covering charity of imagination with which her recording, our commemorated, avenger, never so as in this case an avenger of the wronged beautiful things of life, hangs over and breathes upon her. We see her come out to him—and the extremely remarkable thing is that we see it, on the whole, without doubting that it might have been so. Nothing could thus be more interesting, however it may at moments and in places puzzle us, than the impunity, on our poet's part, of most of these overstretchings of proportion, these violations of the immediate appearance. Browning is deep down below the immediate with the first step of his approach; he has vaulted over the gate, is already far afield, and never, so long as we watch him, has occasion to fall back. We wonder, for after all the real is his quest, the very ideal of the real, the real most finely mixed with life, which is, in the last analysis, the ideal; and we know, with our dimmer vision, no such reality as a Franceschini fighting for his life, fighting for the vindication of his baseness, embodying his squalor, with an audacity of wit, an intensity of colour, a variety of speculation and illustration, that represent well-nigh the maximum play of the human mind. It is in like sort scarce too much to say of the exquisite Pompilia that on her part intelligence and expression are disengaged to a point at which the angels may well begin to envy her; and all again without our once wincing so far as our consistently liking to see and hear and believe is concerned. Caponsacchi regales us, of course, with the rarest fruit of a great character, a great culture and a great case; but Caponsacchi is acceptedly and naturally, needfully and illustratively, splendid. He *is* the soul of man at its finest—having passed through the smoky fires of life and emerging clear and high. Greatest of all the spirits exhibited, however, is that of the more than octogenarian Pope, at whose brooding, pondering, solitary vigil, by the end of a hard grey winter day in the great, bleak, waiting Vatican—"in the plain closet where he does such work"—we assist as intimately as at every other step of the case, and on whose grand meditation we heavily hang. But the Pope is too high above the whole connection, functionally and historically, for us to place him within it dramatically. Our Novel—which please believe I still keep before me!—dispenses with him, as it dispenses with the amazing, bristling, all too indulgently presented Roman advocates, on either side of the case, who combine to put together the most formidable monument we possess to Browning's active curiosity, and the liveliest proof of his almost unlimited power to give on his readers' nerves without giving on his own.

What remains with us all this time, none the less, is the effect of magnification, the exposure of each of these figures, in its degree, to that irridescent wash of personality, of temper and faculty, that our author ladles out to them, as the copious share of each, from his own great reservoir of spiritual health, and which makes us, as I have noted, seek the reason of a perpetual anomaly. Why, bristling so with references to him rather than with references to each other or to any accompanying set of circumstances, do they still establish more truth and beauty than they sacrifice, do they still, according to their chance, help to make 'The Ring and the Book' a great living thing, a great objective mass? I brushed by the answer a moment ago, I think, in speaking of the development in Pompilia of the resource of expression; which brings us round, it seems to me, to the justification of Browning's method. To express his inner self—his outward was a different affair!—and to express it utterly, even if no matter how, was clearly, for his own measure and consciousness of that inner self, to *be* poetic; and the solution of all the deviations and disparities, or, speaking critically, monstrosities, in the mingled tissue of this work, is the fact that, whether or no by such convulsions of soul and sense life got delivered for him, the garment of life—which for him was poetry and poetry alone—got disposed in its due and adequate multitudinous folds. We move with him but in images and references and vast and far correspondences, we eat but of strange compounds and drink but of rare distillations; and very soon, after a course of this, we feel ourselves, however much or however little to our advantage we may on occasion pronounce it, in the world of expression at any cost. That, essentially, is the world of poetry—which, in the cases known to our experience where it seems to us to differ from Browning's world, does so but through the latter's having been, by the vigour and violence, the bold familiarity, of his grasp and pull at it, moved several degrees nearer us, so to speak, than any other of the same general sort with which we are acquainted; so that, intellectually, we back away from it a little, back down before it, again and again, as we try to get off from a picture or a group or a view which is too much upon us and thereby out of focus. Browning is "upon" us, straighter upon us always, somehow, than anyone else of his race—and we thus recoil, we push our chair back from the table he so tremendously spreads, just to see a little better what is on it. That makes a relation with him that it is difficult to express; as if he came up against us each time, on the same side of the street and not on the other side, across the way, where we mostly see the poets elegantly walk and where we greet them without danger of concussion. It is on this same side, as I call it, on our side, on the other hand, that I rather see our encounter with the novelists taking place—we being, as it were, more mixed with them, or they at least, by their desire and necessity, more mixed with us, and our brush of them, in their minor frenzy, a comparatively muffled matter.

We have in the whole thing, at any rate, the element of action which is at the same time constant picture, and the element of picture which is at the same time constant action—and with a fusion, as the mass moves, that is none the less effective, none the less thick and complete, from our not owing it in the least to an artful economy. Another force pushes its way through the waste and rules the scene, making wrong things right and right things a hundred times more so: that breath of Browning's own particular matchless Italy which takes us full in the face and remains from the first the felt, rich, coloured air in which we live. The quantity of that atmosphere that he had to give out is like nothing else in English poetry, any more than in English prose, that I recall; and since I am taking these liberties with him let me take one too, a little, with the fruit of another genius shining at us here in association—with that great placed and timed prose fiction which we owe to George Eliot, and in which her projection of the stage and scenery is so different a matter. Curious enough this difference where so many things make for identity: the quantity of talent, the quantity of knowledge, the high equality (or almost) of culture and curiosity, not to say of "spiritual life." Each writer drags along a farsweeping train, though indeed Browning's spreads so considerably furthest; but his stirs up, to my vision, a perfect cloud of gold-dust, while hers, in Romola, by contrast, leaves the air about as clear, about as white, and withal about as cold, as before she had benevolently entered it. This straight saturation of our author's, this prime assimilation of the elements for which the name of Italy stands, is a single splendid case, however; I can think of no second one that is not below it—if we take it as supremely expressed in those of his lyrics and shorter dramatic monologues that it has most helped to inspire. The Rome and Tuscany of the early 'fifties had become for him so at once a medium, a bath of the senses and perceptions, into which he could sink, in which he could unlimitedly soak, that wherever he might be touched afterwards he gave out some effect of that immersion. This places him to my mind quite apart, makes the rest of our poetic record of a similar experience comparatively pale and abstract. Shelley and Swinburne—to name only his compeers, are, I know, a part of the record; but the author of "Men and Women," of "Pippa Passes," of certain of the "Dramatic Lyrics" and other scattered felicities, not only expresses and reflects the matter, he fairly, he heatedly (if I may use such a term) exudes and perspires it. Shelley, let us say in the connection, is a light, and Swinburne is a sound—Browning alone is a temperature. We feel it, we are in it at a plunge, with the very first pages of the thing before us—to which, I confess, we surrender with a momentum drawn from fifty of their predecessors, pages not less sovereign, elsewhere.

The old Florence of the late spring closes round us; the hand of Italy is at once, with the recital of the old-world litter of Piazza San Lorenzo, with that of the great glare and the great shadow-masses heavy upon us, heavy with that strange weight, that mixed pressure which is somehow to the imagination at once a caress and a menace. Our poet kicks up on the spot and at short notice what I have called his cloud of gold-dust; I can but speak for myself at least—something that I want to feel both as historic and aesthetic truth, both as pictorial and moral interest, something that will repay my fancy tenfold if I can but feel it, hovers before me, and I say to myself that whether or no a great poem is going to "come off," I'll be hanged if one of the vividest of all stories and one of the sharpest of all impressions doesn't. I beckon these things on, I follow them up, I so desire and need them that I, of course, by my imaginative collaboration, contribute to them— from the moment, that is, of my finding myself *really* in relation to the great points. On the other hand, as certainly, it has taken the author of the first volume and of the two admirable chapters of the same— since I can't call them cantos!—entitled respectively "Half-Rome" and "The Other Half-Rome," to put me in relation; where it is that he keeps me more and more, letting the closeness of my state, it must be owned, occasionally drop, letting the finer call on me, even for bad quarters of an hour, considerably languish, but starting up before me again in vivid authority if I really presume to droop or stray. He takes his wilful way with me, but I make it my own, picking over and over, as I have said, like some lingering, talking pedlar's client, his great unloosed pack; and thus it is that by the time I am settled with Pompilia at Arezzo I have lived into all the conditions. They press upon me close, those wonderful, dreadful, beautiful particulars of the Italy of the eve of the eighteenth century—Browning himself moving about, darting hither and thither in them, at his mighty ease. Beautiful, I say, because of the quantity of romantic and aesthetic tradition, from a more romantic and aesthetic age, still visibly, palpably in solution there; and wonderful and dreadful through something of a similar tissue of matchless and ruthless consistencies and immoralities. I make to my hand, as this infatuated reader, *my* Italy of the eve of the eighteenth century—a vast painted and gilded rococo shell roofing over a scenic, an amazingly figured and furnished earth, but shutting out almost the whole of our dearly bought, rudely recovered spiritual sky. You see I have this right, all the while, if I recognise my suggested material, which keeps coming and coming in the measure of my need, and my duty to which is to recognise it, and as handsomely and actively as possible. The great thing is that I have such a group of figures moving across a so constituted scene—figures so typical, so salient, so reeking with the old-world character, so impressed all over with its manners and its morals, and so predestined, we see, to this particular horrid little drama. And let me not be charged with giving it away, the idea of the latent prose fiction, by calling it little and horrid; let me not—for with my contention I can't possibly afford to—appear to agree with those who speak of the Franceschini-Comparini case as a mere vulgar criminal anecdote.

It might have been such but for two reasons—counting only the principal ones; one of these our fact that we see it so, I repeat in Browning's inordinately coloured light, and the other—which is indeed, perhaps, but another face of the same—that, with whatever limitations, it gives us in the rarest manner three characters of the first importance. I hold three a great many—I could have done with it almost, I think, if there had been but one or two; our rich provision shows you at any rate what I mean by speaking of our author's performance as above all a preparation for something. Deeply he felt that with the three—the three built up at us each with an equal genial rage of reiterative touches—there couldn't eventually *not* be something done (artistically done, I mean) if someone would only do it! There they are in their old yellow Arezzo, that miniature milder Florence, as sleepy to my recollection as a little English cathedral city clustered about a close, but dreaming not so peacefully nor so innocently; there is the great fretted fabric of the church on which they are all swarming and grovelling, yet after their fashion interesting parasites, from the high and dry old Archbishop, meanly wise or ignobly edifying, to whom Pompilia resorts in her woe, and who practically pushes her away with a shuffling velvet foot; down through the couple of Franceschini cadets, Canon Girolamo and Abate Paul, mere minions, fairly in the verminous degree, of the overgrown order or too-rank organism; down to Count Guido himself and to Count Caponsacchi, who have taken the tonsure at the outset of their careers, but not the vows, and who lead their lives under some strangest, profanest, pervertedest clerical category. There have been before this the Roman preliminaries, the career of the queer Comparini, the adoption, the assumption of the parentship of the ill-starred little girl, with the sordid cynicism of her marriage out of hand, conveying her presumptive little fortune, her poor handful of even less than contingent cash, to hungry middle-aged Count Guido's stale "rank"; the many-toned note or turbid harmony of all of which recurs to us in the vivid image of the pieties and paganisms of San Lorenzo in Lucina, that *banal* little church in the old upper Corso—banal, that is, at the worst, with the rare Roman *banalité;* bravely banal or banal with style—that we have passed, but with a sense of its reprieve to our sight-seeing, and where the bleeding bodies of the still-breathing Pompilia and her extinct companions are laid out on the greasy marble of the altar steps. To glance at these things, however, is fairly to be tangled, and at once, in the author's complexity of suggestion—to which our own thick-coming fancies respond in no less a measure; so that I have already missed my time to so much even as name properly the tremendous little chapter we should have devoted to the Franceschini interior as revealed at last to Comparini eyes; the sinister scene or ragged ruin of the Aretine "palace," where pride and penury, and, at once, rabid resentment, show their teeth in the dark and the void, and where Pompilia's inspired little character, clear silver hardened, effectually beaten and battered to steel, begins to shine at the blackness with a light that fairly out-faces at last the gleam of wolfish fangs; the character that draws from Guido, in his, alas, too boundless harangue of the fourth volume, some of the sharpest characterisations into which that extraordinary desert, that indescribable waste of intellectual life, as I have called it, from time to time flowers.

> "None of your abnegation of revenge!
> Fly at me frank, tug where I tear again!"
> ....
> "Away with the empty stare! Be holy still,
> And stupid ever! Occupy your patch
> Of private snow that's somewhere in what world
> May now be growing icy round your head
> And aguish at your foot-print—freeze not *me!*"

Or elsewhere:

> "She could play off her sex's armoury,
> Entreat, reproach, be female to my male,
> Try all the shrieking doubles of the hare,
> And yield fair sport so: but the tactics change,
> The hare stands stock-still to enrage the hound!
> ....
> This self-possession to the uttermost,
> How does it differ in aught save degree
> From the terrible patience of God?"

But I find myself, too unresistingly, quoting, and so, frankly, as I cannot justify some of my positions here by another example or two, I must cut short as to what I should have liked to add for that shaft further to be sunk into the dense deposit of social decay forming Count Guido's domestic life; the shaft so soon widening out to his awful mother, evoked for us in our author's single sufficing line:

"The gaunt grey nightmare in the furthest smoke."

The mere use of "furthest" there somehow makes the image! But other single lines glance at us, more flower-like, all along, out of the rank vegetation; such as:

"Fragment of record very strong and old."

Or such as:

"Those old odd corners of an empty heart."

Or such as:

"Leave that live passion, come be dead with me."

And even these already take me too far, or would if I didn't feel it really important just to put in, for your brief attention, the page or two representing to my sense the highest watermark of our author's imagination here; representing not, like too many others, mere imaginative motion, but real imaginative life. Taken from Caponsacchi's address in the second volume it consists of his superb visionary dismissal and disposal of Guido; which let me just preface, however, by the latter's own splendid howl, when at the end of his prodigious final interview with justice, an interview, as given us, all on his own side and involving, well-nigh, a complete conspectus of human history, the man, with the officers of the law at the door and the red scaffold in view, breaks out in the concrete truth of his weakness and terror and his cry, first, to his judges, "Hold me from them! I am yours." And then, frantically, wonderfully:

"I am the Grand-duke's—No, I am the Pope's!

Abate—Cardinal—Christ—Maria—God...
Pompilia, will you let them murder me?"

I have pronounced them all splendid contentious minds; so that the return there, at a jump, to alarmed nature, to passion and pain as we more easily, that is less loquaciously, know them, has again no less a value at Caponsacchi's broken climax of his magnificent plea—"I do but play with an imagined life"—when he drops suddenly straight down from magnanimous speculative heights to his personal sense of the reality:

"O great, just, good God! Miserable me!"

However, the great passage I allude to has everything.

"Let us go away—leave Guido all alone
Back on the world again that knows him now!
I think he will be found (indulged so far!)
Not to die so much as slide out of life,
Pushed by the general horror and common hate
Low, lower—left o' the very ledge of things,
I seem to see him catch convulsively
One by one at all honest forms of life,
At reason, order, decency and use—
To cramp him and get foothold by at least;
And still they disengage them from his clutch.
'What, you are he then had Pompilia once
And so forewent her? Take not up with us!'
And thus I see him slowly and surely edged
Of all the table-land whence life upsprings
Aspiring to be immortality,
As the snake, hatched on hill-top by mischance,
Despite his wriggling, slips, slides, slidders down
Hillside, lies low and prostrate on the smooth
Level of the outer place, lapsed in the vale:
So I lose Guido in the loneliness,
Silence and dusk, till at the doleful end,
At the horizontal line, creation's verge,
From what just is to absolute nothingness—
Lo, what is this he meets, strains onward still?
What other man deep further in the fate,
Who, turning at the prize of a footfall
To flatter him and promise fellowship,
Discovers in the act a frightful face—
Judas, made monstrous by much solitude!
The two are at one now! Let them love their love
That bites and claws like hate, or hate their hate
That mops and mows and makes as it were love!
There, let them each tear each in devil's-fun,
Or fondle this the other while malice aches—
Both teach, both learn detestability!
Kiss him the kiss, Iscariot! Pay that back,
That smatch o' the slaver blistering on your lip—
By the better trick, the insult he spared Christ—
Lure him the lure o' the letters, Aretine!
Lick him o'er slimy-smooth with jelly-filth
O' the verse-and-prose pollution in love's guise!
The cockatrice is with the basilisk!
There let them grapple, denizen's o' the dark,
Foes or friends, but indissolubly bound,
In their one spot out of the ken of God
Or care of man, for ever and ever more!"

I have spoken of the enveloping consciousness—or call it just the struggling, emerging, comparing, at last intensely living conscience—of Caponsacchi as the indicated centre of our situation or determinant of our form, in the matter of the excellent novel; and know, of course, what such an indication lets me in for, responsibly speaking, in the way of a rearrangement of relations, in the way of liberties taken. To lift our subject out of the sphere of anecdote and place it in the sphere of drama, liberally considered, to give it dignity by extracting its finest importance, causing its parts to flower together into some splendid special sense, we supply it with a large lucid reflector, which we find only, as I have already noted, in that mind and soul concerned in the business that have at once the highest sensibility and the highest capacity, or that are, as we may call it, most admirably agitated. There is the awkward fact, the objector may say, that by our record the mind and soul in question are not concerned till a given hour, when many things have already happened and the climax is almost in sight; to which we reply, at our ease, that we simply don't suffer that fact to be awkward. From the moment I am taking liberties I suffer *no* awkwardness; I should be very helpless, quite without resource and without vision, if I did. I said it to begin with: Browning works the whole thing over—the whole thing as originally given him—and we work *him*; helpfully, artfully, boldly, which is our whole blest basis. We therefore turn Caponsacchi on earlier, ever so much earlier; turn him on, with a brave ingenuity, from the very first—that is in Rome, if need be; place him there in the field, at once recipient and agent, vaguely conscious and with splendid brooding apprehension, awaiting the adventure of his life, awaiting his call, his real call (the others have been such vain shows and hollow stopgaps), awaiting, in fine, his terrible great fortune. His direct connection with Pompilia begins, certainly, at Arezzo, only after she had been some time hideously mismated and has suffered all but her direst extremity—that is of the essence: we *take* it; it's all right. But his indirect participation is another affair, and we get it—at a magnificent stroke—by the fact that his view of Franceschini, his fellow-Aretine sordidly "on the make," his measure of undesired, of, indeed, quite execrated, contact with him, brushed against in the motley, hungry Roman traffic, where and while that sinister soul snuffs about on the very vague, or the very foul, scent of *his* fortune, may begin whenever we like. We have only to have it begin right, only to make it, on the part of two men, a relation of strong, irritated perception and restless, righteous, convinced instinct in the one nature, and of equally instinctive hate and envy, jealousy and latent fear, on the other, to see the indirect connection, the one with Pompilia, as I say, throw across our page as portentous a shadow as we need. Then we get Caponsacchi as a recipient up to the brim—as an agent, a predestined one, up to the hilt. I can scarce begin to tell you what I see him give, as we say, or how his sentient and observational life, his fine reactions in presence of such a creature as Guido, such a social type and image and lurid light, as it were, make him comparatively a modern man, breathed upon, to that deep and interesting agitation I have mentioned, by more forces than he yet reckons or knows the names of.

The direct relation—always to Pompilia—is made, at Arezzo, as we know, by Franceschini himself; preparing his own doom, in the false light of his debased wit, by creating an appearance of hidden dealing between his wife and the priest which shall, as promptly as he likes—if he but work it right—compromise and overwhelm them. The particular deepest damnation he conceives for his weaker, his weakest victim is that she shall take the cleric Caponsacchi for her lover, he indubitably willing—to Guido's apprehension; and that her castigation at his hands for this, sufficiently proved upon her, shall be the last luxury of his own baseness. He forges infernally, though grossly enough, an imputed correspondence between them, a series of love letters, scandalous scrawls, of the last erotic intensity; which we in the event see solemnly weighed by his fatuous judges, all fatuous save the grave old Pope, in the scale of Pompilia's guilt and responsibility. It is this atrocity that at the *dénoûment* damns Guido himself most, or well-nigh; but if it fails and recoils, as all his calculations do—it is only his rush of passion that doesn't miss—this is by the fact exactly that, as we have seen, his wife and her friend are, for our perfect persuasion, characters of the deepest dye. There, if you please, is the finest side of our subject; such sides come up, such sides flare out upon us, when we get such characters in such embroilments. Admire with me therefore our felicity in this first-class value of Browning's beautiful, critical, genial vision of his Caponsacchi—vision of him as the tried and tempered and illuminated *man,* a great round smooth, though as yet but little worn gold-piece, an embossed and figured ducat or sequin of the period, placed by the poet in my hand. He gives me that value to spend for him, spend on all the strange old experience, old sights and sounds and stuffs, of the old stored Italy—so we have at least the wit to spend it to high advantage; which is just what I mean by our taking the liberties we spoke of. I see such bits we can get with it; but the difficulty is that I see so many more things than I can have even dreamed of giving you a hint of. I see the Arezzo life and the Arezzo crisis with every "i" dotted and every circumstance presented; and when Guido takes his wife, as a possible trap for her, to the theatre—the theatre of old Arezzo: share with me the tattered vision and inhale the musty air!—I am well in range of Pompilia, the tragically exquisite, in her box, with her husband not there for the hour but posted elsewhere; I look at her in fact over Caponsacchi's shoulder and that of his brother-canon Conti, while this light character, a vivid recruit to our company, manages to toss into her lap, and as coming in guise of overture from his smitten friend, "a paper-twist of comfits." There is a particular famous occasion at the theatre in a work of more or less contemporary fiction—at a petty provincial theatre which isn't even, as you might think, the place where Pendennis had his first glimpse of Miss Fotheringay. The evening at the Rouen playhouse of Flaubert's "Madame Bovary" has a relief not elsewhere equalled—it is the most *done* visit to the play in all literature—but, though "doing" is now so woefully out of favour, my idea would be to give it here a precious *pendant;* which connection, silly Canon Conti, the old fripperies and levities, the whole queer picture and show of manners, is handed over to us, expressly, as inapt for poetic illustration.

What is equally apt for poetic or for the other, indeed, is the thing for which we feel 'The Ring and the Book' preponderantly done—it is at least what comes out clearest, comes out as straightest and strongest and finest, from Browning's genius—the exhibition of the great constringent relation between man and woman at once at its maximum and as the relation most worth while in life for either party; an exhibition forming quite the main substance of our author's message. He has dealt, in his immense variety and vivacity, with other relations, but on this he has thrown his most living weight; it remains the thing of which his own rich experience most convincingly spoke to him. He has testified to it as charged to the brim with the burden of the senses, and has testified to it as almost too clarified, too liberated and sublimated, for traceable application or fair record; he has figured it as never too much either of the flesh or of the spirit for him, so long as the possibility of both of these is in each, but always and ever as the thing absolutely most worth while. It is in the highest and rarest degree clarified and disengaged for Caponsacchi and Pompilia; but what their history most concludes to is how ineffably it was, whatever happened, worth while. Worth while most then for them or for us is the question? Well, let us say worth while assuredly for us, in this noble exercise of our imagination. Which accordingly shows us what we, for all our prose basis, would have found, to repeat my term once more, prepared for us. There isn't a detail of their panting flight to Rome over the autumn Appennines—the long hours when they melt together only *not* to meet—that doesn't positively plead for our perfect prose transcript. And if it be said that the mere massacre at the final end is a lapse to a passivity from the high plane, for our pair of protagonists, of constructive, of heroic vision, this is not a blur from the time everything that happens happens most effectively to Caponsacchi's life. Pompilia's is taken, but she is none the less given; and it is in his consciousness and experience that she most intensely flowers—with all her jubilation for doing so. So that *he* contains the whole—unless indeed, after all, the Pope does, the Pope whom I was leaving out as too transcendent for *our* version. Unless, unless, further and further, I see what I have at this late moment no right to; see, as the very end and splendid climax of all, Caponsacchi sent for to the Vatican and admitted alone to the Papal presence. *There* is a scene if we will; and in the mere mutual confrontation, brief, silent, searching, recognising, consecrating, almost as august on the one part as on the other.

It has been easy in many another case to run to earth the stray prime fancy, the original anecdote or artless tale from which a great imaginative work, starting off after meeting it, has sprung and rebounded again and soared; and perhaps it is right and happy and final that one should have faltered in attempting by a converse curiosity to clip off or tie back the wings that once have spread. You will agree with me none the less, I feel, that Browning's great generous wings are over us still and even now, more than ever now—as also that they shake down on us his blessing.

Preface to *Poems* (1853)

Matthew Arnold

(London: Longman, Brown, Green & Longmans, 1853).

In two small volumes of Poems, published anonymously, one in 1849, the other in 1852, many of the Poems which compose the present volume have already appeared. The rest are now published for the first time.

I have, in the present collection, omitted the Poem from which the volume published in 1852 took its title. I have done so, not because the subject of it was a Sicilian Greek born between two and three thousand years ago, although many persons would think this a sufficient reason. Neither have I done so because I had, in my opinion, failed in the delineation which I intended to effect. I intended to delineate the feelings of one of the last of the Greek religious philosophers, one of the family of Orpheus and Musaeus, having survived his fellows, living on into a time when the habits of Greek thought and feeling had begun fast to change, character to dwindle, the influence of the Sophists to prevail. Into the feelings of a man so situated there entered much that we are accustomed to consider as exclusively modern; how much, the fragments of Empedocles himself which remain to us are sufficient at least to indicate. What those who are familiar only with the great monuments of early Greek genius suppose to be its exclusive characteristics, have disappeared; the calm, the cheerfulness, the disinterested objectivity have disappeared: the dialogue of the mind with itself has commenced; modern problems have presented themselves; we hear already the doubts, we witness the discouragement, of Hamlet and of Faust.

The representation of such a man's feelings must be interesting, if consistently drawn. We all naturally take pleasure, says Aristotle, in any imitation or representation whatever: this is the basis of our love of Poetry: and we take pleasure in them, he adds, because all knowledge is naturally agreeable to us; not to the philosopher only, but to mankind at large. Every representation therefore which is consistently drawn may be supposed to be interesting, inasmuch as it gratifies this natural interest in knowledge of all kinds. What is *not* interesting, is that which does not add to our knowledge of any kind; that which is vaguely conceived and loosely drawn; a representation which is general, indeterminate, and faint, instead of being particular, precise, and firm.

Any accurate representation may therefore be expected to be interesting; but, if the representation be a poetical one, more than this is demanded. It is demanded, not only that it shall interest, but also that it shall inspirit and rejoice the reader: that it shall convey a charm, and infuse delight. For the Muses, as Hesiod says, were born that they might be 'a forgetfulness of evils, and a truce from cares': and it is not enough that the Poet should add to the knowledge of men, it is required of him also that he should add to their happiness. 'All Art,' says Schiller 'is dedicated to Joy, and there is no higher and no more serious problem, than how to make men happy. The right Art is that alone, which creates the highest enjoyment.'

A poetical work, therefore, is not yet justified when it has been shown to be an accurate, and therefore interesting representation; it has to be shown also that it is a representation from which men can derive enjoyment. In presence of the most tragic circumstances, represented in a work of Art, the feeling of enjoyment, as is well known, may still subsist: the representation of the most utter calamity, of the liveliest anguish, is not sufficient to destroy it: the more tragic the situation, the deeper becomes the enjoyment; and the situation is more tragic in proportion as it becomes more terrible.

What then are the situations, from the representation of which, though accurate, no poetical enjoyment can be derived? They are those in which the suffering finds no vent in action; in which a continuous state of mental distress is prolonged, unrelieved by incident, hope, or resistance; in which there is everything to be endured, nothing to be done. In such situations there is inevitably something morbid, in the description of them something monotonous. When they occur in actual life, they are painful, not tragic; the representation of them in poetry is painful also.

To this class of situations, poetically faulty as it appears to me, that of Empedocles, as I have endeavoured to represent him, belongs; and I have therefore excluded the Poem from the present collection.

And why, it may be asked, have I entered into this explanation respecting a matter so unimportant as the admission or exclusion of the Poem in question? I have done so, because I was anxious to avow that the sole reason for its exclusion was that which has been stated above; and that it has not been excluded in deference to the opinion which many critics of the present day appear to entertain against subjects chosen from distant times and countries: against the choice, in short, of any subjects but modern ones.

'The Poet,' it is said,[1] and by an intelligent critic, 'the Poet who would really fix the public attention must leave the exhausted past, and draw his subjects from matters of present import, and *therefore* both of interest and novelty.'

Now this view I believe to be completely false. It is worth examining, inasmuch as it is a fair sample of a class of critical dicta everywhere current at the present day, having a philosophical form and air, but no real basis in fact; and which are calculated to vitiate the judgment of readers of poetry, while they exert, so far as they are adopted, a misleading influence on the practice of those who write it.

What are the eternal objects of Poetry, among all nations and at all times? They are actions; human actions; possessing an inherent interest in themselves, and which are to be communicated in an interesting manner by the art of the Poet. Vainly will the latter imagine that he has everything in his own power; that he can make an intrinsically inferior action equally delightful with a more excellent one by his treatment of it; he may indeed compel us to admire his skill, but his work will possess, within itself, an incurable defect.

The Poet, then, has in the first place to select an excellent action; and what actions are the most excellent? Those, certainly, which most powerfully appeal to the great primary human affections: to those elementary feelings which subsist permanently in the race, and which are independent of time. These feelings are permanent and the same; that which interests them is permanent and the same also. The modernness or antiquity of an action, therefore, has nothing to do with its fitness for poetical representation; this depends upon its inherent qualities. To the elementary part of our nature, to our passions, that which is great and passionate is eternally interesting; and interesting solely in proportion to its greatness and to its passion. A great human action of a thousand years ago is more interesting to it than a smaller human action of to-day, even though upon the representation of this last the most consummate skill may have been expended, and though it has the advantage of appealing by its modern language, familiar manners, and contemporary allusions, to all our transient feelings and interests. These, however, have no right to demand of a poetical work that it shall satisfy them; their claims are to be directed elsewhere. Poetical works belong to the domain of our permanent passions: let them interest these, and the voice of all subordinate claims upon them is at once silenced.

Achilles, Prometheus, Clytemnestra, Dido—what modern poem presents personages as interesting, even to us moderns, as these personages of an 'exhausted past'? We have the domestic epic dealing with the details of modern life which pass daily under our eyes; we have poems representing modern personages in contact with the problems of modern life, moral, intellectual, and social; these works have been produced by poets the most distinguished of their nation and time; yet I fearlessly assert that Hermann and Dorothea, Childe Harold, Jocelyn, The Excursion, leave the reader cold in comparison with the effect produced upon him by the latter books of the Iliad, by the Oresteia, or by the episode of Dido. And why is this? Simply because in the three last-named cases the action is greater, the personages nobler, the situations more intense: and this is the true basis of the interest in a poetical work, and this alone.

It may be urged, however, that past actions may be interesting in themselves, but that they are not to be adopted by the modern Poet, because it is impossible for him to have them clearly present to his own mind, and he cannot therefore feel them deeply, nor represent them forcibly. But this is not necessarily the case. The externals of a past action, indeed, he cannot know with the precision of a contemporary; but his business is with its essentials. The outward man of Oedipus or of Macbeth, the houses in which they lived, the ceremonies of their courts, he cannot accurately figure to himself; but neither do they essentially concern him. His business is with their inward man; with their feelings and behaviour in certain tragic situations, which engage their passions as men; these have in them nothing local and casual; they are as accessible to the modern Poet as to a contemporary.

The date of an action, then, signifies nothing: the action itself, its selection and construction, this is what is all-important. This the Greeks understood far more clearly than we do. The radical difference between their poetical theory and ours consists, as it appears to me, in this: that, with them, the poetical character of the action in itself, and the conduct of it, was the first consideration; with us, attention is fixed mainly on the value of the separate thoughts and images which occur in the treatment of an action. They regarded the whole; we regard the parts. With them, the action predominated over the expression of it; with us, the expression predominates over the action. Not that they failed in expression, or were inattentive to it; on the contrary, they are the highest models of expression, the unapproached masters of the *grand style:* but their expression is so excellent because it is so admirably kept in its right degree of prominence; because it is so simple and so well subordinated; because it draws its force directly from the pregnancy of the matter which it conveys. For what reason was the Greek tragic poet confined to so limited a range of subjects? Because there are so few actions which unite in themselves, in the highest degree, the conditions of excellence: and it was not thought that on any but an excellent subject could an excellent Poem be constructed. A few actions, therefore, eminently adapted for tragedy, maintained almost exclusive possession of the Greek tragic stage; their significance appeared inexhaustible; they were as permanent problems, perpetually offered to the genius of every fresh poet. This too is the reason of what appears to us moderns a certain baldness of expression in Greek tragedy; of the triviality with which we often reproach the remarks of the chorus, where it takes part in the dialogue: that the action itself, the situation of Orestes, or Merope, or Alcmaeon, was to stand the central point of interest, unforgotten, absorbing, principal; that no accessories were for a moment to distract the spectator's attention from this; that the tone of the parts was to be perpetually kept down, in order not to impair the grandiose effect of the whole. The terrible old mythic story on which the drama was founded stood, before he entered the theatre, traced in its bare outlines upon the spectator's mind; it stood in his memory, as a group of statuary, faintly seen, at the end of a long and dark vista: then came the Poet, embodying outlines, developing situations, not a word wasted, not a sentiment capriciously thrown in: stroke upon stroke, the drama proceeded: the light deepened upon the group; more and more it revealed itself to the rivetted gaze of the spectator: until at last, when the final words were spoken, it stood before him in broad sunlight, a model of immortal beauty.

This was what a Greek critic demanded; this was what a Greek poet endeavoured to effect. It signified nothing to what time an action belonged; we do not find that the Persae occupied a particularly high rank among the dramas of Aeschylus because it represented a matter of contemporary interest: this was not what a cultivated Athenian required; he required that the permanent elements of his nature should be moved; and dramas of which the action, though taken from a long-distant mythic time, yet was calculated to accomplish this in a higher degree than that of the Persae, stood higher in his estimation accordingly. The Greeks felt, no doubt, with their exquisite sagacity of taste, that an action of present times was too near them, too much mixed up with what was accidental and passing, to form a sufficiently grand, detached, and self-subsistent object for a tragic poem: such objects belonged to the domain of the comic poet, and of the lighter kinds of poetry. For the more serious kinds, for *pragmatic* poetry, to use an excellent expression of Polybius, they were more difficult and severe in the range of subjects which they permitted. Their theory and practice alike, the admirable treatise of Aristotle, and the unrivalled works of their poets, exclaim with a thousand tongues—'All depends upon the subject; choose a fitting action, penetrate yourself with the feeling of its situations; this done, everything else will follow.'

But for all kinds of poetry alike there was one point on which they were rigidly exacting; the adaptability of the subject to the kind of poetry selected, and the careful construction of the poem.

How different a way of thinking from this is ours! We can hardly at the present day understand what Menander meant, when he told a man who inquired as to the progress of his comedy that he had finished it, not having yet written a single line, because he had constructed the action of it in his mind. A modern critic would have assured him that the merit of his piece depended on the brilliant things which arose under his pen as he went along. We have poems which seem to exist merely for the sake of single lines and passages; not for the sake of producing any total-impression. We have critics who seem to direct their attention merely to detached expressions, to the language about the action, not to the action itself. I verily think that the majority of them do not in their hearts believe that there is such a thing as a total-impression to be derived from a poem at all, or to be demanded from a poet; they think the term a common-place of metaphysical criticism. They will permit the Poet to select any action he pleases, and to suffer that action to go as it will, provided he gratifies them with occasional bursts of fine writing, and with a shower of isolated thoughts and images. That is, they permit him to leave their poetical sense ungratified, provided that he gratifies their rhetorical sense and their curiosity. Of his neglecting to gratify these, there is little danger; he needs rather to be warned against the danger of attempting to gratify these alone; he needs rather to be perpetually reminded to prefer his action to everything else; so to treat this, as to permit its inherent excellences to develop themselves, without interruption from the intrusion of his personal peculiarities: most fortunate, when he most entirely succeeds in effacing himself, and in enabling a noble action to subsist as it did in nature.

But the modern critic not only permits a false practice; he absolutely prescribes false aims.—'A true allegory of the state of one's own mind in a representative history,' the Poet is told, 'is perhaps the highest thing that one can attempt in the way of poetry.'—And accordingly he attempts it. An allegory of the state of one's own mind, the highest problem of an art which imitates actions! No assuredly, it is not, it never can be so: no great poetical work has ever been produced with such an aim. Faust itself, in which something of the kind is attempted, wonderful passages as it contains, and in spite of the unsurpassed beauty of the scenes which relate to Margaret, Faust itself, judged as a whole, and judged strictly as a poetical work, is defective: its illustrious author, the greatest poet of modern times, the greatest critic of all times, would have been the first to acknowledge it; he only defended his work, indeed, by asserting it to be 'something incommensurable.'

The confusion of the present times is great, the multitude of voices counselling different things bewildering, the number of existing works capable of attracting a young writer's attention and of becoming his models, immense: what he wants is a hand to guide him through the confusion, a voice to prescribe to him the aim which he should keep in view, and to explain to him that the value of the literary works which offer themselves to his attention is relative to their power of helping him forward on his road towards this aim. Such a guide the English writer at the present day will nowhere find. Failing this, all that can be looked for, all indeed that can be desired, is, that his attention should be fixed on excellent models; that he may reproduce, at any rate, something of their excellence, by penetrating himself with their works and by catching their spirit, if he cannot be taught to produce what is excellent independently.

Foremost among these models for the English writer stands Shakespeare: a name the greatest perhaps of all poetical names; a name never to be mentioned without reverence. I will venture, however, to express a doubt whether the influence of his works, excellent and fruitful for the readers of poetry, for the great majority, has been of unmixed advantage to the writers of it. Shakespeare indeed chose excellent subjects; the world could afford no better than Macbeth, or Romeo and Juliet, or Othello: he had no theory respecting the necessity of choosing subjects of present import, or the paramount interest attaching to allegories of the state of one's own mind; like all great poets he knew well what constituted a poetical action; like them, wherever he found such an action, he took it; like them, too, he found his best in past times. But to these general characteristics of all great poets, he added a special one of his own; a gift, namely, of happy, abundant, and ingenious expression, eminent and unrivalled: so eminent as irresistibly to strike the attention first in him, and even to throw into comparative shade his other excellences as a poet. Here has been the mischief. These other excellences were his fundamental excellences *as a poet;* what distinguishes the artist from the mere amateur, says Goethe, is *Architectonicè* in the highest sense; that power of execution, which creates, forms, and constitutes: not the profoundness of single thoughts, not the richness of imagery, not the abundance of illustration. But these attractive accessories of a poetical work being more easily seized than the spirit of the whole, and these accessories being possessed by Shakespeare in an unequalled degree, a young writer having recourse to Shakespeare as his model runs great risk of being vanquished and absorbed by them, and, in consequence, of reproducing, according to the measure of his power, these, and these alone. Of this preponderating quality of Shakespeare's genius, accordingly, almost the whole of modern English poetry has, it appears to me, felt the influence. To the exclusive attention on the part of his imitators to this it is in a great degree owing, that of the majority of modern poetical works the details alone are valuable, the composition worthless. In reading them one is perpetually reminded of that terrible sentence on a modern French poet—*il dit tout ce qu'il veut, mais malheureusement il n'a rien à dire.* ["He says all he wishes to, but unfortunately he has nothing to say."]

Let me give an instance of what I mean. I will take it from the works of the very chief among those who seem to have been formed in the school of Shakespeare: of one whose exquisite genius and pathetic death render him for ever interesting. I will take the poem of Isabella, or the Pot of Basil, by Keats. I choose this rather than the Endymion, because the latter work (which a modern critic has classed with the Fairy Queen!), although undoubtedly there blows through it the breath of genius, is yet as a whole so utterly incoherent, as not strictly to merit the name of a poem at all. The poem of Isabella, then, is a perfect treasure-house of graceful and felicitous words and images: almost in every stanza there occurs one of those vivid and picturesque turns of expression, by which the object is made to flash upon the eye of the mind, and which thrill the reader with a sudden delight. This one short poem contains, perhaps, a greater number of happy single expressions which one could quote than all the extant tragedies of Sophocles. But the action, the story? The action in itself is an excellent one; but so feebly is it conceived by the Poet, so loosely constructed, that the effect produced by it, in and for itself, is absolutely null. Let the reader, after he has finished the poem of Keats, turn to the same story in the Decameron: he will then feel how pregnant and interesting the same action has become in the hands of a great artist, who above all things delineates his object; who subordinates expression to that which it is designed to express.

I have said that the imitators of Shakespeare, fixing their attention on his wonderful gift of expression, have directed their imitation to this, neglecting his other excellences. These excellences, the fundamental excellences of poetical art, Shakespeare no doubt possessed them—possessed many of them in a splendid degree; but it may perhaps be doubted whether even he himself did not sometimes give scope to his faculty of expression to the prejudice of a higher poetical duty. For we must never forget that Shakespeare is the great poet he is from his skill in discerning and firmly conceiving an excellent action, from his power of intensely feeling a situation, of intimately associating himself with a character; not from his gift of expression, which rather even leads him astray, degenerating sometimes into a fondness for curiosity of expression, into an irritability of fancy, which seems to make it impossible for him to say a thing plainly, even when the press of the action demands the very directest language, or its level character the very simplest. Mr. [Henry] Hallam, than whom it is impossible to find a saner and more judicious critic, has had the courage (for at the present day it needs courage) to remark, how extremely and faultily difficult Shakespeare's language often is. It is so: you may find main scenes in some of his greatest tragedies, King Lear for instance, where the language is so artificial, so curiously tortured, and so difficult, that every speech has to be read two or three times before its meaning can be comprehended. This over-curiousness of expression is indeed but the excessive employment of a wonderful gift—of the power of saying a thing in a happier way than any other man; nevertheless, it is carried so far that one understands what M. Guizot meant, when he said that Shakespeare appears in his language to have tried all styles except that of simplicity. He has not the severe and scrupulous self-restraint of the ancients, partly no doubt, because he had a far less cultivated and exacting audience: he has indeed a far wider range than they had, a far richer fertility of thought; in this respect he rises above them: in his strong conception of his subject, in the genuine way in which he is penetrated with it, he resembles them, and is unlike the moderns: but in the accurate limitation of it, the conscientious rejection of superfluities, the simple and rigorous development of it from the first line of his work to the last, he falls below them, and comes nearer to the moderns. In his chief works, besides what he has of his own, he has the elementary soundness of the ancients; he has their important action and their large and broad manner: but he has not their purity of method. He is therefore a less safe model; for what he has of his own is personal, and inseparable from his own rich nature; it may be imitated and exaggerated, it cannot be learned or applied as an art; he is above all suggestive; more valuable, therefore, to young writers as men than as artists. But clearness of arrangement, rigour of development, simplicity of style—these may to a certain extent be learned: and these may, I am convinced, be learned best from the ancients, who although infinitely less suggestive than Shakespeare, are thus, to the artist, more instructive.

What, then, it will be asked, are the ancients to be our sole models? the ancients with their comparatively narrow range of experience, and their widely different circumstances? Not, certainly, that which is narrow in the ancients, nor that in which we can no longer sympathize. An action like the action of the Antigone of Sophocles, which turns upon the conflict between the heroine's duty to her brother's corpse and that to the laws of her country, is no longer one in which it is possible that we should feel a deep interest. I am speaking too, it will be remembered, not of the best sources of intellectual stimulus for the general reader, but of the best models of instruction for the individual writer. This last may certainly learn of the ancients, better than anywhere else, three things which it is vitally important for him to know:—the all-importance of the choice of a subject; the necessity of accurate construction; and the subordinate character of expression. He will learn from them how unspeakably superior is the effect of the one moral impression left by a great action treated as a whole, to the effect produced by the most striking single thought or by the happiest image. As he penetrates into the spirit of the great classical works, as he becomes gradually aware of their intense significance, their noble simplicity, and their calm pathos, he will be convinced that it is this effect, unity and profoundness of moral impression, at which the ancient Poets aimed; that it is this which constitutes the grandeur of their works, and which makes them immortal. He will desire to direct his own efforts towards producing the same effect. Above all, he will deliver himself from the jargon of modern criticism, and escape the danger of producing poetical works conceived in the spirit of the passing time, and which partake of its transitoriness.

The present age makes great claims upon us: we owe it service, it will not be satisfied without our admiration. I know not how it is, but their commerce with the ancients appears to me to produce, in those who constantly practise it, a steadying and composing effect upon their judgment, not of literary works only, but of men and events in general. They are like persons who have had a very weighty and impressive experience: they are more truly than others under the empire of facts, and more independent of the language current among those with whom they live. They wish neither to applaud nor to revile their age: they wish to know what it is, what it can give them, and whether this is what they want. What they want, they know very well; they want to educe and cultivate what is best and noblest in themselves: they know, too, that this is no easy task—[*chalepon*], as Pittacus said, [*chalepon esthlon emmenai*] ["It is hard to be excellent."]—and they ask themselves sincerely whether their age and its literature can assist them in the attempt. If they are endeavouring to practise any art, they remember the plain and simple proceedings of the old artists, who attained their grand results by penetrating themselves with some noble and significant action, not by inflating themselves with a belief in the preeminent importance and greatness of their own times. They do not talk of their mission, nor of interpreting their age, nor of the coming Poet; all this, they know, is the mere delirium of vanity; their business is not to praise their age, but to afford to the men who live in it the highest pleasure which they are capable of feeling. If asked to afford this by means of subjects drawn from the age itself, they ask what special fitness the present age has for supplying them: they are told that it is an era of progress, an age commissioned to carry out the great ideas of industrial development and social amelioration. They reply that with all this they can do nothing; that the elements they need for the exercise of their art are great actions, calculated powerfully and delightfully to affect what is permanent in the human soul; that so far as the present age can supply such actions, they will gladly make use of them; but that an age wanting in moral grandeur can with difficulty supply such, and an age of spiritual discomfort with difficulty be powerfully and delightfully affected by them.

A host of voices will indignantly rejoin that the present age is inferior to the past neither in moral grandeur nor in spiritual health. He who possesses the discipline I speak of will content himself with remembering the judgements passed upon the present age, in this respect, by the two men, the one of strongest head, the other of widest culture, whom it has produced; by Goethe and by Niebuhr. It will be sufficient for him that he knows the opinions held by these two great men respecting the present age and its literature; and that he feels assured in his own mind that their aims and demands upon life were such as he would wish, at any rate, his own to be; and their judgement as to what is impeding and disabling such as he may safely follow. He will not, however, maintain a hostile attitude towards the false pretensions of his age; he will content himself with not being overwhelmed by them. He will esteem himself fortunate if he can succeed in banishing from his mind all feelings of contradiction, and irritation, and impatience; in order to delight himself with the contemplation of some noble action of a heroic time, and to enable others, through his representation of it, to delight in it also.

I am far indeed from making any claim, for myself, that I possess this discipline; or for the following Poems, that they breathe its spirit. But I say, that in the sincere endeavour to learn and practise, amid the bewildering confusion of our times, what is sound and true in poetical art, I seemed to myself to find the only sure guidance, the only solid footing, among the ancients. They, at any rate, knew what they wanted in Art, and we do not. It is this uncertainty which is disheartening, and not hostile criticism. How often have I felt this when reading words of disparagement or of cavil: that it is the uncertainty as to what is really to be aimed at which makes our difficulty, not the dissatisfaction of the critic, who himself suffers from the same uncertainty. *Non me tua fervida terrent Dicta: Dii me terrent, et Jupiter hostis.* ["Your hot words do not frighten me . . . The gods frighten me, and Jupiter as my enemy."]

Two kinds of *dilettanti,* says Goethe, there are in poetry: he who neglects the indispensable mechanical part, and thinks he has done enough if he shows spirituality and feeling; and he who seeks to arrive at poetry merely by mechanism, in which he can acquire an artisan's readiness, and is without soul and matter. And he adds, that the first does most harm to Art, and the last to himself. If we must be *dilettanti:* if it is impossible for us, under the circumstances amidst which we live, to think clearly, to feel nobly, and to delineate firmly: if we cannot attain to the mastery of the great artists—let us, at least, have so much respect for our Art as to prefer it to ourselves: let us not bewilder our successors: let us transmit to them the practice of Poetry, with its boundaries and wholesome regulative laws, under which excellent works may again, perhaps, at some future time, be produced, not yet fallen into oblivion through our neglect, not yet condemned and cancelled by the influence of their eternal enemy, Caprice.

---

1. In *The Spectator* of April 2nd, 1853. The words quoted were not used with reference to poems of mine.

Books for Further Reading

Altholz, Joseph L., ed. *The Mind and Art of Victorian England.* Minneapolis: University of Minnesota Press, 1976.

Altick, Richard. *The English Common Reader: A Social History of the Mass Reading Public, 1800-1900.* Chicago: University of Chicago Press, 1957.

Altick. *Victorian People and Ideas.* New York: Norton, 1973.

Appleman, Philip, William A. Madden, and Michael Wolff, eds. *1859: Entering An Age of Crisis.* Bloomington: Indiana University Press, 1959.

Armstrong, Isobel. *Language as Living Form in Nineteenth Century Poetry.* Totowa, N.J.: Barnes & Noble, 1982.

Armstrong, ed. *The Major Victorian Poets: Reconsiderations.* Lincoln: University of Nebraska Press, 1969.

Armstrong, ed. *Victorian Scrutinies: Reviews of Poetry, 1830-1870.* London: Athlone, 1972.

Ball, Patricia M. *The Heart's Events: The Victorian Poetry of Relationships.* London: Athlone, 1976.

Batho, Edith and Bonamy Dobrée. *The Victorians and After, 1830-1914,* second revised edition. London: Cresset, 1950.

Beach, Joseph Warren. *The Concept of Nature in Nineteenth Century Poetry.* New York: Macmillan, 1936.

Briggs, Asa. *The Age of Improvement.* London & New York: Longmans, Green, 1959.

Buckler, William E. *The Victorian Imagination: Essays in Aesthetic Exploration.* New York: New York University Press, 1980.

Buckley, Jerome. *The Triumph of Time: A Study of the Victorian Concepts of Time, History, Progress and Decadence.* Cambridge: Harvard University Press, 1966.

Buckley. *The Victorian Temper: A Study in Literary Culture.* Cambridge: Harvard University Press, 1951.

Burn, W. L. *The Age of Equipoise: A Study of the Mid-Victorian Generation.* New York: Norton, 1965.

Bush, Douglas. *Science and English Poetry: A Historical Sketch, 1590-1950.* New York: Oxford University Press, 1950.

Charlesworth, Barbara. *Dark Passages: The Decadent Consciousness in Victorian Literature.* Madison: University of Wisconsin Press, 1965.

Chesterton, G. K. *The Victorian Age in Literature.* London: Williams & Norgate, 1913; New York: Holt, 1913.

Christ, Carol. *The Finer Optic: The Aesthetic of Particularity in Victorian Poetry.* New Haven: Yale University Press, 1975.

Conrad, Peter. *The Victorian Treasure-House.* London: Collins, 1973.

Books for Further Reading

Cosslett, Tess. *The Scientific Movement and Victorian Literature.* New York: St. Martin's, 1983.

Cruse, Amy. *The Victorians and Their Reading.* Boston & New York: Houghton Mifflin, 1935. Republished as *The Victorians and Their Books.* London: Allen & Unwin, 1935.

Dawson, Carl. *Victorian Noon: English Literature in 1850.* Baltimore & London: Johns Hopkins University Press, 1979.

Drinkwater, John. *Victorian Poetry.* London: Hodder & Stoughton, 1923; New York: Doran, 1924.

Ensor, R. C. K. *England, 1870-1914.* Oxford: Clarendon Press, 1936.

Fairchild, Hoxie N. *Religious Trends in English Poetry. IV: Christianity and Romanticism in the Victorian Era: 1830-1880; V: Gods of a Changing Poetry: 1880-1920.* New York: Columbia University Press, 1957, 1962.

Faverty, Frederic, ed. *The Victorian Poets: A Guide to Research,* second edition. Cambridge: Harvard University Press, 1968.

Fletcher, Pauline. *Gardens and Grim Ravines: The Language of Landscape in Victorian Poetry.* Princeton: Princeton University Press, 1983.

Foakes, R. A. *The Romantic Assertion: A Study in the Language of Nineteenth Century Poetry.* New Haven: Yale University Press, 1958.

Ford, George. *Keats and the Victorians: A Study of His Influence and Rise to Fame, 1821-1895.* New Haven: Yale University Press, 1944; London: Oxford University Press, 1944.

Fredeman, W. E. *Pre-Raphaelitism: A Bibliocritical Study.* Cambridge: Harvard University Press, 1965.

Gaunt, William. *The Pre-Raphaelite Tragedy.* London: Cape, 1942.

Gilbert, Sandra M. and Susan Gubar. *The Madwoman in the Attic: The Woman Writer and The Nineteenth Century Literary Imagination.* New Haven: Yale University Press, 1979.

Heyck, T. W. *The Transformation of Intellectual Life in Victorian England.* New York: St. Martin's, 1982.

Holloway, John. *The Proud Knowledge: Poetry, Insight and the Self, 1620-1920.* London: Routledge & Kegan Paul, 1977.

Hough, Graham. *The Last Romantics.* London: Duckworth, 1949; Totowa, N.J.: Barnes & Noble, 1961.

Houghton, Walter E. *The Victorian Frame of Mind, 1830-1870.* New Haven: Yale University Press, 1957.

Hunt, John Dixon. *The Pre-Raphaelite Imagination, 1848-1900.* Lincoln: University of Nebraska Press, 1977.

Jenkyns, Richard. *The Victorians and Ancient Greece.* Cambridge: Harvard University Press, 1981.

Johnson, E. D. H. *The Alien Vision of Victorian Poetry: Sources of the Poetic Imagination in Tennyson, Browning, and Arnold.* Princeton: Princeton University Press, 1952.

Johnson, Wendell Stacey. *Sex and Marriage in Victorian Poetry.* Ithaca, N.Y.: Cornell University Press, 1975.

Kermode, Frank. *Romantic Image.* London: Routledge & Kegan Paul, 1957; New York: Macmillan, 1957.

Kitson Clark, G. *The Making of Victorian England.* Cambridge: Harvard University Press, 1962.

Knoepflmacher, U. C. and G. B. Tennyson, eds. *Nature and the Victorian Imagination.* Berkeley: University of California Press, 1978.

Langbaum, Robert. *The Poetry of Experience: The Dramatic Monologue in Modern Literary Tradition.* New York: Random House, 1957; London: Chatto & Windus, 1957.

Levine, Richard A., ed. *Backgrounds to Victorian Literature.* San Francisco: Chandler, 1967.

Levine, ed. *The Victorian Experience: The Poets.* Athens: Ohio University Press, 1982.

Longford, Elizabeth. *Queen Victoria: Born to Succeed.* New York: Harper & Row, 1974.

Lucas, F. L. *Ten Victorian Poets,* third edition. Cambridge: Cambridge University Press, 1948.

McGhee, Richard D. *Marriage, Duty and Desire in Victorian Poetry and Drama.* Lawrence: Regents Press of Kansas, 1980.

Mermin, Dorothy. *The Audience in The Poem: Five Victorian Poets.* New Brunswick, N.J.: Rutgers University Press, 1983.

Miller, J. Hillis. *The Disappearance of God: Five Nineteenth Century Writers.* Cambridge: Harvard University Press, 1976.

Miyoshi, Masao. *The Divided Self: A Perspective on the Literature of the Victorians.* New York: New York University Press, 1969.

Nelson, James G. *The Sublime Puritan: Milton and The Victorians.* Madison: University of Wisconsin Press, 1963.

Peckham, Morse. *Beyond the Tragic Vision: The Quest for Identity in the Nineteenth Century.* New York: Braziller, 1962.

Reed, John R. *Victorian Conventions.* Athens: Ohio University Press, 1975.

Roppen, Georg. *Evolution and Poetic Belief: A Study in Some Victorian and Modern Writers.* Oslo: Oslo University Press, 1956.

Schneewind, J. B. *Backgrounds of English Victorian Literature.* New York: Random House, 1970.

Somervell, D. C. *English Thought in the Nineteenth Century.* London: Methuen, 1929.

Stevenson, Lionel. *The Pre-Raphaelite Poets.* Chapel Hill: University of North Carolina Press, 1972.

Sussman, Herbert. *Victorians and The Machine: Literary Response to Technology.* Cambridge: Harvard University Press, 1968.

Tennyson, G. B. *Victorian Devotional Poetry: The Tractarian Mode.* Cambridge: Harvard University Press, 1980.

Thesing, William B. *The London Muse: Victorian Poetic Responses to the City.* Athens: University of Georgia Press, 1982.

Thomson, David. *England in the Nineteenth Century, 1815-1914.* Harmondsworth, U.K.: Penguin, 1950.

Books for Further Reading

Tillotson, Geoffrey. *A View of Victorian Literature.* Oxford: Oxford University Press, 1978.

Tillotson, Kathleen and Geoffrey Tillotson. *Mid-Victorian Studies.* London: Athlone, 1965.

Vicinus, Martha. *The Industrial Muse: A Study of Nineteenth-Century British Working Class Literature.* New York: Barnes & Noble, 1974.

Vicinus, ed. *Suffer and Be Still: Women in the Victorian Age.* Bloomington: Indiana University Press, 1972.

Victorian Poetry. Stratford-upon-Avon Studies No. 15. London: Edward Arnold, 1972.

Warren, Alba H., Jr. *English Poetic Theory, 1825-1865.* Princeton: Princeton University Press, 1950.

Williams, Raymond. *Culture and Society, 1780-1950.* New York: Columbia University Press, 1958; London: Chatto & Windus, 1958.

Wright, Austin, ed. *Victorian Literature: Modern Essays in Criticism.* New York: Oxford University Press, 1961.

Young, G. M. *Victorian England: Portrait of An Age.* London: Oxford University Press, 1936.

Contributors

Lionel Adey	*University of Victoria*
Tirthankar Bose	*University of British Columbia*
Nicholas Coles	*University of Pittsburgh*
Dorothy W. Collin	*University of Western Australia*
Rowland L. Collins	*University of Rochester*
Thomas J. Collins	*University of Western Ontario*
Michael Darling	*Vanier College*
Susan Drain	*Mount Saint Vincent University*
William E. Fredeman	*University of British Columbia*
Ina Rae Hark	*University of South Carolina*
Jack Kolb	*University of California, Los Angeles*
Robert G. Laird	*Carleton University*
David Latham	*University of Lethbridge*
Christopher Murray	*University of Regina*
Ira Bruce Nadel	*University of British Columbia*
Victor A. Neufeldt	*University of Victoria*
Lawrence Poston	*University of Illinois at Chicago*
Peter Quartermain	*Vancouver, British Columbia*
John R. Reed	*Wayne State University*
William Robbins	*University of British Columbia*
Patrick Scott	*University of South Carolina*
Joseph Sendry	*Catholic University of America*
Gardner B. Taplin	*Tulane University*
G. B. Tennyson	*University of California, Los Angeles*
William B. Thesing	*University of South Carolina*
Richard Tobias	*University of Pittsburgh*
Mark A. Weinstein	*University of Nevada, Las Vegas*

Cumulative Index
Dictionary of Literary Biography, Volumes 1-32
Dictionary of Literary Biography Yearbook, 1980-1983
Dictionary of Literary Biography Documentary Series, Volumes 1-4

Cumulative Index

DLB before number: *Dictionary of Literary Biography*, Volumes 1-32
Y before number: *Dictionary of Literary Biography Yearbook*, 1980-1983
DS before number: *Dictionary of Literary Biography Documentary Series*, Volumes 1-4

A

Abbot, Willis J. 1863-1934 .... DLB29
Abbott, Jacob 1803-1879 .... DLB1
Abbott, Robert S. 1868-1940 .... DLB29
Abercrombie, Lascelles 1881-1938 .... DLB19
Abse, Dannie 1923- DLB27
Adair, James 1709?-1783? DLB30
Adamic, Louis 1898-1951 .... DLB9
Adams, Douglas 1952- Y83
Adams, Franklin P. 1881-1960 .... DLB29
Adams, Henry 1838-1918 .... DLB12
Adams, James Truslow 1878-1949 .... DLB17
Adams, John 1734-1826 .... DLB31
Adams, Samuel 1722-1803 .... DLB31
Ade, George 1866-1944 .... DLB11, 25
Adeler, Max (see Clark, Charles Heber)
AE 1867-1935 .... DLB19
Agassiz, Jean Louis Rodolphe 1807-1873 .... DLB1
Agee, James 1909-1955 .... DLB2, 26
Aiken, Conrad 1889-1973 .... DLB9
Ainsworth, William Harrison 1805-1882 .... DLB21
Akins, Zoë 1886-1958 .... DLB26
Albee, Edward 1928- DLB7
Alcott, Amos Bronson 1799-1888 .... DLB1
Alcott, Louisa May 1832-1888 .... DLB1
Alcott, William Andrus 1798-1859 .... DLB1
Aldington, Richard 1892-1962 .... DLB20
Aldis, Dorothy 1896-1966 .... DLB22
Aldiss, Brian W. 1925- DLB14
Alexander, James 1691-1756 .... DLB24
Algren, Nelson 1909-1981 .... DLB9; Y81, 82
Alldritt, Keith 1935- DLB14
Allen, Ethan 1738-1789 .... DLB31

Allen, Hervey 1889-1949 .... DLB9
Allen, James 1739-1808 .... DLB31
Allen, Jay Presson 1922- DLB26
Josiah Allen's Wife (see Holly, Marietta)
Allott, Kenneth 1912-1973 .... DLB20
Allston, Washington 1779-1843 .... DLB1
Alsop, George 1636-post 1673 .... DLB24
Alvarez, A. 1929- DLB14
Ames, Mary Clemmer 1831-1884 .... DLB23
Amis, Kingsley 1922- DLB15, 27
Amis, Martin 1949- DLB14
Ammons, A. R. 1926- DLB5
Anderson, Margaret 1886-1973 .... DLB4
Anderson, Maxwell 1888-1959 .... DLB7
Anderson, Paul Y. 1893-1938 .... DLB29
Anderson, Poul 1926- DLB8
Anderson, Robert 1917- DLB7
Anderson, Sherwood 1876-1941 .... DLB4, 9; DS1
Andrews, Charles M. 1863-1943 .... DLB17
Anhalt, Edward 1914- DLB26
Anthony, Piers 1934- DLB8
Archer, William 1856-1924 .... DLB10
Arden, John 1930- DLB13
Arensberg, Ann 1937- Y82
Arnold, Matthew 1822-1888 .... DLB32
Arnow, Harriette Simpson 1908- DLB6
Arp, Bill (see Smith, Charles Henry)
Arthur, Timothy Shay 1809-1885 .... DLB3
Asch, Nathan 1902-1964 .... DLB4, 28
Ashbery, John 1927- DLB5; Y81
Asher, Sandy 1942- Y83
Ashton, Winifred (see Dane, Clemence)
Asimov, Isaac 1920- DLB8
Atherton, Gertrude 1857-1948 .... DLB9

Cumulative Index

Atkins, Josiah circa 1755-1781 ....DLB31
Auchincloss, Louis 1917- DLB2; Y80
Auden, W. H. 1907-1973 ....DLB10, 20
Austin, Mary 1868-1934 ....DLB9
Ayckbourn, Alan 1939- DLB13
Aytoun, William Edmondstoune 1813-1865........DLB32

B

Bacon, Delia 1811-1859 ....DLB1
Bacon, Thomas circa 1700-1768 ....DLB31
Bagnold, Enid 1889-1981 ....DLB13
Bailey, Paul 1937- DLB14
Bailey, Philip James 1816-1902 ....DLB32
Baillie, Hugh 1890-1966 ....DLB29
Bailyn, Bernard 1922- DLB17
Bainbridge, Beryl 1933- DLB14
Bald, Wambly 1902- DLB4
Balderston, John 1889-1954 ....DLB26
Baldwin, James 1924- DLB2, 7
Baldwin, Joseph Glover 1815-1864 ....DLB3, 11
Ballard, J. G. 1930- DLB14
Bancroft, George 1800-1891 ....DLB1, 30
Bangs, John Kendrick 1862-1922 ....DLB11
Banville, John 1945- DLB14
Baraka, Amiri 1934- DLB5, 7, 16
Barber, John Warner 1798-1885 ....DLB30
Barbour, Ralph Henry 1870-1944 ....DLB22
Barker, A. L. 1918- DLB14
Barker, George 1913- DLB20
Barker, Harley Granville 1877-1946 ....DLB10
Barker, Howard 1946- DLB13
Barks, Coleman 1937- DLB5
Barnard, John 1681-1770 ....DLB24
Barnes, Djuna 1892-1982 ....DLB4, 9
Barnes, Margaret Ayer 1886-1967 ....DLB9
Barnes, Peter 1931- DLB13
Barnes, William 1801-1886 ....DLB32
Barney, Natalie 1876-1972 ....DLB4
Barrie, James M. 1860-1937 ....DLB10
Barry, Philip 1896-1949 ....DLB7

Barstow, Stan 1928- DLB14
Barth, John 1930- DLB2
Barthelme, Donald 1931- DLB2; Y80
Bartlett, John 1820-1905 ....DLB1
Bartol, Cyrus Augustus 1813-1900 ....DLB1
Bartram, John 1699-1777 ....DLB31
Bass, T. J. 1932- Y81
Bassett, John Spencer 1867-1928 ....DLB17
Bassler, Thomas Joseph (see Bass, T. J.)
Baum, L. Frank 1856-1919 ....DLB22
Baumbach, Jonathan 1933- Y80
Bawden, Nina 1925- DLB14
Bax, Clifford 1886-1962 ....DLB10
Beach, Sylvia 1887-1962 ....DLB4
Beagle, Peter S. 1939- Y80
Beal, M. F. 1937- Y81
Beale, Howard K. 1899-1959 ....DLB17
Beard, Charles A. 1874-1948 ....DLB17
Beattie, Ann 1947- Y82
Becker, Carl 1873-1945 ....DLB17
Beckett, Samuel 1906- DLB13, 15
Beecher, Catharine Esther 1800-1878 ....DLB1
Beecher, Henry Ward 1813-1887 ....DLB3
Behan, Brendan 1923-1964 ....DLB13
Behrman, S. N. 1893-1973 ....DLB7
Belasco, David 1853-1931 ....DLB7
Belitt, Ben 1911- DLB5
Belknap, Jeremy 1744-1798 ....DLB30
Bell, Marvin 1937- DLB5
Bellamy, Edward 1850-1898 ....DLB12
Bellamy, Joseph 1719-1790 ....DLB31
Belloc, Hilaire 1870-1953 ....DLB19
Bellow, Saul 1915- DLB2, 28; DS3; Y82
Bemelmans, Ludwig 1898-1962 ....DLB22
Bemis, Samuel Flagg 1891-1973 ....DLB17
Benchley, Robert 1889-1945 ....DLB11
Benedictus, David 1938- DLB14
Benedikt, Michael 1935- DLB5
Benét, Stephen Vincent 1898-1943 ....DLB4
Benford, Gregory 1941- Y82
Benjamin, Park 1809-1864 ....DLB3

Bennett, Arnold 1867-1931................................DLB10
Bennett, James Gordon, Jr. 1841-1918...............DLB23
Berg, Stephen 1934- DLB5
Berger, John 1926- DLB14
Berger, Meyer 1898-1959.................................DLB29
Berger, Thomas 1924- DLB2; Y80
Berrigan, Daniel 1921- DLB5
Berrigan, Ted 1934- DLB5
Berry, Wendell 1934- DLB5, 6
Bessie, Alvah 1904- DLB26
Bester, Alfred 1913- DLB8
Betjeman, John 1906- DLB20
Betts, Doris 1932- Y82
Beveridge, Albert J. 1862-1927............................DLB17
Beverley, Robert circa 1673-1722 ....DLB24, 30
Bierce, Ambrose 1842-1914?...................DLB11, 12, 23
Biggle, Lloyd, Jr. 1923- DLB8
Biglow, Hosea (see Lowell, James Russell)
Billings, Josh (see Shaw, Henry Wheeler)
Binyon, Laurence 1869-1943 ....DLB19
Bird, William 1888-1963..................................DLB4
Bishop, Elizabeth 1911-1979...............................DLB5
Bishop, John Peale 1892-1944 ....DLB4, 9
Black, Winifred 1863-1936................................DLB25
Blackamore, Arthur 1679-?................................DLB24
Blackburn, Paul 1926-1971 ....Y81; DLB16
Blackburn, Thomas 1916-1977 ....DLB27
Blackmore, R. D. 1825-1900 ....DLB18
Blackwood, Caroline 1931- DLB14
Blair, James circa 1655-1743 ....DLB24
Bledsoe, Albert Taylor 1809-1877 ....DLB3
Blish, James 1921-1975....................................DLB8
Block, Rudolph (see Lessing, Bruno)
Blunden, Edmund 1896-1974...........................DLB20
Blunt, Wilfrid Scawen 1840-1922 ....DLB19
Bly, Nellie (see Cochrane, Elizabeth)
Bly, Robert 1926- DLB5
Bodenheim, Maxwell 1892-1954.........................DLB9
Boer, Charles 1939- DLB5
Bogarde, Dirk 1921- DLB14
Bolling, Robert 1738-1775................................DLB31

Bolt, Robert 1924- DLB13
Bolton, Herbert E. 1870-1953............................DLB17
Bond, Edward 1934- DLB13
Boorstin, Daniel J. 1914- DLB17
Booth, Philip 1925- Y82
Borrow, George 1803-1881 ....DLB21
Botta, Anne C. Lynch 1815-1891.........................DLB3
Bottomley, Gordon 1874-1948..........................DLB10
Bottoms, David 1949- Y83
Bottrall, Ronald 1906- DLB20
Boucher, Anthony 1911-1968.............................DLB8
Boucher, Jonathan 1738-1804............................DLB31
Bourjaily, Vance Nye 1922- DLB2
Bova, Ben 1932- Y81
Bovard, Oliver K. 1872-1945............................DLB25
Bowen, Elizabeth 1899-1973 ....DLB15
Bowen, Francis 1811-1890................................DLB1
Bowen, John 1924- DLB13
Bowers, Claude G. 1878-1958...........................DLB17
Bowers, Edgar 1924- DLB5
Bowles, Paul 1910- DLB5, 6
Boyd, James 1888-1944 ....DLB9
Boyd, John 1919- DLB8
Boyd, Thomas 1898-1935..................................DLB9
Boyesen, Hjalmar Hjorth 1848-1895 ....DLB12
Boyle, Kay 1902- DLB4, 9
Brackenridge, Hugh Henry 1748-1816...............DLB11
Brackett, Charles 1892-1969 ....DLB26
Brackett, Leigh 1915-1978..............................DLB8, 26
Bradbury, Malcolm 1932- DLB14
Bradbury, Ray 1920- DLB2, 8
Braddon, Mary Elizabeth 1835-1915 ....DLB18
Bradford, Gamaliel 1863-1932...........................DLB17
Bradford, William 1590-1657 ....DLB24, 30
Bradley, Marion Zimmer 1930- DLB8
Bradley, William Aspenwall 1878-1939.................DLB4
Bradstreet, Anne 1612 or 1613-1672 ....DLB24
Bragg, Melvyn 1939- DLB14
Braine, John 1922- DLB15
Brautigan, Richard 1935- DLB2, 5; Y80
Bray, Thomas 1656-1730 ....DLB24

Bremser, Bonnie 1939-	DLB16
Bremser, Ray 1934-	DLB16
Brenton, Howard 1942-	DLB13
Bridges, Robert 1844-1930	DLB19
Bridie, James 1888-1951	DLB10
Briggs, Charles Frederick 1804-1877	DLB3
Brighouse, Harold 1882-1958	DLB10
Brisbane, Albert 1809-1890	DLB3
Brisbane, Arthur 1864-1936	DLB25
Brodhead, John R. 1814-1873	DLB30
Bromfield, Louis 1896-1956	DLB4, 9
Broner, E. M. 1930-	DLB28
Brontë, Anne 1820-1849	DLB21
Brontë, Charlotte 1816-1855	DLB21
Brontë, Emily 1818-1848	DLB21, 32
Brooke, Rupert 1887-1915	DLB19
Brooke-Rose, Christine 1926-	DLB14
Brooks, Charles Timothy 1813-1883	DLB1
Brooks, Gwendolyn 1917-	DLB5
Brooks, Jeremy 1926-	DLB14
Brooks, Mel 1926-	DLB26
Brophy, Brigid 1929-	DLB14
Brossard, Chandler 1922-	DLB16
Brother Antoninus (see Everson, William)	
Brougham, John 1810-1880	DLB11
Broughton, James 1913-	DLB5
Broughton, Rhoda 1840-1920	DLB18
Broun, Heywood 1888-1939	DLB29
Brown, Bob 1886-1959	DLB4
Brown, Christy 1932-1981	DLB14
Brown, Dee 1908-	Y80
Brown, Fredric 1906-1972	DLB8
Brown, George Mackay 1921-	DLB14, 27
Brown, Harry 1917-	DLB26
Brown, Margaret Wise 1910-1952	DLB22
Brown, Oliver Madox 1855-1874	DLB21
Brown, William Wells 1813-1884	DLB3
Browne, Charles Farrar 1834-1867	DLB11
Browne, Wynyard 1911-1964	DLB13
Browning, Elizabeth Barrett 1806-1861	DLB32
Browning, Robert 1812-1889	DLB32
Brownson, Orestes Augustus 1803-1876	DLB1
Bruckman, Clyde 1894-1955	DLB26
Bryant, William Cullen 1794-1878	DLB3
Buchanan, Robert 1841-1901	DLB18
Buchman, Sidney 1902-1975	DLB26
Buck, Pearl S. 1892-1973	DLB9
Buckley, William F., Jr. 1925-	Y80
Buckner, Robert 1906-	DLB26
Budd, Thomas ?-1698	DLB24
Budrys, A. J. 1931-	DLB8
Buechner, Frederick 1926-	Y80
Bukowski, Charles 1920-	DLB5
Bullins, Ed 1935-	DLB7
Bulwer-Lytton, Edward (also Edward Bulwer) 1803-1873	DLB21
Bumpus, Jerry 1937-	Y81
Bunting, Basil 1900-	DLB20
Burgess, Anthony 1917-	DLB14
Burgess, Gelett 1866-1951	DLB11
Burgess, Thornton W. 1874-1965	DLB22
Burnett, W. R. 1899-1982	DLB9
Burns, Alan 1929-	DLB14
Burroughs, Edgar Rice 1875-1950	DLB8
Burroughs, William S., Jr. 1947-1981	DLB16
Burroughs, William Seward 1914-	DLB2, 8, 16; Y81
Burroway, Janet 1936-	DLB6
Burton, Virginia Lee 1909-1968	DLB22
Busch, Frederick 1941-	DLB6
Butler, Samuel 1835-1902	DLB18
Byatt, A. S. 1936-	DLB14
Byles, Mather 1707-1788	DLB24
Byrd, William II 1674-1744	DLB24
Byrne, John Keyes (see Leonard, Hugh)	

C

Cabell, James Branch 1879-1958	DLB9
Cable, George Washington 1844-1925	DLB12
Cahan, Abraham 1860-1951	DLB9, 25, 28
Caldwell, Erskine 1903-	DLB9

Calhoun, John C. 1782-1850	DLB3
Calisher, Hortense 1911-	DLB2
Calmer, Edgar 1907-	DLB4
Calvert, George Henry 1803-1889	DLB1
Camm, John 1718-1778	DLB31
Campbell, John W., Jr. 1910-1971	DLB8
Campbell, Roy 1901-1957	DLB20
Cannan, Gilbert 1884-1955	DLB10
Cannell, Kathleen 1891-1974	DLB4
Cantwell, Robert 1908-1978	DLB9
Capen, Joseph 1658-1725	DLB24
Capote, Truman 1924-1984	DLB2; Y80
Carroll, Gladys Hasty 1904-	DLB9
Carroll, Lewis 1832-1898	DLB18
Carroll, Paul 1927-	DLB16
Carroll, Paul Vincent 1900-1968	DLB10
Carruth, Hayden 1921-	DLB5
Carter, Angela 1940-	DLB14
Carter, Landon 1710-1778	DLB31
Carter, Lin 1930-	Y81
Caruthers, William Alexander 1802-1846	DLB3
Carver, Jonathan 1710-1780	DLB31
Cary, Joyce 1888-1957	DLB15
Casey, Juanita 1925-	DLB14
Casey, Michael 1947-	DLB5
Cassady, Carolyn 1923-	DLB16
Cassady, Neal 1926-1968	DLB16
Cassill, R. V. 1919-	DLB6
Caswall, Edward 1814-1878	DLB32
Cather, Willa 1873-1947	DLB9; DS1
Catton, Bruce 1899-1978	DLB17
Causley, Charles 1917-	DLB27
Caute, David 1936-	DLB14
Challans, Eileen Mary (see Renault, Mary)	
Chalmers, George 1742-1825	DLB30
Chamberlain, Samuel S. 1851-1916	DLB25
Chamberlin, William Henry 1897-1969	DLB29
Chambers, Charles Haddon 1860-1921	DLB10
Chandler, Harry 1864-1944	DLB29
Channing, Edward 1856-1931	DLB17
Channing, Edward Tyrrell 1790-1856	DLB1
Channing, William Ellery 1780-1842	DLB1
Channing, William Ellery II 1817-1901	DLB1
Channing, William Henry 1810-1884	DLB1
Chappell, Fred 1936-	DLB6
Charles, Gerda 1914-	DLB14
Charyn, Jerome 1937-	Y83
Chase, Borden 1900-1971	DLB26
Chauncy, Charles 1705-1787	DLB24
Chayefsky, Paddy 1923-1981	DLB7; Y81
Cheever, Ezekiel 1615-1708	DLB24
Cheever, John 1912-1982	DLB2; Y80, 82
Cheever, Susan 1943-	Y82
Cheney, Ednah Dow (Littlehale) 1824-1904	DLB1
Cherry, Kelly 1940-	Y83
Cherryh, C. J. 1942-	Y80
Chesnutt, Charles Waddell 1858-1932	DLB12
Chesterton, G. K. 1874-1936	DLB10, 19
Child, Francis James 1825-1896	DLB1
Child, Lydia Maria 1802-1880	DLB1
Childress, Alice 1920-	DLB7
Childs, George W. 1829-1894	DLB23
Chivers, Thomas Holley 1809-1858	DLB3
Chopin, Kate 1851-1904	DLB12
Christie, Agatha 1890-1976	DLB13
Church, Benjamin 1734-1778	DLB31
Churchill, Caryl 1938-	DLB13
Ciardi, John 1916-	DLB5
Clapper, Raymond 1892-1944	DLB29
Clark, Charles Heber 1841-1915	DLB11
Clark, Eleanor 1913-	DLB6
Clark, Lewis Gaylord 1808-1873	DLB3
Clark, Walter Van Tilburg 1909-1971	DLB9
Clarke, Austin 1896-1974	DLB10, 20
Clarke, James Freeman 1810-1888	DLB1
Clausen, Andy 1943-	DLB16
Clemens, Samuel Langhorne 1835-1910	DLB11, 12, 23
Clement, Hal 1922-	DLB8
Clemo, Jack 1916-	DLB27
Clifton, Lucille 1936-	DLB5
Clough, Arthur Hugh 1819-1861	DLB32

Coates, Robert M. 1897-1973	DLB4, 9
Coatsworth, Elizabeth 1893-	DLB22
Cobb, Frank I. 1869-1923	DLB25
Cobb, Irvin S. 1876-1944	DLB11, 25
Cochran, Thomas C. 1902-	DLB17
Cochrane, Elizabeth 1867-1922	DLB25
Cockerill, John A. 1845-1896	DLB23
Cohen, Arthur A. 1928-	DLB28
Colden, Cadwallader 1688-1776	DLB24, 30
Cole, Barry 1936-	DLB14
Colegate, Isabel 1931-	DLB14
Coleman, Emily Holmes 1899-1974	DLB4
Coleridge, Mary 1861-1907	DLB19
Collins, Mortimer 1827-1876	DLB21
Collins, Wilkie 1824-1889	DLB18
Colman, Benjamin 1673-1747	DLB24
Colum, Padraic 1881-1972	DLB19
Colwin, Laurie 1944-	Y80
Commager, Henry Steele 1902-	DLB17
Connell, Evan S., Jr. 1924-	DLB2; Y81
Connelly, Marc 1890-1980	DLB7; Y80
Conquest, Robert 1917-	DLB27
Conrad, Joseph 1857-1924	DLB10
Conroy, Jack 1899-	Y81
Conroy, Pat 1945-	DLB6
Conway, Moncure Daniel 1832-1907	DLB1
Cook, Ebenezer circa 1667-circa 1732	DLB24
Cooke, John Esten 1830-1886	DLB3
Cooke, Philip Pendleton 1816-1850	DLB3
Cooke, Rose Terry 1827-1892	DLB12
Cooper, Giles 1918-1966	DLB13
Cooper, James Fenimore 1789-1851	DLB3
Cooper, Kent 1880-1965	DLB29
Coover, Robert 1932-	DLB2; Y81
Coppel, Alfred 1921-	Y83
Corman, Cid 1924-	DLB5
Corn, Alfred 1943-	Y80
Corrington, John William 1932-	DLB6
Corso, Gregory 1930-	DLB5, 16
Costain, Thomas B. 1885-1965	DLB9
Cotton, John 1584-1652	DLB24
Coward, Noel 1899-1973	DLB10
Cowles, Gardner 1861-1946	DLB29
Cowley, Malcolm 1898-	DLB4; Y81
Coxe, Louis 1918-	DLB5
Cozzens, James Gould 1903-1978	DLB9; DS2
Craddock, Charles Egbert (see Murfree, Mary N.)	
Cradock, Thomas 1718-1770	DLB31
Cranch, Christopher Pearse 1813-1892	DLB1
Crane, Hart 1899-1932	DLB4
Crane, Stephen 1871-1900	DLB12
Craven, Avery 1885-1980	DLB17
Crawford, Charles 1752-circa 1815	DLB31
Crayon, Geoffrey (see Irving, Washington)	
Creel, George 1876-1953	DLB25
Creeley, Robert 1926-	DLB5, 16
Creelman, James 1859-1915	DLB23
Cregan, David 1931-	DLB13
Crews, Harry 1935-	DLB6
Crichton, Michael 1942-	Y81
Cristofer, Michael 1946-	DLB7
Crockett, David 1786-1836	DLB3, 11
Croly, Jane Cunningham 1829-1901	DLB23
Crosby, Caresse 1892-1970 and Crosby, Harry 1898-1929	DLB4
Crothers, Rachel 1878-1958	DLB7
Crowley, John 1942-	Y82
Crowley, Mart 1935-	DLB7
Croy, Homer 1883-1965	DLB4
Cullen, Countee 1903-1946	DLB4
Cummings, E. E. 1894-1962	DLB4
Cummings, Ray 1887-1957	DLB8
Cunningham, J. V. 1911-	DLB5
Cuomo, George 1929-	Y80
Cuppy, Will 1884-1949	DLB11
Curti, Merle E. 1897-	DLB17
Curtis, George William 1824-1892	DLB1

D

Dall, Caroline Wells (Healey) 1822-1912	DLB1
D'Alton, Louis 1900-1951	DLB10

Daly, T. A. 1871-1948	DLB11
Dana, Charles A. 1819-1897	DLB3, 23
Dana, Richard Henry, Jr. 1815-1882	DLB1
Dane, Clemence 1887-1965	DLB10
Danforth, John 1660-1730	DLB24
Danforth, Samuel I 1626-1674	DLB24
Danforth, Samuel II 1666-1727	DLB24
Daniels, Josephus 1862-1948	DLB29
Daryush, Elizabeth 1887-1977	DLB20
d'Aulaire, Edgar Parin 1898- and d'Aulaire, Ingri 1904-	DLB22
Daves, Delmer 1904-1977	DLB26
Davidson, Avram 1923-	DLB8
Davidson, John 1857-1909	DLB19
Davidson, Lionel 1922-	DLB14
Davie, Donald 1922-	DLB27
Davies, Samuel 1723-1761	DLB31
Davies, W. H. 1871-1940	DLB19
Daviot, Gordon 1896-1952	DLB10
Davis, Charles A. 1795-1867	DLB11
Davis, Clyde Brion 1894-1962	DLB9
Davis, H. L. 1894-1960	DLB9
Davis, Margaret Thomson 1926-	DLB14
Davis, Ossie 1917-	DLB7
Davis, Richard Harding 1864-1916	DLB12, 23
Davison, Peter 1928-	DLB5
Dawson, William 1704-1752	DLB31
Day, Clarence 1874-1935	DLB11
Day, Dorothy 1897-1980	DLB29
Day Lewis, C. 1904-1972	DLB15, 20
Deal, Borden 1922-	DLB6
de Angeli, Marguerite 1889-	DLB22
De Bow, James D. B. 1820-1867	DLB3
de Camp, L. Sprague 1907-	DLB8
De Forest, John William 1826-1906	DLB12
de Graff, Robert 1895-1981	Y81
de la Mare, Walter 1873-1956	DLB19
Delaney, Shelagh 1939-	DLB13
Delany, Samuel R. 1942-	DLB8
Delbanco, Nicholas 1942-	DLB6
DeLillo, Don 1936-	DLB6
Dell, Floyd 1887-1969	DLB9
del Rey, Lester 1915-	DLB8
Dennis, Nigel 1912-	DLB13, 15
Denton, Daniel circa 1626-1703	DLB24
Derby, George Horatio 1823-1861	DLB11
Derleth, August 1909-1971	DLB9
De Voto, Bernard 1897-1955	DLB9
De Vries, Peter 1910-	DLB6; Y82
de Young, M. H. 1849-1925	DLB25
Diamond, I. A. L. 1920-	DLB26
Dick, Philip K. 1928-	DLB8
Dickens, Charles 1812-1870	DLB21
Dickey, James 1923-	DLB5; Y82
Dickey, William 1928-	DLB5
Dickinson, Emily 1830-1886	DLB1
Dickinson, John 1732-1808	DLB31
Dickinson, Jonathan 1688-1747	DLB24
Dickinson, Patric 1914-	DLB27
Dickson, Gordon R. 1923-	DLB8
Didion, Joan 1934-	DLB2; Y81
Di Donato, Pietro 1911-	DLB9
Dillard, Annie 1945-	Y80
Dillard, R. H. W. 1937-	DLB5
Diogenes, Jr. (see Brougham, John)	
DiPrima, Diane 1934-	DLB5, 16
Disch, Thomas M. 1940-	DLB8
Disney, Walt 1901-1966	DLB22
Disraeli, Benjamin 1804-1881	DLB21
Dix, Dorothea Lynde 1802-1887	DLB1
Dix, Dorothy (see Gilmer, Elizabeth Meriwether)	
Dixon, Richard Watson 1833-1900	DLB19
Dobell, Sydney 1824-1874	DLB32
Doctorow, E. L. 1931-	DLB2, 28; Y80
Dodd, William E. 1869-1940	DLB17
Dodgson, Charles Lutwidge (see Carroll, Lewis)	
Doesticks, Q. K. Philander, P. B. (see Thomson, Mortimer)	
Donald, David H. 1920-	DLB17
Donleavy, J. P. 1926-	DLB6
Donnelly, Ignatius 1831-1901	DLB12
Doolittle, Hilda 1886-1961	DLB4

Dorn, Edward 1929-	DLB5
Dorr, Rheta Childe 1866-1948	DLB25
Dos Passos, John 1896-1970	DLB4, 9; DS1
Doughty, Charles M. 1843-1926	DLB19
Douglas, Keith 1920-1944	DLB27
Douglass, Frederick 1817?-1895	DLB1
Douglass, William circa 1691-1752	DLB24
Downing, J., Major (see Davis, Charles A.)	
Downing, Major Jack (see Smith, Seba)	
Dowson, Ernest 1867-1900	DLB19
Doyle, Arthur Conan 1859-1930	DLB18
Doyle, Kirby 1932-	DLB16
Drabble, Margaret 1939-	DLB14
Draper, John W. 1811-1882	DLB30
Draper, Lyman C. 1815-1891	DLB30
Dreiser, Theodore 1871-1945	DLB9, 12; DS1
Drinkwater, John 1882-1937	DLB10, 19
Duffy, Maureen 1933-	DLB14
Dugan, Alan 1923-	DLB5
Dukes, Ashley 1885-1959	DLB10
Duncan, Robert 1919-	DLB5, 16
Duncan, Ronald 1914-1982	DLB13
Dunlap, William 1766-1839	DLB30
Dunne, Finley Peter 1867-1936	DLB11, 23
Dunne, John Gregory 1932-	Y80
Dunne, Philip 1908-	DLB26
Dunning, Ralph Cheever 1878-1930	DLB4
Dunning, William A. 1857-1922	DLB17
Plunkett, Edward John Moreton Drax, Lord Dunsany 1878-1957	DLB10
Duranty, Walter 1884-1957	DLB29
Durrell, Lawrence 1912-	DLB15, 27
Duyckinck, Evert A. 1816-1878	DLB3
Duyckinck, George L. 1823-1863	DLB3
Dwight, John Sullivan 1813-1893	DLB1
Dyer, Charles 1928-	DLB13
Dylan, Bob 1941-	DLB16

E

Eager, Edward 1911-1964	DLB22
Eastlake, William 1917-	DLB6
Edgar, David 1948-	DLB13
Edmonds, Walter D. 1903-	DLB9
Edwards, Jonathan 1703-1758	DLB24
Effinger, George Alec 1947-	DLB8
Eggleston, Edward 1837-1902	DLB12
Eigner, Larry 1927-	DLB5
Eklund, Gordon 1945-	Y83
Elder, Lonne, III 1931-	DLB7
Eliot, George 1819-1880	DLB21
Eliot, John 1604-1690	DLB24
Eliot, T. S. 1888-1965	DLB7, 10
Elkin, Stanley 1930-	DLB2, 28; Y80
Ellet, Elizabeth F. 1818?-1877	DLB30
Elliott, Janice 1931-	DLB14
Elliott, William 1788-1863	DLB3
Ellison, Harlan 1934-	DLB8
Ellison, Ralph 1914-	DLB2
Emerson, Ralph Waldo 1803-1882	DLB1
Empson, William 1906-	DLB20
Enright, D. J. 1920-	DLB27
Enright, Elizabeth 1909-1968	DLB22
Epstein, Julius 1909- and Epstein, Philip 1909-1952	DLB26
Erskine, John 1879-1951	DLB9
Ervine, St. John Greer 1883-1971	DLB10
Eshleman, Clayton 1935-	DLB5
Estes, Eleanor 1906-	DLB22
Ets, Marie Hall 1893-	DLB22
Evans, Mary Ann (see George Eliot)	
Evans, Nathaniel 1742-1767	DLB31
Everett, Edward 1794-1865	DLB1
Everson, William 1912-	DLB5, 16
Ewing, Juliana Horatia 1841-1885	DLB21
Exley, Frederick 1929-	Y81

F

Faber, Frederick William 1814-1863	DLB32
Fairfax, Beatrice (see Manning, Marie)	
Fancher, Betsy 1928-	Y83

Fante, John 1909-1983	Y83
Farley, Walter 1920-	DLB22
Farmer, Philip José 1918-	DLB8
Farrell, James T. 1904-1979	DLB4, 9; DS2
Farrell, J. G. 1935-1979	DLB14
Fast, Howard 1914-	DLB9
Faulkner, William 1897-1962	DLB9, 11; DS2
Faust, Irvin 1924-	DLB2, 28; Y80
Fearing, Kenneth 1902-1961	DLB9
Federman, Raymond 1928-	Y80
Feiffer, Jules 1929-	DLB7
Feinstein, Elaine 1930-	DLB14
Felton, Cornelius Conway 1807-1862	DLB1
Ferber, Edna 1885-1968	DLB9, 28
Ferguson, Sir Samuel 1810-1886	DLB32
Ferlinghetti, Lawrence 1919-	DLB5, 16
Fiedler, Leslie 1917-	DLB28
Field, Eugene 1850-1895	DLB23
Field, Rachel 1894-1942	DLB9, 22
Fields, James Thomas 1817-1881	DLB1
Figes, Eva 1932-	DLB14
Finney, Jack 1911-	DLB8
Finney, Walter Braden (see Finney, Jack)	
Firmin, Giles 1615-1697	DLB24
Fisher, Dorothy Canfield 1879-1958	DLB9
Fisher, Vardis 1895-1968	DLB9
Fiske, John 1608-1677	DLB24
Fitch, Thomas circa 1700-1774	DLB31
Fitch, William Clyde 1865-1909	DLB7
FitzGerald, Edward 1809-1883	DLB32
Fitzgerald, F. Scott 1896-1940	DLB4, 9; Y81; DS1
Fitzgerald, Penelope 1916-	DLB14
Fitzgerald, Robert 1910-	Y80
Fitzgerald, Thomas 1819-1891	DLB23
Fitzhugh, William circa 1651-1701	DLB24
Flanagan, Thomas 1923-	Y80
Flanner, Janet 1892-1978	DLB4
Flavin, Martin 1883-1967	DLB9
Flecker, James Elroy 1884-1915	DLB10, 19
Fleeson, Doris 1901-1970	DLB29
Fletcher, John Gould 1886-1950	DLB4
Flint, F. S. 1885-1960	DLB19
Follen, Eliza Lee (Cabot) 1787-1860	DLB1
Follett, Ken 1949-	Y81
Foote, Horton 1916-	DLB26
Foote, Shelby 1916-	DLB2, 17
Forbes, Ester 1891-1967	DLB22
Force, Peter 1790-1868	DLB30
Forché, Carolyn 1950-	DLB5
Ford, Charles Henri 1913-	DLB4
Ford, Corey 1902-1969	DLB11
Ford, Jesse Hill 1928-	DLB6
Foreman, Carl 1914-1984	DLB26
Fornés, María Irene 1930-	DLB7
Fortune, T. Thomas 1856-1928	DLB23
Foster, John 1648-1681	DLB24
Foster, Michael 1904-1956	DLB9
Fowles, John 1926-	DLB14
Fox, John, Jr. 1862 or 1863-1919	DLB9
Fox, William Price 1926-	DLB2; Y81
Fraenkel, Michael 1896-1957	DLB4
France, Richard 1938-	DLB7
Francis, Convers 1795-1863	DLB1
Frank, Waldo 1889-1967	DLB9
Franklin, Benjamin 1706-1790	DLB24
Frantz, Ralph Jules 1902-1979	DLB4
Fraser, G. S. 1915-1980	DLB27
Frayn, Michael 1933-	DLB13, 14
Frederic, Harold 1856-1898	DLB12, 23
Freeman, Douglas Southall 1886-1953	DLB17
Freeman, Legh Richmond 1842-1915	DLB23
Freeman, Mary Wilkins 1852-1930	DLB12
Friedman, Bruce Jay 1930-	DLB2, 28
Friel, Brian 1929-	DLB13
Friend, Krebs 1895?-1967?	DLB4
Frothingham, Octavius Brooks 1822-1895	DLB1
Froude, James Anthony 1818-1894	DLB18
Fry, Christopher 1907-	DLB13
Fuchs, Daniel 1909-	DLB9, 26, 28
Fuller, Henry Blake 1857-1929	DLB12
Fuller, Roy 1912-	DLB15, 20
Fuller, Samuel 1912-	DLB26

Fuller, Sarah Margaret, Marchesa D'Ossoli 1810-1850 ....DLB1

Furness, William Henry 1802-1896 ....DLB1

Furthman, Jules 1888-1966 ....DLB26

G

Gaddis, William 1922- DLB2

Gag, Wanda 1893-1946 ....DLB22

Gaines, Ernest J. 1933- DLB2; Y80

Gale, Zona 1874-1938 ....DLB9

Gallico, Paul 1897-1976 ....DLB9

Galsworthy, John 1867-1933 ....DLB10

Galvin, Brendan 1938- DLB5

Gannett, Frank E. 1876-1957 ....DLB29

Gardam, Jane 1928- DLB14

Garden, Alexander circa 1685-1756 ....DLB31

Gardner, John 1933-1982 ....DLB2; Y82

Garis, Howard R. 1873-1962 ....DLB22

Garland, Hamlin 1860-1940 ....DLB12

Garraty, John A. 1920- DLB17

Garrett, George 1929- DLB2, 5; Y83

Garrison, William Lloyd 1805-1879 ....DLB1

Gascoyne, David 1916- DLB20

Gaskell, Elizabeth Cleghorn 1810-1865 ....DLB21

Gass, William Howard 1924- DLB2

Gates, Doris 1901- DLB22

Gay, Ebenezer 1696-1787 ....DLB24

Gayarre, Charles E. A. 1805-1895 ....DLB30

Geddes, Virgil 1897- DLB4

Gelber, Jack 1932- DLB7

Gellhorn, Martha 1908- Y82

Gems, Pam 1925- DLB13

Genovese, Eugene D. 1930- DLB17

Gent, Peter 1942- Y82

George, Henry 1839-1897 ....DLB23

Gernsback, Hugo 1884-1967 ....DLB8

Gerrold, David 1944- DLB8

Geston, Mark S. 1946- DLB8

Gibbons, Floyd 1887-1939 ....DLB25

Gibson, Wilfrid 1878-1962 ....DLB19

Gibson, William 1914- DLB7

Gillespie, A. Lincoln, Jr. 1895-1950 ....DLB4

Gilliam, Florence ?-? DLB4

Gilliatt, Penelope 1932- DLB14

Gillott, Jacky 1939-1980 ....DLB14

Gilman, Caroline H. 1794-1888 ....DLB3

Gilmer, Elizabeth Meriwether 1861-1951 ....DLB29

Gilroy, Frank D. 1925- DLB7

Ginsberg, Allen 1926- DLB5, 16

Giovanni, Nikki 1943- DLB5

Gipson, Lawrence Henry 1880-1971 ....DLB17

Gissing, George 1857-1903 ....DLB18

Glanville, Brian 1931- DLB15

Glasgow, Ellen 1873-1945 ....DLB9, 12

Glaspell, Susan 1882-1948 ....DLB7, 9

Glass, Montague 1877-1934 ....DLB11

Glück, Louise 1943- DLB5

Goddard, Morrill 1865-1937 ....DLB25

Godfrey, Thomas 1736-1763 ....DLB31

Godwin, Gail 1937- DLB6

Godwin, Parke 1816-1904 ....DLB3

Gogarty, Oliver St. John 1878-1957 ....DLB15, 19

Gold, Herbert 1924- DLB2; Y81

Gold, Michael 1893-1967 ....DLB9, 28

Goldberg, Dick 1947- DLB7

Golding, William 1911- DLB15

Goodrich, Frances 1891- and
  Hackett, Albert 1900- DLB26

Goodrich, Samuel Griswold 1793-1860 ....DLB1

Goodwin, Stephen 1943- Y82

Gookin, Daniel 1612-1687 ....DLB24

Gordon, Caroline 1895-1981 ....DLB4, 9; Y81

Gordon, Giles 1940- DLB14

Gordon, Mary 1949- DLB6; Y81

Gordone, Charles 1925- DLB7

Goyen, William 1915-1983 ....DLB2; Y83

Grady, Henry W. 1850-1889 ....DLB23

Graham, W. S. 1918- DLB20

Gramatky, Hardie 1907-1979 ....DLB22

Granich, Irwin (see Gold, Michael)

Grant, Harry J. 1881-1963 ....DLB29

Grant, James Edward 1905-1966........................DLB26
Grasty, Charles H. 1863-1924 ....DLB25
Grau, Shirley Ann 1929- DLB2
Graves, John 1920- Y83
Graves, Robert 1895- DLB20
Gray, Asa 1810-1888..DLB1
Gray, David 1838-1861..DLB32
Gray, Simon 1936- DLB13
Grayson, William J. 1788-1863..........................DLB3
Greeley, Horace 1811-1872 ....DLB3
Green, Gerald 1922- DLB28
Green, Henry 1905-1973..................................DLB15
Green, Jonas 1712-1767 ....DLB31
Green, Joseph 1706-1780 ....DLB31
Green, Julien 1900- DLB4
Green, Paul 1894-1981 ....DLB7, 9; Y81
Greene, Asa 1789-1838......................................DLB11
Greene, Graham 1904- DLB13, 15
Greenhow, Robert 1800-1854..........................DLB30
Greenough, Horatio 1805-1852 ....DLB1
Greenwood, Walter 1903-1974........................DLB10
Greer, Ben 1948- DLB6
Persse, Isabella Augusta,
 Lady Gregory 1852-1932 ....DLB10
Grey, Zane 1872-1939..DLB9
Grieve, C. M. (see MacDiarmid, Hugh)
Griffiths, Trevor 1935- DLB13
Grigson, Geoffrey 1905- DLB27
Griswold, Rufus 1815-1857...............................DLB3
Gross, Milt 1895-1953.......................................DLB11
Grubb, Davis 1919-1980 ....DLB6
Gruelle, Johnny 1880-1938 ....DLB22
Guare, John 1938- DLB7
Guest, Barbara 1920- DLB5
Guiterman, Arthur 1871-1943 ....DLB11
Gunn, James E. 1923- DLB8
Gunn, Neil M. 1891-1973..................................DLB15
Gunn, Thom 1929- DLB27
Guthrie, A. B., Jr. 1901- DLB6
Guthrie, Ramon 1896-1973 ....DLB4
Gwynne, Erskine 1898-1948..............................DLB4

Gysin, Brion 1916- DLB16

H

H. D. (see Doolittle, Hilda)

Hailey, Arthur 1920- Y82
Haines, John 1924- DLB5
Hake, Thomas Gordon 1809-1895 ....DLB32
Haldeman, Joe 1943- DLB8
Hale, Edward Everett 1822-1909.....................DLB1
Hale, Nancy 1908- Y80
Hale, Sara Josepha (Buell) 1788-1879 ....DLB1
Haliburton, Thomas Chandler 1796-1865 ....DLB11
Hall, Donald 1928- DLB5
Hallam, Arthur Henry 1811-1833 ....DLB32
Halleck, Fitz-Greene 1790-1867 ....DLB3
Halper, Albert 1904- DLB9
Halstead, Murat 1829-1908..............................DLB23
Hamburger, Michael 1924- DLB27
Hamilton, Alexander 1712-1756.....................DLB31
Hamilton, Cicely 1872-1952 ....DLB10
Hamilton, Edmond 1904-1977........................DLB8
Hamilton, Patrick 1904-1962...........................DLB10
Hammon, Jupiter 1711-died between
 1790 and 1806 ....DLB31
Hammond, John ?-1663 ....DLB24
Hamner, Earl 1923- DLB6
Hampton, Christopher 1946- DLB13
Handlin, Oscar 1915- DLB17
Hankin, St. John 1869-1909.............................DLB10
Hanley, Clifford 1922- DLB14
Hannah, Barry 1942- DLB6
Hannay, James 1827-1873................................DLB21
Hansberry, Lorraine 1930-1965.......................DLB7
Hardwick, Elizabeth 1916- DLB6
Hardy, Thomas 1840-1928 ....DLB18, 19
Hare, David 1947- DLB13
Hargrove, Marion 1919- DLB11
Harness, Charles L. 1915- DLB8
Harris, George Washington 1814-1869 ....DLB3, 11

Harris, Joel Chandler 1848-1908	DLB11, 23
Harris, Mark 1922-	DLB2; Y80
Harrison, Harry 1925-	DLB8
Harrison, Jim 1937-	Y82
Hart, Albert Bushnell 1854-1943	DLB17
Hart, Moss 1904-1961	DLB7
Hart, Oliver 1723-1795	DLB31
Harte, Bret 1836-1902	DLB12
Hartley, L. P. 1895-1972	DLB15
Harwood, Ronald 1934-	DLB13
Hauser, Marianne 1910-	Y83
Hawker, Robert Stephen 1803-1875	DLB32
Hawkes, John 1925-	DLB2; Y80
Hawthorne, Nathaniel 1804-1864	DLB1
Hay, John 1838-1905	DLB12
Hayden, Robert 1913-1980	DLB5
Hayes, John Michael 1919-	DLB26
Hayne, Paul Hamilton 1830-1886	DLB3
Hazzard, Shirley 1931-	Y82
Headley, Joel T. 1813-1897	DLB30
Hearn, Lafcadio 1850-1904	DLB12
Hearst, William Randolph 1863-1951	DLB25
Heath, Catherine 1924-	DLB14
Heath-Stubbs, John 1918-	DLB27
Hecht, Anthony 1923-	DLB5
Hecht, Ben 1894-1964	DLB7, 9, 25, 26, 28
Hecker, Isaac Thomas 1819-1888	DLB1
Hedge, Frederic Henry 1805-1890	DLB1
Heidish, Marcy 1947-	Y82
Heinlein, Robert A. 1907-	DLB8
Heller, Joseph 1923-	DLB2, 28; Y80
Hellman, Lillian 1906-1984	DLB7
Hemingway, Ernest 1899-1961	DLB4, 9; Y81; DS1
Henchman, Daniel 1689-1761	DLB24
Henderson, Zenna 1917-	DLB8
Henley, William Ernest 1849-1903	DLB19
Henry, Buck 1930-	DLB26
Henry, Marguerite 1902-	DLB22
Henry, Robert Selph 1889-1970	DLB17
Henty, G. A. 1832-1902	DLB18
Hentz, Caroline Lee 1800-1856	DLB3
Herbert, Alan Patrick 1890-1971	DLB10
Herbert, Frank 1920-	DLB8
Herbert, Henry William 1807-1858	DLB3
Herbst, Josephine 1892-1969	DLB9
Hergesheimer, Joseph 1880-1954	DLB9
Herrick, Robert 1868-1938	DLB9, 12
Herrick, William 1915-	Y83
Herrmann, John 1900-1959	DLB4
Hersey, John 1914-	DLB6
Hewat, Alexander circa 1743-circa 1824	DLB30
Hewitt, John 1907-	DLB27
Heyen, William 1940-	DLB5
Heyward, Dorothy 1890-1961 and Heyward, DuBose 1885-1940	DLB7
Heyward, DuBose 1885-1940	DLB9
Higgins, Aidan 1927-	DLB14
Higgins, Colin 1941-	DLB26
Higgins, George V. 1939-	DLB2; Y81
Higginson, Thomas Wentworth 1822-1911	DLB1
Hildreth, Richard 1807-1865	DLB1, 30
Hill, Susan 1942-	DLB14
Himes, Chester 1909-	DLB2
Hoagland, Edward 1932-	DLB6
Hobson, Laura Z. 1900-	DLB28
Hochman, Sandra 1936-	DLB5
Hodgman, Helen 1945-	DLB14
Hodgson, Ralph 1871-1962	DLB19
Hoffenstein, Samuel 1890-1947	DLB11
Hoffman, Charles Fenno 1806-1884	DLB3
Hoffman, Daniel 1923-	DLB5
Hofstadter, Richard 1916-1970	DLB17
Hogan, Desmond 1950-	DLB14
Holbrook, David 1923-	DLB14
Hollander, John 1929-	DLB5
Holley, Marietta 1836-1926	DLB11
Holloway, John 1920-	DLB27
Holmes, John Clellon 1926-	DLB16
Holmes, Oliver Wendell 1809-1894	DLB1
Home, William Douglas 1912-	DLB13

Honig, Edwin 1919- DLB5
Hooker, Thomas 1586-1647................................DLB24
Hooper, Johnson Jones 1815-1862..................DLB3, 11
Hopkins, Samuel 1721-1803................................DLB31
Hopkinson, Francis 1737-1791............................DLB31
Horne, Richard Henry (Hengist) 1802 or
    1803-1884..DLB32
Horovitz, Israel 1939- DLB7
Hough, Emerson 1857-1923...................................DLB9
Houghton, Stanley 1881-1913..............................DLB10
Housman, A. E. 1859-1936..................................DLB19
Housman, Laurence 1865-1959............................DLB10
Howard, Maureen 1930- Y83
Howard, Richard 1929- DLB5
Howard, Roy W. 1883-1964.................................DLB29
Howard, Sidney 1891-1939..............................DLB7, 26
Howe, E. W. 1853-1937..................................DLB12, 25
Howe, Henry 1816-1893......................................DLB30
Howe, Julia Ward 1819-1910.................................DLB1
Howell, Clark, Sr. 1863-1936................................DLB25
Howell, Evan P. 1839-1905..................................DLB23
Howells, William Dean 1837-1920.......................DLB12
Hoyem, Andrew 1935- DLB5
Hubbard, Kin 1868-1930......................................DLB11
Hubbard, William circa 1621-1704......................DLB24
Hughes, David 1930- DLB14
Hughes, Langston 1902-1967..............................DLB4, 7
Hughes, Richard 1900-1976.................................DLB15
Hughes, Thomas 1822-1896.................................DLB18
Hugo, Richard 1923-1982......................................DLB5
Hulme, T. E. 1883-1917.......................................DLB19
Humphrey, William 1924- DLB6
Humphreys, Emyr 1919- DLB15
Huncke, Herbert 1915- DLB16
Hunter, Evan 1926- Y82
Hunter, Jim 1939- DLB14
Hunter, N. C. 1908-1971......................................DLB10
Huston, John 1906- DLB26
Hutchinson, Thomas 1711-1780.....................DLB30, 31

I

Ignatow, David 1914- DLB5
Imbs, Bravig 1904-1946...DLB4
Inge, William 1913-1973..DLB7
Ingraham, Joseph Holt 1809-1860........................DLB3
Irving, John 1942- DLB6; Y82
Irving, Washington 1783-1859....................DLB3, 11, 30
Irwin, Will 1873-1948..DLB25
Isherwood, Christopher 1904- DLB15

J

Jackson, Shirley 1919-1965....................................DLB6
Jacob, Piers Anthony Dillingham (see Anthony,
    Piers)
Jacobson, Dan 1929- DLB14
Jakes, John 1932- Y83
James, Henry 1843-1916......................................DLB12
James, John circa 1633-1729...............................DLB24
Jameson, J. Franklin 1859-1937..........................DLB17
Jay, John 1745-1829..DLB31
Jefferson, Thomas 1743-1826..............................DLB31
Jellicoe, Ann 1927- DLB13
Jenkins, Robin 1912- DLB14
Jenkins, William Fitzgerald (see Leinster, Murray)
Jennings, Elizabeth 1926- DLB27
Jensen, Merrill 1905-1980...................................DLB17
Jerome, Jerome K. 1859-1927.............................DLB10
Jewett, Sarah Orne 1849-1909............................DLB12
Jewsbury, Geraldine 1812-1880..........................DLB21
Joans, Ted 1928- DLB16
Johnson, B. S. 1933-1973....................................DLB14
Johnson, Diane 1934- Y80
Johnson, Edward 1598-1672...............................DLB24
Johnson, Gerald W. 1890-1980...........................DLB29
Johnson, Lionel 1867-1902..................................DLB19
Johnson, Nunnally 1897-1977.............................DLB26
Johnson, Pamela Hansford 1912- DLB15

Cumulative Index

Johnson, Samuel 1696-1772 .... DLB24
Johnson, Samuel 1822-1882 .... DLB1
Johnston, Denis 1901- DLB10
Johnston, Jennifer 1930- DLB14
Johnston, Mary 1870-1936 .... DLB9
Jolas, Eugene 1894-1952 .... DLB4
Jones, Charles C., Jr. 1831-1893 .... DLB30
Jones, David 1895-1974 .... DLB20
Jones, Ebenezer 1820-1860 .... DLB32
Jones, Ernest 1819-1868 .... DLB32
Jones, Glyn 1905- DLB15
Jones, Gwyn 1907- DLB15
Jones, Henry Arthur 1851-1929 .... DLB10
Jones, Hugh circa 1692-1760 .... DLB24
Jones, James 1921-1977 .... DLB2
Jones, LeRoi (see Baraka, Amiri)
Jones, Lewis 1897-1939 .... DLB15
Jones, Major Joseph (see Thompson, William Tappan)
Jones, Preston 1936-1979 .... DLB7
Jong, Erica 1942- DLB2, 5, 28
Josephson, Matthew 1899-1978 .... DLB4
Josipovici, Gabriel 1940- DLB14
Josselyn, John ?-1675 .... DLB24
Joyce, James 1882-1941 .... DLB10, 19
Judd, Sylvester 1813-1853 .... DLB1
June, Jennie (see Croly, Jane Cunningham)
Justice, Donald 1925- Y83

K

Kalechofsky, Roberta 1931- DLB28
Kandel, Lenore 1932- DLB16
Kanin, Garson 1912- DLB7
Kantor, Mackinlay 1904-1977 .... DLB9
Kaplan, Johanna 1942- DLB28
Katz, Steve 1935- Y83
Kaufman, Bob 1925- DLB16
Kaufman, George S. 1889-1961 .... DLB7
Kavanagh, Patrick 1904-1967 .... DLB15, 20
Keane, John B. 1928- DLB13

Keble, John 1792-1866 .... DLB32
Keeble, John 1944- Y83
Keeffe, Barrie 1945- DLB13
Keeley, James 1867-1934 .... DLB25
Kelley, Edith Summers 1884-1956 .... DLB9
Kellogg, Ansel Nash 1832-1886 .... DLB23
Kelly, George 1887-1974 .... DLB7
Kelly, Robert 1935- DLB5
Kemble, Fanny 1809-1893 .... DLB32
Kemelman, Harry 1908- DLB28
Kennedy, John Pendleton 1795-1870 ...... DLB3
Kennedy, X. J. 1929- DLB5
Kent, Frank R. 1877-1958 .... DLB29
Kerouac, Jack 1922-1969 .... DLB2, 16; DS3
Kerouac, Jan 1952- DLB16
Kerr, Orpheus C. (see Newell, Robert Henry)
Kesey, Ken 1935- DLB2, 16
Kiely, Benedict 1919- DLB15
Kiley, Jed 1889-1962 .... DLB4
King, Clarence 1842-1901 .... DLB12
King, Francis 1923- DLB15
King, Grace 1852-1932 .... DLB12
King, Stephen 1947- Y80
Kingsley, Charles 1819-1875 .... DLB21, 32
Kingsley, Henry 1830-1876 .... DLB21
Kingsley, Sidney 1906- DLB7
Kingston, Maxine Hong 1940- Y80
Kinnell, Galway 1927- DLB5
Kinsella, Thomas 1928- DLB27
Kipling, Rudyard 1865-1936 .... DLB19
Kirkland, Caroline 1801-1864 .... DLB3
Kirkland, Joseph 1830-1893 .... DLB12
Kirkup, James 1918- DLB27
Kizer, Carolyn 1925- DLB5
Klappert, Peter 1942- DLB5
Klass, Philip (see Tenn, William)
Knickerbocker, Diedrich (see Irving, Washington)
Knight, Damon 1922- DLB8
Knight, John S. 1894-1981 .... DLB29
Knight, Sarah Kemble 1666-1727 .... DLB24
Knoblock, Edward 1874-1945 .... DLB10

Knowles, John 1926-	DLB6
Knox, Frank 1874-1944	DLB29
Knox, John Armoy 1850-1906	DLB23
Kober, Arthur 1900-1975	DLB11
Koch, Howard 1902-	DLB26
Koch, Kenneth 1925-	DLB5
Koenigsberg, Moses 1879-1945	DLB25
Koestler, Arthur 1905-1983	Y83
Komroff, Manuel 1890-1974	DLB4
Kopit, Arthur 1937-	DLB7
Kops, Bernard 1926?-	DLB13
Kornbluth, C. M. 1923-1958	DLB8
Kosinski, Jerzy 1933-	DLB2; Y82
Kraf, Elaine 1946-	Y81
Krasna, Norman 1909-	DLB26
Kreymborg, Alfred 1883-1966	DLB4
Krim, Seymour 1922-	DLB16
Krock, Arthur 1886-1974	DLB29
Kubrick, Stanley 1928-	DLB26
Kumin, Maxine 1925-	DLB5
Kupferberg, Tuli 1923-	DLB16
Kuttner, Henry 1915-1958	DLB8
Kyger, Joanne 1934-	DLB16

L

La Farge, Oliver 1901-1963	DLB9
Lafferty, R. A. 1914-	DLB8
Laird, Carobeth 1895-	Y82
Lamantia, Philip 1927-	DLB16
L'Amour, Louis 1908?-	Y80
Landesman, Jay 1919- and Landesman, Fran 1927-	DLB16
Lane, Charles 1800-1870	DLB1
Laney, Al 1896-	DLB4
Lanham, Edwin 1904-1979	DLB4
Lardner, Ring 1885-1933	DLB11, 25
Lardner, Ring, Jr. 1915-	DLB26
Larkin, Philip 1922-	DLB27
Lathrop, Dorothy P. 1891-1980	DLB22
Laumer, Keith 1925-	DLB8

Laurents, Arthur 1918-	DLB26
Laurie, Annie (see Black, Winifred)	
Lavin, Mary 1912-	DLB15
Lawrence, David 1888-1973	DLB29
Lawrence, D. H. 1885-1930	DLB10, 19
Lawson, John ?-1711	DLB24
Lawson, Robert 1892-1957	DLB22
Lawson, Victor F. 1850-1925	DLB25
Lea, Tom 1907-	DLB6
Leacock, John 1729-1802	DLB31
Lear, Edward 1812-1888	DLB32
Leary, Timothy 1920-	DLB16
Lederer, Charles 1910-1976	DLB26
Ledwidge, Francis 1887-1917	DLB20
Lee, Don L. (see Madhubuti, Haki R.)	
Lee, Harper 1926-	DLB6
Lee, Laurie 1914-	DLB27
Le Fanu, Joseph Sheridan 1814-1873	DLB21
Le Gallienne, Richard 1866-1947	DLB4
Legare, Hugh Swinton 1797-1843	DLB3
Legare, James M. 1823-1859	DLB3
Le Guin, Ursula K. 1929-	DLB8
Lehmann, John 1907-	DLB27
Lehmann, Rosamond 1901-	DLB15
Leiber, Fritz 1910-	DLB8
Leinster, Murray 1896-1975	DLB8
Leitch, Maurice 1933-	DLB14
Leland, Charles G. 1824-1903	DLB11
Lenski, Lois 1893-1974	DLB22
Leonard, Hugh 1926-	DLB13
Lerner, Max 1902-	DLB29
Lessing, Bruno 1870-1940	DLB28
Lessing, Doris 1919-	DLB15
Lever, Charles 1806-1872	DLB21
Levertov, Denise 1923-	DLB5
Levin, Meyer 1905-1981	DLB9, 28; Y81
Levine, Philip 1928-	DLB5
Levy, Benn Wolfe 1900-1973	Y81; DLB13
Lewis, Alfred H. 1857-1914	DLB25
Lewis, Alun 1915-1944	DLB20
Lewis, C. Day (see Day Lewis, C.)	

Lewis, Charles B. 1842-1924	DLB11
Lewis, C. S. 1898-1963	DLB15
Lewis, Henry Clay 1825-1850	DLB3
Lewis, Richard circa 1700-1734	DLB24
Lewis, Sinclair 1885-1951	DLB9; DS1
Lewis, Wyndham 1882-1957	DLB15
Lewisohn, Ludwig 1882-1955	DLB4, 9, 28
Liebling, A. J. 1904-1963	DLB4
Linebarger, Paul Myron Anthony (see Smith, Cordwainer)	
Link, Arthur S. 1920-	DLB17
Linton, Eliza Lynn 1822-1898	DLB18
Linton, William James 1812-1897	DLB32
Lippmann, Walter 1889-1974	DLB29
Lipton, Lawrence 1898-1975	DLB16
Littlewood, Joan 1914-	DLB13
Lively, Penelope 1933-	DLB14
Livings, Henry 1929-	DLB13
Livingston, William 1723-1790	DLB31
Llewellyn, Richard 1906-	DLB15
Lochridge, Betsy Hopkins (see Fancher, Betsy)	
Locke, David Ross 1833-1888	DLB11, 23
Lockridge, Ross, Jr. 1914-1948	Y80
Lodge, David 1935-	DLB14
Loeb, Harold 1891-1974	DLB4
Logan, James 1674-1751	DLB24
Logan, John 1923-	DLB5
Logue, Christopher 1926-	DLB27
London, Jack 1876-1916	DLB8, 12
Longfellow, Henry Wadsworth 1807-1882	DLB1
Longfellow, Samuel 1819-1892	DLB1
Longstreet, Augustus Baldwin 1790-1870	DLB3, 11
Lonsdale, Frederick 1881-1954	DLB10
Loos, Anita 1893-1981	DLB11, 26; Y81
Lopate, Phillip 1943-	Y80
Lossing, Benson J. 1813-1891	DLB30
Lovingood, Sut (see Harris, George Washington)	
Lowell, James Russell 1819-1891	DLB1, 11
Lowell, Robert 1917-1977	DLB5
Lowenfels, Walter 1897-1976	DLB4
Lowry, Malcolm 1909-1957	DLB15
Loy, Mina 1882-1966	DLB4
Ludlum, Robert 1927-	Y82
Luke, Peter 1919-	DLB13
Lurie, Alison 1926-	DLB2
Lytle, Andrew 1902-	DLB6
Lytton, Edward (see Bulwer-Lytton, Edward)	
Lytton, Edward Robert Bulwer 1831-1891	DLB32

M

MacArthur, Charles 1895-1956	DLB7, 25
Macaulay, Thomas Babington 1800-1859	DLB32
MacCaig, Norman 1910-	DLB27
MacDiarmid, Hugh 1892-1978	DLB20
MacDonald, George 1824-1905	DLB18
MacDonald, John D. 1916-	DLB8
Macfadden, Bernarr 1868-1955	DLB25
MacInnes, Colin 1914-1976	DLB14
Macken, Walter 1915-1967	DLB13
MacLean, Katherine Anne 1925-	DLB8
MacLeish, Archibald 1892-1982	DLB4, 7; Y82
Macleod, Norman 1906-	DLB4
MacNamara, Brinsley 1890-1963	DLB10
MacNeice, Louis 1907-1963	DLB10, 20
Madden, David 1933-	DLB6
Madhubuti, Haki R. 1942-	DLB5
Mailer, Norman 1923-	DLB2, 16, 28; Y80, 83; DS3
Makemie, Francis circa 1658-1708	DLB24
Malamud, Bernard 1914-	DLB2, 28; Y80
Mallock, W. H. 1849-1923	DLB18
Malone, Dumas 1892-	DLB17
Malzberg, Barry N. 1939-	DLB8
Mamet, David 1947-	DLB7
Manfred, Frederick 1912-	DLB6
Mangan, Sherry 1904-1961	DLB4
Mankiewicz, Herman 1897-1953	DLB26
Mankowitz, Wolf 1924-	DLB15
Mann, Horace 1796-1859	DLB1
Manning, Marie 1873?-1945	DLB29
Mano, D. Keith 1942-	DLB6
March, William 1893-1954	DLB9

Marcus, Frank 1928-	DLB13
Markfield, Wallace 1926-	DLB2, 28
Marquand, John P. 1893-1960	DLB9
Marquis, Don 1878-1937	DLB11, 25
Marryat, Frederick 1792-1848	DLB21
Marsh, George Perkins 1801-1882	DLB1
Marsh, James 1794-1842	DLB1
Marshall, Edward 1932-	DLB16
Martin, Abe (see Hubbard, Kin)	
Martineau, Harriet 1802-1876	DLB21
Martyn, Edward 1859-1923	DLB10
Masefield, John 1878-1967	DLB10, 19
Massey, Gerald 1828-1907	DLB32
Mather, Cotton 1663-1728	DLB24, 30
Mather, Increase 1639-1723	DLB24
Mather, Richard 1596-1669	DLB24
Matheson, Richard 1926-	DLB8
Mathews, Cornelius 1817-1889	DLB3
Mathias, Roland 1915-	DLB27
Matthews, Jack 1925-	DLB6
Matthews, William 1942-	DLB5
Matthiessen, Peter 1927-	DLB6
Maugham, W. Somerset 1874-1965	DLB10
Maury, James 1718-1769	DLB31
Mavor, Elizabeth 1927-	DLB14
Mavor, Osborne Henry (see Bridie, James)	
Maxwell, William 1908-	Y80
Mayer, O. B. 1818-1891	DLB3
Mayes, Wendell 1919-	DLB26
Mayhew, Henry 1812-1887	DLB18
Mayhew, Jonathan 1720-1766	DLB31
McAlmon, Robert 1896-1956	DLB4
McCaffrey, Anne 1926-	DLB8
McCarthy, Cormac 1933-	DLB6
McCarthy, Mary 1912-	DLB2; Y81
McCay, Winsor 1871-1934	DLB22
McClatchy, C. K. 1858-1936	DLB25
McCloskey, Robert 1914-	DLB22
McClure, Joanna 1930-	DLB16
McClure, Michael 1932-	DLB16
McCormick, Anne O'Hare 1880-1954	DLB29
McCormick, Robert R. 1880-1955	DLB29
McCoy, Horace 1897-1955	DLB9
McCullagh, Joseph B. 1842-1896	DLB23
McCullers, Carson 1917-1967	DLB2, 7
McDonald, Forrest 1927-	DLB17
McEwan, Ian 1948-	DLB14
McGahern, John 1934-	DLB14
McGeehan, W. O. 1879-1933	DLB25
McGill, Ralph 1898-1969	DLB29
McGinley, Phyllis 1905-1978	DLB11
McGuane, Thomas 1939-	DLB2; Y80
McIlvanney, William 1936-	DLB14
McIntyre, O. O. 1884-1938	DLB25
McKay, Claude 1889-1948	DLB4
McKean, William V. 1820-1903	DLB23
McLaverty, Michael 1907-	DLB15
McLean, John R. 1848-1916	DLB23
McLean, William L. 1852-1931	DLB25
McMurtry, Larry 1936-	DLB2; Y80
McNally, Terrence 1939-	DLB7
Mead, Taylor ?-	DLB16
Medoff, Mark 1940-	DLB7
Meek, Alexander Beaufort 1814-1865	DLB3
Meinke, Peter 1932-	DLB5
Meltzer, David 1937-	DLB16
Melville, Herman 1819-1891	DLB3
Mencken, H. L. 1880-1956	DLB11, 29
Mercer, David 1928-1980	DLB13
Mercer, John 1704-1768	DLB31
Meredith, George 1828-1909	DLB18
Meredith, William 1919-	DLB5
Merrill, James 1926-	DLB5
Merton, Thomas 1915-1968	Y81
Merwin, W. S. 1927-	DLB5
Mew, Charlotte 1869-1928	DLB19
Mewshaw, Michael 1943-	Y80
Meyer, Eugene 1875-1959	DLB29
Meynell, Alice 1847-1922	DLB19
Micheline, Jack 1929-	DLB16
Michener, James A. 1907?-	DLB6
Micklejohn, George circa 1717-1818	DLB31

Middleton, Stanley 1919-	DLB14
Millar, Kenneth 1915-1983	DLB2; Y83
Miller, Arthur 1915-	DLB7
Miller, Caroline 1903-	DLB9
Miller, Henry 1891-1980	DLB4, 9; Y80
Miller, Jason 1939-	DLB7
Miller, Perry 1905-1963	DLB17
Miller, Walter M., Jr. 1923-	DLB8
Miller, Webb 1892-1940	DLB29
Millhauser, Steven 1943-	DLB2
Milne, A. A. 1882-1956	DLB10
Milnes (Lord Houghton), Richard Monckton 1809-1885	DLB32
Mitchel, Jonathan 1624-1668	DLB24
Mitchell, Donald Grant 1822-1908	DLB1
Mitchell, James Leslie 1901-1935	DLB15
Mitchell, Julian 1935-	DLB14
Mitchell, Langdon 1862-1935	DLB7
Mitchell, Margaret 1900-1949	DLB9
Monkhouse, Allan 1858-1936	DLB10
Monro, Harold 1879-1932	DLB19
Monsarrat, Nicholas 1910-1979	DLB15
Montgomery, John 1919-	DLB16
Montgomery, Marion 1925-	DLB6
Moody, Joshua circa 1633-1697	DLB24
Moody, William Vaughn 1869-1910	DLB7
Moorcock, Michael 1939-	DLB14
Moore, Catherine L. 1911-	DLB8
Moore, George 1852-1933	DLB10, 18
Moore, T. Sturge 1870-1944	DLB19
Moore, Ward 1903-1978	DLB8
Morgan, Berry 1919-	DLB6
Morgan, Edmund S. 1916-	DLB17
Morgan, Edwin 1920-	DLB27
Morison, Samuel Eliot 1887-1976	DLB17
Morley, Christopher 1890-1957	DLB9
Morris, Richard B. 1904-	DLB17
Morris, William 1834-1896	DLB18
Morris, Willie 1934-	Y80
Morris, Wright 1910-	DLB2; Y81
Morrison, Toni 1931-	DLB6; Y81
Mortimer, John 1923-	DLB13
Morton, Nathaniel 1613-1685	DLB24
Morton, Thomas circa 1579-circa 1647	DLB24
Mosley, Nicholas 1923-	DLB14
Moss, Arthur 1889-1969	DLB4
Moss, Howard 1922-	DLB5
Motley, John Lothrop 1814-1877	DLB1, 30
Mowrer, Edgar Ansel 1892-1977	DLB29
Mowrer, Paul Scott 1887-1971	DLB29
Muir, Edwin 1887-1959	DLB20
Muir, Helen 1937-	DLB14
Munford, Robert circa 1737-1783	DLB31
Munsey, Frank A. 1854-1925	DLB25
Murdoch, Iris 1919-	DLB14
Murfree, Mary N. 1850-1922	DLB12
Murray, Gilbert 1866-1957	DLB10
Myers, L. H. 1881-1944	DLB15

N

Nabokov, Vladimir 1899-1977	DLB2; Y80; DS3
Nasby, Petroleum Vesuvius (see Locke, David Ross)	
Nash, Ogden 1902-1971	DLB11
Nathan, Robert 1894-	DLB9
Naughton, Bill 1910-	DLB13
Neagoe, Peter 1881-1960	DLB4
Neal, John 1793-1876	DLB1
Neal, Joseph C. 1807-1847	DLB11
Neihardt, John G. 1881-1973	DLB9
Nelson, William Rockhill 1841-1915	DLB23
Nemerov, Howard 1920-	DLB5, 6; Y83
Neugeboren, Jay 1938-	DLB28
Nevins, Allan 1890-1971	DLB17
Newbolt, Henry 1862-1938	DLB19
Newby, P. H. 1918-	DLB15
Newcomb, Charles King 1820-1894	DLB1
Newell, Robert Henry 1836-1901	DLB11
Newman, Frances 1883-1928	Y80
Newman, John Henry 1801-1890	DLB18, 32
Nichols, Dudley 1895-1960	DLB26
Nichols, John 1940-	Y82

Nichols, Mary Sargeant (Neal) Gove 1810-1884 ...DLB1
Nichols, Peter 1927- DLB13
Nichols, Roy F. 1896-1973................................DLB17
Nicholson, Norman 1914- DLB27
Niebuhr, Reinhold 1892-1971............................DLB17
Nieman, Lucius W. 1857-1935...........................DLB25
Niggli, Josefina 1910- Y80
Nims, John Frederick 1913- DLB5
Nin, Anaïs 1903-1977..DLB2, 4
Nissenson, Hugh 1933- DLB28
Niven, Larry 1938- DLB8
Nolan, William F. 1928- DLB8
Noland, C. F. M. 1810?-1858............................DLB11
Noone, John 1936- DLB14
Nordhoff, Charles 1887-1947 ....DLB9
Norris, Charles G. 1881-1945............................DLB9
Norris, Frank 1870-1902...................................DLB12
Norris, Leslie 1921- DLB27
Norse, Harold 1916- DLB16
Norton, Alice Mary (see Norton, Andre)
Norton, Andre 1912- DLB8
Norton, Andrews 1786-1853.............................DLB1
Norton, Caroline 1808-1877..............................DLB21
Norton, Charles Eliot 1827-1908 ....DLB1
Norton, John 1606-1663...................................DLB24
Nourse, Alan E. 1928- DLB8
Noyes, Alfred 1880-1958...................................DLB20
Noyes, Crosby S. 1825-1908..............................DLB23
Noyes, Nicholas 1647-1717...............................DLB24
Noyes, Theodore W. 1858-1946 ....DLB29
Nye, Bill 1850-1896...DLB11, 23
Nye, Robert 1939- DLB14

O

Oakes, Urian circa 1631-1681............................DLB24
Oates, Joyce Carol 1938- DLB2, 5; Y81
O'Brien, Edna 1932- DLB14
O'Brien, Kate 1897-1974..................................DLB15
O'Brien, Tim 1946- Y80
O'Casey, Sean 1880-1964..................................DLB10

Ochs, Adolph S. 1858-1935...............................DLB25
O'Connor, Flannery 1925-1964.......................DLB2; Y80
Odell, Jonathan 1737-1818...............................DLB31
Odets, Clifford 1906-1963................................DLB7, 26
O'Faolain, Julia 1932- DLB14
O'Faolain, Sean 1900- DLB15
O'Hara, Frank 1926-1966 ....DLB5, 16
O'Hara, John 1905-1970 ....DLB9; DS2
O. Henry (see Porter, William S.)
Older, Fremont 1856-1935................................DLB25
Oliphant, Laurence 1829-1888.........................DLB18
Oliphant, Margaret 1828-1897.........................DLB18
Oliver, Chad 1928- DLB8
Oliver, Mary 1935- DLB5
Olsen, Tillie 1913?- DLB28; Y80
Olson, Charles 1910-1970 ....DLB5, 16
O'Neill, Eugene 1888-1953...............................DLB7
Oppen, George 1908- DLB5
Oppenheim, James 1882-1932 ....DLB28
Oppenheimer, Joel 1930- DLB5
Orlovitz, Gil 1918-1973 ....DLB2, 5
Orlovsky, Peter 1933- DLB16
Ormond, John 1923- DLB27
Ornitz, Samuel 1890-1957................................DLB28
Orton, Joe 1933-1967 ....DLB13
Orwell, George 1903-1950................................DLB15
Osborne, John 1929- DLB13
Otis, James, Jr. 1725-1783................................DLB31
Ottendorfer, Oswald 1826-1900........................DLB23
Ouida 1839-1908...DLB18
Owen, Guy 1925- DLB5
Owen, Wilfred 1893-1918 ....DLB20
Owsley, Frank L. 1890-1956.............................DLB17
Ozick, Cynthia 1928- DLB28; Y82

P

Pack, Robert 1929- DLB5
Padgett, Ron 1942- DLB5
Page, Thomas Nelson 1853-1922.....................DLB12
Pain, Philip ?-circa 1666 ....DLB24

Paine, Thomas 1737-1809 ....DLB31
Paley, Grace 1922- DLB28
Palfrey, John Gorham 1796-1881 ....DLB1, 30
Panama, Norman 1914- and
    Melvin Frank 1913- DLB26
Pangborn, Edgar 1909-1976 ....DLB8
Panshin, Alexei 1940- DLB8
Parke, John 1754-1789 ....DLB31
Parker, Dorothy 1893-1967 ....DLB11
Parker, Theodore 1810-1860 ....DLB1
Parkman, Francis, Jr. 1823-1893 ....DLB1, 30
Parrington, Vernon L. 1871-1929 ....DLB17
Parton, James 1822-1891 ....DLB30
Pastan, Linda 1932- DLB5
Pastorius, Francis Daniel 1651-circa 1720 ....DLB24
Patchen, Kenneth 1911-1972 ....DLB16
Patrick, John 1906- DLB7
Patterson, Eleanor Medill 1881-1948 ....DLB29
Patterson, Joseph Medill 1879-1946 ....DLB29
Paul, Elliot 1891-1958 ....DLB4
Paulding, James Kirke 1778-1860 ....DLB3
Payn, James 1830-1898 ....DLB18
Peabody, Elizabeth Palmer 1804-1894 ....DLB1
Pead, Deuel ?-1727 ....DLB24
Peake, Mervyn DLB15
Peck, George W. 1840-1916 ....DLB23
Penn, William 1644-1718 ....DLB24
Penner, Jonathan 1940- Y83
Pennington, Lee 1939- Y82
Percy, Walker 1916- DLB2; Y80
Perelman, S. J. 1904-1979 ....DLB11
Perkoff, Stuart Z. 1930-1974 ....DLB16
Peterkin, Julia 1880-1961 ....DLB9
Petersham, Maud 1889-1971 and
    Petersham, Miska 1888-1960 ....DLB22
Phillips, David Graham 1867-1911 ....DLB9, 12
Phillips, Jayne Anne 1952- Y80
Phillips, Stephen 1864-1915 ....DLB10
Phillips, Ulrich B. 1877-1934 ....DLB17
Phillpotts, Eden 1862-1960 ....DLB10
Phoenix, John (see Derby, George Horatio)

Pinckney, Josephine 1895-1957 ....DLB6
Pinero, Arthur Wing 1855-1934 ....DLB10
Pinsky, Robert 1940- Y82
Pinter, Harold 1930- DLB13
Piper, H. Beam 1904-1964 ....DLB8
Piper, Watty DLB22
Pisar, Samuel 1929- Y83
Pitkin, Timothy 1766-1847 ....DLB30
Pitter, Ruth 1897- DLB20
Plante, David 1940- Y83
Plath, Sylvia 1932-1963 ....DLB5, 6
Plomer, William 1903-1973 ....DLB20
Plumly, Stanley 1939- DLB5
Plunkett, James 1920- DLB14
Plymell, Charles 1935- DLB16
Poe, Edgar Allan 1809-1849 ....DLB3
Pohl, Frederik 1919- DLB8
Poliakoff, Stephen 1952- DLB13
Pollard, Edward A. 1832-1872 ....DLB30
Polonsky, Abraham 1910- DLB26
Poole, Ernest 1880-1950 ....DLB9
Poore, Benjamin Perley 1820-1887 ....DLB23
Porter, Eleanor H. 1868-1920 ....DLB9
Porter, Katherine Anne 1890-1980 ....DLB4, 9; Y80
Porter, William S. 1862-1910 ....DLB12
Porter, William T. 1809-1858 ....DLB3
Portis, Charles 1933- DLB6
Potok, Chaim 1929- DLB28
Potter, David M. 1910-1971 ....DLB17
Pound, Ezra 1885-1972 ....DLB4
Powell, Anthony 1905- DLB15
Pownall, David 1938- DLB14
Powys, John Cowper 1872-1963 ....DLB15
Prescott, William Hickling 1796-1859 ....DLB1, 30
Price, Reynolds 1933- DLB2
Price, Richard 1949- Y81
Priest, Christopher 1943- DLB14
Priestley, J. B. 1894-1984 ....DLB10
Prime, Benjamin Young 1733-1791 ....DLB31
Prince, F. T. 1912- DLB20
Prince, Thomas 1687-1758 ....DLB24

Pritchett, V. S. 1900-	DLB15
Procter, Adelaide Anne 1825-1864	DLB32
Propper, Dan 1937-	DLB16
Proud, Robert 1728-1813	DLB30
Pulitzer, Joseph 1847-1911	DLB23
Pulitzer, Joseph, Jr. 1885-1955	DLB29
Purdy, James 1923-	DLB2
Putnam, George Palmer 1814-1872	DLB3
Putnam, Samuel 1892-1950	DLB4
Puzo, Mario 1920-	DLB6
Pyle, Ernie 1900-1945	DLB29
Pym, Barbara 1913-1980	DLB14
Pynchon, Thomas 1937-	DLB2

Q

Quad, M. (see Lewis, Charles B.)	
Quin, Ann 1936-1973	DLB14
Quincy, Samuel of Georgia birth date and death date unknown	DLB31
Quincy, Samuel of Massachusetts 1734-1789	DLB31

R

Rabe, David 1940-	DLB7
Raine, Kathleen 1908-	DLB20
Ralph, Julian 1853-1903	DLB23
Ramée, Marie Louise de la (see Ouida)	
Ramsay, David 1749-1815	DLB30
Randall, Henry S. 1811-1876	DLB30
Randall, James G. 1881-1953	DLB17
Raphael, Frederic 1931-	DLB14
Rattigan, Terence 1911-1977	DLB13
Rawlings, Marjorie Kinnan 1896-1953	DLB9, 22
Ray, David 1932-	DLB5
Read, Herbert 1893-1968	DLB20
Read, Opie 1852-1939	DLB23
Read, Piers Paul 1941-	DLB14
Reade, Charles 1814-1884	DLB21
Rechy, John 1934-	Y82
Reed, Henry 1914-	DLB27

Reed, Ishmael 1938-	DLB2, 5
Reed, Sampson 1800-1880	DLB1
Reid, Alastair 1926-	DLB27
Reid, Helen Rogers 1882-1970	DLB29
Reid, James birth date and death date unknown	DLB31
Reid, Mayne 1818-1883	DLB21
Reid, Whitelaw 1837-1912	DLB23
Remington, Frederic 1861-1909	DLB12
Renault, Mary 1905-1983	Y83
Rexroth, Kenneth 1905-1982	DLB16; Y82
Rey, H. A. 1898-1977	DLB22
Reynolds, G. W. M. 1814-1879	DLB21
Reynolds, Mack 1917-	DLB8
Reznikoff, Charles 1894-1976	DLB28
Rice, Elmer 1892-1967	DLB4, 7
Rice, Grantland 1880-1954	DLB29
Rich, Adrienne 1929-	DLB5
Richards, I. A. 1893-1979	DLB27
Richardson, Jack 1935-	DLB7
Richter, Conrad 1890-1968	DLB9
Rickword, Edgell 1898-1982	DLB20
Riddell, John (see Ford, Corey)	
Ridler, Anne 1912-	DLB27
Riis, Jacob 1849-1914	DLB23
Ripley, George 1802-1880	DLB1
Riskin, Robert 1897-1955	DLB26
Ritchie, Anna Mowatt 1819-1870	DLB3
Ritchie, Anne Thackeray 1837-1919	DLB18
Rivkin, Allen 1903-	DLB26
Robbins, Tom 1936-	Y80
Roberts, Elizabeth Madox 1881-1941	DLB9
Roberts, Kenneth 1885-1957	DLB9
Robinson, Lennox 1886-1958	DLB10
Robinson, Mabel Louise 1874-1962	DLB22
Rodgers, W. R. 1909-1969	DLB20
Roethke, Theodore 1908-1963	DLB5
Rogers, Will 1879-1935	DLB11
Roiphe, Anne 1935-	Y80
Rolvaag, O. E. 1876-1931	DLB9
Root, Waverley 1903-1982	DLB4

Rose, Reginald 1920-	DLB26
Rosen, Norma 1925-	DLB28
Rosenberg, Isaac 1890-1918	DLB20
Rosenfeld, Isaac 1918-1956	DLB28
Rosenthal, M. L. 1917-	DLB5
Ross, Leonard Q. (see Rosten, Leo)	
Rossen, Robert 1908-1966	DLB26
Rossner, Judith 1935-	DLB6
Rosten, Leo 1908-	DLB11
Roth, Henry 1906?-	DLB28
Roth, Philip 1933-	DLB2, 28; Y82
Rothenberg, Jerome 1931-	DLB5
Rowlandson, Mary circa 1635-circa 1678	DLB24
Rubens, Bernice 1928-	DLB14
Rudkin, David 1956-	DLB13
Rumaker, Michael 1932-	DLB16
Runyon, Damon 1880-1946	DLB11
Russ, Joanna 1937-	DLB8
Russell, Charles Edward 1860-1941	DLB25
Russell, George William (see AE)	
Rutherford, Mark 1831-1913	DLB18
Ryan, Michael 1946-	Y82
Ryskind, Morrie 1895-	DLB26

S

Saberhagen, Fred 1930-	DLB8
Sackler, Howard 1929-1982	DLB7
Saffin, John circa 1626-1710	DLB24
Sage, Robert 1899-1962	DLB4
St. Johns, Adela Rogers 1894-	DLB29
Salemson, Harold J. 1910-	DLB4
Salinger, J. D. 1919-	DLB2
Sanborn, Franklin Benjamin 1831-1917	DLB1
Sandburg, Carl 1878-1967	DLB17
Sanders, Ed 1939-	DLB16
Sandoz, Mari 1896-1966	DLB9
Sandys, George 1578-1644	DLB24
Sargent, Pamela 1948-	DLB8
Saroyan, William 1908-1981	DLB7, 9; Y81
Sarton, May 1912-	Y81
Sassoon, Siegfried 1886-1967	DLB20
Saunders, James 1925-	DLB13
Saunders, John Monk 1897-1940	DLB26
Savage, James 1784-1873	DLB30
Savage, Marmion W. 1803-1872	DLB21
Sawyer, Ruth 1880-1970	DLB22
Sayers, Dorothy L. 1893-1957	DLB10
Scannell, Vernon 1922-	DLB27
Schaeffer, Susan Fromberg 1941-	DLB28
Schlesinger, Arthur M., Jr. 1917-	DLB17
Schmitz, James H. 1911-	DLB8
Schreiner, Olive 1855-1920	DLB18
Schulberg, Budd 1914-	DLB6, 26, 28; Y81
Schurz, Carl 1829-1906	DLB23
Schuyler, George S. 1895-1977	DLB29
Schuyler, James 1923-	DLB5
Schwartz, Delmore 1913-1966	DLB28
Schwartz, Jonathan 1938-	Y82
Scott, Evelyn 1893-1963	DLB9
Scott, Harvey W. 1838-1910	DLB23
Scott, Paul 1920-1978	DLB14
Scott, Tom 1918-	DLB27
Scott, William Bell 1811-1890	DLB32
Scripps, E. W. 1854-1926	DLB25
Seabrook, William 1886-1945	DLB4
Seabury, Samuel 1729-1796	DLB31
Sedgwick, Catharine Maria 1789-1867	DLB1
Seid, Ruth (see Sinclair, Jo)	
Selby, Hubert, Jr. 1928-	DLB2
Seredy, Kate 1899-1975	DLB22
Serling, Rod 1924-1975	DLB26
Settle, Mary Lee 1918-	DLB6
Sewall, Joseph 1688-1769	DLB24
Sewall, Samuel 1652-1730	DLB24
Sexton, Anne 1928-1974	DLB5
Shaara, Michael 1929-	Y83
Shaffer, Anthony 1926-	DLB13
Shaffer, Peter 1926-	DLB13
Shairp, Mordaunt 1887-1939	DLB10
Sharpe, Tom 1928-	DLB14
Shaw, Bernard 1856-1950	DLB10

Shaw, Henry Wheeler 1818-1885	DLB11
Shaw, Irwin 1913-	DLB6
Shaw, Robert 1927-1978	DLB13, 14
Shea, John Gilmary 1824-1892	DLB30
Sheckley, Robert 1928-	DLB8
Sheed, Wilfred 1930-	DLB6
Sheldon, Alice B. (see Tiptree, James, Jr.)	
Sheldon, Edward 1886-1946	DLB7
Shepard, Sam 1943-	DLB7
Shepard, Thomas I 1604 or 1605-1649	DLB24
Shepard, Thomas II 1635-1677	DLB24
Sherriff, R. C. 1896-1975	DLB10
Sherwood, Robert 1896-1955	DLB7, 26
Shiels, George 1886-1949	DLB10
Shillaber, Benjamin Penhallow 1814-1890	DLB1, 11
Shirer, William L. 1904-	DLB4
Shorthouse, Joseph Henry 1834-1903	DLB18
Shulman, Max 1919-	DLB11
Shute, Henry A. 1856-1943	DLB9
Shuttle, Penelope 1947-	DLB14
Sigourney, Lydia Howard (Huntley) 1791-1865	DLB1
Silkin, Jon 1930-	DLB27
Silliphant, Stirling 1918-	DLB26
Sillitoe, Alan 1928-	DLB14
Silman, Roberta 1934-	DLB28
Silverberg, Robert 1935-	DLB8
Simak, Clifford D. 1904-	DLB8
Simms, William Gilmore 1806-1870	DLB3, 30
Simon, Neil 1927-	DLB7
Simons, Katherine Drayton Mayrant 1890-1969	Y83
Simpson, Louis 1923-	DLB5
Simpson, N. F. 1919-	DLB13
Sinclair, Andrew 1935-	DLB14
Sinclair, Jo 1913-	DLB28
Sinclair, Upton 1878-1968	DLB9
Singer, Isaac Bashevis 1904-	DLB6, 28
Singmaster, Elsie 1879-1958	DLB9
Sissman, L. E. 1928-1976	DLB5
Sisson, C. H. 1914-	DLB27
Sitwell, Edith 1887-1964	DLB20
Skelton, Robin 1925-	DLB27
Slavitt, David 1935-	DLB5, 6
Slick, Sam (see Haliburton, Thomas Chandler)	
Smith, Alexander 1830-1867	DLB32
Smith, Betty 1896-1972	Y82
Smith, Carol Sturm 1938-	Y81
Smith, Charles Henry 1826-1903	DLB11
Smith, Cordwainer 1913-1966	DLB8
Smith, Dave 1942-	DLB5
Smith, Dodie 1896-	DLB10
Smith, E. E. 1890-1965	DLB8
Smith, Elizabeth Oakes (Prince) 1806-1893	DLB1
Smith, George O. 1911-1981	DLB8
Smith, H. Allen 1906-1976	DLB11, 29
Smith, John 1580-1631	DLB24, 30
Smith, Josiah 1704-1781	DLB24
Smith, Lee 1944-	Y83
Smith, Mark 1935-	Y82
Smith, Michael 1698-circa 1771	DLB31
Smith, Red 1905-1982	DLB29
Smith, Seba 1792-1868	DLB1, 11
Smith, Stevie 1902-1971	DLB20
Smith, Sydney Goodsir 1915-1975	DLB27
Smith, William 1727-1803	DLB31
Smith, William 1728-1793	DLB30
Smith, William Jay 1918-	DLB5
Snodgrass, W. D. 1926-	DLB5
Snow, C. P. 1905-1980	DLB15
Snyder, Gary 1930-	DLB5, 16
Solano, Solita 1888-1975	DLB4
Solomon, Carl 1928-	DLB16
Sontag, Susan 1933-	DLB2
Sorrentino, Gilbert 1929-	DLB5; Y80
Southern, Terry 1924-	DLB2
Spark, Muriel 1918-	DLB15
Sparks, Jared 1789-1866	DLB1, 30
Spencer, Elizabeth 1921-	DLB6
Spender, Stephen 1909-	DLB20
Spicer, Jack 1925-1965	DLB5, 16
Spielberg, Peter 1929-	Y81
Spinrad, Norman 1940-	DLB8
Squibob (see Derby, George Horatio)	

Stafford, Jean 1915-1979	DLB2
Stafford, William 1914-	DLB5
Stallings, Laurence 1894-1968	DLB7, 9
Stampp, Kenneth M. 1912-	DLB17
Stanford, Ann 1916-	DLB5
Stanton, Frank L. 1857-1927	DLB25
Stapledon, Olaf 1886-1950	DLB15
Starkweather, David 1935-	DLB7
Steadman, Mark 1930-	DLB6
Stearns, Harold E. 1891-1943	DLB4
Steele, Max 1922-	Y80
Steere, Richard circa 1643-1721	DLB24
Stegner, Wallace 1909-	DLB9
Stein, Gertrude 1874-1946	DLB4
Stein, Leo 1872-1947	DLB4
Steinbeck, John 1902-1968	DLB7, 9; DS2
Stephens, Ann 1813-1886	DLB3
Stephens, James 1882?-1950	DLB19
Sterling, James 1701-1763	DLB24
Stern, Stewart 1922-	DLB26
Stevenson, Robert Louis 1850-1894	DLB18
Stewart, Donald Ogden 1894-1980	DLB4, 11, 26
Stewart, George R. 1895-1980	DLB8
Stiles, Ezra 1727-1795	DLB31
Still, James 1906-	DLB9
Stith, William 1707-1755	DLB31
Stoddard, Richard Henry 1825-1903	DLB3
Stoddard, Solomon 1643-1729	DLB24
Stokes, Thomas L. 1898-1958	DLB29
Stone, Melville 1848-1929	DLB25
Stone, Samuel 1602-1663	DLB24
Stoppard, Tom 1937-	DLB13
Storey, Anthony 1928-	DLB14
Storey, David 1933-	DLB13, 14
Story, Thomas circa 1670-1742	DLB31
Story, William Wetmore 1819-1895	DLB1
Stoughton, William 1631-1701	DLB24
Stowe, Harriet Beecher 1811-1896	DLB1, 12
Stowe, Leland 1899-	DLB29
Strand, Mark 1934-	DLB5
Streeter, Edward 1891-1976	DLB11
Stribling, T. S. 1881-1965	DLB9
Strother, David Hunter 1816-1888	DLB3
Stuart, Jesse 1907-	DLB9
Stubbs, Harry Clement (see Clement, Hal)	
Sturgeon, Theodore 1918-	DLB8
Sturges, Preston 1898-1959	DLB26
Styron, William 1925-	DLB2; Y80
Suckow, Ruth 1892-1960	DLB9
Suggs, Simon (see Hooper, Johnson Jones)	
Sukenick, Ronald 1932-	Y81
Sullivan, C. Gardner 1886-1965	DLB26
Sullivan, Frank 1892-1976	DLB11
Summers, Hollis 1916-	DLB6
Surtees, Robert Smith 1803-1864	DLB21
Sutro, Alfred 1863-1933	DLB10
Swados, Harvey 1920-1972	DLB2
Swain, Charles 1801-1874	DLB32
Swenson, May 1919-	DLB5
Swope, Herbert Bayard 1882-1958	DLB25
Symons, Arthur 1865-1945	DLB19
Synge, John Millington 1871-1909	DLB10, 19

T

Tarkington, Booth 1869-1946	DLB9
Tate, Allen 1896-1979	DLB4
Tate, James 1943-	DLB5
Taylor, Bayard 1825-1878	DLB3
Taylor, Bert Leston 1866-1921	DLB25
Taylor, Charles H. 1846-1921	DLB25
Taylor, Edward circa 1642-1729	DLB24
Taylor, Henry 1942-	DLB5
Taylor, Sir Henry 1800-1886	DLB32
Taylor, Peter 1917-	Y81
Tenn, William 1919-	DLB8
Tennant, Emma 1937-	DLB14
Tennyson, Alfred 1809-1892	DLB32
Tennyson, Frederick 1807-1898	DLB32
Terhune, Albert Payson 1872-1942	DLB9
Terry, Megan 1932-	DLB7
Terson, Peter 1932-	DLB13

Tesich, Steve 1943-	Y83
Thackeray, William Makepeace 1811-1863	DLB21
Theroux, Paul 1941-	DLB2
Thoma, Richard 1902-	DLB4
Thomas, Dylan 1914-1953	DLB13, 20
Thomas, Edward 1878-1917	DLB19
Thomas, Gwyn 1913-1981	DLB15
Thomas, John 1900-1932	DLB4
Thomas, R. S. 1915-	DLB27
Thompson, Dorothy 1893-1961	DLB29
Thompson, Francis 1859-1907	DLB19
Thompson, John R. 1823-1873	DLB3
Thompson, Ruth Plumly 1891-1976	DLB22
Thompson, William Tappan 1812-1882	DLB3, 11
Thomson, Mortimer 1831-1875	DLB11
Thoreau, Henry David 1817-1862	DLB1
Thorpe, Thomas Bangs 1815-1878	DLB3, 11
Thurber, James 1894-1961	DLB4, 11, 22
Ticknor, George 1791-1871	DLB1
Timrod, Henry 1828-1867	DLB3
Tiptree, James, Jr. 1915-	DLB8
Titus, Edward William 1870-1952	DLB4
Toklas, Alice B. 1877-1967	DLB4
Tolkien, J. R. R. 1892-1973	DLB15
Tompson, Benjamin 1642-1714	DLB24
Tonks, Rosemary 1932-	DLB14
Toole, John Kennedy 1937-1969	Y81
Tracy, Honor 1913-	DLB15
Traven, B. 1882? or 1890?-1969	DLB9
Travers, Ben 1886-1980	DLB10
Tremain, Rose 1943-	DLB14
Trescot, William Henry 1822-1898	DLB30
Trevor, William 1928-	DLB14
Trilling, Lionel 1905-1975	DLB28
Trocchi, Alexander 1925-	DLB15
Trollope, Anthony 1815-1882	DLB21
Trollope, Frances 1779-1863	DLB21
Troop, Elizabeth 1931-	DLB14
Trumbo, Dalton 1905-1976	DLB26
Trumbull, Benjamin 1735-1820	DLB30
Trumbull, John 1750-1831	DLB31
Tucker, George 1775-1861	DLB3, 30
Tucker, Nathaniel Beverley 1784-1851	DLB3
Tunis, John R. 1889-1975	DLB22
Tuohy, Frank 1925-	DLB14
Tupper, Martin F. 1810-1889	DLB32
Turner, Charles (Tennyson) 1808-1879	DLB32
Turner, Frederick Jackson 1861-1932	DLB17
Twain, Mark (see Clemens, Samuel Langhorne)	
Tyler, Anne 1941-	DLB6; Y82

U

Upchurch, Boyd B. (see Boyd, John)	
Updike, John 1932-	DLB2, 5; Y80, 82; DS3
Upton, Charles 1948-	DLB16
Ustinov, Peter 1921-	DLB13

V

Vail, Laurence 1891-1968	DLB4
Van Anda, Carr 1864-1945	DLB25
Vance, Jack 1916?-	DLB8
van Druten, John 1901-1957	DLB10
Van Duyn, Mona 1921-	DLB5
Vane, Sutton 1888-1963	DLB10
van Itallie, Jean-Claude 1936-	DLB7
Vann, Robert L. 1879-1940	DLB29
Van Vechten, Carl 1880-1964	DLB4, 9
van Vogt, A. E. 1912-	DLB8
Varley, John 1947-	Y81
Vega, Janine Pommy 1942-	DLB16
Very, Jones 1813-1880	DLB1
Vidal, Gore 1925-	DLB6
Viereck, Peter 1916-	DLB5
Villard, Henry 1835-1900	DLB23
Villard, Oswald Garrison 1872-1949	DLB25
Vonnegut, Kurt 1922-	DLB2, 8; Y80; DS3

W

Wagoner, David 1926-	DLB5

Wain, John 1925-	DLB15, 27
Wakoski, Diane 1937-	DLB5
Walcott, Derek 1930-	Y81
Waldman, Anne 1945-	DLB16
Walker, Alice 1944-	DLB6
Wallant, Edward Lewis 1926-1962	DLB2, 28
Walsh, Ernest 1895-1926	DLB4
Wambaugh, Joseph 1937-	DLB6; Y83
Ward, Artemus (see Browne, Charles Farrar)	
Ward, Douglas Turner 1930-	DLB7
Ward, Lynd 1905-	DLB22
Ward, Mrs. Humphry 1851-1920	DLB18
Ward, Nathaniel circa 1578-1652	DLB24
Ware, William 1797-1852	DLB1
Warner, Rex 1905-	DLB15
Warner, Susan B. 1819-1885	DLB3
Warren, Lella 1899-1982	Y83
Warren, Mercy Otis 1728-1814	DLB31
Warren, Robert Penn 1905-	DLB2; Y80
Washington, George 1732-1799	DLB31
Wasson, David Atwood 1823-1887	DLB1
Waterhouse, Keith 1929-	DLB13
Watkins, Vernon 1906-1967	DLB20
Watterson, Henry 1840-1921	DLB25
Watts, Alan 1915-1973	DLB16
Waugh, Auberon 1939-	DLB14
Waugh, Evelyn 1903-1966	DLB15
Webb, Walter Prescott 1888-1963	DLB17
Webster, Noah 1758-1843	DLB1
Weems, Mason Locke 1759-1825	DLB30
Weidman, Jerome 1913-	DLB28
Weinbaum, Stanley Grauman 1902-1935	DLB8
Weiss, John 1818-1879	DLB1
Weiss, Theodore 1916-	DLB5
Welch, Lew 1926-1971?	DLB16
Weldon, Fay 1931-	DLB14
Wells, Carolyn 1862-1942	DLB11
Wells, Charles Jeremiah circa 1800-1879	DLB32
Wells-Barnett, Ida B. 1862-1931	DLB23
Welty, Eudora 1909-	DLB2
Wescott, Glenway 1901-	DLB4, 9
Wesker, Arnold 1932-	DLB13
West, Anthony 1914-	DLB15
West, Jessamyn 1902-1984	DLB6
West, Nathanael 1903-1940	DLB4, 9, 28
West, Paul 1930-	DLB14
West, Rebecca 1892-1983	Y83
Whalen, Philip 1923-	DLB16
Wharton, Edith 1862-1937	DLB4, 9, 12
Wharton, William 1920s?-	Y80
Wheatley, Phillis circa 1754-1784	DLB31
Wheeler, Charles Stearns 1816-1843	DLB1
Wheeler, Monroe 1900-	DLB4
Wheelwright, John circa 1592-1679	DLB24
Whetstone, Colonel Pete (see Noland, C. F. M.)	
Whipple, Edwin Percy 1819-1886	DLB1
Whitaker, Alexander 1585-1617	DLB24
Whitcher, Frances Miriam 1814-1852	DLB11
White, Andrew 1579-1656	DLB24
White, E. B. 1899-	DLB11, 22
White, Horace 1834-1916	DLB23
White, William Allen 1868-1944	DLB9, 25
White, William Anthony Parker (see Boucher, Anthony)	
White, William Hale (see Rutherford, Mark)	
Whitehead, James 1936-	Y81
Whiting, John 1917-1963	DLB13
Whiting, Samuel 1597-1679	DLB24
Whitlock, Brand 1869-1934	DLB12
Whitman, Sarah Helen (Power) 1803-1878	DLB1
Whitman, Walt 1819-1892	DLB3
Whittemore, Reed 1919-	DLB5
Whittier, John Greenleaf 1807-1892	DLB1
Wieners, John 1934-	DLB16
Wigglesworth, Michael 1631-1705	DLB24
Wilbur, Richard 1921-	DLB5
Wild, Peter 1940-	DLB5
Wilde, Oscar 1854-1900	DLB10, 19
Wilde, Richard Henry 1789-1847	DLB3
Wilder, Billy 1906-	DLB26
Wilder, Laura Ingalls 1867-1957	DLB22
Wilder, Thornton 1897-1975	DLB4, 7, 9
Wiley, Bell Irvin 1906-1980	DLB17

Wilhelm, Kate 1928-	DLB8
Willard, Nancy 1936-	DLB5
Willard, Samuel 1640-1707	DLB24
Williams, C. K. 1936-	DLB5
Williams, Emlyn 1905-	DLB10
Williams, Garth 1912-	DLB22
Williams, Heathcote 1941-	DLB13
Williams, Isaac 1802-1865	DLB32
Williams, Joan 1928-	DLB6
Williams, John A. 1925-	DLB2
Williams, John E. 1922-	DLB6
Williams, Jonathan 1929-	DLB5
Williams, Raymond 1921-	DLB14
Williams, Roger circa 1603-1683	DLB24
Williams, T. Harry 1909-1979	DLB17
Williams, Tennessee 1911-1983	DLB7; DS4; Y83
Williams, William Appleman 1921-	DLB17
Williams, William Carlos 1883-1963	DLB4, 16
Williams, Wirt 1921-	DLB6
Williamson, Jack 1908-	DLB8
Willingham, Calder Baynard, Jr. 1922-	DLB2
Willis, Nathaniel Parker 1806-1867	DLB3
Wilson, A. N. 1950-	DLB14
Wilson, Angus 1913-	DLB15
Wilson, Colin 1931-	DLB14
Wilson, Harry Leon 1867-1939	DLB9
Wilson, John 1588-1667	DLB24
Wilson, Lanford 1937-	DLB7
Wilson, Margaret 1882-1973	DLB9
Winchell, Walter 1897-1972	DLB29
Windham, Donald 1920-	DLB6
Winthrop, John 1588-1649	DLB24, 30
Winthrop, John, Jr. 1606-1676	DLB24
Wise, John 1652-1725	DLB24
Wister, Owen 1860-1938	DLB9
Witherspoon, John 1723-1794	DLB31
Woiwode, Larry 1941-	DLB6
Wolcott, Roger 1679-1767	DLB24
Wolfe, Gene 1931-	DLB8
Wolfe, Thomas 1900-1938	DLB9; DS2
Wood, Benjamin 1820-1900	DLB23
Wood, Charles 1932-	DLB13
Wood, Mrs. Henry 1814-1887	DLB18
Wood, William ?-?	DLB24
Woodbridge, Benjamin 1622-1684	DLB24
Woodmason, Charles circa 1720-death date unknown	DLB31
Woodson, Carter G. 1875-1950	DLB17
Woodward, C. Vann 1908-	DLB17
Woollcott, Alexander 1887-1943	DLB29
Woolman, John 1720-1772	DLB31
Woolson, Constance Fenimore 1840-1894	DLB12
Worcester, Joseph Emerson 1784-1865	DLB1
Wouk, Herman 1915-	Y82
Wright, Charles 1935-	Y82
Wright, Harold Bell 1872-1944	DLB9
Wright, James 1927-1980	DLB5
Wright, Louis B. 1899-	DLB17
Wright, Richard 1908-1960	DS2
Wylie, Elinor 1885-1928	DLB9
Wylie, Philip 1902-1971	DLB9

Y

Yates, Richard 1926-	DLB2; Y81
Yeats, William Butler 1865-1939	DLB10, 19
Yezierska, Anzia 1885-1970	DLB28
Yonge, Charlotte Mary 1823-1901	DLB18
Young, Stark 1881-1963	DLB9
Young, Waldemar 1880-1938	DLB26

Z

Zangwill, Israel 1864-1926	DLB10
Zebrowski, George 1945-	DLB8
Zelazny, Roger 1937-	DLB8
Zenger, John Peter 1697-1746	DLB24
Zimmer, Paul 1934-	DLB5
Zindel, Paul 1936-	DLB7
Zubly, John Joachim 1724-1781	DLB31
Zukofsky, Louis 1904-1978	DLB5